DAREDEVIL

VISIONARIES: FRANK MILLER
VOLUME 2

FRANK MILLER
cover art

STEVE BUCCELLATO
with CLARISSA MARRERO, ROB TOKAR and BRIAN BUCCELLATO
color separations

JG ROSHELL of COMICRAFT design

JOE QUESADA
editor in chief

DAREDEVIL© VISIONARIES: FRANK MILLER VOL. 2. Contains material
originally published in magazine form as DAREDEVIL (Vol. 1) #168-182.
Second Printing, March 2002. ISBN # 0-7851-0771-1. Published by MAR-
VEL COMICS, a division of MARVEL ENTERTAINMENT GROUP, INC. OFFICE
OF PUBLICATION: 10 EAST 40th STREET, NEW YORK, NY 10016. Copyright ©
1981, 1982, 2001 and 2002 Marvel Characters, Inc. All rights reserved. Price
$24.95 in the U.S. and $39.95 in Canada (GST #R127032852). No similarity
between any of the names, characters, persons, and/or institutions in this publication with those of any living or dead person or institutions is intended, and any
such similarity which may exist is purely coincidental. This publication may not be
sold except by authorized dealers and is sold subject to the conditions that it shall
not be sold or distributed with any part of its cover or markings removed, nor in a
mutilated condition. DAREDEVIL (including all prominent characters featured in this
publication and the distinctive likenesses thereof) is a trademark of MARVEL CHARAC-
TERS, INC. Printed in Canada. PETER CUNEO, Chief Executive Officer; AVI ARAD, Chief
Creative Officer; GUI KARYO, Chief Information Officer; STAN LEE, Chairman Emeritus.

10 9 8 7 6 5 4 3 2

DEVIL

page 5 #168 "Elektra"

page 28 #169 "Devils"

page 51 #170 "The Kingpin Must Die"

page 74 #171 "In the Kingpin's Clutches"

page 97 #172 "Gangwar!"

page 120 #173 "Lady Killer"

page 143 #174 "The Assassination of Matt Murdock"

page 164 #175 "Gantlet"

page 186 #176 "Hunters"

page 208 #177 "Where Angels Fear to Tread"

page 230 #178 "Paper Chase"

page 252 #179 "Spiked!"

page 276 #180 "The Damned"

page 299 #181 "Last Hand"

page 338 #182 "She's Alive!"

INTRODUCTION: DIANA SCHUTZ

IT WAS DECEMBER 1981. A few months earlier I had driven my '65 pumpkin-colored Volkswagen — the *original* "bug" — from Montreal to California and had begun working at Berkeley's Comics & Comix store on fabled Telegraph Avenue.

It was a very good time for comics. The direct-sale comics specialty market was *booming*. New, "independent" publishers were proliferating, offering the first alternative to the Big Two since the heyday of the undergrounds; customers were buying *X-Men* by the case lots; and *Daredevil* was the hottest book on the racks.

Written and drawn by a young upstart named Frank Miller, *Daredevil* was bristling with innovation: cinematic storytelling without endlessly wordy captions; writing rich with atmosphere, visually heightened by a liberal use of black on the page; Eisnerian titles and credits (before many of us younger comics fans had even heard of *The Spirit*); first-person narrative, which would eventually segue into a total dispensation with thought balloons, and captions used instead to reflect each individual's innermost points of view. Not to mention one of the first truly liberated and liberat*ing* female characters ever to be found in four-color: the beautiful, strong, yet tragic Elektra, Matt Murdock's first and most powerful love. It was all pretty much brand new to the medium back then, and all the result of a kid from Vermont who'd moved to New York City to pursue his dream of working in comics.

SOMETHING ELSE ABOUT FRANK'S *DAREDEVIL*: the comic boasted a lot of female readers — decidedly unusual for the times and rivaling only Claremont's *X-Men* in that regard — and some of those gals even wrote letters of comment. You can find them in the back pages of the original issues: gals like Liz Holden, Teresa Conway, "verde" (who I always suspected was female), and ... Diana Schutz.

Oh, yeah, I was a fangirl — *and* a letterhack — and here it was December '81 and Frank Miller was flying to Berkeley, California to sign copies of the about-to-be-released and much-heralded *Daredevil* #181, the climax of the Elektra story line! The autograph party was being sponsored *not* by Comics & Comix, but by our competition, Best of Two Worlds. Nonetheless, I was determined, as only a fan can be, to meet my hero. And so, the day before Frank's signing, I wandered across the street to the rival store, ready to pump my buddy Rory Root, who worked there, for information about when the writer-artist would be arriving, where he was staying, how I could meet him.

As I approached the shop, a tall, lanky young guy strode out, hands buried deep in the pockets of his long trench coat, head bowed, his walk determined, his face grim. No Californian, he — this was a bona fide New Yorker (if not a native). I'd never seen a photo of Frank, but somehow I just ... *knew* this had to be him.

I was forced to run to catch up; those long legs of his were moving at New York City speeds. "Excuse me," I breathlessly proffered, "are you Frank Miller?"

Pause. *Long* pause.

"Yesss," he answered, carefully. Summoning up whatever courage hadn't withered under that uncompromising stare of his, I was about to launch into my comics resumé, by way of introduction, beginning with my job at the "other" Berkeley store. I got as far as my name, whereupon Frank enthusiastically shook my hand and asked me some question about a letter of mine he'd just received.

He actually *read* the damn letters! And he *knew* who I was! It was a fangirl's dream come true!

We went for a long walk that day that ended in a three-way late-night conversation with letterer Tom Orzechowski in my tiny Oakland kitchen. It was the beginning of a now nineteen-year friendship, which, four years ago, blossomed into a professional relationship as well, when I became Frank's editor at Dark Horse.

I ENVY THOSE OF YOU READING THESE *DAREDEVIL*S for the first time; they're buzzing with energy, the energy of a then 24-year-old creator whose already remarkable talent would only continue, astonishingly, to grow. And those of you *re*reading this volume of work will learn that the stories haven't dulled with age, that they still crackle with the vitality of a young man following his dream and discovering his strength therein.

In preparation for writing this introduction, I reread these *Daredevil*s myself just yesterday, for the first time in nineteen years. In every way, they are timeless. Like the dreams of all of us when we are still young.

Like a friendship that lasts a lifetime.

Diana Schutz
Portland, Oregon
November 26, 2000

DAREDEVIL #168

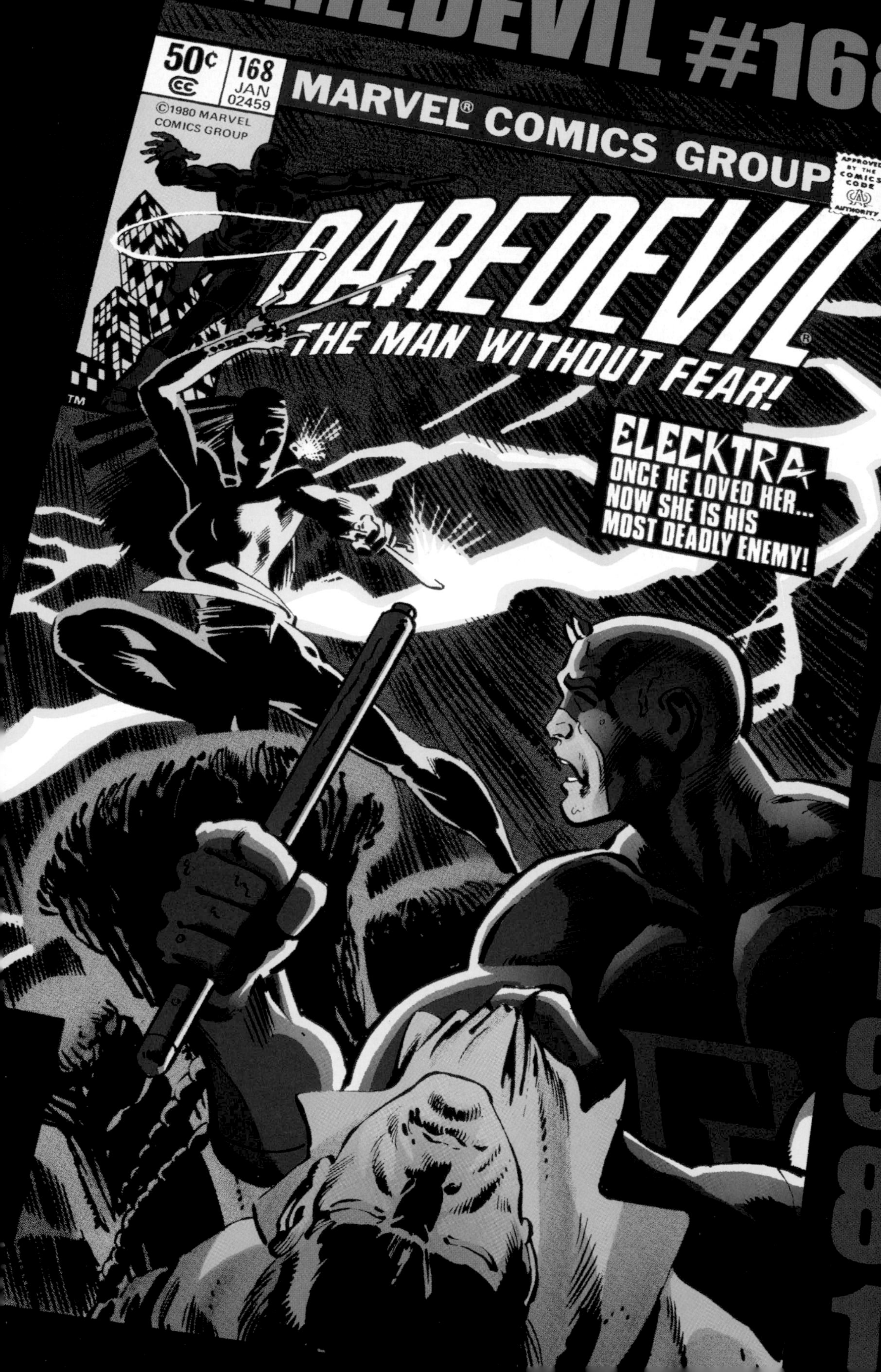
50¢
CC
168
JAN
02459
©1980 MARVEL
COMICS GROUP
MARVEL® COMICS GROUP
APPROVED BY THE COMICS CODE AUTHORITY
DAREDEVIL®
THE MAN WITHOUT FEAR!
TM
ELECKTRA
ONCE HE LOVED HER...
NOW SHE IS HIS
MOST DEADLY ENEMY!

JAN 1981

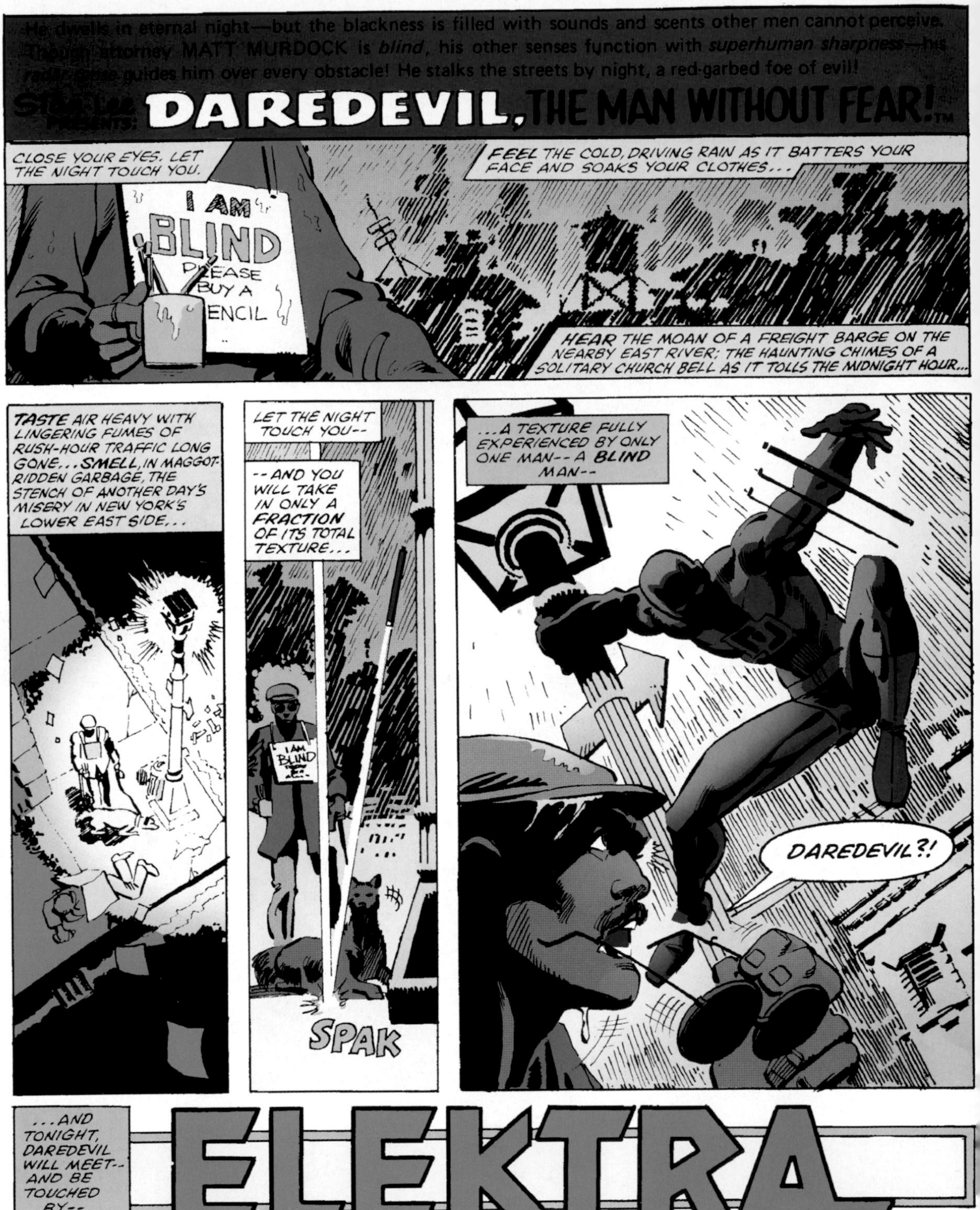
He dwells in eternal night—but the blackness is filled with sounds and scents other men cannot perceive. Though attorney MATT MURDOCK is blind, his other senses function with superhuman sharpness—his radar sense guides him over every obstacle! He stalks the streets by night, a red-garbed foe of evil!
Stan Lee PRESENTS: DAREDEVIL, THE MAN WITHOUT FEAR!™
CLOSE YOUR EYES. LET THE NIGHT TOUCH YOU.
I AM BLIND PLEASE BUY A PENCIL
FEEL THE COLD, DRIVING RAIN AS IT BATTERS YOUR FACE AND SOAKS YOUR CLOTHES...
HEAR THE MOAN OF A FREIGHT BARGE ON THE NEARBY EAST RIVER; THE HAUNTING CHIMES OF A SOLITARY CHURCH BELL AS IT TOLLS THE MIDNIGHT HOUR...
TASTE AIR HEAVY WITH LINGERING FUMES OF RUSH-HOUR TRAFFIC LONG GONE... SMELL, IN MAGGOT-RIDDEN GARBAGE, THE STENCH OF ANOTHER DAY'S MISERY IN NEW YORK'S LOWER EAST SIDE...
LET THE NIGHT TOUCH YOU--
--AND YOU WILL TAKE IN ONLY A FRACTION OF ITS TOTAL TEXTURE...
I AM BLIND
SPAK
...A TEXTURE FULLY EXPERIENCED BY ONLY ONE MAN--A BLIND MAN--
DAREDEVIL?!
...AND TONIGHT, DAREDEVIL WILL MEET--AND BE TOUCHED BY--
ELEKTRA

FRANK MILLER, ARTIST AND WRITER / KLAUS JANSON, INKER / EMBELLISHER / DR. MARTIN, COLORIST / JOE ROSEN, LETTERER / DENNY O'NEIL, EDITOR / JIM SHOOTER, ED-IN-CHIEF

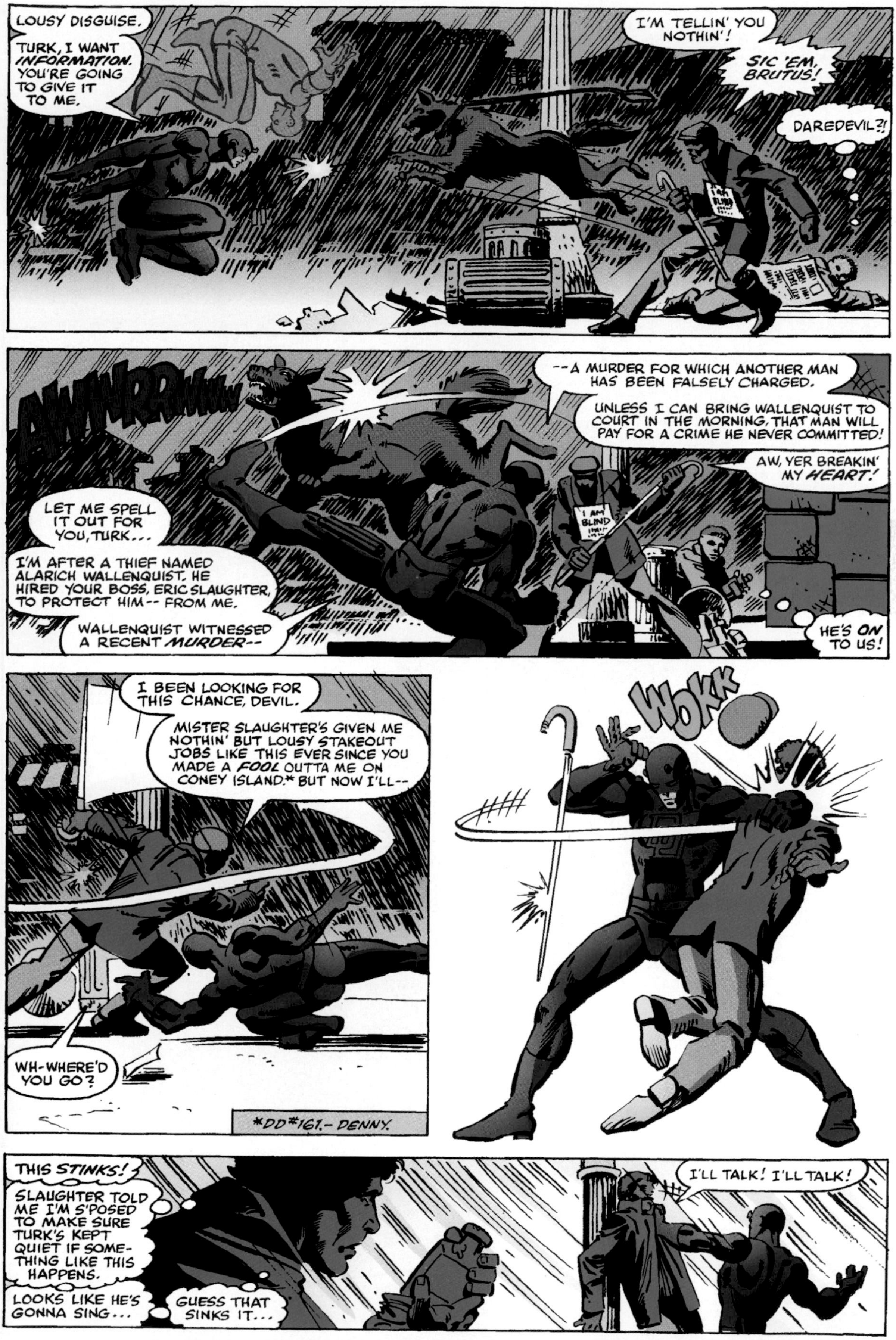
LOUSY DISGUISE.
TURK, I WANT *INFORMATION.* YOU'RE GOING TO GIVE IT TO ME.
I'M TELLIN' YOU NOTHIN'!
SIC 'EM, BRUTUS!
DAREDEVIL?!
AWWRRR
LET ME SPELL IT OUT FOR YOU, TURK...
I'M AFTER A THIEF NAMED ALARICH WALLENQUIST. HE HIRED YOUR BOSS, ERIC SLAUGHTER, TO PROTECT HIM-- FROM ME.
WALLENQUIST WITNESSED A RECENT *MURDER*--
--A MURDER FOR WHICH ANOTHER MAN HAS BEEN FALSELY CHARGED.
UNLESS I CAN BRING WALLENQUIST TO COURT IN THE MORNING, THAT MAN WILL PAY FOR A CRIME HE NEVER COMMITTED!
AW, YER BREAKIN' MY *HEART!*
I AM BLIND
HE'S *ON* TO US!
I BEEN LOOKING FOR THIS CHANCE, DEVIL.
MISTER SLAUGHTER'S GIVEN ME NOTHIN' BUT LOUSY STAKEOUT JOBS LIKE THIS EVER SINCE YOU MADE A *FOOL* OUTTA ME ON CONEY ISLAND.* BUT NOW I'LL--
WH-WHERE'D YOU GO?
*DD#161.- DENNY.
WOKK
THIS *STINKS!*
SLAUGHTER TOLD ME I'M S'POSED TO MAKE SURE TURK'S KEPT QUIET IF SOMETHING LIKE THIS HAPPENS.
LOOKS LIKE HE'S GONNA SING...
GUESS THAT SINKS IT...
I'LL TALK! I'LL TALK!

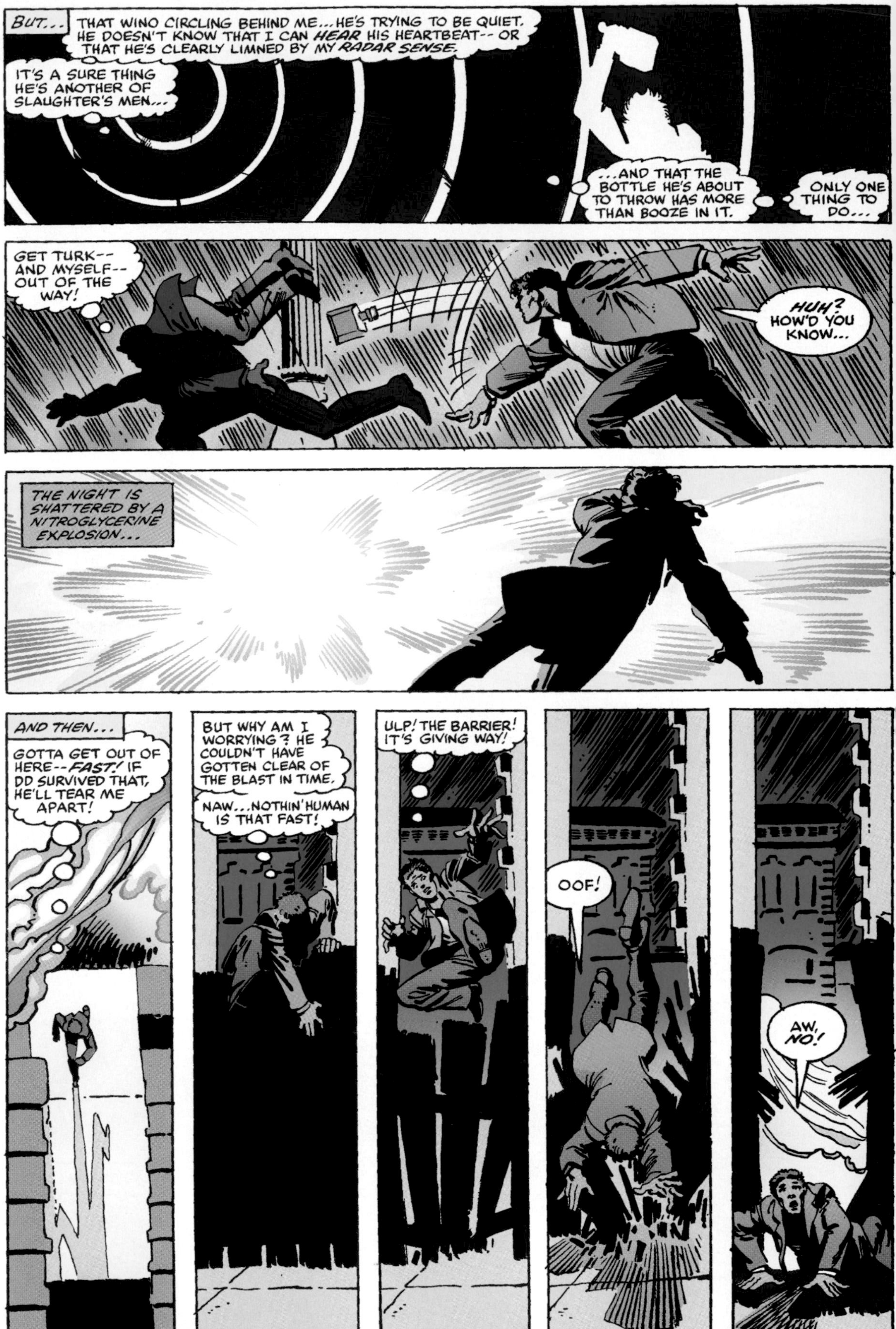
BUT...
THAT WINO CIRCLING BEHIND ME... HE'S TRYING TO BE QUIET. HE DOESN'T KNOW THAT I CAN HEAR HIS HEARTBEAT-- OR THAT HE'S CLEARLY LIMNED BY MY RADAR SENSE.
IT'S A SURE THING HE'S ANOTHER OF SLAUGHTER'S MEN...
...AND THAT THE BOTTLE HE'S ABOUT TO THROW HAS MORE THAN BOOZE IN IT.
ONLY ONE THING TO DO...
GET TURK-- AND MYSELF-- OUT OF THE WAY!
HUH? HOW'D YOU KNOW...
THE NIGHT IS SHATTERED BY A NITROGLYCERINE EXPLOSION...
AND THEN...
GOTTA GET OUT OF HERE--FAST! IF DD SURVIVED THAT, HE'LL TEAR ME APART!
BUT WHY AM I WORRYING? HE COULDN'T HAVE GOTTEN CLEAR OF THE BLAST IN TIME.
NAW... NOTHIN' HUMAN IS THAT FAST!
ULP! THE BARRIER! IT'S GIVING WAY!
OOF!
AW, NO!

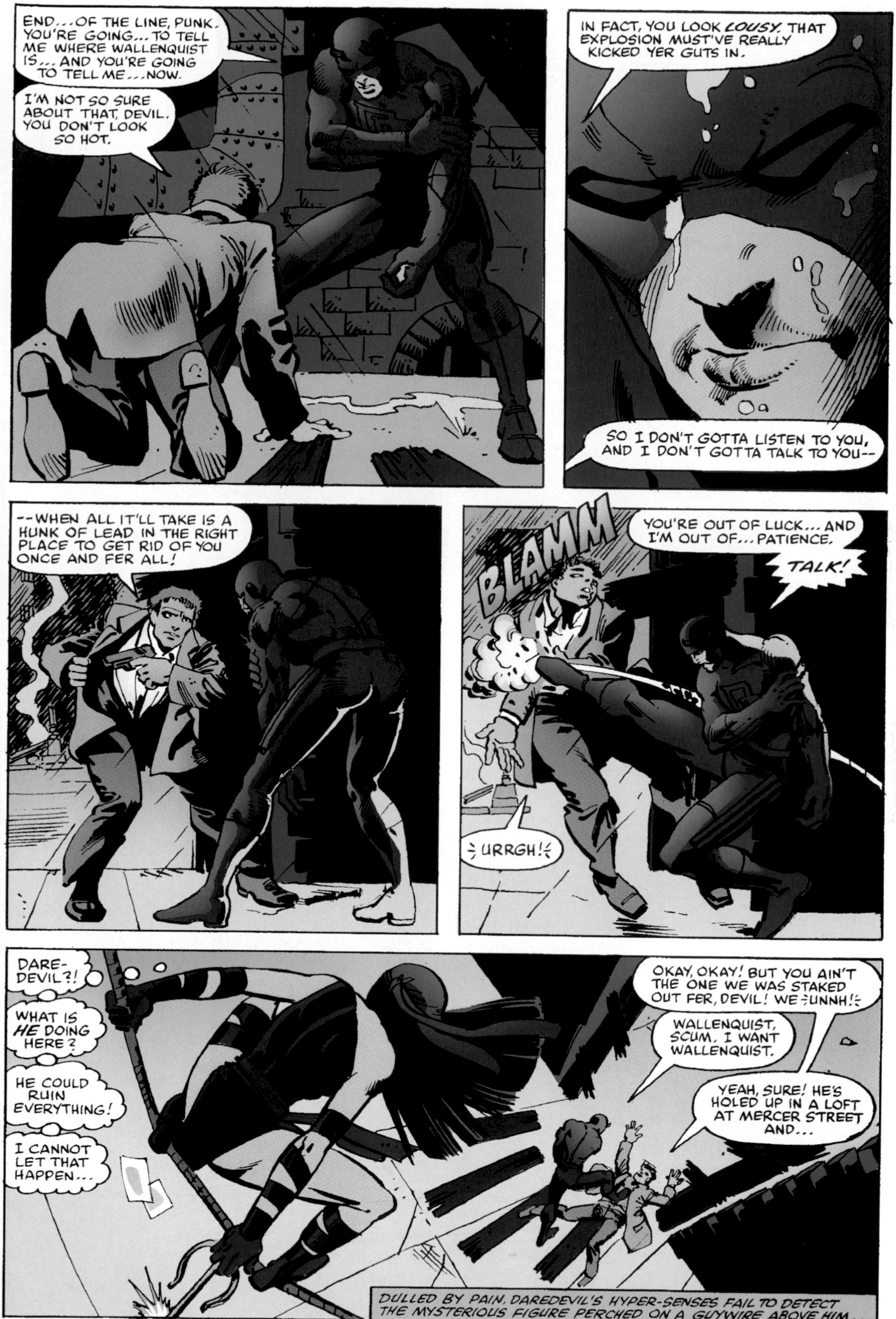

END... OF THE LINE, PUNK. YOU'RE GOING... TO TELL ME WHERE WALLENQUIST IS... AND YOU'RE GOING TO TELL ME... NOW.
I'M NOT SO SURE ABOUT THAT, DEVIL. YOU DON'T LOOK SO HOT.
IN FACT, YOU LOOK LOUSY. THAT EXPLOSION MUST'VE REALLY KICKED YER GUTS IN.
SO I DON'T GOTTA LISTEN TO YOU, AND I DON'T GOTTA TALK TO YOU--
--WHEN ALL IT'LL TAKE IS A HUNK OF LEAD IN THE RIGHT PLACE TO GET RID OF YOU ONCE AND FER ALL!
BLAMM
YOU'RE OUT OF LUCK... AND I'M OUT OF... PATIENCE.
TALK!
URRGH!
DARE-DEVIL?!
WHAT IS HE DOING HERE?
HE COULD RUIN EVERYTHING!
I CANNOT LET THAT HAPPEN...
OKAY, OKAY! BUT YOU AIN'T THE ONE WE WAS STAKED OUT FER, DEVIL! WE UNNH!
WALLENQUIST, SCUM. I WANT WALLENQUIST.
YEAH, SURE! HE'S HOLED UP IN A LOFT AT MERCER STREET AND...
DULLED BY PAIN, DAREDEVIL'S HYPER-SENSES FAIL TO DETECT THE MYSTERIOUS FIGURE PERCHED ON A GUYWIRE ABOVE HIM...

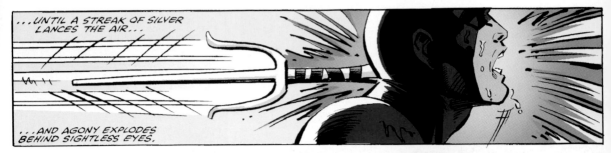

...UNTIL A STREAK OF SILVER LANCES THE AIR...

...AND AGONY EXPLODES BEHIND SIGHTLESS EYES.

HE REELS, DIMLY AWARE OF A WOMAN'S FORM--

--A MOMENT BEFORE SHE STRIKES HIM A BLOW THAT ROCKS HIS BRAIN AND STRETCHES THE CORDS IN HIS NECK.

HE FALLS. HE STRUGGLES TO REMAIN CONSCIOUS. SOMEHOW, HE HEARS FLEEING FOOTSTEPS...

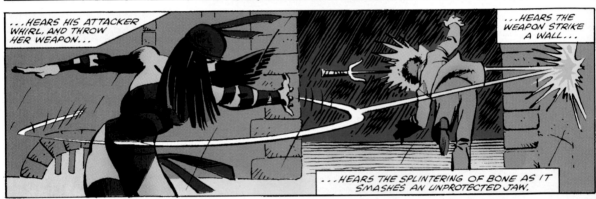

...HEARS HIS ATTACKER WHIRL, AND THROW HER WEAPON...

...HEARS THE WEAPON STRIKE A WALL...

...HEARS THE SPLINTERING OF BONE AS IT SMASHES AN UNPROTECTED JAW.

THEN, HE HEARS HER SPEAK...

THERE IS A BOUNTY OUT IN EUROPE FOR ALARICH WALLENQUIST, BILGE--

-- A BOUNTY I INTEND TO COLLECT.

YOU ARE GOING TO HELP ME CAPTURE HIM, OR I AM GOING TO KILL YOU.

IT IS AS SIMPLE AS THAT.

THAT VOICE--

ELEKTRA?!

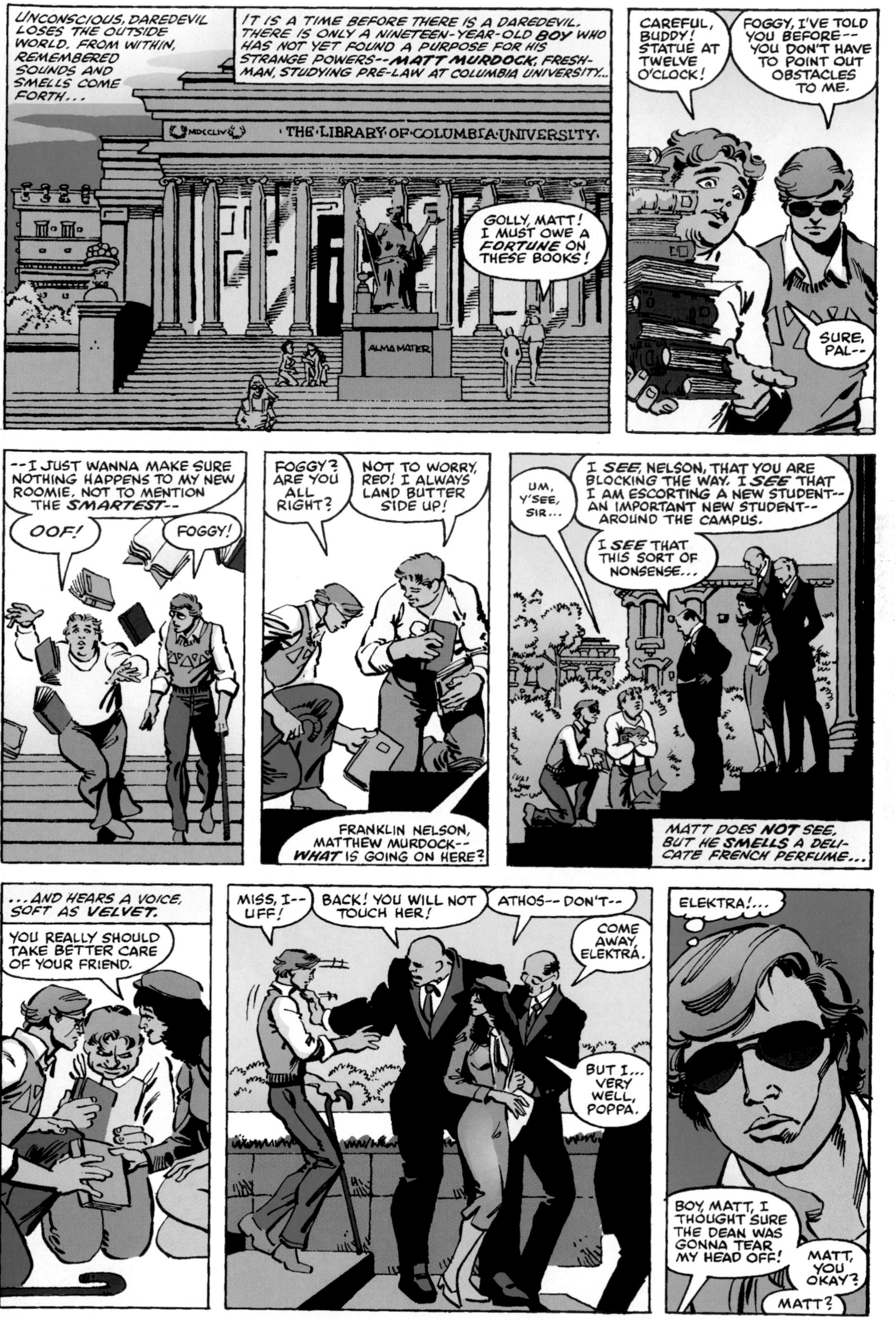
UNCONSCIOUS, DAREDEVIL LOSES THE OUTSIDE WORLD. FROM WITHIN, REMEMBERED SOUNDS AND SMELLS COME FORTH...
IT IS A TIME BEFORE THERE IS A DAREDEVIL. THERE IS ONLY A NINETEEN-YEAR-OLD BOY WHO HAS NOT YET FOUND A PURPOSE FOR HIS STRANGE POWERS--MATT MURDOCK, FRESHMAN, STUDYING PRE-LAW AT COLUMBIA UNIVERSITY...
MDCCLIV
THE·LIBRARY·OF·COLUMBIA·UNIVERSITY
ALMA MATER
GOLLY, MATT! I MUST OWE A FORTUNE ON THESE BOOKS!
CAREFUL, BUDDY! STATUE AT TWELVE O'CLOCK!
FOGGY, I'VE TOLD YOU BEFORE-- YOU DON'T HAVE TO POINT OUT OBSTACLES TO ME.
SURE, PAL--
--I JUST WANNA MAKE SURE NOTHING HAPPENS TO MY NEW ROOMIE, NOT TO MENTION THE SMARTEST--
OOF!
FOGGY!
FOGGY? ARE YOU ALL RIGHT?
NOT TO WORRY, RED! I ALWAYS LAND BUTTER SIDE UP!
FRANKLIN NELSON, MATTHEW MURDOCK-- WHAT IS GOING ON HERE?
UM, Y'SEE, SIR...
I SEE, NELSON, THAT YOU ARE BLOCKING THE WAY. I SEE THAT I AM ESCORTING A NEW STUDENT-- AN IMPORTANT NEW STUDENT-- AROUND THE CAMPUS.
I SEE THAT THIS SORT OF NONSENSE...
MATT DOES NOT SEE, BUT HE SMELLS A DELICATE FRENCH PERFUME...
...AND HEARS A VOICE, SOFT AS VELVET.
YOU REALLY SHOULD TAKE BETTER CARE OF YOUR FRIEND.
MISS, I-- UFF!
BACK! YOU WILL NOT TOUCH HER!
ATHOS-- DON'T--
COME AWAY, ELEKTRA.
BUT I... VERY WELL, POPPA.
ELEKTRA!...
BOY, MATT, I THOUGHT SURE THE DEAN WAS GONNA TEAR MY HEAD OFF!
MATT, YOU OKAY?
MATT?

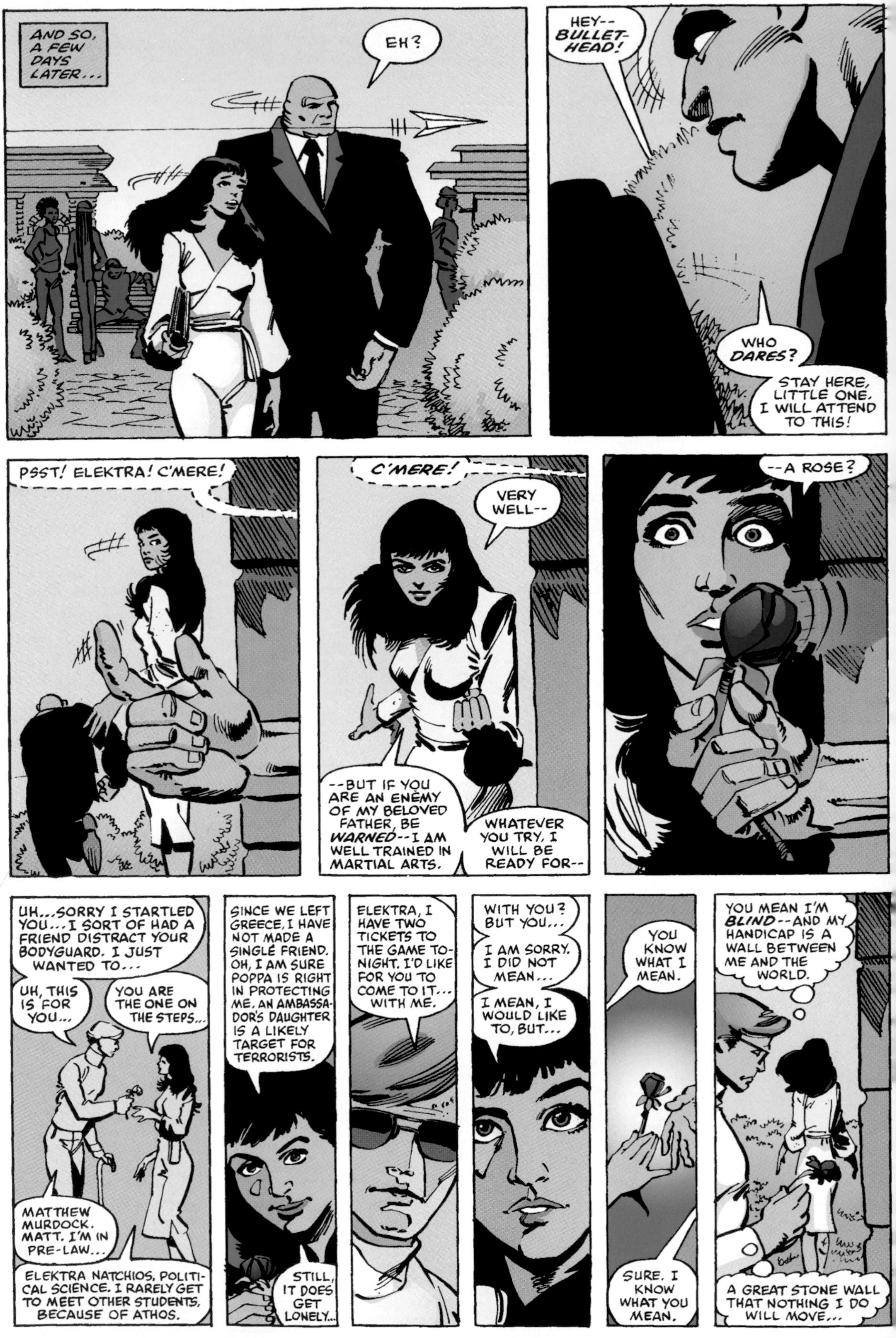
AND SO, A FEW DAYS LATER...
EH?
HEY-- BULLET-HEAD!
WHO DARES?
STAY HERE, LITTLE ONE. I WILL ATTEND TO THIS!
PSST! ELEKTRA! C'MERE!
C'MERE!
VERY WELL--
--BUT IF YOU ARE AN ENEMY OF MY BELOVED FATHER, BE WARNED--I AM WELL TRAINED IN MARTIAL ARTS.
WHATEVER YOU TRY, I WILL BE READY FOR--
--A ROSE?
UH...SORRY I STARTLED YOU...I SORT OF HAD A FRIEND DISTRACT YOUR BODYGUARD. I JUST WANTED TO...
UH, THIS IS FOR YOU...
YOU ARE THE ONE ON THE STEPS...
MATTHEW MURDOCK. MATT. I'M IN PRE-LAW...
ELEKTRA NATCHIOS, POLITICAL SCIENCE. I RARELY GET TO MEET OTHER STUDENTS, BECAUSE OF ATHOS.
SINCE WE LEFT GREECE, I HAVE NOT MADE A SINGLE FRIEND. OH, I AM SURE POPPA IS RIGHT IN PROTECTING ME. AN AMBASSADOR'S DAUGHTER IS A LIKELY TARGET FOR TERRORISTS.
STILL, IT DOES GET LONELY...
ELEKTRA, I HAVE TWO TICKETS TO THE GAME TONIGHT. I'D LIKE FOR YOU TO COME TO IT... WITH ME.
WITH YOU? BUT YOU...
I AM SORRY. I DID NOT MEAN...
I MEAN, I WOULD LIKE TO, BUT...
YOU KNOW WHAT I MEAN.
SURE. I KNOW WHAT YOU MEAN.
YOU MEAN I'M BLIND--AND MY HANDICAP IS A WALL BETWEEN ME AND THE WORLD.
A GREAT STONE WALL THAT NOTHING I DO WILL MOVE...

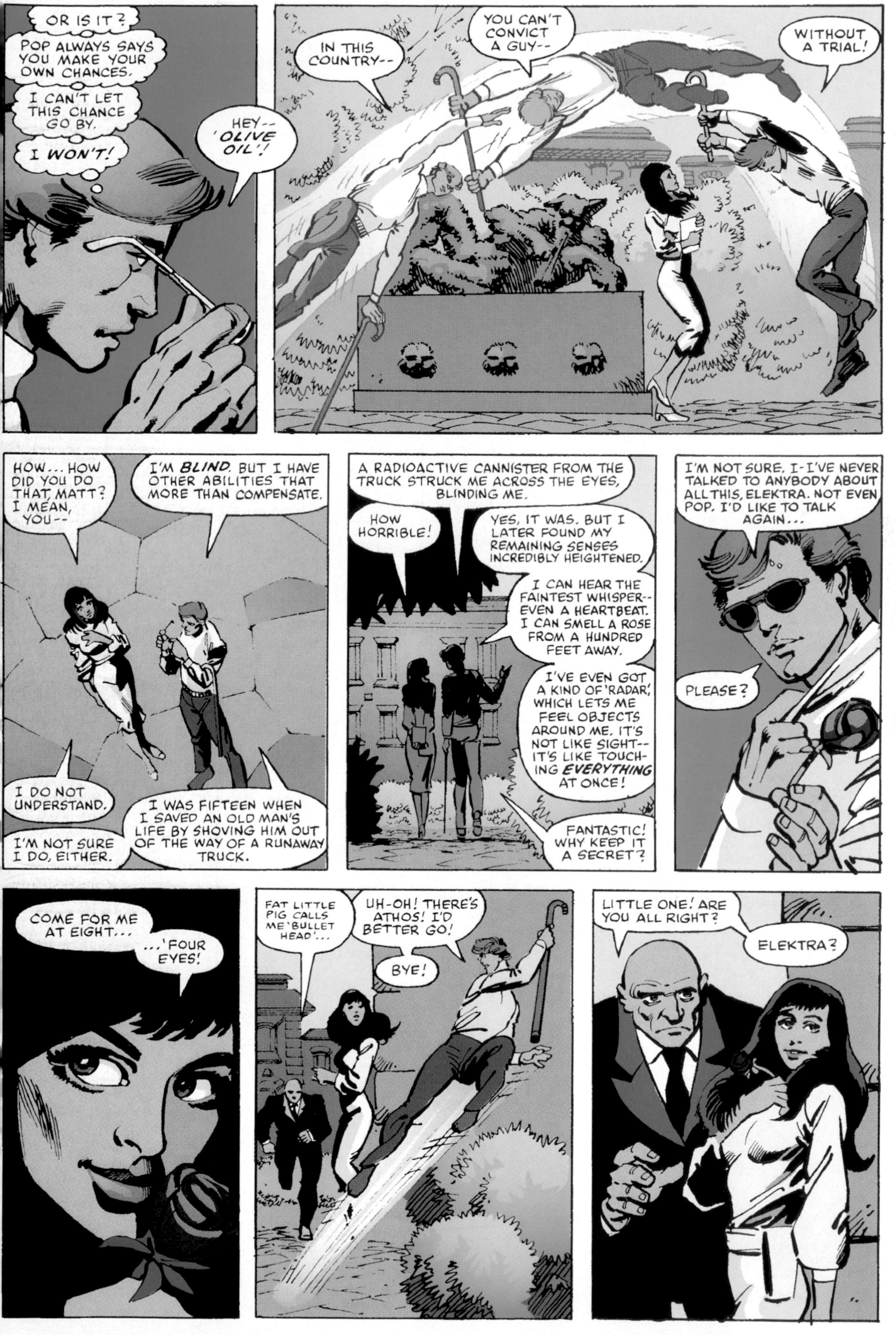
OR IS IT?
POP ALWAYS SAYS YOU MAKE YOUR OWN CHANCES.
I CAN'T LET THIS CHANCE GO BY.
I WON'T!
HEY-- 'OLIVE OIL'!
IN THIS COUNTRY--
YOU CAN'T CONVICT A GUY--
WITHOUT A TRIAL!
HOW... HOW DID YOU DO THAT, MATT? I MEAN, YOU--
I'M BLIND. BUT I HAVE OTHER ABILITIES THAT MORE THAN COMPENSATE.
I DO NOT UNDERSTAND.
I'M NOT SURE I DO, EITHER.
I WAS FIFTEEN WHEN I SAVED AN OLD MAN'S LIFE BY SHOVING HIM OUT OF THE WAY OF A RUNAWAY TRUCK.
A RADIOACTIVE CANNISTER FROM THE TRUCK STRUCK ME ACROSS THE EYES, BLINDING ME.
HOW HORRIBLE!
YES, IT WAS. BUT I LATER FOUND MY REMAINING SENSES INCREDIBLY HEIGHTENED.
I CAN HEAR THE FAINTEST WHISPER-- EVEN A HEARTBEAT. I CAN SMELL A ROSE FROM A HUNDRED FEET AWAY.
I'VE EVEN GOT A KIND OF 'RADAR', WHICH LETS ME FEEL OBJECTS AROUND ME. IT'S NOT LIKE SIGHT-- IT'S LIKE TOUCHING EVERYTHING AT ONCE!
FANTASTIC! WHY KEEP IT A SECRET?
I'M NOT SURE. I-I'VE NEVER TALKED TO ANYBODY ABOUT ALL THIS, ELEKTRA. NOT EVEN POP. I'D LIKE TO TALK AGAIN...
PLEASE?
COME FOR ME AT EIGHT...
...'FOUR EYES!
FAT LITTLE PIG CALLS ME 'BULLET HEAD'...
UH-OH! THERE'S ATHOS! I'D BETTER GO!
BYE!
LITTLE ONE! ARE YOU ALL RIGHT?
ELEKTRA?

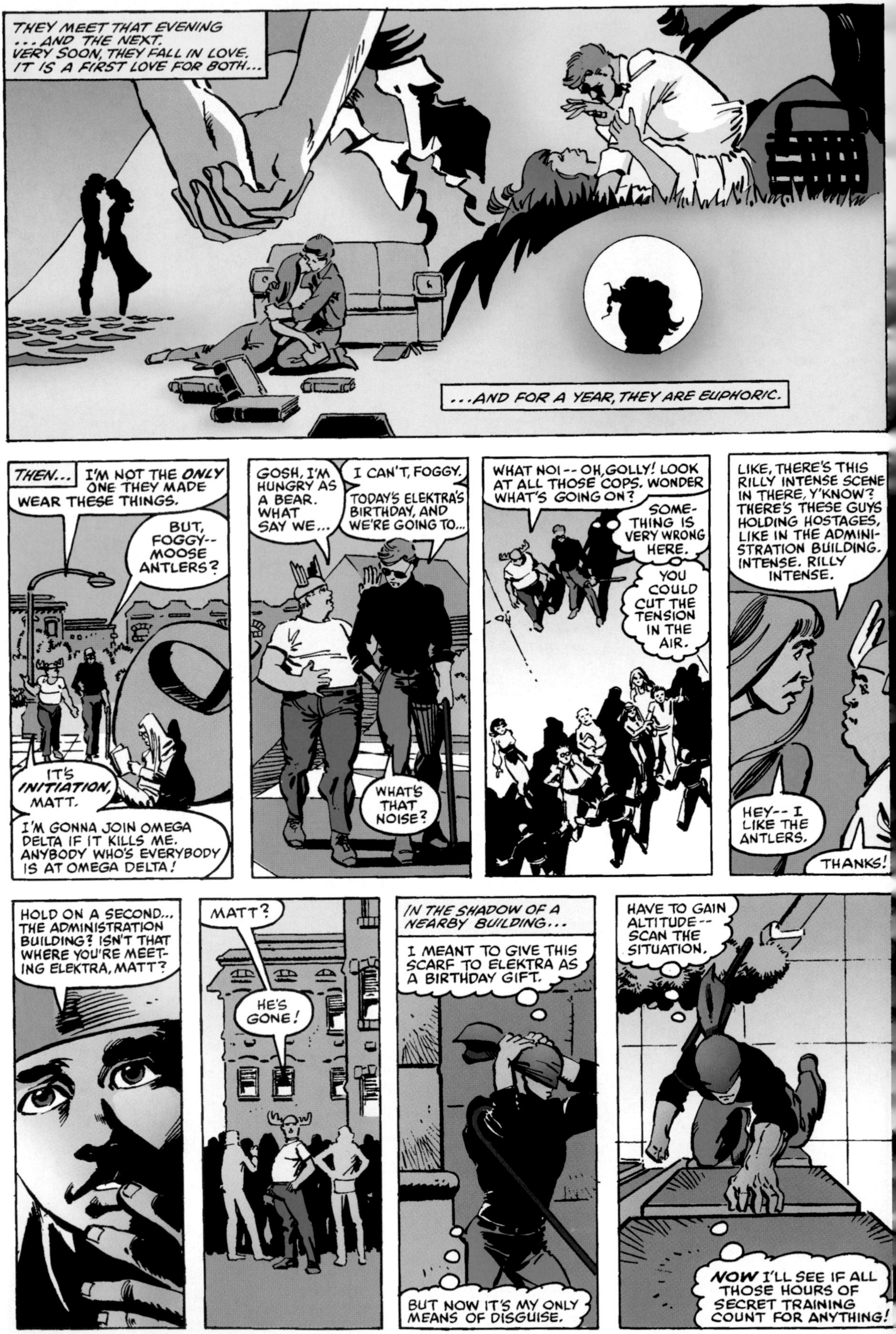

THEY MEET THAT EVENING ...AND THE NEXT. VERY SOON, THEY FALL IN LOVE. IT IS A FIRST LOVE FOR BOTH...
...AND FOR A YEAR, THEY ARE EUPHORIC.
THEN...
I'M NOT THE ONLY ONE THEY MADE WEAR THESE THINGS.
BUT, FOGGY-- MOOSE ANTLERS?
IT'S INITIATION, MATT.
I'M GONNA JOIN OMEGA DELTA IF IT KILLS ME. ANYBODY WHO'S EVERYBODY IS AT OMEGA DELTA!
GOSH, I'M HUNGRY AS A BEAR. WHAT SAY WE...
I CAN'T, FOGGY.
TODAY'S ELEKTRA'S BIRTHDAY, AND WE'RE GOING TO...
WHAT'S THAT NOISE?
WHAT NOI-- OH, GOLLY! LOOK AT ALL THOSE COPS. WONDER WHAT'S GOING ON?
SOMETHING IS VERY WRONG HERE.
YOU COULD CUT THE TENSION IN THE AIR.
LIKE, THERE'S THIS RILLY INTENSE SCENE IN THERE, Y'KNOW? THERE'S THESE GUYS HOLDING HOSTAGES, LIKE IN THE ADMINISTRATION BUILDING. INTENSE. RILLY INTENSE.
HEY-- I LIKE THE ANTLERS.
THANKS!
HOLD ON A SECOND... THE ADMINISTRATION BUILDING? ISN'T THAT WHERE YOU'RE MEETING ELEKTRA, MATT?
MATT?
HE'S GONE!
IN THE SHADOW OF A NEARBY BUILDING...
I MEANT TO GIVE THIS SCARF TO ELEKTRA AS A BIRTHDAY GIFT.
BUT NOW IT'S MY ONLY MEANS OF DISGUISE.
HAVE TO GAIN ALTITUDE-- SCAN THE SITUATION.
NOW I'LL SEE IF ALL THOSE HOURS OF SECRET TRAINING COUNT FOR ANYTHING!

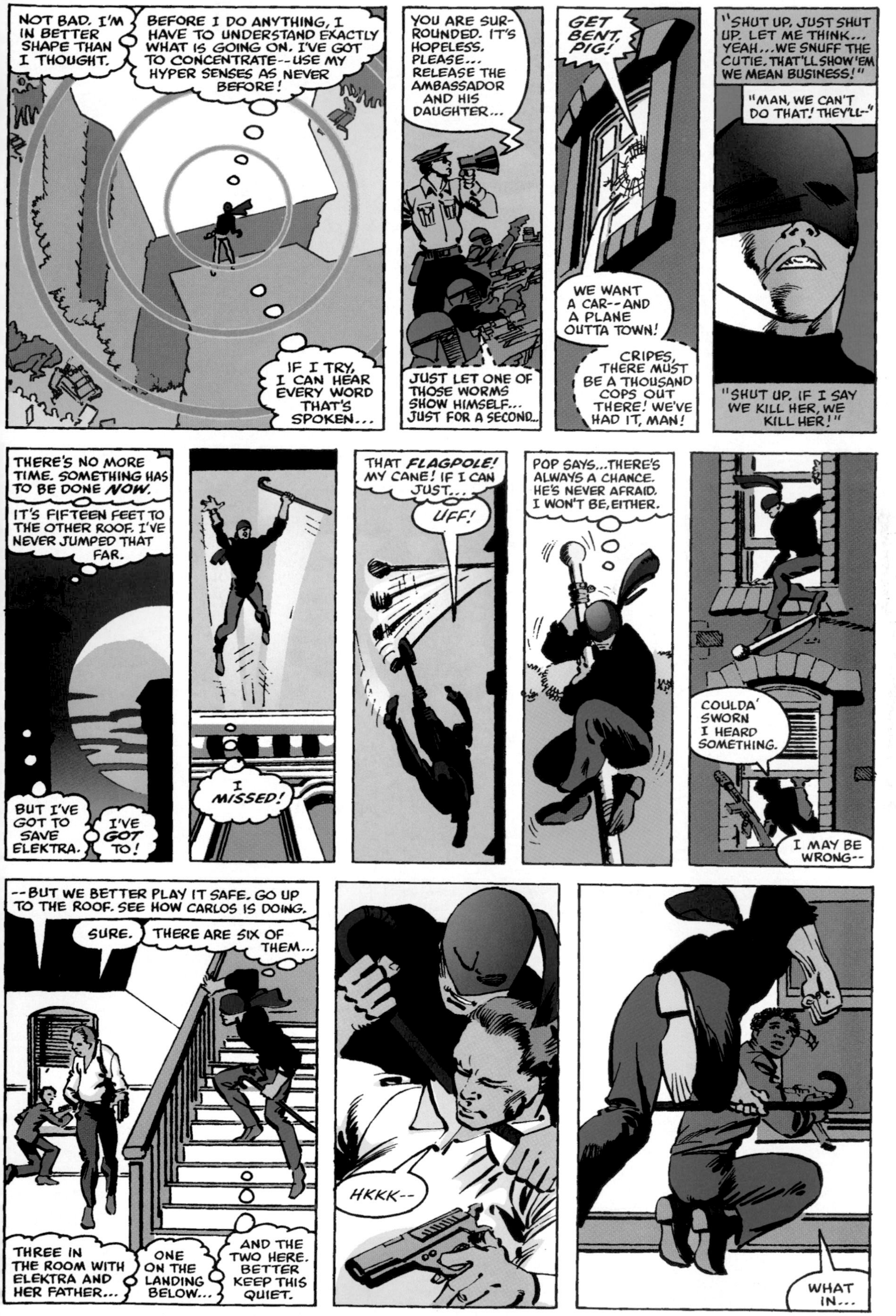
NOT BAD. I'M IN BETTER SHAPE THAN I THOUGHT.
BEFORE I DO ANYTHING, I HAVE TO UNDERSTAND EXACTLY WHAT IS GOING ON. I'VE GOT TO CONCENTRATE--USE MY HYPER SENSES AS NEVER BEFORE!
IF I TRY, I CAN HEAR EVERY WORD THAT'S SPOKEN...
YOU ARE SURROUNDED. IT'S HOPELESS. PLEASE... RELEASE THE AMBASSADOR AND HIS DAUGHTER...
JUST LET ONE OF THOSE WORMS SHOW HIMSELF... JUST FOR A SECOND...
GET BENT, PIG!
WE WANT A CAR--AND A PLANE OUTTA TOWN!
CRIPES, THERE MUST BE A THOUSAND COPS OUT THERE! WE'VE HAD IT, MAN!
"SHUT UP. JUST SHUT UP. LET ME THINK... YEAH... WE SNUFF THE CUTIE. THAT'LL SHOW 'EM WE MEAN BUSINESS!"
"MAN, WE CAN'T DO THAT! THEY'LL--"
"SHUT UP. IF I SAY WE KILL HER, WE KILL HER!"
THERE'S NO MORE TIME. SOMETHING HAS TO BE DONE NOW.
IT'S FIFTEEN FEET TO THE OTHER ROOF. I'VE NEVER JUMPED THAT FAR.
BUT I'VE GOT TO SAVE ELEKTRA.
I'VE GOT TO!
I MISSED!
THAT FLAGPOLE! MY CANE! IF I CAN JUST...
UFF!
POP SAYS...THERE'S ALWAYS A CHANCE. HE'S NEVER AFRAID. I WON'T BE, EITHER.
COULDA' SWORN I HEARD SOMETHING.
I MAY BE WRONG--
--BUT WE BETTER PLAY IT SAFE. GO UP TO THE ROOF. SEE HOW CARLOS IS DOING.
SURE.
THERE ARE SIX OF THEM...
THREE IN THE ROOM WITH ELEKTRA AND HER FATHER...
ONE ON THE LANDING BELOW...
AND THE TWO HERE. BETTER KEEP THIS QUIET.
HKKK--
WHAT IN...

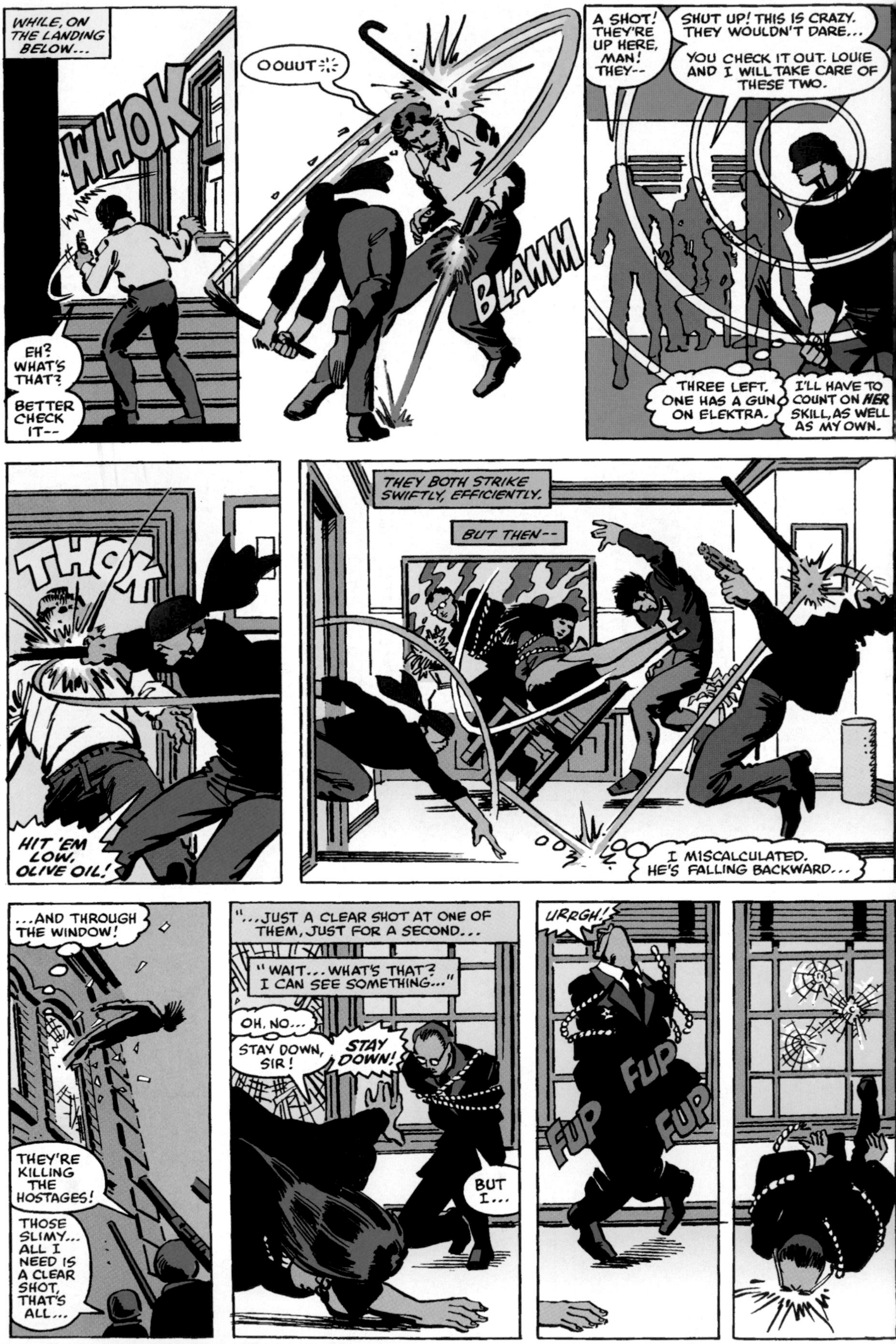

WHILE, ON THE LANDING BELOW...
WHOK
EH? WHAT'S THAT?
BETTER CHECK IT--
OOUUT
BLAMM
A SHOT! THEY'RE UP HERE, MAN! THEY--
SHUT UP! THIS IS CRAZY. THEY WOULDN'T DARE...
YOU CHECK IT OUT. LOUIE AND I WILL TAKE CARE OF THESE TWO.
THREE LEFT. ONE HAS A GUN ON ELEKTRA.
I'LL HAVE TO COUNT ON HER SKILL, AS WELL AS MY OWN.
THOK
HIT 'EM LOW, OLIVE OIL!
THEY BOTH STRIKE SWIFTLY, EFFICIENTLY.
BUT THEN--
I MISCALCULATED. HE'S FALLING BACKWARD...
...AND THROUGH THE WINDOW!
THEY'RE KILLING THE HOSTAGES!
THOSE SLIMY... ALL I NEED IS A CLEAR SHOT, THAT'S ALL...
"...JUST A CLEAR SHOT AT ONE OF THEM, JUST FOR A SECOND...
"WAIT... WHAT'S THAT? I CAN SEE SOMETHING..."
OH, NO...
STAY DOWN, SIR!
STAY DOWN!
BUT I...
URRGH!
FUP
FUP
FUP

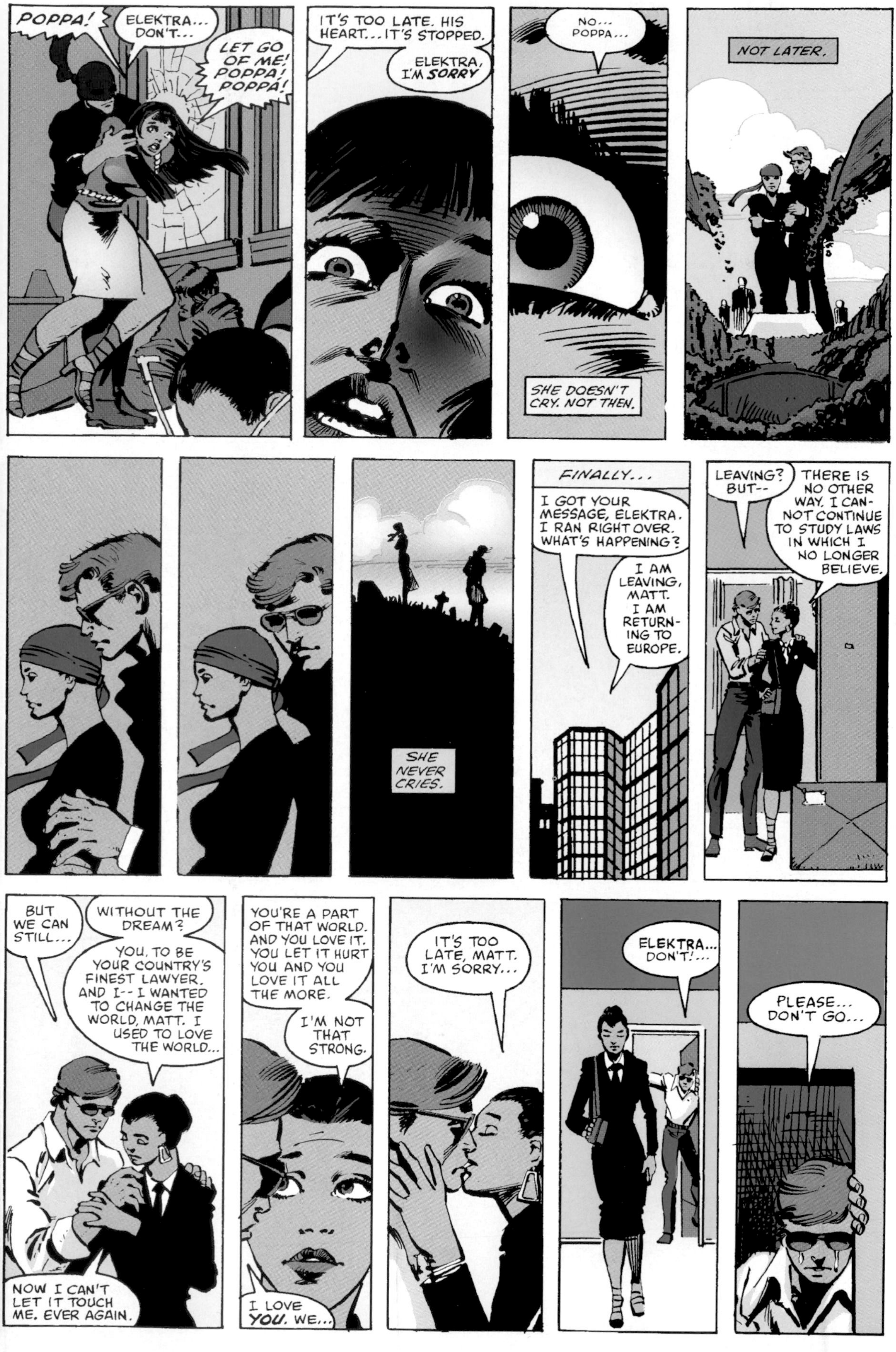

POPPA!
ELEKTRA... DON'T...
LET GO OF ME! POPPA! POPPA!
IT'S TOO LATE. HIS HEART... IT'S STOPPED.
ELEKTRA, I'M SORRY
NO... POPPA...
SHE DOESN'T CRY. NOT THEN.
NOT LATER.
SHE NEVER CRIES.
FINALLY...
I GOT YOUR MESSAGE, ELEKTRA. I RAN RIGHT OVER. WHAT'S HAPPENING?
I AM LEAVING, MATT. I AM RETURNING TO EUROPE.
LEAVING? BUT--
THERE IS NO OTHER WAY. I CANNOT CONTINUE TO STUDY LAWS IN WHICH I NO LONGER BELIEVE.
BUT WE CAN STILL...
WITHOUT THE DREAM?
YOU, TO BE YOUR COUNTRY'S FINEST LAWYER. AND I-- I WANTED TO CHANGE THE WORLD, MATT. I USED TO LOVE THE WORLD...
NOW I CAN'T LET IT TOUCH ME. EVER AGAIN.
YOU'RE A PART OF THAT WORLD. AND YOU LOVE IT. YOU LET IT HURT YOU AND YOU LOVE IT ALL THE MORE.
I'M NOT THAT STRONG.
I LOVE YOU. WE...
IT'S TOO LATE, MATT. I'M SORRY...
ELEKTRA... DON'T!...
PLEASE... DON'T GO...

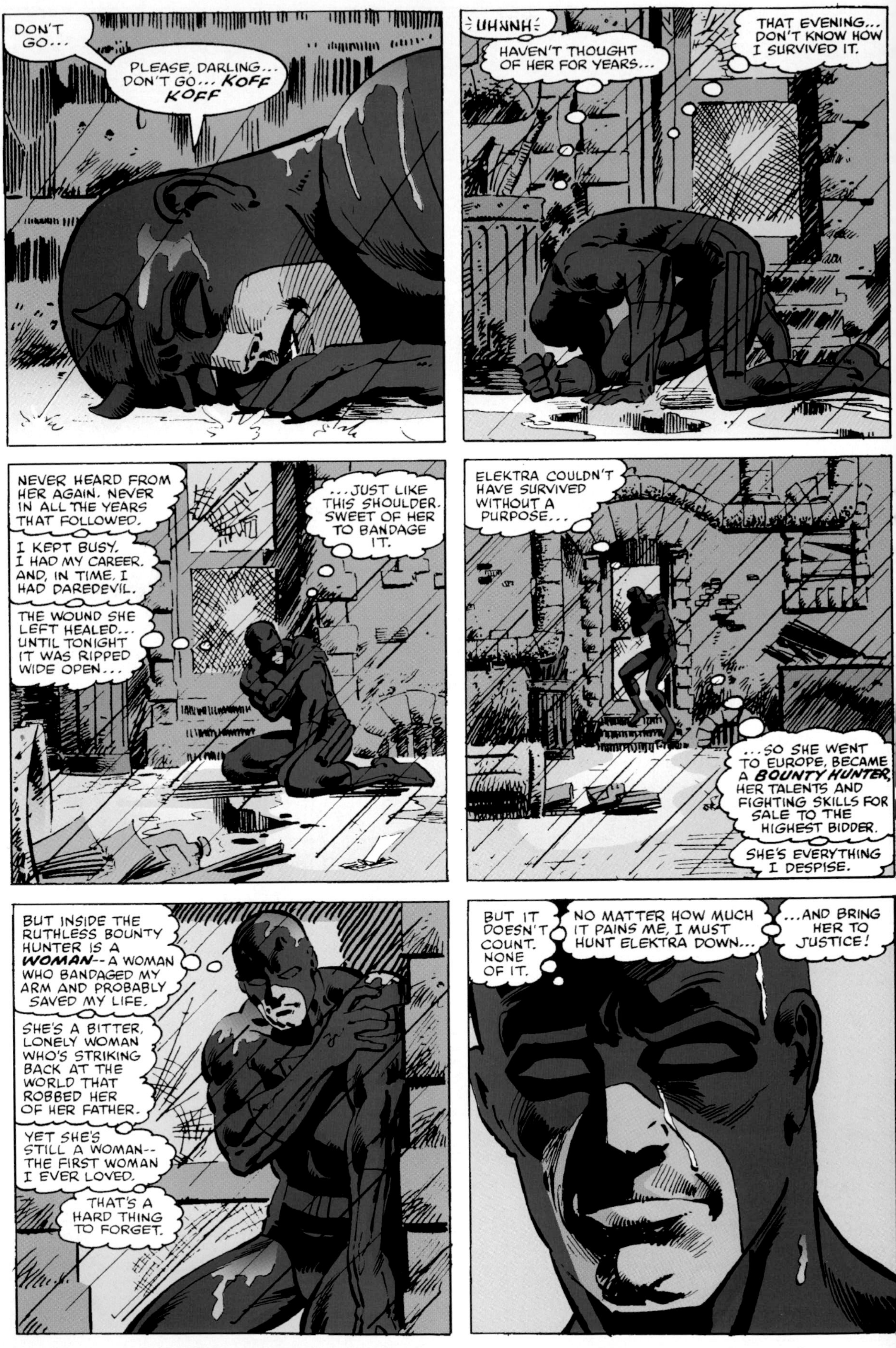
DON'T GO...
PLEASE, DARLING... DON'T GO... KOFF KOFF
UHNNH
HAVEN'T THOUGHT OF HER FOR YEARS...
THAT EVENING... DON'T KNOW HOW I SURVIVED IT.
NEVER HEARD FROM HER AGAIN. NEVER IN ALL THE YEARS THAT FOLLOWED.
I KEPT BUSY. I HAD MY CAREER. AND, IN TIME, I HAD DAREDEVIL.
THE WOUND SHE LEFT HEALED... UNTIL TONIGHT IT WAS RIPPED WIDE OPEN...
...JUST LIKE THIS SHOULDER. SWEET OF HER TO BANDAGE IT.
ELEKTRA COULDN'T HAVE SURVIVED WITHOUT A PURPOSE...
...SO SHE WENT TO EUROPE, BECAME A BOUNTY HUNTER, HER TALENTS AND FIGHTING SKILLS FOR SALE TO THE HIGHEST BIDDER.
SHE'S EVERYTHING I DESPISE.
BUT INSIDE THE RUTHLESS BOUNTY HUNTER IS A WOMAN-- A WOMAN WHO BANDAGED MY ARM AND PROBABLY SAVED MY LIFE.
SHE'S A BITTER, LONELY WOMAN WHO'S STRIKING BACK AT THE WORLD THAT ROBBED HER OF HER FATHER.
YET SHE'S STILL A WOMAN-- THE FIRST WOMAN I EVER LOVED.
THAT'S A HARD THING TO FORGET.
BUT IT DOESN'T COUNT. NONE OF IT.
NO MATTER HOW MUCH IT PAINS ME, I MUST HUNT ELEKTRA DOWN...
...AND BRING HER TO JUSTICE!

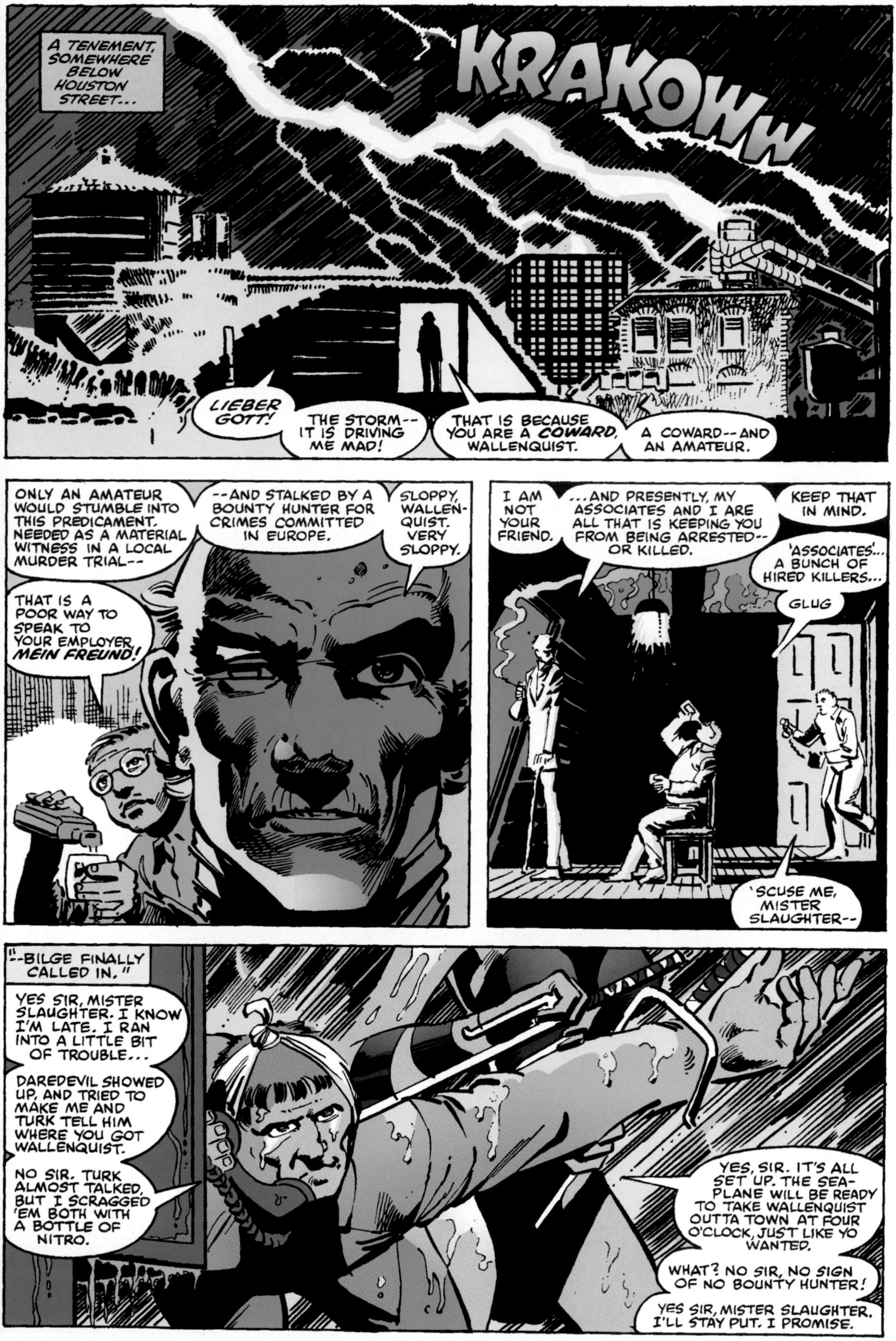
A TENEMENT, SOMEWHERE BELOW HOUSTON STREET...
KRAKOWW
LIEBER GOTT!
THE STORM-- IT IS DRIVING ME MAD!
THAT IS BECAUSE YOU ARE A COWARD, WALLENQUIST.
A COWARD--AND AN AMATEUR.
ONLY AN AMATEUR WOULD STUMBLE INTO THIS PREDICAMENT. NEEDED AS A MATERIAL WITNESS IN A LOCAL MURDER TRIAL--
--AND STALKED BY A BOUNTY HUNTER FOR CRIMES COMMITTED IN EUROPE.
SLOPPY, WALLENQUIST. VERY SLOPPY.
THAT IS A POOR WAY TO SPEAK TO YOUR EMPLOYER, MEIN FREUND!
I AM NOT YOUR FRIEND.
...AND PRESENTLY, MY ASSOCIATES AND I ARE ALL THAT IS KEEPING YOU FROM BEING ARRESTED-- OR KILLED.
KEEP THAT IN MIND.
'ASSOCIATES'... A BUNCH OF HIRED KILLERS...
GLUG
'SCUSE ME, MISTER SLAUGHTER--
"--BILGE FINALLY CALLED IN."
YES SIR, MISTER SLAUGHTER. I KNOW I'M LATE. I RAN INTO A LITTLE BIT OF TROUBLE...
DAREDEVIL SHOWED UP, AND TRIED TO MAKE ME AND TURK TELL HIM WHERE YOU GOT WALLENQUIST.
NO SIR. TURK ALMOST TALKED, BUT I SCRAGGED 'EM BOTH WITH A BOTTLE OF NITRO.
YES, SIR. IT'S ALL SET UP. THE SEA-PLANE WILL BE READY TO TAKE WALLENQUIST OUTTA TOWN AT FOUR O'CLOCK, JUST LIKE YO WANTED.
WHAT? NO SIR, NO SIGN OF NO BOUNTY HUNTER!
YES SIR, MISTER SLAUGHTER. I'LL STAY PUT. I PROMISE.

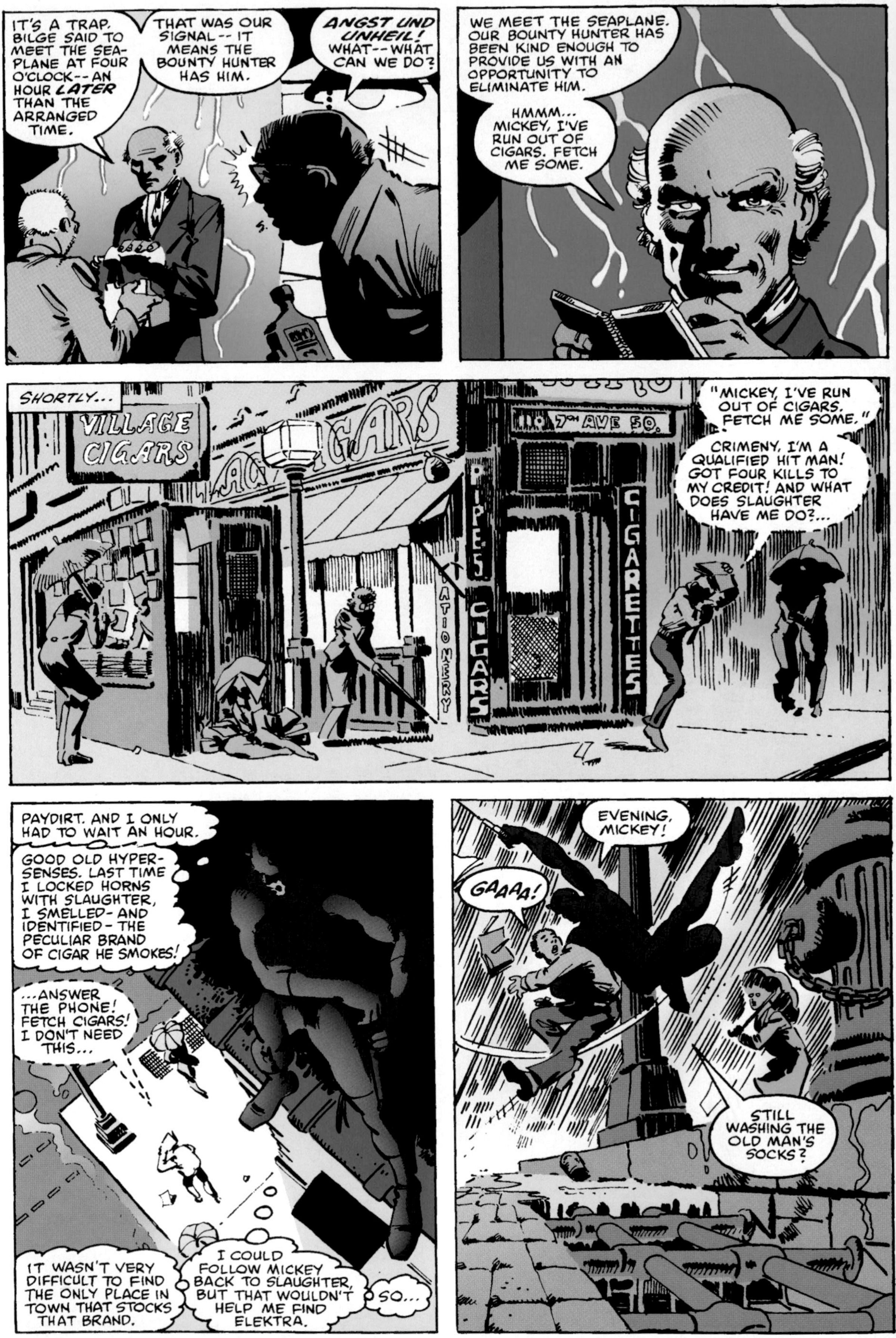
IT'S A TRAP. BILGE SAID TO MEET THE SEA-PLANE AT FOUR O'CLOCK--AN HOUR LATER THAN THE ARRANGED TIME.
THAT WAS OUR SIGNAL--IT MEANS THE BOUNTY HUNTER HAS HIM.
ANGST UND UNHEIL! WHAT--WHAT CAN WE DO?
WE MEET THE SEAPLANE. OUR BOUNTY HUNTER HAS BEEN KIND ENOUGH TO PROVIDE US WITH AN OPPORTUNITY TO ELIMINATE HIM.
HMMM... MICKEY, I'VE RUN OUT OF CIGARS. FETCH ME SOME.
SHORTLY...
VILLAGE CIGARS
7TH AVE SO.
PIPES
CIGARS
CIGARETTES
STATIONERY
"MICKEY, I'VE RUN OUT OF CIGARS. FETCH ME SOME."
CRIMENY, I'M A QUALIFIED HIT MAN! GOT FOUR KILLS TO MY CREDIT! AND WHAT DOES SLAUGHTER HAVE ME DO?...
PAYDIRT. AND I ONLY HAD TO WAIT AN HOUR.
GOOD OLD HYPER-SENSES. LAST TIME I LOCKED HORNS WITH SLAUGHTER, I SMELLED- AND IDENTIFIED- THE PECULIAR BRAND OF CIGAR HE SMOKES!
...ANSWER THE PHONE! FETCH CIGARS! I DON'T NEED THIS...
IT WASN'T VERY DIFFICULT TO FIND THE ONLY PLACE IN TOWN THAT STOCKS THAT BRAND.
I COULD FOLLOW MICKEY BACK TO SLAUGHTER, BUT THAT WOULDN'T HELP ME FIND ELEKTRA.
SO...
EVENING, MICKEY!
GAAAA!
STILL WASHING THE OLD MAN'S SOCKS?

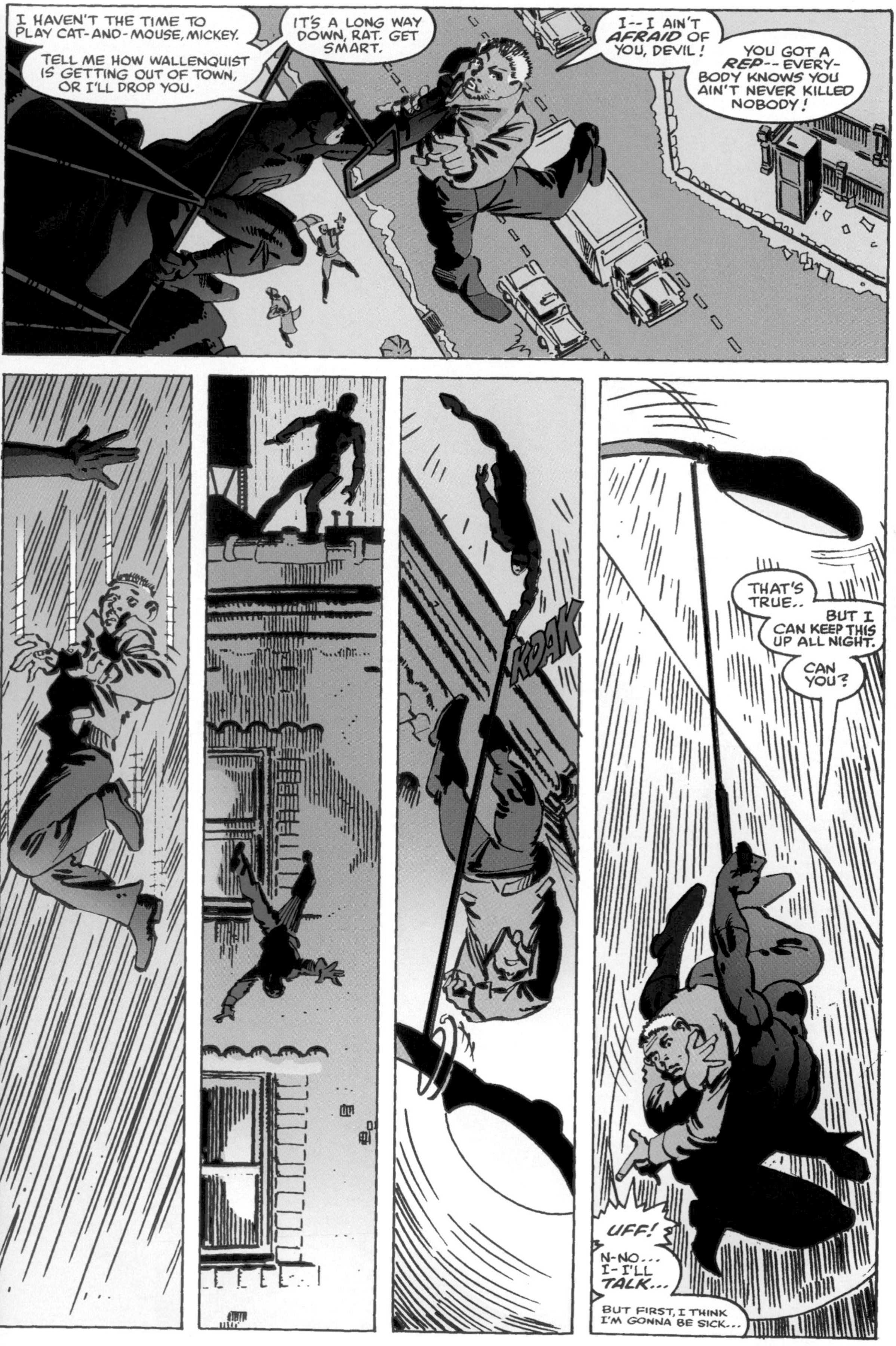
I HAVEN'T THE TIME TO PLAY CAT-AND-MOUSE, MICKEY.
TELL ME HOW WALLENQUIST IS GETTING OUT OF TOWN, OR I'LL DROP YOU.
IT'S A LONG WAY DOWN, RAT. GET SMART.
I-- I AIN'T AFRAID OF YOU, DEVIL!
YOU GOT A REP-- EVERYBODY KNOWS YOU AIN'T NEVER KILLED NOBODY!
KDAK
THAT'S TRUE..
BUT I CAN KEEP THIS UP ALL NIGHT.
CAN YOU?
UFF!
N-NO... I- I'LL TALK...
BUT FIRST, I THINK I'M GONNA BE SICK...

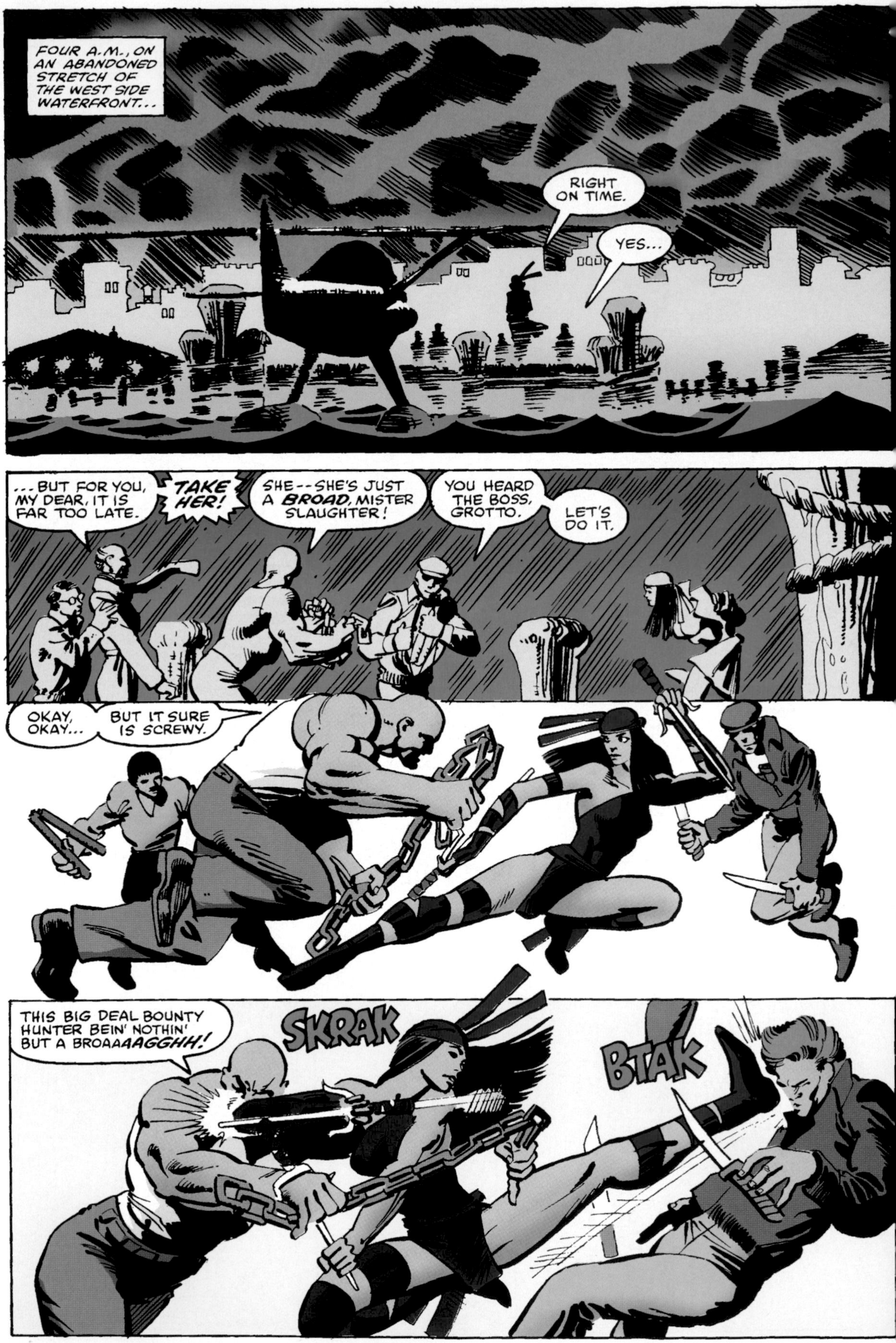
FOUR A.M., ON AN ABANDONED STRETCH OF THE WEST SIDE WATERFRONT...
RIGHT ON TIME.
YES...
...BUT FOR YOU, MY DEAR, IT IS FAR TOO LATE.
TAKE HER!
SHE--SHE'S JUST A BROAD, MISTER SLAUGHTER!
YOU HEARD THE BOSS, GROTTO.
LET'S DO IT.
OKAY, OKAY...
BUT IT SURE IS SCREWY.
THIS BIG DEAL BOUNTY HUNTER BEIN' NOTHIN' BUT A BROAAAAGGHH!
SKRAK
BTAK

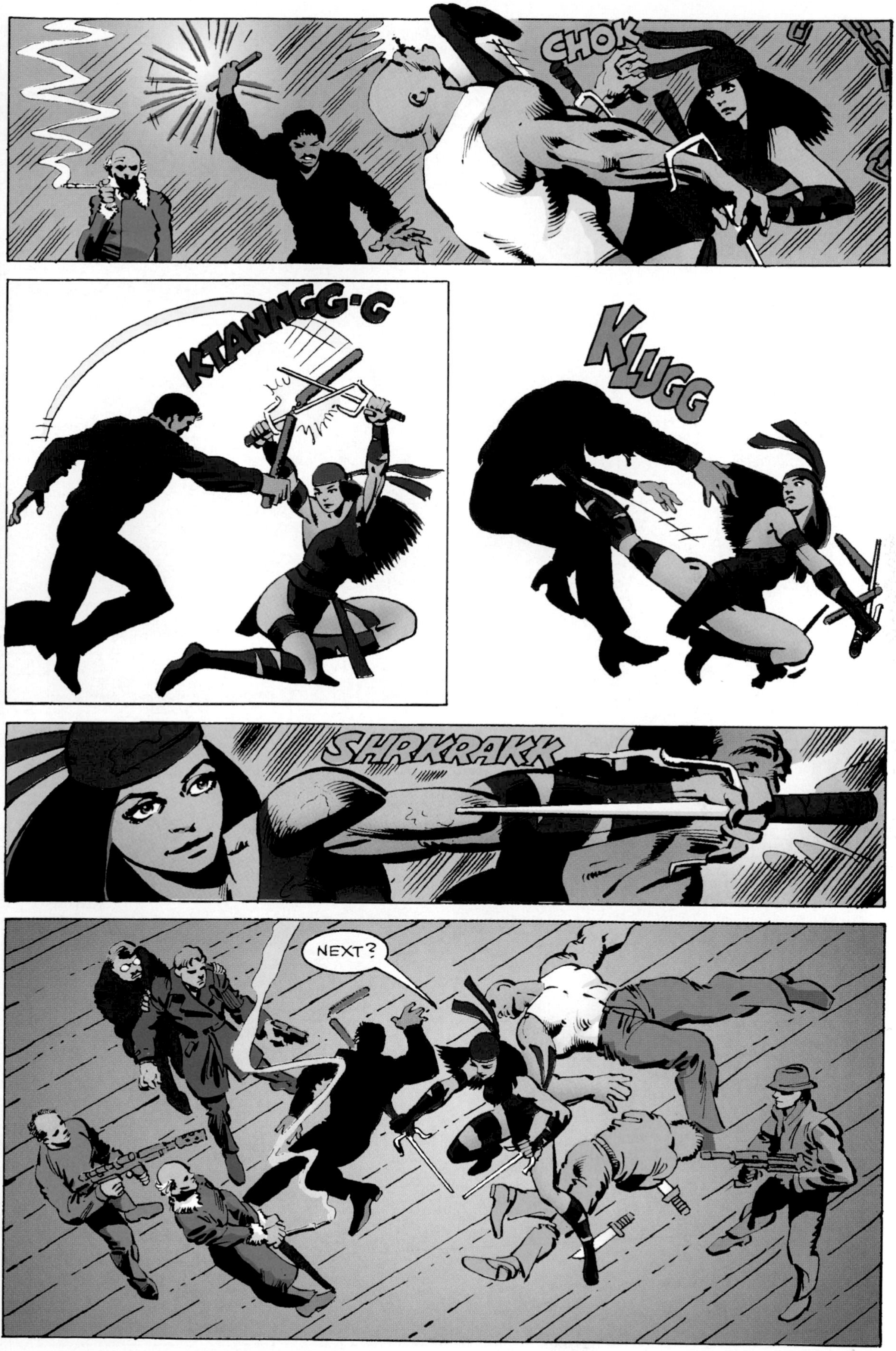
CHOK
KTANNGG-G
KLUGG
SHRKRAKK
NEXT?

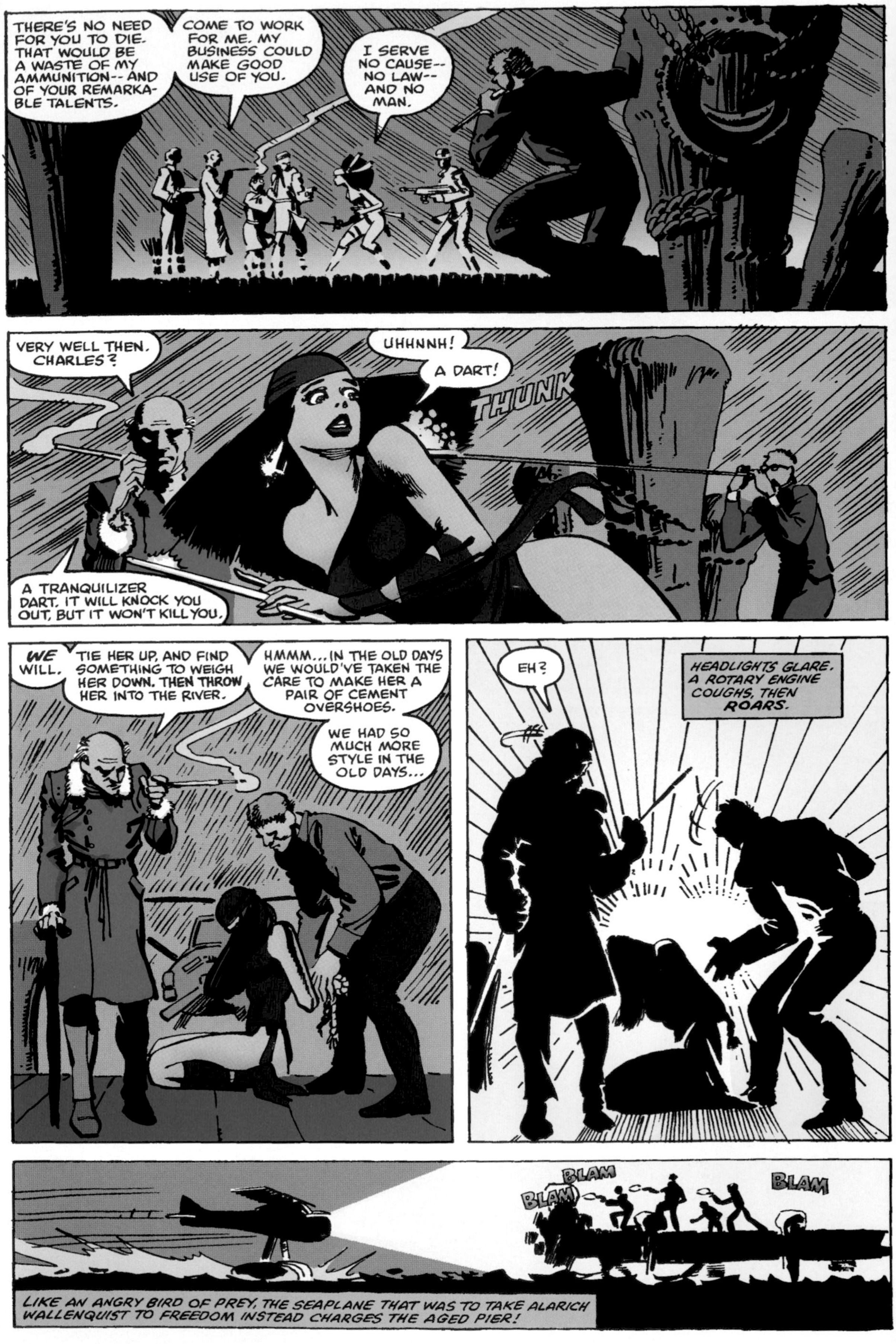
THERE'S NO NEED FOR YOU TO DIE. THAT WOULD BE A WASTE OF MY AMMUNITION-- AND OF YOUR REMARKABLE TALENTS.
COME TO WORK FOR ME. MY BUSINESS COULD MAKE GOOD USE OF YOU.
I SERVE NO CAUSE-- NO LAW-- AND NO MAN.
VERY WELL THEN. CHARLES?
UHHNNH!
A DART!
THUNK
A TRANQUILIZER DART. IT WILL KNOCK YOU OUT, BUT IT WON'T KILL YOU.
WE WILL.
TIE HER UP, AND FIND SOMETHING TO WEIGH HER DOWN. THEN THROW HER INTO THE RIVER.
HMMM... IN THE OLD DAYS WE WOULD'VE TAKEN THE CARE TO MAKE HER A PAIR OF CEMENT OVERSHOES.
WE HAD SO MUCH MORE STYLE IN THE OLD DAYS...
EH?
HEADLIGHTS GLARE. A ROTARY ENGINE COUGHS, THEN ROARS.
BLAM
BLAM
BLAM
LIKE AN ANGRY BIRD OF PREY, THE SEAPLANE THAT WAS TO TAKE ALARICH WALLENQUIST TO FREEDOM INSTEAD CHARGES THE AGED PIER!

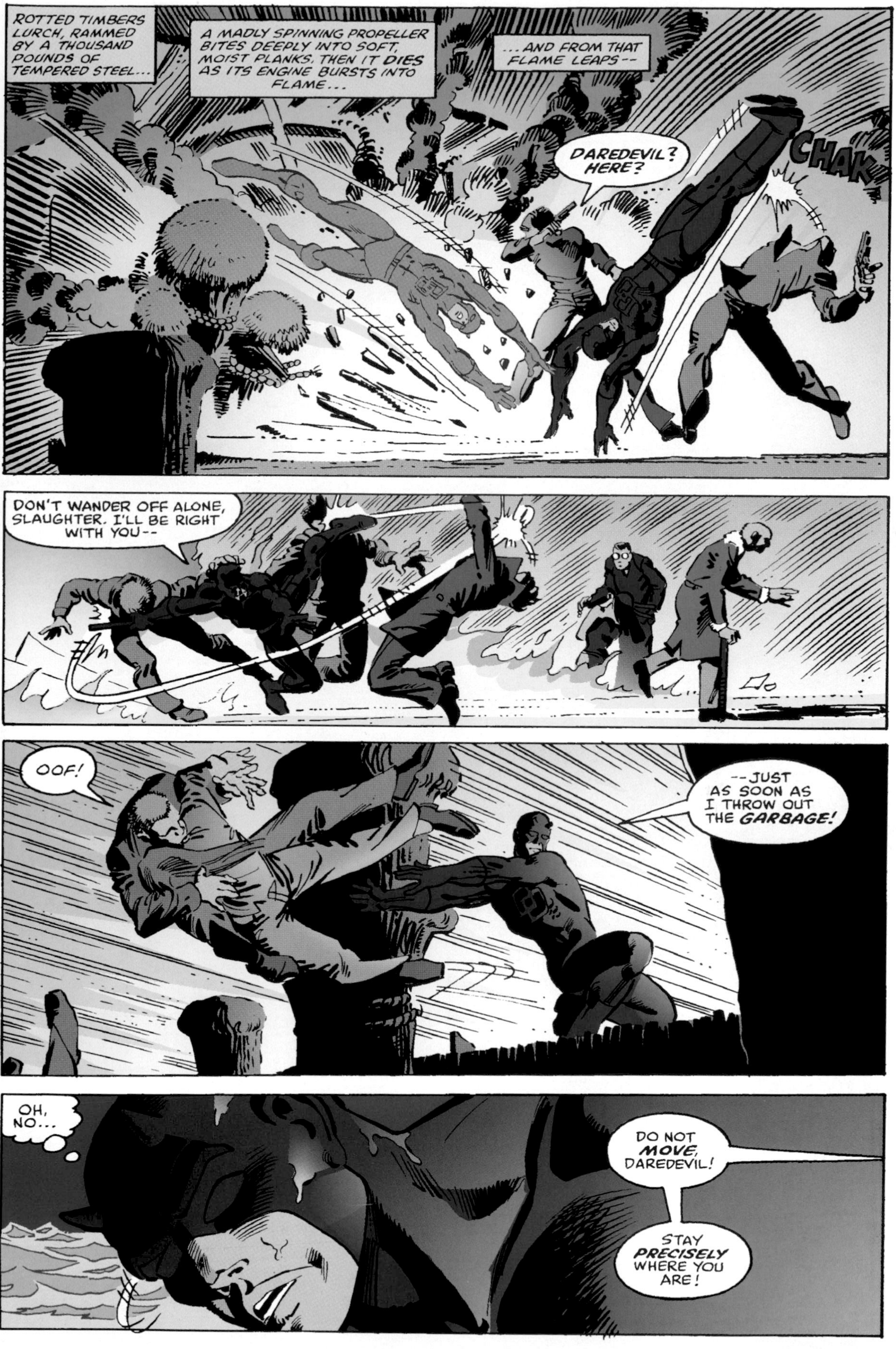
ROTTED TIMBERS LURCH, RAMMED BY A THOUSAND POUNDS OF TEMPERED STEEL...
A MADLY SPINNING PROPELLER BITES DEEPLY INTO SOFT, MOIST PLANKS. THEN IT DIES AS ITS ENGINE BURSTS INTO FLAME...
...AND FROM THAT FLAME LEAPS--
DAREDEVIL? HERE?
CHAK
DON'T WANDER OFF ALONE, SLAUGHTER. I'LL BE RIGHT WITH YOU--
OOF!
--JUST AS SOON AS I THROW OUT THE GARBAGE!
OH, NO...
DO NOT MOVE, DAREDEVIL!
STAY PRECISELY WHERE YOU ARE!

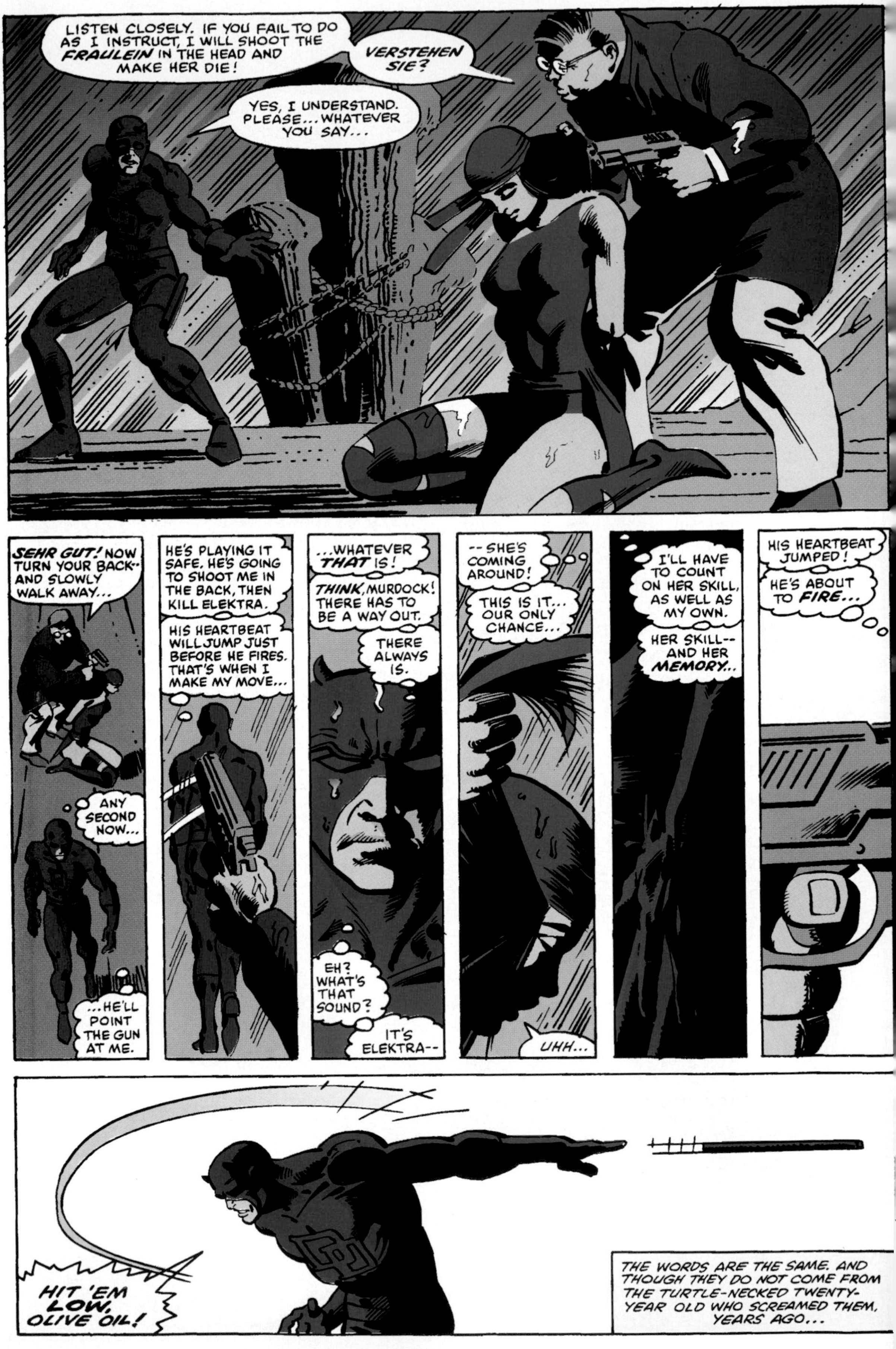
LISTEN CLOSELY. IF YOU FAIL TO DO AS I INSTRUCT, I WILL SHOOT THE FRAULEIN IN THE HEAD AND MAKE HER DIE!
VERSTEHEN SIE?
YES, I UNDERSTAND. PLEASE... WHATEVER YOU SAY...
SEHR GUT! NOW TURN YOUR BACK-- AND SLOWLY WALK AWAY...
ANY SECOND NOW...
...HE'LL POINT THE GUN AT ME.
HE'S PLAYING IT SAFE. HE'S GOING TO SHOOT ME IN THE BACK, THEN KILL ELEKTRA.
HIS HEARTBEAT WILL JUMP JUST BEFORE HE FIRES. THAT'S WHEN I MAKE MY MOVE...
...WHATEVER THAT IS!
THINK, MURDOCK! THERE HAS TO BE A WAY OUT.
THERE ALWAYS IS.
EH? WHAT'S THAT SOUND?
IT'S ELEKTRA--
--SHE'S COMING AROUND!
THIS IS IT... OUR ONLY CHANCE...
UHH...
I'LL HAVE TO COUNT ON HER SKILL, AS WELL AS MY OWN.
HER SKILL-- AND HER MEMORY...
HIS HEARTBEAT JUMPED!
HE'S ABOUT TO FIRE...
HIT 'EM LOW, OLIVE OIL!
THE WORDS ARE THE SAME. AND THOUGH THEY DO NOT COME FROM THE TURTLE-NECKED TWENTY-YEAR OLD WHO SCREAMED THEM, YEARS AGO...

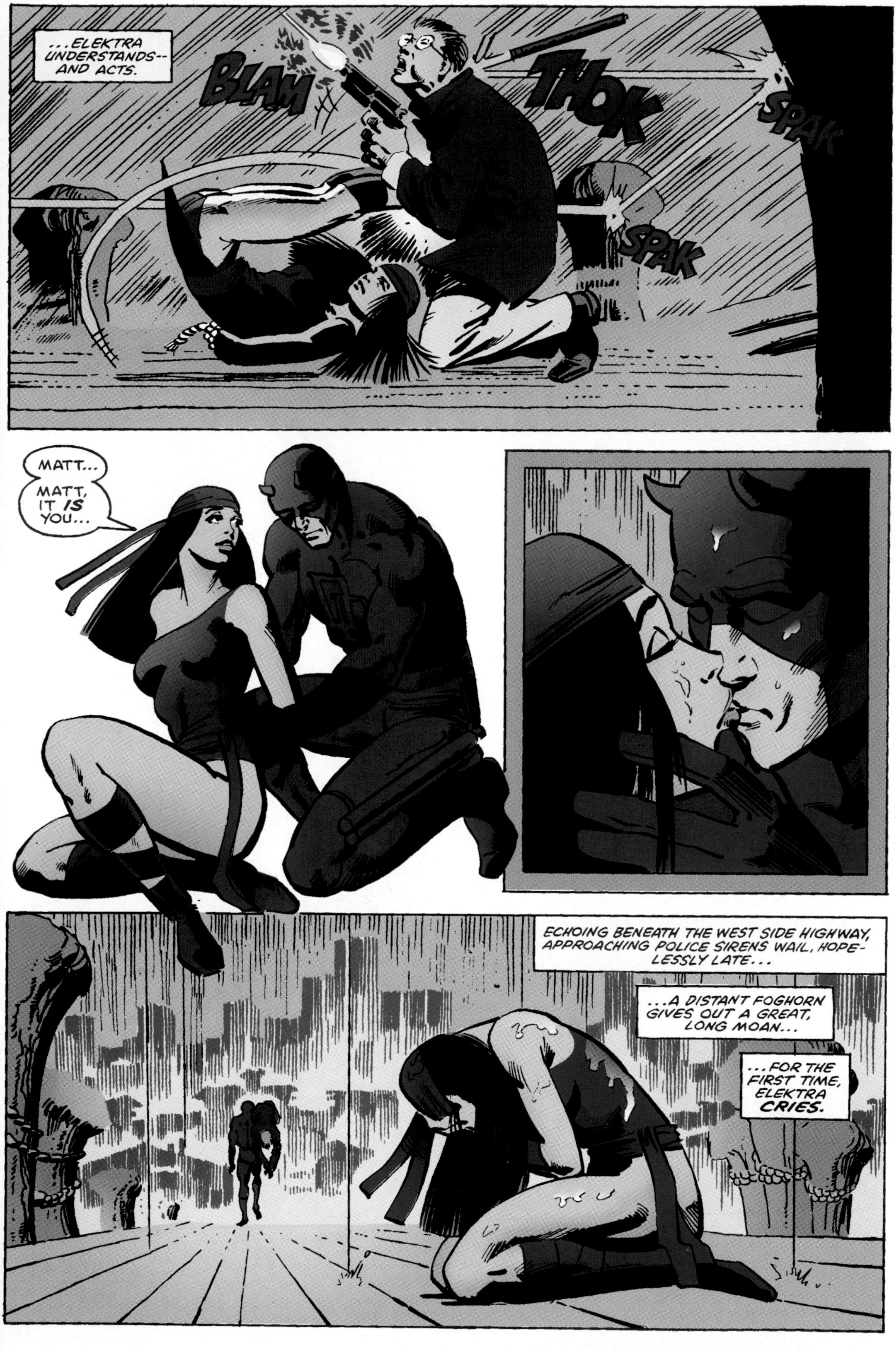
...ELEKTRA UNDERSTANDS-- AND ACTS.
BLAM
THOK
SPAK
SPAK
MATT... MATT, IT IS YOU...
ECHOING BENEATH THE WEST SIDE HIGHWAY, APPROACHING POLICE SIRENS WAIL, HOPE-LESSLY LATE...
...A DISTANT FOGHORN GIVES OUT A GREAT, LONG MOAN...
...FOR THE FIRST TIME, ELEKTRA CRIES.

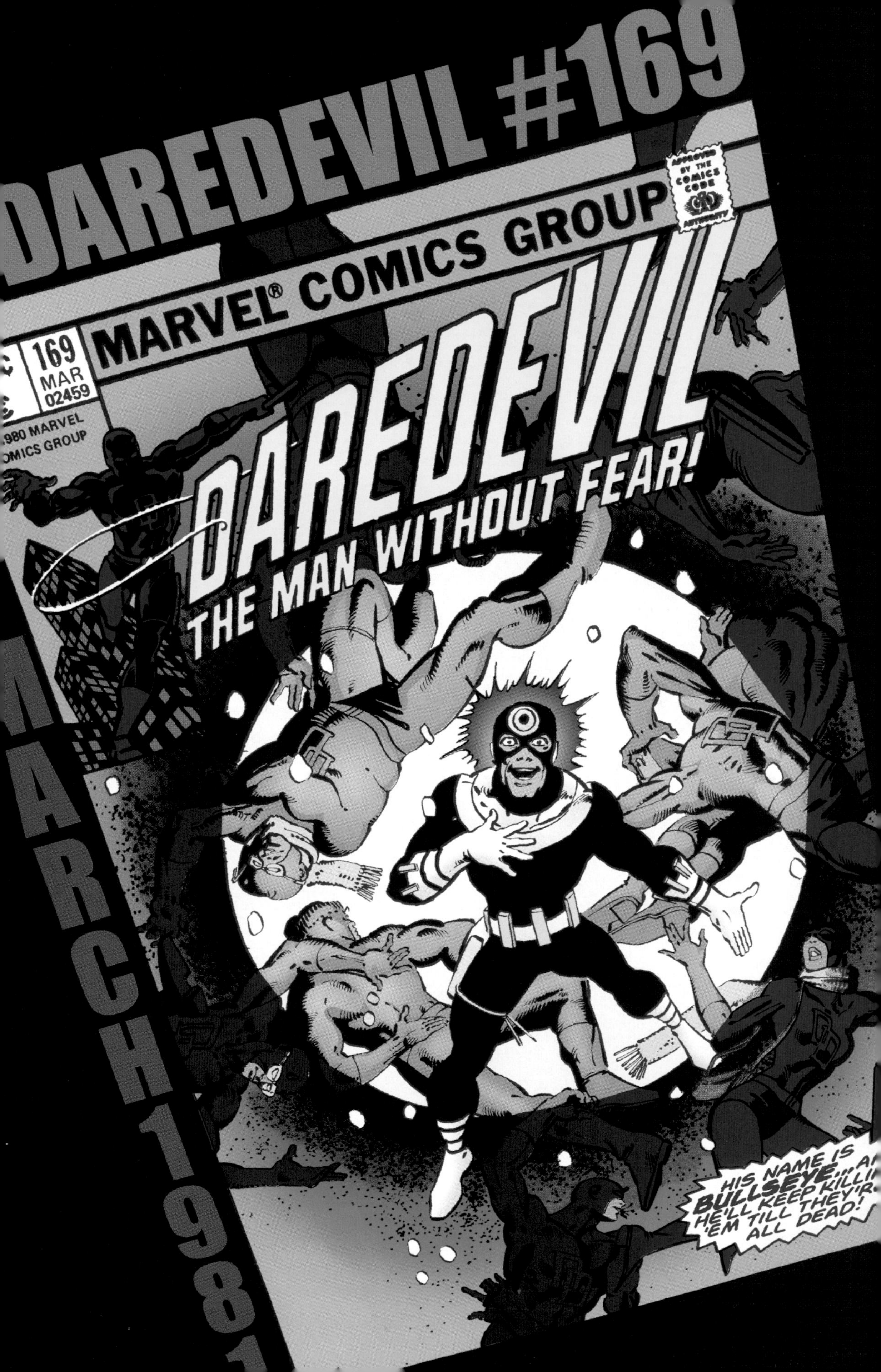
DAREDEVIL #169
MARVEL® COMICS GROUP
APPROVED BY THE COMICS CODE AUTHORITY
169 MAR 02459
1980 MARVEL COMICS GROUP
DAREDEVIL
THE MAN WITHOUT FEAR!
HIS NAME IS BULLSEYE...!
HE'LL KEEP KILLI
'EM TILL THEY'R
ALL DEAD!
MARCH 1981

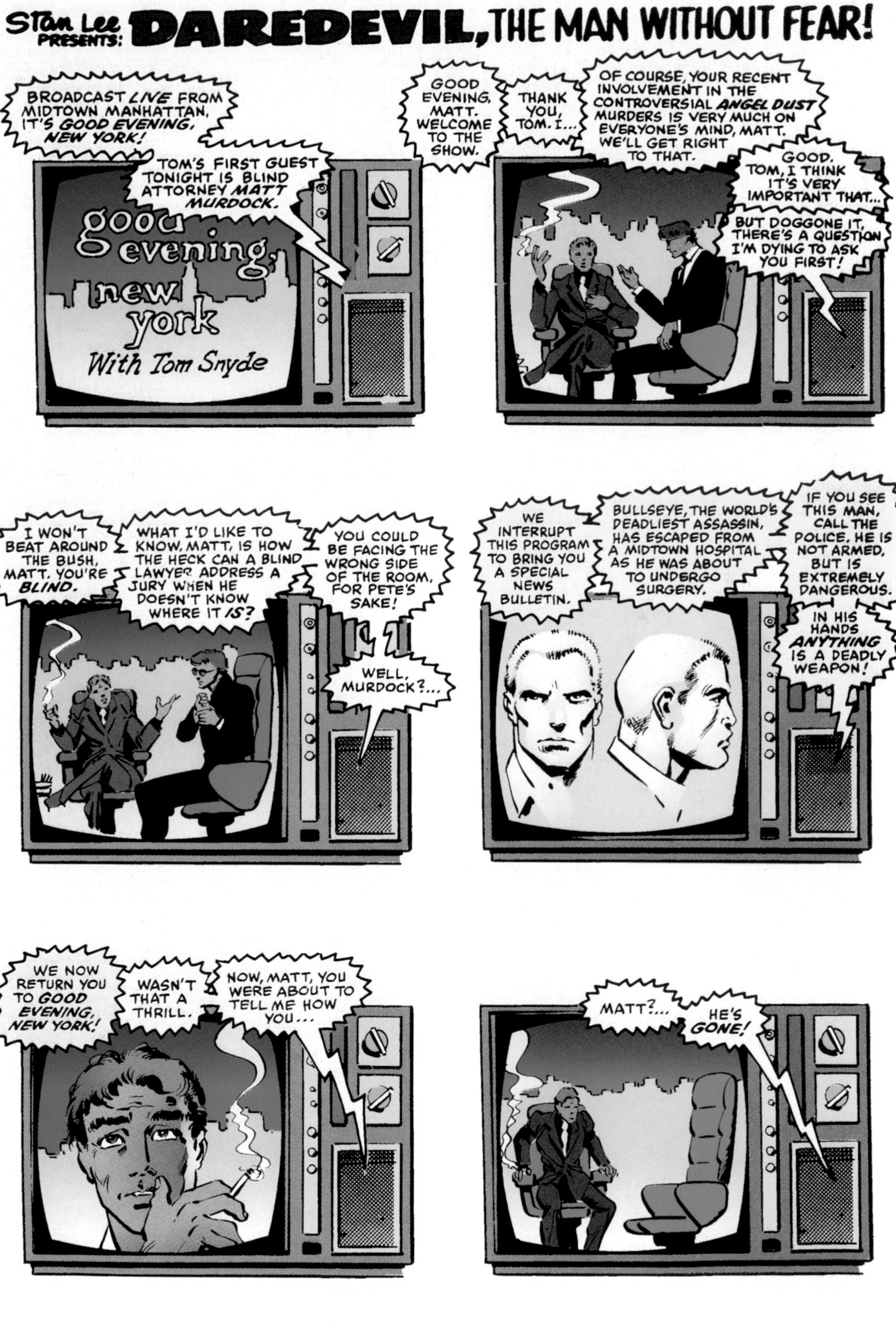

STAN LEE PRESENTS: DAREDEVIL, THE MAN WITHOUT FEAR!
BROADCAST LIVE FROM MIDTOWN MANHATTAN, IT'S GOOD EVENING, NEW YORK!
TOM'S FIRST GUEST TONIGHT IS BLIND ATTORNEY MATT MURDOCK.
good evening, new york
With Tom Snyde
GOOD EVENING, MATT. WELCOME TO THE SHOW.
THANK YOU, TOM. I...
OF COURSE, YOUR RECENT INVOLVEMENT IN THE CONTROVERSIAL ANGEL DUST MURDERS IS VERY MUCH ON EVERYONE'S MIND, MATT. WE'LL GET RIGHT TO THAT.
GOOD. TOM, I THINK IT'S VERY IMPORTANT THAT...
BUT DOGGONE IT, THERE'S A QUESTION I'M DYING TO ASK YOU FIRST!
I WON'T BEAT AROUND THE BUSH, MATT. YOU'RE BLIND.
WHAT I'D LIKE TO KNOW, MATT, IS HOW THE HECK CAN A BLIND LAWYER ADDRESS A JURY WHEN HE DOESN'T KNOW WHERE IT IS?
YOU COULD BE FACING THE WRONG SIDE OF THE ROOM, FOR PETE'S SAKE!
WELL, MURDOCK?...
WE INTERRUPT THIS PROGRAM TO BRING YOU A SPECIAL NEWS BULLETIN.
BULLSEYE, THE WORLD'S DEADLIEST ASSASSIN, HAS ESCAPED FROM A MIDTOWN HOSPITAL AS HE WAS ABOUT TO UNDERGO SURGERY.
IF YOU SEE THIS MAN, CALL THE POLICE. HE IS NOT ARMED, BUT IS EXTREMELY DANGEROUS.
IN HIS HANDS ANYTHING IS A DEADLY WEAPON!
WE NOW RETURN YOU TO GOOD EVENING, NEW YORK!
WASN'T THAT A THRILL.
NOW, MATT, YOU WERE ABOUT TO TELL ME HOW YOU...
MATT?...
HE'S GONE!

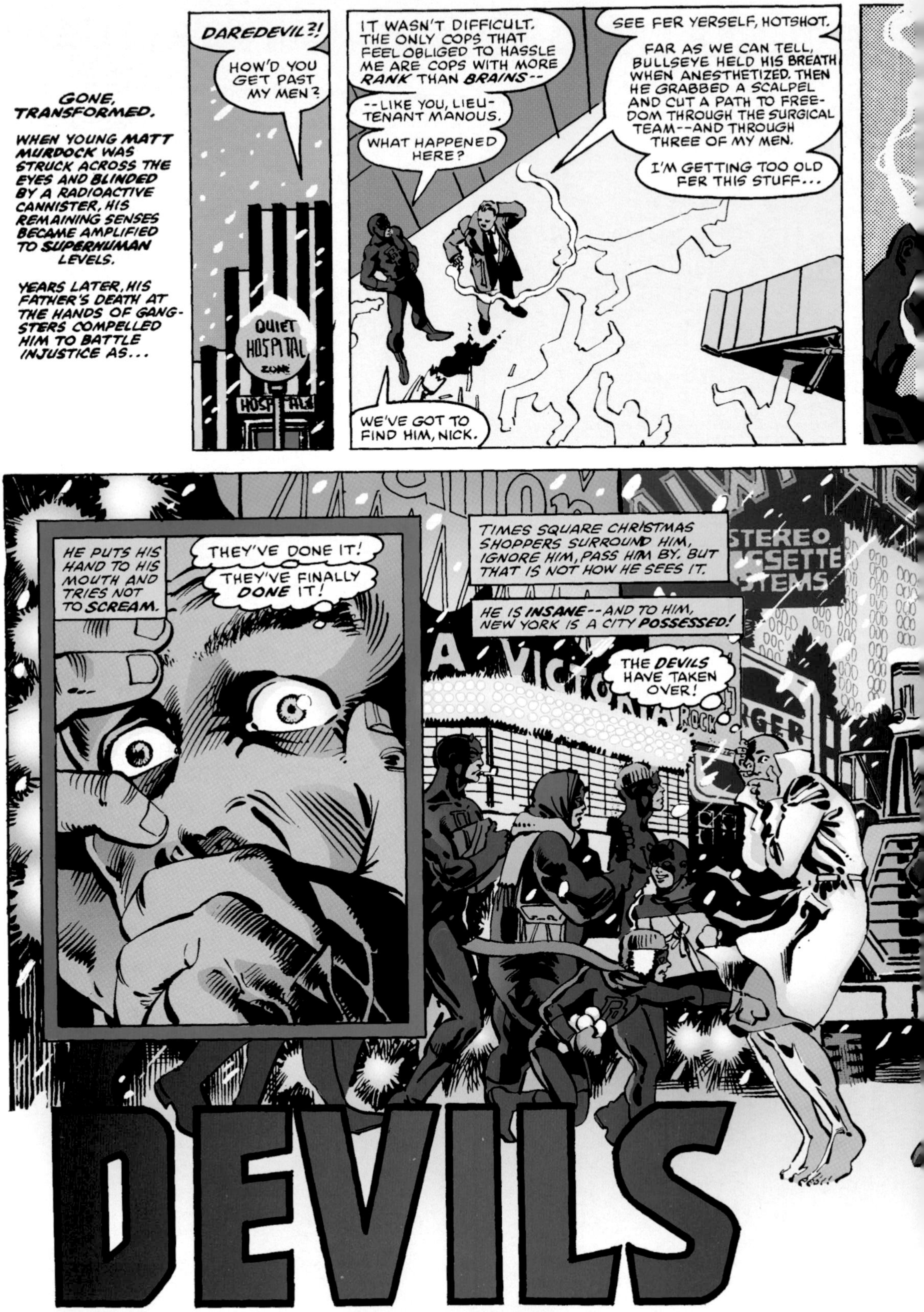
GONE, TRANSFORMED.
WHEN YOUNG MATT MURDOCK WAS STRUCK ACROSS THE EYES AND BLINDED BY A RADIOACTIVE CANNISTER, HIS REMAINING SENSES BECAME AMPLIFIED TO SUPERHUMAN LEVELS.
YEARS LATER, HIS FATHER'S DEATH AT THE HANDS OF GANGSTERS COMPELLED HIM TO BATTLE INJUSTICE AS...
DAREDEVIL?!
HOW'D YOU GET PAST MY MEN?
QUIET HOSPITAL ZONE
IT WASN'T DIFFICULT. THE ONLY COPS THAT FEEL OBLIGED TO HASSLE ME ARE COPS WITH MORE RANK THAN BRAINS--
--LIKE YOU, LIEUTENANT MANOUS.
WHAT HAPPENED HERE?
SEE FER YERSELF, HOTSHOT.
FAR AS WE CAN TELL, BULLSEYE HELD HIS BREATH WHEN ANESTHETIZED. THEN HE GRABBED A SCALPEL AND CUT A PATH TO FREEDOM THROUGH THE SURGICAL TEAM--AND THROUGH THREE OF MY MEN.
I'M GETTING TOO OLD FER THIS STUFF...
WE'VE GOT TO FIND HIM, NICK.
HE PUTS HIS HAND TO HIS MOUTH AND TRIES NOT TO SCREAM.
THEY'VE DONE IT!
THEY'VE FINALLY DONE IT!
TIMES SQUARE CHRISTMAS SHOPPERS SURROUND HIM, IGNORE HIM, PASS HIM BY. BUT THAT IS NOT HOW HE SEES IT.
HE IS INSANE--AND TO HIM, NEW YORK IS A CITY POSSESSED!
STEREO
THE DEVILS HAVE TAKEN OVER!
DEVILS
FRANK MILLER WRITER/PENCILLER • KLAUS JANSON INKER • GLYNIS WEIN COLORIST • JOE ROSEN LETTERER • DENNY O'NEIL EDITOR • JIM SHOOTER ED-IN-CHIEF

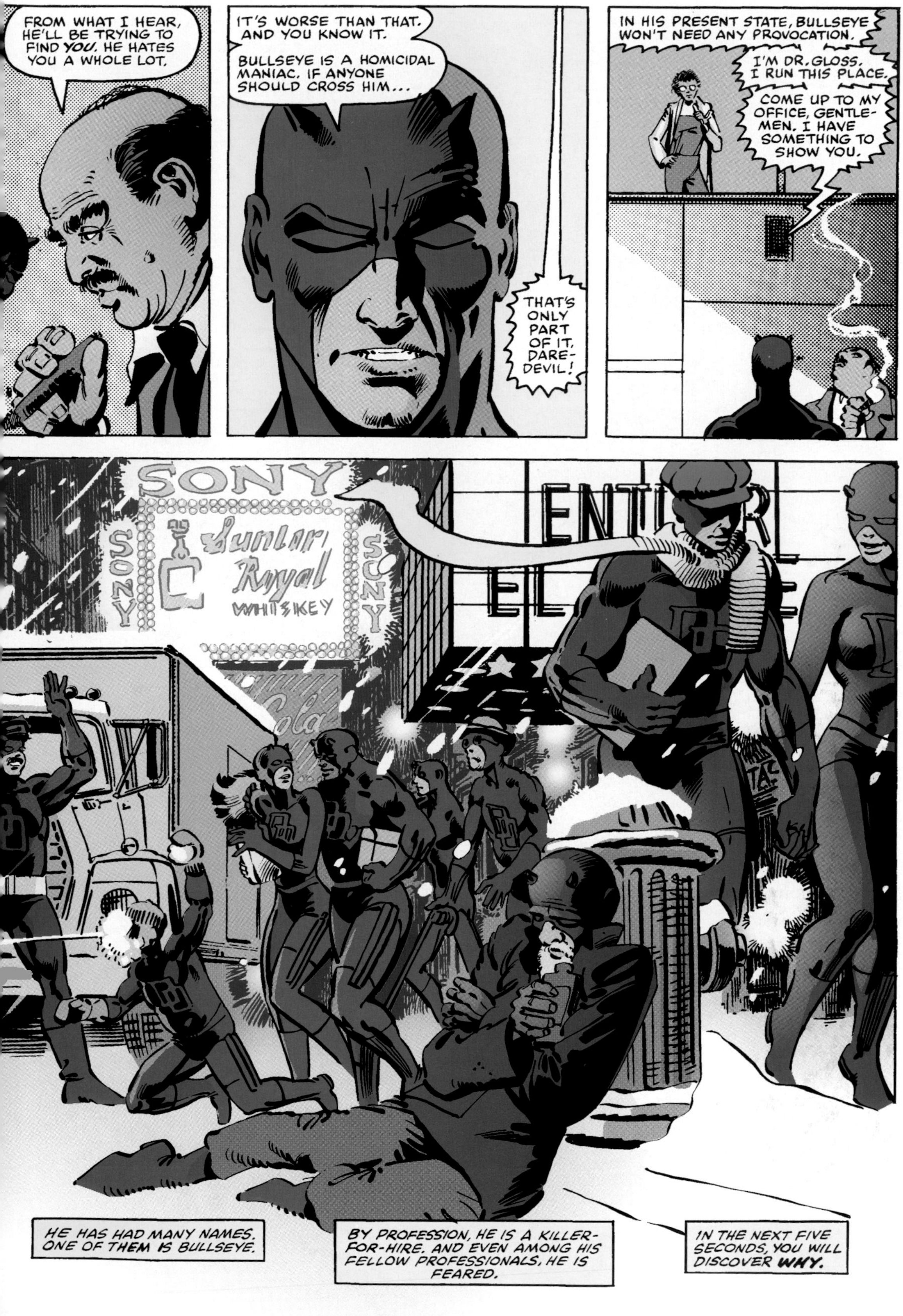
FROM WHAT I HEAR, HE'LL BE TRYING TO FIND YOU. HE HATES YOU A WHOLE LOT.
IT'S WORSE THAN THAT. AND YOU KNOW IT.
BULLSEYE IS A HOMICIDAL MANIAC. IF ANYONE SHOULD CROSS HIM...
THAT'S ONLY PART OF IT, DAREDEVIL!
IN HIS PRESENT STATE, BULLSEYE WON'T NEED ANY PROVOCATION.
I'M DR. GLOSS. I RUN THIS PLACE.
COME UP TO MY OFFICE, GENTLEMEN. I HAVE SOMETHING TO SHOW YOU.
SONY
Suntori Royal WHISKEY
SONY
SONY
HE HAS HAD MANY NAMES. ONE OF THEM IS BULLSEYE.
BY PROFESSION, HE IS A KILLER-FOR-HIRE. AND EVEN AMONG HIS FELLOW PROFESSIONALS, HE IS FEARED.
IN THE NEXT FIVE SECONDS, YOU WILL DISCOVER WHY.

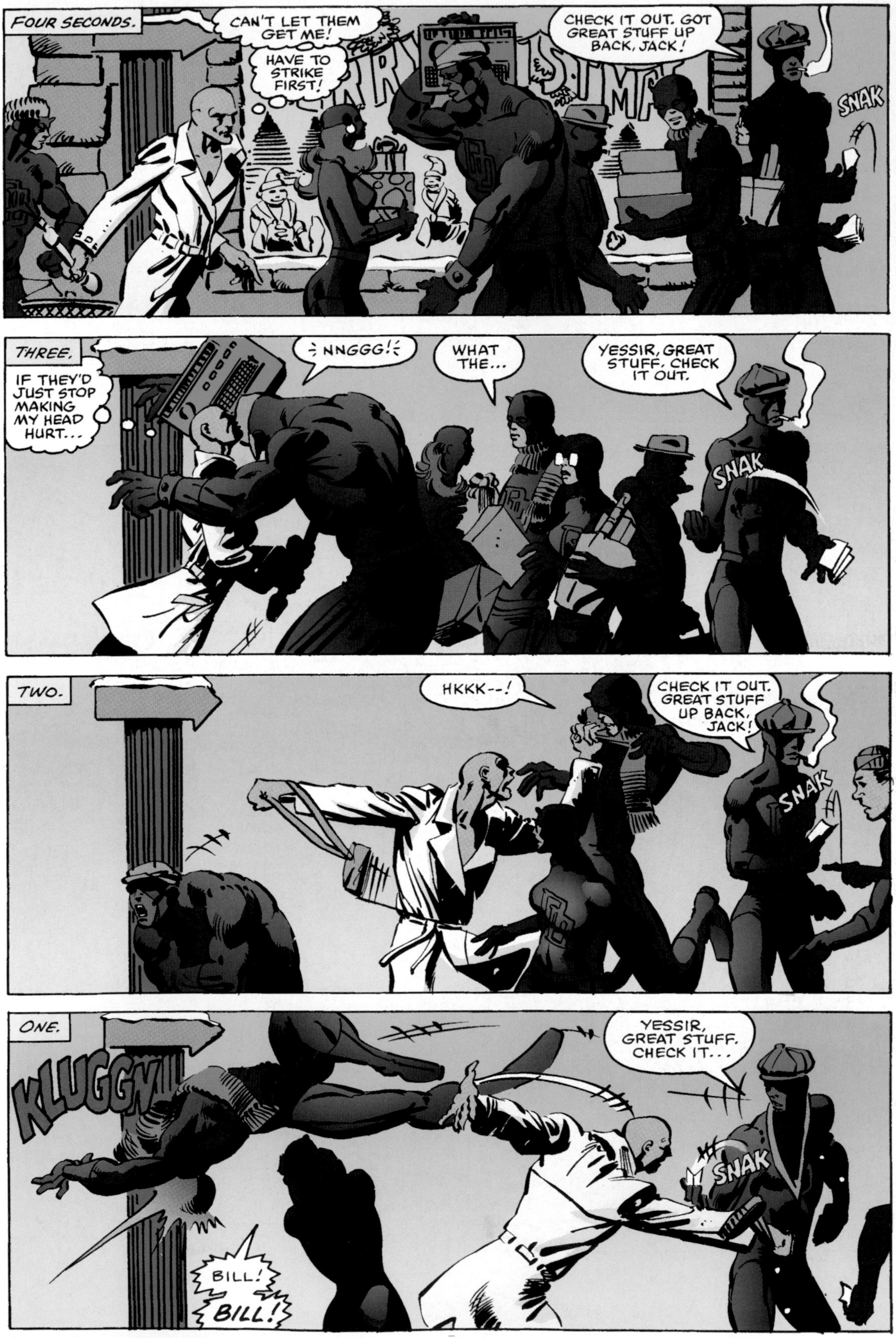
FOUR SECONDS.
CAN'T LET THEM GET ME!
HAVE TO STRIKE FIRST!
CHECK IT OUT. GOT GREAT STUFF UP BACK, JACK!
SNAK
THREE.
IF THEY'D JUST STOP MAKING MY HEAD HURT...
NNGGG!
WHAT THE...
YESSIR, GREAT STUFF, CHECK IT OUT.
SNAK
TWO.
HKKK--!
CHECK IT OUT. GREAT STUFF UP BACK, JACK!
SNAK
ONE.
KLUGGN
YESSIR, GREAT STUFF. CHECK IT...
SNAK
BILL!
BILL!

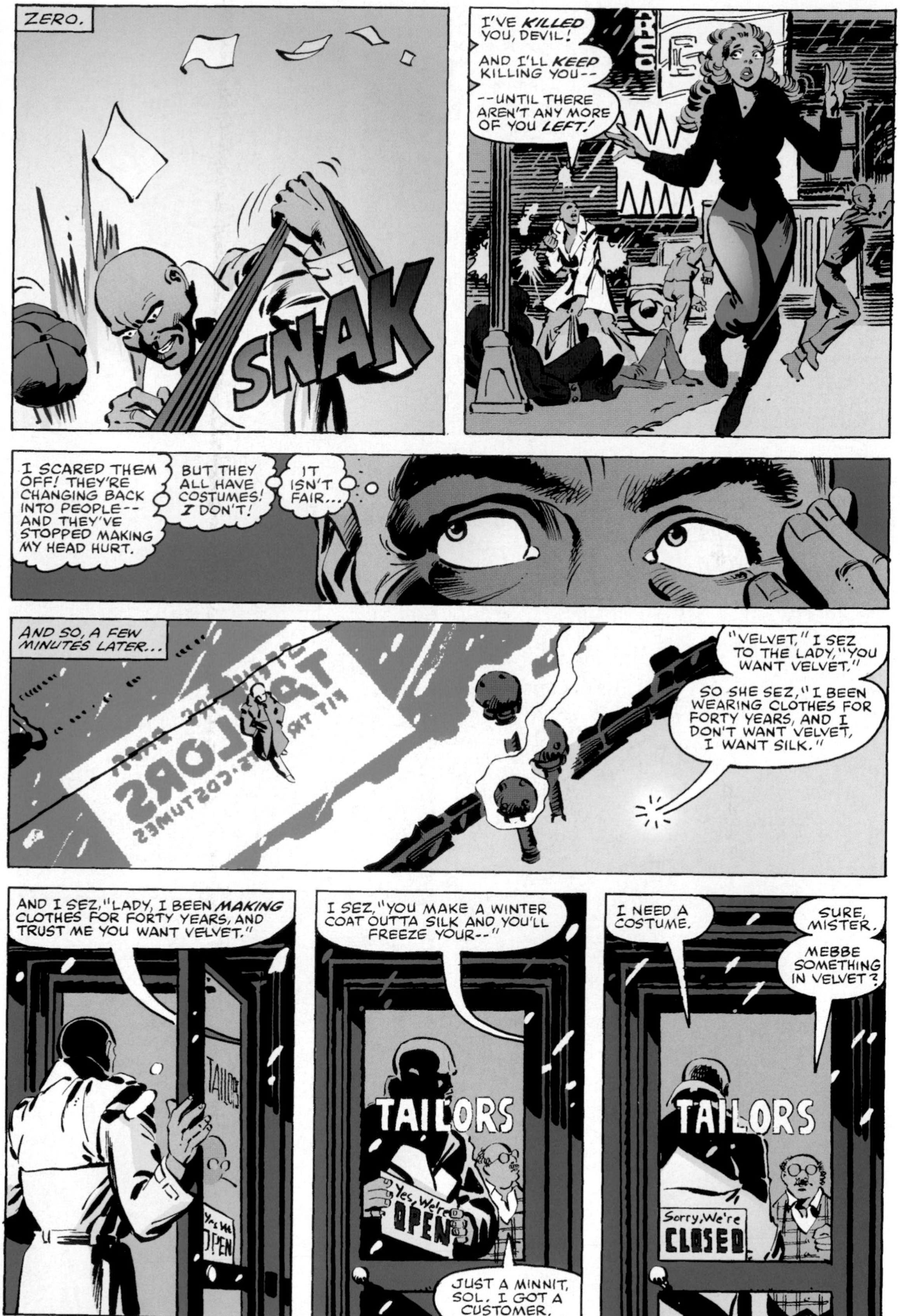
ZERO.
SNAK
I'VE KILLED YOU, DEVIL!
AND I'LL KEEP KILLING YOU--
--UNTIL THERE AREN'T ANY MORE OF YOU LEFT!
I SCARED THEM OFF! THEY'RE CHANGING BACK INTO PEOPLE-- AND THEY'VE STOPPED MAKING MY HEAD HURT.
BUT THEY ALL HAVE COSTUMES! I DON'T!
IT ISN'T FAIR...
AND SO, A FEW MINUTES LATER...
"VELVET," I SEZ TO THE LADY, "YOU WANT VELVET."
SO SHE SEZ, "I BEEN WEARING CLOTHES FOR FORTY YEARS, AND I DON'T WANT VELVET, I WANT SILK."
AND I SEZ, "LADY, I BEEN MAKING CLOTHES FOR FORTY YEARS, AND TRUST ME YOU WANT VELVET."
I SEZ, "YOU MAKE A WINTER COAT OUTTA SILK AND YOU'LL FREEZE YOUR--"
TAILORS
Yes, We're OPEN
JUST A MINNIT, SOL. I GOT A CUSTOMER.
I NEED A COSTUME.
SURE, MISTER.
MEBBE SOMETHING IN VELVET?
TAILORS
Sorry, We're CLOSED

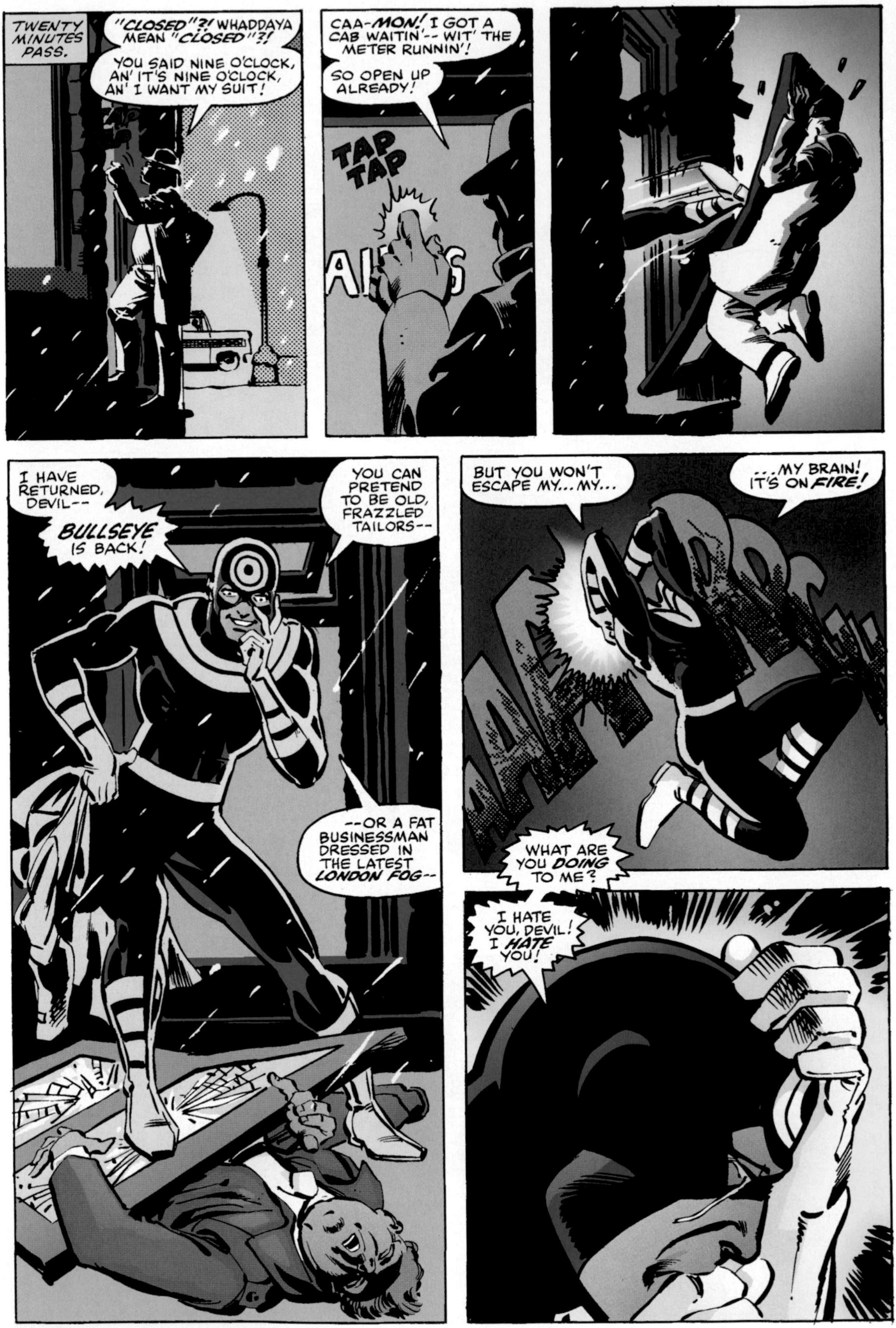

TWENTY MINUTES PASS.
"CLOSED"?! WHADDAYA MEAN "CLOSED"?!
YOU SAID NINE O'CLOCK, AN' IT'S NINE O'CLOCK, AN' I WANT MY SUIT!
CAA-MON! I GOT A CAB WAITIN'-- WIT' THE METER RUNNIN'!
SO OPEN UP ALREADY!
TAP TAP
I HAVE RETURNED, DEVIL--
BULLSEYE IS BACK!
YOU CAN PRETEND TO BE OLD, FRAZZLED TAILORS--
--OR A FAT BUSINESSMAN DRESSED IN THE LATEST LONDON FOG--
BUT YOU WON'T ESCAPE MY... MY...
...MY BRAIN! IT'S ON FIRE!
WHAT ARE YOU DOING TO ME?
I HATE YOU, DEVIL! I HATE YOU!

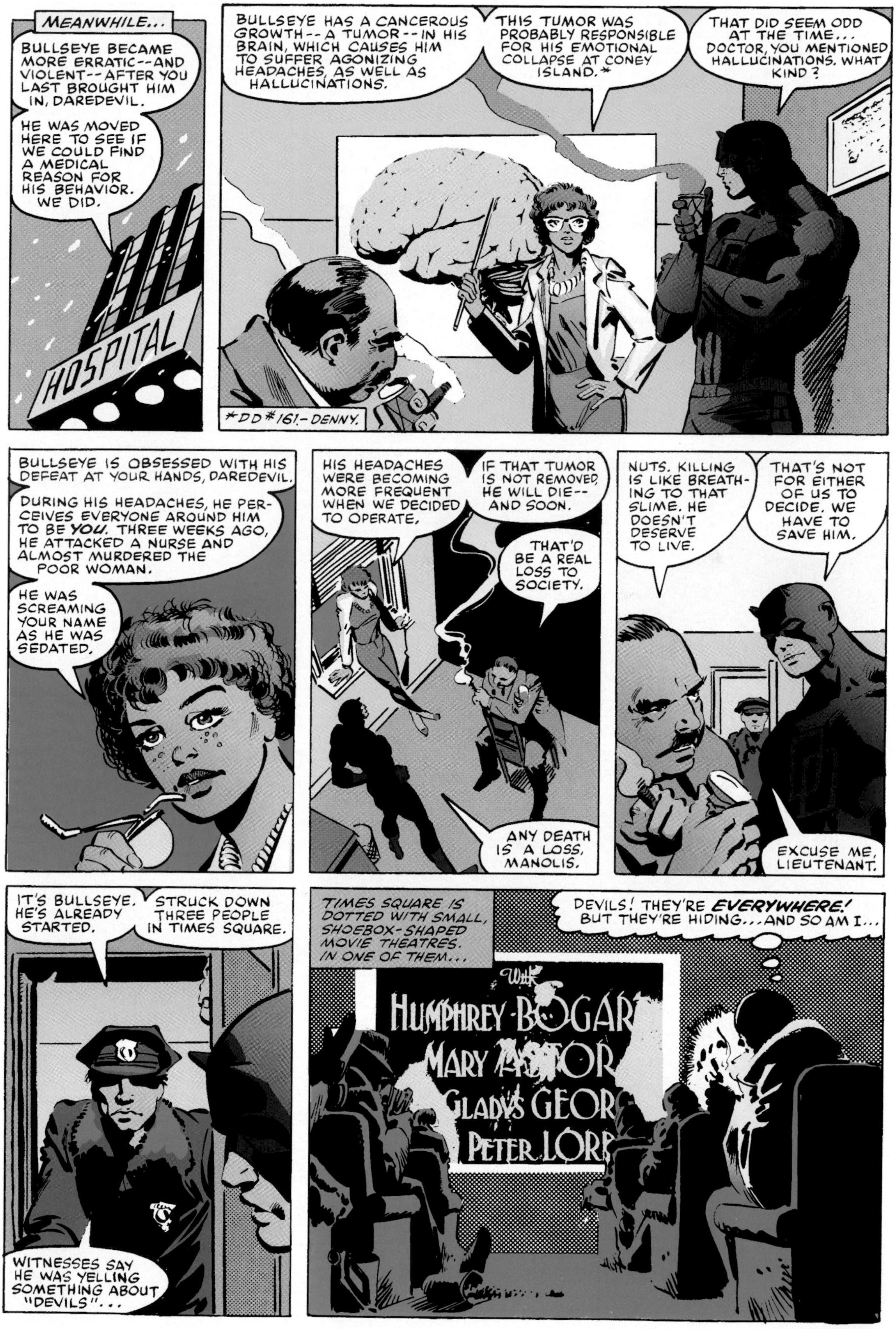
MEANWHILE...
BULLSEYE BECAME MORE ERRATIC--AND VIOLENT--AFTER YOU LAST BROUGHT HIM IN, DAREDEVIL.
HE WAS MOVED HERE TO SEE IF WE COULD FIND A MEDICAL REASON FOR HIS BEHAVIOR. WE DID.
HOSPITAL
BULLSEYE HAS A CANCEROUS GROWTH--A TUMOR--IN HIS BRAIN, WHICH CAUSES HIM TO SUFFER AGONIZING HEADACHES, AS WELL AS HALLUCINATIONS.
THIS TUMOR WAS PROBABLY RESPONSIBLE FOR HIS EMOTIONAL COLLAPSE AT CONEY ISLAND.*
THAT DID SEEM ODD AT THE TIME... DOCTOR, YOU MENTIONED HALLUCINATIONS. WHAT KIND?
*DD #161.-DENNY.
BULLSEYE IS OBSESSED WITH HIS DEFEAT AT YOUR HANDS, DAREDEVIL.
DURING HIS HEADACHES, HE PERCEIVES EVERYONE AROUND HIM TO BE YOU. THREE WEEKS AGO, HE ATTACKED A NURSE AND ALMOST MURDERED THE POOR WOMAN.
HE WAS SCREAMING YOUR NAME AS HE WAS SEDATED.
HIS HEADACHES WERE BECOMING MORE FREQUENT WHEN WE DECIDED TO OPERATE.
IF THAT TUMOR IS NOT REMOVED, HE WILL DIE--AND SOON.
THAT'D BE A REAL LOSS TO SOCIETY.
ANY DEATH IS A LOSS, MANOLIS.
NUTS. KILLING IS LIKE BREATHING TO THAT SLIME. HE DOESN'T DESERVE TO LIVE.
THAT'S NOT FOR EITHER OF US TO DECIDE. WE HAVE TO SAVE HIM.
EXCUSE ME, LIEUTENANT.
IT'S BULLSEYE. HE'S ALREADY STARTED.
STRUCK DOWN THREE PEOPLE IN TIMES SQUARE.
WITNESSES SAY HE WAS YELLING SOMETHING ABOUT "DEVILS"...
TIMES SQUARE IS DOTTED WITH SMALL, SHOEBOX-SHAPED MOVIE THEATRES. IN ONE OF THEM...
DEVILS! THEY'RE EVERYWHERE! BUT THEY'RE HIDING...AND SO AM I...
With
HUMPHREY BOGAR
MARY ASTOR
GLADYS GEOR
PETER LORR

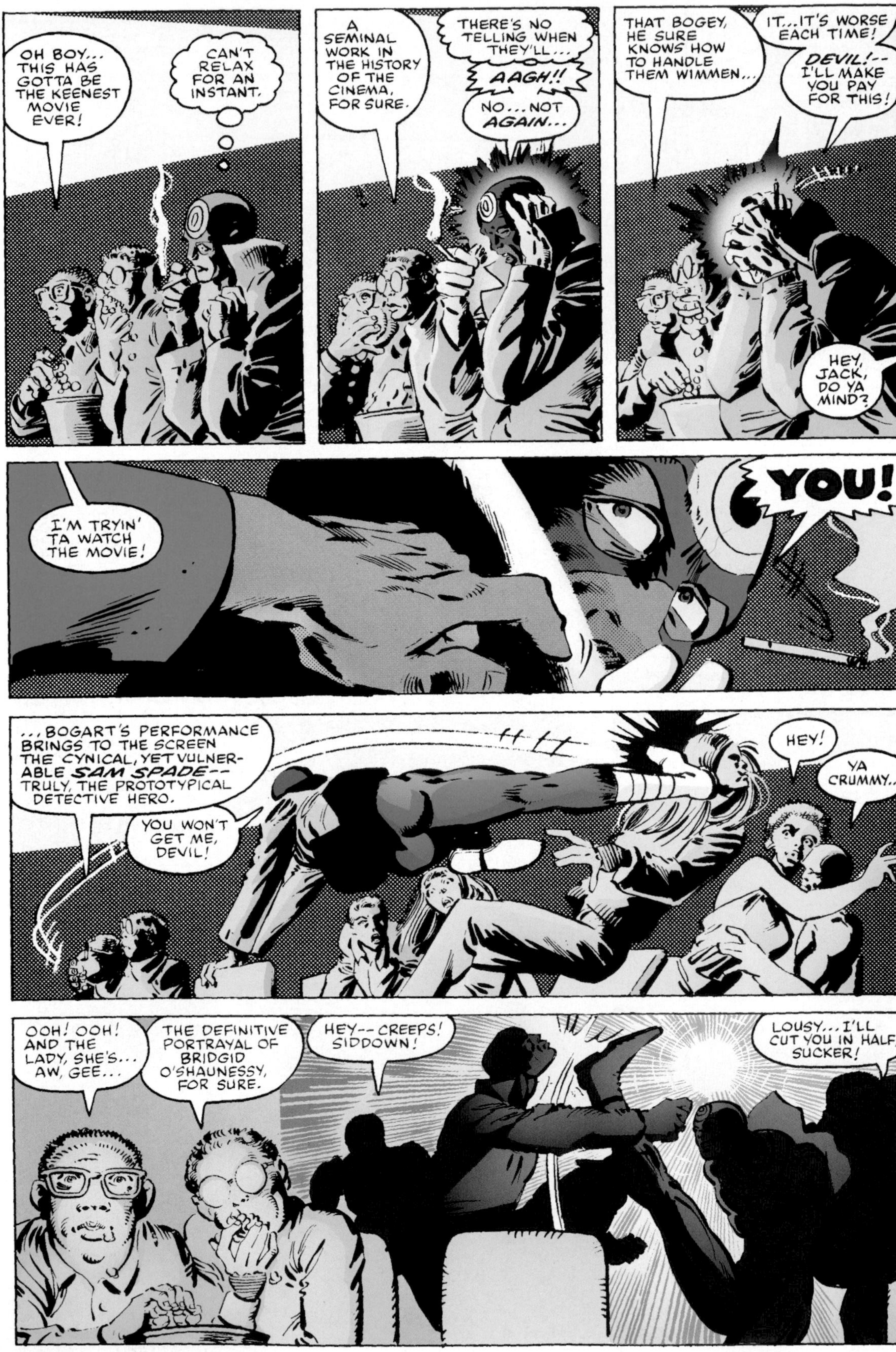

OH BOY... THIS HAS GOTTA BE THE KEENEST MOVIE EVER!
CAN'T RELAX FOR AN INSTANT.
A SEMINAL WORK IN THE HISTORY OF THE CINEMA, FOR SURE.
THERE'S NO TELLING WHEN THEY'LL...
AAGH!!
NO... NOT AGAIN...
THAT BOGEY, HE SURE KNOWS HOW TO HANDLE THEM WIMMEN...
IT... IT'S WORSE EACH TIME!
DEVIL!-- I'LL MAKE YOU PAY FOR THIS!
HEY, JACK, DO YA MIND?
I'M TRYIN' TA WATCH THE MOVIE!
YOU!
..., BOGART'S PERFORMANCE BRINGS TO THE SCREEN THE CYNICAL, YET VULNERABLE SAM SPADE-- TRULY, THE PROTOTYPICAL DETECTIVE HERO.
YOU WON'T GET ME, DEVIL!
HEY!
YA CRUMMY...
OOH! OOH! AND THE LADY, SHE'S... AW, GEE...
THE DEFINITIVE PORTRAYAL OF BRIDGID O'SHAUNESSY, FOR SURE.
HEY-- CREEPS! SIDDOWN!
LOUSY... I'LL CUT YOU IN HALF, SUCKER!

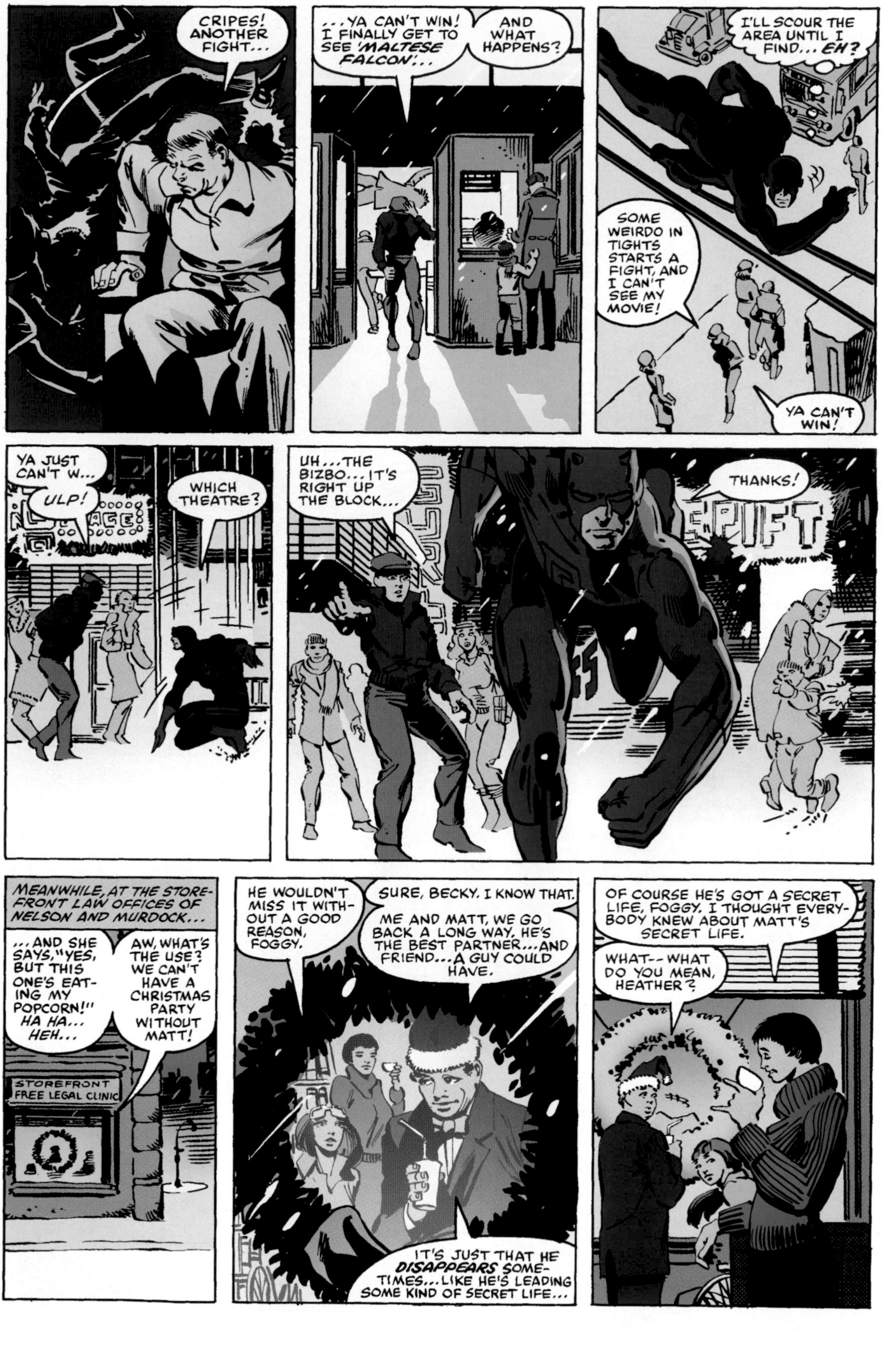
CRIPES! ANOTHER FIGHT...
...YA CAN'T WIN! I FINALLY GET TO SEE '*MALTESE FALCON*'...
AND WHAT HAPPENS?
I'LL SCOUR THE AREA UNTIL I FIND... *EH?*
SOME WEIRDO IN TIGHTS STARTS A FIGHT, AND I CAN'T SEE MY MOVIE!
YA CAN'T WIN!
YA JUST CAN'T W...
ULP!
WHICH THEATRE?
UH... THE BIZBO... IT'S RIGHT UP THE BLOCK...
THANKS!
MEANWHILE, AT THE STOREFRONT LAW OFFICES OF NELSON AND MURDOCK...
...AND SHE SAYS, "YES, BUT THIS ONE'S EATING MY POPCORN!" HA HA... HEH...
AW, WHAT'S THE USE? WE CAN'T HAVE A CHRISTMAS PARTY WITHOUT MATT!
STOREFRONT FREE LEGAL CLINIC
HE WOULDN'T MISS IT WITHOUT A GOOD REASON, FOGGY.
SURE, BECKY. I KNOW THAT.
ME AND MATT, WE GO BACK A LONG WAY. HE'S THE BEST PARTNER... AND FRIEND... A GUY COULD HAVE.
IT'S JUST THAT HE *DISAPPEARS* SOMETIMES... LIKE HE'S LEADING SOME KIND OF SECRET LIFE...
OF COURSE HE'S GOT A SECRET LIFE, FOGGY. I THOUGHT EVERYBODY KNEW ABOUT MATT'S SECRET LIFE.
WHAT-- WHAT DO YOU MEAN, HEATHER?

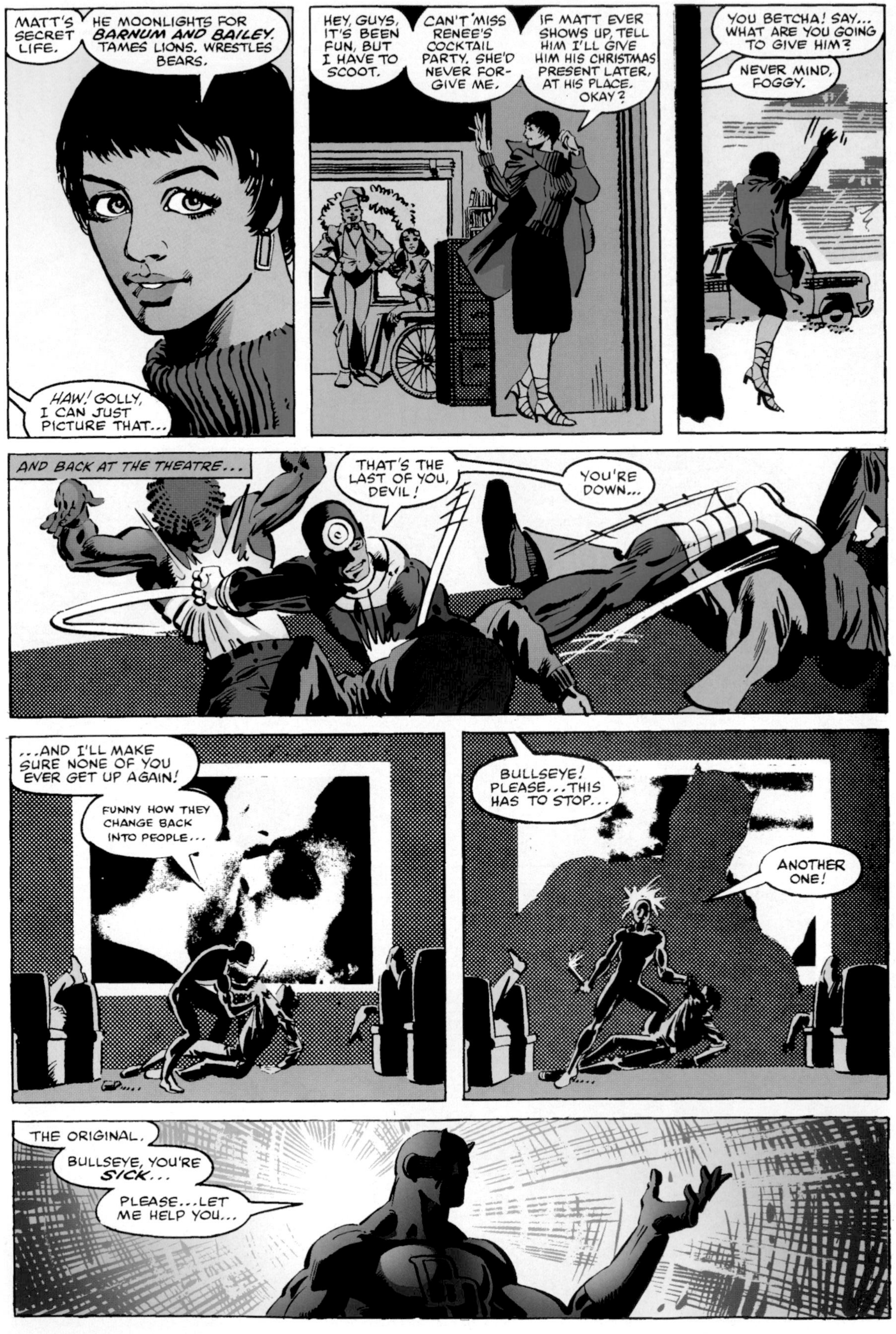
MATT'S SECRET LIFE.
HE MOONLIGHTS FOR BARNUM AND BAILEY. TAMES LIONS. WRESTLES BEARS.
HAW! GOLLY, I CAN JUST PICTURE THAT...
HEY, GUYS, IT'S BEEN FUN, BUT I HAVE TO SCOOT.
CAN'T MISS RENEE'S COCKTAIL PARTY. SHE'D NEVER FOR-GIVE ME.
IF MATT EVER SHOWS UP, TELL HIM I'LL GIVE HIM HIS CHRISTMAS PRESENT LATER, AT HIS PLACE. OKAY?
YOU BETCHA! SAY... WHAT ARE YOU GOING TO GIVE HIM?
NEVER MIND, FOGGY.
AND BACK AT THE THEATRE...
THAT'S THE LAST OF YOU, DEVIL!
YOU'RE DOWN...
...AND I'LL MAKE SURE NONE OF YOU EVER GET UP AGAIN!
FUNNY HOW THEY CHANGE BACK INTO PEOPLE...
BULLSEYE! PLEASE... THIS HAS TO STOP...
ANOTHER ONE!
THE ORIGINAL.
BULLSEYE, YOU'RE SICK...
PLEASE... LET ME HELP YOU...

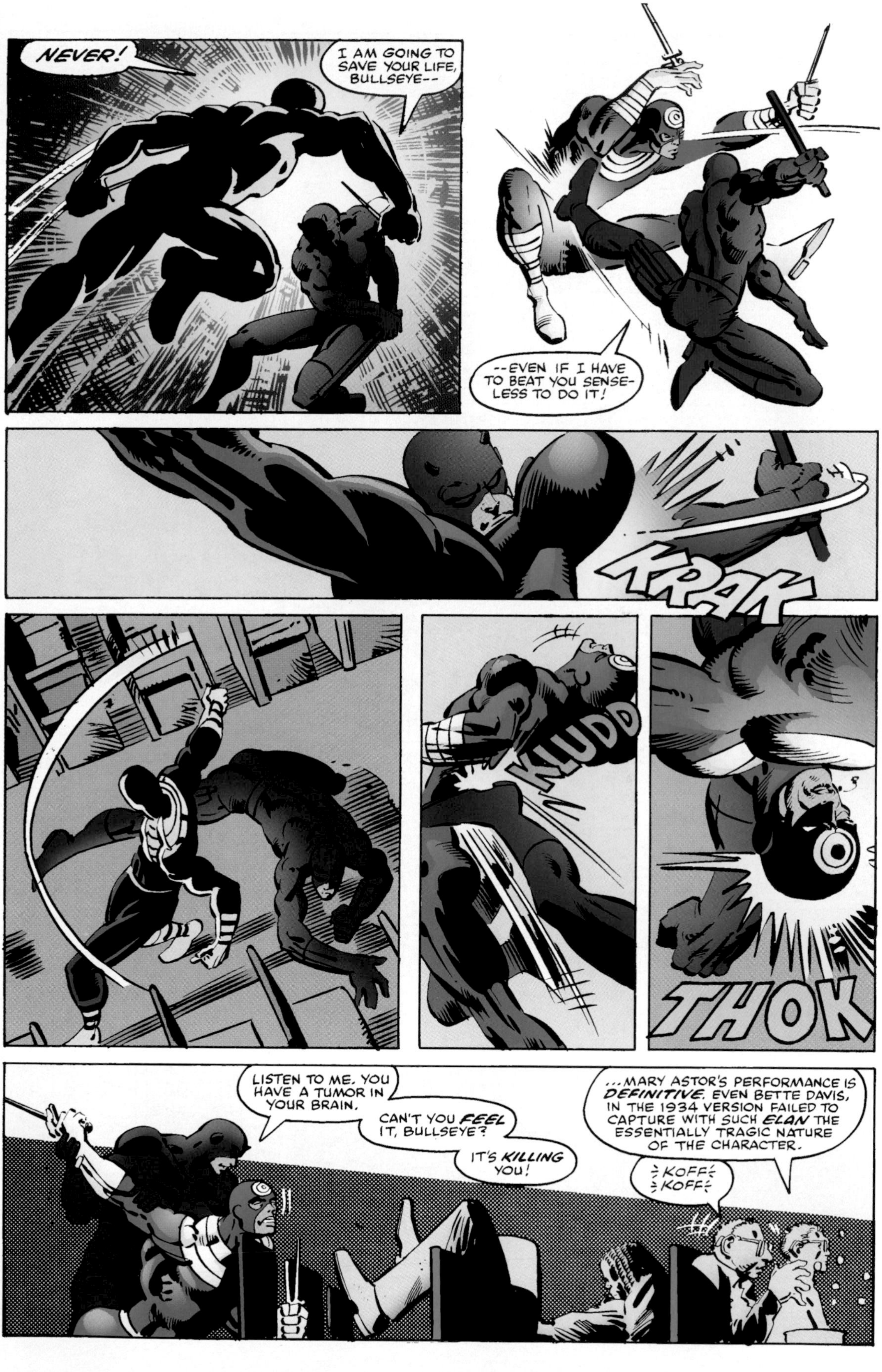

NEVER!
I AM GOING TO SAVE YOUR LIFE, BULLSEYE--
--EVEN IF I HAVE TO BEAT YOU SENSELESS TO DO IT!
KRAK
KLUDD
THOK
LISTEN TO ME. YOU HAVE A TUMOR IN YOUR BRAIN.
CAN'T YOU FEEL IT, BULLSEYE?
IT'S KILLING YOU!
...MARY ASTOR'S PERFORMANCE IS DEFINITIVE. EVEN BETTE DAVIS, IN THE 1934 VERSION FAILED TO CAPTURE WITH SUCH ELAN THE ESSENTIALLY TRAGIC NATURE OF THE CHARACTER.
KOFF KOFF

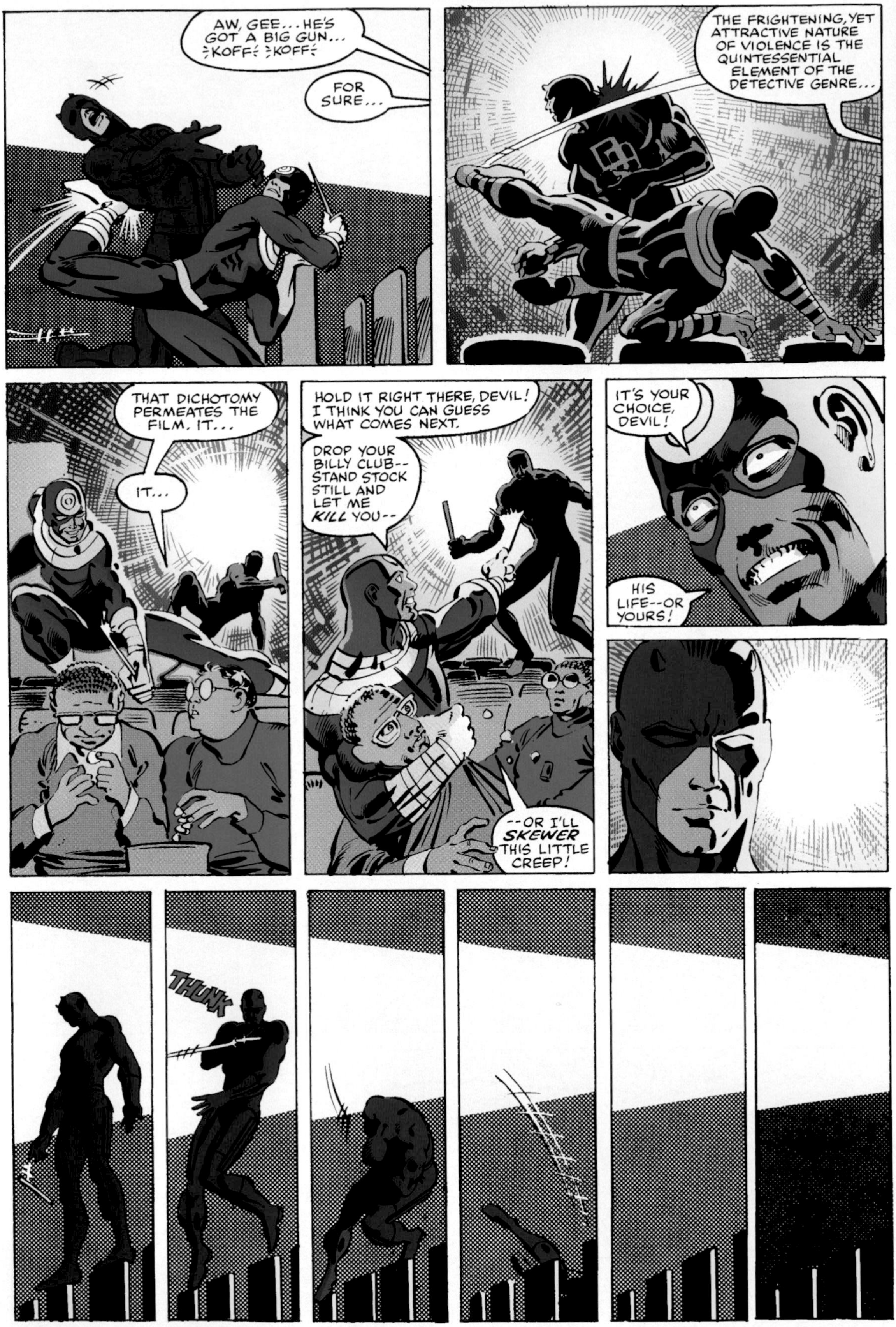
AW, GEE... HE'S GOT A BIG GUN... KOFF KOFF
FOR SURE...
THE FRIGHTENING, YET ATTRACTIVE NATURE OF VIOLENCE IS THE QUINTESSENTIAL ELEMENT OF THE DETECTIVE GENRE...
THAT DICHOTOMY PERMEATES THE FILM. IT...
IT...
HOLD IT RIGHT THERE, DEVIL! I THINK YOU CAN GUESS WHAT COMES NEXT.
DROP YOUR BILLY CLUB-- STAND STOCK STILL AND LET ME KILL YOU--
--OR I'LL SKEWER THIS LITTLE CREEP!
IT'S YOUR CHOICE, DEVIL!
HIS LIFE--OR YOURS!
THUNK

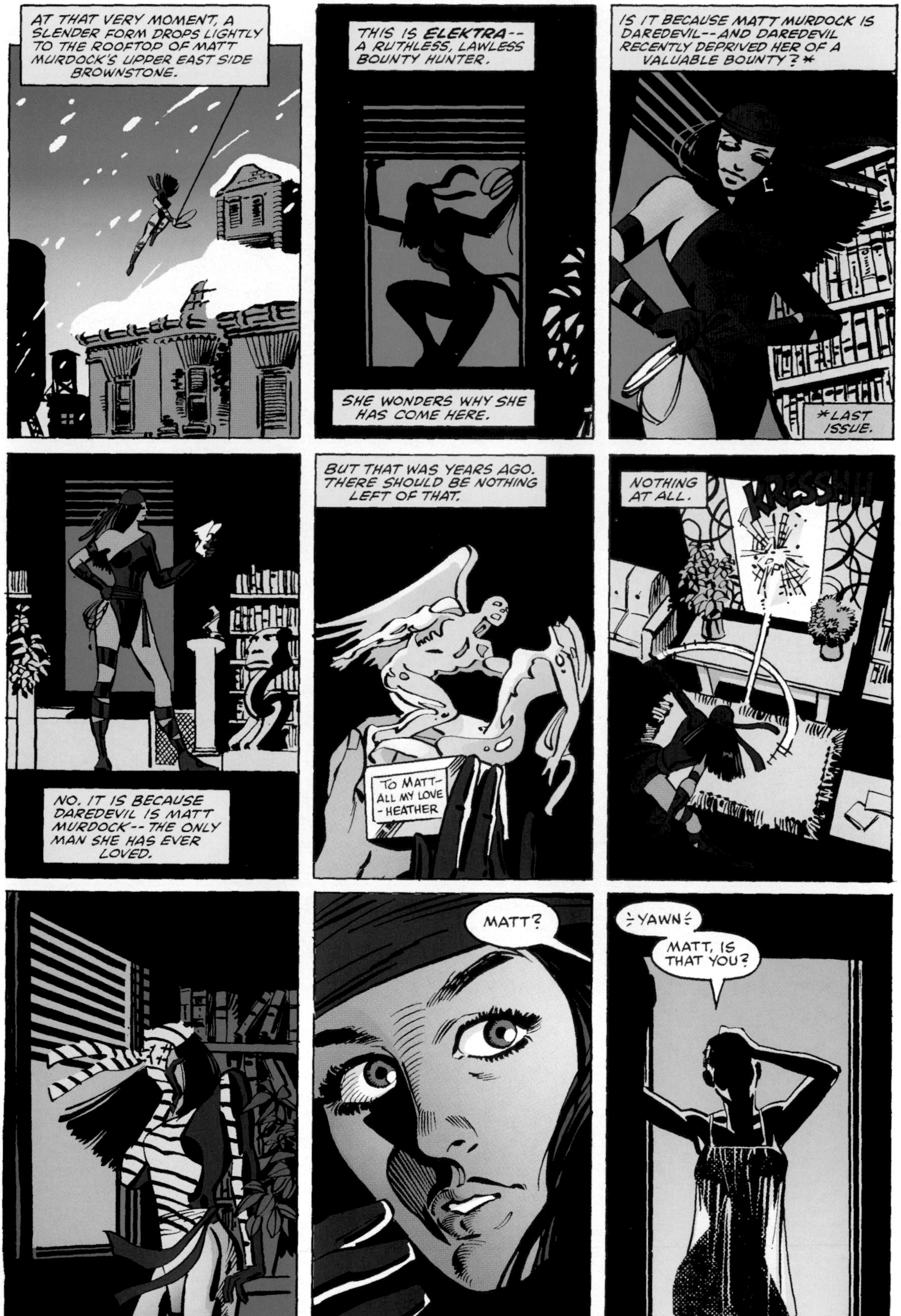
AT THAT VERY MOMENT, A SLENDER FORM DROPS LIGHTLY TO THE ROOFTOP OF MATT MURDOCK'S UPPER EAST SIDE BROWNSTONE.
THIS IS ELEKTRA-- A RUTHLESS, LAWLESS BOUNTY HUNTER.
SHE WONDERS WHY SHE HAS COME HERE.
IS IT BECAUSE MATT MURDOCK IS DAREDEVIL--AND DAREDEVIL RECENTLY DEPRIVED HER OF A VALUABLE BOUNTY?*
*LAST ISSUE.
NO. IT IS BECAUSE DAREDEVIL IS MATT MURDOCK--THE ONLY MAN SHE HAS EVER LOVED.
BUT THAT WAS YEARS AGO. THERE SHOULD BE NOTHING LEFT OF THAT.
TO MATT- ALL MY LOVE -HEATHER
NOTHING AT ALL.
KRESSHH
MATT?
YAWN
MATT, IS THAT YOU?

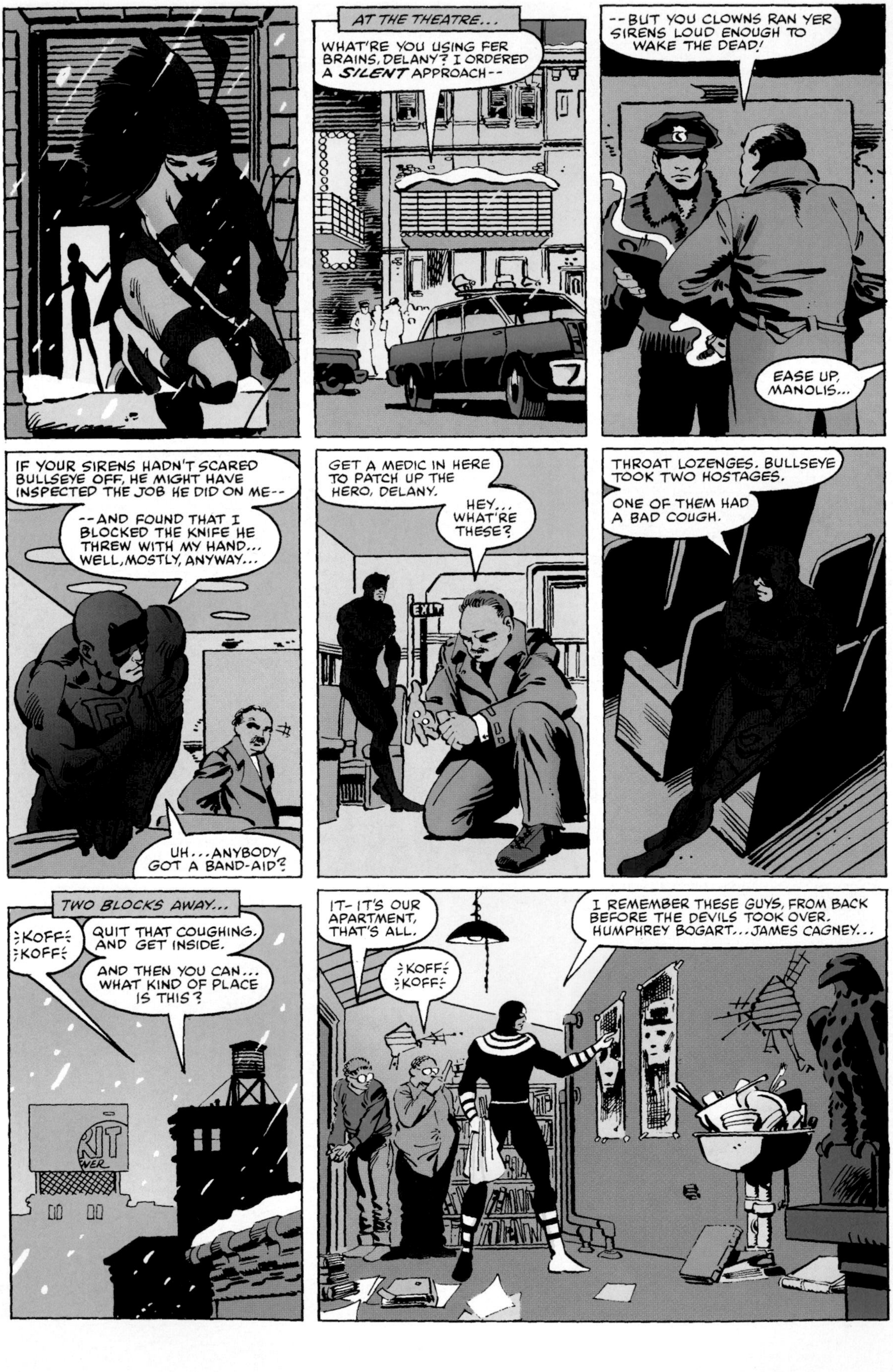
AT THE THEATRE...
WHAT'RE YOU USING FER BRAINS, DELANY? I ORDERED A SILENT APPROACH--
--BUT YOU CLOWNS RAN YER SIRENS LOUD ENOUGH TO WAKE THE DEAD!
EASE UP, MANOLIS...
IF YOUR SIRENS HADN'T SCARED BULLSEYE OFF, HE MIGHT HAVE INSPECTED THE JOB HE DID ON ME--
--AND FOUND THAT I BLOCKED THE KNIFE HE THREW WITH MY HAND... WELL, MOSTLY, ANYWAY...
UH... ANYBODY GOT A BAND-AID?
GET A MEDIC IN HERE TO PATCH UP THE HERO, DELANY.
HEY... WHAT'RE THESE?
EXIT
THROAT LOZENGES. BULLSEYE TOOK TWO HOSTAGES.
ONE OF THEM HAD A BAD COUGH.
TWO BLOCKS AWAY...
KOFF KOFF
QUIT THAT COUGHING. AND GET INSIDE.
AND THEN YOU CAN... WHAT KIND OF PLACE IS THIS?
IT- IT'S OUR APARTMENT, THAT'S ALL.
KOFF KOFF
I REMEMBER THESE GUYS, FROM BACK BEFORE THE DEVILS TOOK OVER. HUMPHREY BOGART... JAMES CAGNEY...

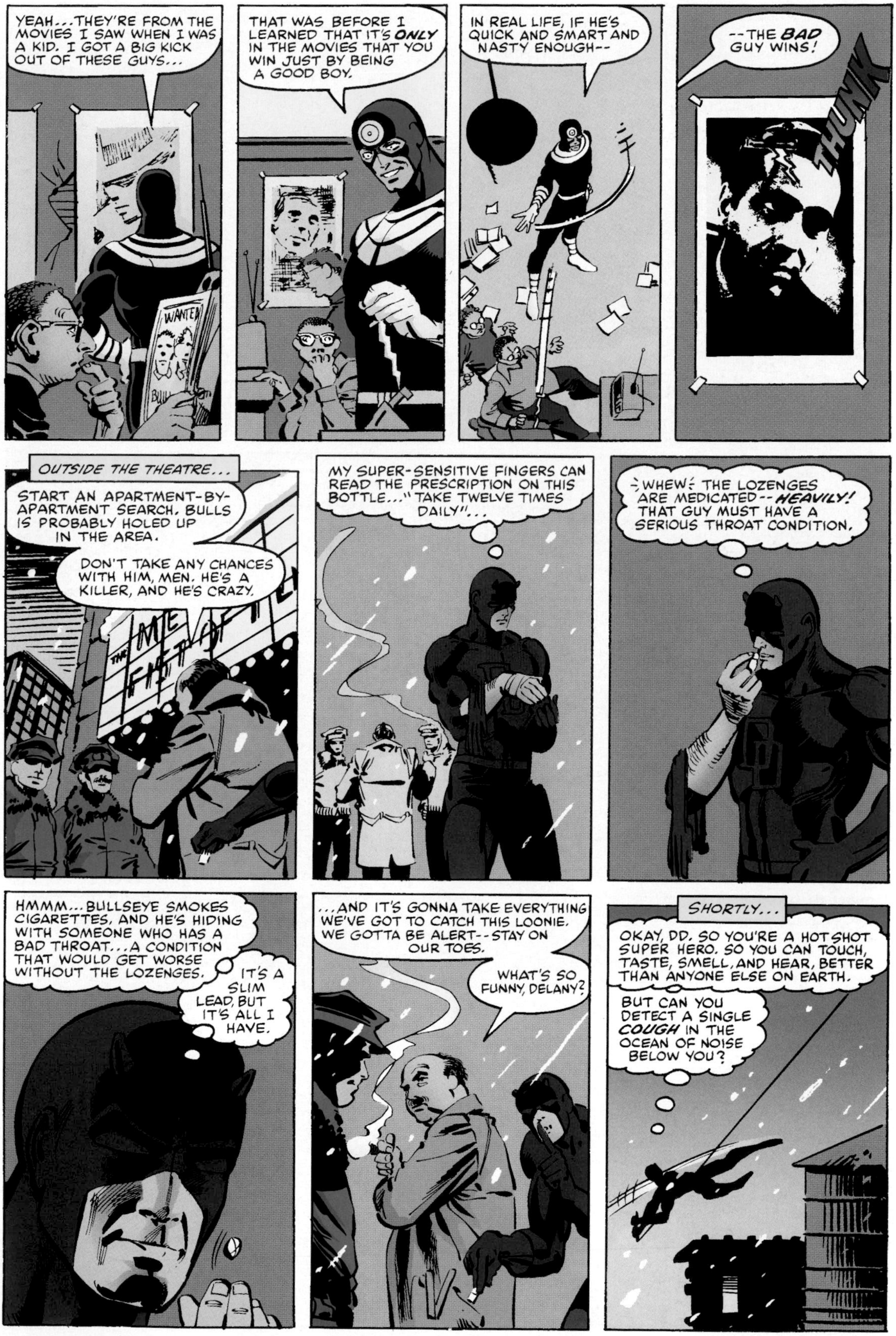
YEAH...THEY'RE FROM THE MOVIES I SAW WHEN I WAS A KID. I GOT A BIG KICK OUT OF THESE GUYS...
WANTED
THAT WAS BEFORE I LEARNED THAT IT'S ONLY IN THE MOVIES THAT YOU WIN JUST BY BEING A GOOD BOY.
IN REAL LIFE, IF HE'S QUICK AND SMART AND NASTY ENOUGH--
--THE BAD GUY WINS!
THUNK
OUTSIDE THE THEATRE...
START AN APARTMENT-BY-APARTMENT SEARCH. BULLS IS PROBABLY HOLED UP IN THE AREA.
DON'T TAKE ANY CHANCES WITH HIM, MEN. HE'S A KILLER, AND HE'S CRAZY.
MY SUPER-SENSITIVE FINGERS CAN READ THE PRESCRIPTION ON THIS BOTTLE..."TAKE TWELVE TIMES DAILY"...
WHEW! THE LOZENGES ARE MEDICATED--HEAVILY! THAT GUY MUST HAVE A SERIOUS THROAT CONDITION.
HMMM...BULLSEYE SMOKES CIGARETTES, AND HE'S HIDING WITH SOMEONE WHO HAS A BAD THROAT...A CONDITION THAT WOULD GET WORSE WITHOUT THE LOZENGES.
IT'S A SLIM LEAD, BUT IT'S ALL I HAVE.
...AND IT'S GONNA TAKE EVERYTHING WE'VE GOT TO CATCH THIS LOONIE. WE GOTTA BE ALERT--STAY ON OUR TOES.
WHAT'S SO FUNNY, DELANY?
SHORTLY...
OKAY, DD. SO YOU'RE A HOT SHOT SUPER HERO. SO YOU CAN TOUCH, TASTE, SMELL, AND HEAR, BETTER THAN ANYONE ELSE ON EARTH.
BUT CAN YOU DETECT A SINGLE COUGH IN THE OCEAN OF NOISE BELOW YOU?

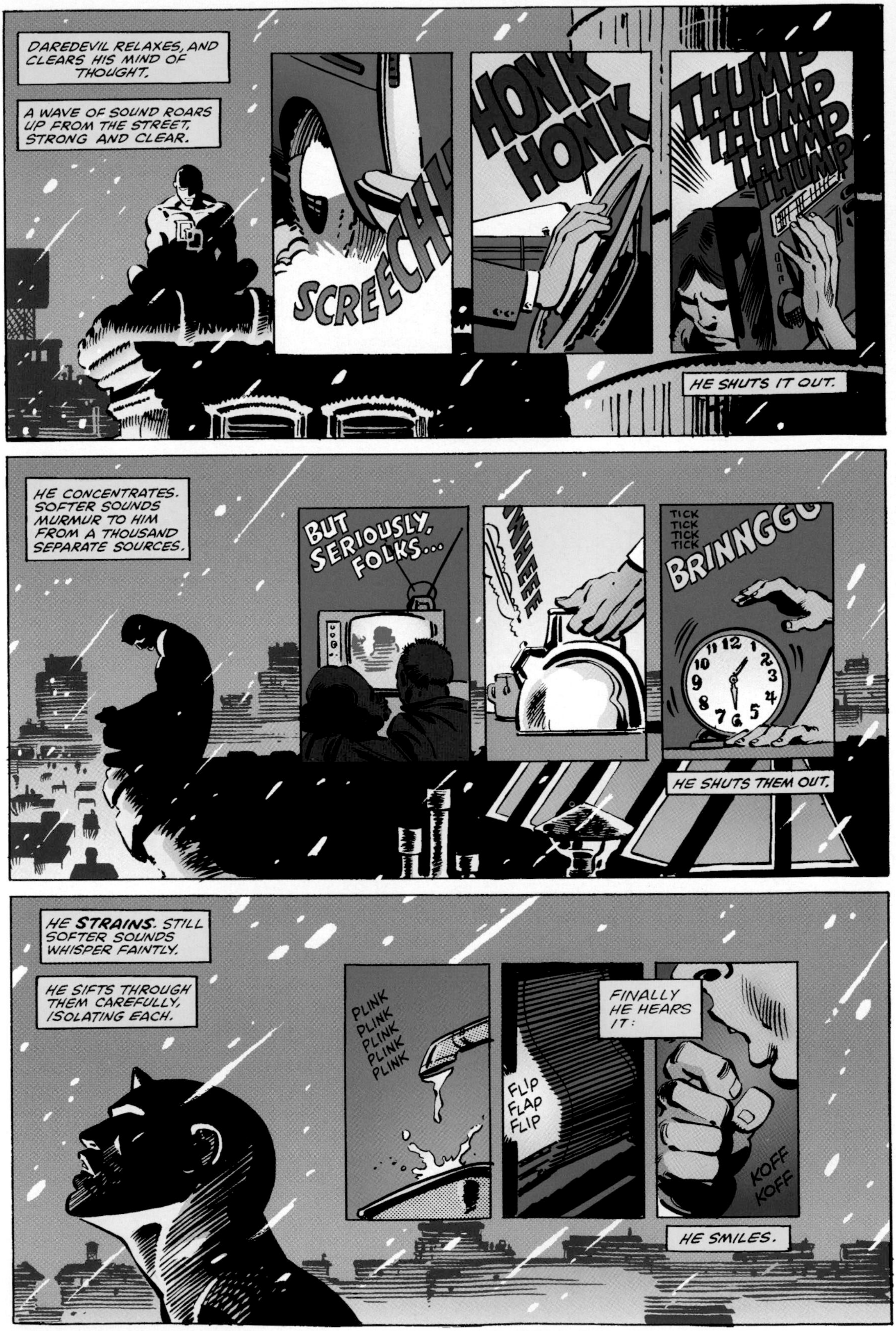
DAREDEVIL RELAXES, AND CLEARS HIS MIND OF THOUGHT.
A WAVE OF SOUND ROARS UP FROM THE STREET, STRONG AND CLEAR.
SCREECH
HONK HONK
THUMP THUMP THUMP THUMP
HE SHUTS IT OUT.
HE CONCENTRATES. SOFTER SOUNDS MURMUR TO HIM FROM A THOUSAND SEPARATE SOURCES.
BUT SERIOUSLY, FOLKS...
TICK TICK TICK TICK
BRINNGG
HE SHUTS THEM OUT.
HE STRAINS. STILL SOFTER SOUNDS WHISPER FAINTLY.
HE SIFTS THROUGH THEM CAREFULLY, ISOLATING EACH.
PLINK PLINK PLINK PLINK PLINK
FLIP FLAP FLIP
FINALLY HE HEARS IT:
KOFF KOFF
HE SMILES.

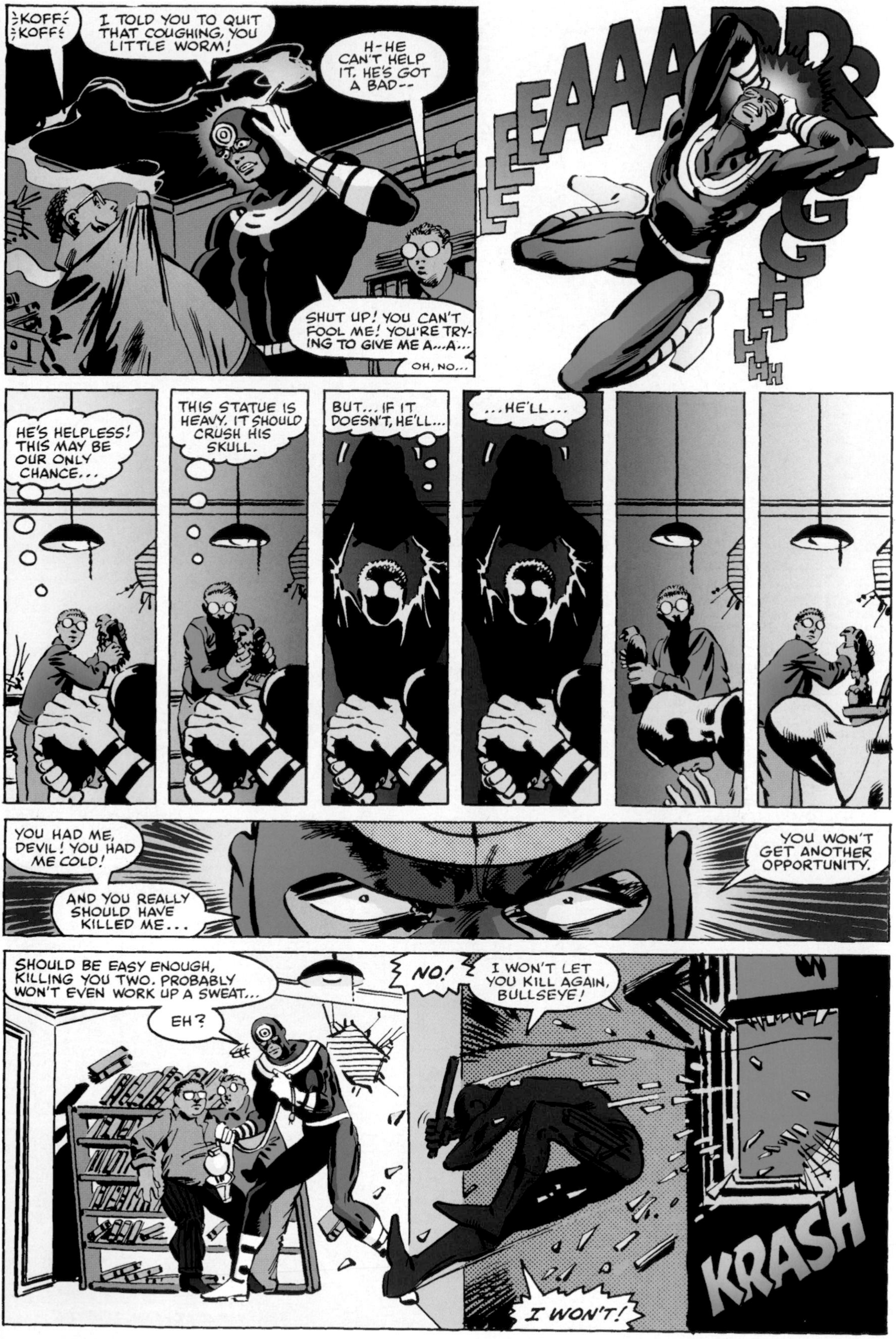

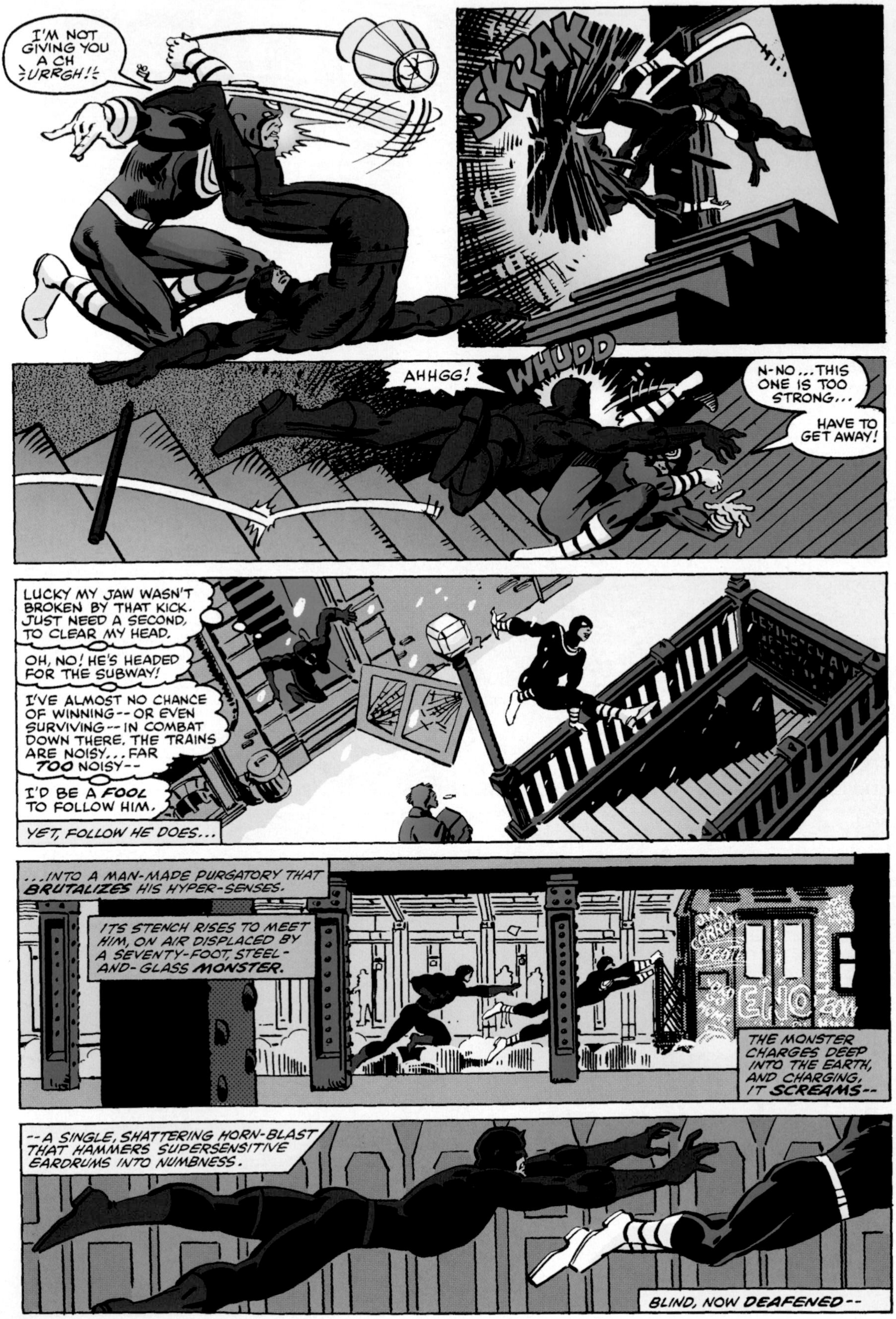
I'M NOT GIVING YOU A CH URRGH!!
SKRAK
AHHGG!
WHUDD
N-NO... THIS ONE IS TOO STRONG...
HAVE TO GET AWAY!
LUCKY MY JAW WASN'T BROKEN BY THAT KICK. JUST NEED A SECOND, TO CLEAR MY HEAD.
OH, NO! HE'S HEADED FOR THE SUBWAY!
I'VE ALMOST NO CHANCE OF WINNING--OR EVEN SURVIVING--IN COMBAT DOWN THERE. THE TRAINS ARE NOISY... FAR TOO NOISY--
I'D BE A FOOL TO FOLLOW HIM.
YET, FOLLOW HE DOES...
...INTO A MAN-MADE PURGATORY THAT BRUTALIZES HIS HYPER-SENSES.
ITS STENCH RISES TO MEET HIM, ON AIR DISPLACED BY A SEVENTY-FOOT, STEEL-AND-GLASS MONSTER.
THE MONSTER CHARGES DEEP INTO THE EARTH, AND CHARGING, IT SCREAMS--
--A SINGLE, SHATTERING HORN-BLAST THAT HAMMERS SUPERSENSITIVE EARDRUMS INTO NUMBNESS.
BLIND, NOW DEAFENED--

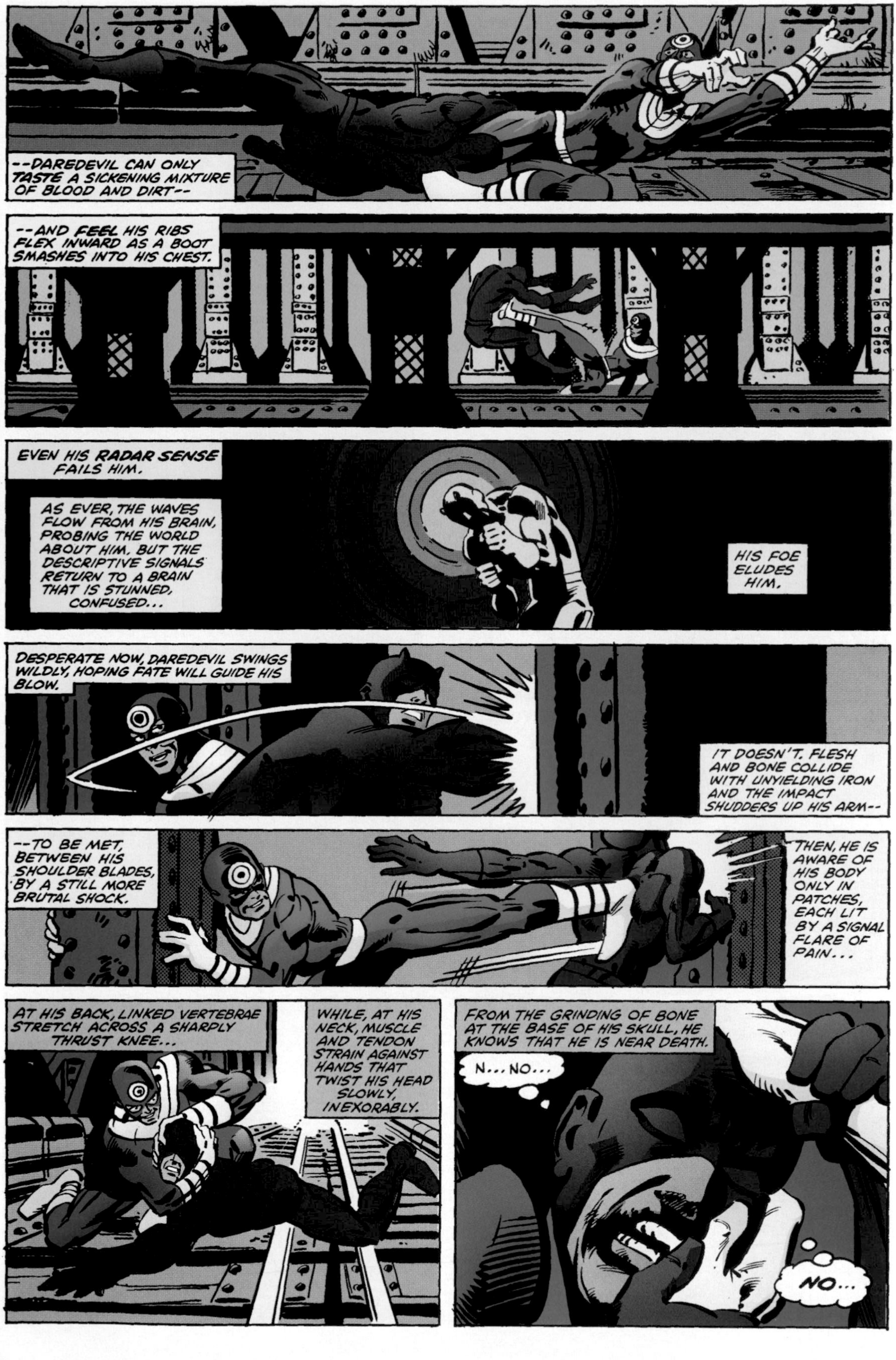
--DAREDEVIL CAN ONLY TASTE A SICKENING MIXTURE OF BLOOD AND DIRT--
--AND FEEL HIS RIBS FLEX INWARD AS A BOOT SMASHES INTO HIS CHEST.
EVEN HIS RADAR SENSE FAILS HIM.
AS EVER, THE WAVES FLOW FROM HIS BRAIN, PROBING THE WORLD ABOUT HIM. BUT THE DESCRIPTIVE SIGNALS RETURN TO A BRAIN THAT IS STUNNED, CONFUSED...
HIS FOE ELUDES HIM.
DESPERATE NOW, DAREDEVIL SWINGS WILDLY, HOPING FATE WILL GUIDE HIS BLOW.
IT DOESN'T. FLESH AND BONE COLLIDE WITH UNYIELDING IRON AND THE IMPACT SHUDDERS UP HIS ARM--
--TO BE MET, BETWEEN HIS SHOULDER BLADES, BY A STILL MORE BRUTAL SHOCK.
THEN, HE IS AWARE OF HIS BODY ONLY IN PATCHES, EACH LIT BY A SIGNAL FLARE OF PAIN...
AT HIS BACK, LINKED VERTEBRAE STRETCH ACROSS A SHARPLY THRUST KNEE...
WHILE, AT HIS NECK, MUSCLE AND TENDON STRAIN AGAINST HANDS THAT TWIST HIS HEAD SLOWLY, INEXORABLY.
FROM THE GRINDING OF BONE AT THE BASE OF HIS SKULL, HE KNOWS THAT HE IS NEAR DEATH.
N...NO...
NO...

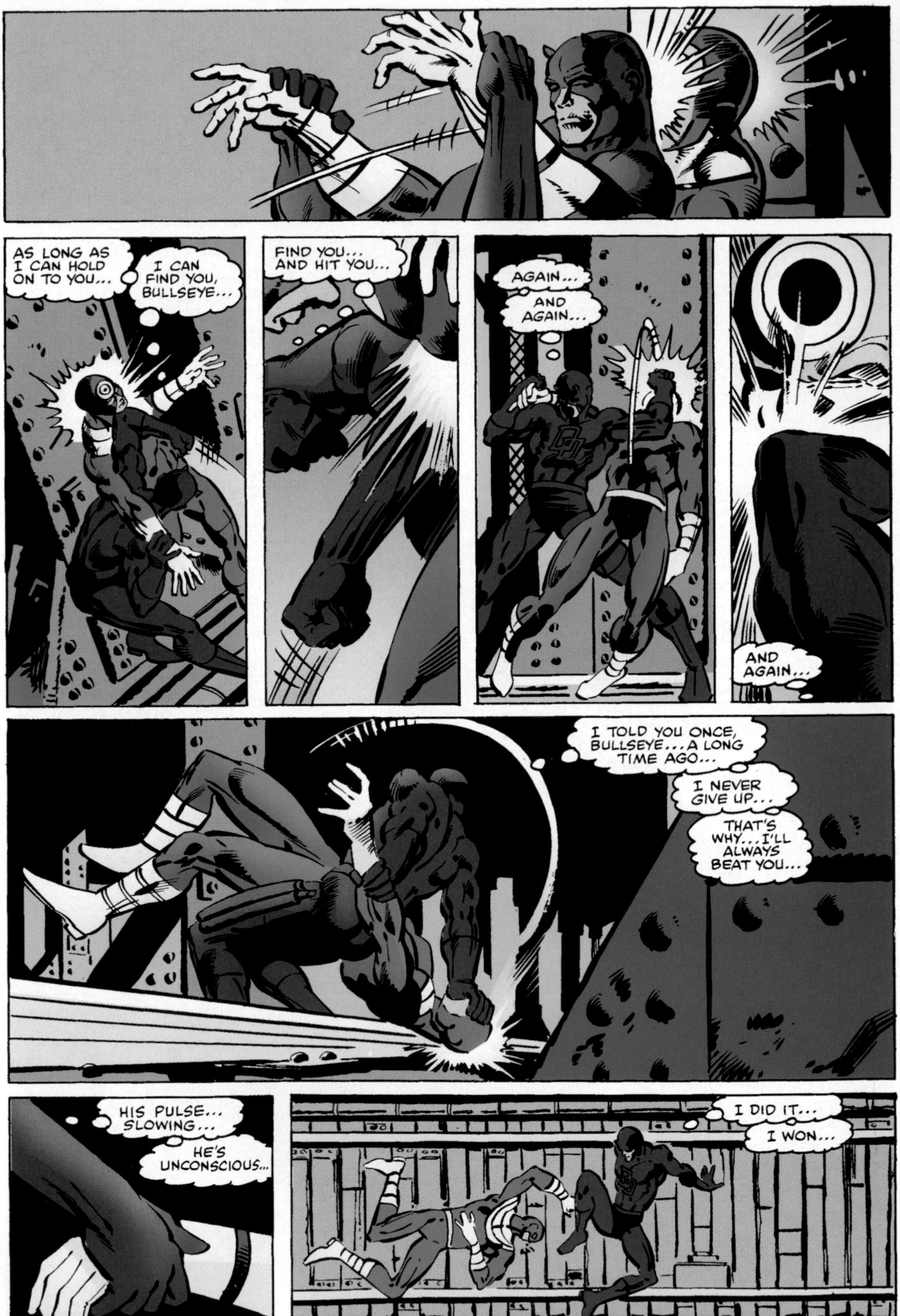
AS LONG AS I CAN HOLD ON TO YOU...
I CAN FIND YOU, BULLSEYE...
FIND YOU... AND HIT YOU...
AGAIN...
AND AGAIN...
AND AGAIN...
I TOLD YOU ONCE, BULLSEYE... A LONG TIME AGO...
I NEVER GIVE UP...
THAT'S WHY... I'LL ALWAYS BEAT YOU...
HIS PULSE... SLOWING...
HE'S UNCONSCIOUS...
I DID IT...
I WON...

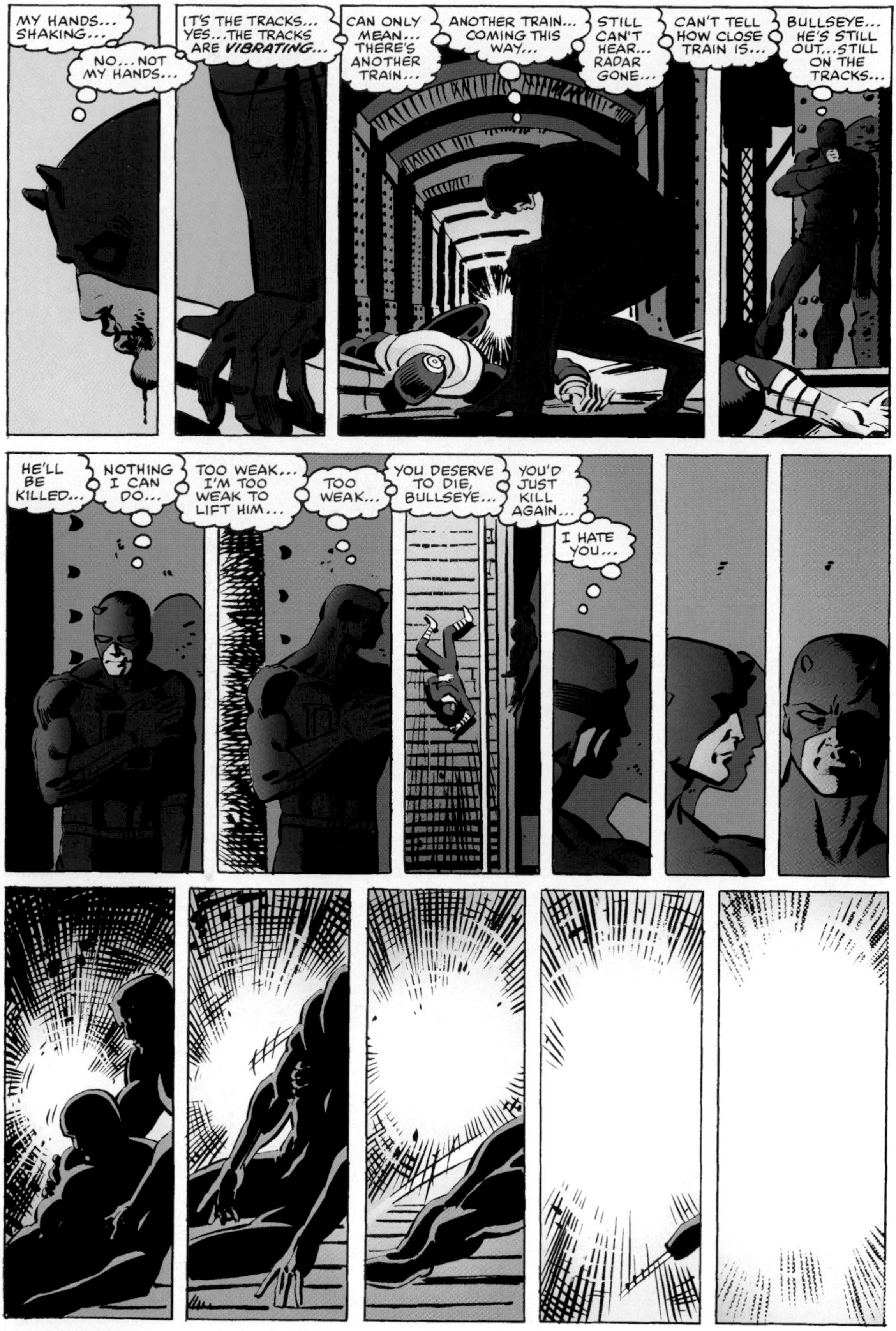
MY HANDS... SHAKING...
NO... NOT MY HANDS...
IT'S THE TRACKS... YES... THE TRACKS ARE *VIBRATING*...
CAN ONLY MEAN... THERE'S ANOTHER TRAIN...
ANOTHER TRAIN... COMING THIS WAY...
STILL CAN'T HEAR... RADAR GONE...
CAN'T TELL HOW CLOSE TRAIN IS...
BULLSEYE... HE'S STILL OUT... STILL ON THE TRACKS...
HE'LL BE KILLED...
NOTHING I CAN DO...
TOO WEAK... I'M TOO WEAK TO LIFT HIM...
TOO WEAK...
YOU DESERVE TO DIE, BULLSEYE...
YOU'D JUST KILL AGAIN...
I HATE YOU...

DAWN.

WHY'D YOU DO IT, DAREDEVIL?

YOU SHOULD HAVE LET HIM DIE!

STOP YELLING, MANOLIS. I HAVE AN EAR ACHE.

DO YOU KNOW WHAT'S GONNA HAPPEN NOW? DO YOU?

IF THAT OPERATION DOWN THERE IS SUCCESSFUL, BULLSEYE WILL LIVE--AND HE'LL HIRE HIMSELF SOME SLICK, HIGH-PRICED LAWYER--

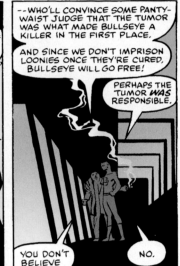

--WHO'LL CONVINCE SOME PANTY-WAIST JUDGE THAT THE TUMOR WAS WHAT MADE BULLSEYE A KILLER IN THE FIRST PLACE,

AND SINCE WE DON'T IMPRISON LOONIES ONCE THEY'RE CURED, BULLSEYE WILL GO FREE!

PERHAPS THE TUMOR *WAS* RESPONSIBLE.

YOU DON'T BELIEVE THAT.

NO.

NICK, MEN LIKE BULLSEYE WOULD RULE THE WORLD--

--WERE IT NOT FOR A STRUCTURE OF *LAWS* THAT SOCIETY HAS CREATED TO KEEP SUCH MEN IN CHECK.

THE MOMENT ONE MAN TAKES ANOTHER MAN'S LIFE IN HIS OWN HANDS, HE IS REJECTING THE LAW--AND WORKING TO DESTROY THAT STRUCTURE.

IF BULLSEYE IS A MENACE TO SOCIETY, IT IS SOCIETY THAT MUST MAKE HIM PAY THE PRICE. NOT YOU. AND NOT ME.

I--I WANTED HIM TO DIE, NICK, I DETEST WHAT HE DOES... WHAT HE *IS.*

BUT I'M NOT GOD-- I'M NOT THE LAW--

--AND I'M NOT A MURDERER.

HE'S GONNA GO FREE. HE'S GONNA KILL AGAIN.

AND NEXT TIME IT'LL BE YOUR FAULT.

DAREDEVIL DOES NOT ANSWER. HE TURNS AND SLOWLY WALKS OFF, PRAYING THAT TONIGHT HE HAS DONE THE RIGHT THING...

...AS FROM BEHIND HIM, HE HEARS THE SURGEON'S VOICE:

SKRIKK

GENTLEMEN, THE OPERATION IS A SUCCESS.

THE PATIENT WILL LIVE.

END.

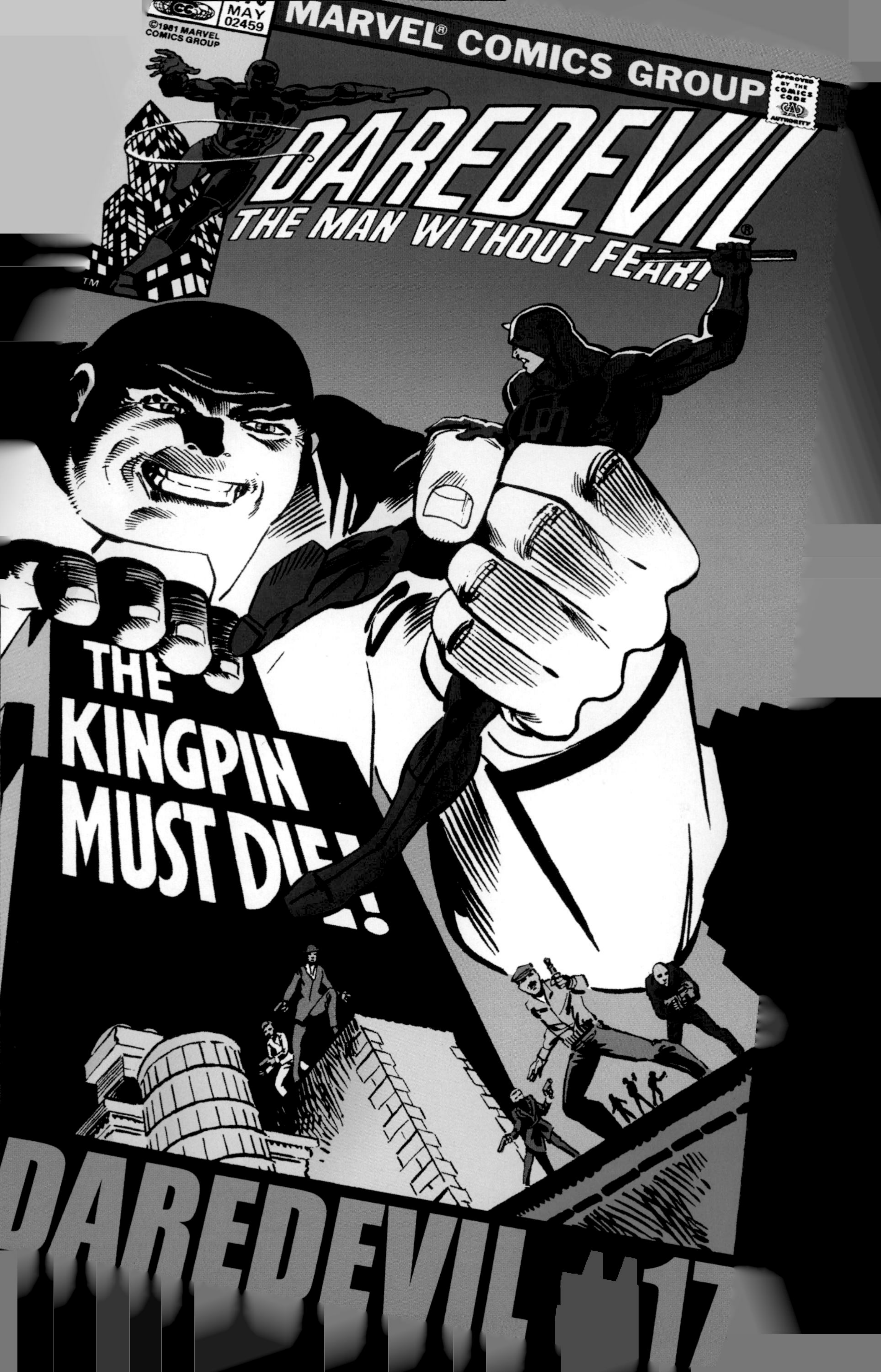

MAY
02459
©1981 MARVEL COMICS GROUP
MARVEL® COMICS GROUP
APPROVED BY THE COMICS CODE AUTHORITY
DAREDEVIL®
THE MAN WITHOUT FEAR!
TM
THE KINGPIN MUST DIE!
DAREDEVIL

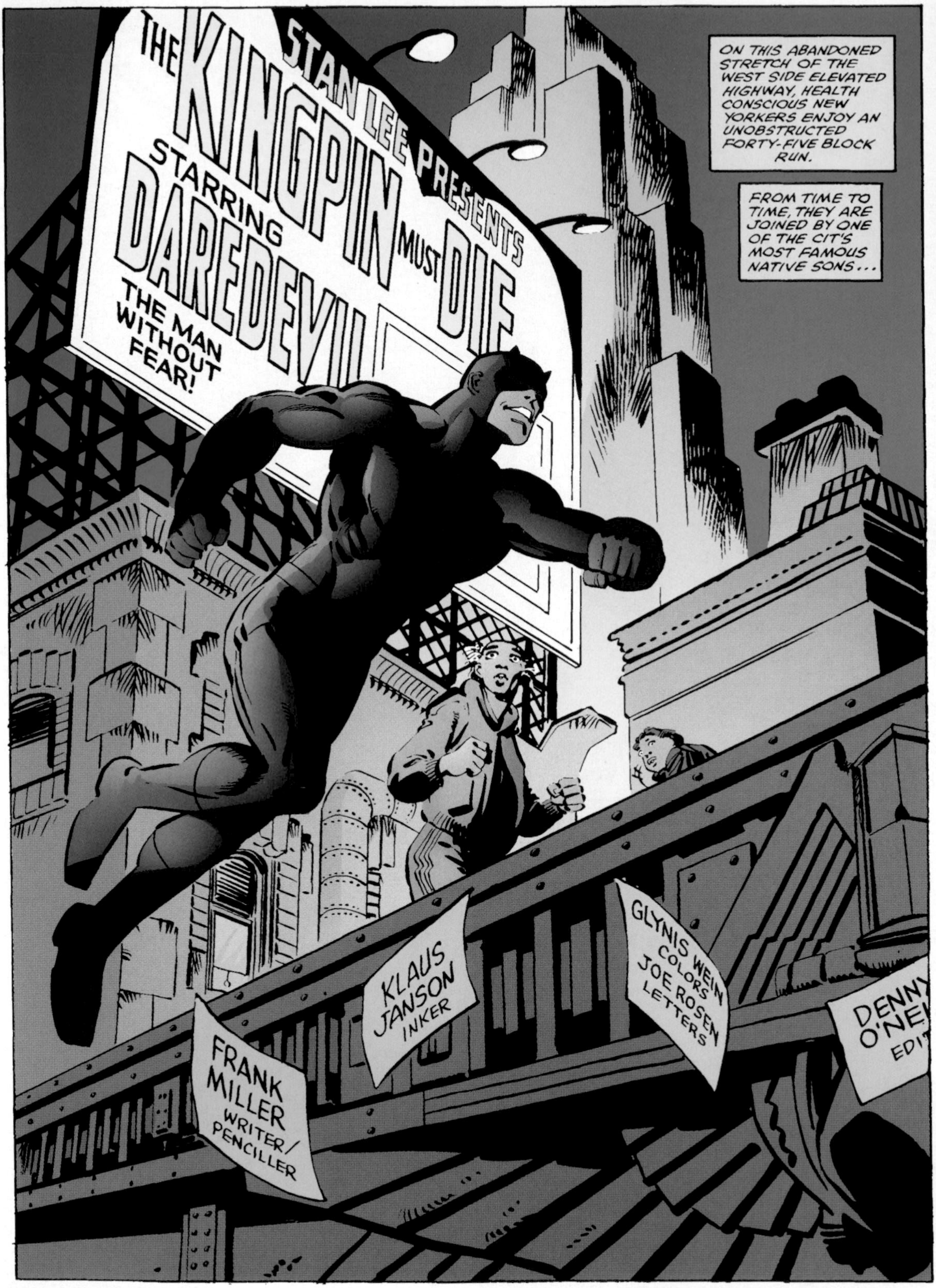
STAN LEE PRESENTS
THE KINGPIN MUST DIE
STARRING DAREDEVIL
THE MAN WITHOUT FEAR!
ON THIS ABANDONED STRETCH OF THE WEST SIDE ELEVATED HIGHWAY, HEALTH CONSCIOUS NEW YORKERS ENJOY AN UNOBSTRUCTED FORTY-FIVE BLOCK RUN.
FROM TIME TO TIME, THEY ARE JOINED BY ONE OF THE CIT'S MOST FAMOUS NATIVE SONS...
FRANK MILLER WRITER/ PENCILLER
KLAUS JANSON INKER
GLYNIS WEIN COLORS
JOE ROSEN LETTERS

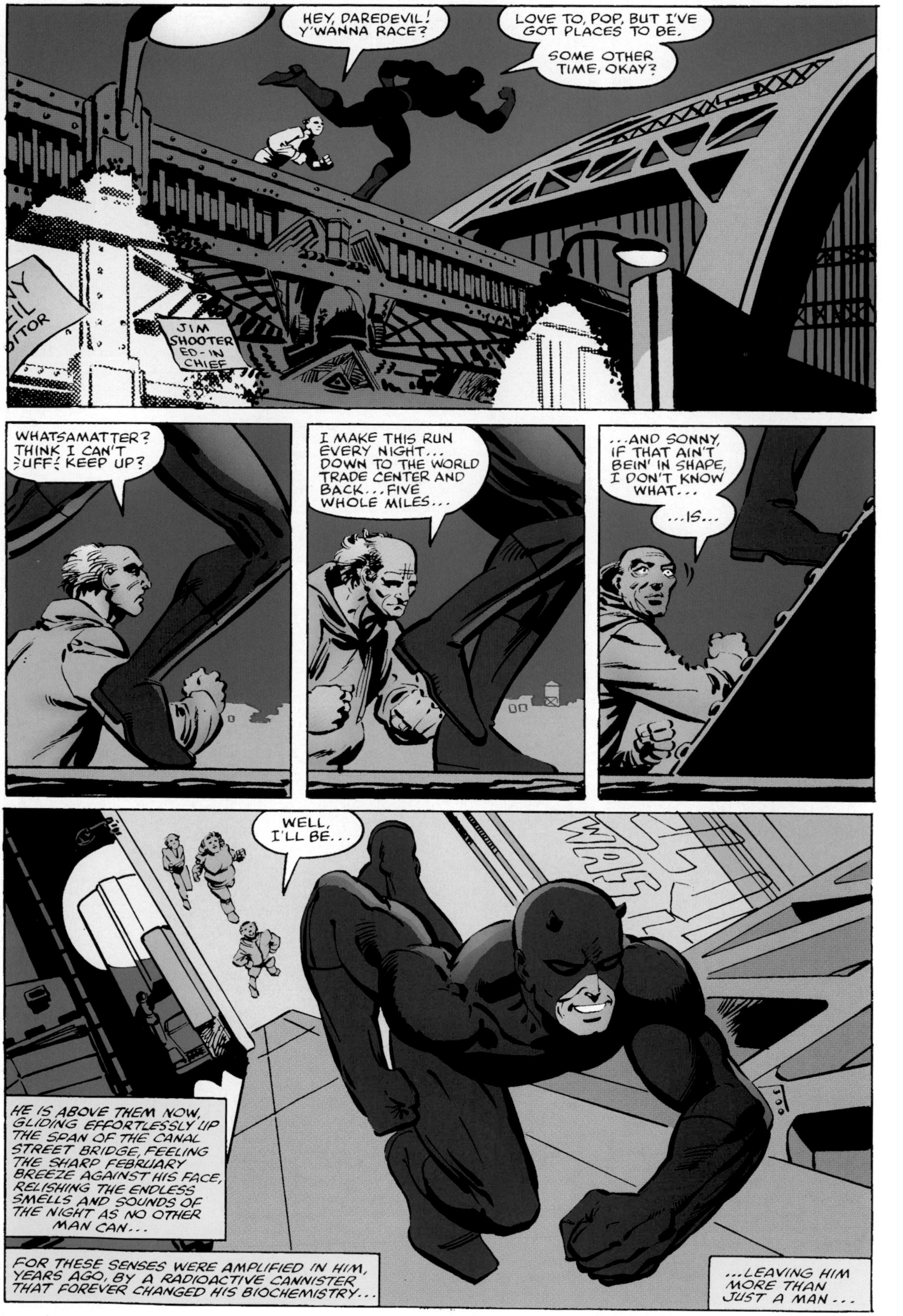
HEY, DAREDEVIL! Y'WANNA RACE?
LOVE TO, POP, BUT I'VE GOT PLACES TO BE.
SOME OTHER TIME, OKAY?
JIM SHOOTER ED-IN CHIEF
WHATSAMATTER? THINK I CAN'T ≷UFF≶ KEEP UP?
I MAKE THIS RUN EVERY NIGHT... DOWN TO THE WORLD TRADE CENTER AND BACK...FIVE WHOLE MILES...
...AND SONNY, IF THAT AIN'T BEIN' IN SHAPE, I DON'T KNOW WHAT...
...IS...
WELL, I'LL BE...
HE IS ABOVE THEM NOW, GLIDING EFFORTLESSLY UP THE SPAN OF THE CANAL STREET BRIDGE, FEELING THE SHARP FEBRUARY BREEZE AGAINST HIS FACE, RELISHING THE ENDLESS SMELLS AND SOUNDS OF THE NIGHT AS NO OTHER MAN CAN...
FOR THESE SENSES WERE AMPLIFIED IN HIM, YEARS AGO, BY A RADIOACTIVE CANNISTER THAT FOREVER CHANGED HIS BIOCHEMISTRY...
...LEAVING HIM MORE THAN JUST A MAN...

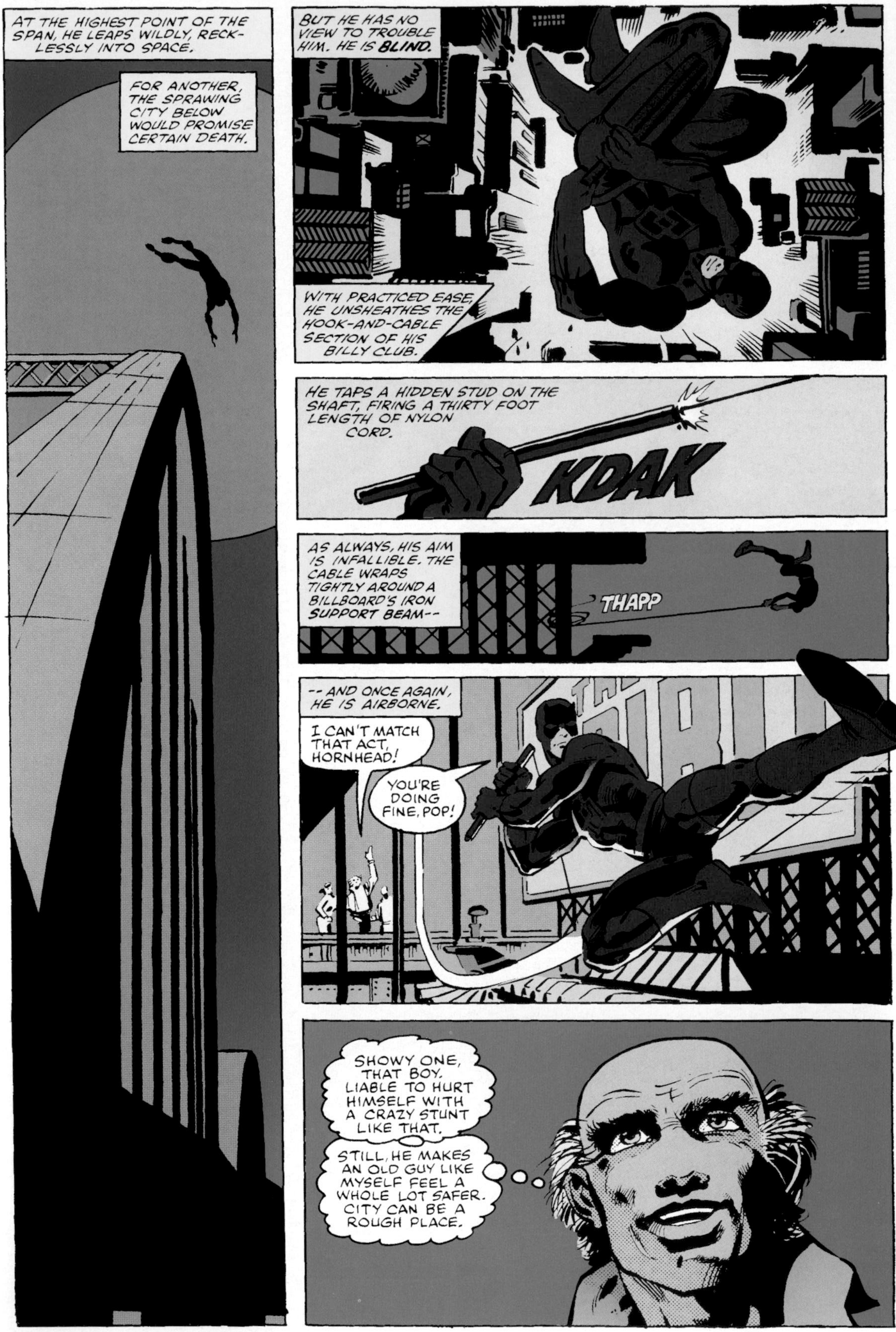
AT THE HIGHEST POINT OF THE SPAN, HE LEAPS WILDLY, RECKLESSLY INTO SPACE.
FOR ANOTHER, THE SPRAWING CITY BELOW WOULD PROMISE CERTAIN DEATH.
BUT HE HAS NO VIEW TO TROUBLE HIM. HE IS BLIND.
WITH PRACTICED EASE, HE UNSHEATHES THE HOOK-AND-CABLE SECTION OF HIS BILLY CLUB.
HE TAPS A HIDDEN STUD ON THE SHAFT, FIRING A THIRTY FOOT LENGTH OF NYLON CORD.
KDAK
AS ALWAYS, HIS AIM IS INFALLIBLE. THE CABLE WRAPS TIGHTLY AROUND A BILLBOARD'S IRON SUPPORT BEAM--
THAPP
-- AND ONCE AGAIN, HE IS AIRBORNE.
I CAN'T MATCH THAT ACT, HORNHEAD!
YOU'RE DOING FINE, POP!
SHOWY ONE, THAT BOY. LIABLE TO HURT HIMSELF WITH A CRAZY STUNT LIKE THAT.
STILL, HE MAKES AN OLD GUY LIKE MYSELF FEEL A WHOLE LOT SAFER. CITY CAN BE A ROUGH PLACE.

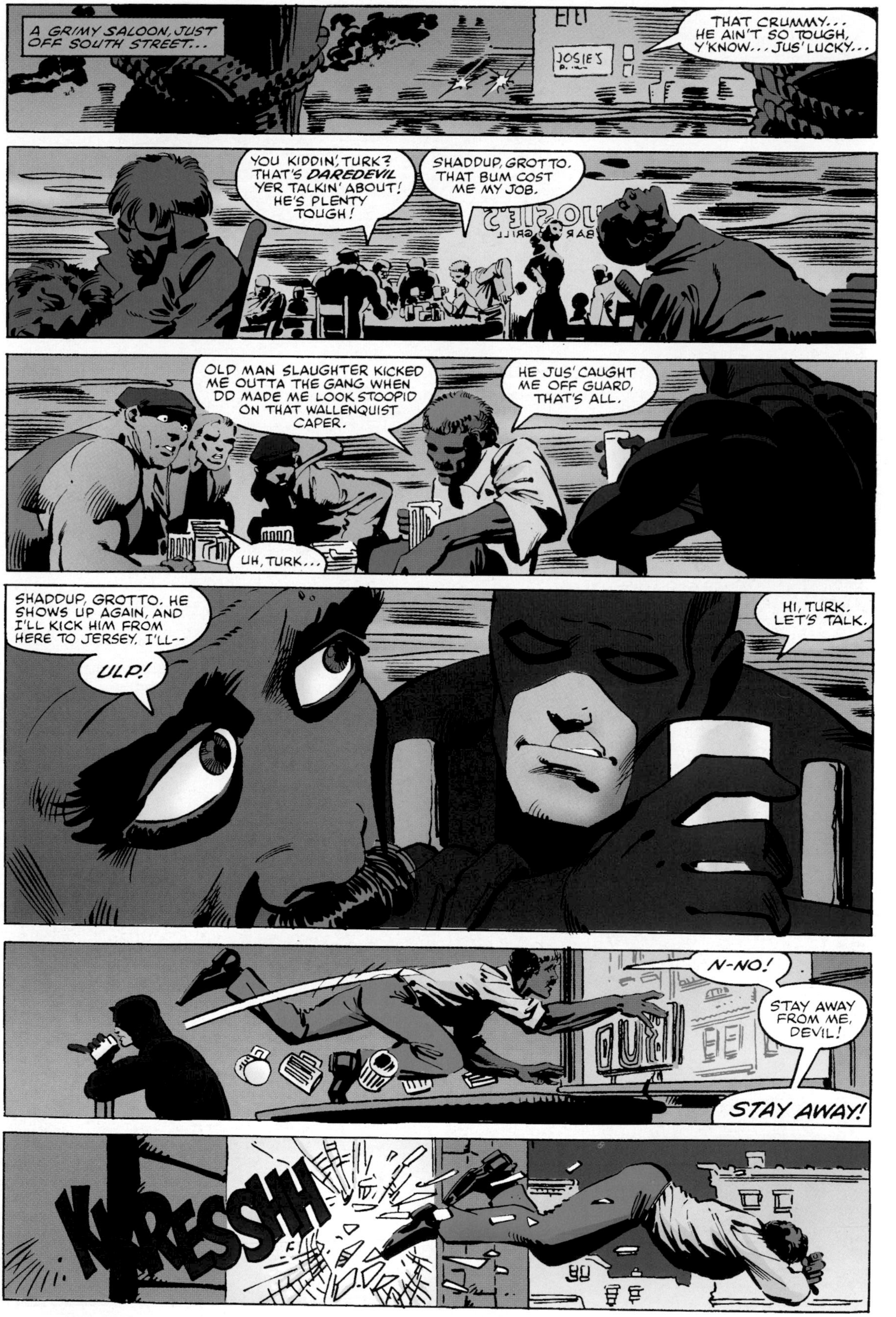
A GRIMY SALOON, JUST OFF SOUTH STREET...
JOSIE'S
THAT CRUMMY... HE AIN'T SO TOUGH, Y'KNOW... JUS' LUCKY...
YOU KIDDIN', TURK? THAT'S DAREDEVIL YER TALKIN' ABOUT! HE'S PLENTY TOUGH!
SHADDUP, GROTTO. THAT BUM COST ME MY JOB.
JOSIE'S BAR GRILL
OLD MAN SLAUGHTER KICKED ME OUTTA THE GANG WHEN DD MADE ME LOOK STOOPID ON THAT WALLENQUIST CAPER.
HE JUS' CAUGHT ME OFF GUARD, THAT'S ALL.
UH, TURK...
SHADDUP, GROTTO. HE SHOWS UP AGAIN, AND I'LL KICK HIM FROM HERE TO JERSEY. I'LL--
ULP!
HI, TURK. LET'S TALK.
N-NO!
STAY AWAY FROM ME, DEVIL!
STAY AWAY!
KRESSH

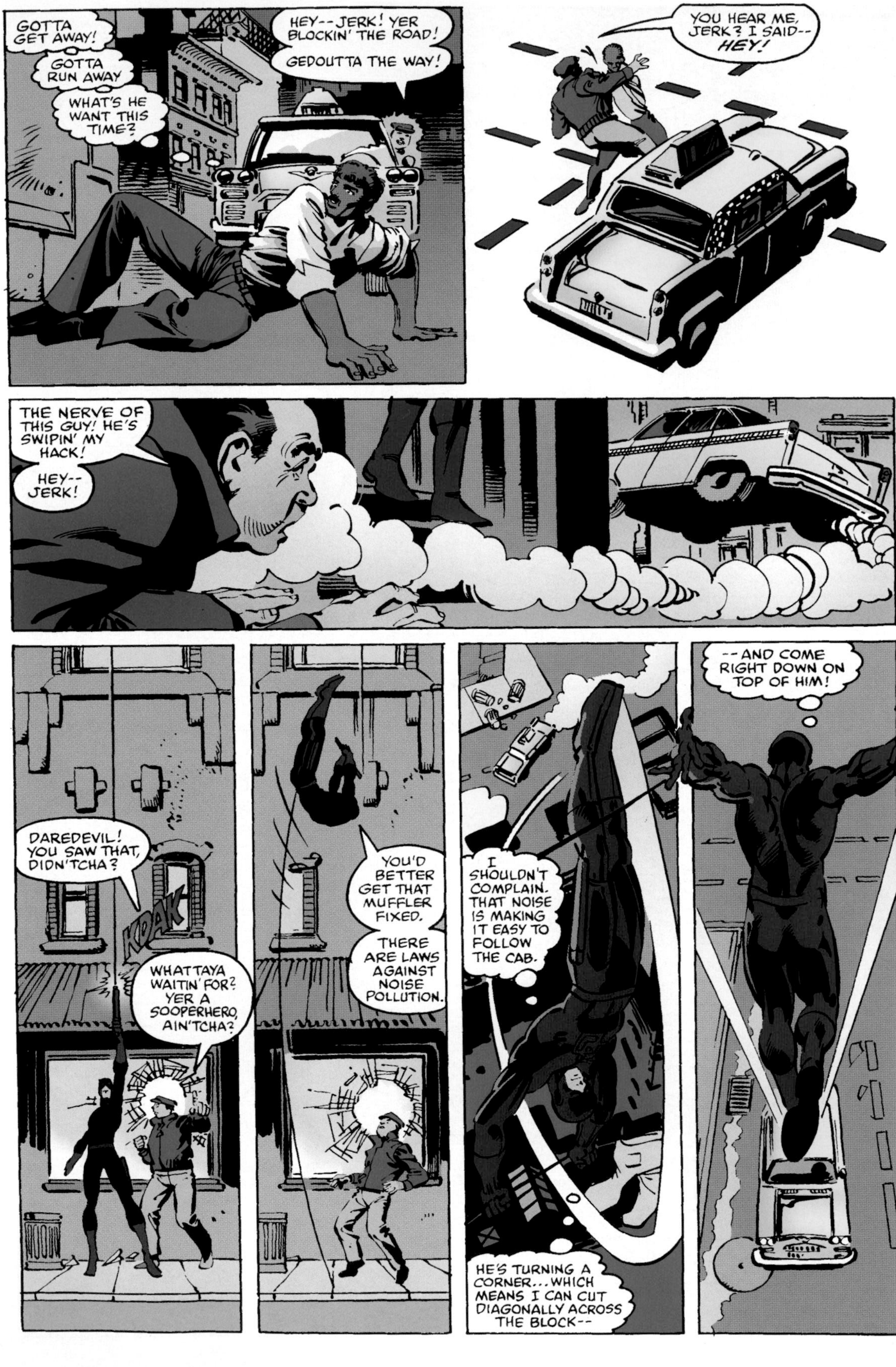

GOTTA GET AWAY!
GOTTA RUN AWAY
WHAT'S HE WANT THIS TIME?
HEY--JERK! YER BLOCKIN' THE ROAD!
GEDOUTTA THE WAY!
YOU HEAR ME, JERK? I SAID-- HEY!
THE NERVE OF THIS GUY! HE'S SWIPIN' MY HACK!
HEY-- JERK!
DAREDEVIL! YOU SAW THAT, DIDN'TCHA?
KDAK
WHATTAYA WAITIN' FOR? YER A SOOPERHERO, AIN'TCHA?
YOU'D BETTER GET THAT MUFFLER FIXED.
THERE ARE LAWS AGAINST NOISE POLLUTION.
I SHOULDN'T COMPLAIN. THAT NOISE IS MAKING IT EASY TO FOLLOW THE CAB.
HE'S TURNING A CORNER... WHICH MEANS I CAN CUT DIAGONALLY ACROSS THE BLOCK--
--AND COME RIGHT DOWN ON TOP OF HIM!

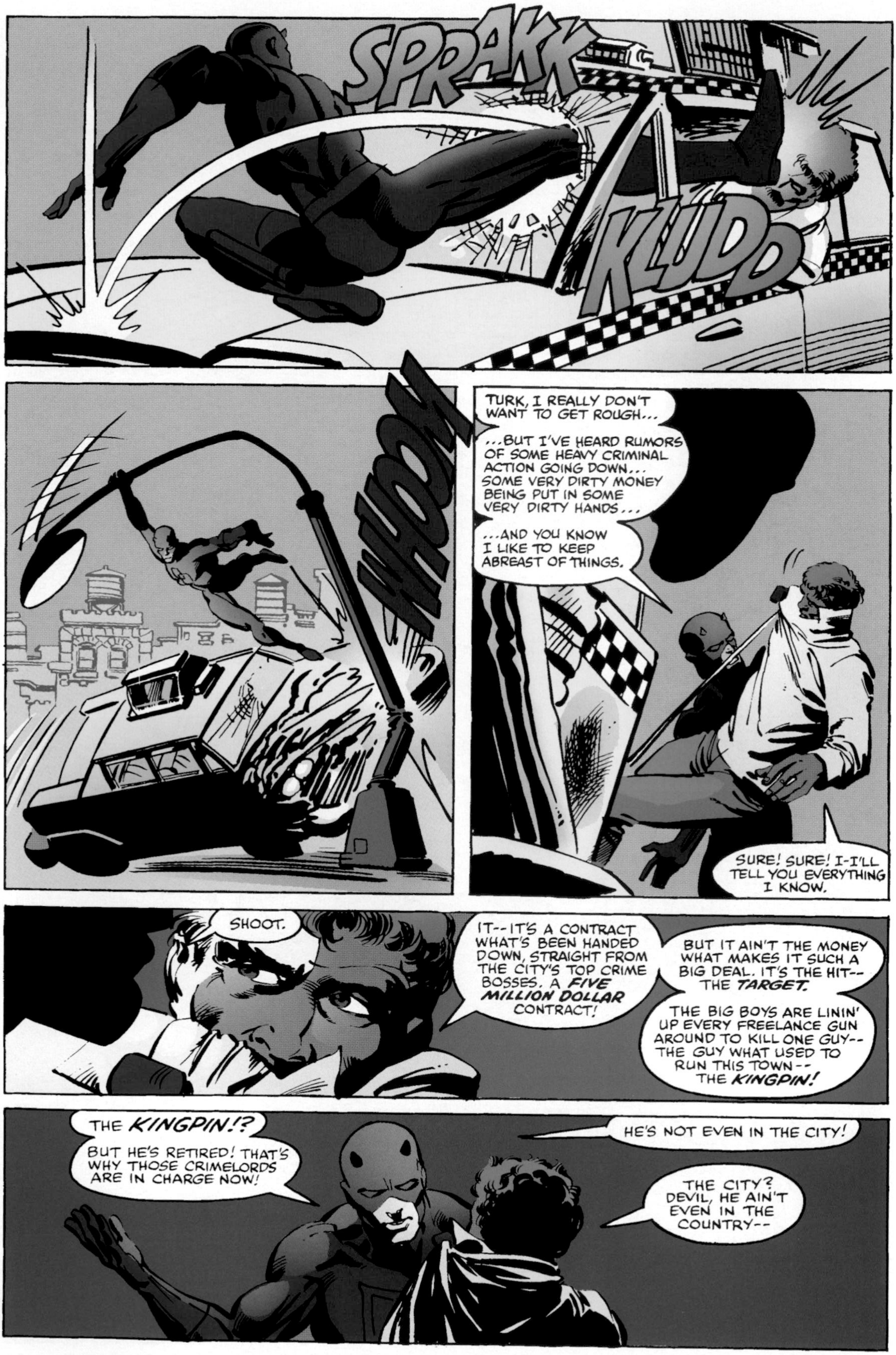
SPRAKK
KLUDD
WHOOSH
TURK, I REALLY DON'T WANT TO GET ROUGH...
...BUT I'VE HEARD RUMORS OF SOME HEAVY CRIMINAL ACTION GOING DOWN... SOME VERY DIRTY MONEY BEING PUT IN SOME VERY DIRTY HANDS...
...AND YOU KNOW I LIKE TO KEEP ABREAST OF THINGS.
SURE! SURE! I-I'LL TELL YOU EVERYTHING I KNOW.
SHOOT.
IT--IT'S A CONTRACT WHAT'S BEEN HANDED DOWN, STRAIGHT FROM THE CITY'S TOP CRIME BOSSES. A FIVE MILLION DOLLAR CONTRACT!
BUT IT AIN'T THE MONEY WHAT MAKES IT SUCH A BIG DEAL. IT'S THE HIT-- THE TARGET.
THE BIG BOYS ARE LININ' UP EVERY FREELANCE GUN AROUND TO KILL ONE GUY-- THE GUY WHAT USED TO RUN THIS TOWN-- THE KINGPIN!
THE KINGPIN!?
BUT HE'S RETIRED! THAT'S WHY THOSE CRIMELORDS ARE IN CHARGE NOW!
HE'S NOT EVEN IN THE CITY!
THE CITY? DEVIL, HE AIN'T EVEN IN THE COUNTRY--

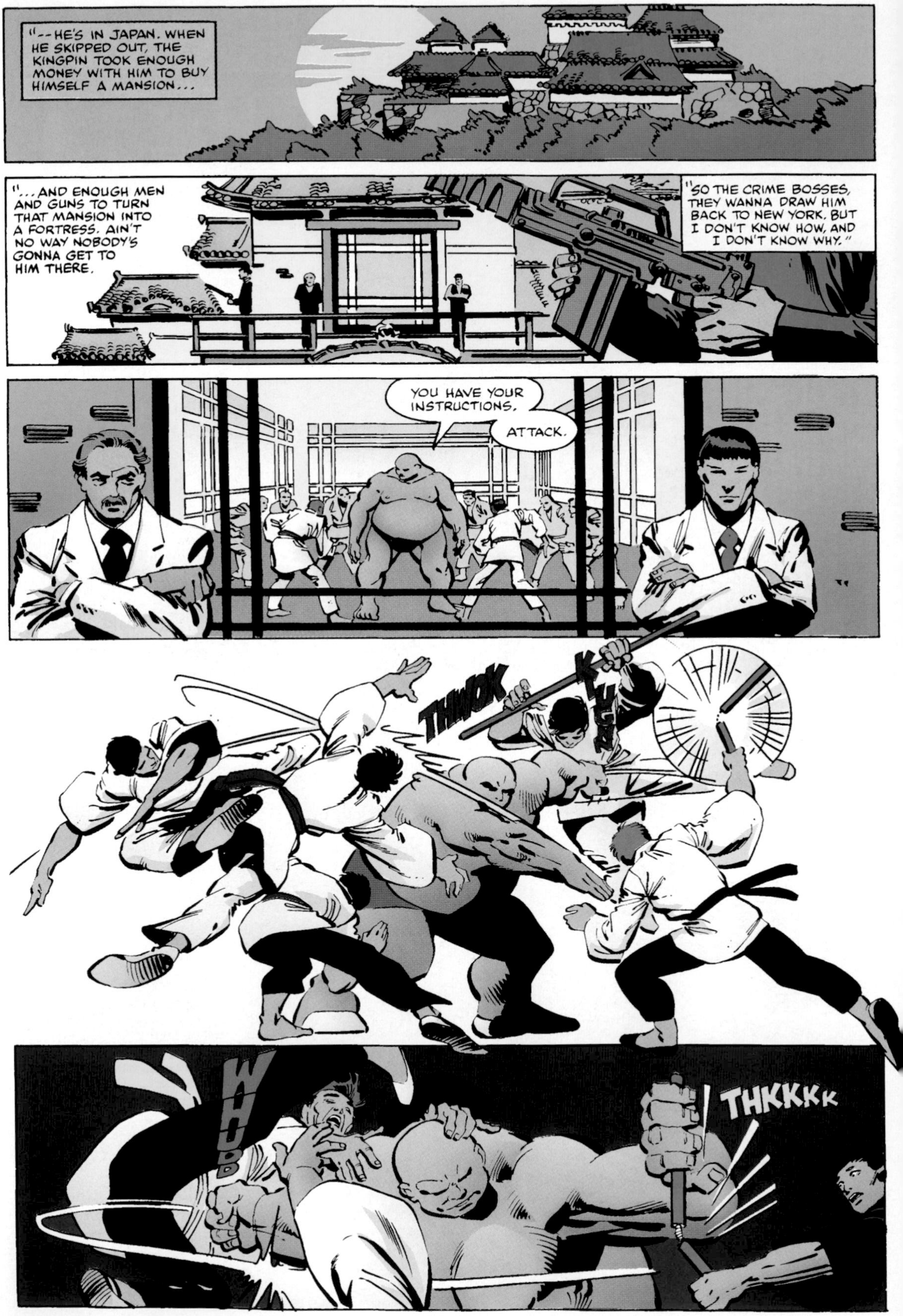
"--HE'S IN JAPAN. WHEN HE SKIPPED OUT, THE KINGPIN TOOK ENOUGH MONEY WITH HIM TO BUY HIMSELF A MANSION...
"...AND ENOUGH MEN AND GUNS TO TURN THAT MANSION INTO A FORTRESS. AIN'T NO WAY NOBODY'S GONNA GET TO HIM THERE.
"SO THE CRIME BOSSES, THEY WANNA DRAW HIM BACK TO NEW YORK. BUT I DON'T KNOW HOW, AND I DON'T KNOW WHY."
YOU HAVE YOUR INSTRUCTIONS.
ATTACK.
THWOK
THKKKK

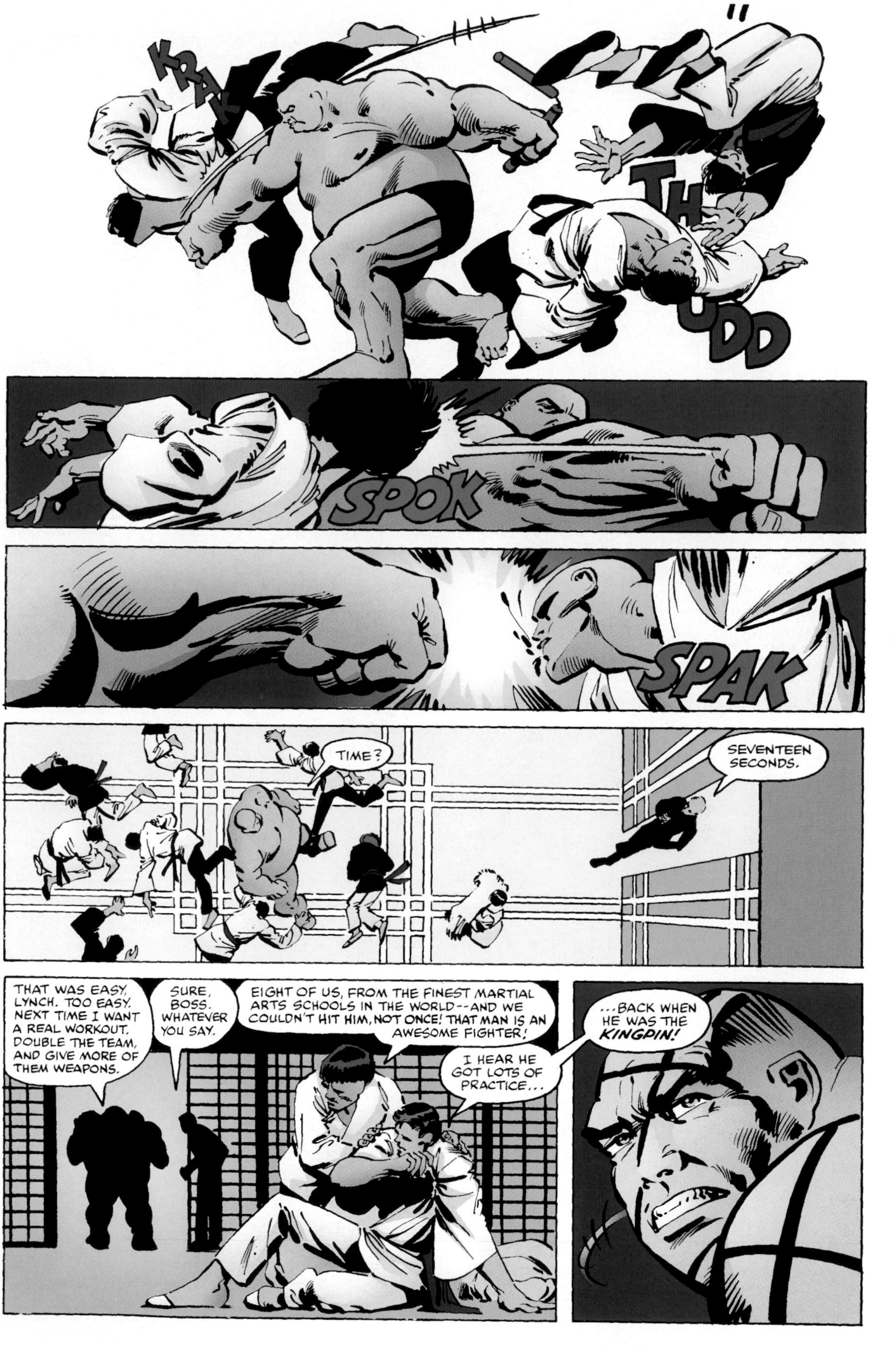

KRAK
THUDD
SPOK
SPAK
TIME?
SEVENTEEN SECONDS.
THAT WAS EASY, LYNCH. TOO EASY. NEXT TIME I WANT A REAL WORKOUT. DOUBLE THE TEAM, AND GIVE MORE OF THEM WEAPONS.
SURE, BOSS. WHATEVER YOU SAY.
EIGHT OF US, FROM THE FINEST MARTIAL ARTS SCHOOLS IN THE WORLD--AND WE COULDN'T HIT HIM, NOT ONCE! THAT MAN IS AN AWESOME FIGHTER!
I HEAR HE GOT LOTS OF PRACTICE...
...BACK WHEN HE WAS THE *KINGPIN!*

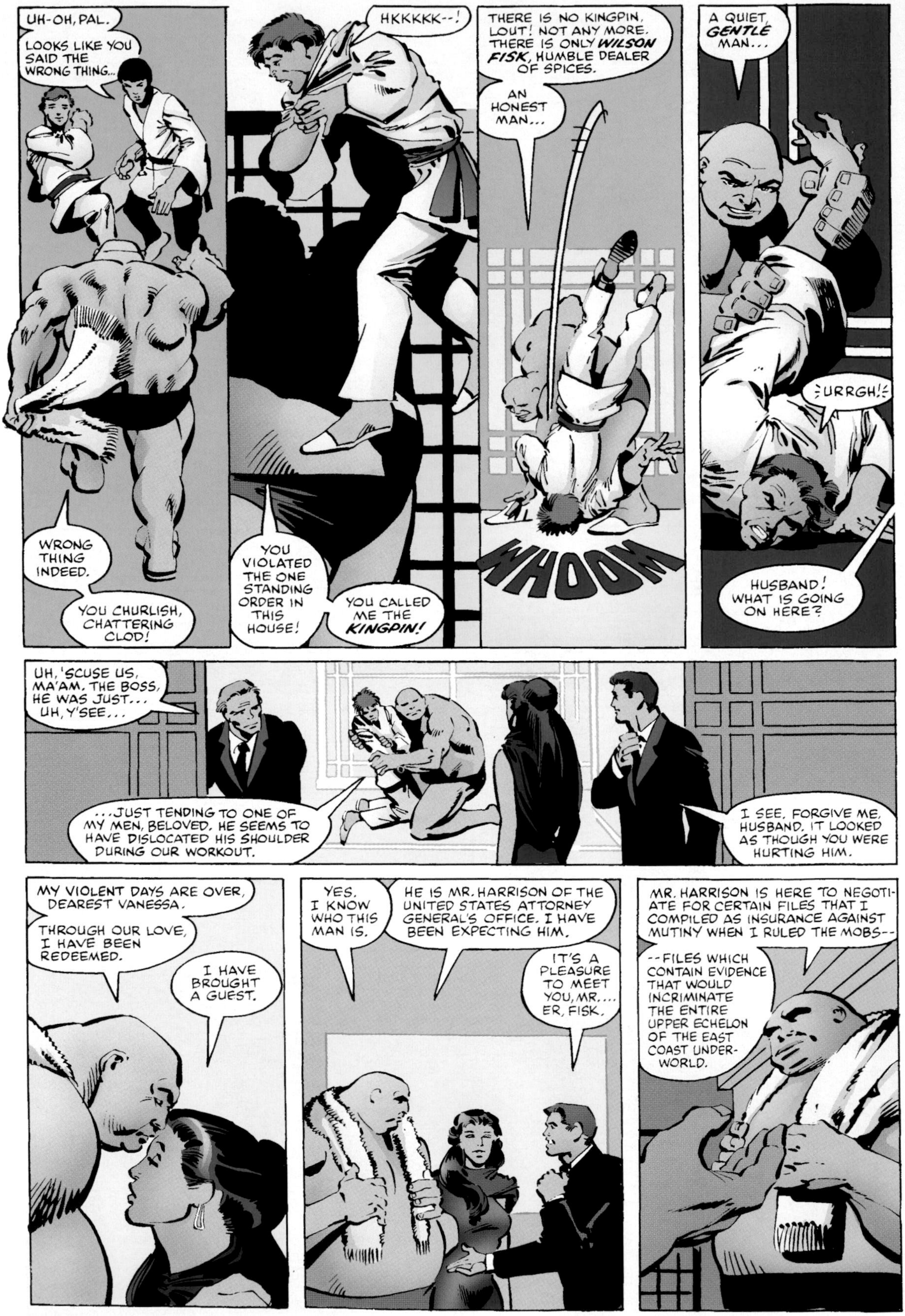
UH-OH, PAL.
LOOKS LIKE YOU SAID THE WRONG THING...
WRONG THING INDEED.
YOU CHURLISH, CHATTERING CLOD!
HKKKKK--!
YOU VIOLATED THE ONE STANDING ORDER IN THIS HOUSE!
YOU CALLED ME THE KINGPIN!
THERE IS NO KINGPIN, LOUT! NOT ANY MORE. THERE IS ONLY WILSON FISK, HUMBLE DEALER OF SPICES.
AN HONEST MAN...
WHOOM
A QUIET, GENTLE MAN...
URRGH!
HUSBAND! WHAT IS GOING ON HERE?
UH, 'SCUSE US, MA'AM. THE BOSS, HE WAS JUST... UH, Y'SEE...
...JUST TENDING TO ONE OF MY MEN, BELOVED. HE SEEMS TO HAVE DISLOCATED HIS SHOULDER DURING OUR WORKOUT.
I SEE. FORGIVE ME, HUSBAND. IT LOOKED AS THOUGH YOU WERE HURTING HIM.
MY VIOLENT DAYS ARE OVER, DEAREST VANESSA.
THROUGH OUR LOVE, I HAVE BEEN REDEEMED.
I HAVE BROUGHT A GUEST.
YES. I KNOW WHO THIS MAN IS.
HE IS MR. HARRISON OF THE UNITED STATES ATTORNEY GENERAL'S OFFICE. I HAVE BEEN EXPECTING HIM.
IT'S A PLEASURE TO MEET YOU, MR.... ER, FISK.
MR. HARRISON IS HERE TO NEGOTIATE FOR CERTAIN FILES THAT I COMPILED AS INSURANCE AGAINST MUTINY WHEN I RULED THE MOBS--
--FILES WHICH CONTAIN EVIDENCE THAT WOULD INCRIMINATE THE ENTIRE UPPER ECHELON OF THE EAST COAST UNDER-WORLD.

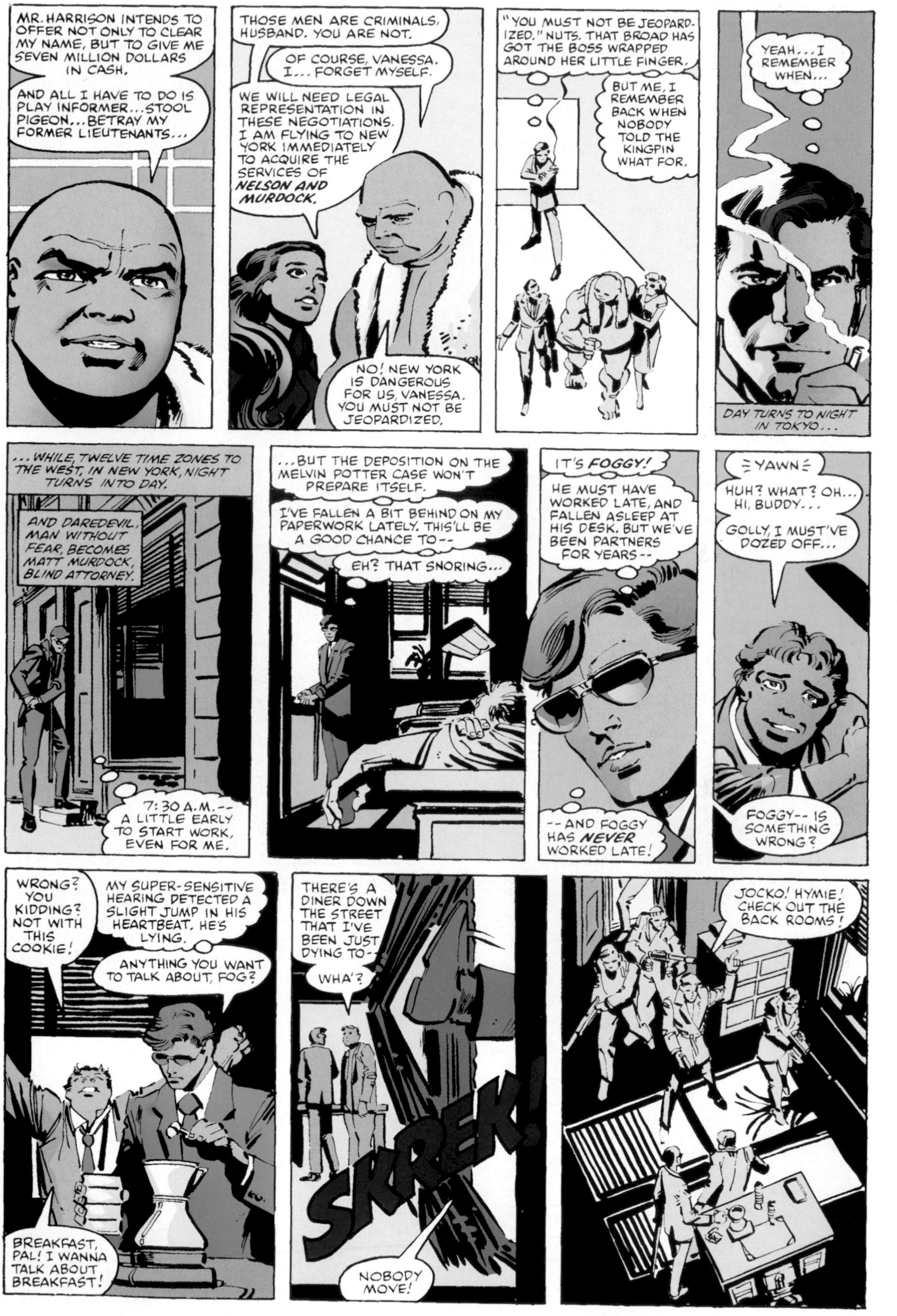
MR. HARRISON INTENDS TO OFFER NOT ONLY TO CLEAR MY NAME, BUT TO GIVE ME SEVEN MILLION DOLLARS IN CASH.
AND ALL I HAVE TO DO IS PLAY INFORMER...STOOL PIGEON...BETRAY MY FORMER LIEUTENANTS...
THOSE MEN ARE CRIMINALS, HUSBAND. YOU ARE NOT.
OF COURSE, VANESSA. I... FORGET MYSELF.
WE WILL NEED LEGAL REPRESENTATION IN THESE NEGOTIATIONS. I AM FLYING TO NEW YORK IMMEDIATELY TO ACQUIRE THE SERVICES OF NELSON AND MURDOCK.
NO! NEW YORK IS DANGEROUS FOR US, VANESSA. YOU MUST NOT BE JEOPARDIZED.
"YOU MUST NOT BE JEOPARDIZED." NUTS. THAT BROAD HAS GOT THE BOSS WRAPPED AROUND HER LITTLE FINGER.
BUT ME, I REMEMBER BACK WHEN NOBODY TOLD THE KINGPIN WHAT FOR.
YEAH...I REMEMBER WHEN...
DAY TURNS TO NIGHT IN TOKYO...
...WHILE, TWELVE TIME ZONES TO THE WEST, IN NEW YORK, NIGHT TURNS INTO DAY.
AND DAREDEVIL, MAN WITHOUT FEAR, BECOMES MATT MURDOCK, BLIND ATTORNEY.
7:30 A.M.-- A LITTLE EARLY TO START WORK, EVEN FOR ME.
...BUT THE DEPOSITION ON THE MELVIN POTTER CASE WON'T PREPARE ITSELF.
I'VE FALLEN A BIT BEHIND ON MY PAPERWORK LATELY. THIS'LL BE A GOOD CHANCE TO--
EH? THAT SNORING...
IT'S FOGGY!
HE MUST HAVE WORKED LATE, AND FALLEN ASLEEP AT HIS DESK. BUT WE'VE BEEN PARTNERS FOR YEARS--
--AND FOGGY HAS NEVER WORKED LATE!
YAWN
HUH? WHAT? OH... HI, BUDDY...
GOLLY, I MUST'VE DOZED OFF...
FOGGY-- IS SOMETHING WRONG?
WRONG? YOU KIDDING? NOT WITH THIS COOKIE!
MY SUPER-SENSITIVE HEARING DETECTED A SLIGHT JUMP IN HIS HEARTBEAT. HE'S LYING.
ANYTHING YOU WANT TO TALK ABOUT, FOG?
BREAKFAST, PAL! I WANNA TALK ABOUT BREAKFAST!
THERE'S A DINER DOWN THE STREET THAT I'VE BEEN JUST DYING TO--
WHA'?
SKREEK!
NOBODY MOVE!
JOCKO! HYMIE! CHECK OUT THE BACK ROOMS!

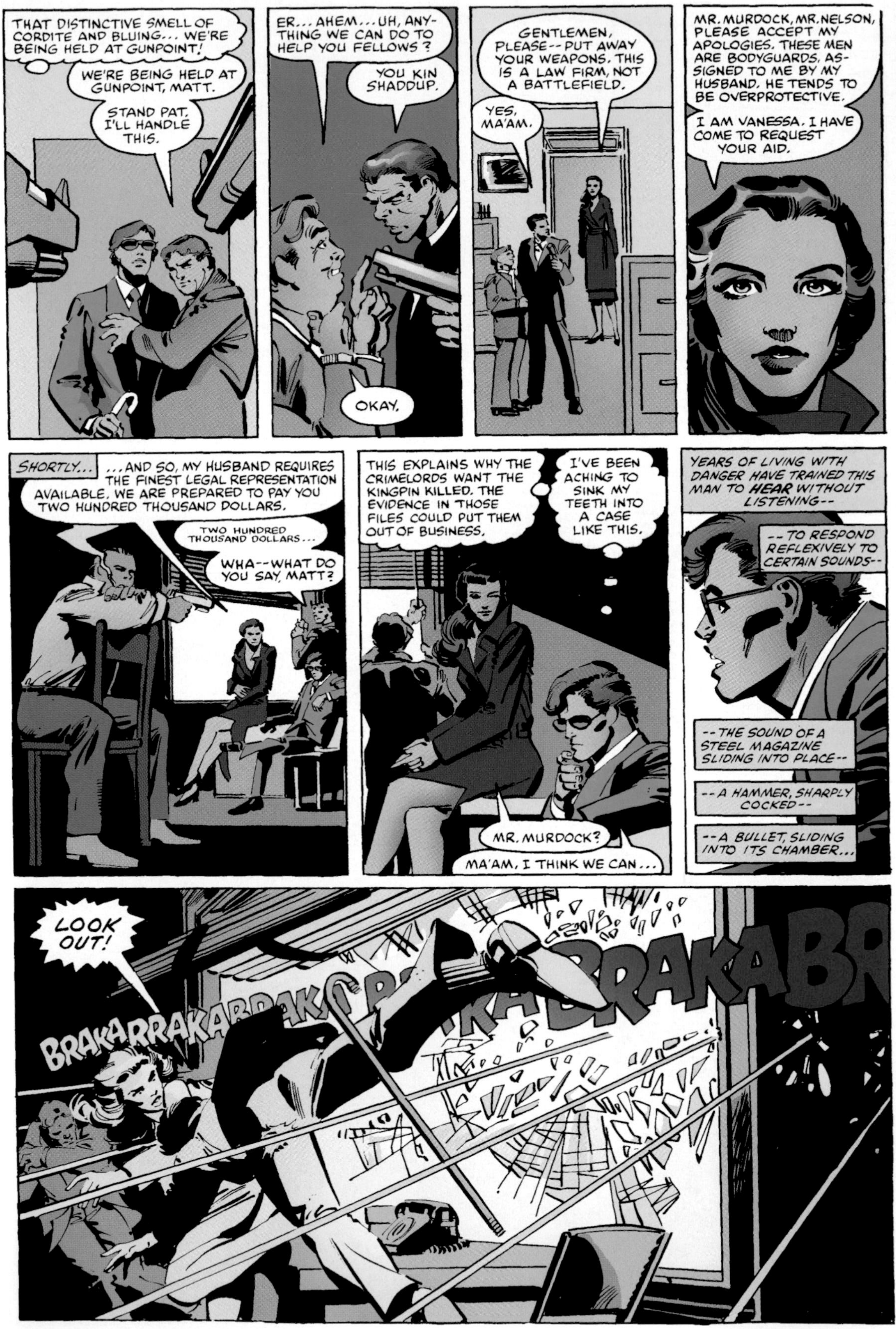
THAT DISTINCTIVE SMELL OF CORDITE AND BLUING... WE'RE BEING HELD AT GUNPOINT!
WE'RE BEING HELD AT GUNPOINT, MATT.
STAND PAT. I'LL HANDLE THIS.
ER... AHEM... UH, ANYTHING WE CAN DO TO HELP YOU FELLOWS?
YOU KIN SHADDUP.
OKAY.
GENTLEMEN, PLEASE--PUT AWAY YOUR WEAPONS. THIS IS A LAW FIRM, NOT A BATTLEFIELD.
YES, MA'AM.
MR. MURDOCK, MR. NELSON, PLEASE ACCEPT MY APOLOGIES. THESE MEN ARE BODYGUARDS, ASSIGNED TO ME BY MY HUSBAND. HE TENDS TO BE OVERPROTECTIVE.
I AM VANESSA. I HAVE COME TO REQUEST YOUR AID.
SHORTLY...
...AND SO, MY HUSBAND REQUIRES THE FINEST LEGAL REPRESENTATION AVAILABLE. WE ARE PREPARED TO PAY YOU TWO HUNDRED THOUSAND DOLLARS.
TWO HUNDRED THOUSAND DOLLARS...
WHA--WHAT DO YOU SAY, MATT?
THIS EXPLAINS WHY THE CRIMELORDS WANT THE KINGPIN KILLED. THE EVIDENCE IN THOSE FILES COULD PUT THEM OUT OF BUSINESS.
I'VE BEEN ACHING TO SINK MY TEETH INTO A CASE LIKE THIS.
MR. MURDOCK?
MA'AM, I THINK WE CAN...
YEARS OF LIVING WITH DANGER HAVE TRAINED THIS MAN TO HEAR WITHOUT LISTENING--
--TO RESPOND REFLEXIVELY TO CERTAIN SOUNDS--
--THE SOUND OF A STEEL MAGAZINE SLIDING INTO PLACE--
--A HAMMER, SHARPLY COCKED--
--A BULLET, SLIDING INTO ITS CHAMBER...
LOOK OUT!
BRAKA BRAKA BRAKA BRAKA BRAKA BR

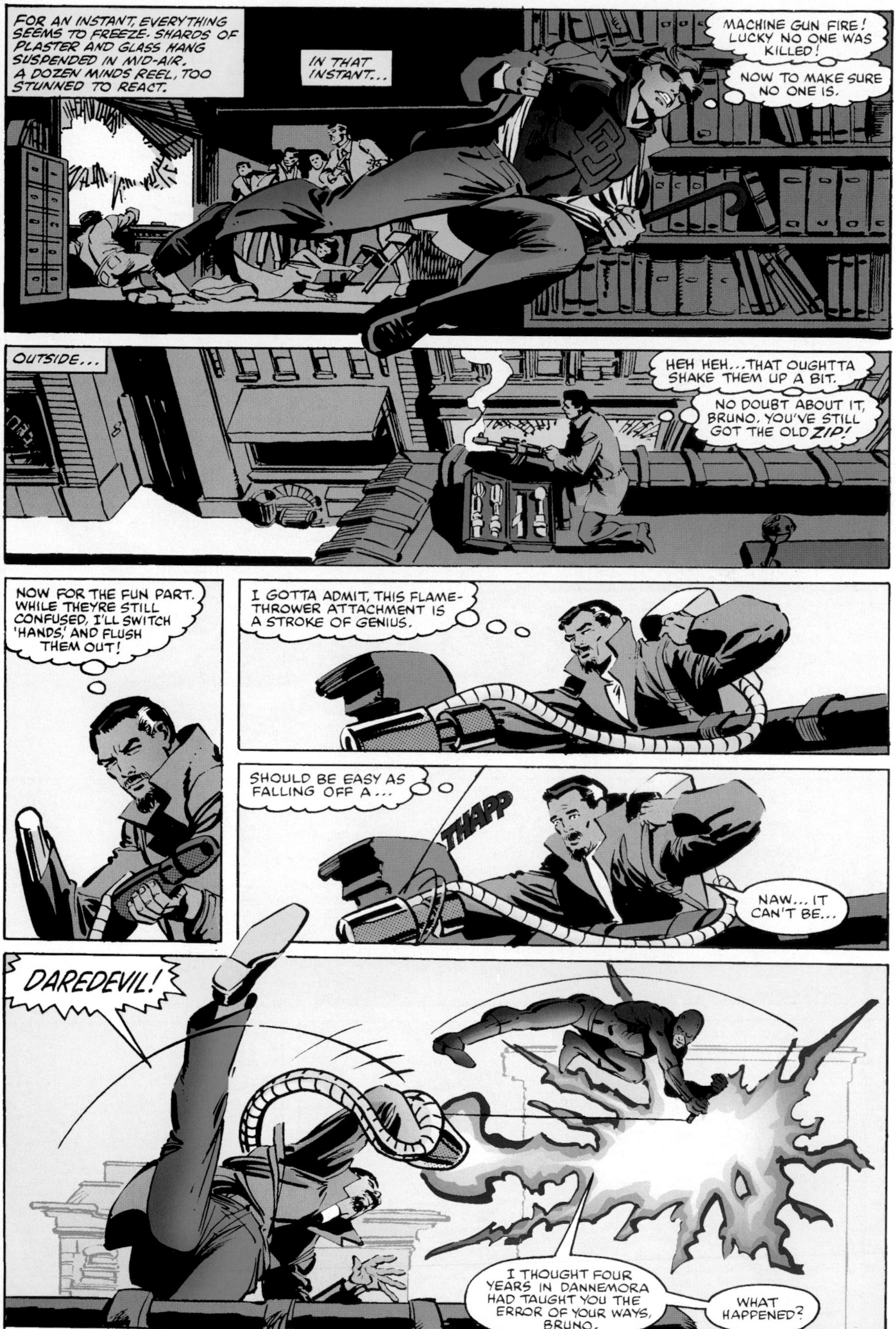
FOR AN INSTANT, EVERYTHING SEEMS TO FREEZE. SHARDS OF PLASTER AND GLASS HANG SUSPENDED IN MID-AIR. A DOZEN MINDS REEL, TOO STUNNED TO REACT.
IN THAT INSTANT...
MACHINE GUN FIRE! LUCKY NO ONE WAS KILLED!
NOW TO MAKE SURE NO ONE IS.
OUTSIDE...
HEH HEH...THAT OUGHTTA SHAKE THEM UP A BIT.
NO DOUBT ABOUT IT, BRUNO. YOU'VE STILL GOT THE OLD ZIP!
NOW FOR THE FUN PART. WHILE THEY'RE STILL CONFUSED, I'LL SWITCH 'HANDS,' AND FLUSH THEM OUT!
I GOTTA ADMIT, THIS FLAME-THROWER ATTACHMENT IS A STROKE OF GENIUS.
SHOULD BE EASY AS FALLING OFF A...
THAPP
NAW... IT CAN'T BE...
DAREDEVIL!
I THOUGHT FOUR YEARS IN DANNEMORA HAD TAUGHT YOU THE ERROR OF YOUR WAYS, BRUNO.
WHAT HAPPENED?

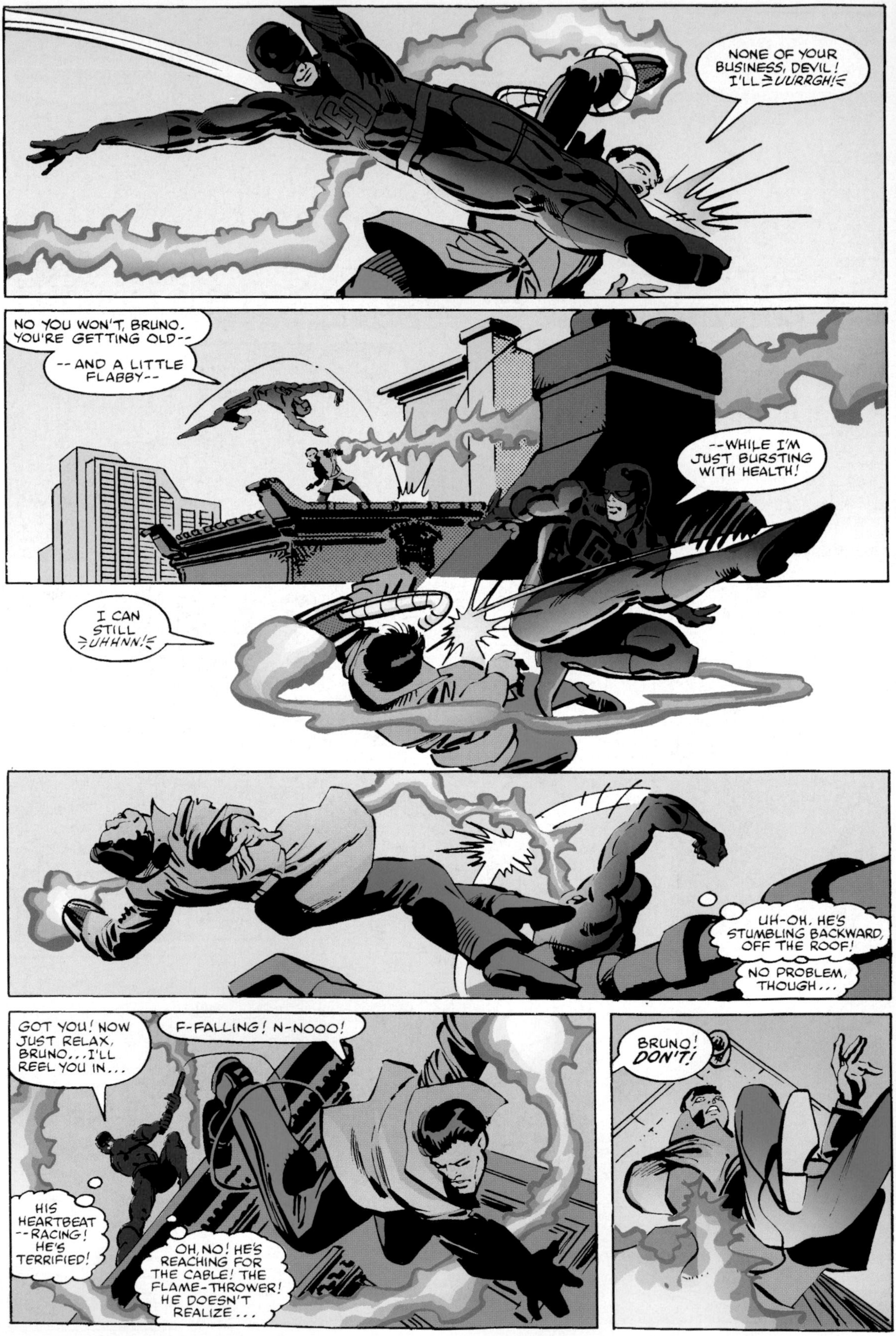
NONE OF YOUR BUSINESS, DEVIL! I'LL UURRGH!
NO YOU WON'T, BRUNO. YOU'RE GETTING OLD--
--AND A LITTLE FLABBY--
--WHILE I'M JUST BURSTING WITH HEALTH!
I CAN STILL UHHNN!
UH-OH. HE'S STUMBLING BACKWARD, OFF THE ROOF!
NO PROBLEM, THOUGH...
GOT YOU! NOW JUST RELAX, BRUNO... I'LL REEL YOU IN...
F-FALLING! N-NOOO!
HIS HEARTBEAT --RACING! HE'S TERRIFIED!
OH, NO! HE'S REACHING FOR THE CABLE! THE FLAME-THROWER! HE DOESN'T REALIZE...
BRUNO! DON'T!

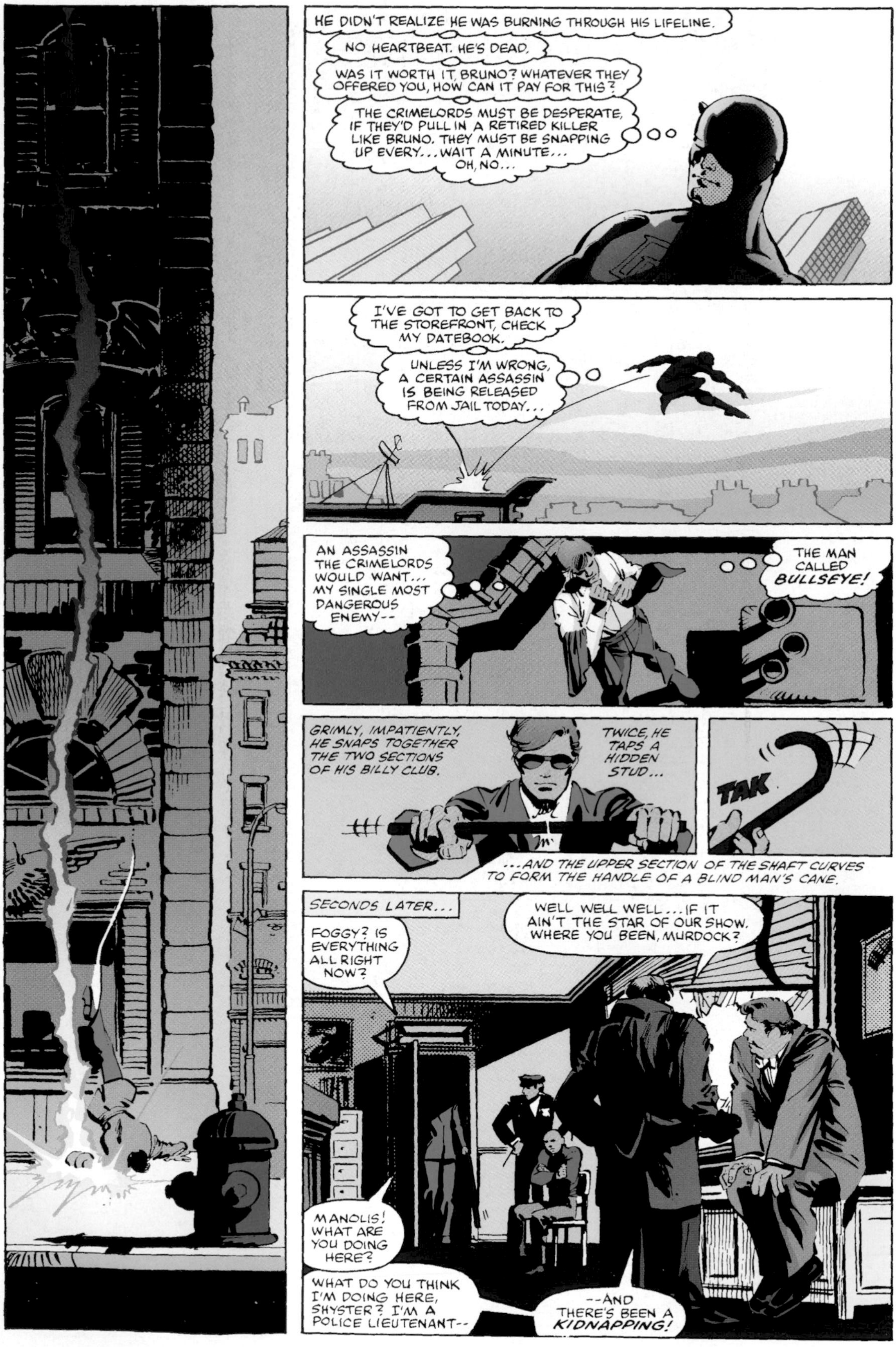
HE DIDN'T REALIZE HE WAS BURNING THROUGH HIS LIFELINE.
NO HEARTBEAT. HE'S DEAD.
WAS IT WORTH IT, BRUNO? WHATEVER THEY OFFERED YOU, HOW CAN IT PAY FOR THIS?
THE CRIMELORDS MUST BE DESPERATE, IF THEY'D PULL IN A RETIRED KILLER LIKE BRUNO. THEY MUST BE SNAPPING UP EVERY... WAIT A MINUTE... OH, NO...
I'VE GOT TO GET BACK TO THE STOREFRONT, CHECK MY DATEBOOK.
UNLESS I'M WRONG, A CERTAIN ASSASSIN IS BEING RELEASED FROM JAIL TODAY...
AN ASSASSIN THE CRIMELORDS WOULD WANT... MY SINGLE MOST DANGEROUS ENEMY--
THE MAN CALLED BULLSEYE!
GRIMLY, IMPATIENTLY, HE SNAPS TOGETHER THE TWO SECTIONS OF HIS BILLY CLUB.
TWICE, HE TAPS A HIDDEN STUD...
TAK
...AND THE UPPER SECTION OF THE SHAFT CURVES TO FORM THE HANDLE OF A BLIND MAN'S CANE.
SECONDS LATER...
FOGGY? IS EVERYTHING ALL RIGHT NOW?
WELL WELL WELL... IF IT AIN'T THE STAR OF OUR SHOW. WHERE YOU BEEN, MURDOCK?
MANOLIS! WHAT ARE YOU DOING HERE?
WHAT DO YOU THINK I'M DOING HERE, SHYSTER? I'M A POLICE LIEUTENANT--
--AND THERE'S BEEN A KIDNAPPING!

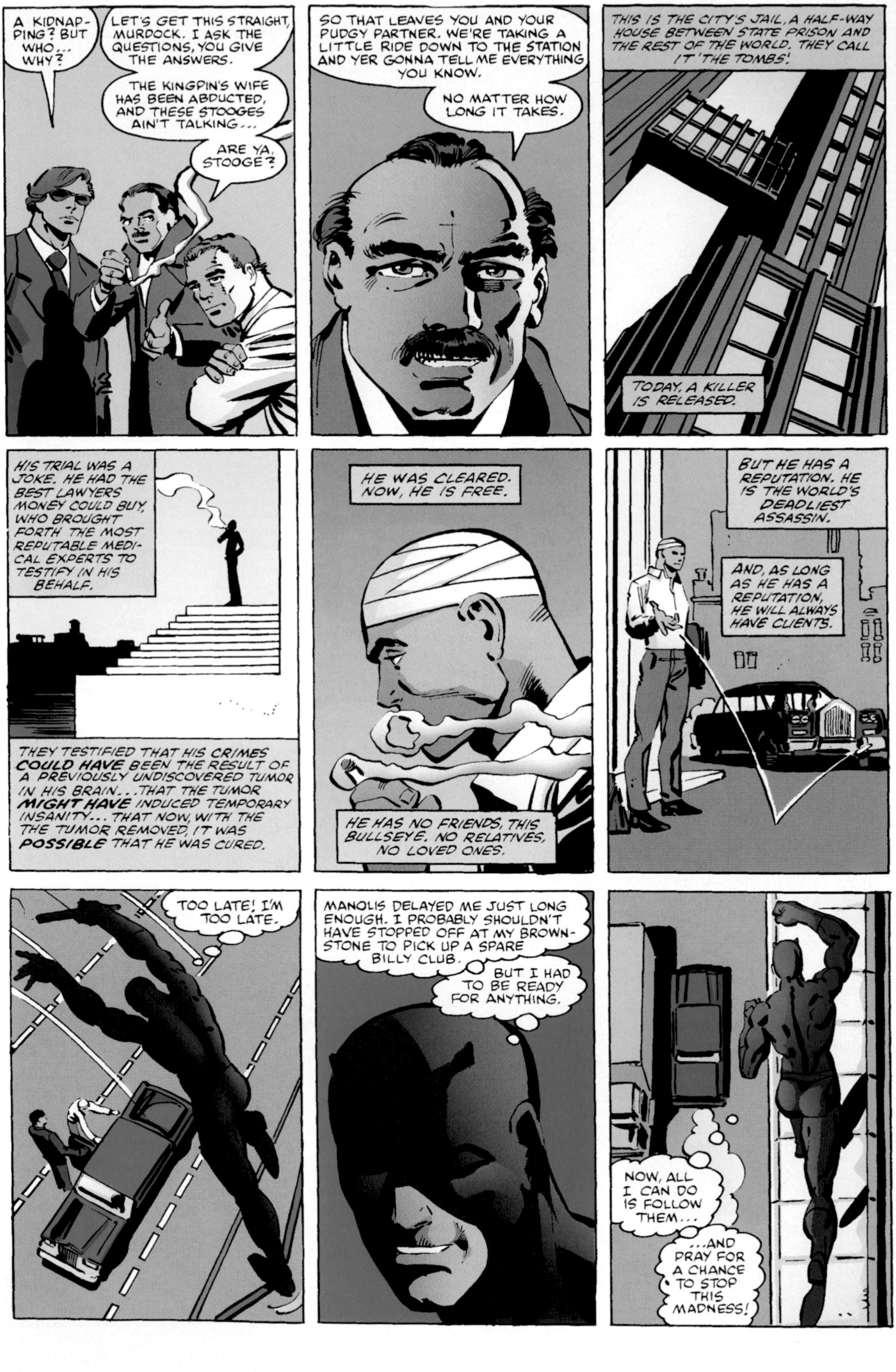
A KIDNAPPING? BUT WHO... WHY?
LET'S GET THIS STRAIGHT, MURDOCK. I ASK THE QUESTIONS, YOU GIVE THE ANSWERS.
THE KINGPIN'S WIFE HAS BEEN ABDUCTED, AND THESE STOOGES AIN'T TALKING...
ARE YA, STOOGE?
SO THAT LEAVES YOU AND YOUR PUDGY PARTNER. WE'RE TAKING A LITTLE RIDE DOWN TO THE STATION AND YER GONNA TELL ME EVERYTHING YOU KNOW.
NO MATTER HOW LONG IT TAKES.
THIS IS THE CITY'S JAIL, A HALF-WAY HOUSE BETWEEN STATE PRISON AND THE REST OF THE WORLD. THEY CALL IT 'THE TOMBS'.
TODAY, A KILLER IS RELEASED.
HIS TRIAL WAS A JOKE. HE HAD THE BEST LAWYERS MONEY COULD BUY, WHO BROUGHT FORTH THE MOST REPUTABLE MEDICAL EXPERTS TO TESTIFY IN HIS BEHALF.
THEY TESTIFIED THAT HIS CRIMES COULD HAVE BEEN THE RESULT OF A PREVIOUSLY UNDISCOVERED TUMOR IN HIS BRAIN...THAT THE TUMOR MIGHT HAVE INDUCED TEMPORARY INSANITY... THAT NOW, WITH THE THE TUMOR REMOVED, IT WAS POSSIBLE THAT HE WAS CURED.
HE WAS CLEARED. NOW, HE IS FREE.
HE HAS NO FRIENDS, THIS BULLSEYE. NO RELATIVES, NO LOVED ONES.
BUT HE HAS A REPUTATION. HE IS THE WORLD'S DEADLIEST ASSASSIN.
AND, AS LONG AS HE HAS A REPUTATION, HE WILL ALWAYS HAVE CLIENTS.
TOO LATE! I'M TOO LATE.
MANOLIS DELAYED ME JUST LONG ENOUGH. I PROBABLY SHOULDN'T HAVE STOPPED OFF AT MY BROWNSTONE TO PICK UP A SPARE BILLY CLUB.
BUT I HAD TO BE READY FOR ANYTHING.
NOW, ALL I CAN DO IS FOLLOW THEM...
...AND PRAY FOR A CHANCE TO STOP THIS MADNESS!

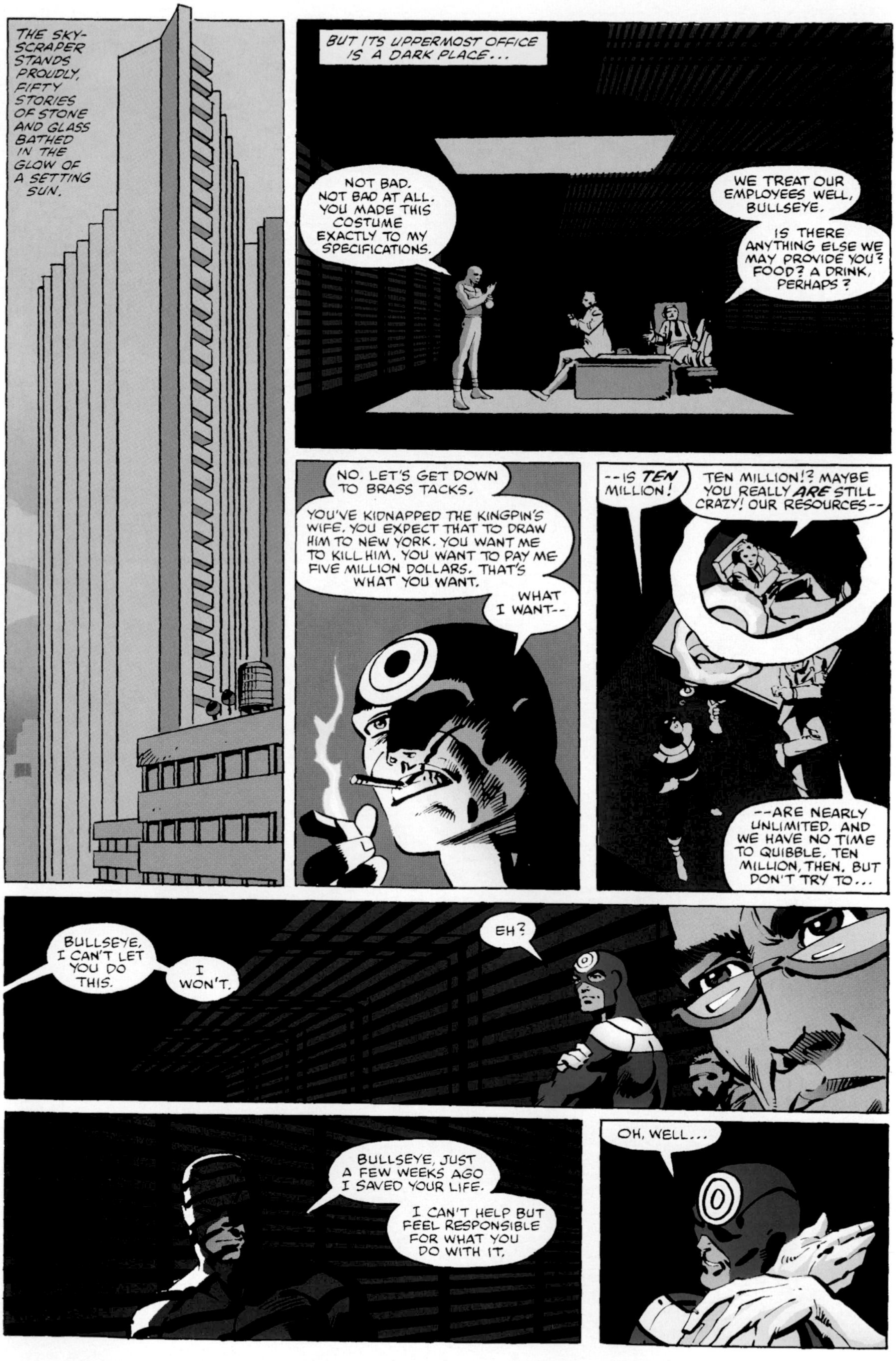
THE SKY-SCRAPER STANDS PROUDLY, FIFTY STORIES OF STONE AND GLASS BATHED IN THE GLOW OF A SETTING SUN.
BUT ITS UPPERMOST OFFICE IS A DARK PLACE...
NOT BAD. NOT BAD AT ALL. YOU MADE THIS COSTUME EXACTLY TO MY SPECIFICATIONS.
WE TREAT OUR EMPLOYEES WELL, BULLSEYE.
IS THERE ANYTHING ELSE WE MAY PROVIDE YOU? FOOD? A DRINK, PERHAPS?
NO. LET'S GET DOWN TO BRASS TACKS.
YOU'VE KIDNAPPED THE KINGPIN'S WIFE. YOU EXPECT THAT TO DRAW HIM TO NEW YORK. YOU WANT ME TO KILL HIM. YOU WANT TO PAY ME FIVE MILLION DOLLARS. THAT'S WHAT YOU WANT.
WHAT I WANT--
--IS TEN MILLION!
TEN MILLION!? MAYBE YOU REALLY ARE STILL CRAZY! OUR RESOURCES--
--ARE NEARLY UNLIMITED. AND WE HAVE NO TIME TO QUIBBLE. TEN MILLION, THEN. BUT DON'T TRY TO...
BULLSEYE, I CAN'T LET YOU DO THIS.
I WON'T.
EH?
BULLSEYE, JUST A FEW WEEKS AGO I SAVED YOUR LIFE.
I CAN'T HELP BUT FEEL RESPONSIBLE FOR WHAT YOU DO WITH IT.
OH, WELL...

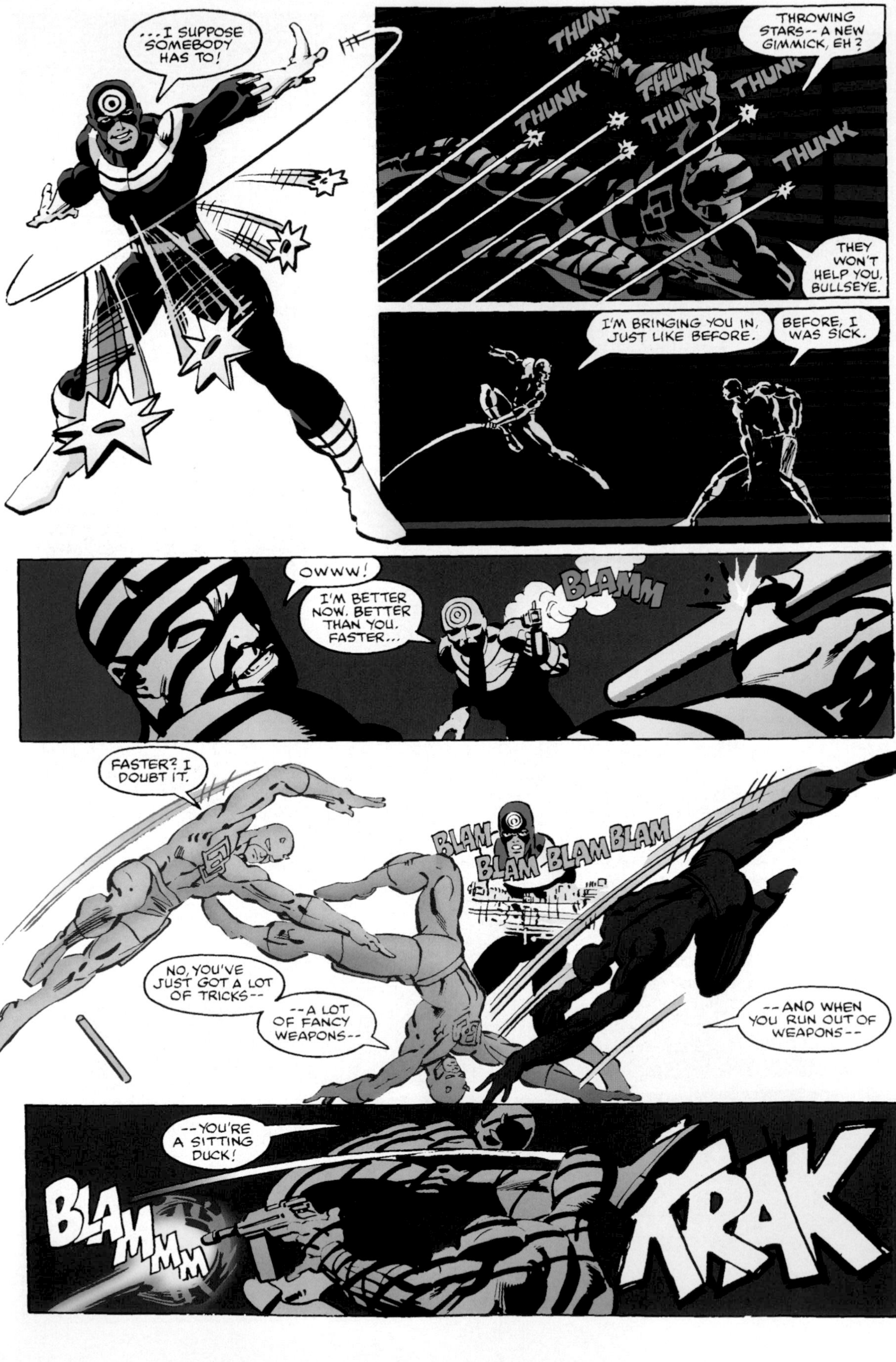
...I SUPPOSE SOMEBODY HAS TO!
THUNK
THUNK
THUNK
THUNK
THUNK
THUNK
THUNK
THROWING STARS-- A NEW GIMMICK, EH?
THEY WON'T HELP YOU, BULLSEYE.
I'M BRINGING YOU IN, JUST LIKE BEFORE.
BEFORE, I WAS SICK.
OWWW!
I'M BETTER NOW. BETTER THAN YOU. FASTER...
BLAMM
FASTER? I DOUBT IT.
BLAM BLAM BLAM BLAM
NO, YOU'VE JUST GOT A LOT OF TRICKS--
--A LOT OF FANCY WEAPONS--
--AND WHEN YOU RUN OUT OF WEAPONS--
--YOU'RE A SITTING DUCK!
BLAMMMM
TRAK

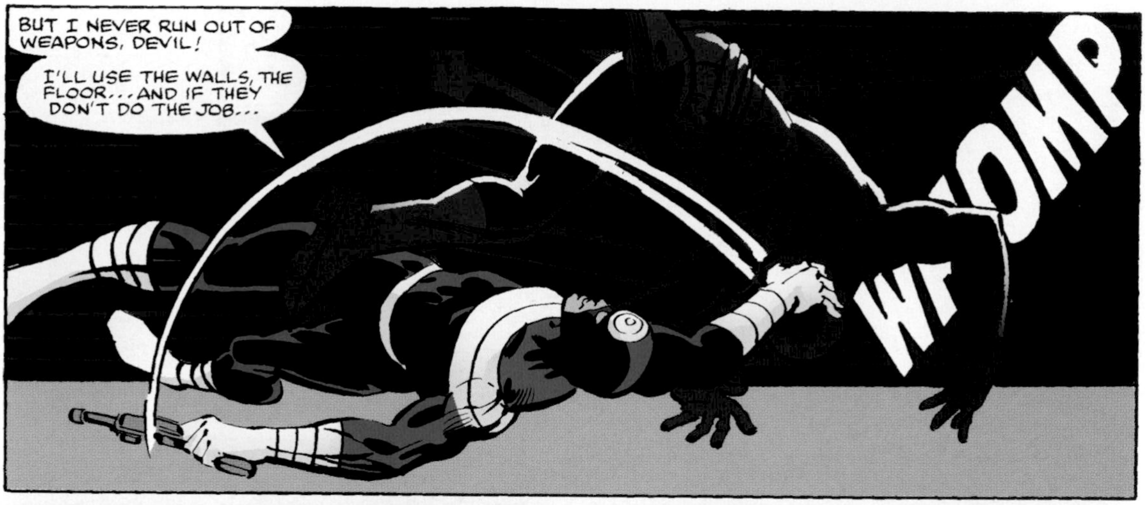
BUT I NEVER RUN OUT OF WEAPONS, DEVIL!
I'LL USE THE WALLS, THE FLOOR...AND IF THEY DON'T DO THE JOB...
WHOMP

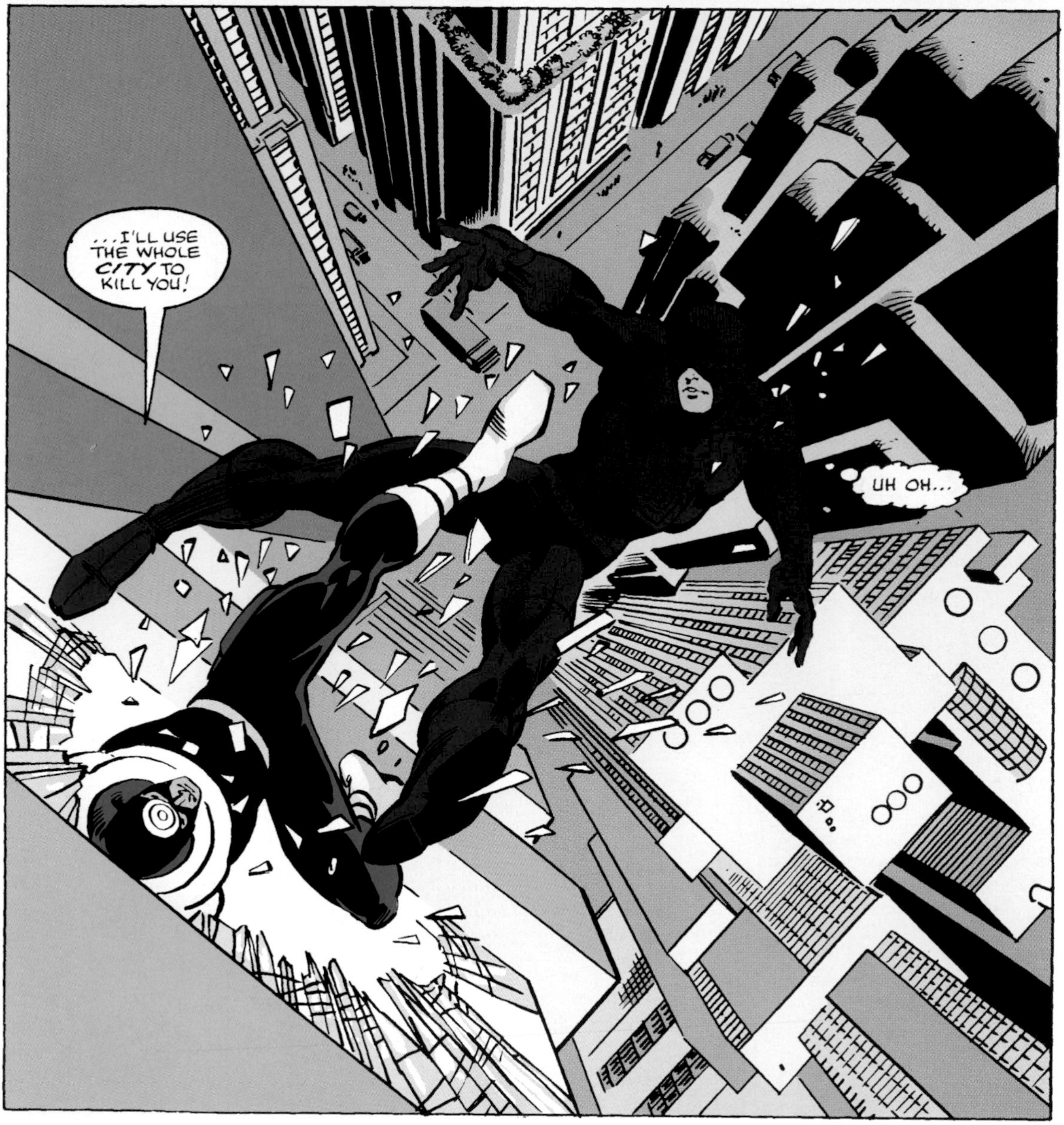
...I'LL USE THE WHOLE CITY TO KILL YOU!
UH OH...

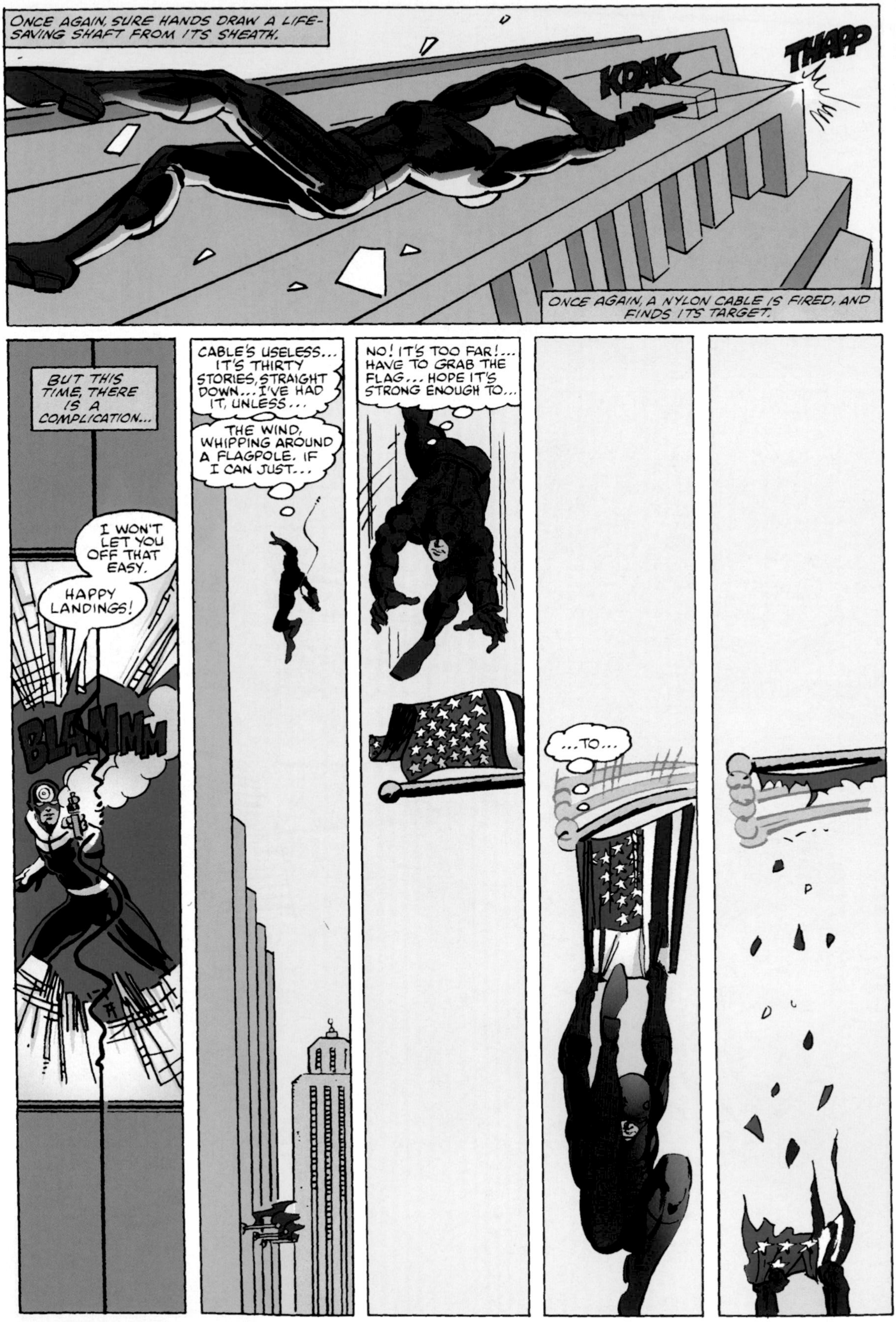
ONCE AGAIN, SURE HANDS DRAW A LIFE-SAVING SHAFT FROM ITS SHEATH.
KDAK
THAPP
ONCE AGAIN, A NYLON CABLE IS FIRED, AND FINDS ITS TARGET.
BUT THIS TIME, THERE IS A COMPLICATION...
I WON'T LET YOU OFF THAT EASY.
HAPPY LANDINGS!
BLAMMM
CABLE'S USELESS... IT'S THIRTY STORIES, STRAIGHT DOWN... I'VE HAD IT, UNLESS...
THE WIND, WHIPPING AROUND A FLAGPOLE. IF I CAN JUST...
NO! IT'S TOO FAR!... HAVE TO GRAB THE FLAG... HOPE IT'S STRONG ENOUGH TO...
...TO...

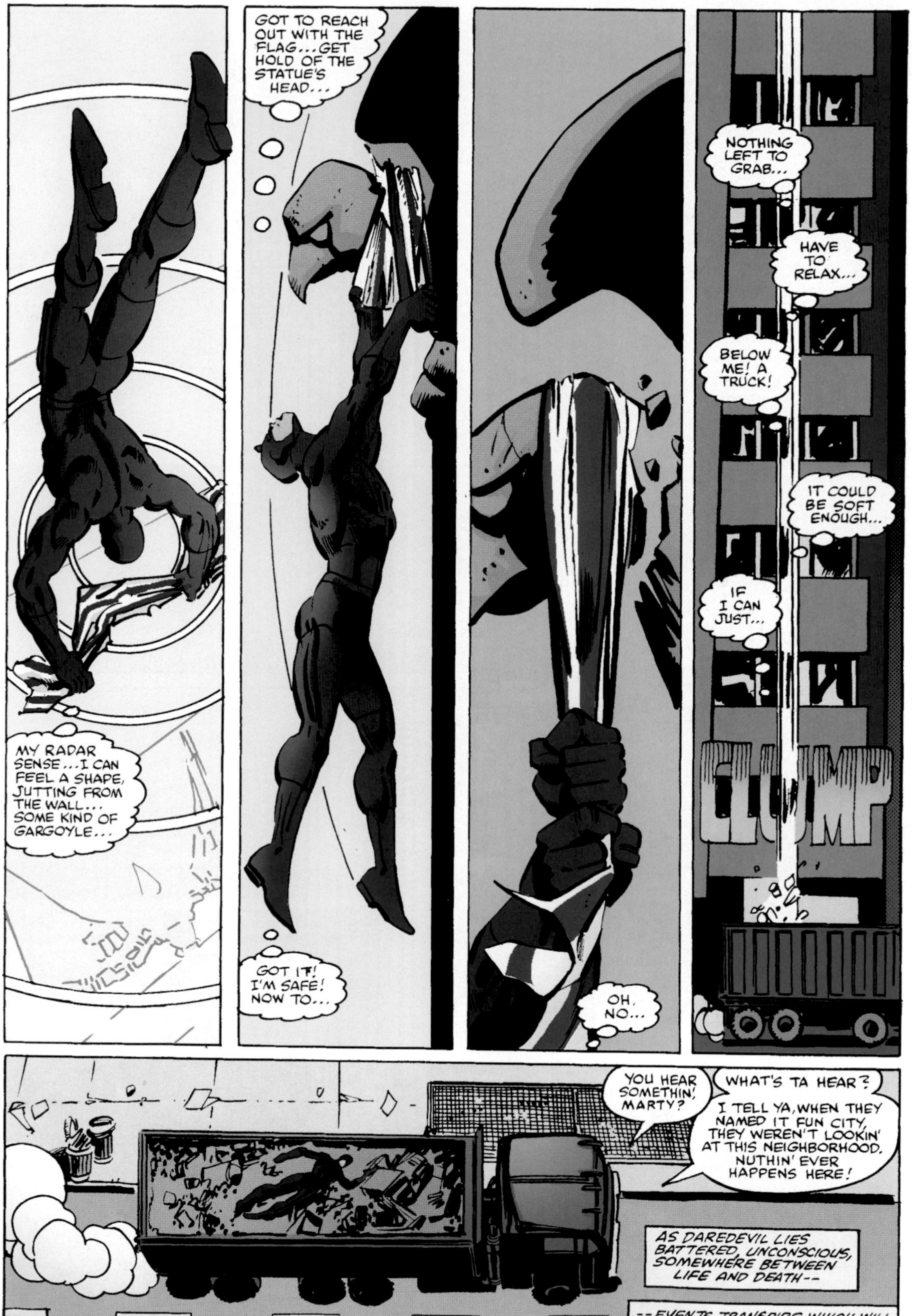
MY RADAR SENSE... I CAN FEEL A SHAPE, JUTTING FROM THE WALL... SOME KIND OF GARGOYLE...
GOT TO REACH OUT WITH THE FLAG... GET HOLD OF THE STATUE'S HEAD...
GOT IT! I'M SAFE! NOW TO...
OH, NO...
NOTHING LEFT TO GRAB...
HAVE TO RELAX...
BELOW ME! A TRUCK!
IT COULD BE SOFT ENOUGH...
IF I CAN JUST...
CLUMP
YOU HEAR SOMETHIN', MARTY?
WHAT'S TA HEAR?
I TELL YA, WHEN THEY NAMED IT FUN CITY, THEY WEREN'T LOOKIN' AT THIS NEIGHBORHOOD. NUTHIN' EVER HAPPENS HERE!
AS DAREDEVIL LIES BATTERED, UNCONSCIOUS, SOMEWHERE BETWEEN LIFE AND DEATH--
--EVENTS TRANSPIRE WHICH WILL PLACE IN DEADLY PERIL THE CITY HE HAS SWORN TO PROTECT...

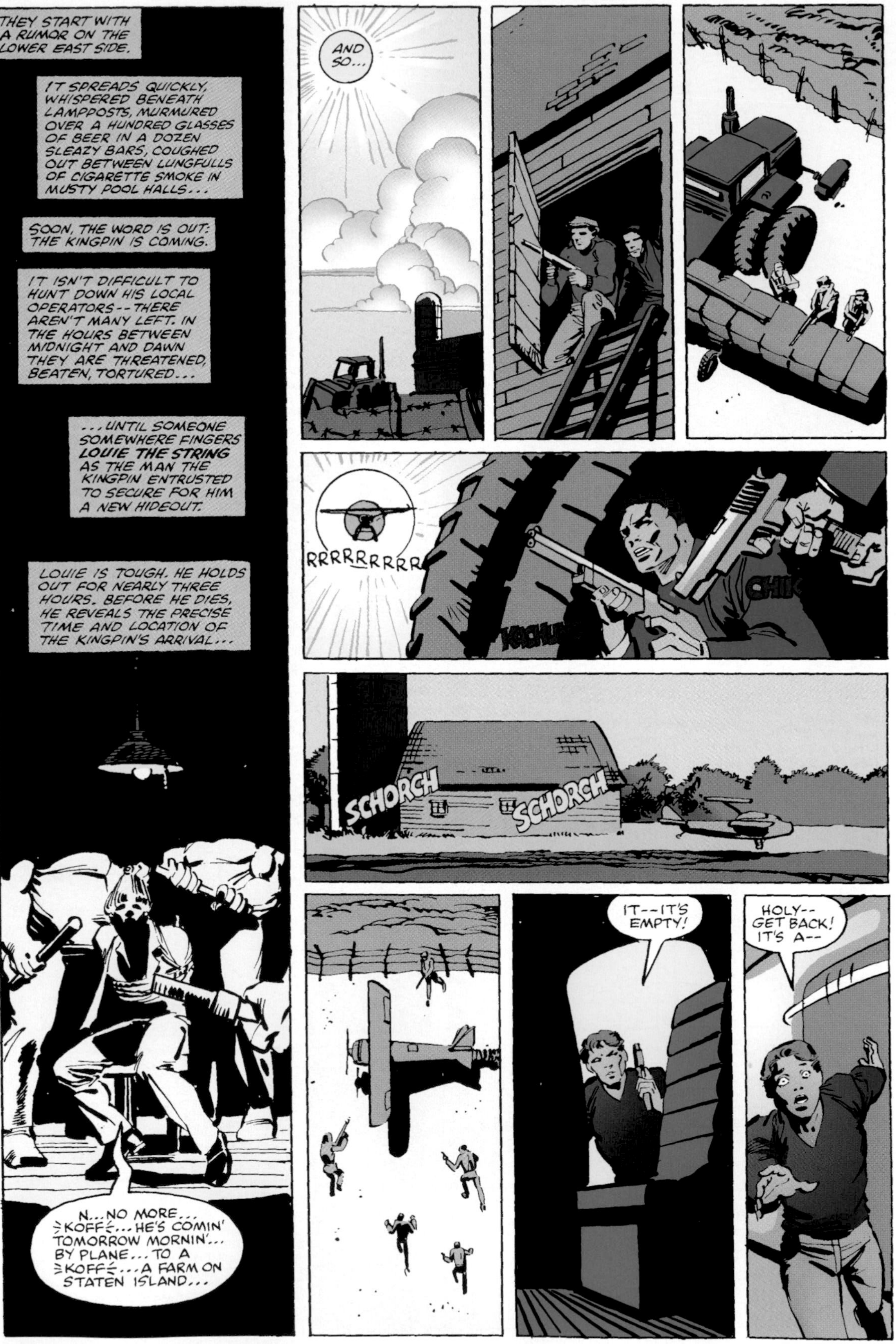

THEY START WITH A RUMOR ON THE LOWER EAST SIDE.
IT SPREADS QUICKLY, WHISPERED BENEATH LAMPPOSTS, MURMURED OVER A HUNDRED GLASSES OF BEER IN A DOZEN SLEAZY BARS, COUGHED OUT BETWEEN LUNGFULLS OF CIGARETTE SMOKE IN MUSTY POOL HALLS...
SOON, THE WORD IS OUT: THE KINGPIN IS COMING.
IT ISN'T DIFFICULT TO HUNT DOWN HIS LOCAL OPERATORS--THERE AREN'T MANY LEFT. IN THE HOURS BETWEEN MIDNIGHT AND DAWN THEY ARE THREATENED, BEATEN, TORTURED...
...UNTIL SOMEONE SOMEWHERE FINGERS LOUIE THE STRING AS THE MAN THE KINGPIN ENTRUSTED TO SECURE FOR HIM A NEW HIDEOUT.
LOUIE IS TOUGH. HE HOLDS OUT FOR NEARLY THREE HOURS. BEFORE HE DIES, HE REVEALS THE PRECISE TIME AND LOCATION OF THE KINGPIN'S ARRIVAL...
N...NO MORE... ≡KOFF≡... HE'S COMIN' TOMORROW MORNIN'... BY PLANE... TO A ≡KOFF≡... A FARM ON STATEN ISLAND...
AND SO...
RRRRRRRRR
KACHUK
CHIK
SCHORCH
SCHORCH
IT--IT'S EMPTY!
HOLY-- GET BACK! IT'S A--

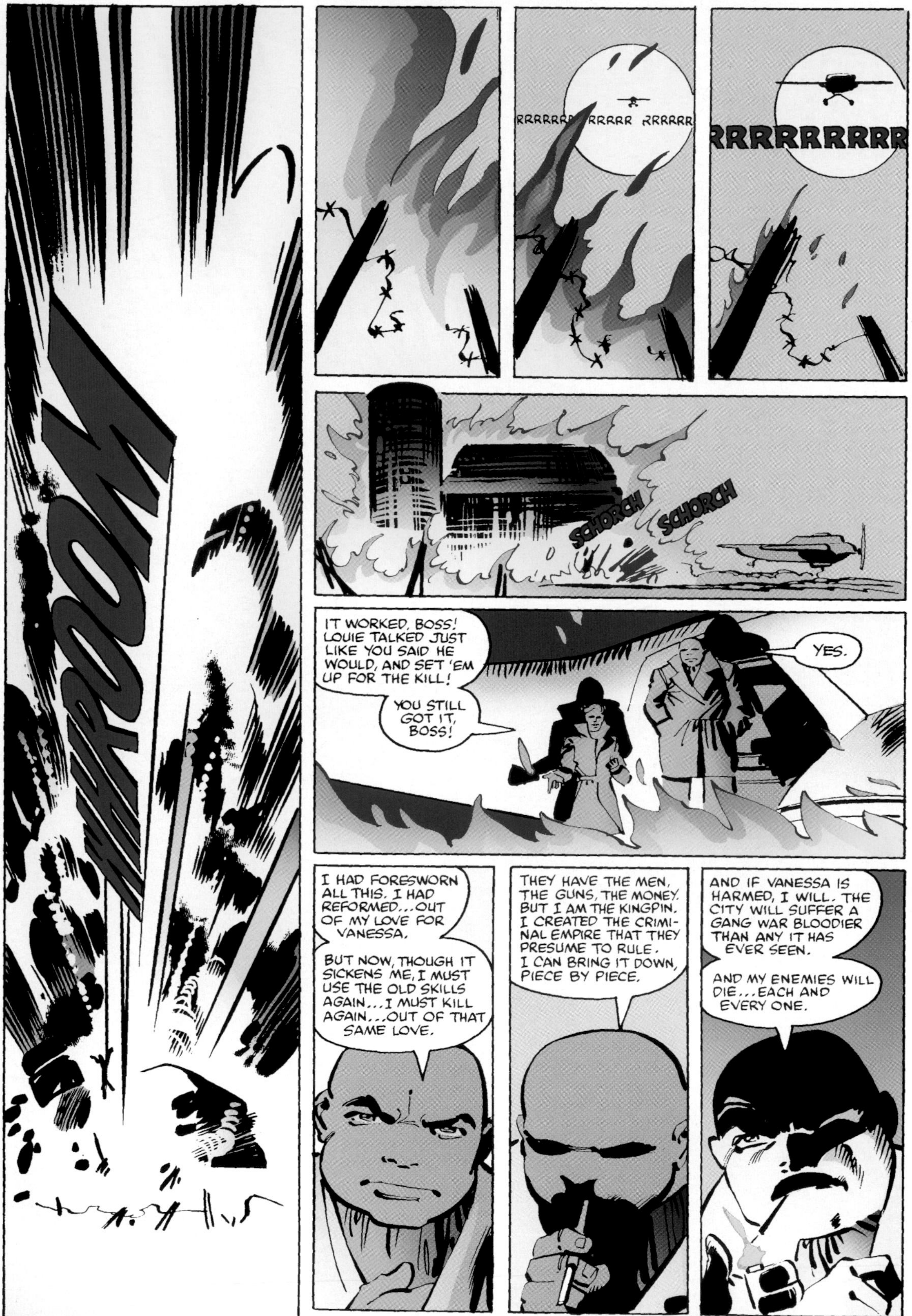
WHOOM
RRRRRRR RRRRR RRRRRR
RRRRRRRRRR
SCHORCH
SCHORCH
IT WORKED, BOSS! LOUIE TALKED JUST LIKE YOU SAID HE WOULD, AND SET 'EM UP FOR THE KILL!
YOU STILL GOT IT, BOSS!
YES.
I HAD FORESWORN ALL THIS. I HAD REFORMED... OUT OF MY LOVE FOR VANESSA.
BUT NOW, THOUGH IT SICKENS ME, I MUST USE THE OLD SKILLS AGAIN... I MUST KILL AGAIN... OUT OF THAT SAME LOVE.
THEY HAVE THE MEN, THE GUNS, THE MONEY. BUT I AM THE KINGPIN. I CREATED THE CRIMINAL EMPIRE THAT THEY PRESUME TO RULE. I CAN BRING IT DOWN, PIECE BY PIECE.
AND IF VANESSA IS HARMED, I WILL. THE CITY WILL SUFFER A GANG WAR BLOODIER THAN ANY IT HAS EVER SEEN.
AND MY ENEMIES WILL DIE... EACH AND EVERY ONE.

TO BE CONTINUED!

JUNE 1981

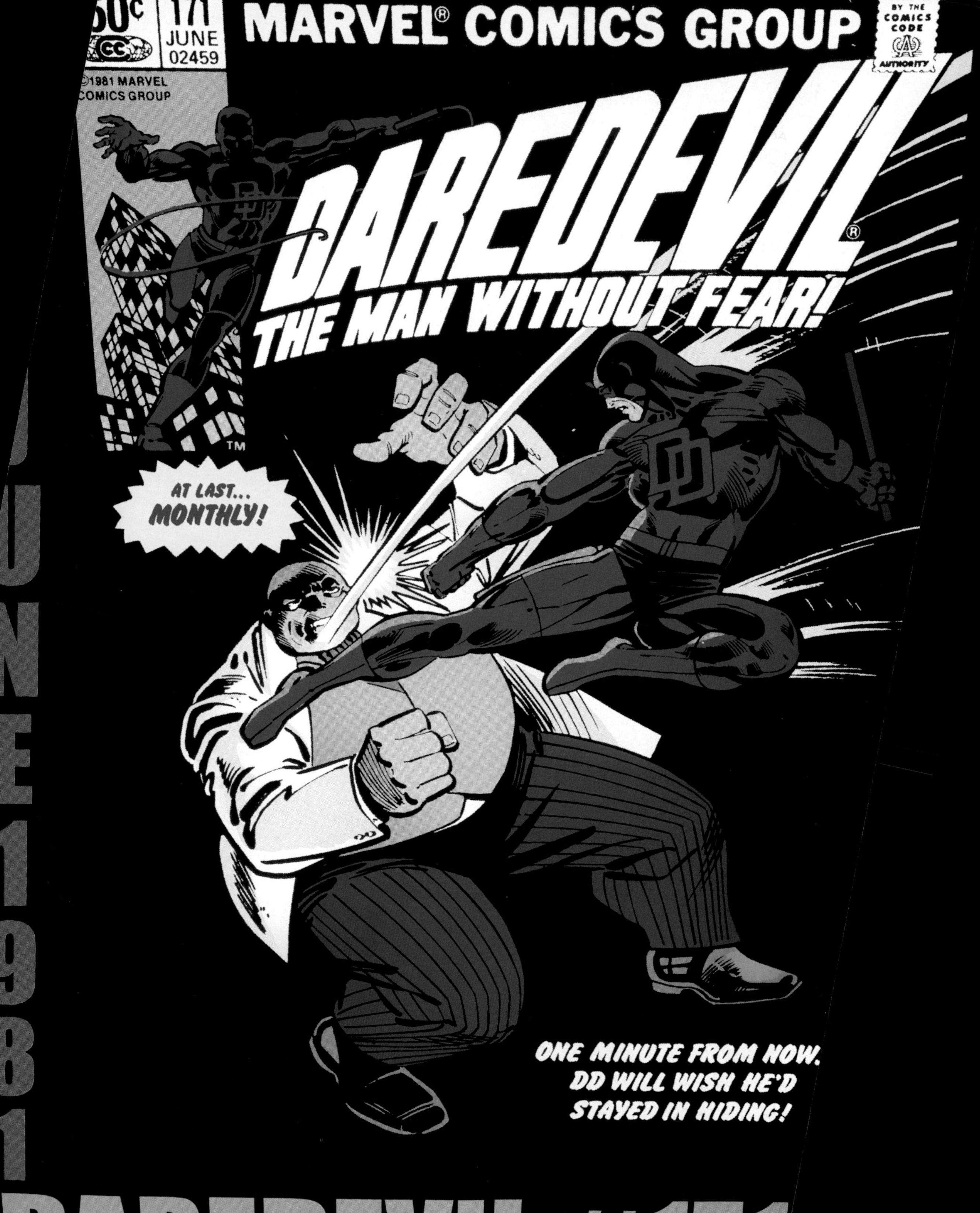

50¢
171
JUNE
02459
CC
MARVEL® COMICS GROUP
APPROVED BY THE COMICS CODE AUTHORITY
©1981 MARVEL COMICS GROUP
DAREDEVIL®
THE MAN WITHOUT FEAR!
TM
AT LAST... MONTHLY!
ONE MINUTE FROM NOW. DD WILL WISH HE'D STAYED IN HIDING!

DAREDEVIL #171

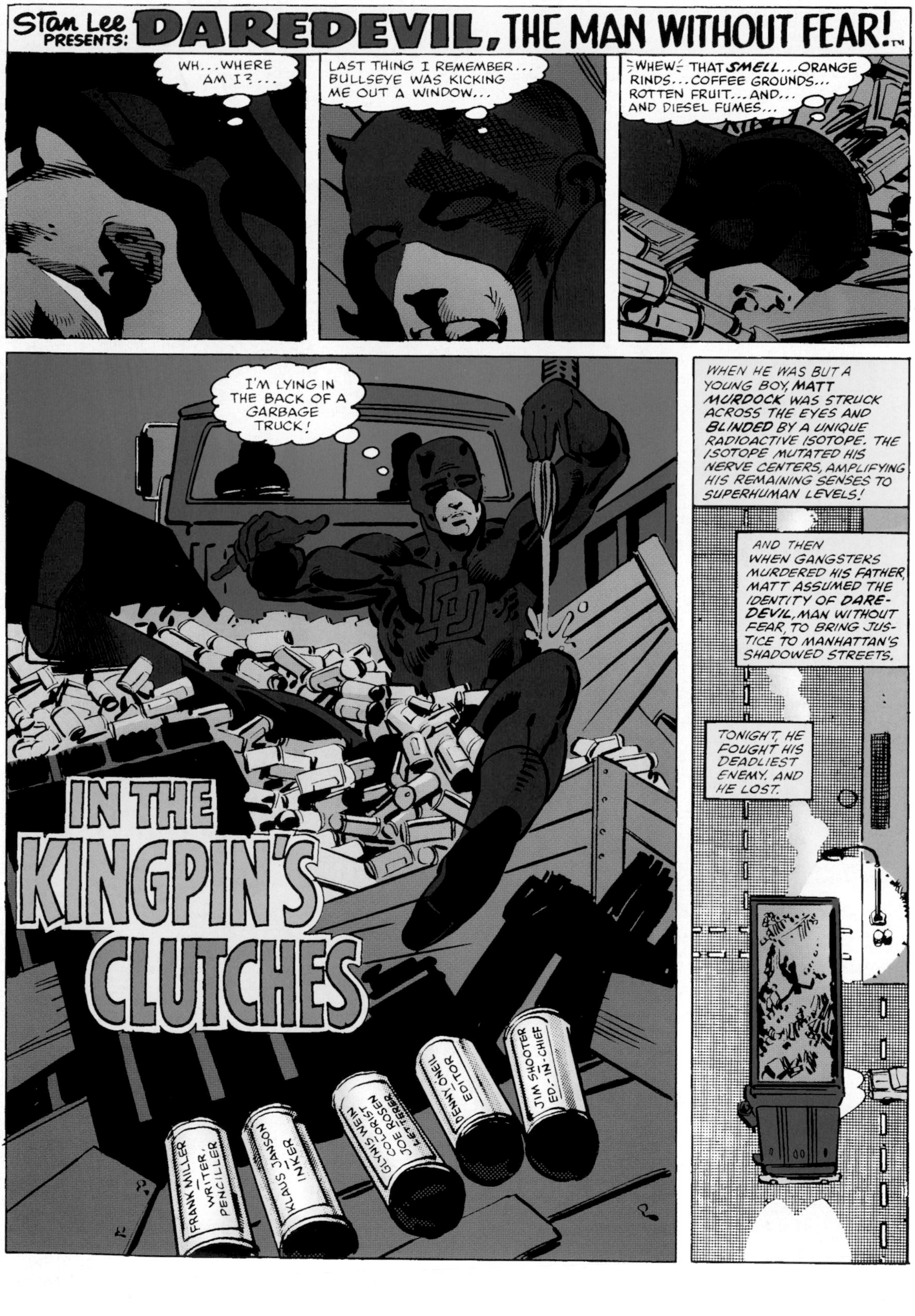

STAN LEE PRESENTS: DAREDEVIL, THE MAN WITHOUT FEAR!™
WH... WHERE AM I?...
LAST THING I REMEMBER... BULLSEYE WAS KICKING ME OUT A WINDOW...
WHEW -- THAT SMELL... ORANGE RINDS... COFFEE GROUNDS... ROTTEN FRUIT... AND... AND DIESEL FUMES...
I'M LYING IN THE BACK OF A GARBAGE TRUCK!
WHEN HE WAS BUT A YOUNG BOY, MATT MURDOCK WAS STRUCK ACROSS THE EYES AND BLINDED BY A UNIQUE RADIOACTIVE ISOTOPE. THE ISOTOPE MUTATED HIS NERVE CENTERS, AMPLIFYING HIS REMAINING SENSES TO SUPERHUMAN LEVELS!
AND THEN WHEN GANGSTERS MURDERED HIS FATHER, MATT ASSUMED THE IDENTITY OF DAREDEVIL, MAN WITHOUT FEAR, TO BRING JUSTICE TO MANHATTAN'S SHADOWED STREETS.
TONIGHT, HE FOUGHT HIS DEADLIEST ENEMY. AND HE LOST.
IN THE KINGPIN'S CLUTCHES
FRANK MILLER WRITER, PENCILLER
KLAUS JANSON INKER
GLYNIS WEIN COLORIST
JOE ROSEN LETTERER
DENNY O'NEIL EDITOR
JIM SHOOTER ED.-IN-CHIEF

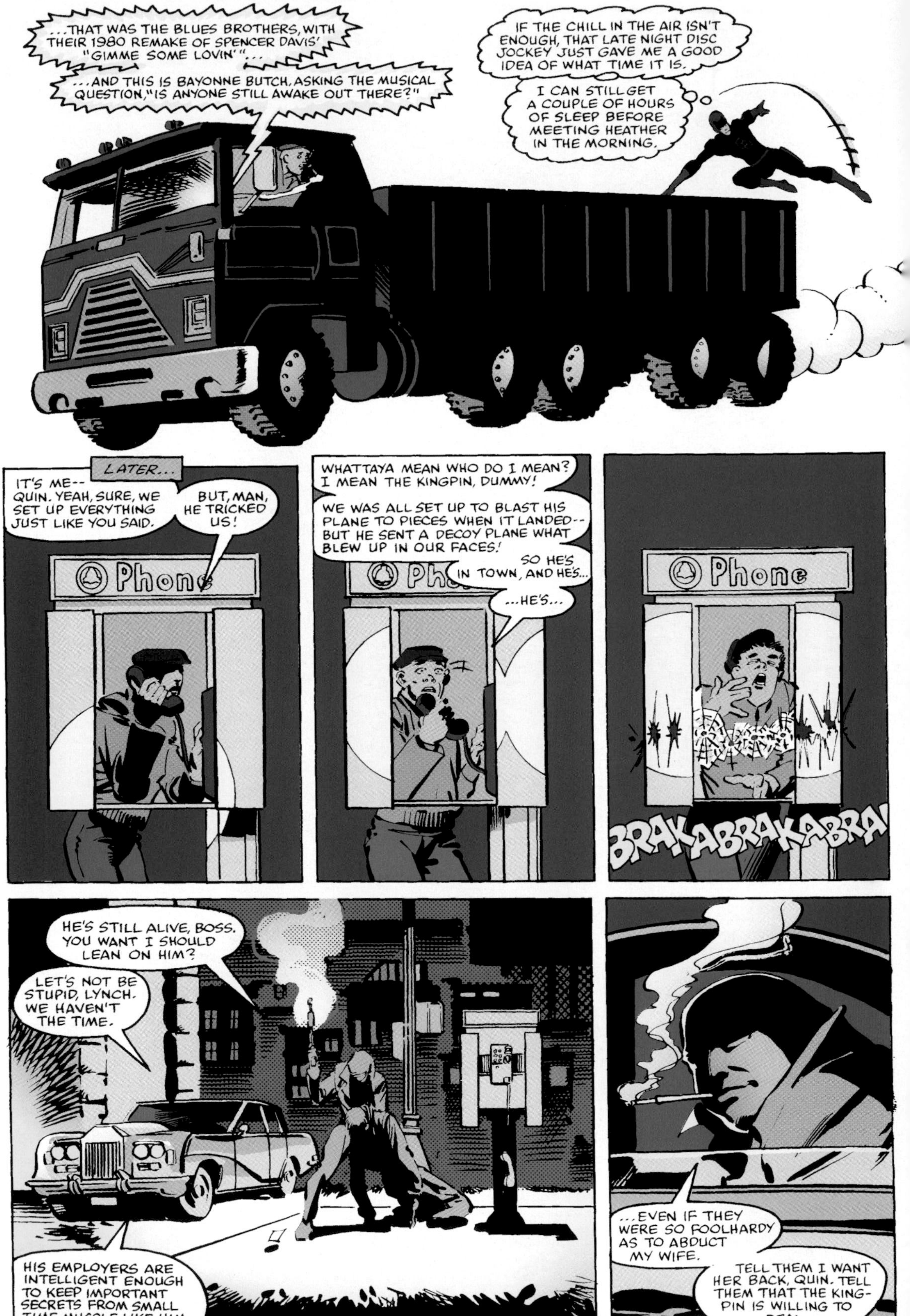
...THAT WAS THE BLUES BROTHERS, WITH THEIR 1980 REMAKE OF SPENCER DAVIS' "GIMME SOME LOVIN'"...
...AND THIS IS BAYONNE BUTCH, ASKING THE MUSICAL QUESTION, "IS ANYONE STILL AWAKE OUT THERE?"
IF THE CHILL IN THE AIR ISN'T ENOUGH, THAT LATE NIGHT DISC JOCKEY JUST GAVE ME A GOOD IDEA OF WHAT TIME IT IS.
I CAN STILL GET A COUPLE OF HOURS OF SLEEP BEFORE MEETING HEATHER IN THE MORNING.
LATER...
IT'S ME-- QUIN. YEAH, SURE, WE SET UP EVERYTHING JUST LIKE YOU SAID.
BUT, MAN, HE TRICKED US!
Phone
WHATTAYA MEAN WHO DO I MEAN? I MEAN THE KINGPIN, DUMMY!
WE WAS ALL SET UP TO BLAST HIS PLANE TO PIECES WHEN IT LANDED-- BUT HE SENT A DECOY PLANE WHAT BLEW UP IN OUR FACES!
SO HE'S IN TOWN, AND HE'S...
...HE'S...
Phone
BRAKABRAKABRA!
HE'S STILL ALIVE, BOSS. YOU WANT I SHOULD LEAN ON HIM?
LET'S NOT BE STUPID, LYNCH. WE HAVEN'T THE TIME.
HIS EMPLOYERS ARE INTELLIGENT ENOUGH TO KEEP IMPORTANT SECRETS FROM SMALL TIME MUSCLE LIKE HIM...
...EVEN IF THEY WERE SO FOOLHARDY AS TO ABDUCT MY WIFE.
TELL THEM I WANT HER BACK, QUIN. TELL THEM THAT THE KING-PIN IS WILLING TO DEAL.

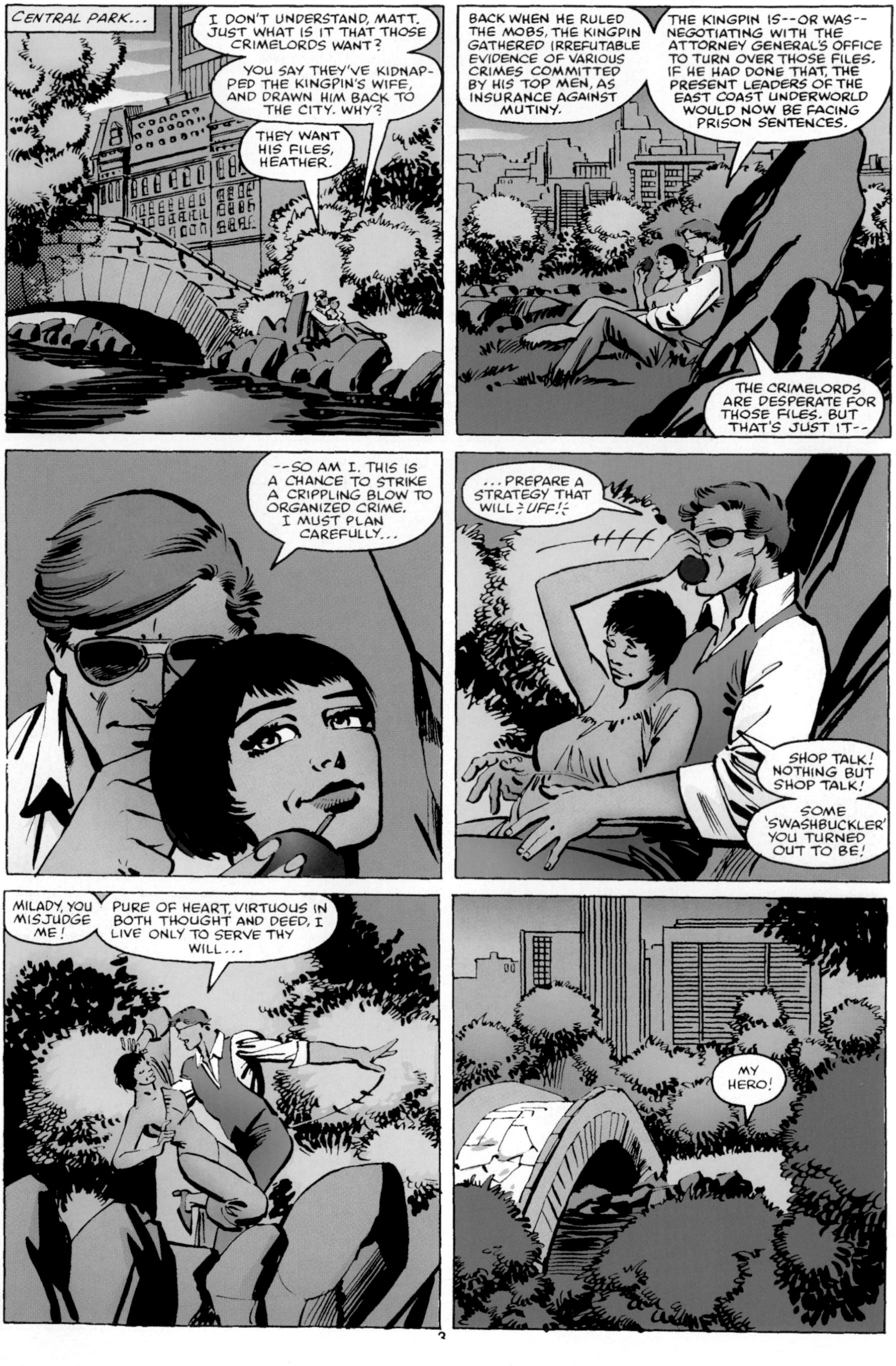
CENTRAL PARK...
I DON'T UNDERSTAND, MATT. JUST WHAT IS IT THAT THOSE CRIMELORDS WANT?
YOU SAY THEY'VE KIDNAPPED THE KINGPIN'S WIFE, AND DRAWN HIM BACK TO THE CITY. WHY?
THEY WANT HIS FILES, HEATHER.
BACK WHEN HE RULED THE MOBS, THE KINGPIN GATHERED IRREFUTABLE EVIDENCE OF VARIOUS CRIMES COMMITTED BY HIS TOP MEN, AS INSURANCE AGAINST MUTINY.
THE KINGPIN IS--OR WAS--NEGOTIATING WITH THE ATTORNEY GENERAL'S OFFICE TO TURN OVER THOSE FILES. IF HE HAD DONE THAT, THE PRESENT LEADERS OF THE EAST COAST UNDERWORLD WOULD NOW BE FACING PRISON SENTENCES.
THE CRIMELORDS ARE DESPERATE FOR THOSE FILES. BUT THAT'S JUST IT--
--SO AM I. THIS IS A CHANCE TO STRIKE A CRIPPLING BLOW TO ORGANIZED CRIME. I MUST PLAN CAREFULLY...
...PREPARE A STRATEGY THAT WILL -UFF!-
SHOP TALK! NOTHING BUT SHOP TALK!
SOME 'SWASHBUCKLER' YOU TURNED OUT TO BE!
MILADY, YOU MISJUDGE ME!
PURE OF HEART, VIRTUOUS IN BOTH THOUGHT AND DEED, I LIVE ONLY TO SERVE THY WILL...
MY HERO!

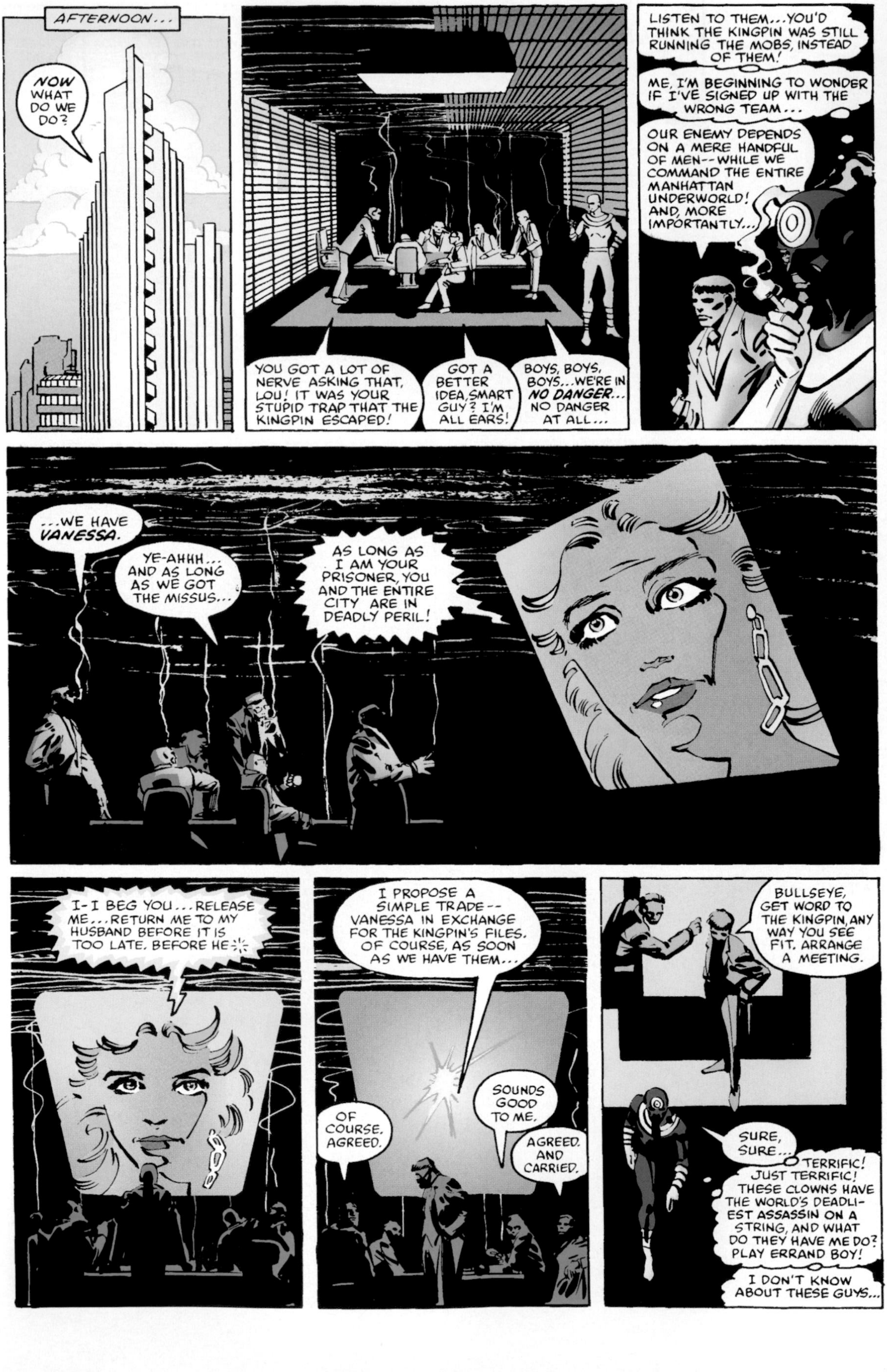
AFTERNOON...
NOW WHAT DO WE DO?
YOU GOT A LOT OF NERVE ASKING THAT, LOU! IT WAS YOUR STUPID TRAP THAT THE KINGPIN ESCAPED!
GOT A BETTER IDEA, SMART GUY? I'M ALL EARS!
BOYS, BOYS, BOYS... WE'RE IN NO DANGER... NO DANGER AT ALL...
LISTEN TO THEM... YOU'D THINK THE KINGPIN WAS STILL RUNNING THE MOBS, INSTEAD OF THEM!
ME, I'M BEGINNING TO WONDER IF I'VE SIGNED UP WITH THE WRONG TEAM...
OUR ENEMY DEPENDS ON A MERE HANDFUL OF MEN--WHILE WE COMMAND THE ENTIRE MANHATTAN UNDERWORLD! AND, MORE IMPORTANTLY...
...WE HAVE VANESSA.
YE-AHHH... AND AS LONG AS WE GOT THE MISSUS...
AS LONG AS I AM YOUR PRISONER, YOU AND THE ENTIRE CITY ARE IN DEADLY PERIL!
I-I BEG YOU... RELEASE ME... RETURN ME TO MY HUSBAND BEFORE IT IS TOO LATE. BEFORE HE--
I PROPOSE A SIMPLE TRADE-- VANESSA IN EXCHANGE FOR THE KINGPIN'S FILES. OF COURSE, AS SOON AS WE HAVE THEM...
OF COURSE. AGREED.
SOUNDS GOOD TO ME.
AGREED. AND CARRIED.
BULLSEYE, GET WORD TO THE KINGPIN, ANY WAY YOU SEE FIT. ARRANGE A MEETING.
SURE, SURE...
TERRIFIC! JUST TERRIFIC! THESE CLOWNS HAVE THE WORLD'S DEADLIEST ASSASSIN ON A STRING, AND WHAT DO THEY HAVE ME DO? PLAY ERRAND BOY!
I DON'T KNOW ABOUT THESE GUYS...

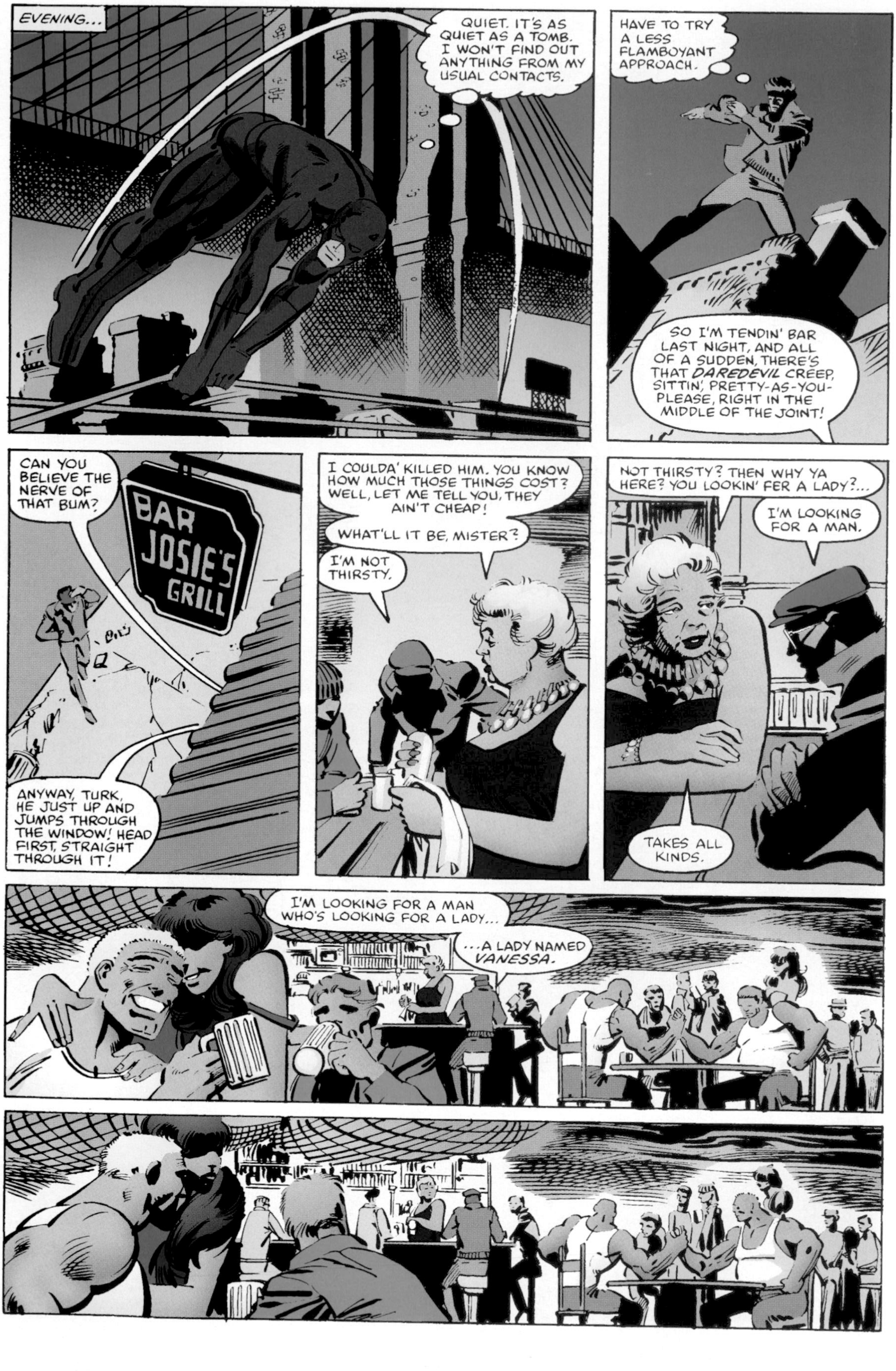
EVENING...
QUIET. IT'S AS QUIET AS A TOMB. I WON'T FIND OUT ANYTHING FROM MY USUAL CONTACTS.
HAVE TO TRY A LESS FLAMBOYANT APPROACH.
SO I'M TENDIN' BAR LAST NIGHT, AND ALL OF A SUDDEN, THERE'S THAT DAREDEVIL CREEP, SITTIN', PRETTY-AS-YOU-PLEASE, RIGHT IN THE MIDDLE OF THE JOINT!
CAN YOU BELIEVE THE NERVE OF THAT BUM?
BAR JOSIE'S GRILL
ANYWAY, TURK, HE JUST UP AND JUMPS THROUGH THE WINDOW! HEAD FIRST, STRAIGHT THROUGH IT!
I COULDA' KILLED HIM. YOU KNOW HOW MUCH THOSE THINGS COST? WELL, LET ME TELL YOU, THEY AIN'T CHEAP!
WHAT'LL IT BE, MISTER?
I'M NOT THIRSTY.
NOT THIRSTY? THEN WHY YA HERE? YOU LOOKIN' FER A LADY?...
I'M LOOKING FOR A MAN.
TAKES ALL KINDS.
I'M LOOKING FOR A MAN WHO'S LOOKING FOR A LADY...
...A LADY NAMED VANESSA.

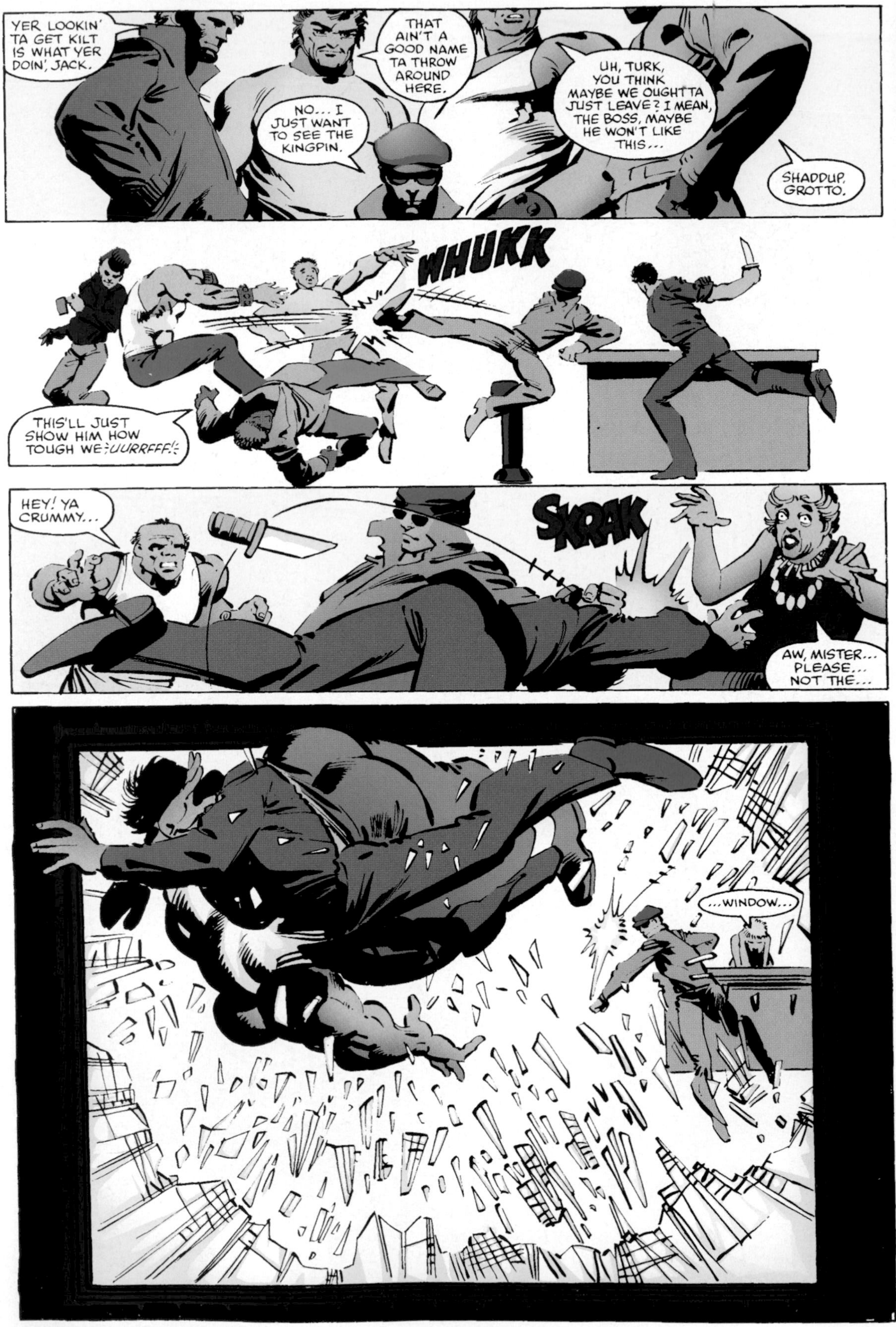
YER LOOKIN' TA GET KILT IS WHAT YER DOIN', JACK.
NO... I JUST WANT TO SEE THE KINGPIN.
THAT AIN'T A GOOD NAME TA THROW AROUND HERE.
UH, TURK, YOU THINK MAYBE WE OUGHTTA JUST LEAVE? I MEAN, THE BOSS, MAYBE HE WON'T LIKE THIS...
SHADDUP, GROTTO.
WHUKK
THIS'LL JUST SHOW HIM HOW TOUGH WE UURRFFF!
HEY! YA CRUMMY...
SKRAK
AW, MISTER... PLEASE... NOT THE...
...WINDOW...

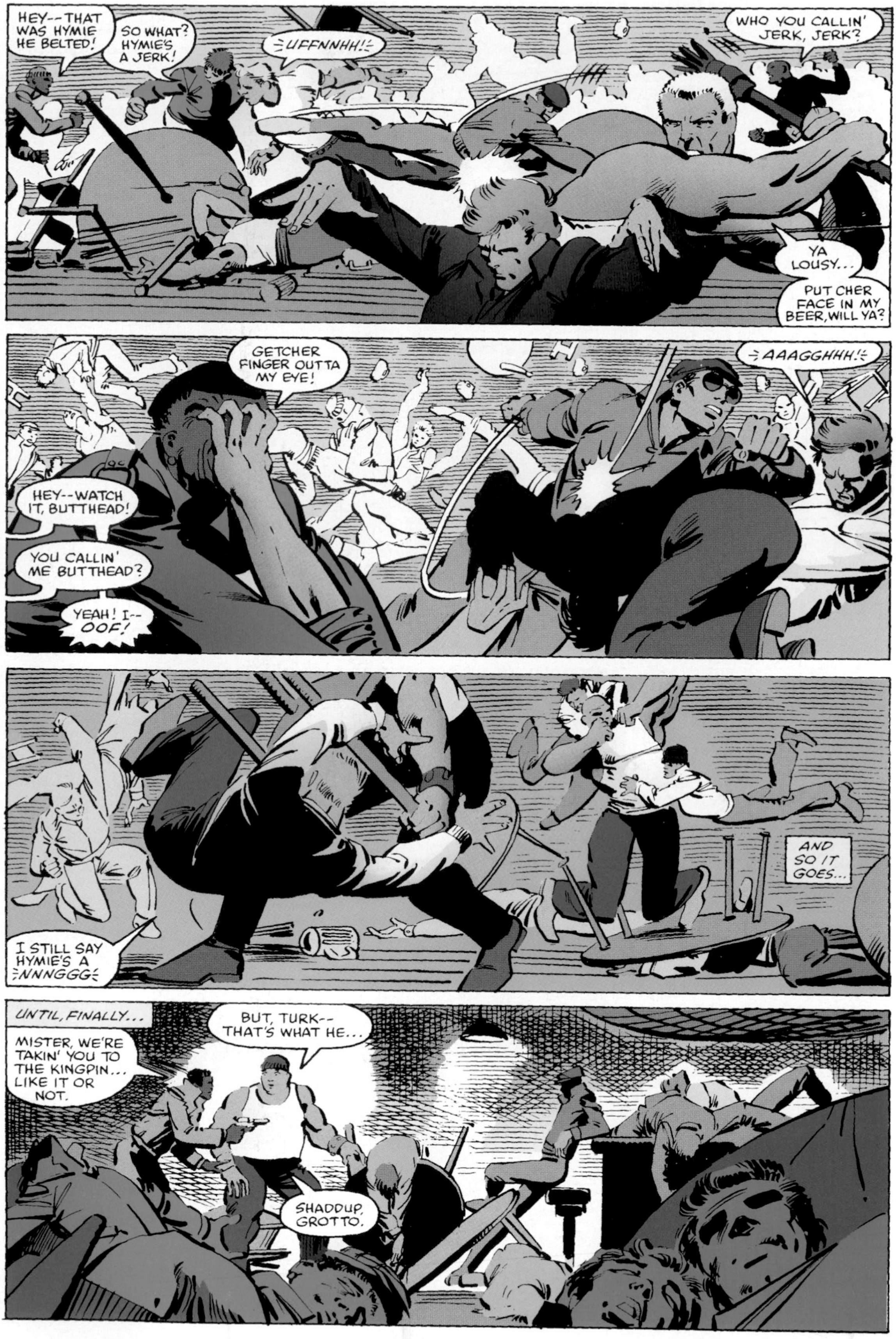
HEY--THAT WAS HYMIE HE BELTED!
SO WHAT? HYMIE'S A JERK!
UFFNNHH!
WHO YOU CALLIN' JERK, JERK?
YA LOUSY...
PUT CHER FACE IN MY BEER, WILL YA?
GETCHER FINGER OUTTA MY EYE!
AAAGGHHH!
HEY--WATCH IT, BUTTHEAD!
YOU CALLIN' ME BUTTHEAD?
YEAH! I-- OOF!
AND SO IT GOES...
I STILL SAY HYMIE'S A NNNGGG
UNTIL, FINALLY...
MISTER, WE'RE TAKIN' YOU TO THE KINGPIN... LIKE IT OR NOT.
BUT, TURK-- THAT'S WHAT HE...
SHADDUP, GROTTO.

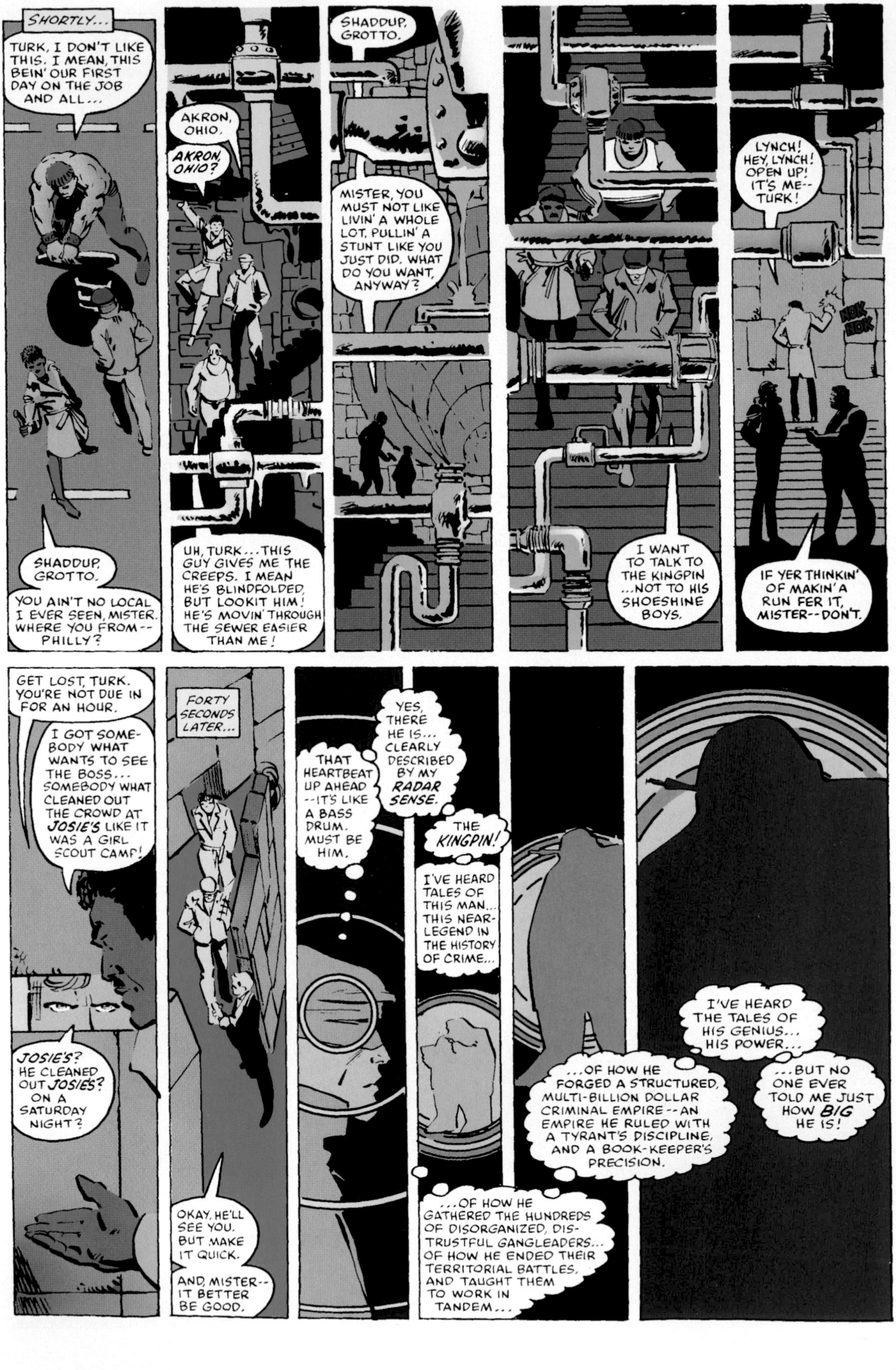
SHORTLY...
TURK, I DON'T LIKE THIS. I MEAN, THIS BEIN' OUR FIRST DAY ON THE JOB AND ALL...
SHADDUP, GROTTO.
YOU AIN'T NO LOCAL I EVER SEEN, MISTER. WHERE YOU FROM--PHILLY?
AKRON, OHIO.
AKRON, OHIO?
UH, TURK... THIS GUY GIVES ME THE CREEPS. I MEAN HE'S BLINDFOLDED, BUT LOOKIT HIM! HE'S MOVIN' THROUGH THE SEWER EASIER THAN ME!
SHADDUP, GROTTO.
MISTER, YOU MUST NOT LIKE LIVIN' A WHOLE LOT, PULLIN' A STUNT LIKE YOU JUST DID. WHAT DO YOU WANT, ANYWAY?
I WANT TO TALK TO THE KINGPIN ...NOT TO HIS SHOESHINE BOYS.
LYNCH! HEY, LYNCH! OPEN UP! IT'S ME--TURK!
HOK HOK
IF YER THINKIN' OF MAKIN' A RUN FER IT, MISTER--DON'T.
GET LOST, TURK. YOU'RE NOT DUE IN FOR AN HOUR.
I GOT SOMEBODY WHAT WANTS TO SEE THE BOSS... SOMEBODY WHAT CLEANED OUT THE CROWD AT JOSIE'S LIKE IT WAS A GIRL SCOUT CAMP!
JOSIE'S? HE CLEANED OUT JOSIE'S? ON A SATURDAY NIGHT?
FORTY SECONDS LATER...
OKAY, HE'LL SEE YOU. BUT MAKE IT QUICK.
AND, MISTER--IT BETTER BE GOOD.
THAT HEARTBEAT UP AHEAD --IT'S LIKE A BASS DRUM. MUST BE HIM.
YES, THERE HE IS... CLEARLY DESCRIBED BY MY RADAR SENSE.
THE KINGPIN!
I'VE HEARD TALES OF THIS MAN... THIS NEAR-LEGEND IN THE HISTORY OF CRIME...
...OF HOW HE GATHERED THE HUNDREDS OF DISORGANIZED, DISTRUSTFUL GANGLEADERS... OF HOW HE ENDED THEIR TERRITORIAL BATTLES, AND TAUGHT THEM TO WORK IN TANDEM...
...OF HOW HE FORGED A STRUCTURED, MULTI-BILLION DOLLAR CRIMINAL EMPIRE--AN EMPIRE HE RULED WITH A TYRANT'S DISCIPLINE, AND A BOOK-KEEPER'S PRECISION.
I'VE HEARD THE TALES OF HIS GENIUS... HIS POWER...
...BUT NO ONE EVER TOLD ME JUST HOW BIG HE IS!

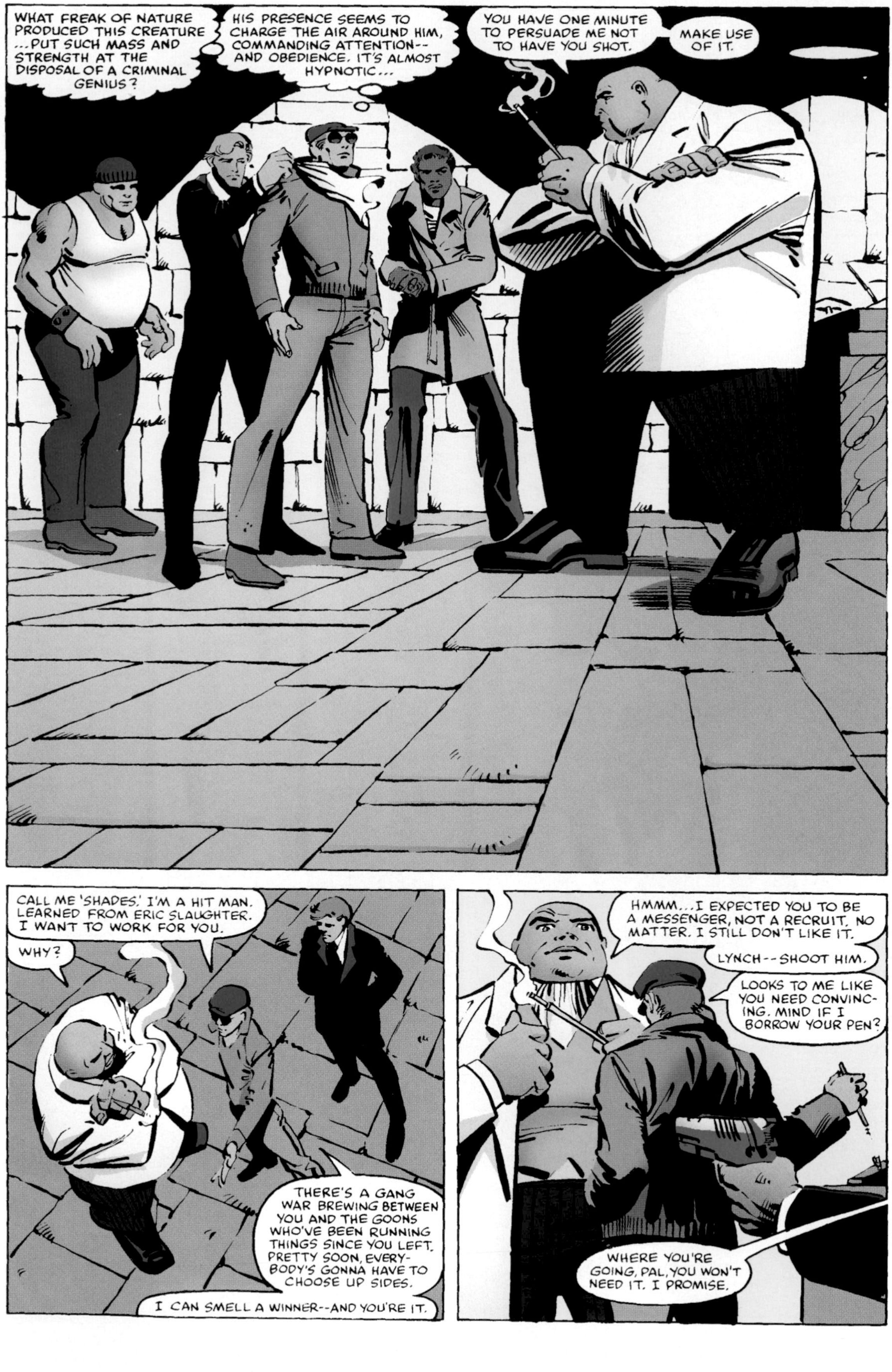
WHAT FREAK OF NATURE PRODUCED THIS CREATURE ...PUT SUCH MASS AND STRENGTH AT THE DISPOSAL OF A CRIMINAL GENIUS?
HIS PRESENCE SEEMS TO CHARGE THE AIR AROUND HIM, COMMANDING ATTENTION-- AND OBEDIENCE. IT'S ALMOST HYPNOTIC...
YOU HAVE ONE MINUTE TO PERSUADE ME NOT TO HAVE YOU SHOT.
MAKE USE OF IT.
CALL ME 'SHADES.' I'M A HIT MAN. LEARNED FROM ERIC SLAUGHTER. I WANT TO WORK FOR YOU.
WHY?
THERE'S A GANG WAR BREWING BETWEEN YOU AND THE GOONS WHO'VE BEEN RUNNING THINGS SINCE YOU LEFT. PRETTY SOON, EVERY-BODY'S GONNA HAVE TO CHOOSE UP SIDES.
I CAN SMELL A WINNER--AND YOU'RE IT.
HMMM...I EXPECTED YOU TO BE A MESSENGER, NOT A RECRUIT. NO MATTER. I STILL DON'T LIKE IT.
LYNCH--SHOOT HIM.
LOOKS TO ME LIKE YOU NEED CONVINC-ING. MIND IF I BORROW YOUR PEN?
WHERE YOU'RE GOING, PAL, YOU WON'T NEED IT. I PROMISE.

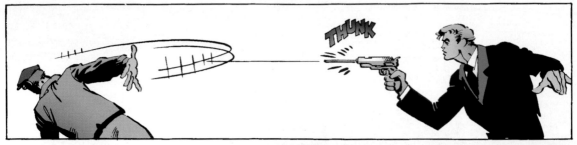

THUNK

WELL?

YOU'RE HIRED.

LORD... NEVER SAW ANYONE MOVE THAT FAST... NEVER...

EH?

IT...IT WAS *BULLSEYE*, BOSS, HE CAUGHT UP WITH ME AND THE BOYS OUTSIDE OF SWEENEYS...

SAID...SAID HE HAD A MESSAGE... FOR YOU, BOSS...

WHAT IS IT, DUKE? QUICKLY.

HE SAYS IF...IF YOU WANT YOUR WIFE BACK...YOU GOTTA...

YOU GOTTA MEET HIS BOSSES ALONE...UN ...UNARMED...

...AT A CON...CON- STRUCTION SITE ON NINTH AVENUE AND ...AND FORTIETH... TOMORROW NIGHT... MIDNIGH...

HKKK--!

HE'S CROAKED.

SLOW ACTING POISON, NO DOUBT.

YEAH, BOSS?

THERE'S A BODY IN MY OFFICE. COME FETCH IT, AND POST ANOTHER GUARD AT THE VAULT TONIGHT.

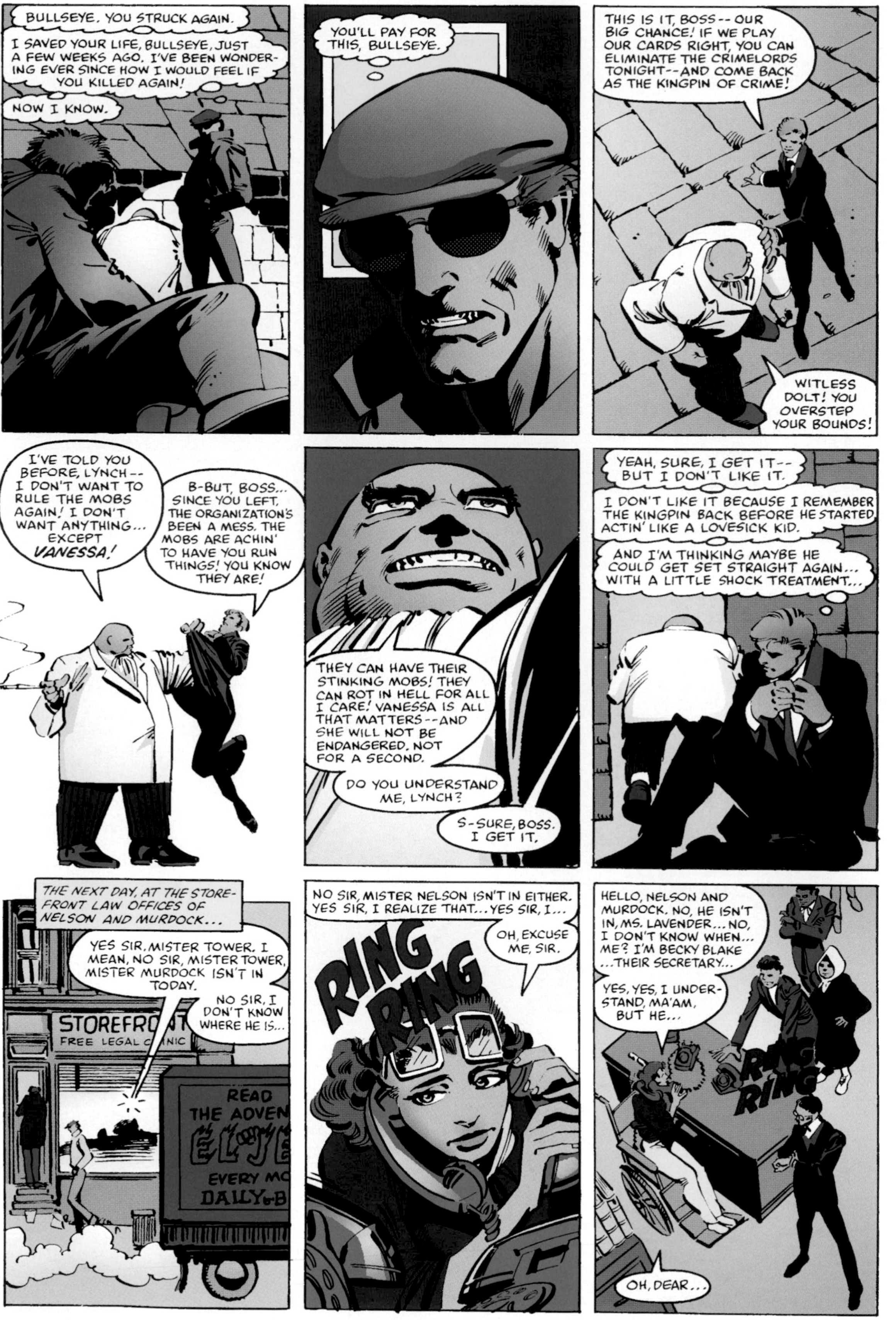
BULLSEYE. YOU STRUCK AGAIN.
I SAVED YOUR LIFE, BULLSEYE, JUST A FEW WEEKS AGO. I'VE BEEN WONDERING EVER SINCE HOW I WOULD FEEL IF YOU KILLED AGAIN!
NOW I KNOW.
YOU'LL PAY FOR THIS, BULLSEYE.
THIS IS IT, BOSS -- OUR BIG CHANCE! IF WE PLAY OUR CARDS RIGHT, YOU CAN ELIMINATE THE CRIMELORDS TONIGHT--AND COME BACK AS THE KINGPIN OF CRIME!
WITLESS DOLT! YOU OVERSTEP YOUR BOUNDS!
I'VE TOLD YOU BEFORE, LYNCH -- I DON'T WANT TO RULE THE MOBS AGAIN! I DON'T WANT ANYTHING... EXCEPT VANESSA!
B-BUT, BOSS... SINCE YOU LEFT, THE ORGANIZATION'S BEEN A MESS. THE MOBS ARE ACHIN' TO HAVE YOU RUN THINGS! YOU KNOW THEY ARE!
THEY CAN HAVE THEIR STINKING MOBS! THEY CAN ROT IN HELL FOR ALL I CARE! VANESSA IS ALL THAT MATTERS--AND SHE WILL NOT BE ENDANGERED. NOT FOR A SECOND.
DO YOU UNDERSTAND ME, LYNCH?
S-SURE, BOSS. I GET IT.
YEAH, SURE, I GET IT-- BUT I DON'T LIKE IT.
I DON'T LIKE IT BECAUSE I REMEMBER THE KINGPIN BACK BEFORE HE STARTED ACTIN' LIKE A LOVESICK KID.
AND I'M THINKING MAYBE HE COULD GET SET STRAIGHT AGAIN... WITH A LITTLE SHOCK TREATMENT...
THE NEXT DAY, AT THE STOREFRONT LAW OFFICES OF NELSON AND MURDOCK...
YES SIR, MISTER TOWER. I MEAN, NO SIR, MISTER TOWER, MISTER MURDOCK ISN'T IN TODAY.
NO SIR, I DON'T KNOW WHERE HE IS...
STOREFRONT
FREE LEGAL C INIC
READ THE ADVEN
EVERY MO
DAILY B
NO SIR, MISTER NELSON ISN'T IN EITHER. YES SIR, I REALIZE THAT... YES SIR, I...
OH, EXCUSE ME, SIR.
RING RING
HELLO, NELSON AND MURDOCK. NO, HE ISN'T IN, MS. LAVENDER... NO, I DON'T KNOW WHEN... ME? I'M BECKY BLAKE ...THEIR SECRETARY...
YES, YES, I UNDERSTAND, MA'AM, BUT HE...
RING RING
OH, DEAR...

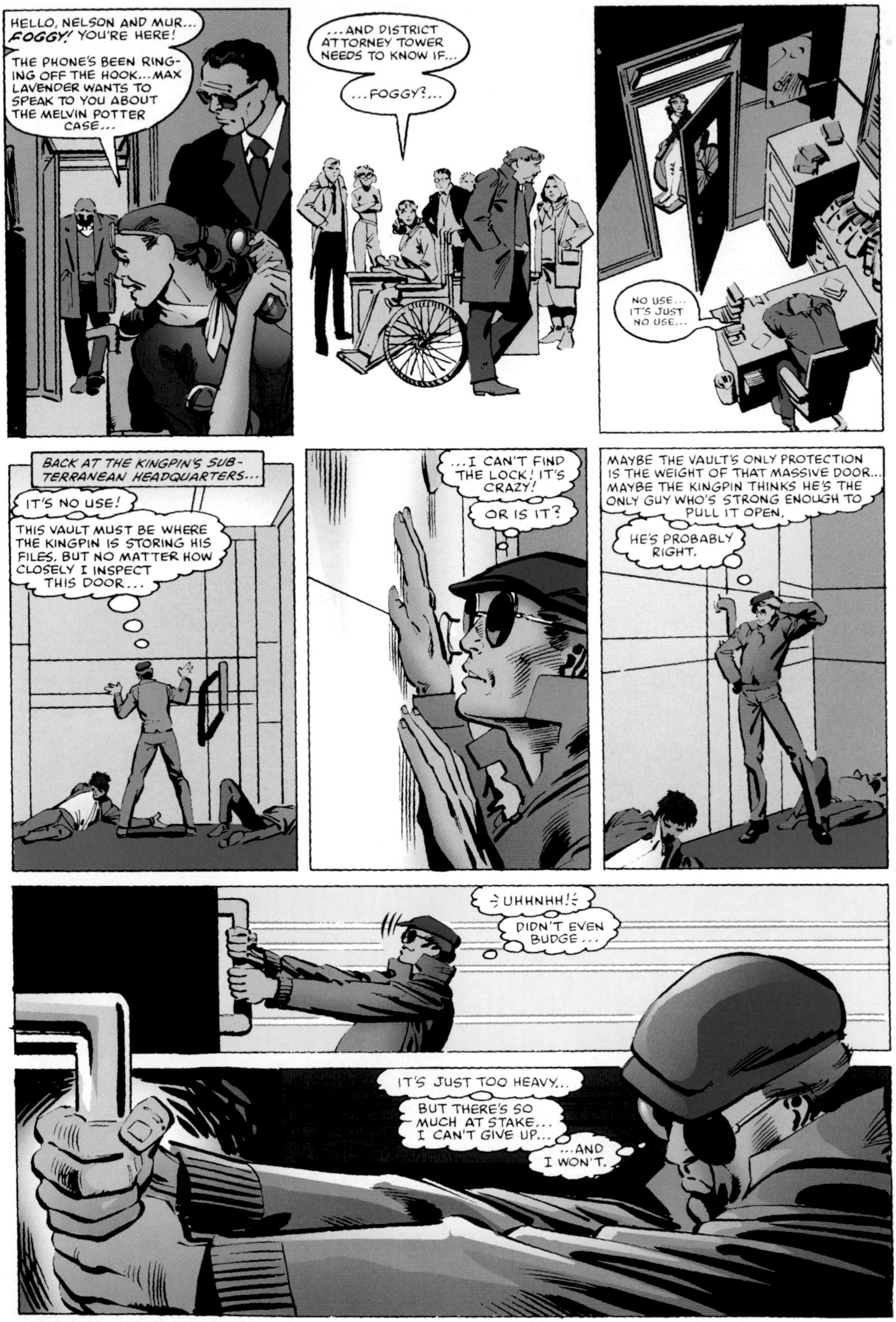

HELLO, NELSON AND MUR... FOGGY! YOU'RE HERE!
THE PHONE'S BEEN RINGING OFF THE HOOK... MAX LAVENDER WANTS TO SPEAK TO YOU ABOUT THE MELVIN POTTER CASE...
...AND DISTRICT ATTORNEY TOWER NEEDS TO KNOW IF...
...FOGGY?...
NO USE... IT'S JUST NO USE...
BACK AT THE KINGPIN'S SUBTERRANEAN HEADQUARTERS...
IT'S NO USE!
THIS VAULT MUST BE WHERE THE KINGPIN IS STORING HIS FILES. BUT NO MATTER HOW CLOSELY I INSPECT THIS DOOR...
...I CAN'T FIND THE LOCK! IT'S CRAZY!
OR IS IT?
MAYBE THE VAULT'S ONLY PROTECTION IS THE WEIGHT OF THAT MASSIVE DOOR... MAYBE THE KINGPIN THINKS HE'S THE ONLY GUY WHO'S STRONG ENOUGH TO PULL IT OPEN.
HE'S PROBABLY RIGHT.
UHHNHH!
DIDN'T EVEN BUDGE...
IT'S JUST TOO HEAVY...
BUT THERE'S SO MUCH AT STAKE... I CAN'T GIVE UP...
...AND I WON'T.

IT IS HOPELESS, HE KNOWS, SO HE DOESN'T HOPE.

HE SIMPLY PULLS--

--UNTIL HIS SHOULDER BLADES BULGE AGAINST THE KNOTTED MUSCLES OF HIS BACK--

--UNTIL HIS BREATH HISSES HOTLY THROUGH CLENCHED TEETH--

--UNTIL CORDED SINEW STRETCHES, NEAR BREAKING--

--UNTIL HIS ARMS SHAKE, AND THREATEN TO YANK FREE OF THEIR SOCKETS...

...AND SOMEHOW, SOMEWHERE BEYOND THE PAIN...

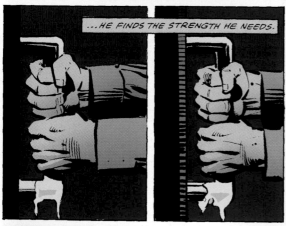

...HE FINDS THE STRENGTH HE NEEDS.

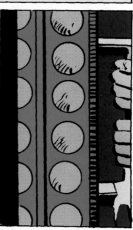

HANDS FEEL BIG AS BASKETBALLS. CAN BARELY MOVE MY ARMS. BUT THERE'S NO TIME TO RELAX.

NOW IT'S JUST A MATTER OF TAKING THESE FILES, AND GETTING OUT OF THIS PLACE ALIVE.

I WISH I WASN'T BLIND, JUST FOR AN HOUR--SO I COULD SEE DISTRICT ATTORNEY TOWER'S FACE WHEN I HAND HIM THIS!

UH-OH...STEPS, ECHOING DOWN THE HALLWAY...

BIG STEPS.

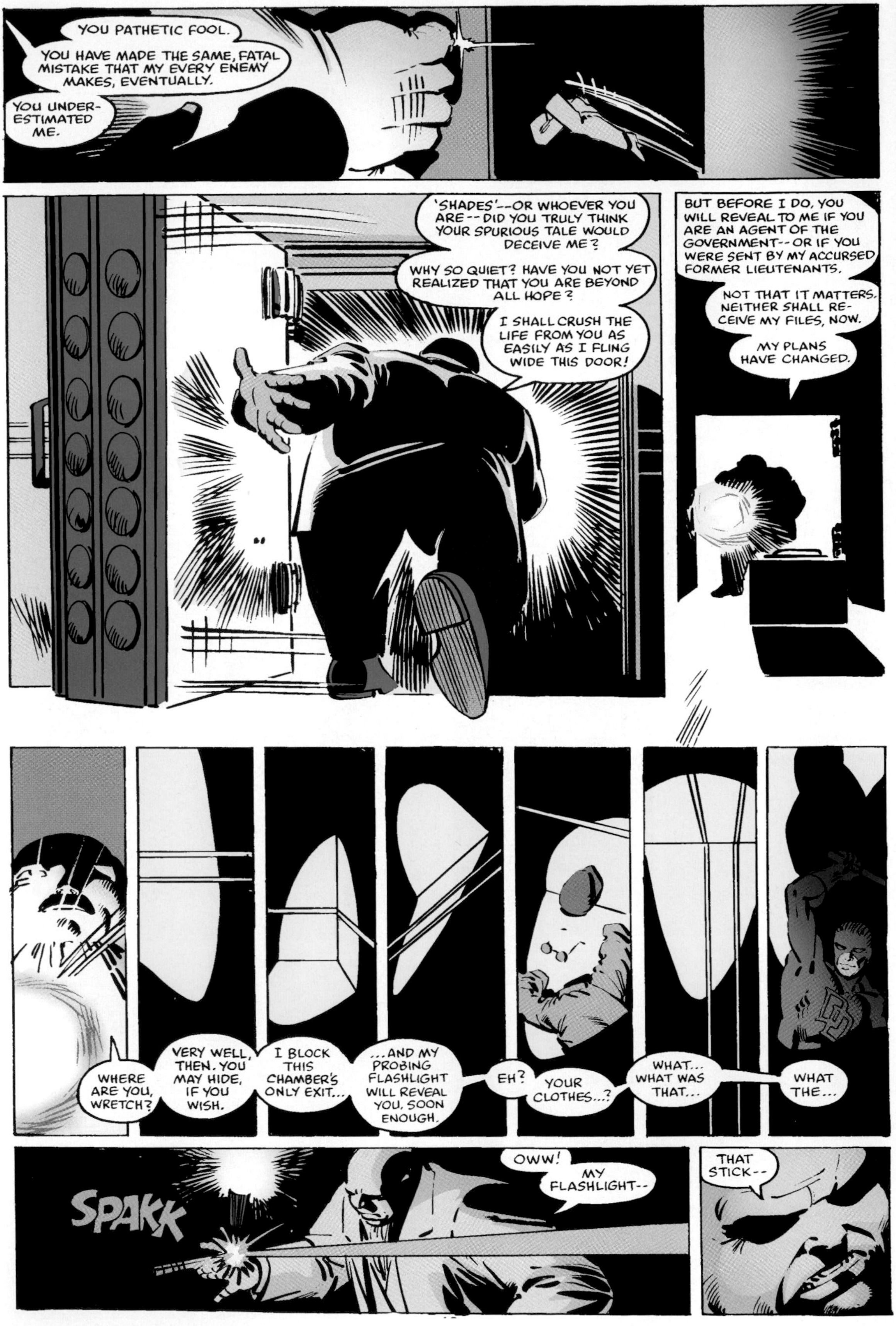
YOU PATHETIC FOOL.
YOU HAVE MADE THE SAME, FATAL MISTAKE THAT MY EVERY ENEMY MAKES, EVENTUALLY.
YOU UNDER-ESTIMATED ME.
'SHADES'--OR WHOEVER YOU ARE--DID YOU TRULY THINK YOUR SPURIOUS TALE WOULD DECEIVE ME?
WHY SO QUIET? HAVE YOU NOT YET REALIZED THAT YOU ARE BEYOND ALL HOPE?
I SHALL CRUSH THE LIFE FROM YOU AS EASILY AS I FLING WIDE THIS DOOR!
BUT BEFORE I DO, YOU WILL REVEAL TO ME IF YOU ARE AN AGENT OF THE GOVERNMENT--OR IF YOU WERE SENT BY MY ACCURSED FORMER LIEUTENANTS.
NOT THAT IT MATTERS. NEITHER SHALL RECEIVE MY FILES, NOW.
MY PLANS HAVE CHANGED.
WHERE ARE YOU, WRETCH?
VERY WELL, THEN. YOU MAY HIDE, IF YOU WISH.
I BLOCK THIS CHAMBER'S ONLY EXIT...
...AND MY PROBING FLASHLIGHT WILL REVEAL YOU, SOON ENOUGH.
EH?
YOUR CLOTHES...?
WHAT... WHAT WAS THAT...
WHAT THE...
SPAKK
OWW!
MY FLASHLIGHT--
THAT STICK--

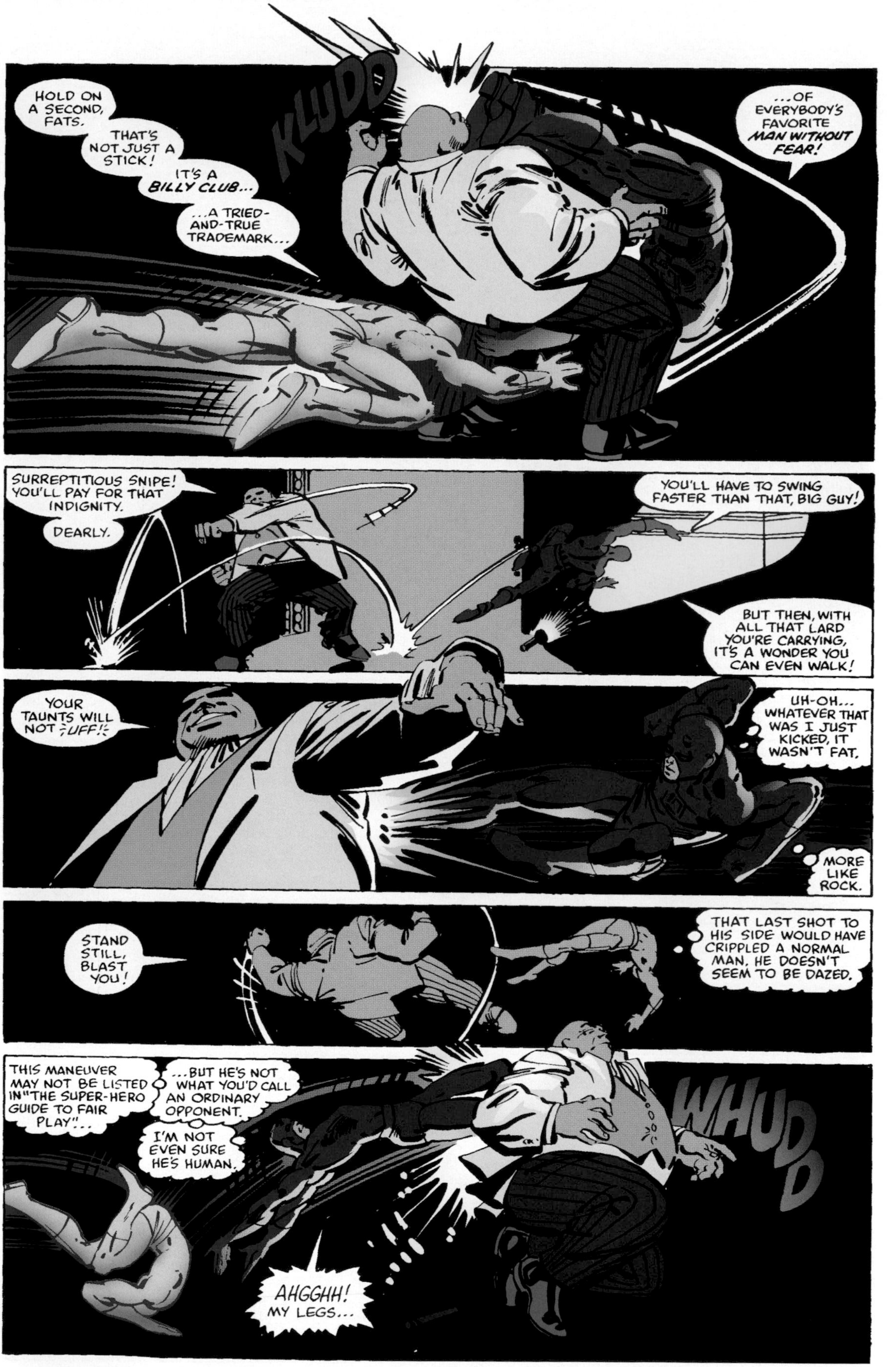
HOLD ON A SECOND, FATS.
THAT'S NOT JUST A STICK!
IT'S A BILLY CLUB...
...A TRIED-AND-TRUE TRADEMARK...
KLUDD
...OF EVERYBODY'S FAVORITE MAN WITHOUT FEAR!
SURREPTITIOUS SNIPE! YOU'LL PAY FOR THAT INDIGNITY.
DEARLY.
YOU'LL HAVE TO SWING FASTER THAN THAT, BIG GUY!
BUT THEN, WITH ALL THAT LARD YOU'RE CARRYING, IT'S A WONDER YOU CAN EVEN WALK!
YOUR TAUNTS WILL NOT ¡UFF!¡
UH-OH... WHATEVER THAT WAS I JUST KICKED, IT WASN'T FAT.
MORE LIKE ROCK.
STAND STILL, BLAST YOU!
THAT LAST SHOT TO HIS SIDE WOULD HAVE CRIPPLED A NORMAL MAN. HE DOESN'T SEEM TO BE DAZED.
THIS MANEUVER MAY NOT BE LISTED IN "THE SUPER-HERO GUIDE TO FAIR PLAY"...
...BUT HE'S NOT WHAT YOU'D CALL AN ORDINARY OPPONENT.
I'M NOT EVEN SURE HE'S HUMAN.
WHUDD
AHGGHH! MY LEGS...

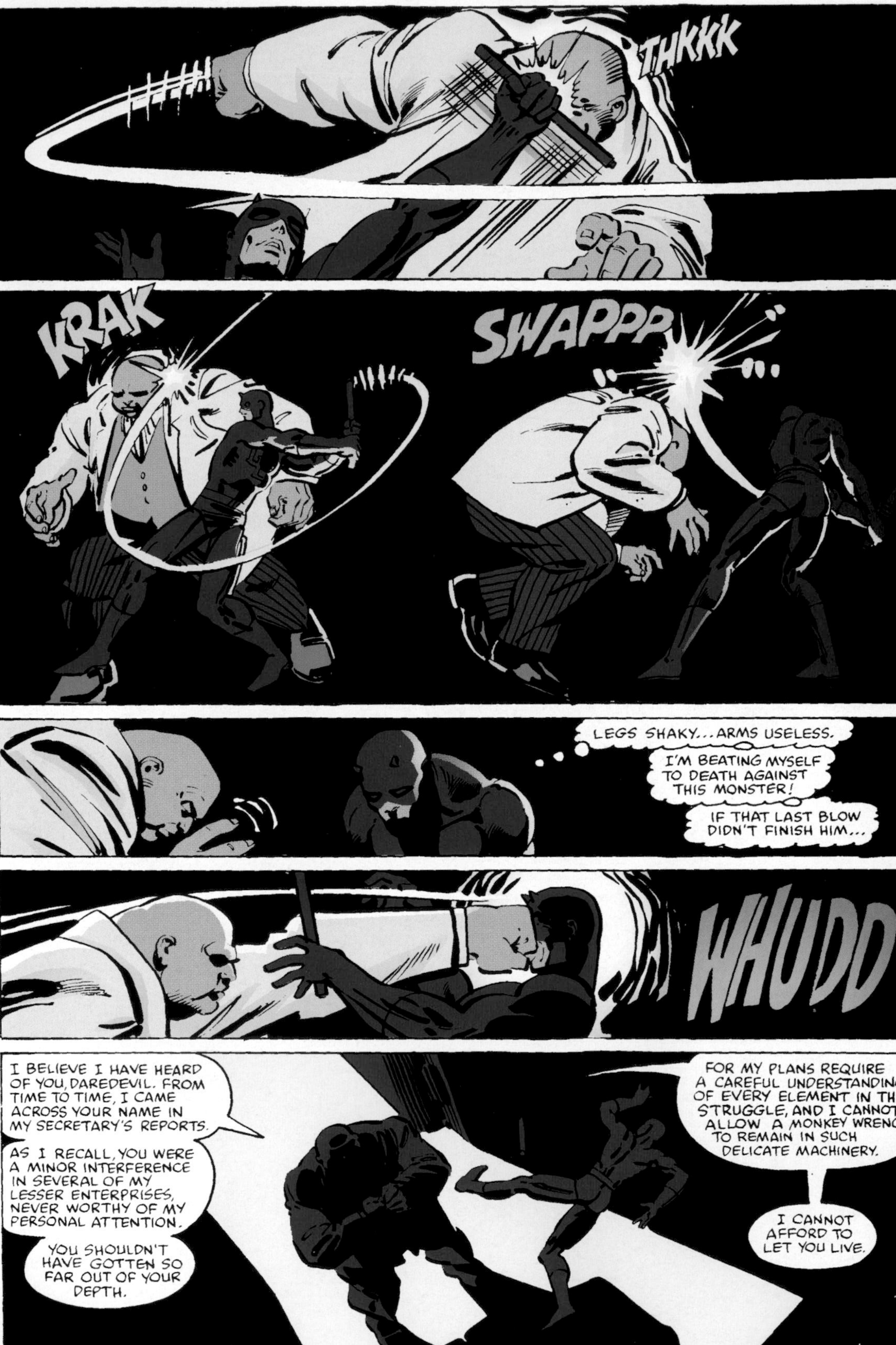
THKKK
KRAK
SWAPPP
LEGS SHAKY... ARMS USELESS.
I'M BEATING MYSELF TO DEATH AGAINST THIS MONSTER!
IF THAT LAST BLOW DIDN'T FINISH HIM...
WHUDD
I BELIEVE I HAVE HEARD OF YOU, DAREDEVIL. FROM TIME TO TIME, I CAME ACROSS YOUR NAME IN MY SECRETARY'S REPORTS.
AS I RECALL, YOU WERE A MINOR INTERFERENCE IN SEVERAL OF MY LESSER ENTERPRISES, NEVER WORTHY OF MY PERSONAL ATTENTION.
YOU SHOULDN'T HAVE GOTTEN SO FAR OUT OF YOUR DEPTH.
FOR MY PLANS REQUIRE A CAREFUL UNDERSTANDING OF EVERY ELEMENT IN THIS STRUGGLE, AND I CANNOT ALLOW A MONKEY WRENCH TO REMAIN IN SUCH DELICATE MACHINERY.
I CANNOT AFFORD TO LET YOU LIVE.

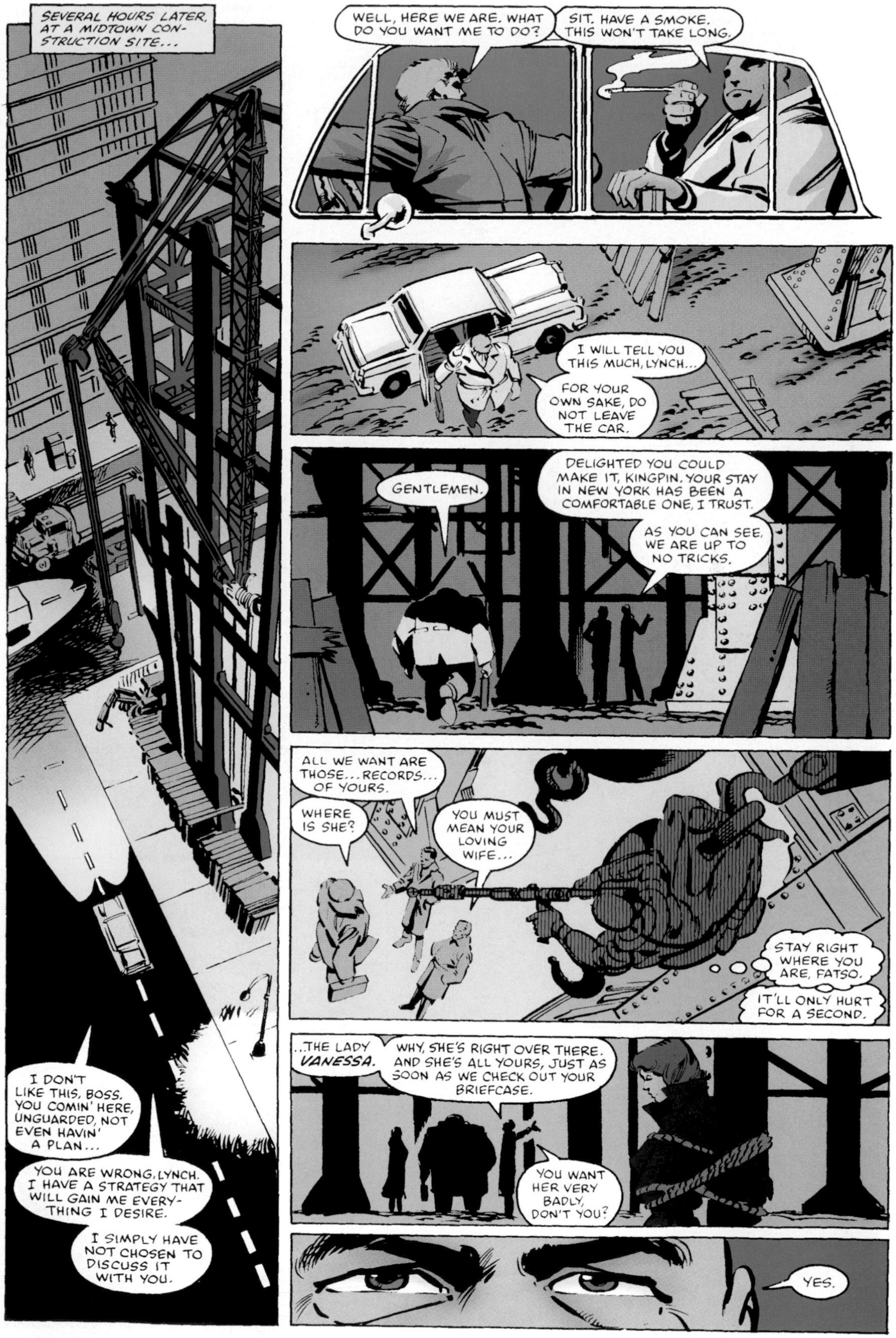
SEVERAL HOURS LATER, AT A MIDTOWN CONSTRUCTION SITE...
I DON'T LIKE THIS, BOSS. YOU COMIN' HERE, UNGUARDED, NOT EVEN HAVIN' A PLAN...
YOU ARE WRONG, LYNCH. I HAVE A STRATEGY THAT WILL GAIN ME EVERYTHING I DESIRE.
I SIMPLY HAVE NOT CHOSEN TO DISCUSS IT WITH YOU.
WELL, HERE WE ARE. WHAT DO YOU WANT ME TO DO?
SIT. HAVE A SMOKE. THIS WON'T TAKE LONG.
I WILL TELL YOU THIS MUCH, LYNCH...
FOR YOUR OWN SAKE, DO NOT LEAVE THE CAR.
GENTLEMEN.
DELIGHTED YOU COULD MAKE IT, KINGPIN. YOUR STAY IN NEW YORK HAS BEEN A COMFORTABLE ONE, I TRUST.
AS YOU CAN SEE, WE ARE UP TO NO TRICKS.
ALL WE WANT ARE THOSE... RECORDS... OF YOURS.
WHERE IS SHE?
YOU MUST MEAN YOUR LOVING WIFE...
STAY RIGHT WHERE YOU ARE, FATSO.
IT'LL ONLY HURT FOR A SECOND.
...THE LADY VANESSA.
WHY, SHE'S RIGHT OVER THERE. AND SHE'S ALL YOURS, JUST AS SOON AS WE CHECK OUT YOUR BRIEFCASE.
YOU WANT HER VERY BADLY, DON'T YOU?
YES.

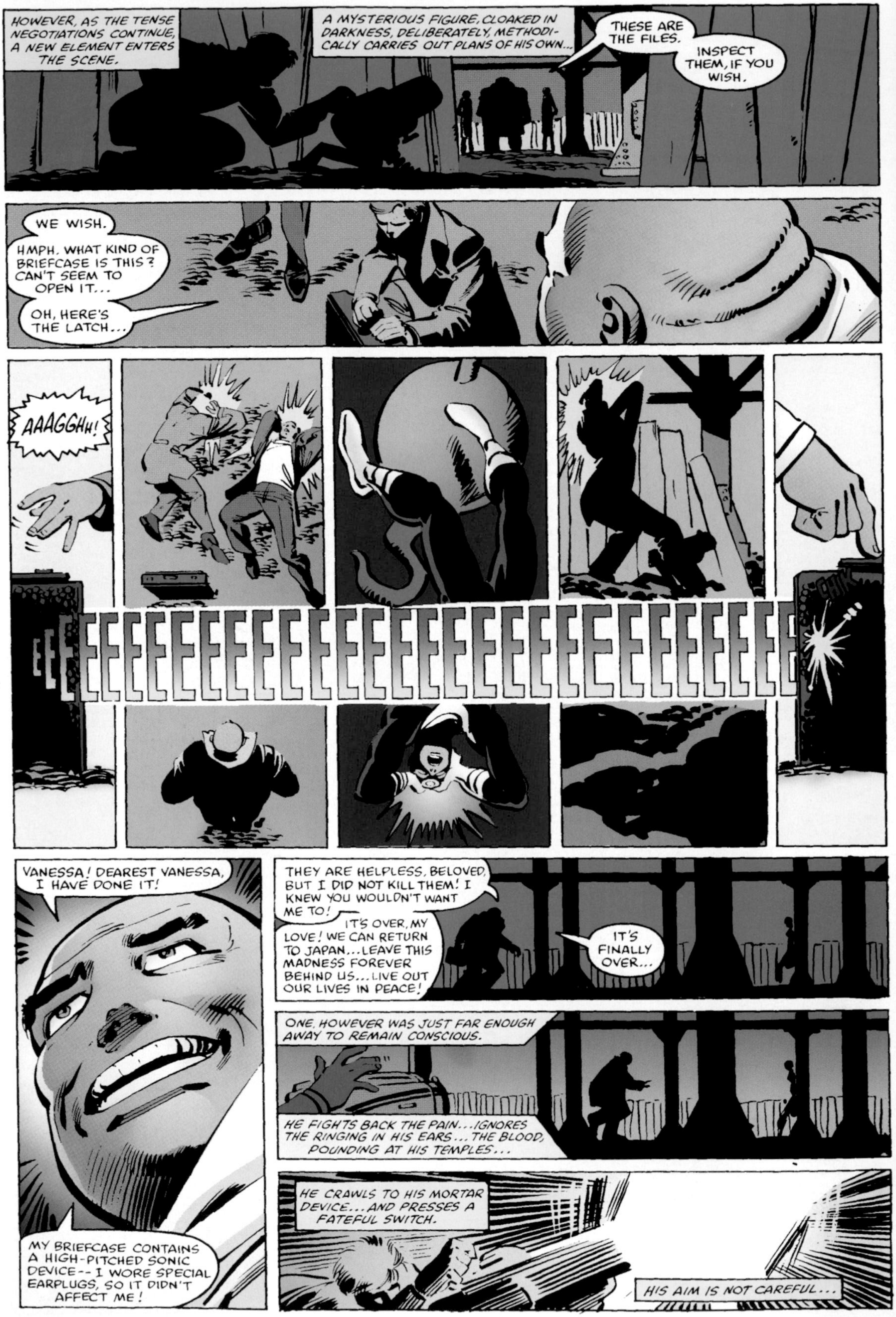
HOWEVER, AS THE TENSE NEGOTIATIONS CONTINUE, A NEW ELEMENT ENTERS THE SCENE.
A MYSTERIOUS FIGURE, CLOAKED IN DARKNESS, DELIBERATELY, METHODICALLY CARRIES OUT PLANS OF HIS OWN...
THESE ARE THE FILES.
INSPECT THEM, IF YOU WISH.
WE WISH.
HMPH. WHAT KIND OF BRIEFCASE IS THIS? CAN'T SEEM TO OPEN IT...
OH, HERE'S THE LATCH...
AAAGGHH!
EEEEEEEEEEEEEEEEEEEEEEEEEEE
CHIK
VANESSA! DEAREST VANESSA, I HAVE DONE IT!
MY BRIEFCASE CONTAINS A HIGH-PITCHED SONIC DEVICE-- I WORE SPECIAL EARPLUGS, SO IT DIDN'T AFFECT ME!
THEY ARE HELPLESS, BELOVED, BUT I DID NOT KILL THEM! I KNEW YOU WOULDN'T WANT ME TO!
IT'S OVER, MY LOVE! WE CAN RETURN TO JAPAN... LEAVE THIS MADNESS FOREVER BEHIND US... LIVE OUT OUR LIVES IN PEACE!
IT'S FINALLY OVER...
ONE, HOWEVER WAS JUST FAR ENOUGH AWAY TO REMAIN CONSCIOUS.
HE FIGHTS BACK THE PAIN... IGNORES THE RINGING IN HIS EARS... THE BLOOD, POUNDING AT HIS TEMPLES...
HE CRAWLS TO HIS MORTAR DEVICE... AND PRESSES A FATEFUL SWITCH.
HIS AIM IS NOT CAREFUL...

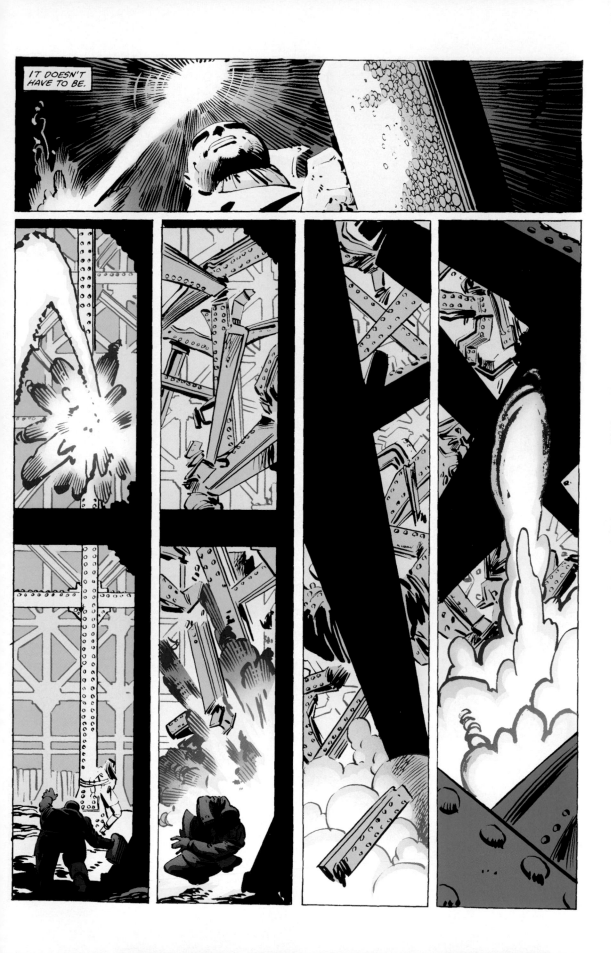

IT DOESN'T HAVE TO BE.

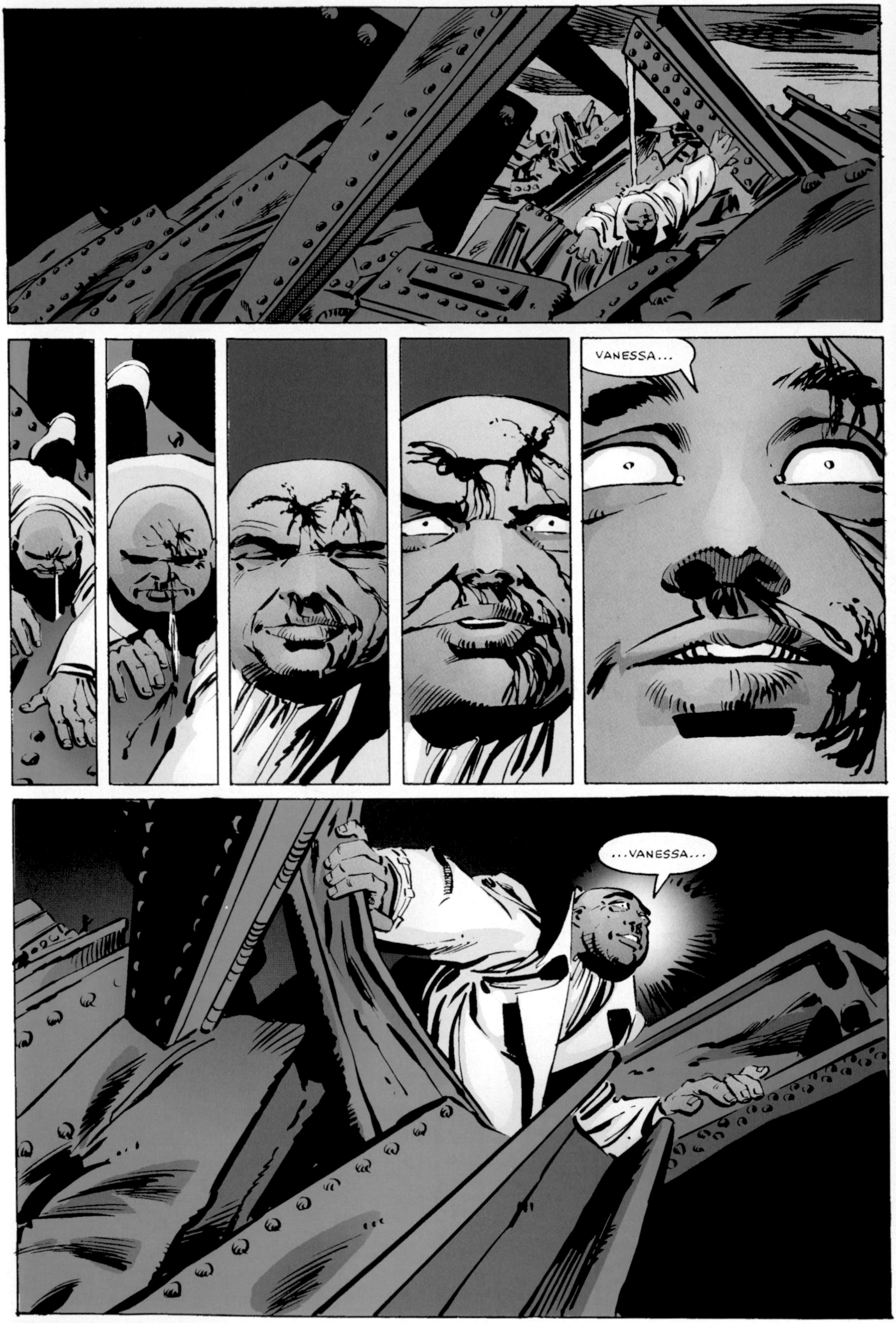
VANESSA...
...VANESSA...

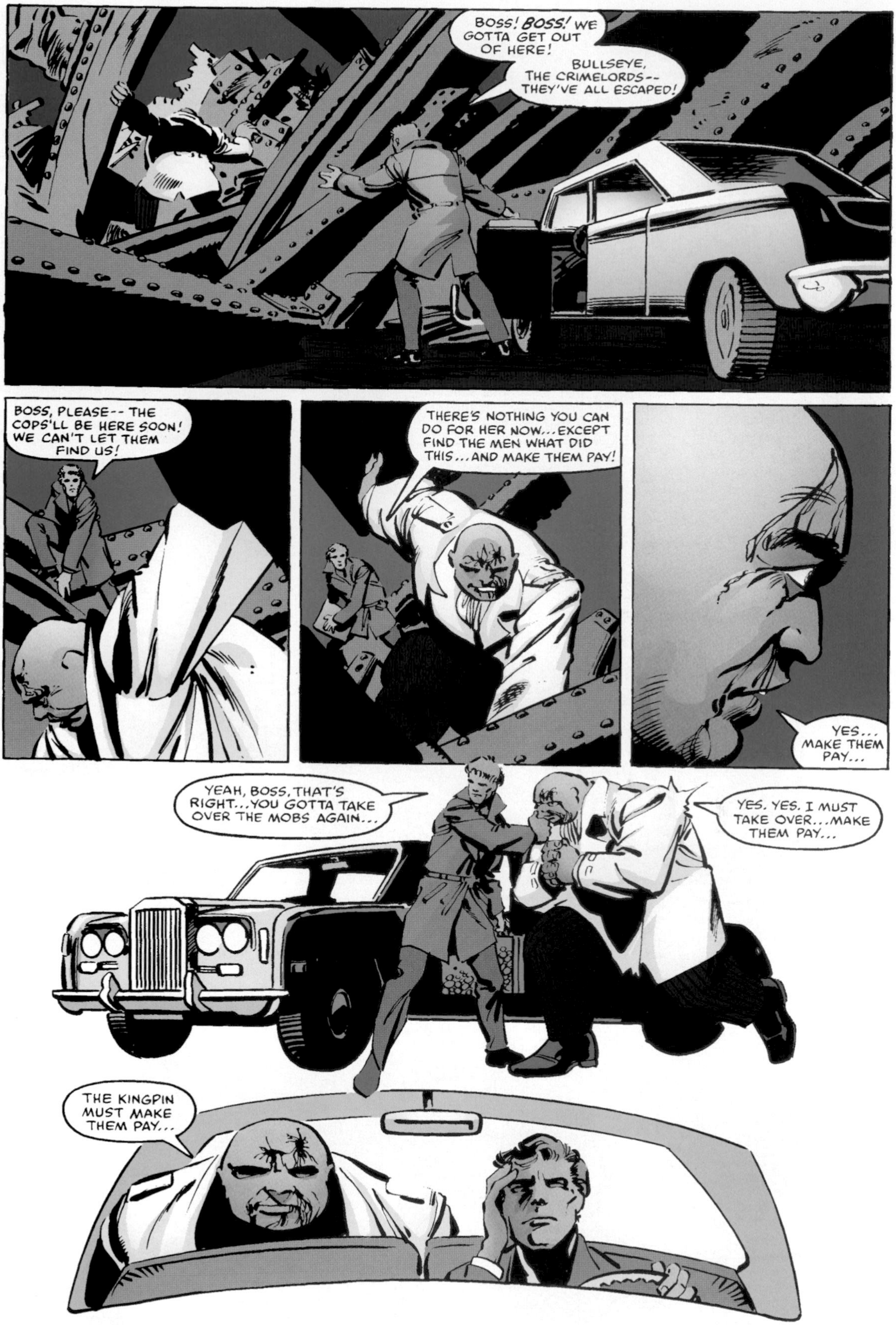
BOSS! BOSS! WE GOTTA GET OUT OF HERE!
BULLSEYE, THE CRIMELORDS-- THEY'VE ALL ESCAPED!
BOSS, PLEASE-- THE COPS'LL BE HERE SOON! WE CAN'T LET THEM FIND US!
THERE'S NOTHING YOU CAN DO FOR HER NOW... EXCEPT FIND THE MEN WHAT DID THIS... AND MAKE THEM PAY!
YES... MAKE THEM PAY...
YEAH, BOSS, THAT'S RIGHT... YOU GOTTA TAKE OVER THE MOBS AGAIN...
YES. YES. I MUST TAKE OVER... MAKE THEM PAY...
THE KINGPIN MUST MAKE THEM PAY...

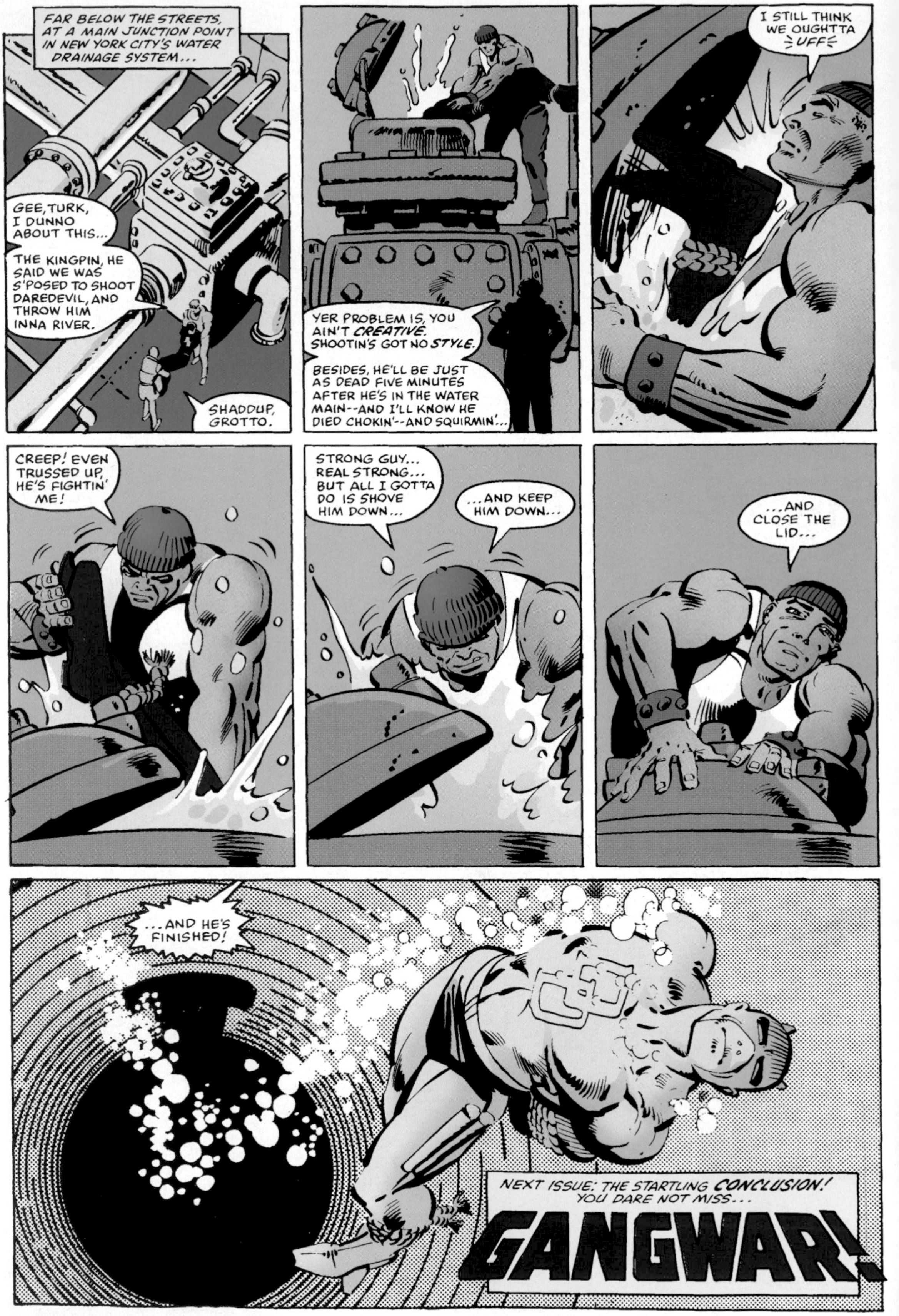
FAR BELOW THE STREETS, AT A MAIN JUNCTION POINT IN NEW YORK CITY'S WATER DRAINAGE SYSTEM...
GEE, TURK, I DUNNO ABOUT THIS...
THE KINGPIN, HE SAID WE WAS S'POSED TO SHOOT DAREDEVIL, AND THROW HIM INNA RIVER.
SHADDUP, GROTTO.
YER PROBLEM IS, YOU AIN'T CREATIVE. SHOOTIN'S GOT NO STYLE.
BESIDES, HE'LL BE JUST AS DEAD FIVE MINUTES AFTER HE'S IN THE WATER MAIN--AND I'LL KNOW HE DIED CHOKIN'--AND SQUIRMIN'...
I STILL THINK WE OUGHTTA UFF
CREEP! EVEN TRUSSED UP, HE'S FIGHTIN' ME!
STRONG GUY... REAL STRONG... BUT ALL I GOTTA DO IS SHOVE HIM DOWN...
...AND KEEP HIM DOWN...
...AND CLOSE THE LID...
...AND HE'S FINISHED!
NEXT ISSUE: THE STARTLING CONCLUSION! YOU DARE NOT MISS...
GANGWAR!

DAREDEVIL #172

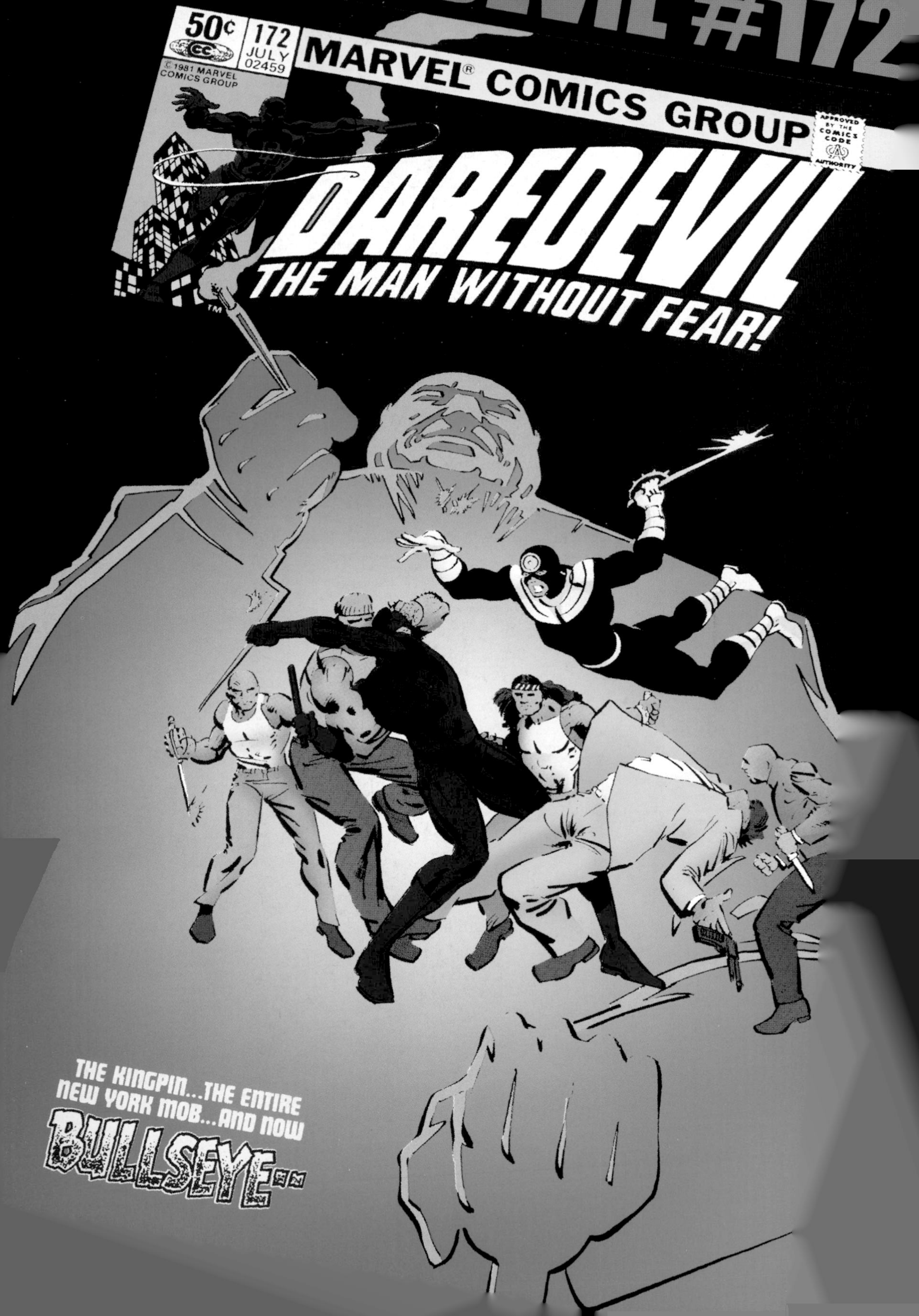
50¢
172
JULY
02459
©1981 MARVEL COMICS GROUP
MARVEL® COMICS GROUP
APPROVED BY THE COMICS CODE AUTHORITY
DAREDEVIL
THE MAN WITHOUT FEAR!
THE KINGPIN...THE ENTIRE NEW YORK MOB...AND NOW
BULLSEYE--

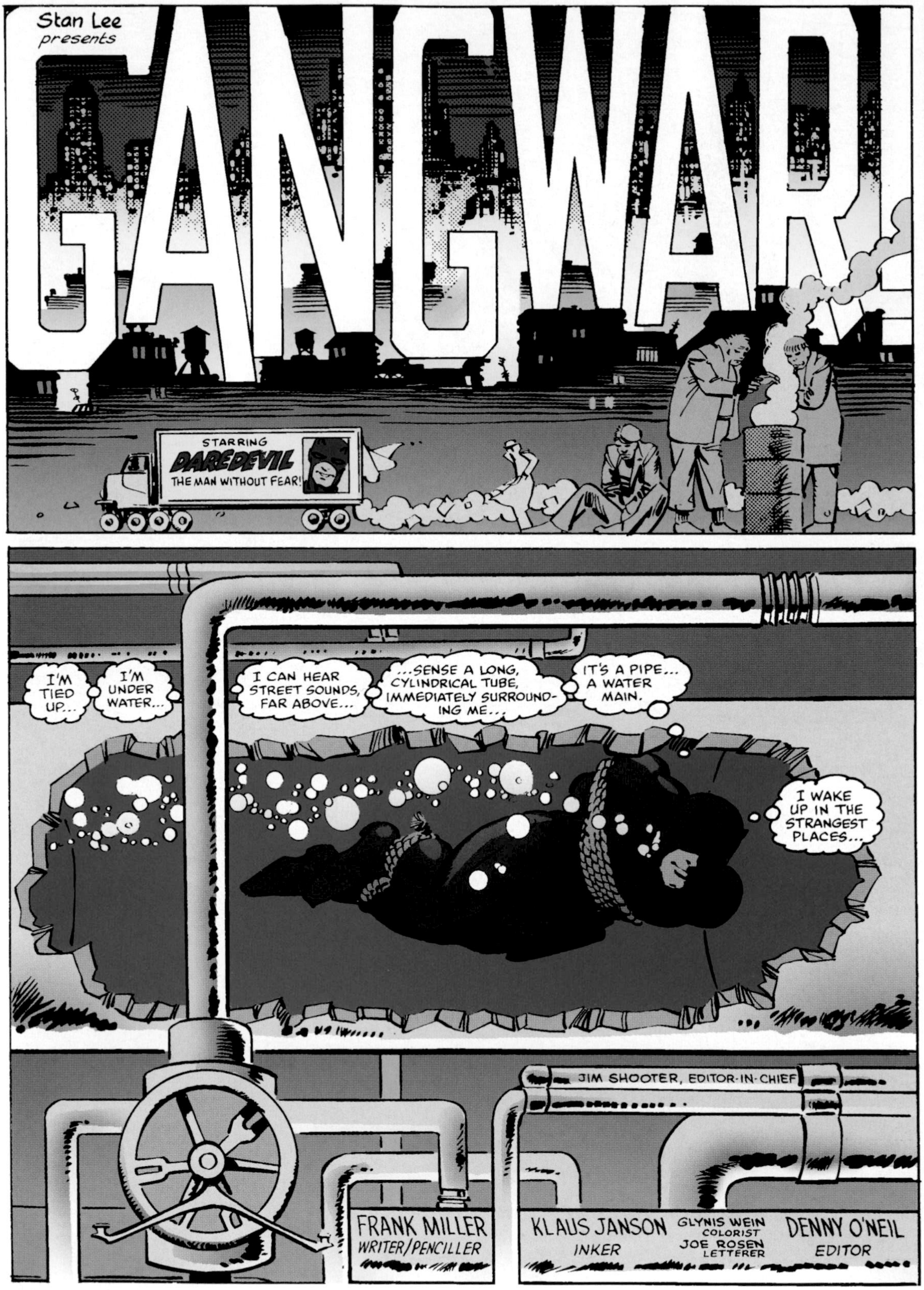
Stan Lee
presents
GANGWAR!
STARRING
DAREDEVIL
THE MAN WITHOUT FEAR!
I'M TIED UP...
I'M UNDER WATER...
I CAN HEAR STREET SOUNDS, FAR ABOVE...
...SENSE A LONG, CYLINDRICAL TUBE, IMMEDIATELY SURROUNDING ME...
IT'S A PIPE... A WATER MAIN.
I WAKE UP IN THE STRANGEST PLACES...
JIM SHOOTER, EDITOR-IN-CHIEF
FRANK MILLER WRITER/PENCILLER
KLAUS JANSON INKER
GLYNIS WEIN COLORIST
JOE ROSEN LETTERER
DENNY O'NEIL EDITOR

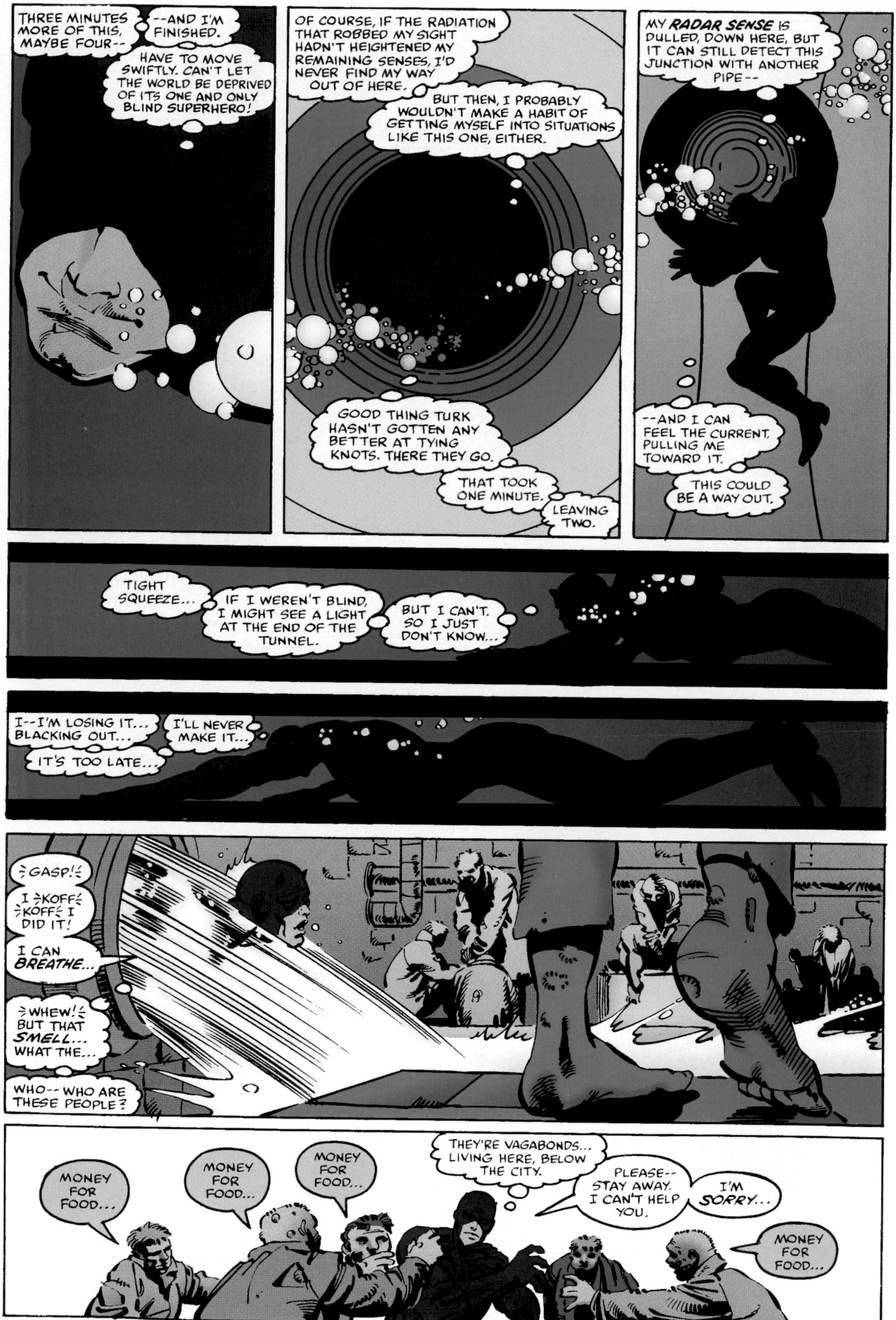
THREE MINUTES MORE OF THIS, MAYBE FOUR--
--AND I'M FINISHED.
HAVE TO MOVE SWIFTLY. CAN'T LET THE WORLD BE DEPRIVED OF ITS ONE AND ONLY BLIND SUPERHERO!
OF COURSE, IF THE RADIATION THAT ROBBED MY SIGHT HADN'T HEIGHTENED MY REMAINING SENSES, I'D NEVER FIND MY WAY OUT OF HERE.
BUT THEN, I PROBABLY WOULDN'T MAKE A HABIT OF GETTING MYSELF INTO SITUATIONS LIKE THIS ONE, EITHER.
GOOD THING TURK HASN'T GOTTEN ANY BETTER AT TYING KNOTS. THERE THEY GO.
THAT TOOK ONE MINUTE.
LEAVING TWO.
MY RADAR SENSE IS DULLED, DOWN HERE, BUT IT CAN STILL DETECT THIS JUNCTION WITH ANOTHER PIPE--
--AND I CAN FEEL THE CURRENT, PULLING ME TOWARD IT.
THIS COULD BE A WAY OUT.
TIGHT SQUEEZE...
IF I WEREN'T BLIND, I MIGHT SEE A LIGHT AT THE END OF THE TUNNEL.
BUT I CAN'T. SO I JUST DON'T KNOW...
I--I'M LOSING IT... BLACKING OUT...
I'LL NEVER MAKE IT...
IT'S TOO LATE...
GASP!
I KOFF KOFF I DID IT!
I CAN BREATHE...
WHEW! BUT THAT SMELL... WHAT THE...
WHO-- WHO ARE THESE PEOPLE?
MONEY FOR FOOD...
MONEY FOR FOOD...
MONEY FOR FOOD...
THEY'RE VAGABONDS... LIVING HERE, BELOW THE CITY.
PLEASE-- STAY AWAY. I CAN'T HELP YOU.
I'M SORRY...
MONEY FOR FOOD...

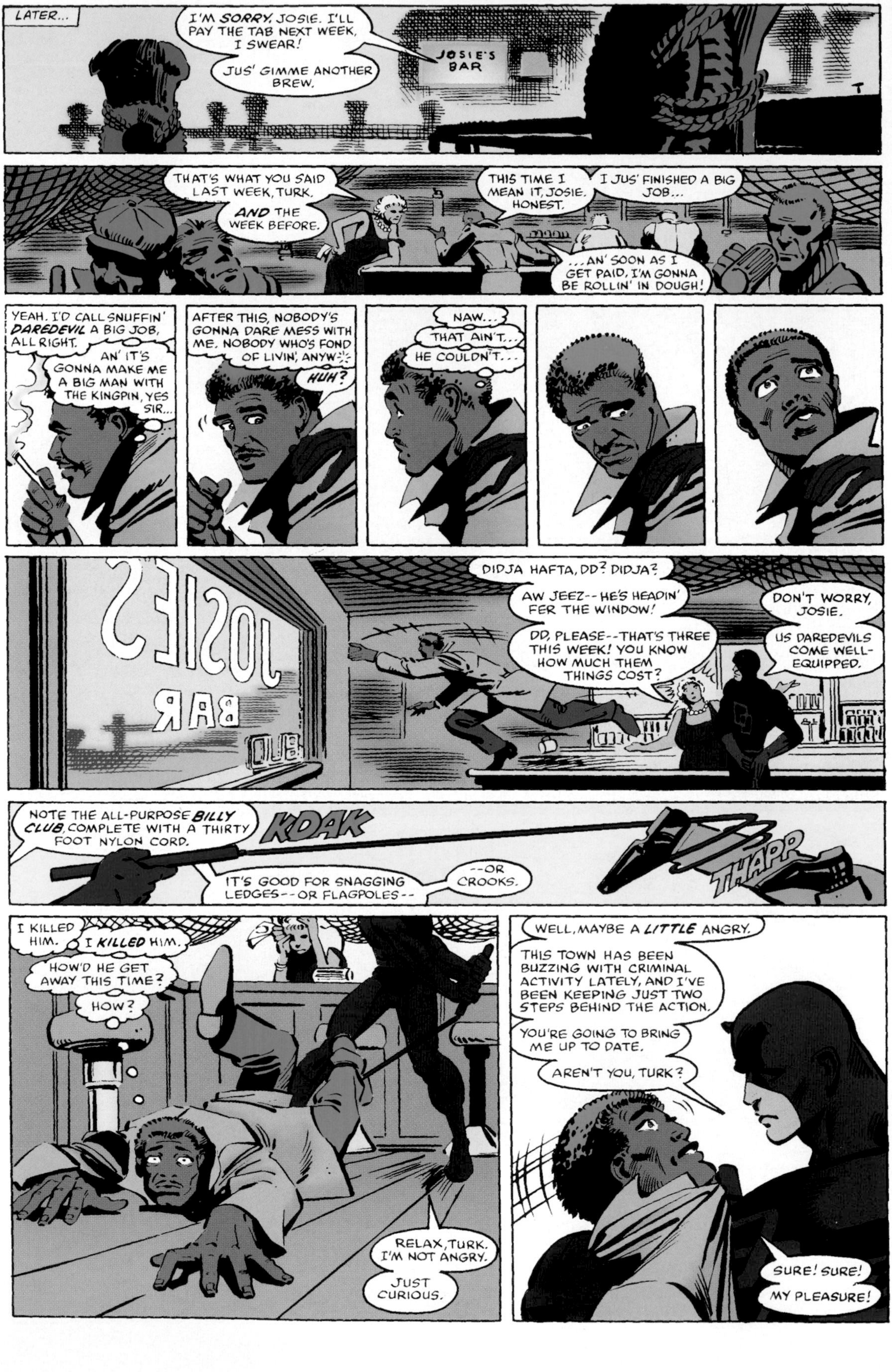
LATER...
I'M SORRY, JOSIE. I'LL PAY THE TAB NEXT WEEK, I SWEAR!
JUS' GIMME ANOTHER BREW.
JOSIE'S BAR
THAT'S WHAT YOU SAID LAST WEEK, TURK.
AND THE WEEK BEFORE.
THIS TIME I MEAN IT, JOSIE. HONEST.
I JUS' FINISHED A BIG JOB...
...AN' SOON AS I GET PAID, I'M GONNA BE ROLLIN' IN DOUGH!
YEAH. I'D CALL SNUFFIN' DAREDEVIL A BIG JOB, ALL RIGHT.
AN' IT'S GONNA MAKE ME A BIG MAN WITH THE KINGPIN, YES SIR...
AFTER THIS, NOBODY'S GONNA DARE MESS WITH ME. NOBODY WHO'S FOND OF LIVIN', ANYW
HUH?
NAW...
THAT AIN'T...
HE COULDN'T...
DIDJA HAFTA, DD? DIDJA?
AW JEEZ--HE'S HEADIN' FER THE WINDOW!
DD, PLEASE--THAT'S THREE THIS WEEK! YOU KNOW HOW MUCH THEM THINGS COST?
DON'T WORRY, JOSIE.
US DAREDEVILS COME WELL-EQUIPPED.
NOTE THE ALL-PURPOSE BILLY CLUB, COMPLETE WITH A THIRTY FOOT NYLON CORD.
KDAK
THAPP
IT'S GOOD FOR SNAGGING LEDGES--OR FLAGPOLES--
--OR CROOKS.
I KILLED HIM.
I KILLED HIM.
HOW'D HE GET AWAY THIS TIME?
HOW?
RELAX, TURK. I'M NOT ANGRY.
JUST CURIOUS.
WELL, MAYBE A LITTLE ANGRY.
THIS TOWN HAS BEEN BUZZING WITH CRIMINAL ACTIVITY LATELY, AND I'VE BEEN KEEPING JUST TWO STEPS BEHIND THE ACTION.
YOU'RE GOING TO BRING ME UP TO DATE.
AREN'T YOU, TURK?
SURE! SURE!
MY PLEASURE!

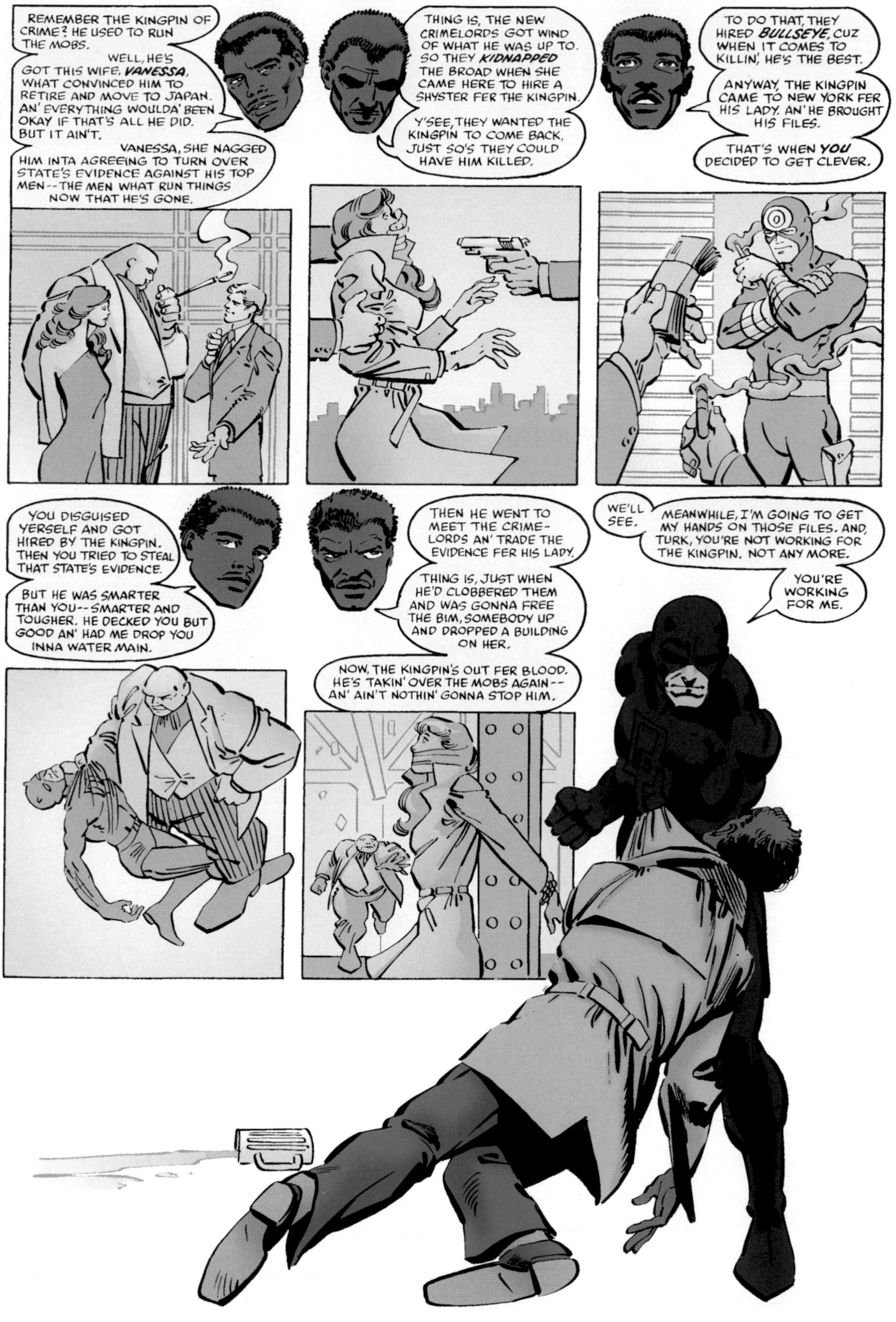

REMEMBER THE KINGPIN OF CRIME? HE USED TO RUN THE MOBS.
WELL, HE'S GOT THIS WIFE, VANESSA, WHAT CONVINCED HIM TO RETIRE AND MOVE TO JAPAN. AN' EVERYTHING WOULDA' BEEN OKAY IF THAT'S ALL HE DID. BUT IT AIN'T.
VANESSA, SHE NAGGED HIM INTA AGREEING TO TURN OVER STATE'S EVIDENCE AGAINST HIS TOP MEN--THE MEN WHAT RUN THINGS NOW THAT HE'S GONE.
THING IS, THE NEW CRIMELORDS GOT WIND OF WHAT HE WAS UP TO. SO THEY KIDNAPPED THE BROAD WHEN SHE CAME HERE TO HIRE A SHYSTER FER THE KINGPIN.
Y'SEE, THEY WANTED THE KINGPIN TO COME BACK, JUST SO'S THEY COULD HAVE HIM KILLED.
TO DO THAT, THEY HIRED BULLSEYE, CUZ WHEN IT COMES TO KILLIN', HE'S THE BEST.
ANYWAY, THE KINGPIN CAME TO NEW YORK FER HIS LADY. AN' HE BROUGHT HIS FILES.
THAT'S WHEN YOU DECIDED TO GET CLEVER.
YOU DISGUISED YERSELF AND GOT HIRED BY THE KINGPIN. THEN YOU TRIED TO STEAL THAT STATE'S EVIDENCE.
BUT HE WAS SMARTER THAN YOU--SMARTER AND TOUGHER. HE DECKED YOU BUT GOOD AN' HAD ME DROP YOU INNA WATER MAIN.
THEN HE WENT TO MEET THE CRIME-LORDS AN' TRADE THE EVIDENCE FER HIS LADY.
THING IS, JUST WHEN HE'D CLOBBERED THEM AND WAS GONNA FREE THE BIM, SOMEBODY UP AND DROPPED A BUILDING ON HER.
NOW, THE KINGPIN'S OUT FER BLOOD. HE'S TAKIN' OVER THE MOBS AGAIN-- AN' AIN'T NOTHIN' GONNA STOP HIM.
WE'LL SEE.
MEANWHILE, I'M GOING TO GET MY HANDS ON THOSE FILES. AND, TURK, YOU'RE NOT WORKING FOR THE KINGPIN. NOT ANY MORE.
YOU'RE WORKING FOR ME.

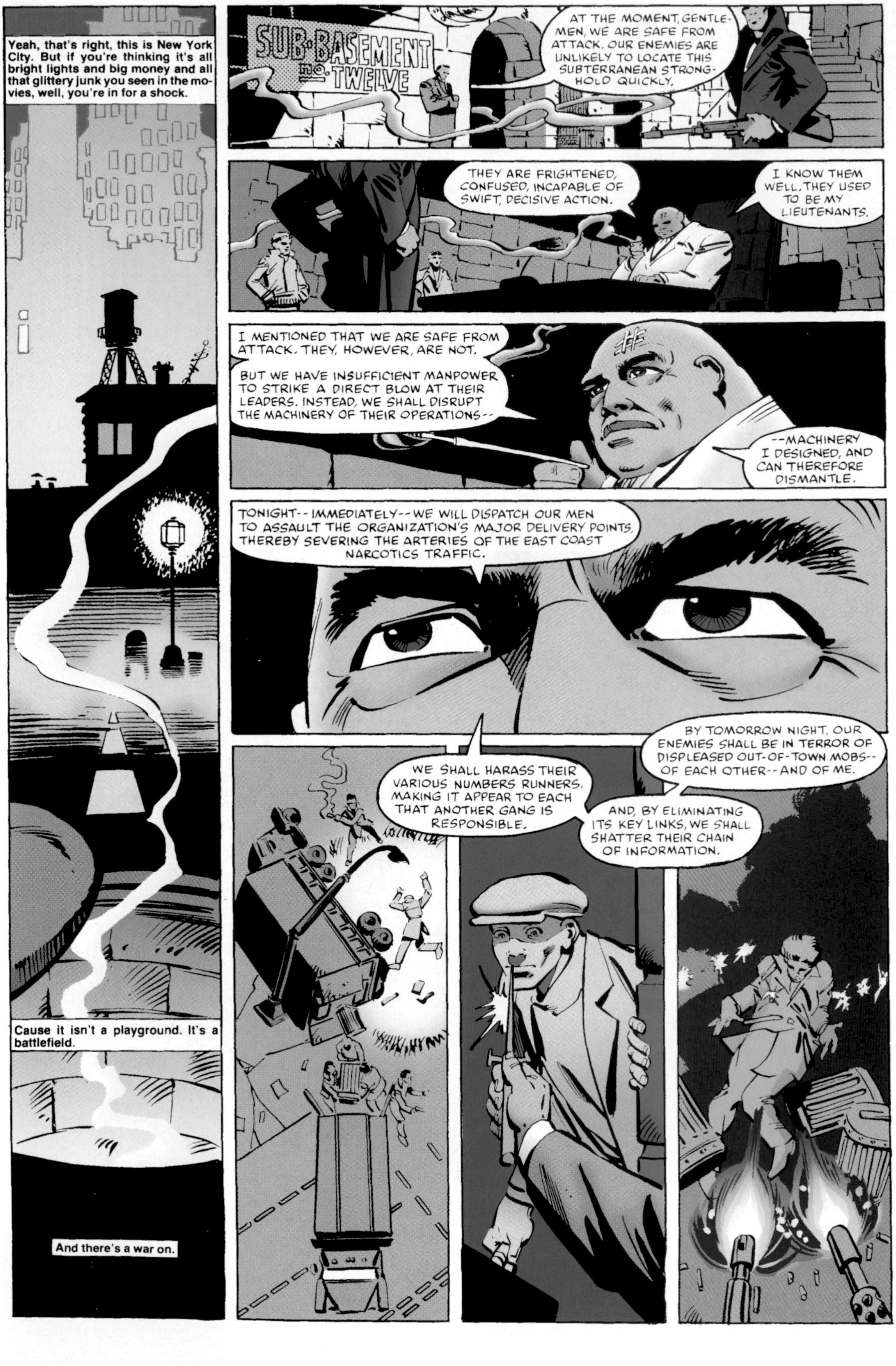
Yeah, that's right, this is New York City. But if you're thinking it's all bright lights and big money and all that glittery junk you seen in the movies, well, you're in for a shock.
SUB-BASEMENT no. TWELVE
AT THE MOMENT, GENTLEMEN, WE ARE SAFE FROM ATTACK. OUR ENEMIES ARE UNLIKELY TO LOCATE THIS SUBTERRANEAN STRONGHOLD QUICKLY.
THEY ARE FRIGHTENED, CONFUSED, INCAPABLE OF SWIFT, DECISIVE ACTION.
I KNOW THEM WELL. THEY USED TO BE MY LIEUTENANTS.
I MENTIONED THAT WE ARE SAFE FROM ATTACK. THEY, HOWEVER, ARE NOT.
BUT WE HAVE INSUFFICIENT MANPOWER TO STRIKE A DIRECT BLOW AT THEIR LEADERS. INSTEAD, WE SHALL DISRUPT THE MACHINERY OF THEIR OPERATIONS--
--MACHINERY I DESIGNED, AND CAN THEREFORE DISMANTLE.
TONIGHT--IMMEDIATELY--WE WILL DISPATCH OUR MEN TO ASSAULT THE ORGANIZATION'S MAJOR DELIVERY POINTS, THEREBY SEVERING THE ARTERIES OF THE EAST COAST NARCOTICS TRAFFIC.
Cause it isn't a playground. It's a battlefield.
WE SHALL HARASS THEIR VARIOUS NUMBERS RUNNERS, MAKING IT APPEAR TO EACH THAT ANOTHER GANG IS RESPONSIBLE.
BY TOMORROW NIGHT, OUR ENEMIES SHALL BE IN TERROR OF DISPLEASED OUT-OF-TOWN MOBS--OF EACH OTHER--AND OF ME.
AND, BY ELIMINATING ITS KEY LINKS, WE SHALL SHATTER THEIR CHAIN OF INFORMATION.
And there's a war on.

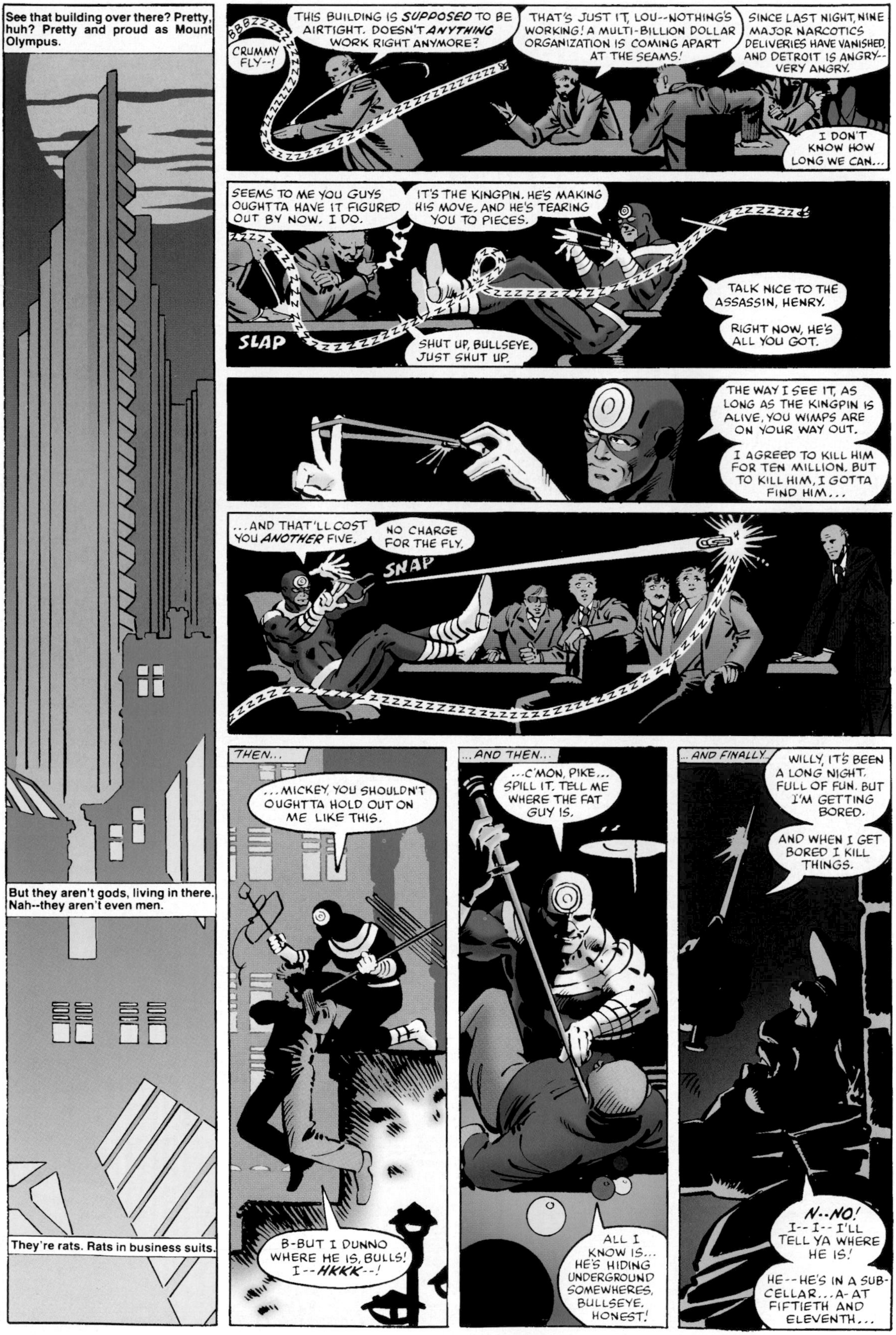

See that building over there? Pretty, huh? Pretty and proud as Mount Olympus.
BBBZZZZZ
CRUMMY FLY--!
THIS BUILDING IS SUPPOSED TO BE AIRTIGHT. DOESN'T ANYTHING WORK RIGHT ANYMORE?
THAT'S JUST IT, LOU--NOTHING'S WORKING! A MULTI-BILLION DOLLAR ORGANIZATION IS COMING APART AT THE SEAMS!
SINCE LAST NIGHT, NINE MAJOR NARCOTICS DELIVERIES HAVE VANISHED, AND DETROIT IS ANGRY--VERY ANGRY.
I DON'T KNOW HOW LONG WE CAN...
SEEMS TO ME YOU GUYS OUGHTTA HAVE IT FIGURED OUT BY NOW. I DO.
IT'S THE KINGPIN. HE'S MAKING HIS MOVE, AND HE'S TEARING YOU TO PIECES.
SLAP
SHUT UP, BULLSEYE. JUST SHUT UP.
TALK NICE TO THE ASSASSIN, HENRY.
RIGHT NOW, HE'S ALL YOU GOT.
THE WAY I SEE IT, AS LONG AS THE KINGPIN IS ALIVE, YOU WIMPS ARE ON YOUR WAY OUT.
I AGREED TO KILL HIM FOR TEN MILLION. BUT TO KILL HIM, I GOTTA FIND HIM...
...AND THAT'LL COST YOU ANOTHER FIVE.
NO CHARGE FOR THE FLY.
SNAP
But they aren't gods, living in there. Nah--they aren't even men.
They're rats. Rats in business suits.
THEN...
...MICKEY, YOU SHOULDN'T OUGHTTA HOLD OUT ON ME LIKE THIS.
B-BUT I DUNNO WHERE HE IS, BULLS! I--HKKK--!
...AND THEN...
...C'MON, PIKE... SPILL IT. TELL ME WHERE THE FAT GUY IS.
ALL I KNOW IS... HE'S HIDING UNDERGROUND SOMEWHERES, BULLSEYE. HONEST!
...AND FINALLY...
WILLY, IT'S BEEN A LONG NIGHT, FULL OF FUN. BUT I'M GETTING BORED.
AND WHEN I GET BORED I KILL THINGS.
N--NO! I-- I-- I'LL TELL YA WHERE HE IS!
HE--HE'S IN A SUB-CELLAR... A-AT FIFTIETH AND ELEVENTH...

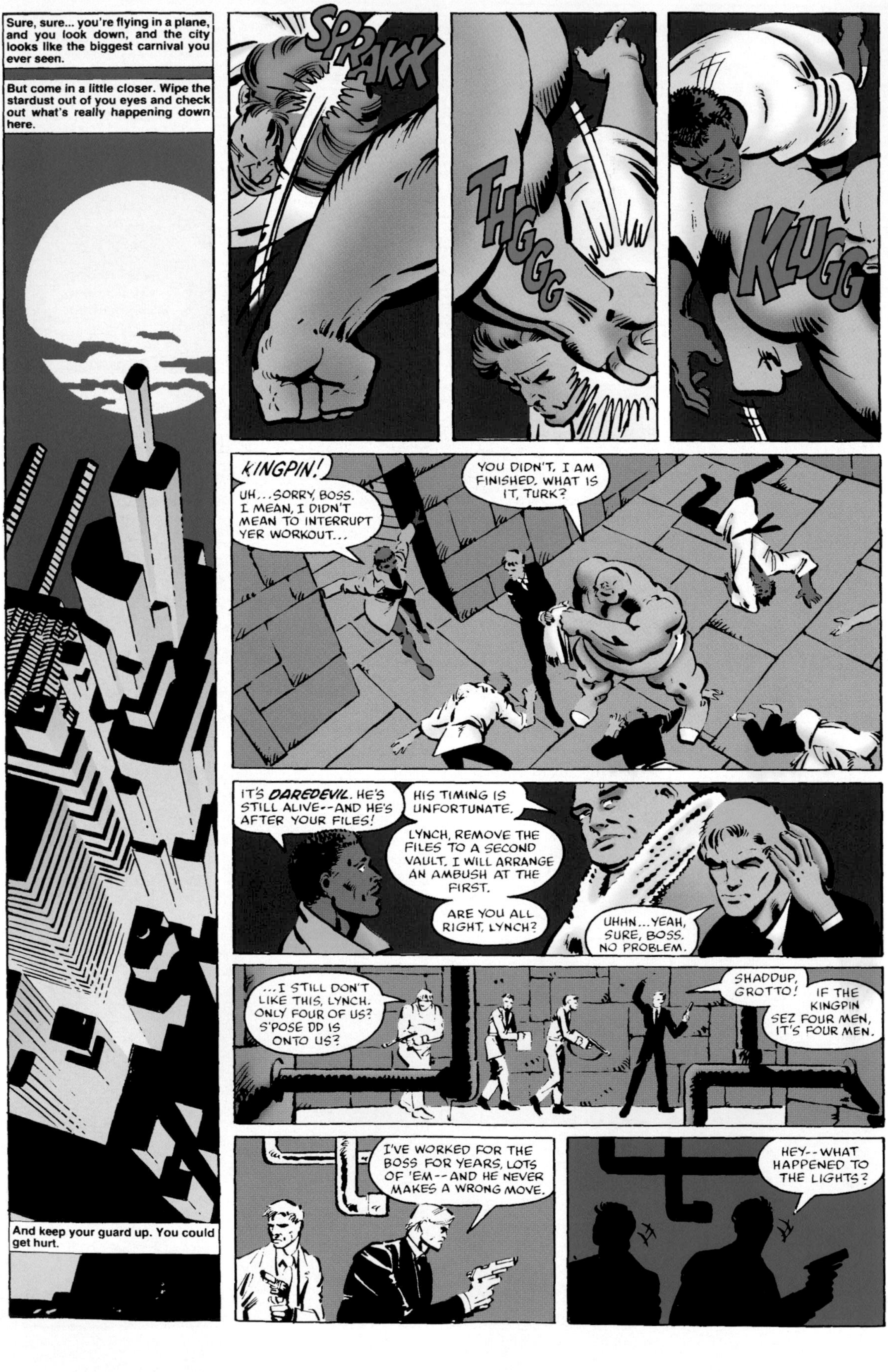
Sure, sure... you're flying in a plane, and you look down, and the city looks like the biggest carnival you ever seen.
But come in a little closer. Wipe the stardust out of you eyes and check out what's really happening down here.
And keep your guard up. You could get hurt.
SPRAKK
THGGG
KLUGG
KINGPIN!
UH...SORRY, BOSS. I MEAN, I DIDN'T MEAN TO INTERRUPT YER WORKOUT...
YOU DIDN'T. I AM FINISHED. WHAT IS IT, TURK?
IT'S DAREDEVIL. HE'S STILL ALIVE--AND HE'S AFTER YOUR FILES!
HIS TIMING IS UNFORTUNATE.
LYNCH, REMOVE THE FILES TO A SECOND VAULT. I WILL ARRANGE AN AMBUSH AT THE FIRST.
ARE YOU ALL RIGHT, LYNCH?
UHHN...YEAH, SURE, BOSS. NO PROBLEM.
...I STILL DON'T LIKE THIS, LYNCH. ONLY FOUR OF US? S'POSE DD IS ONTO US?
SHADDUP, GROTTO!
IF THE KINGPIN SEZ FOUR MEN, IT'S FOUR MEN.
I'VE WORKED FOR THE BOSS FOR YEARS. LOTS OF 'EM--AND HE NEVER MAKES A WRONG MOVE.
HEY--WHAT HAPPENED TO THE LIGHTS?

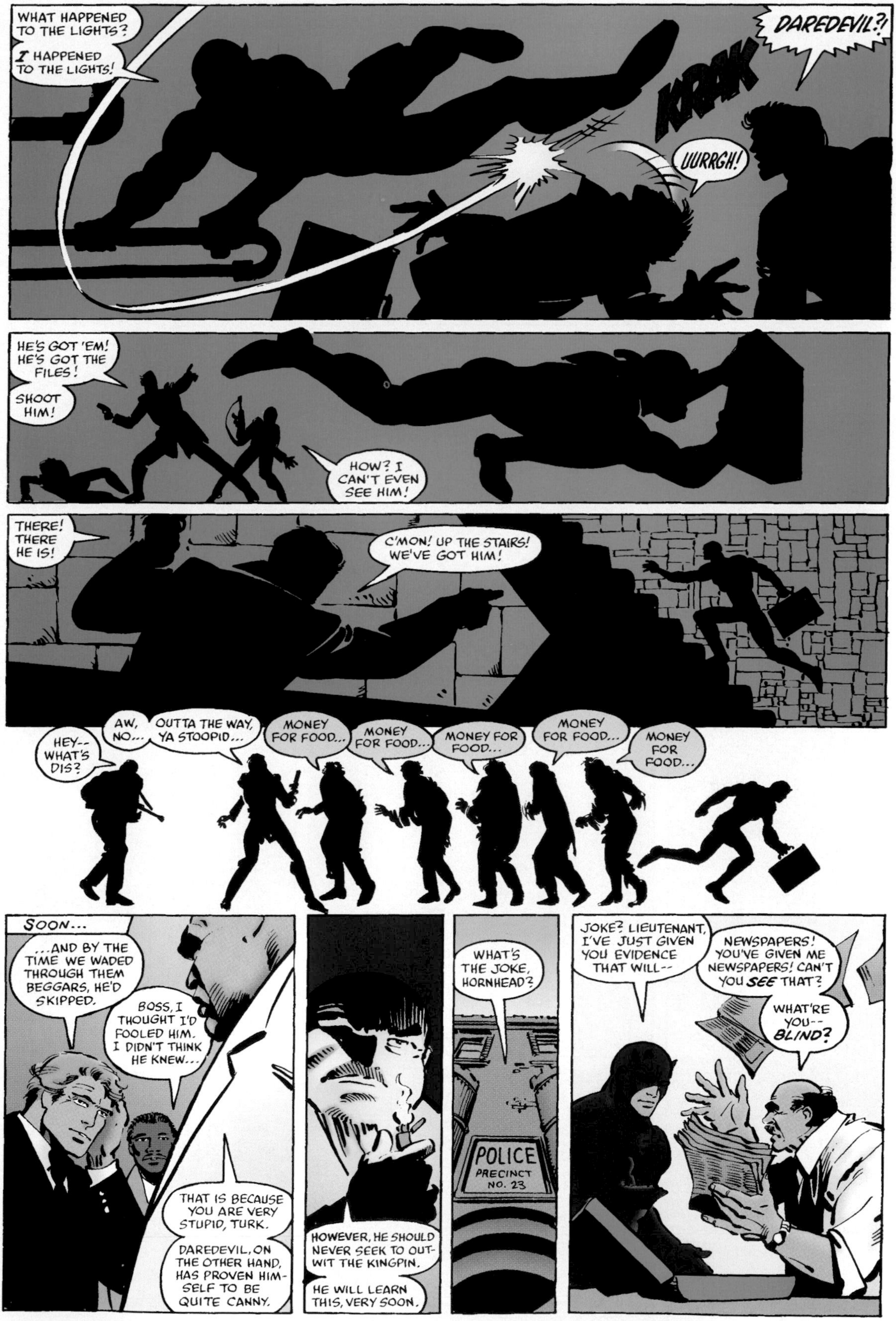
WHAT HAPPENED TO THE LIGHTS?
I HAPPENED TO THE LIGHTS!
DAREDEVIL?!
KRAK
UURRGH!
HE'S GOT 'EM! HE'S GOT THE FILES!
SHOOT HIM!
HOW? I CAN'T EVEN SEE HIM!
THERE! THERE HE IS!
C'MON! UP THE STAIRS! WE'VE GOT HIM!
HEY-- WHAT'S DIS?
AW, NO...
OUTTA THE WAY, YA STOOPID...
MONEY FOR FOOD...
MONEY FOR FOOD...
MONEY FOR FOOD...
MONEY FOR FOOD...
MONEY FOR FOOD...
SOON...
...AND BY THE TIME WE WADED THROUGH THEM BEGGARS, HE'D SKIPPED.
BOSS, I THOUGHT I'D FOOLED HIM. I DIDN'T THINK HE KNEW...
THAT IS BECAUSE YOU ARE VERY STUPID, TURK.
DAREDEVIL, ON THE OTHER HAND, HAS PROVEN HIMSELF TO BE QUITE CANNY.
HOWEVER, HE SHOULD NEVER SEEK TO OUTWIT THE KINGPIN.
HE WILL LEARN THIS, VERY SOON.
WHAT'S THE JOKE, HORNHEAD?
POLICE PRECINCT NO. 23
JOKE? LIEUTENANT, I'VE JUST GIVEN YOU EVIDENCE THAT WILL--
NEWSPAPERS! YOU'VE GIVEN ME NEWSPAPERS! CAN'T YOU SEE THAT?
WHAT'RE YOU-- BLIND?

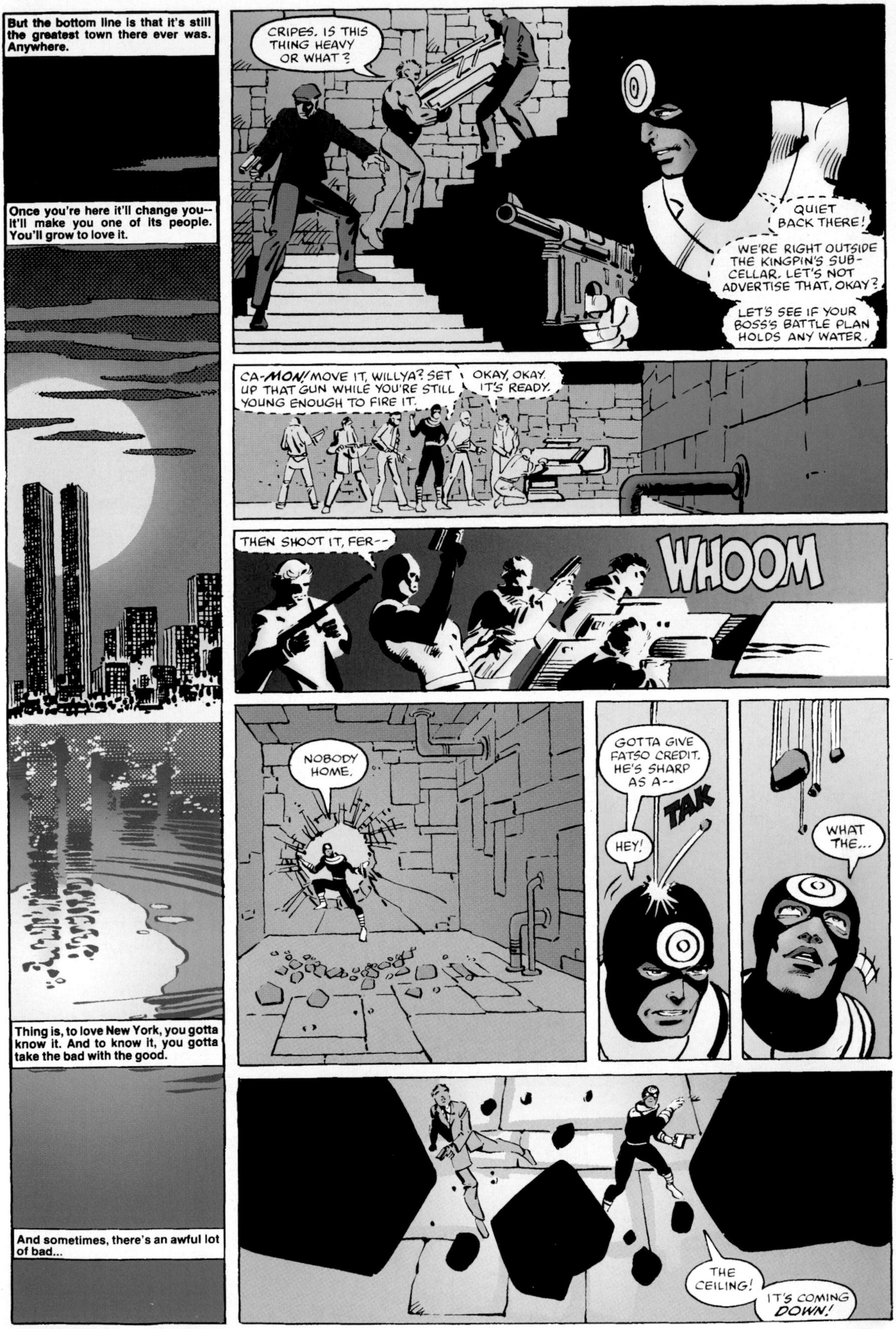

But the bottom line is that it's still the greatest town there ever was. Anywhere.
CRIPES. IS THIS THING HEAVY OR WHAT?
QUIET BACK THERE!
WE'RE RIGHT OUTSIDE THE KINGPIN'S SUB-CELLAR. LET'S NOT ADVERTISE THAT, OKAY?
LET'S SEE IF YOUR BOSS'S BATTLE PLAN HOLDS ANY WATER.
Once you're here it'll change you-- it'll make you one of its people. You'll grow to love it.
CA-MON! MOVE IT, WILLYA? SET UP THAT GUN WHILE YOU'RE STILL YOUNG ENOUGH TO FIRE IT.
OKAY, OKAY. IT'S READY.
THEN SHOOT IT, FER--
WHOOM
NOBODY HOME.
GOTTA GIVE FATSO CREDIT. HE'S SHARP AS A--
TAK
HEY!
WHAT THE...
Thing is, to love New York, you gotta know it. And to know it, you gotta take the bad with the good.
And sometimes, there's an awful lot of bad...
THE CEILING!
IT'S COMING DOWN!

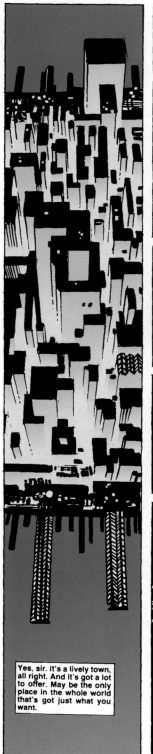

Yes, sir. it's a lively town, all right. And it's got a lot to offer. May be the only place in the whole world that's got just what you want.

But it's up to you to get it. And if you screw up? Well, somebody's sure gonna let you know...

CLOWNS! THAT'S WHAT YOU ARE!

EASY, BULLSEYE. TAKE IT EASY.

REMEMBER WHICH SIDE YOUR BREAD IS BUTTERED ON.

THE KINGPIN PLAYED YOU FOR *SUCKERS!*

HE PLANTED THE LOCATION OF HIS HIDEOUT IN THE HEAD OF A VERY *TALKATIVE* HOOD--

--THEN RIGGED THE JOINT TO COLLAPSE ON THE FIRST PERSON TO ENTER IT!

AND ME, I WAS JUST STUPID ENOUGH TO GO ALONG WITH YOU SAPS!

OKAY! OKAY! WE MISCALCULATED. IT HAPPENS.

BUT DON'T WORRY. AS SOON AS OUR COLLEAGUES ARRIVE, WE WILL HOLD AN EMERGENCY CONFERENCE--

--AND APPOINT A COMMITTEE THAT WILL...

THEY WILL NOT ARRIVE.

EACH OF YOUR COLLEAGUES HAS BEEN APPROACHED TONIGHT. SOME OF THEM NOW WORK FOR ME.

THE REST ARE DEAD.

THE *KINGPIN?!* HERE?

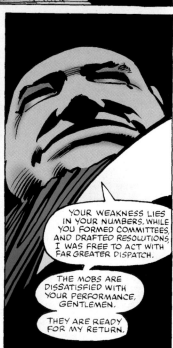

YOUR WEAKNESS LIES IN YOUR NUMBERS. WHILE YOU FORMED COMMITTEES, AND DRAFTED RESOLUTIONS, I WAS FREE TO ACT WITH FAR GREATER DISPATCH.

THE MOBS ARE DISSATISFIED WITH YOUR PERFORMANCE, GENTLEMEN.

THEY ARE READY FOR MY RETURN.

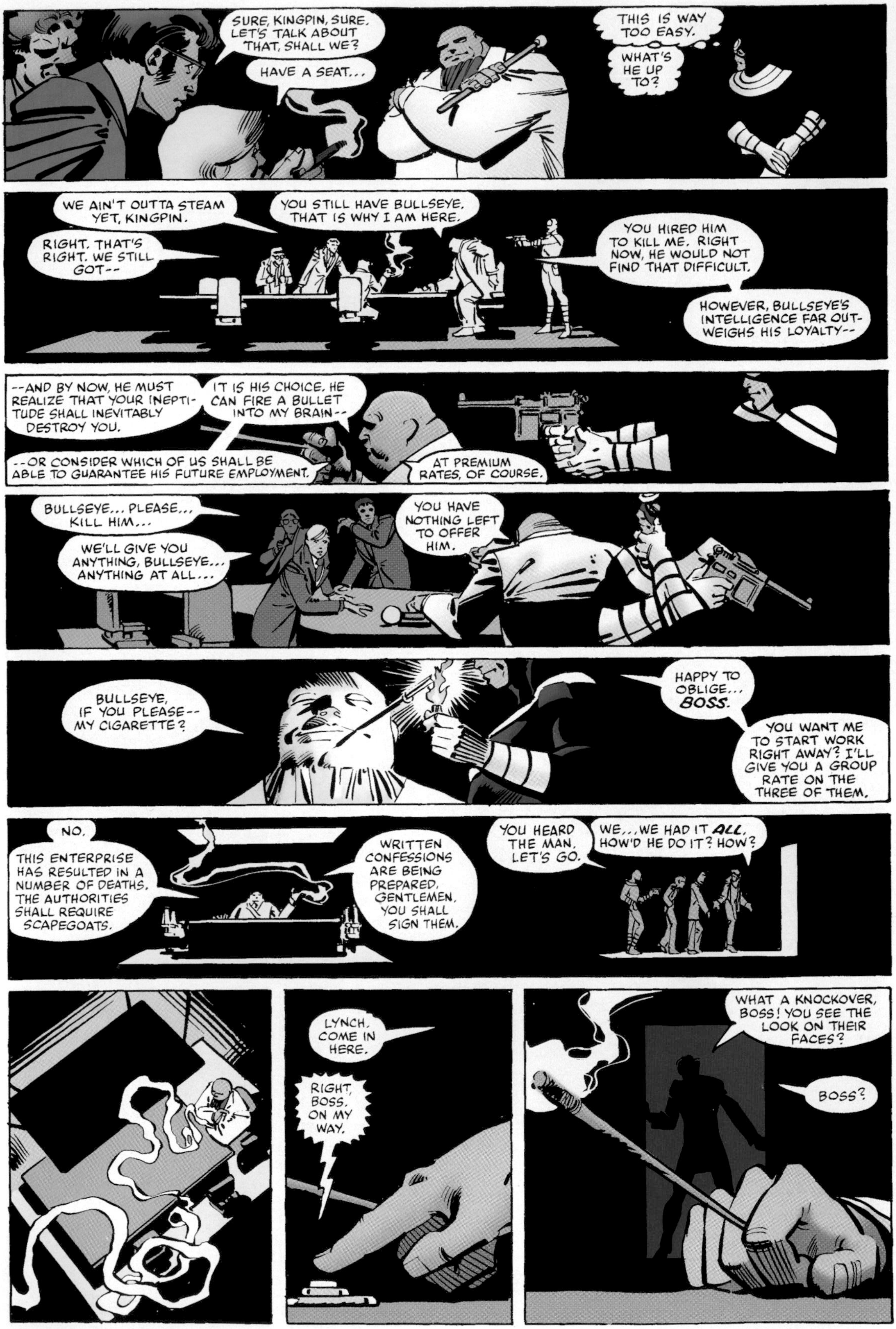
SURE, KINGPIN, SURE, LET'S TALK ABOUT THAT, SHALL WE?
HAVE A SEAT...
THIS IS WAY TOO EASY.
WHAT'S HE UP TO?
WE AIN'T OUTTA STEAM YET, KINGPIN.
RIGHT. THAT'S RIGHT. WE STILL GOT--
YOU STILL HAVE BULLSEYE. THAT IS WHY I AM HERE.
YOU HIRED HIM TO KILL ME. RIGHT NOW, HE WOULD NOT FIND THAT DIFFICULT.
HOWEVER, BULLSEYE'S INTELLIGENCE FAR OUT-WEIGHS HIS LOYALTY--
--AND BY NOW, HE MUST REALIZE THAT YOUR INEPTI-TUDE SHALL INEVITABLY DESTROY YOU.
IT IS HIS CHOICE. HE CAN FIRE A BULLET INTO MY BRAIN--
--OR CONSIDER WHICH OF US SHALL BE ABLE TO GUARANTEE HIS FUTURE EMPLOYMENT.
AT PREMIUM RATES, OF COURSE.
BULLSEYE... PLEASE... KILL HIM...
WE'LL GIVE YOU ANYTHING, BULLSEYE... ANYTHING AT ALL...
YOU HAVE NOTHING LEFT TO OFFER HIM.
BULLSEYE, IF YOU PLEASE-- MY CIGARETTE?
HAPPY TO OBLIGE... BOSS.
YOU WANT ME TO START WORK RIGHT AWAY? I'LL GIVE YOU A GROUP RATE ON THE THREE OF THEM.
NO.
THIS ENTERPRISE HAS RESULTED IN A NUMBER OF DEATHS. THE AUTHORITIES SHALL REQUIRE SCAPEGOATS.
WRITTEN CONFESSIONS ARE BEING PREPARED, GENTLEMEN. YOU SHALL SIGN THEM.
YOU HEARD THE MAN. LET'S GO.
WE... WE HAD IT ALL. HOW'D HE DO IT? HOW?
LYNCH. COME IN HERE.
RIGHT, BOSS. ON MY WAY.
WHAT A KNOCKOVER, BOSS! YOU SEE THE LOOK ON THEIR FACES?
BOSS?

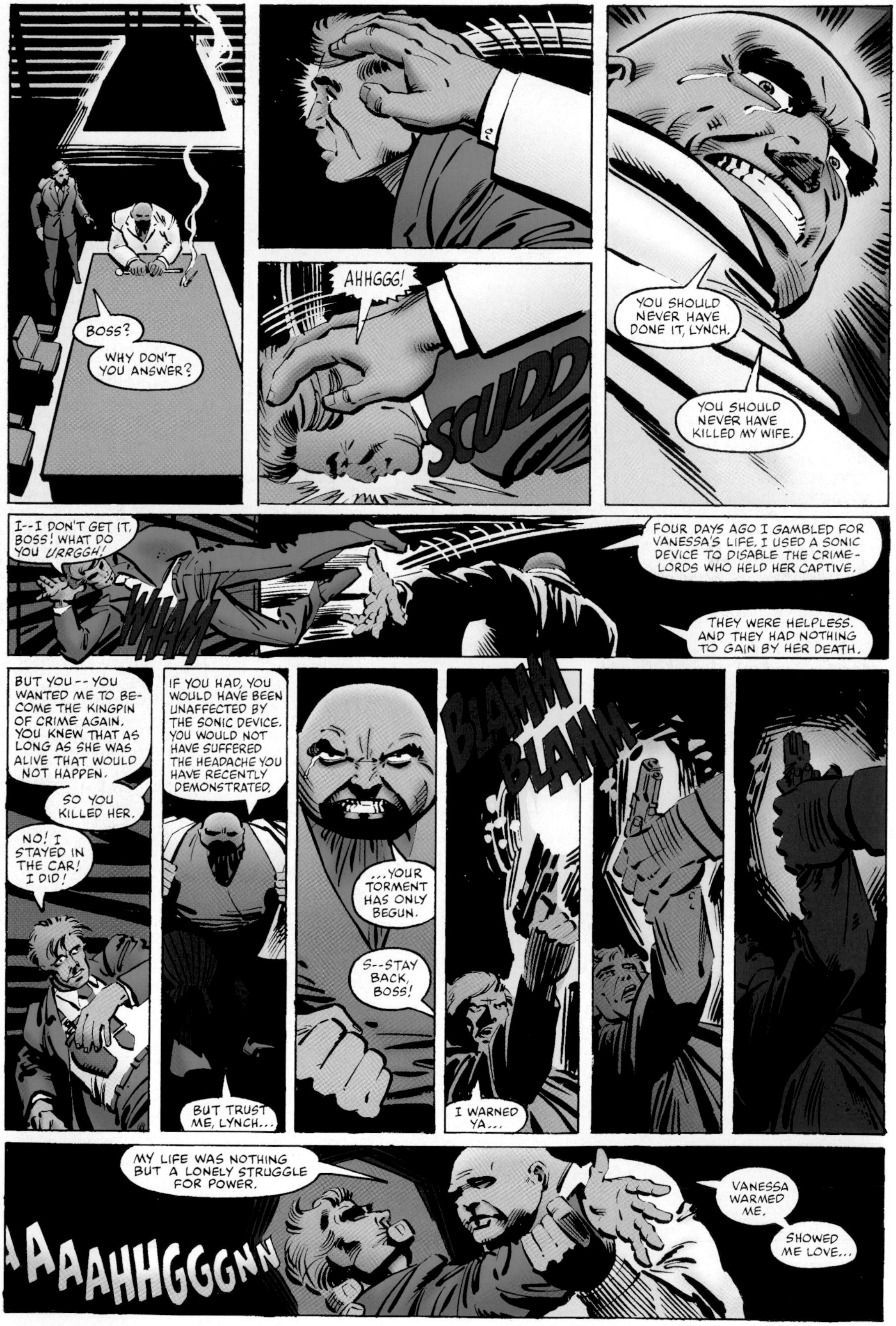
BOSS?
WHY DON'T YOU ANSWER?
AHHGGG!
SCUDD
YOU SHOULD NEVER HAVE DONE IT, LYNCH.
YOU SHOULD NEVER HAVE KILLED MY WIFE.
I--I DON'T GET IT, BOSS! WHAT DO YOU URRGGH!
WHAM
FOUR DAYS AGO I GAMBLED FOR VANESSA'S LIFE. I USED A SONIC DEVICE TO DISABLE THE CRIME-LORDS WHO HELD HER CAPTIVE.
THEY WERE HELPLESS. AND THEY HAD NOTHING TO GAIN BY HER DEATH.
BUT YOU--YOU WANTED ME TO BECOME THE KINGPIN OF CRIME AGAIN. YOU KNEW THAT AS LONG AS SHE WAS ALIVE THAT WOULD NOT HAPPEN.
SO YOU KILLED HER.
NO! I STAYED IN THE CAR! I DID!
IF YOU HAD, YOU WOULD HAVE BEEN UNAFFECTED BY THE SONIC DEVICE. YOU WOULD NOT HAVE SUFFERED THE HEADACHE YOU HAVE RECENTLY DEMONSTRATED.
BUT TRUST ME, LYNCH...
...YOUR TORMENT HAS ONLY BEGUN.
S--STAY BACK, BOSS!
BLAMM BLAMM
I WARNED YA...
MY LIFE WAS NOTHING BUT A LONELY STRUGGLE FOR POWER.
AAAAHHGGGNN
VANESSA WARMED ME.
SHOWED ME LOVE...

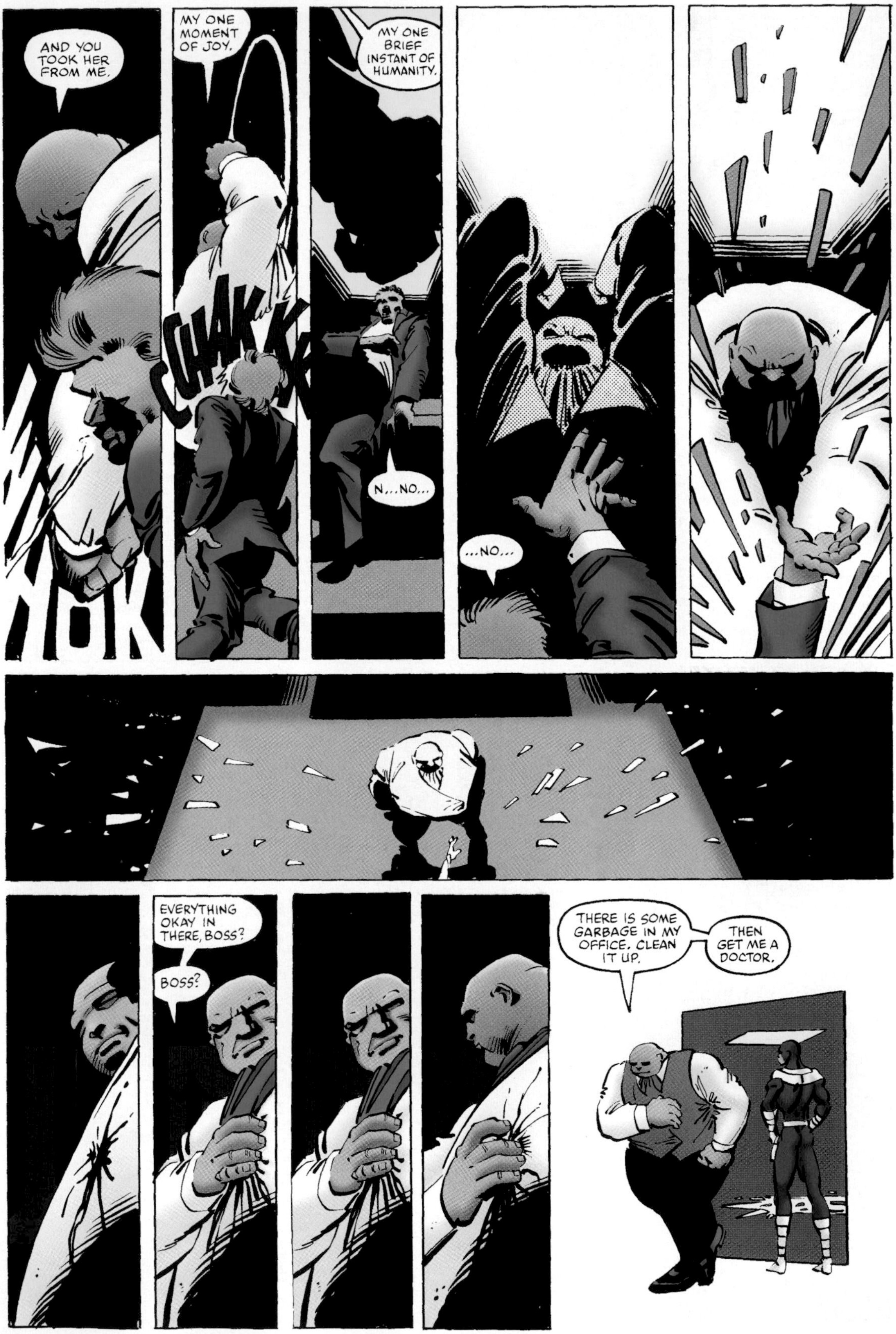
AND YOU TOOK HER FROM ME.
MY ONE MOMENT OF JOY.
CHAK
MY ONE BRIEF INSTANT OF HUMANITY.
N...NO...
...NO...
EVERYTHING OKAY IN THERE, BOSS?
BOSS?
THERE IS SOME GARBAGE IN MY OFFICE. CLEAN IT UP.
THEN GET ME A DOCTOR.

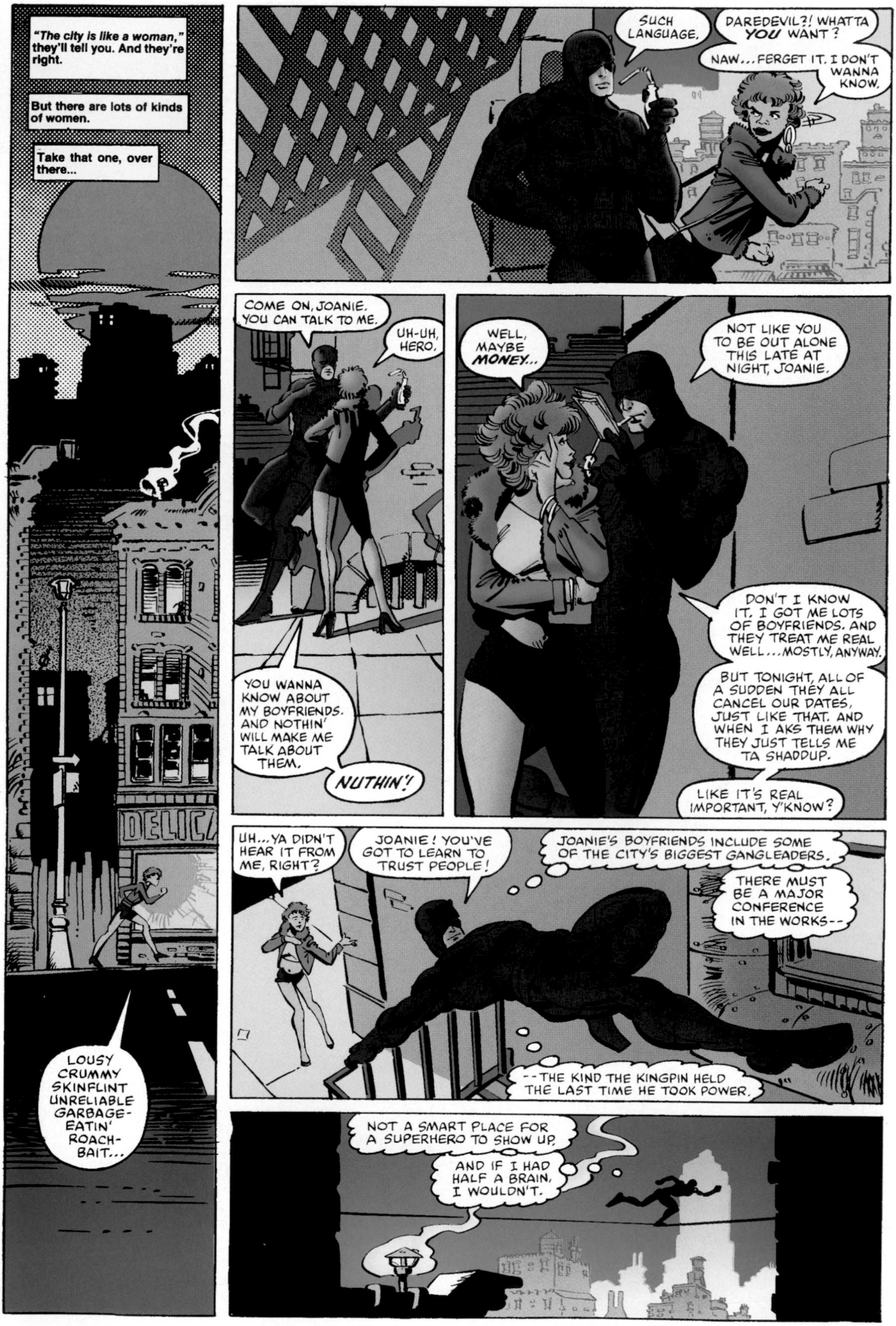

"The city is like a woman," they'll tell you. And they're right.
But there are lots of kinds of women.
Take that one, over there...
LOUSY CRUMMY SKINFLINT UNRELIABLE GARBAGE-EATIN' ROACH-BAIT...
DELIC
SUCH LANGUAGE.
DAREDEVIL?! WHATTA YOU WANT?
NAW... FERGET IT. I DON'T WANNA KNOW.
COME ON, JOANIE. YOU CAN TALK TO ME.
UH-UH, HERO.
YOU WANNA KNOW ABOUT MY BOYFRIENDS. AND NOTHIN' WILL MAKE ME TALK ABOUT THEM.
NUTHIN'!
WELL, MAYBE MONEY...
NOT LIKE YOU TO BE OUT ALONE THIS LATE AT NIGHT, JOANIE.
DON'T I KNOW IT. I GOT ME LOTS OF BOYFRIENDS. AND THEY TREAT ME REAL WELL... MOSTLY, ANYWAY.
BUT TONIGHT, ALL OF A SUDDEN THEY ALL CANCEL OUR DATES, JUST LIKE THAT. AND WHEN I AKS THEM WHY THEY JUST TELLS ME TA SHADDUP.
LIKE IT'S REAL IMPORTANT, Y'KNOW?
UH... YA DIDN'T HEAR IT FROM ME, RIGHT?
JOANIE! YOU'VE GOT TO LEARN TO TRUST PEOPLE!
JOANIE'S BOYFRIENDS INCLUDE SOME OF THE CITY'S BIGGEST GANGLEADERS.
THERE MUST BE A MAJOR CONFERENCE IN THE WORKS--
--THE KIND THE KINGPIN HELD THE LAST TIME HE TOOK POWER.
NOT A SMART PLACE FOR A SUPERHERO TO SHOW UP,
AND IF I HAD HALF A BRAIN, I WOULDN'T.

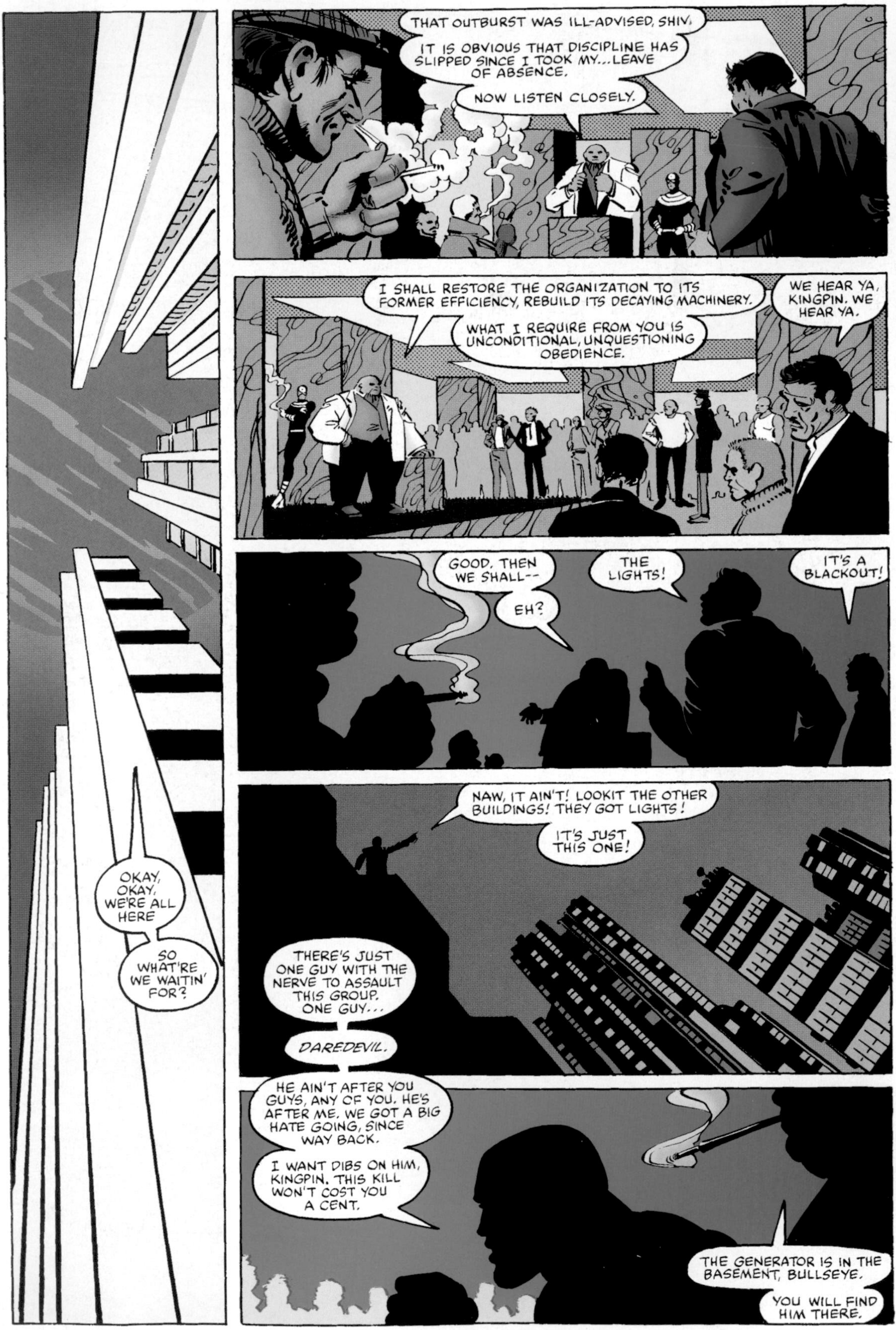
THAT OUTBURST WAS ILL-ADVISED, SHIV.
IT IS OBVIOUS THAT DISCIPLINE HAS SLIPPED SINCE I TOOK MY... LEAVE OF ABSENCE.
NOW LISTEN CLOSELY.
I SHALL RESTORE THE ORGANIZATION TO ITS FORMER EFFICIENCY, REBUILD ITS DECAYING MACHINERY.
WHAT I REQUIRE FROM YOU IS UNCONDITIONAL, UNQUESTIONING OBEDIENCE.
WE HEAR YA, KINGPIN. WE HEAR YA.
GOOD. THEN WE SHALL--
EH?
THE LIGHTS!
IT'S A BLACKOUT!
NAW, IT AIN'T! LOOKIT THE OTHER BUILDINGS! THEY GOT LIGHTS!
IT'S JUST THIS ONE!
OKAY, OKAY, WE'RE ALL HERE
SO WHAT'RE WE WAITIN' FOR?
THERE'S JUST ONE GUY WITH THE NERVE TO ASSAULT THIS GROUP. ONE GUY...
DAREDEVIL.
HE AIN'T AFTER YOU GUYS, ANY OF YOU. HE'S AFTER ME. WE GOT A BIG HATE GOING, SINCE WAY BACK.
I WANT DIBS ON HIM, KINGPIN. THIS KILL WON'T COST YOU A CENT.
THE GENERATOR IS IN THE BASEMENT, BULLSEYE.
YOU WILL FIND HIM THERE.

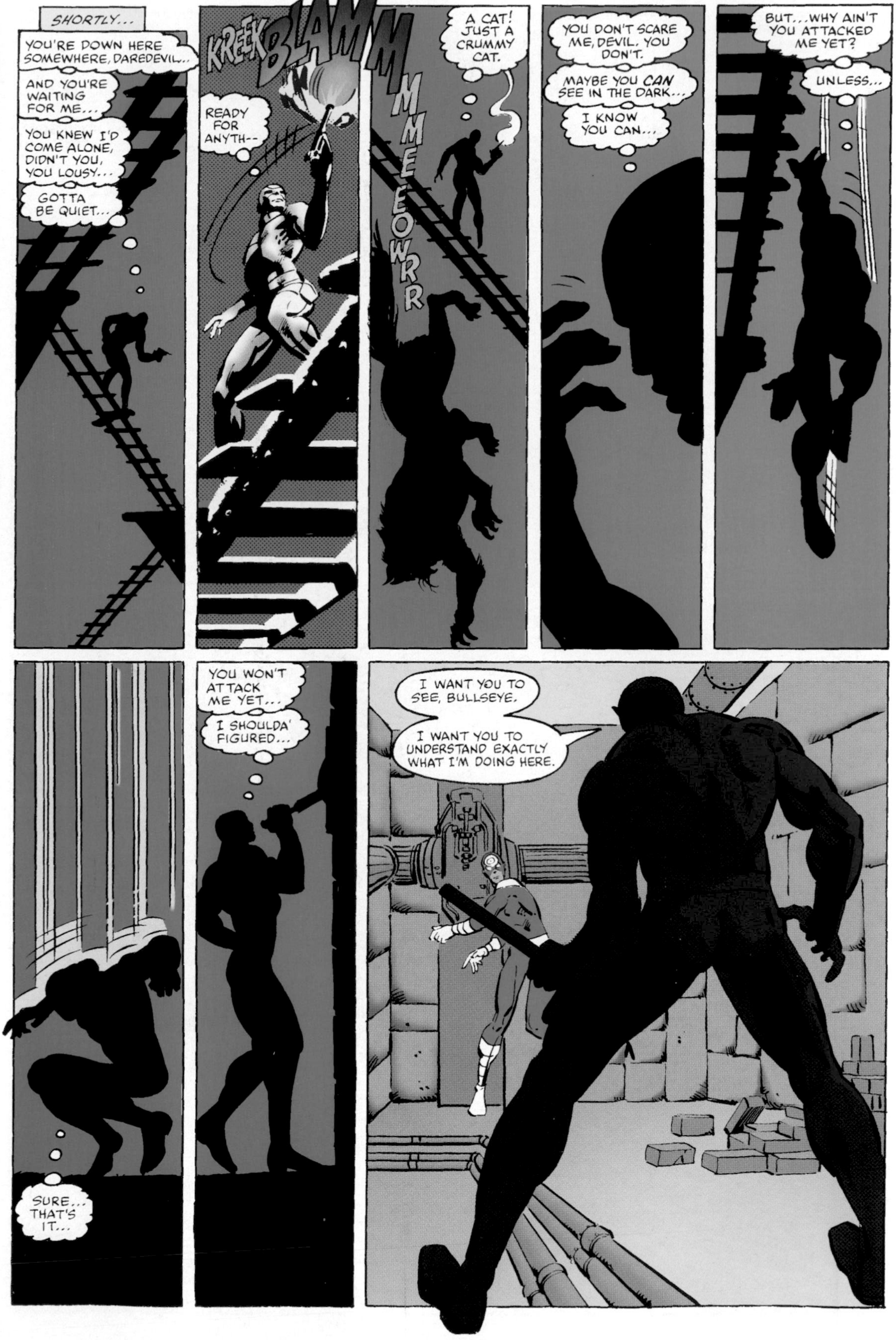

SHORTLY...
YOU'RE DOWN HERE SOMEWHERE, DAREDEVIL...
AND YOU'RE WAITING FOR ME...
YOU KNEW I'D COME ALONE, DIDN'T YOU, YOU LOUSY...
GOTTA BE QUIET...
KREEK BLAMM
READY FOR ANYTH--
MMMEEOWRR
A CAT! JUST A CRUMMY CAT.
YOU DON'T SCARE ME, DEVIL. YOU DON'T.
MAYBE YOU CAN SEE IN THE DARK...
I KNOW YOU CAN...
BUT...WHY AIN'T YOU ATTACKED ME YET?
UNLESS...
SURE... THAT'S IT...
YOU WON'T ATTACK ME YET...
I SHOULDA' FIGURED...
I WANT YOU TO SEE, BULLSEYE.
I WANT YOU TO UNDERSTAND EXACTLY WHAT I'M DOING HERE.

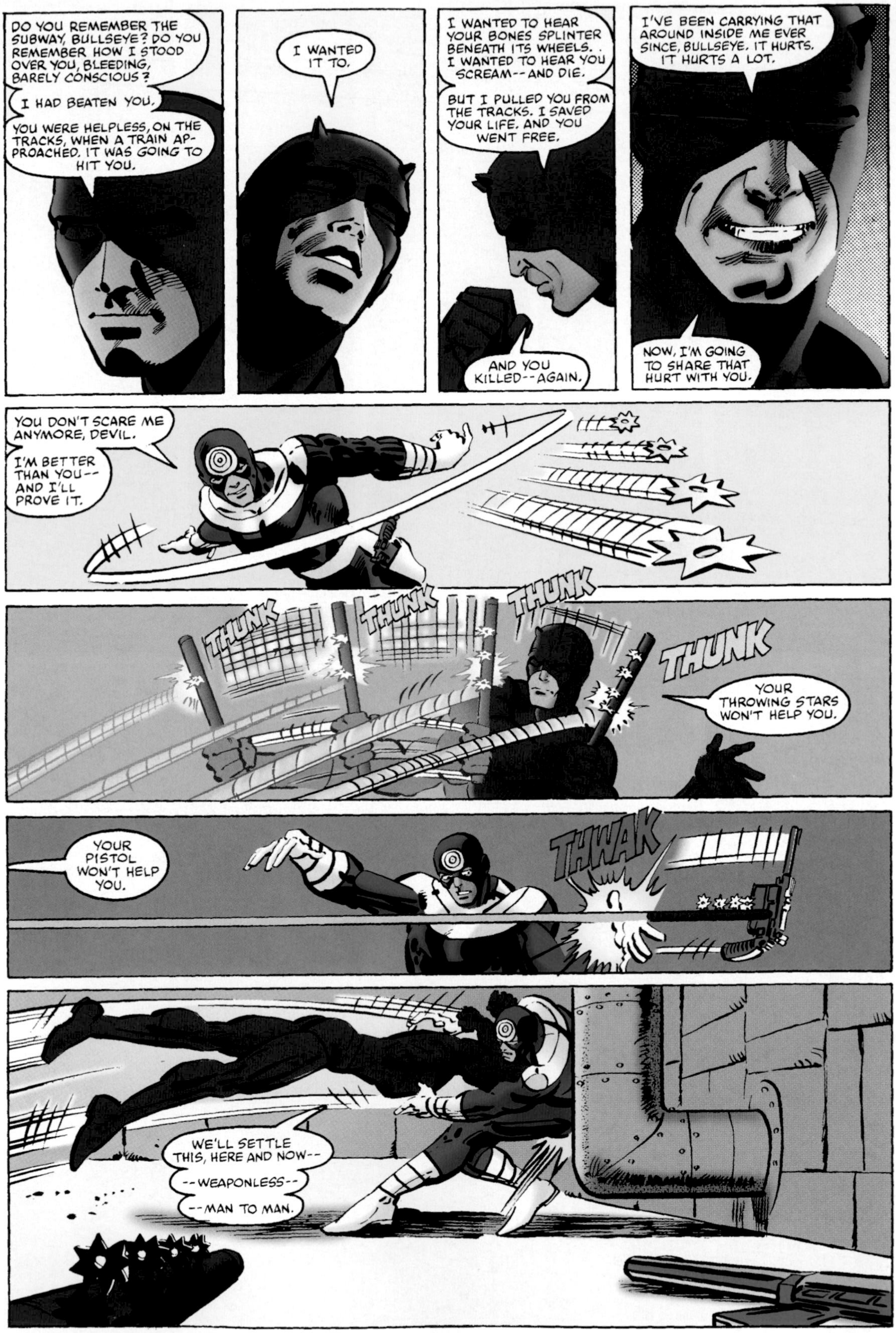
DO YOU REMEMBER THE SUBWAY, BULLSEYE? DO YOU REMEMBER HOW I STOOD OVER YOU, BLEEDING, BARELY CONSCIOUS?
I HAD BEATEN YOU.
YOU WERE HELPLESS, ON THE TRACKS, WHEN A TRAIN APPROACHED. IT WAS GOING TO HIT YOU.
I WANTED IT TO.
I WANTED TO HEAR YOUR BONES SPLINTER BENEATH ITS WHEELS. . I WANTED TO HEAR YOU SCREAM--AND DIE.
BUT I PULLED YOU FROM THE TRACKS. I SAVED YOUR LIFE. AND YOU WENT FREE.
AND YOU KILLED--AGAIN.
I'VE BEEN CARRYING THAT AROUND INSIDE ME EVER SINCE, BULLSEYE. IT HURTS. IT HURTS A LOT.
NOW, I'M GOING TO SHARE THAT HURT WITH YOU.
YOU DON'T SCARE ME ANYMORE, DEVIL.
I'M BETTER THAN YOU--AND I'LL PROVE IT.
THUNK
THUNK
THUNK
THUNK
YOUR THROWING STARS WON'T HELP YOU.
YOUR PISTOL WON'T HELP YOU.
THWAK
WE'LL SETTLE THIS, HERE AND NOW--
--WEAPONLESS--
--MAN TO MAN.

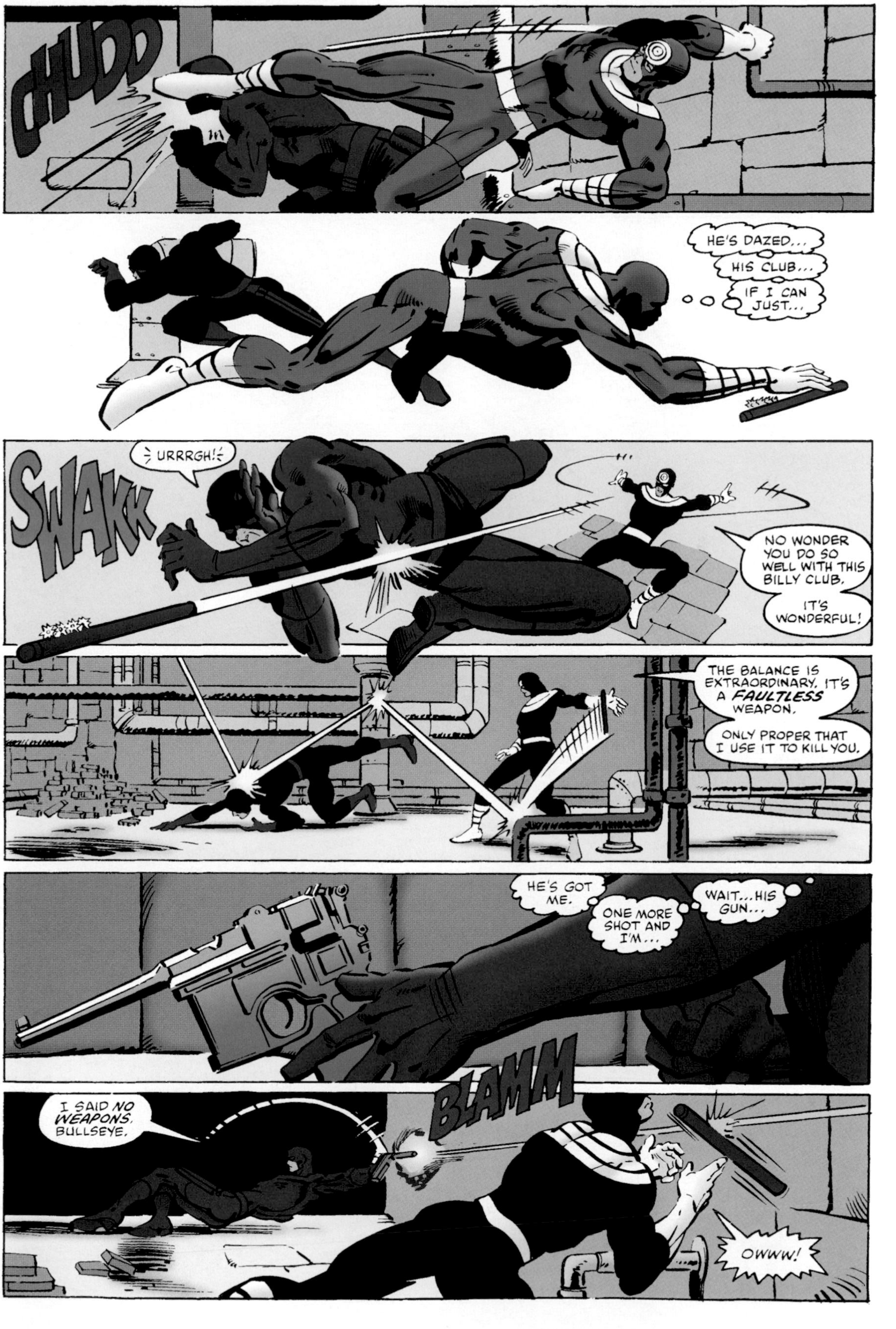
CHUDD
HE'S DAZED...
HIS CLUB...
IF I CAN JUST...
SWAKK
URRRGH!
NO WONDER YOU DO SO WELL WITH THIS BILLY CLUB.
IT'S WONDERFUL!
THE BALANCE IS EXTRAORDINARY. IT'S A FAULTLESS WEAPON.
ONLY PROPER THAT I USE IT TO KILL YOU.
HE'S GOT ME.
ONE MORE SHOT AND I'M...
WAIT... HIS GUN...
BLAMM
I SAID NO WEAPONS, BULLSEYE.
OWWW!

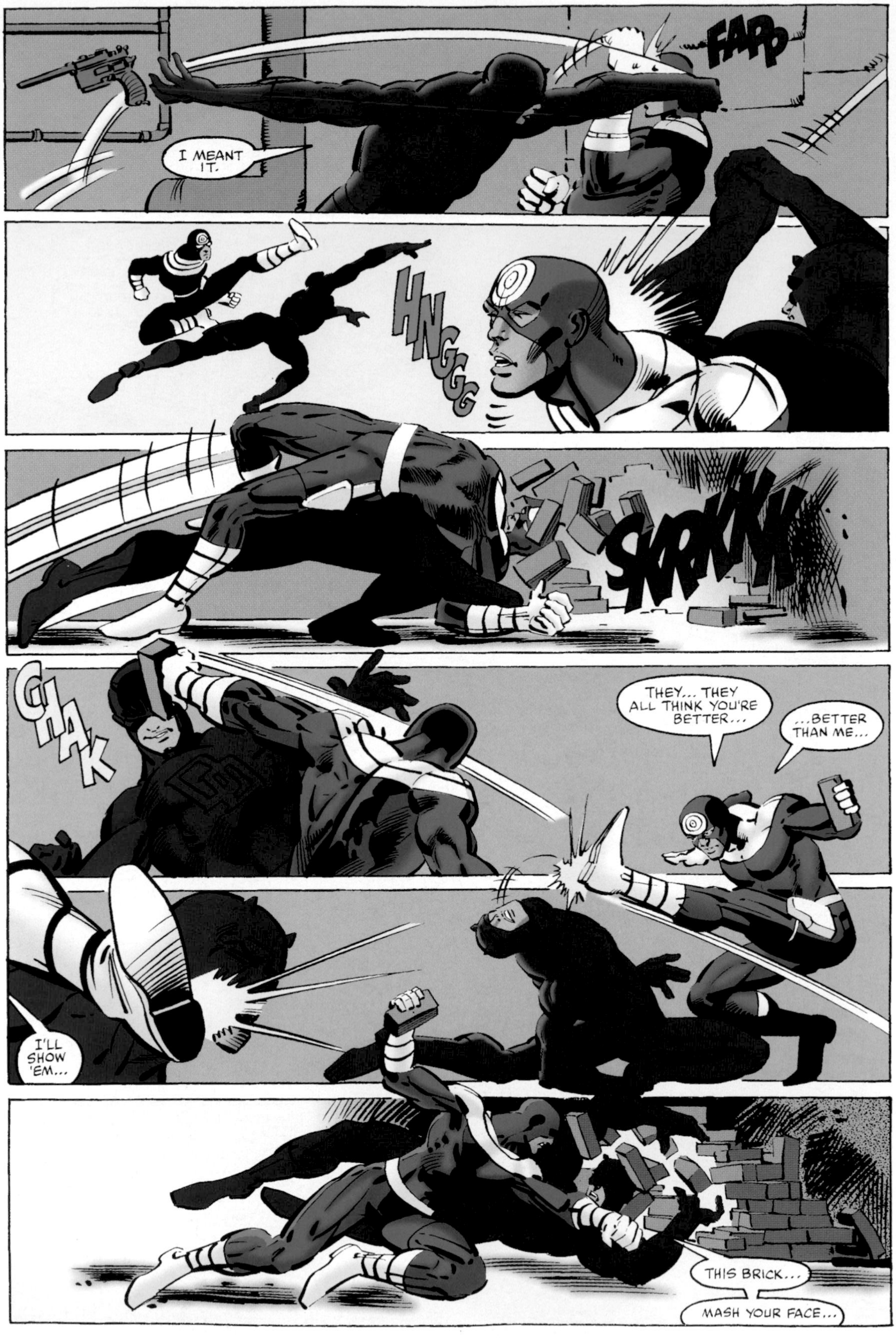
FAPP
I MEANT IT.
HNGGG
SKRKKK
CHAK
THEY... THEY ALL THINK YOU'RE BETTER...
...BETTER THAN ME...
I'LL SHOW 'EM...
THIS BRICK...
MASH YOUR FACE...

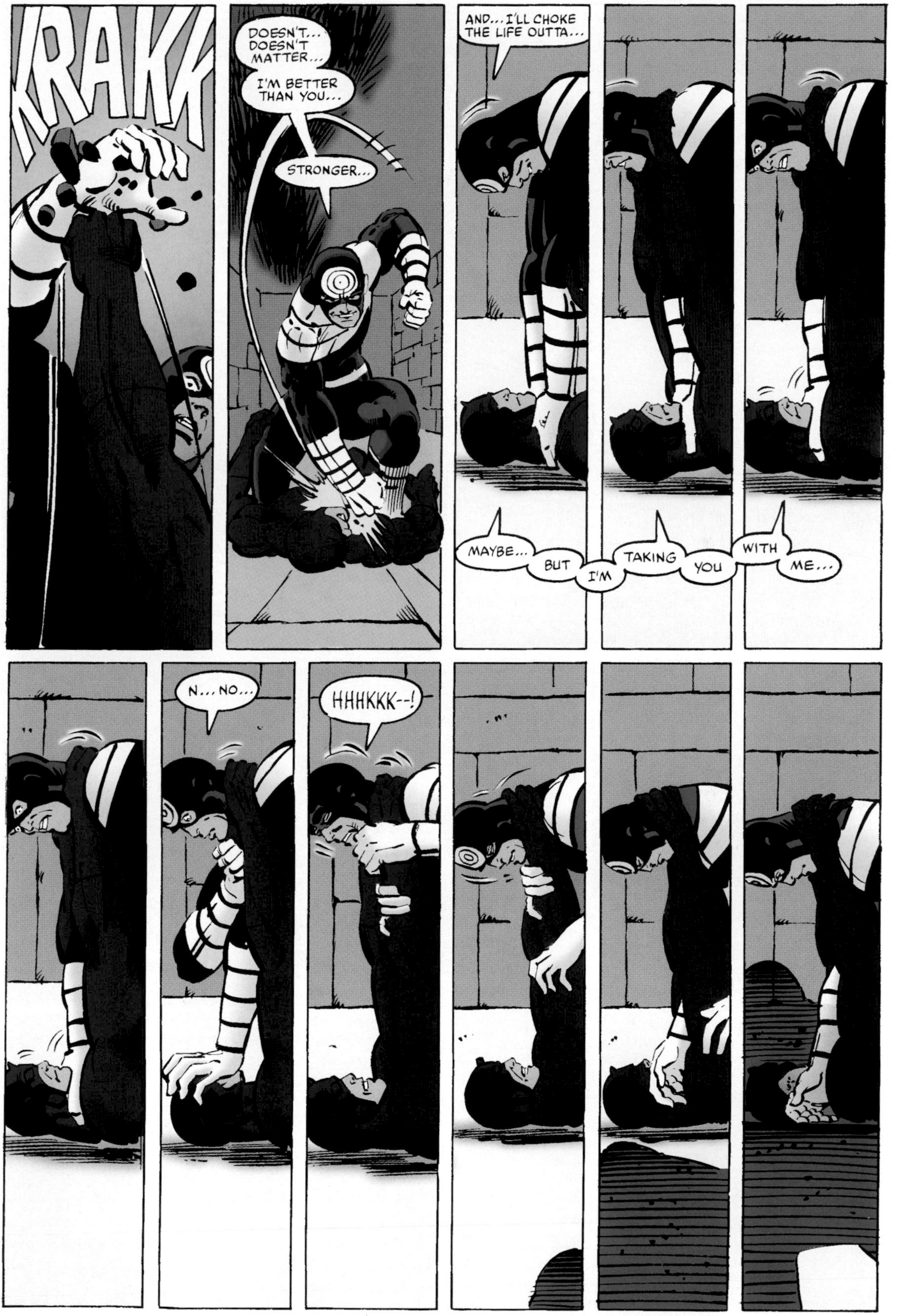
KRAKK
DOESN'T... DOESN'T MATTER...
I'M BETTER THAN YOU...
STRONGER...
AND... I'LL CHOKE THE LIFE OUTTA...
MAYBE...
BUT
I'M
TAKING
YOU
WITH
ME...
N... NO...
HHHKKK--!

DON'T TWITCH A MUSCLE.

SO FOCUSSED ON BULLSEYE... DIDN'T NOTICE THEM.

BUT THERE'S STILL A CHANCE. IF I CAN STALL THEM, JUST LONG ENOUGH FOR ME TO CATCH MY BREATH...

BULLSEYE IS STILL BREATHING. YOU MAY FINISH HIM.

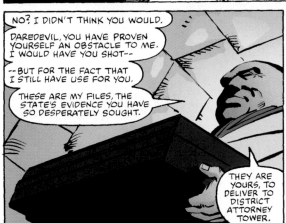

NO? I DIDN'T THINK YOU WOULD.

DAREDEVIL, YOU HAVE PROVEN YOURSELF AN OBSTACLE TO ME. I WOULD HAVE YOU SHOT--

--BUT FOR THE FACT THAT I STILL HAVE USE FOR YOU.

THESE ARE MY FILES, THE STATE'S EVIDENCE YOU HAVE SO DESPERATELY SOUGHT.

THEY ARE YOURS, TO DELIVER TO DISTRICT ATTORNEY TOWER.

MINUTES AFTER HE RECEIVES THEM, HE WILL ISSUE WARRANTS TO ARREST THE ENTIRE UPPER ECHELON OF THE EAST COAST UNDERWORLD.

--AND I SHALL REPLACE THEM WITH MY MEN.

SOON, THEY WILL BE IMPRISONED--

YOU SHALL ELIMINATE MY COMPETITION FOR ME.

I KNOW WHAT YOU'RE THINKING, DAREDEVIL.

YOU'RE PLANNING SOME DESPERATE, FUTILE ATTACK-- YOU SEEK TO BRING ME IN, AS WELL. YOU ARE A VERY PASSIONATE MAN.

CONSIDER THE GREATER GOOD TO SOCIETY...

...AND YOU SHALL SEE THAT YOU REALLY HAVE NO CHOICE, AFTER ALL.

BUT IT IS NOT YOUR PASSION THAT I NOW ADDRESS. IT IS YOUR INTELLECT.

CONSIDER YOUR POSITION. YOU HAVE BULLSEYE -- I'LL THROW HIM IN AS A COURTESY--

--AND I SHALL BE LEFT WITH A SHATTERED ORGANI- ZATION TO REBUILD. FOR A TIME, YOUR SIDE WILL BE THAT MUCH STRONGER.

YOU WIN, KINGPIN.

THIS TIME.

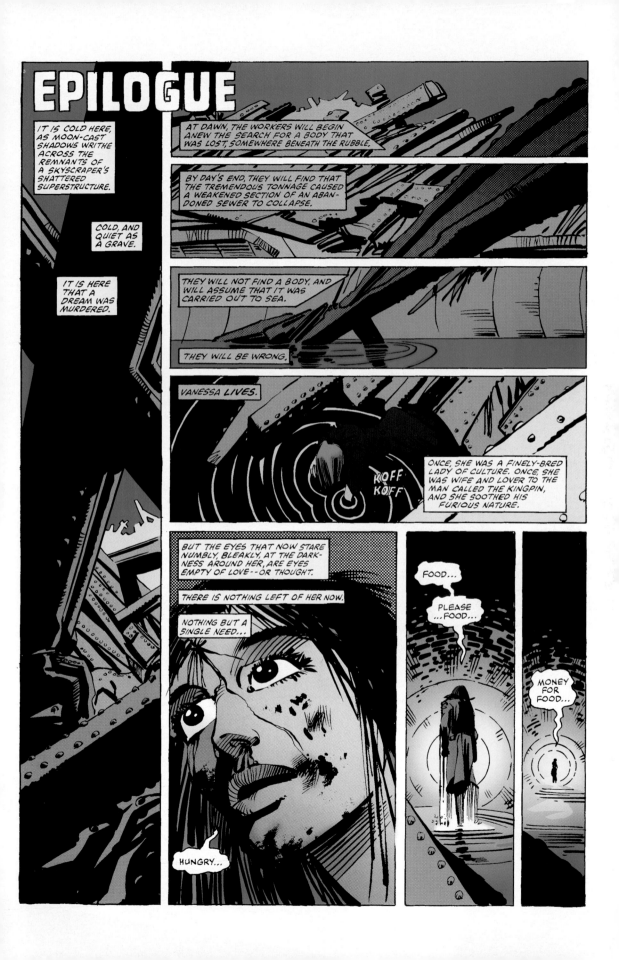

EPILOGUE

IT IS COLD HERE, AS MOON-CAST SHADOWS WRITHE ACROSS THE REMNANTS OF A SKYSCRAPER'S SHATTERED SUPERSTRUCTURE.

COLD, AND QUIET AS A GRAVE.

IT IS HERE THAT A DREAM WAS MURDERED.

AT DAWN, THE WORKERS WILL BEGIN ANEW THE SEARCH FOR A BODY THAT WAS LOST, SOMEWHERE BENEATH THE RUBBLE.

BY DAY'S END, THEY WILL FIND THAT THE TREMENDOUS TONNAGE CAUSED A WEAKENED SECTION OF AN ABANDONED SEWER TO COLLAPSE.

THEY WILL NOT FIND A BODY, AND WILL ASSUME THAT IT WAS CARRIED OUT TO SEA.

THEY WILL BE WRONG.

VANESSA *LIVES.*

KOFF KOFF

ONCE, SHE WAS A FINELY-BRED LADY OF CULTURE. ONCE, SHE WAS WIFE AND LOVER TO THE MAN CALLED THE KINGPIN, AND SHE SOOTHED HIS FURIOUS NATURE.

BUT THE EYES THAT NOW STARE NUMBLY, BLEAKLY, AT THE DARKNESS AROUND HER, ARE EYES EMPTY OF LOVE -- OR THOUGHT.

THERE IS NOTHING LEFT OF HER NOW.

NOTHING BUT A SINGLE NEED...

HUNGRY...

FOOD...

PLEASE ...FOOD...

MONEY FOR FOOD...

DAREDEVIL #173

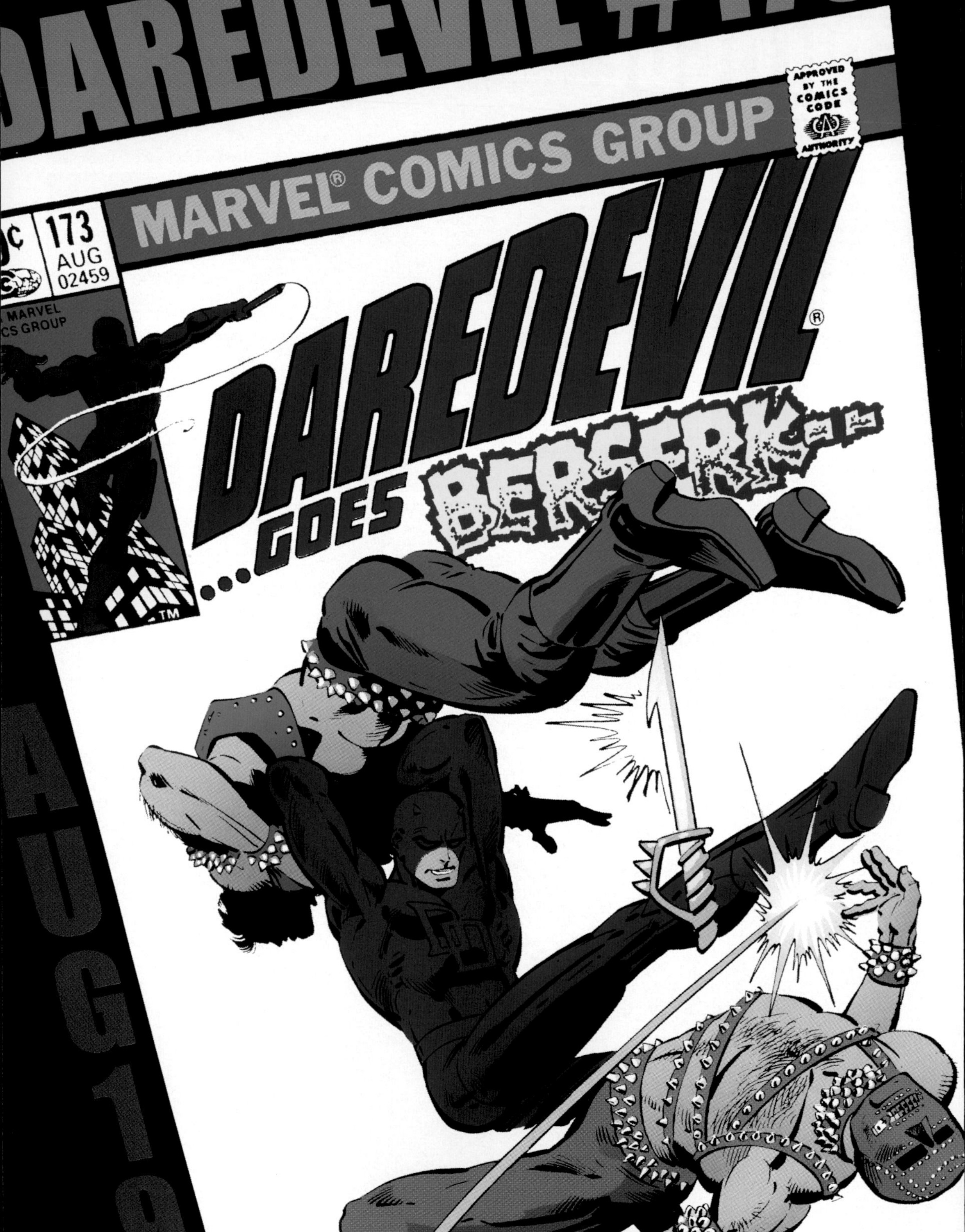

MARVEL® COMICS GROUP
APPROVED BY THE COMICS CODE AUTHORITY
173
AUG
02459
DAREDEVIL®
...GOES BERSERK

AUG 1981

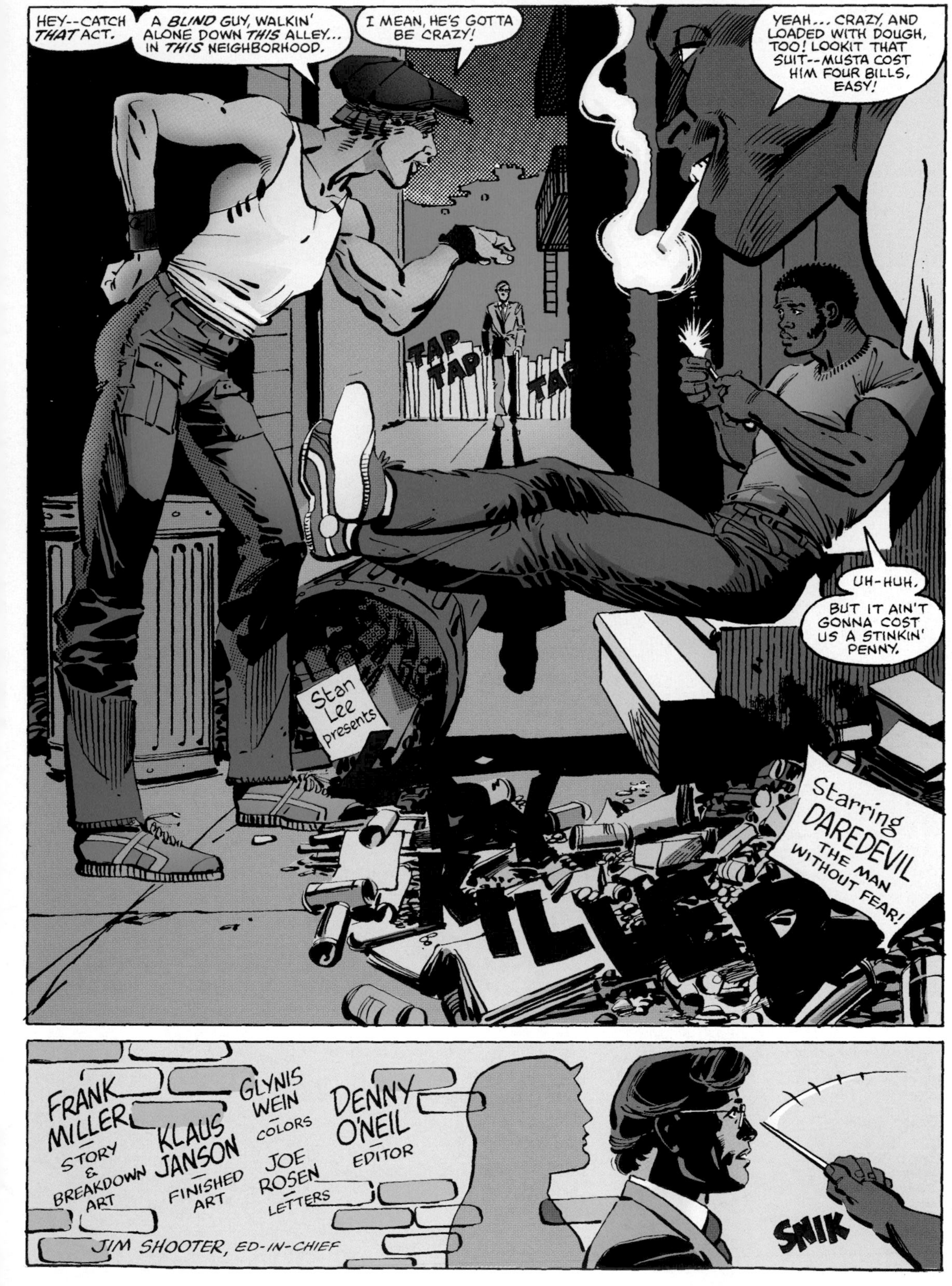
HEY--CATCH *THAT* ACT.
A *BLIND* GUY, WALKIN' ALONE DOWN *THIS* ALLEY... IN *THIS* NEIGHBORHOOD.
I MEAN, HE'S GOTTA BE CRAZY!
YEAH... CRAZY, AND LOADED WITH DOUGH, TOO! LOOKIT THAT SUIT--MUSTA COST HIM FOUR BILLS, EASY!
TAP TAP TAP
UH-HUH. BUT IT AIN'T GONNA COST US A STINKIN' PENNY.
Stan Lee presents
Starring DAREDEVIL THE MAN WITHOUT FEAR!
FRANK MILLER STORY & BREAKDOWN ART
KLAUS JANSON FINISHED ART
GLYNIS WEIN COLORS
JOE ROSEN LETTERS
DENNY O'NEIL EDITOR
JIM SHOOTER, ED-IN-CHIEF
SNIK

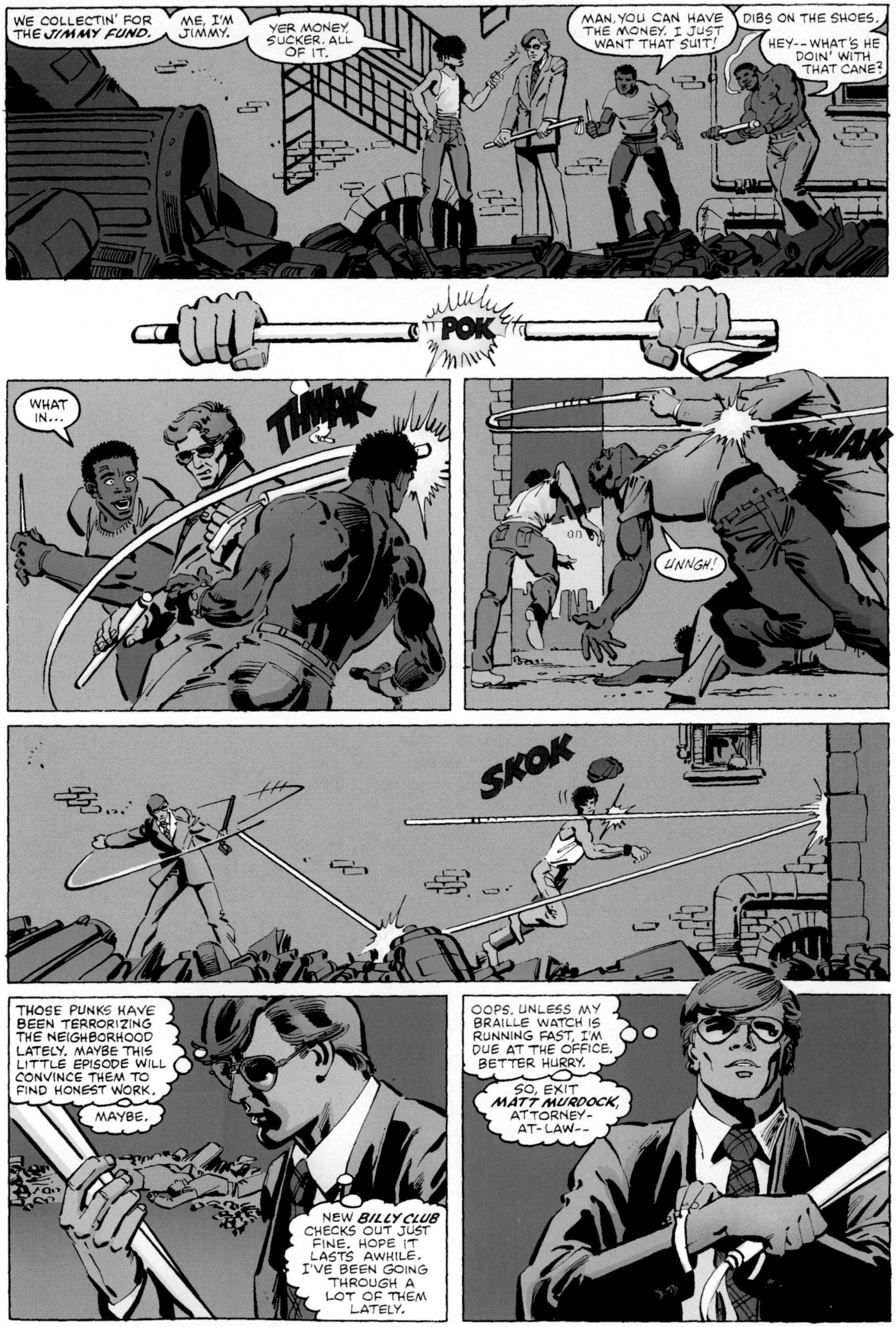
WE COLLECTIN' FOR THE JIMMY FUND.
ME, I'M JIMMY.
YER MONEY, SUCKER. ALL OF IT.
MAN, YOU CAN HAVE THE MONEY. I JUST WANT THAT SUIT!
DIBS ON THE SHOES.
HEY--WHAT'S HE DOIN' WITH THAT CANE?
POK
WHAT IN...
THWAK
THWAK
UNNGH!
SKOK
THOSE PUNKS HAVE BEEN TERRORIZING THE NEIGHBORHOOD LATELY. MAYBE THIS LITTLE EPISODE WILL CONVINCE THEM TO FIND HONEST WORK.
MAYBE.
NEW BILLY CLUB CHECKS OUT JUST FINE. HOPE IT LASTS AWHILE. I'VE BEEN GOING THROUGH A LOT OF THEM LATELY.
OOPS. UNLESS MY BRAILLE WATCH IS RUNNING FAST, I'M DUE AT THE OFFICE. BETTER HURRY.
SO, EXIT MATT MURDOCK, ATTORNEY-AT-LAW--

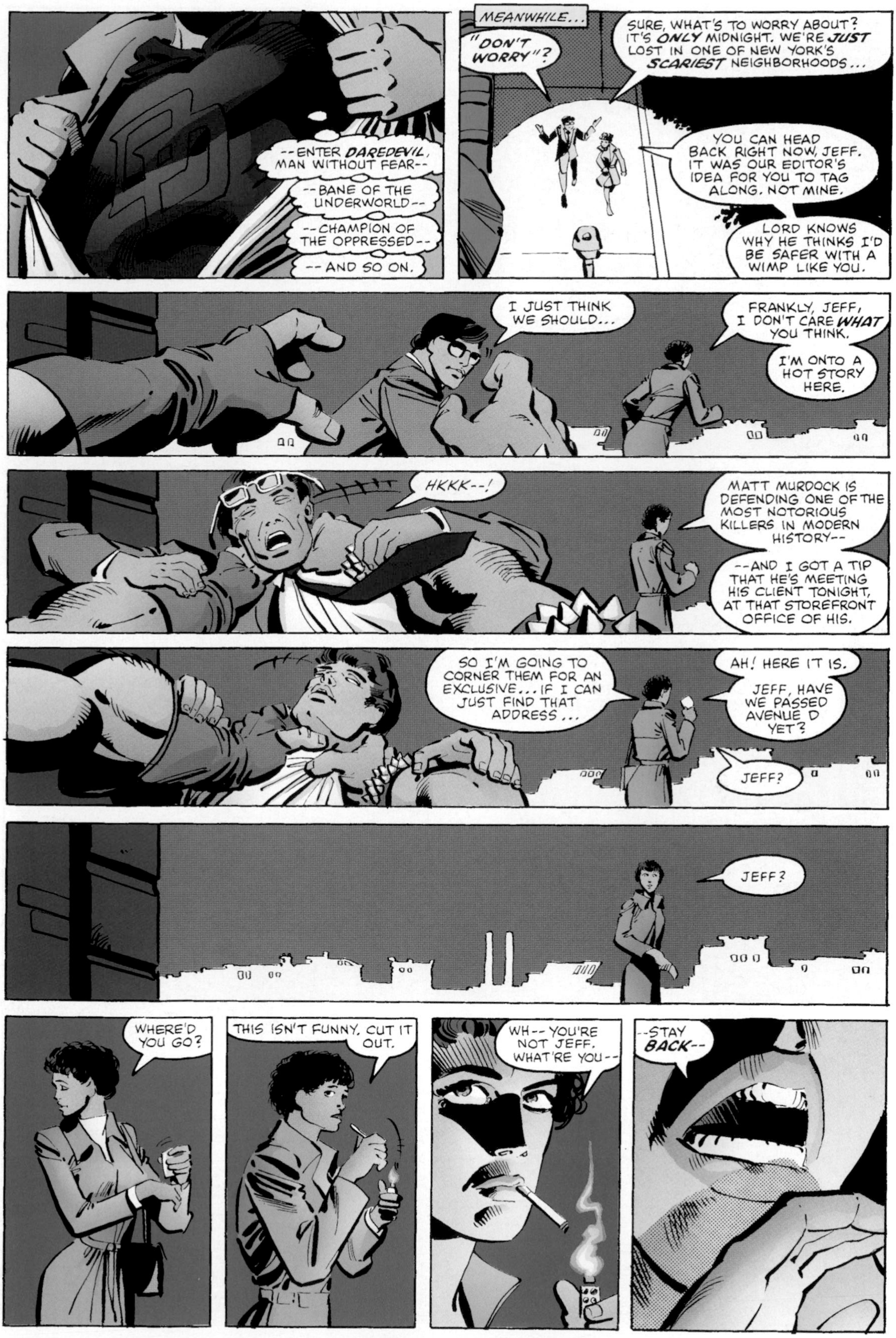
--ENTER DAREDEVIL, MAN WITHOUT FEAR--
--BANE OF THE UNDERWORLD--
--CHAMPION OF THE OPPRESSED--
--AND SO ON.
MEANWHILE...
"DON'T WORRY"?
SURE, WHAT'S TO WORRY ABOUT? IT'S ONLY MIDNIGHT. WE'RE JUST LOST IN ONE OF NEW YORK'S SCARIEST NEIGHBORHOODS...
YOU CAN HEAD BACK RIGHT NOW, JEFF. IT WAS OUR EDITOR'S IDEA FOR YOU TO TAG ALONG. NOT MINE.
LORD KNOWS WHY HE THINKS I'D BE SAFER WITH A WIMP LIKE YOU.
I JUST THINK WE SHOULD...
FRANKLY, JEFF, I DON'T CARE WHAT YOU THINK.
I'M ONTO A HOT STORY HERE.
HKKK--!
MATT MURDOCK IS DEFENDING ONE OF THE MOST NOTORIOUS KILLERS IN MODERN HISTORY--
--AND I GOT A TIP THAT HE'S MEETING HIS CLIENT TONIGHT, AT THAT STOREFRONT OFFICE OF HIS.
SO I'M GOING TO CORNER THEM FOR AN EXCLUSIVE... IF I CAN JUST FIND THAT ADDRESS...
AH! HERE IT IS.
JEFF, HAVE WE PASSED AVENUE D YET?
JEFF?
JEFF?
WHERE'D YOU GO?
THIS ISN'T FUNNY. CUT IT OUT.
WH-- YOU'RE NOT JEFF. WHAT'RE YOU--
--STAY BACK--

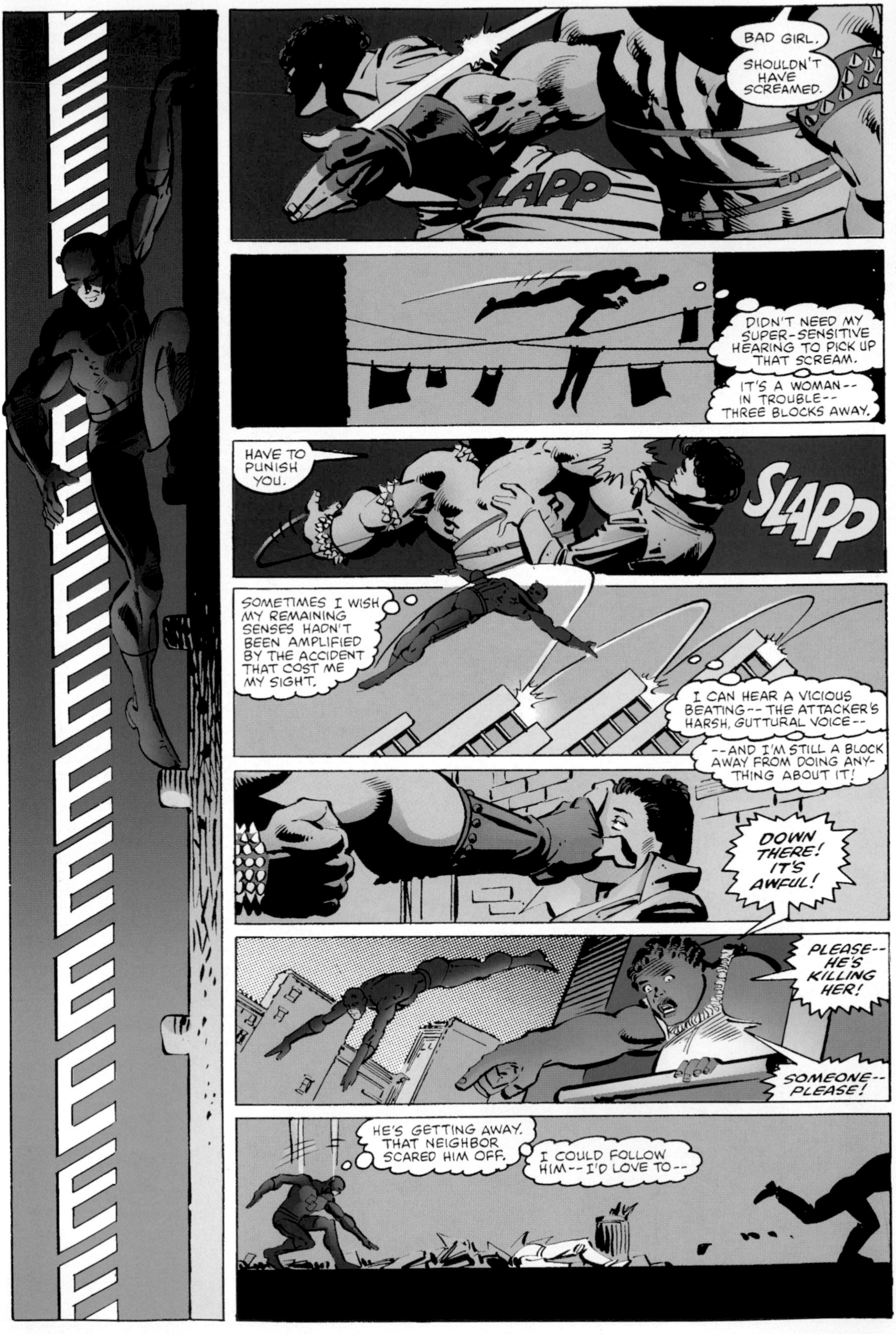
BAD GIRL.
SHOULDN'T HAVE SCREAMED.
SLAPP
DIDN'T NEED MY SUPER-SENSITIVE HEARING TO PICK UP THAT SCREAM.
IT'S A WOMAN-- IN TROUBLE-- THREE BLOCKS AWAY.
HAVE TO PUNISH YOU.
SLAPP
SOMETIMES I WISH MY REMAINING SENSES HADN'T BEEN AMPLIFIED BY THE ACCIDENT THAT COST ME MY SIGHT.
I CAN HEAR A VICIOUS BEATING-- THE ATTACKER'S HARSH, GUTTURAL VOICE--
--AND I'M STILL A BLOCK AWAY FROM DOING ANYTHING ABOUT IT!
DOWN THERE! IT'S AWFUL!
PLEASE-- HE'S KILLING HER!
SOMEONE-- PLEASE!
HE'S GETTING AWAY. THAT NEIGHBOR SCARED HIM OFF.
I COULD FOLLOW HIM-- I'D LOVE TO--

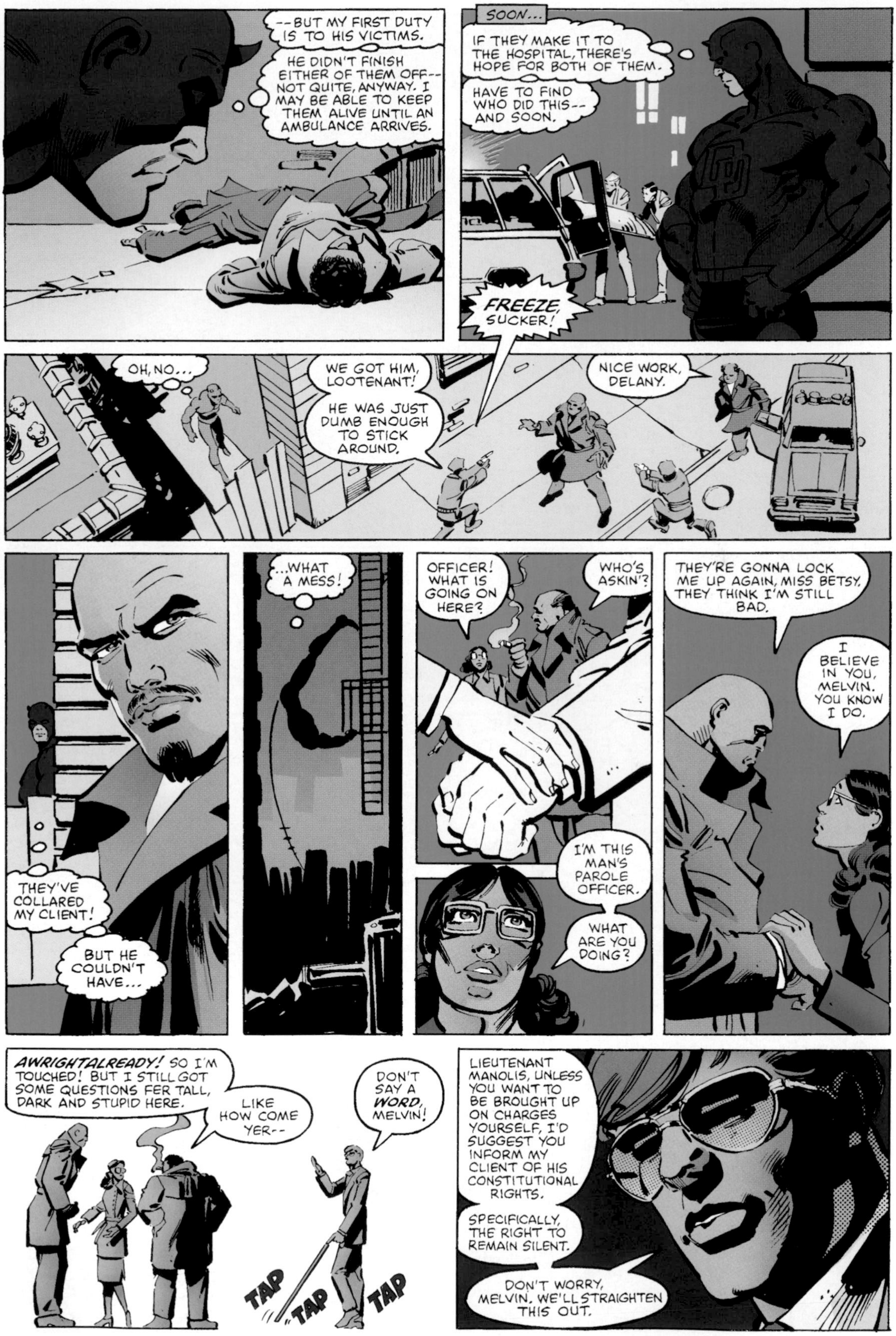
--BUT MY FIRST DUTY IS TO HIS VICTIMS.
HE DIDN'T FINISH EITHER OF THEM OFF--NOT QUITE, ANYWAY. I MAY BE ABLE TO KEEP THEM ALIVE UNTIL AN AMBULANCE ARRIVES.
SOON...
IF THEY MAKE IT TO THE HOSPITAL, THERE'S HOPE FOR BOTH OF THEM.
HAVE TO FIND WHO DID THIS--AND SOON.
FREEZE, SUCKER!
OH, NO...
WE GOT HIM, LOOTENANT!
HE WAS JUST DUMB ENOUGH TO STICK AROUND.
NICE WORK, DELANY.
THEY'VE COLLARED MY CLIENT!
BUT HE COULDN'T HAVE...
...WHAT A MESS!
OFFICER! WHAT IS GOING ON HERE?
WHO'S ASKIN'?
I'M THIS MAN'S PAROLE OFFICER.
WHAT ARE YOU DOING?
THEY'RE GONNA LOCK ME UP AGAIN, MISS BETSY. THEY THINK I'M STILL BAD.
I BELIEVE IN YOU, MELVIN. YOU KNOW I DO.
AWRIGHTALREADY! SO I'M TOUCHED! BUT I STILL GOT SOME QUESTIONS FER TALL, DARK AND STUPID HERE.
LIKE HOW COME YER--
DON'T SAY A WORD, MELVIN!
TAP TAP TAP
LIEUTENANT MANOLIS, UNLESS YOU WANT TO BE BROUGHT UP ON CHARGES YOURSELF, I'D SUGGEST YOU INFORM MY CLIENT OF HIS CONSTITUTIONAL RIGHTS.
SPECIFICALLY, THE RIGHT TO REMAIN SILENT.
DON'T WORRY, MELVIN. WE'LL STRAIGHTEN THIS OUT.

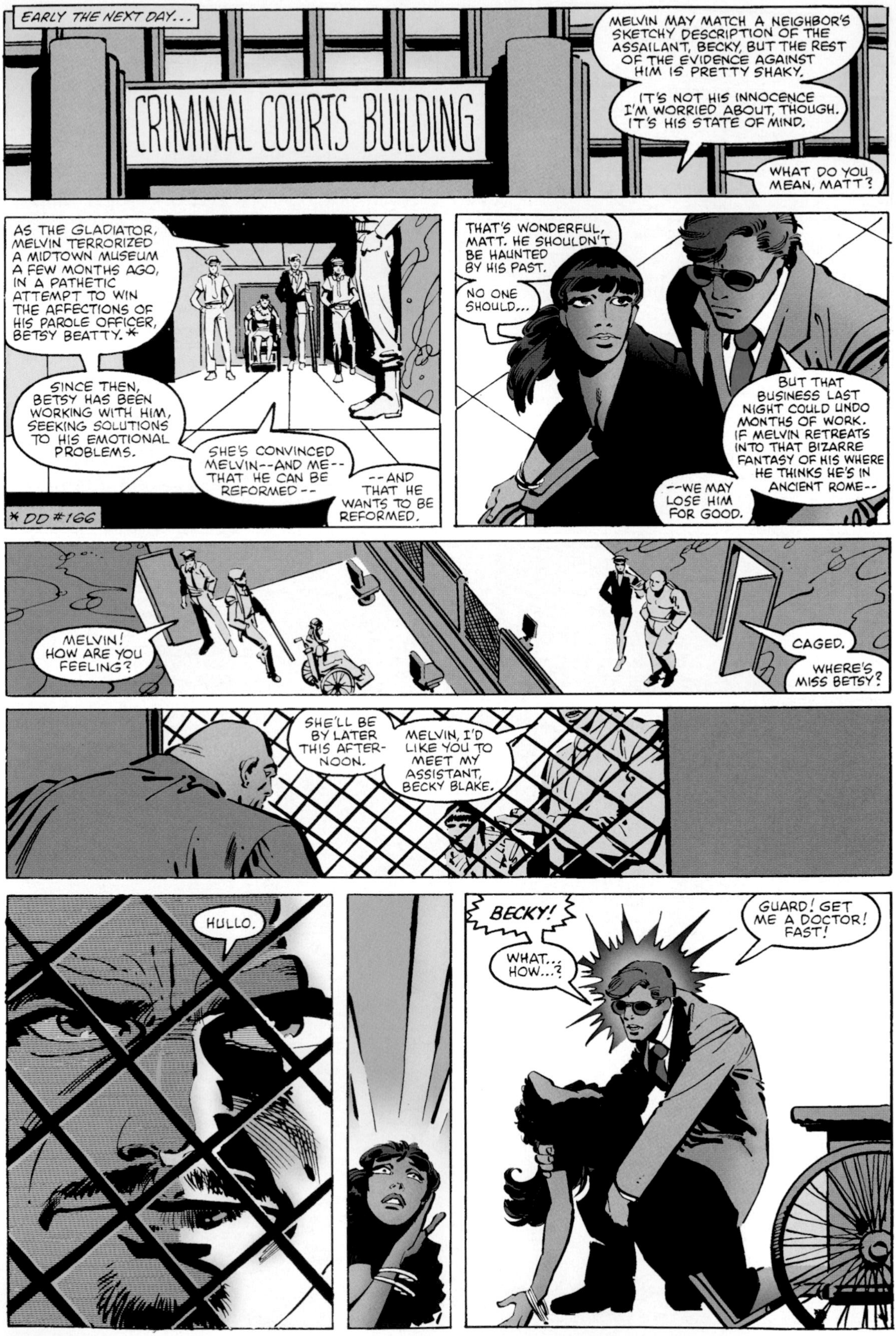
EARLY THE NEXT DAY...
CRIMINAL COURTS BUILDING
MELVIN MAY MATCH A NEIGHBOR'S SKETCHY DESCRIPTION OF THE ASSAILANT, BECKY, BUT THE REST OF THE EVIDENCE AGAINST HIM IS PRETTY SHAKY.
IT'S NOT HIS INNOCENCE I'M WORRIED ABOUT, THOUGH. IT'S HIS STATE OF MIND.
WHAT DO YOU MEAN, MATT?
AS THE GLADIATOR, MELVIN TERRORIZED A MIDTOWN MUSEUM A FEW MONTHS AGO, IN A PATHETIC ATTEMPT TO WIN THE AFFECTIONS OF HIS PAROLE OFFICER, BETSY BEATTY.*
SINCE THEN, BETSY HAS BEEN WORKING WITH HIM, SEEKING SOLUTIONS TO HIS EMOTIONAL PROBLEMS.
SHE'S CONVINCED MELVIN--AND ME--THAT HE CAN BE REFORMED--
--AND THAT HE WANTS TO BE REFORMED.
*DD #166
THAT'S WONDERFUL, MATT. HE SHOULDN'T BE HAUNTED BY HIS PAST.
NO ONE SHOULD...
BUT THAT BUSINESS LAST NIGHT COULD UNDO MONTHS OF WORK. IF MELVIN RETREATS INTO THAT BIZARRE FANTASY OF HIS WHERE HE THINKS HE'S IN ANCIENT ROME--
--WE MAY LOSE HIM FOR GOOD.
MELVIN! HOW ARE YOU FEELING?
CAGED.
WHERE'S MISS BETSY?
SHE'LL BE BY LATER THIS AFTER-NOON.
MELVIN, I'D LIKE YOU TO MEET MY ASSISTANT, BECKY BLAKE.
HULLO.
BECKY!
WHAT... HOW...?
GUARD! GET ME A DOCTOR! FAST!

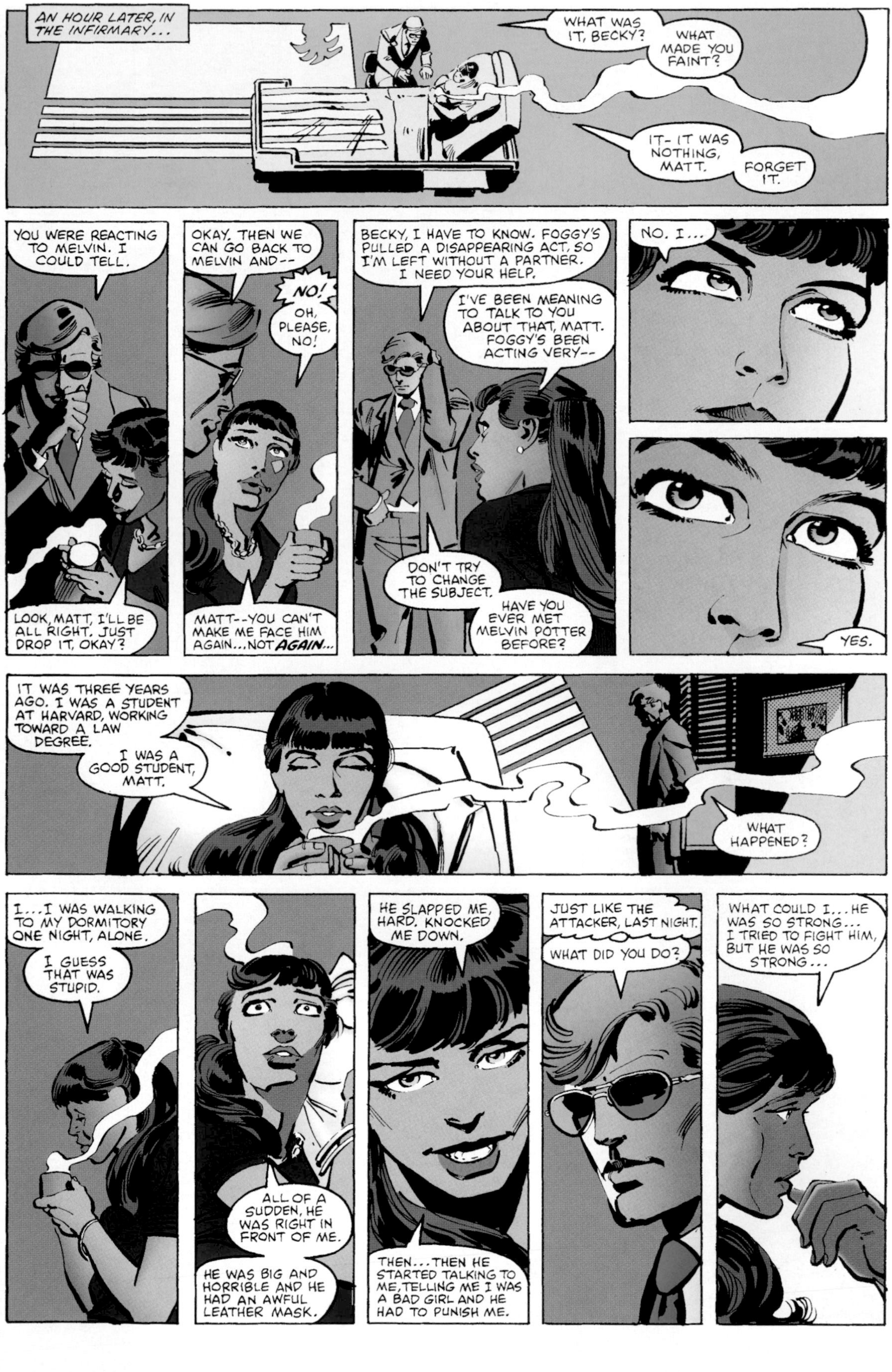
AN HOUR LATER, IN THE INFIRMARY...
WHAT WAS IT, BECKY?
WHAT MADE YOU FAINT?
IT- IT WAS NOTHING, MATT.
FORGET IT.
YOU WERE REACTING TO MELVIN. I COULD TELL.
LOOK, MATT, I'LL BE ALL RIGHT. JUST DROP IT, OKAY?
OKAY. THEN WE CAN GO BACK TO MELVIN AND--
NO! OH, PLEASE, NO!
MATT--YOU CAN'T MAKE ME FACE HIM AGAIN...NOT AGAIN...
BECKY, I HAVE TO KNOW. FOGGY'S PULLED A DISAPPEARING ACT, SO I'M LEFT WITHOUT A PARTNER. I NEED YOUR HELP.
I'VE BEEN MEANING TO TALK TO YOU ABOUT THAT, MATT. FOGGY'S BEEN ACTING VERY--
DON'T TRY TO CHANGE THE SUBJECT.
HAVE YOU EVER MET MELVIN POTTER BEFORE?
NO. I...
YES.
IT WAS THREE YEARS AGO. I WAS A STUDENT AT HARVARD, WORKING TOWARD A LAW DEGREE.
I WAS A GOOD STUDENT, MATT.
WHAT HAPPENED?
I...I WAS WALKING TO MY DORMITORY ONE NIGHT, ALONE.
I GUESS THAT WAS STUPID.
ALL OF A SUDDEN, HE WAS RIGHT IN FRONT OF ME.
HE WAS BIG AND HORRIBLE AND HE HAD AN AWFUL LEATHER MASK.
HE SLAPPED ME, HARD. KNOCKED ME DOWN.
THEN...THEN HE STARTED TALKING TO ME, TELLING ME I WAS A BAD GIRL AND HE HAD TO PUNISH ME.
JUST LIKE THE ATTACKER, LAST NIGHT.
WHAT DID YOU DO?
WHAT COULD I...HE WAS SO STRONG... I TRIED TO FIGHT HIM, BUT HE WAS SO STRONG...

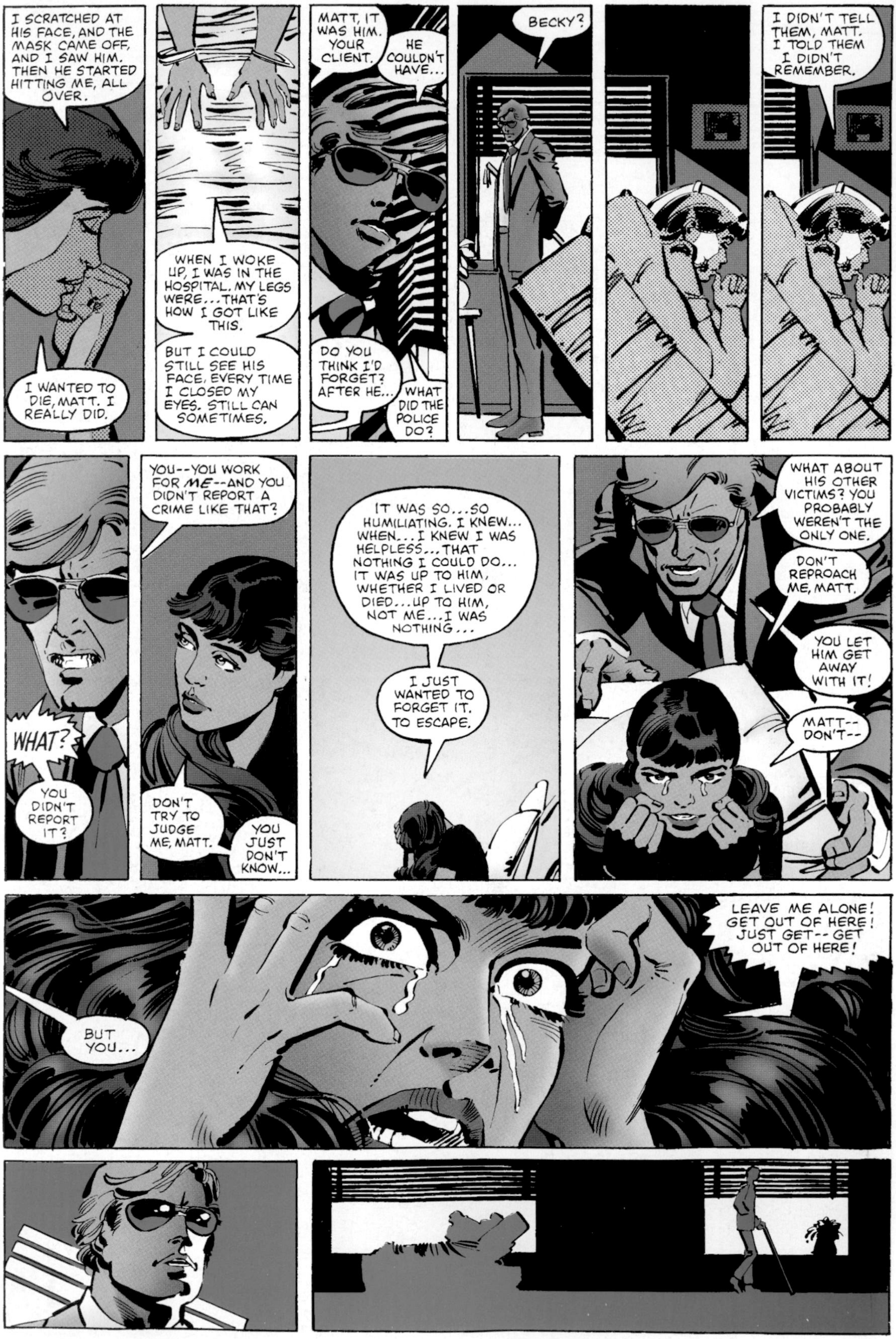
I SCRATCHED AT HIS FACE, AND THE MASK CAME OFF, AND I SAW HIM. THEN HE STARTED HITTING ME, ALL OVER.
I WANTED TO DIE, MATT. I REALLY DID.
WHEN I WOKE UP, I WAS IN THE HOSPITAL. MY LEGS WERE... THAT'S HOW I GOT LIKE THIS.
BUT I COULD STILL SEE HIS FACE, EVERY TIME I CLOSED MY EYES. STILL CAN SOMETIMES.
MATT, IT WAS HIM. YOUR CLIENT.
HE COULDN'T HAVE...
DO YOU THINK I'D FORGET? AFTER HE...
WHAT DID THE POLICE DO?
BECKY?
I DIDN'T TELL THEM, MATT. I TOLD THEM I DIDN'T REMEMBER.
WHAT?
YOU DIDN'T REPORT IT?
YOU--YOU WORK FOR ME--AND YOU DIDN'T REPORT A CRIME LIKE THAT?
DON'T TRY TO JUDGE ME, MATT.
YOU JUST DON'T KNOW...
IT WAS SO...SO HUMILIATING. I KNEW... WHEN... I KNEW I WAS HELPLESS... THAT NOTHING I COULD DO... IT WAS UP TO HIM, WHETHER I LIVED OR DIED... UP TO HIM, NOT ME... I WAS NOTHING...
I JUST WANTED TO FORGET IT. TO ESCAPE.
WHAT ABOUT HIS OTHER VICTIMS? YOU PROBABLY WEREN'T THE ONLY ONE.
DON'T REPROACH ME, MATT.
YOU LET HIM GET AWAY WITH IT!
MATT-- DON'T--
BUT YOU...
LEAVE ME ALONE! GET OUT OF HERE! JUST GET-- GET OUT OF HERE!

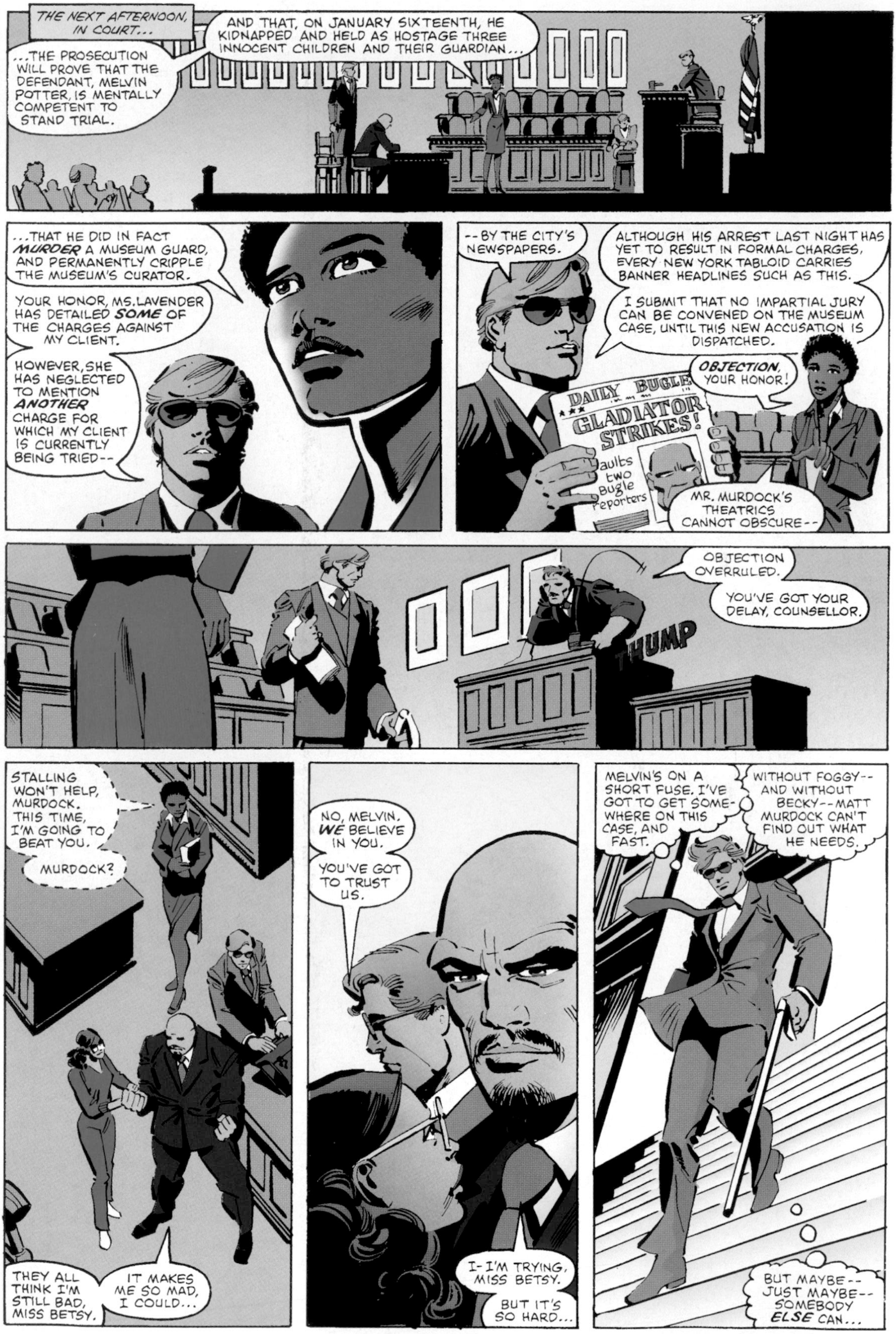
THE NEXT AFTERNOON, IN COURT...
...THE PROSECUTION WILL PROVE THAT THE DEFENDANT, MELVIN POTTER, IS MENTALLY COMPETENT TO STAND TRIAL.
AND THAT, ON JANUARY SIXTEENTH, HE KIDNAPPED AND HELD AS HOSTAGE THREE INNOCENT CHILDREN AND THEIR GUARDIAN...
...THAT HE DID IN FACT MURDER A MUSEUM GUARD, AND PERMANENTLY CRIPPLE THE MUSEUM'S CURATOR.
YOUR HONOR, MS. LAVENDER HAS DETAILED SOME OF THE CHARGES AGAINST MY CLIENT.
HOWEVER, SHE HAS NEGLECTED TO MENTION ANOTHER CHARGE FOR WHICH MY CLIENT IS CURRENTLY BEING TRIED--
--BY THE CITY'S NEWSPAPERS.
ALTHOUGH HIS ARREST LAST NIGHT HAS YET TO RESULT IN FORMAL CHARGES, EVERY NEW YORK TABLOID CARRIES BANNER HEADLINES SUCH AS THIS.
I SUBMIT THAT NO IMPARTIAL JURY CAN BE CONVENED ON THE MUSEUM CASE, UNTIL THIS NEW ACCUSATION IS DISPATCHED.
DAILY BUGLE
GLADIATOR STRIKES!
aults two Bugle reporters
OBJECTION, YOUR HONOR!
MR. MURDOCK'S THEATRICS CANNOT OBSCURE--
OBJECTION OVERRULED.
YOU'VE GOT YOUR DELAY, COUNSELLOR.
THUMP
STALLING WON'T HELP, MURDOCK. THIS TIME, I'M GOING TO BEAT YOU.
MURDOCK?
THEY ALL THINK I'M STILL BAD, MISS BETSY.
IT MAKES ME SO MAD, I COULD...
NO, MELVIN. WE BELIEVE IN YOU.
YOU'VE GOT TO TRUST US.
I- I'M TRYING, MISS BETSY.
BUT IT'S SO HARD...
MELVIN'S ON A SHORT FUSE. I'VE GOT TO GET SOMEWHERE ON THIS CASE, AND FAST.
WITHOUT FOGGY-- AND WITHOUT BECKY--MATT MURDOCK CAN'T FIND OUT WHAT HE NEEDS.
BUT MAYBE-- JUST MAYBE-- SOMEBODY ELSE CAN...

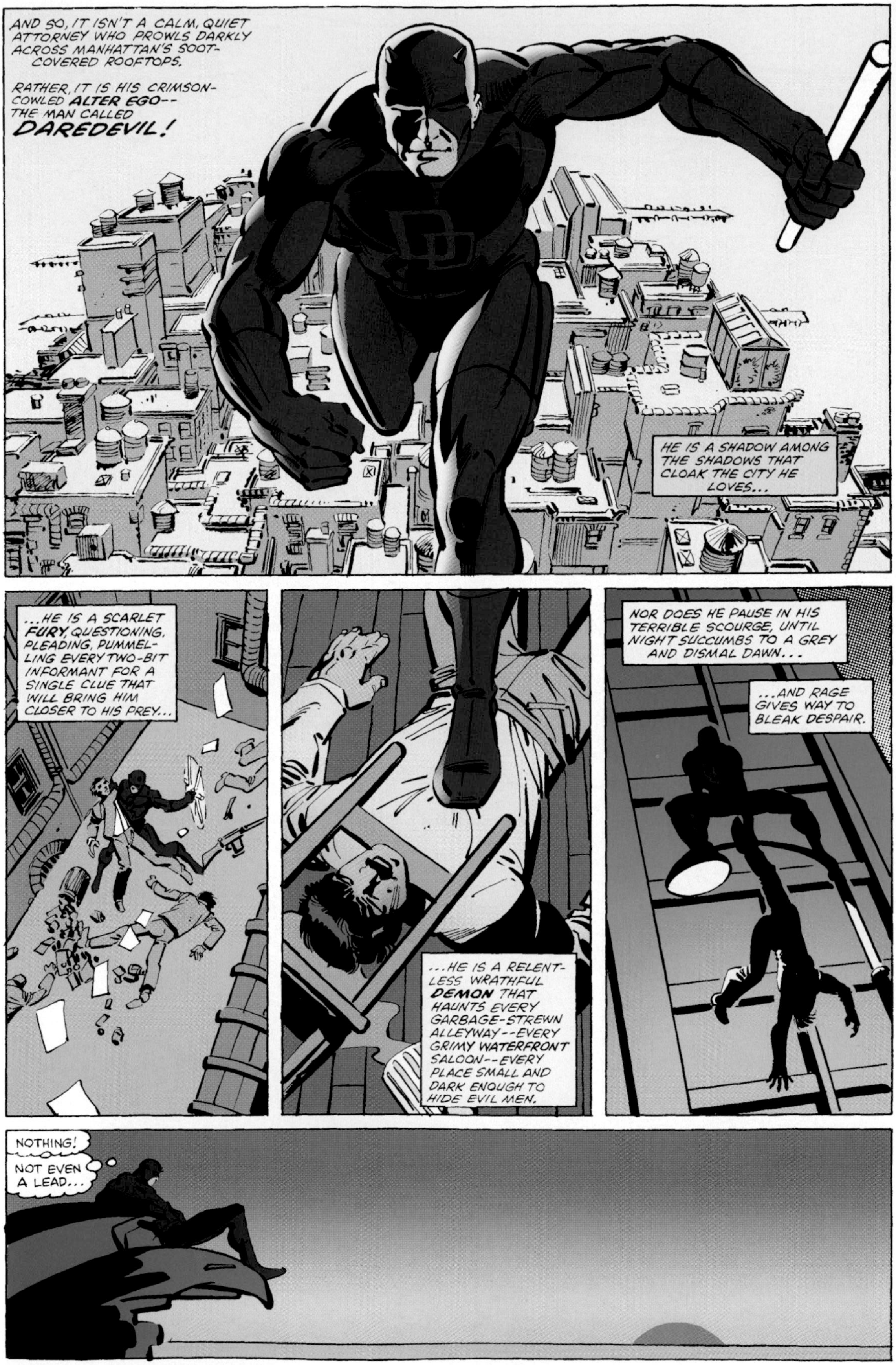
AND SO, IT ISN'T A CALM, QUIET ATTORNEY WHO PROWLS DARKLY ACROSS MANHATTAN'S SOOT-COVERED ROOFTOPS.
RATHER, IT IS HIS CRIMSON-COWLED ALTER EGO-- THE MAN CALLED DAREDEVIL!
HE IS A SHADOW AMONG THE SHADOWS THAT CLOAK THE CITY HE LOVES...
...HE IS A SCARLET FURY, QUESTIONING, PLEADING, PUMMELLING EVERY TWO-BIT INFORMANT FOR A SINGLE CLUE THAT WILL BRING HIM CLOSER TO HIS PREY...
...HE IS A RELENTLESS WRATHFUL DEMON THAT HAUNTS EVERY GARBAGE-STREWN ALLEYWAY--EVERY GRIMY WATERFRONT SALOON--EVERY PLACE SMALL AND DARK ENOUGH TO HIDE EVIL MEN.
NOR DOES HE PAUSE IN HIS TERRIBLE SCOURGE, UNTIL NIGHT SUCCUMBS TO A GREY AND DISMAL DAWN...
...AND RAGE GIVES WAY TO BLEAK DESPAIR.
NOTHING!
NOT EVEN A LEAD...

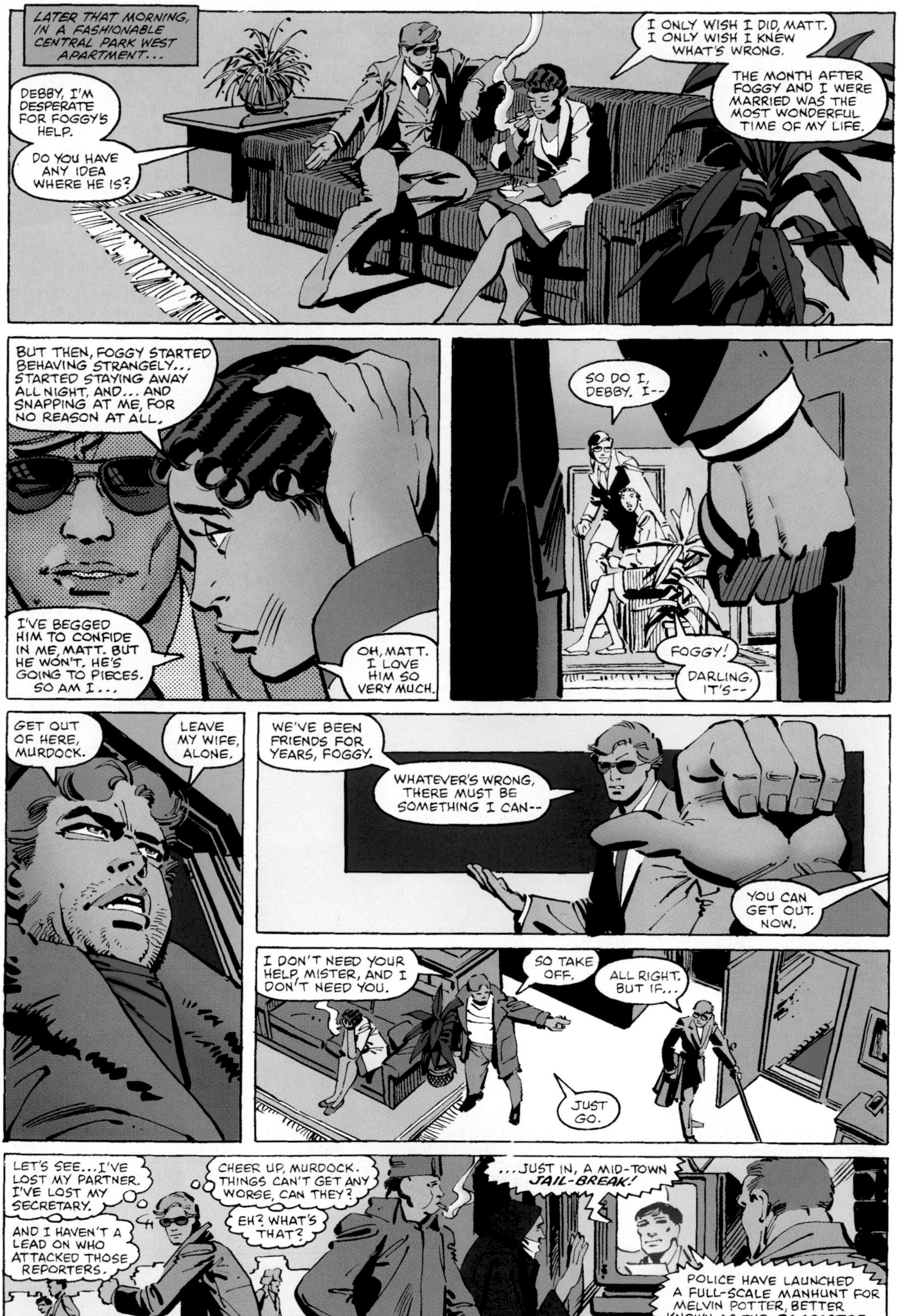
LATER THAT MORNING, IN A FASHIONABLE CENTRAL PARK WEST APARTMENT...
DEBBY, I'M DESPERATE FOR FOGGY'S HELP.
DO YOU HAVE ANY IDEA WHERE HE IS?
I ONLY WISH I DID, MATT. I ONLY WISH I KNEW WHAT'S WRONG.
THE MONTH AFTER FOGGY AND I WERE MARRIED WAS THE MOST WONDERFUL TIME OF MY LIFE.
BUT THEN, FOGGY STARTED BEHAVING STRANGELY... STARTED STAYING AWAY ALL NIGHT, AND... AND SNAPPING AT ME, FOR NO REASON AT ALL.
I'VE BEGGED HIM TO CONFIDE IN ME, MATT. BUT HE WON'T. HE'S GOING TO PIECES. SO AM I...
OH, MATT. I LOVE HIM SO VERY MUCH.
SO DO I, DEBBY. I--
FOGGY!
DARLING, IT'S--
GET OUT OF HERE, MURDOCK.
LEAVE MY WIFE, ALONE.
WE'VE BEEN FRIENDS FOR YEARS, FOGGY.
WHATEVER'S WRONG, THERE MUST BE SOMETHING I CAN--
YOU CAN GET OUT. NOW.
I DON'T NEED YOUR HELP, MISTER, AND I DON'T NEED YOU.
SO TAKE OFF.
ALL RIGHT. BUT IF...
JUST GO.
LET'S SEE... I'VE LOST MY PARTNER. I'VE LOST MY SECRETARY.
AND I HAVEN'T A LEAD ON WHO ATTACKED THOSE REPORTERS.
CHEER UP, MURDOCK. THINGS CAN'T GET ANY WORSE, CAN THEY?
EH? WHAT'S THAT?
...JUST IN, A MID-TOWN JAIL-BREAK!
POLICE HAVE LAUNCHED A FULL-SCALE MANHUNT FOR MELVIN POTTER, BETTER KNOWN AS THE GLADIATOR...

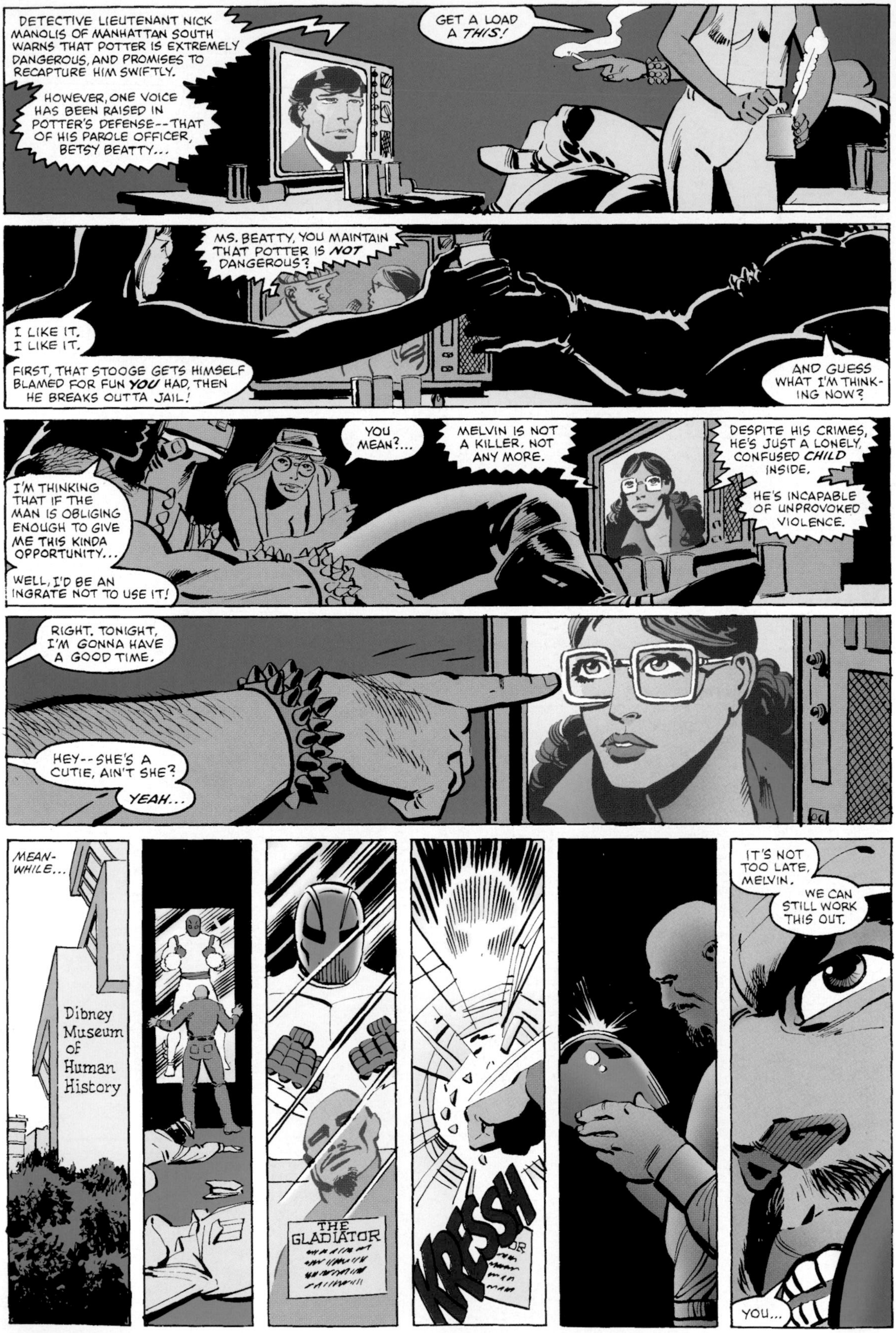
DETECTIVE LIEUTENANT NICK MANOLIS OF MANHATTAN SOUTH WARNS THAT POTTER IS EXTREMELY DANGEROUS, AND PROMISES TO RECAPTURE HIM SWIFTLY.
HOWEVER, ONE VOICE HAS BEEN RAISED IN POTTER'S DEFENSE--THAT OF HIS PAROLE OFFICER, BETSY BEATTY...
GET A LOAD A THIS!
MS. BEATTY, YOU MAINTAIN THAT POTTER IS NOT DANGEROUS?
I LIKE IT. I LIKE IT.
FIRST, THAT STOOGE GETS HIMSELF BLAMED FOR FUN YOU HAD, THEN HE BREAKS OUTTA JAIL!
AND GUESS WHAT I'M THINKING NOW?
I'M THINKING THAT IF THE MAN IS OBLIGING ENOUGH TO GIVE ME THIS KINDA OPPORTUNITY...
WELL, I'D BE AN INGRATE NOT TO USE IT!
YOU MEAN?...
MELVIN IS NOT A KILLER. NOT ANY MORE.
DESPITE HIS CRIMES, HE'S JUST A LONELY, CONFUSED CHILD INSIDE.
HE'S INCAPABLE OF UNPROVOKED VIOLENCE.
RIGHT. TONIGHT, I'M GONNA HAVE A GOOD TIME.
HEY--SHE'S A CUTIE, AIN'T SHE?
YEAH...
MEAN-WHILE...
Dibney Museum of Human History
THE GLADIATOR
KRESSH
IT'S NOT TOO LATE, MELVIN.
WE CAN STILL WORK THIS OUT.
YOU...

GO AWAY, MATT. I'M JUST DOING WHAT I GOT TO.

MELVIN, WE'VE COME SO FAR. I KNOW HOW MUCH YOU WANT TO BE WELL...TO GO STRAIGHT.

WE CAN HELP YOU, BETSY AND I.

I BEEN TRYING, MATT. I BEEN SITTING IN THAT COURTROOM, LISTENING TO THEM SAY THOSE THINGS ABOUT ME, FEELING MY GUTS CHURN UP, WANTING TO RIP THEM ALL TO PIECES...

THEY HATE ME. THEY ALL HATE ME...SO I'M GONNA HATE THEM BACK!

I'M NOT LETTING YOU OFF THAT EASY.

IF YOU WANT TO BECOME THE GLADIATOR AGAIN, YOU'LL HAVE TO GET PAST ME.

PAST YOU?!

LOOK AT YOU-- YOU'RE JUST A SKINNY LITTLE BLIND GUY! I'D BREAK YOU IN HALF!

IT'D BE EASY...

IS THAT WHAT YOU WANT?

WHY NOT? I'M THE GLADIATOR! THE GLADIATOR!

WHEN I'M WEARING MY ARMOR, I'M UNBEATABLE, I'M...

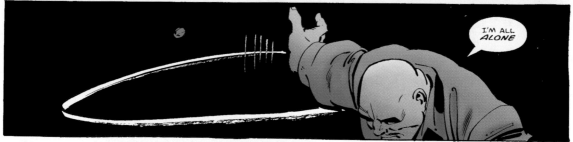

I'M ALL ALONE

HELP ME... PLEASE...

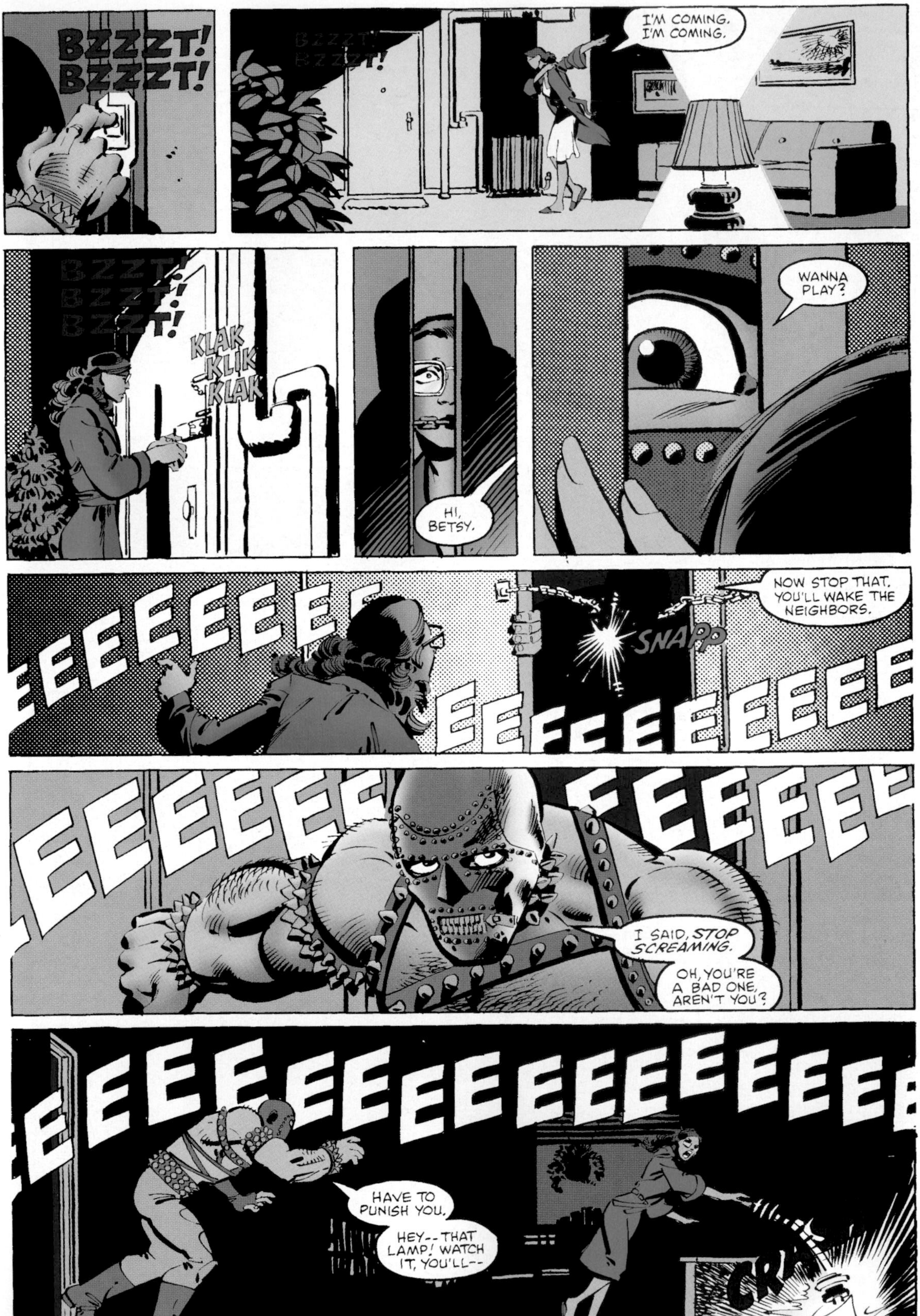
BZZZT! BZZZT!
BZZZT! BZZZT!
I'M COMING. I'M COMING.
BZZZT! BZZZT! BZZZT!
KLAK KLIK KLAK
HI, BETSY.
WANNA PLAY?
EEEEEEEE
NOW STOP THAT. YOU'LL WAKE THE NEIGHBORS.
SNAPP
EEEEEEEEEEE
EEEEEEEEEEEE
I SAID, STOP SCREAMING.
OH, YOU'RE A BAD ONE, AREN'T YOU?
EEEEEEEEEEEEEEEEE
HAVE TO PUNISH YOU.
HEY-- THAT LAMP! WATCH IT, YOU'LL--

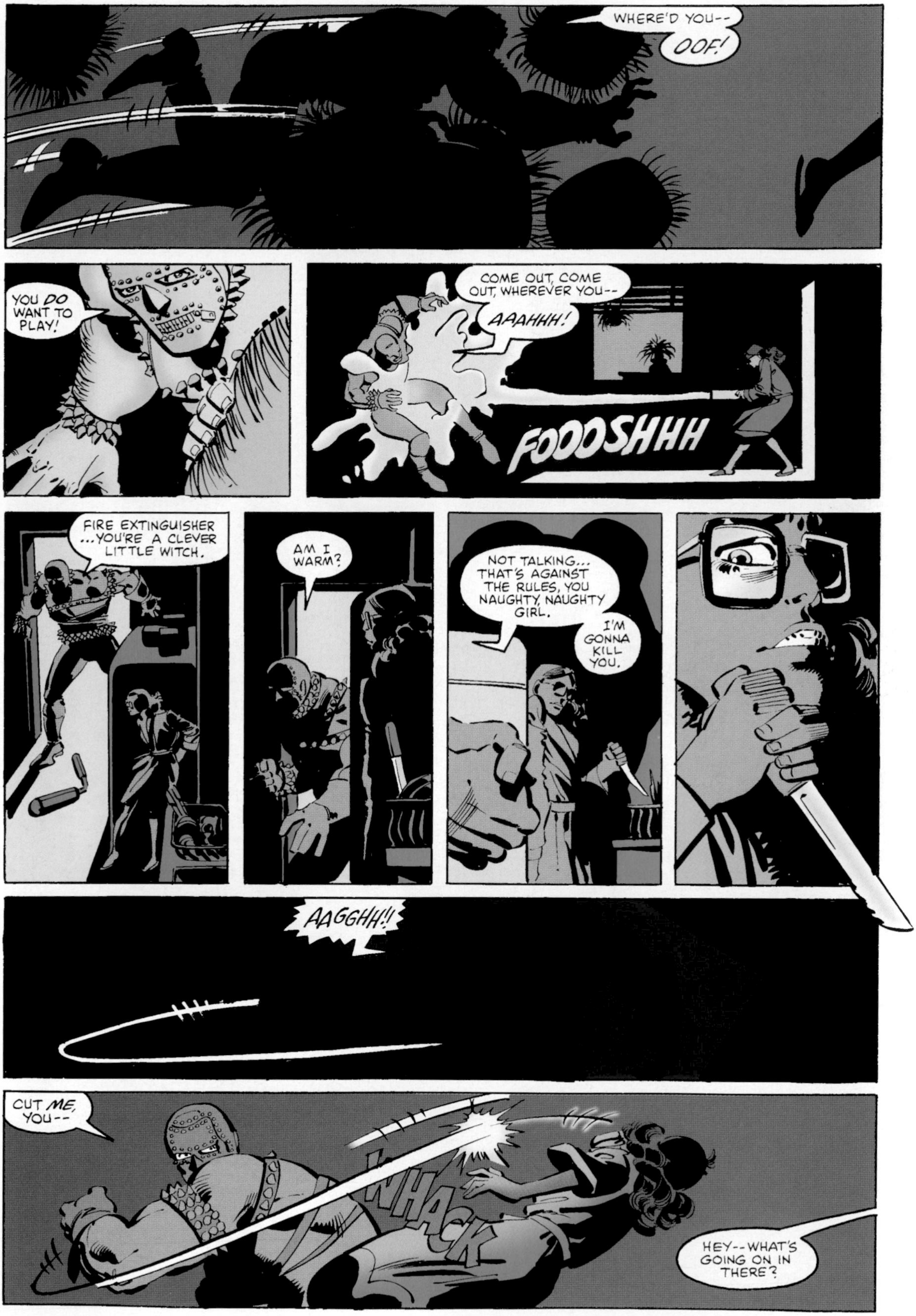
WHERE'D YOU--
OOF!
YOU DO WANT TO PLAY!
COME OUT, COME OUT, WHEREVER YOU--
AAAHHH!
FOOOSHHH
FIRE EXTINGUISHER ...YOU'RE A CLEVER LITTLE WITCH.
AM I WARM?
NOT TALKING... THAT'S AGAINST THE RULES, YOU NAUGHTY, NAUGHTY GIRL.
I'M GONNA KILL YOU.
AAGGHH!!
CUT ME, YOU--
WHACK
HEY--WHAT'S GOING ON IN THERE?

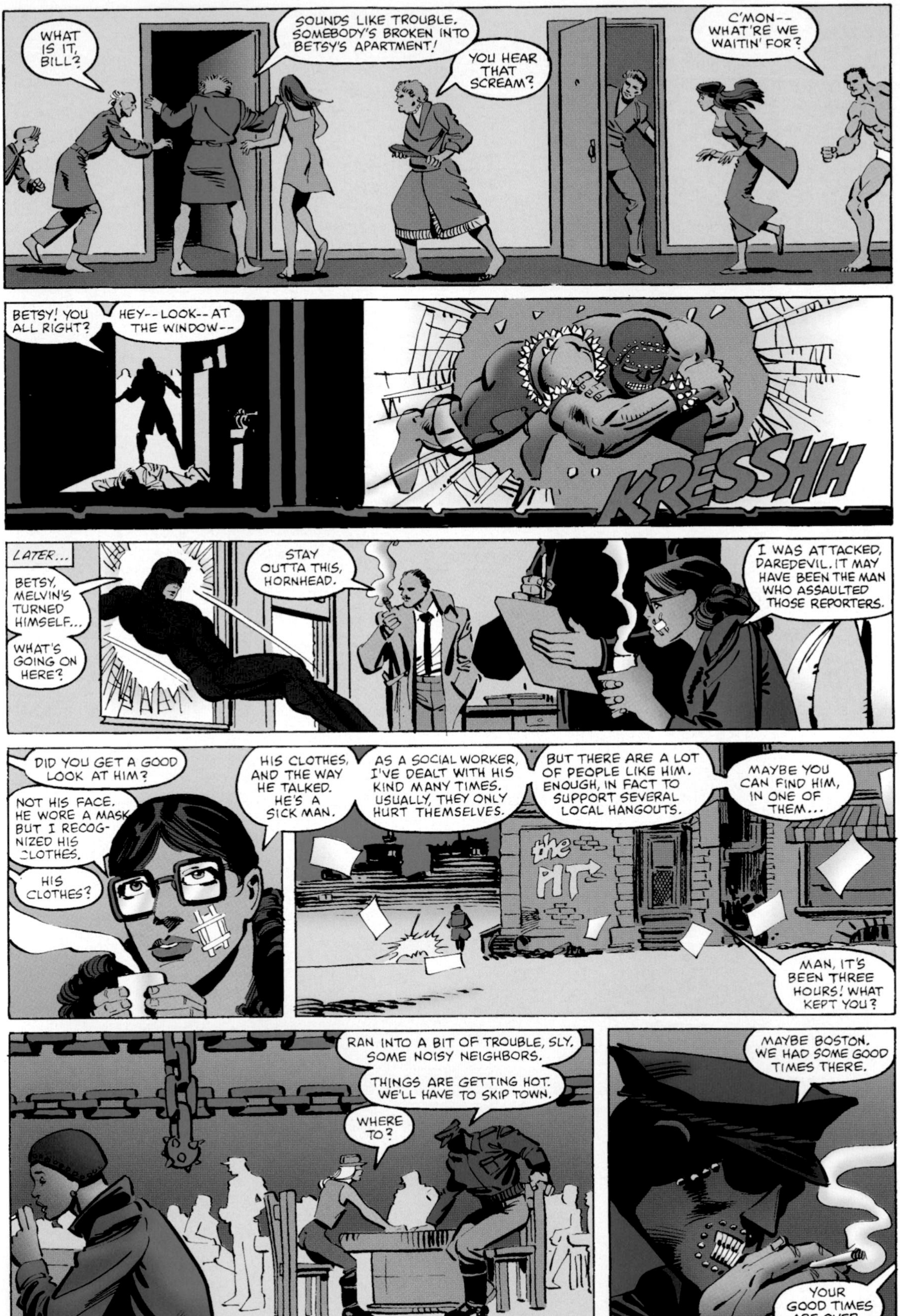
WHAT IS IT, BILL?
SOUNDS LIKE TROUBLE. SOMEBODY'S BROKEN INTO BETSY'S APARTMENT!
YOU HEAR THAT SCREAM?
C'MON-- WHAT'RE WE WAITIN' FOR?
BETSY! YOU ALL RIGHT?
HEY-- LOOK-- AT THE WINDOW--
KRESSHH
LATER...
BETSY, MELVIN'S TURNED HIMSELF...
WHAT'S GOING ON HERE?
STAY OUTTA THIS, HORNHEAD.
I WAS ATTACKED, DAREDEVIL. IT MAY HAVE BEEN THE MAN WHO ASSAULTED THOSE REPORTERS.
DID YOU GET A GOOD LOOK AT HIM?
NOT HIS FACE. HE WORE A MASK BUT I RECOGNIZED HIS CLOTHES.
HIS CLOTHES?
HIS CLOTHES, AND THE WAY HE TALKED. HE'S A SICK MAN.
AS A SOCIAL WORKER, I'VE DEALT WITH HIS KIND MANY TIMES. USUALLY, THEY ONLY HURT THEMSELVES.
BUT THERE ARE A LOT OF PEOPLE LIKE HIM. ENOUGH, IN FACT TO SUPPORT SEVERAL LOCAL HANGOUTS.
MAYBE YOU CAN FIND HIM, IN ONE OF THEM...
the PIT
MAN, IT'S BEEN THREE HOURS! WHAT KEPT YOU?
RAN INTO A BIT OF TROUBLE, SLY. SOME NOISY NEIGHBORS.
THINGS ARE GETTING HOT. WE'LL HAVE TO SKIP TOWN.
WHERE TO?
MAYBE BOSTON. WE HAD SOME GOOD TIMES THERE.
YOUR GOOD TIMES ARE OVER.

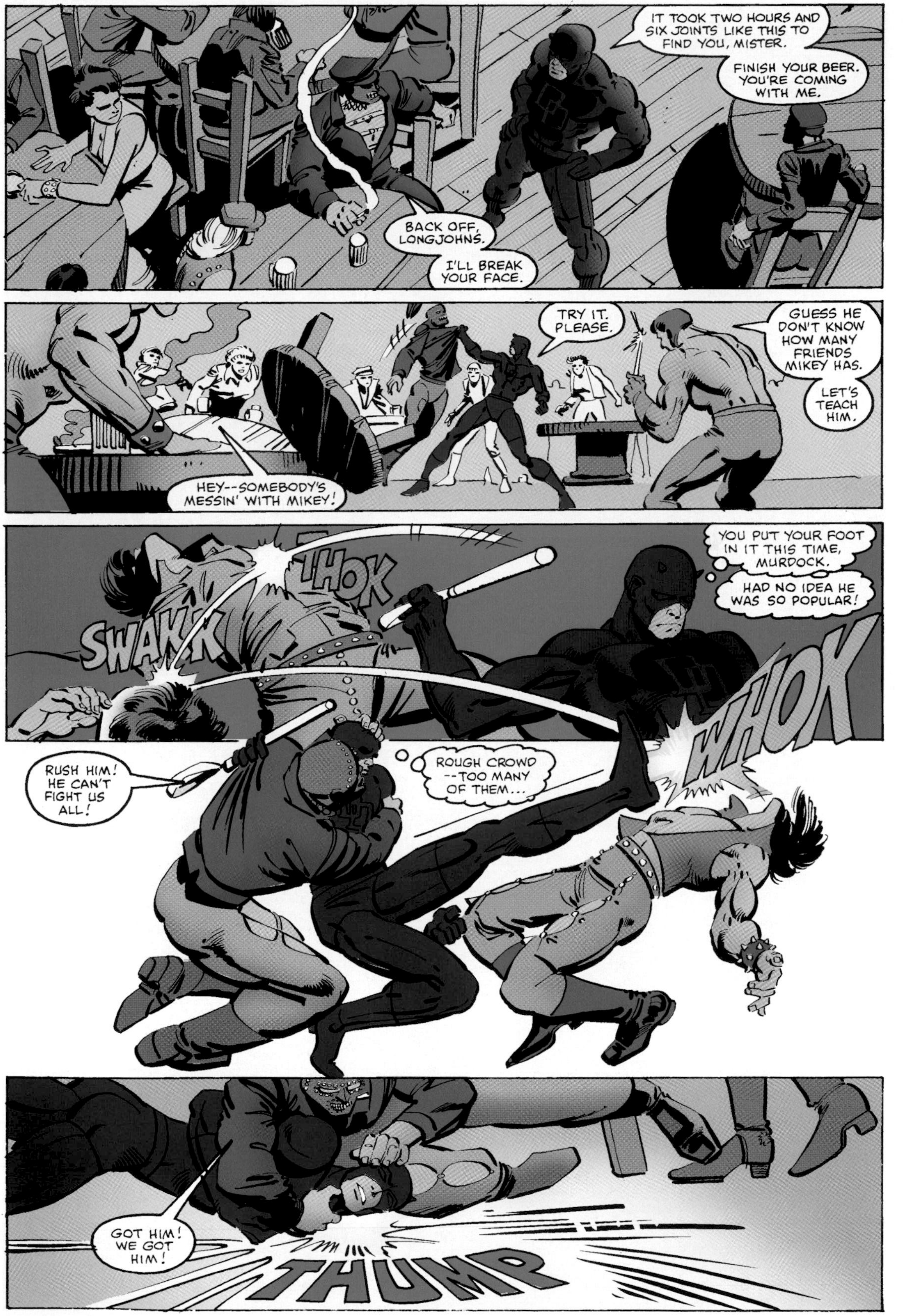
IT TOOK TWO HOURS AND SIX JOINTS LIKE THIS TO FIND YOU, MISTER.
FINISH YOUR BEER. YOU'RE COMING WITH ME.
BACK OFF, LONGJOHNS.
I'LL BREAK YOUR FACE.
TRY IT. PLEASE.
GUESS HE DON'T KNOW HOW MANY FRIENDS MIKEY HAS.
LET'S TEACH HIM.
HEY--SOMEBODY'S MESSIN' WITH MIKEY!
YOU PUT YOUR FOOT IN IT THIS TIME, MURDOCK.
HAD NO IDEA HE WAS SO POPULAR!
THOK
SWAKK
WHOK
RUSH HIM! HE CAN'T FIGHT US ALL!
ROUGH CROWD --TOO MANY OF THEM...
GOT HIM! WE GOT HIM!
THUMP

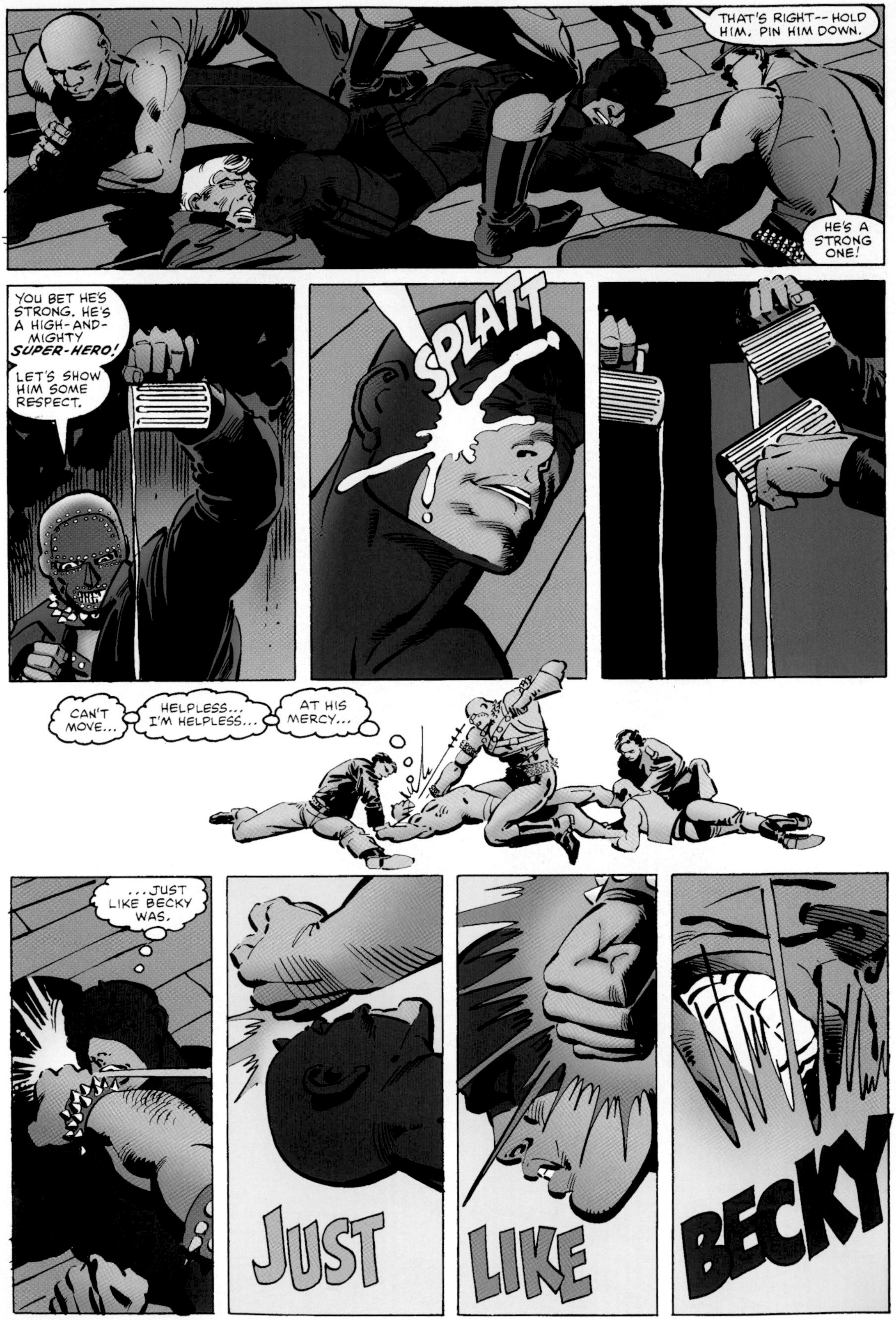
THAT'S RIGHT-- HOLD HIM. PIN HIM DOWN.
HE'S A STRONG ONE!
YOU BET HE'S STRONG. HE'S A HIGH-AND-MIGHTY SUPER-HERO!
LET'S SHOW HIM SOME RESPECT.
SPLATT
CAN'T MOVE...
HELPLESS... I'M HELPLESS...
AT HIS MERCY...
...JUST LIKE BECKY WAS.
JUST
LIKE
BECKY

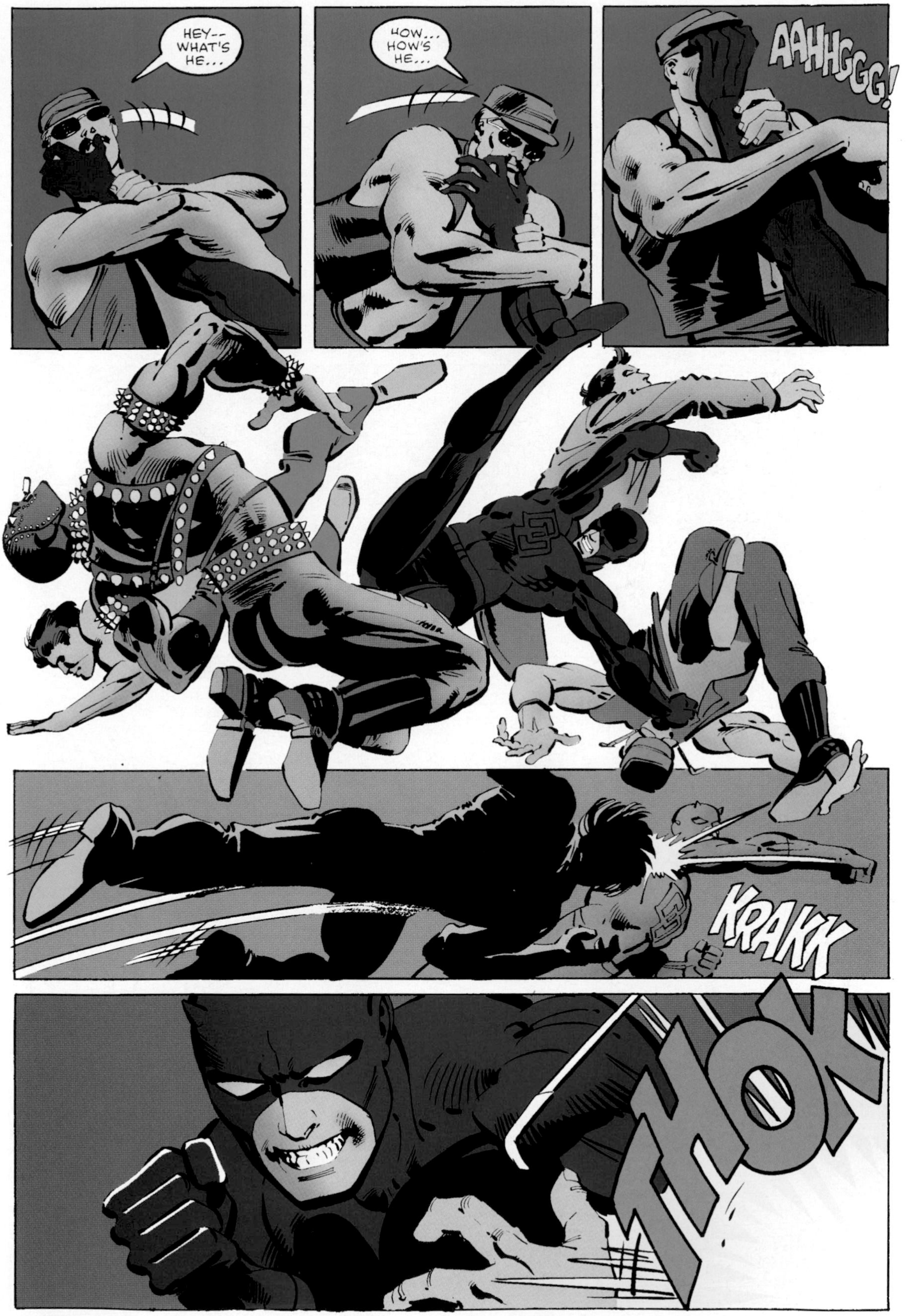
HEY-- WHAT'S HE...
HOW... HOW'S HE...
AAHHGGG!
KRAKK
THOK

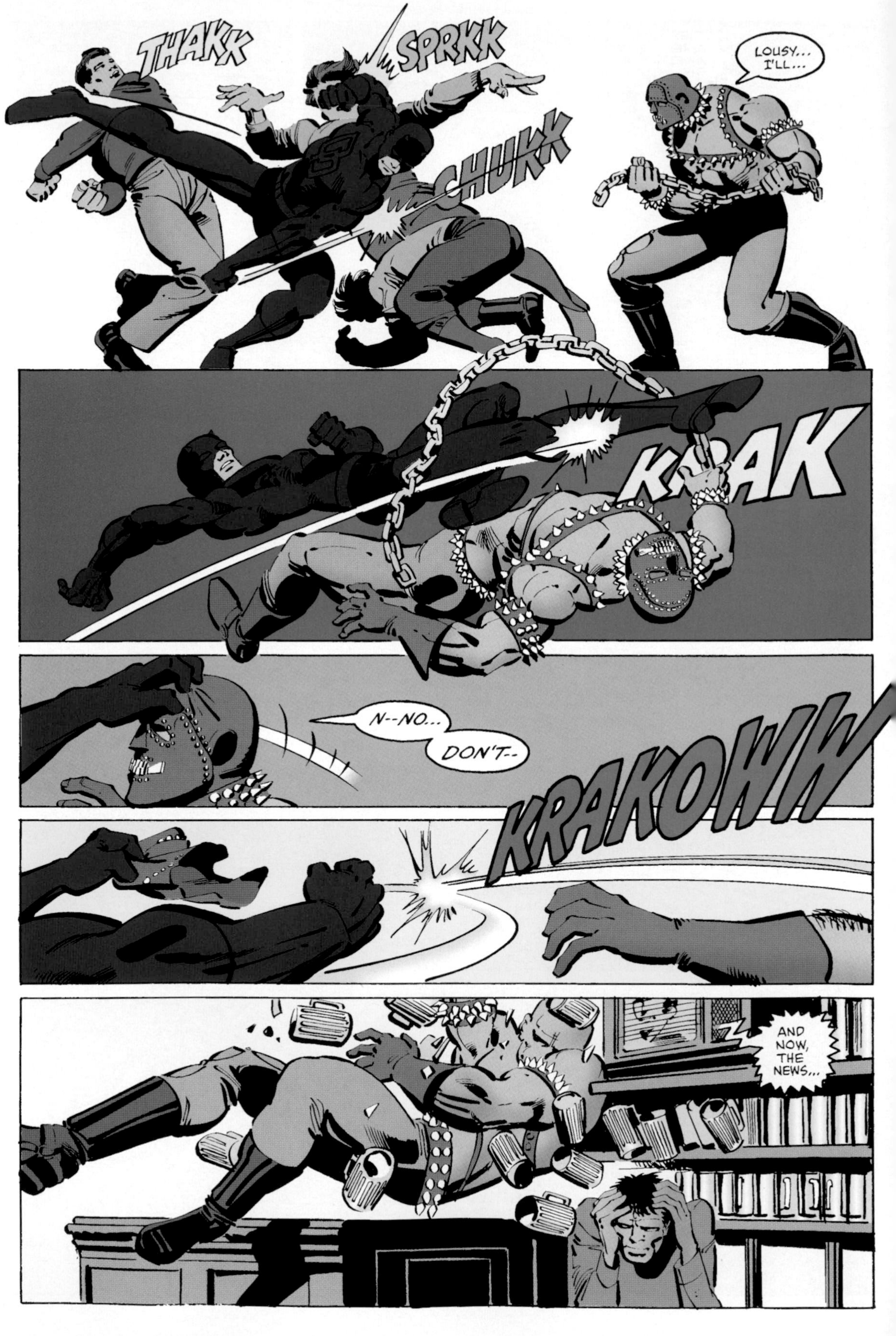
THAKK
SPRKK
CHUKK
LOUSY... I'LL...
KRAK
N--NO...
DON'T--
KRAKOWW
AND NOW, THE NEWS...

THINGS HAVE BEEN HAPPENING TONIGHT, HAVEN'T THEY, FLOYD?

THEY SURE HAVE, EARL.

MELVIN POTTER'S PAROLE OFFICER BRAVELY FENDED OFF AN ATTACK...

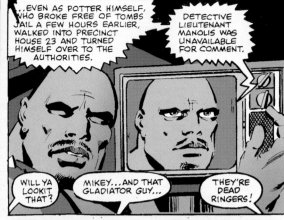

..EVEN AS POTTER HIMSELF, WHO BROKE FREE OF TOMBS JAIL A FEW HOURS EARLIER, WALKED INTO PRECINCT HOUSE 23 AND TURNED HIMSELF OVER TO THE AUTHORITIES.

DETECTIVE LIEUTENANT MANOLIS WAS UNAVAILABLE FOR COMMENT.

WILL YA LOOKIT THAT?

MIKEY...AND THAT GLADIATOR GUY...

THEY'RE DEAD RINGERS!

THE NEXT DAY...

DAILY BUGLE FINAL

DEAD RINGERS!

Melvin Potter cleared on assault rap.

Lookalike Michael Reese arrested.

Reporter victims will live.

BZZZT! BZZZT!

DAILY BUGLE DEAD RINGERS

MATT! I--

MATT, YOUR FACE...

BECKY, SOMETHING HAPPENED LAST NIGHT THAT MADE ME UNDERSTAND AT LEAST A PART OF WHAT YOU WENT THROUGH, THREE YEARS AGO.

AND I WISH I COULD SAY THAT IT'S ALL RIGHT--THAT EVERYTHING IS ALL RIGHT, NOW.

BUT I CAN'T.

THE MAN WHO BATTERED YOU HAS BEEN ARRESTED. BUT THERE ISN'T ENOUGH EVIDENCE TO CONVICT HIM...WITHOUT YOUR TESTIMONY.

YOU MAY BE THE ONLY VICTIM WHO HAS SEEN HIS FACE, BECKY.

IF YOU DON'T CALL THE POLICE --AND REPORT WHAT HAPPENED TO YOU -- HE'LL GO FREE.

HE'LL GO FREE-- AND YOU'LL SPEND THE REST OF YOUR LIFE IMPRISONED BY THAT ONE HIDEOUS MEMORY.

BECKY, HE ROBBED YOU OF THE USE OF YOUR LEGS. NOTHING CAN CHANGE THAT.

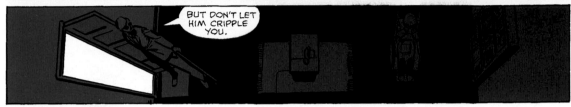

BUT DON'T LET HIM CRIPPLE YOU.

KLIK
whrrr
KLIK
whrrr
KLIK
whrrr

GET ME THE POLICE.

NEXT ISSUE: THE RETURN OF ELEKTRA

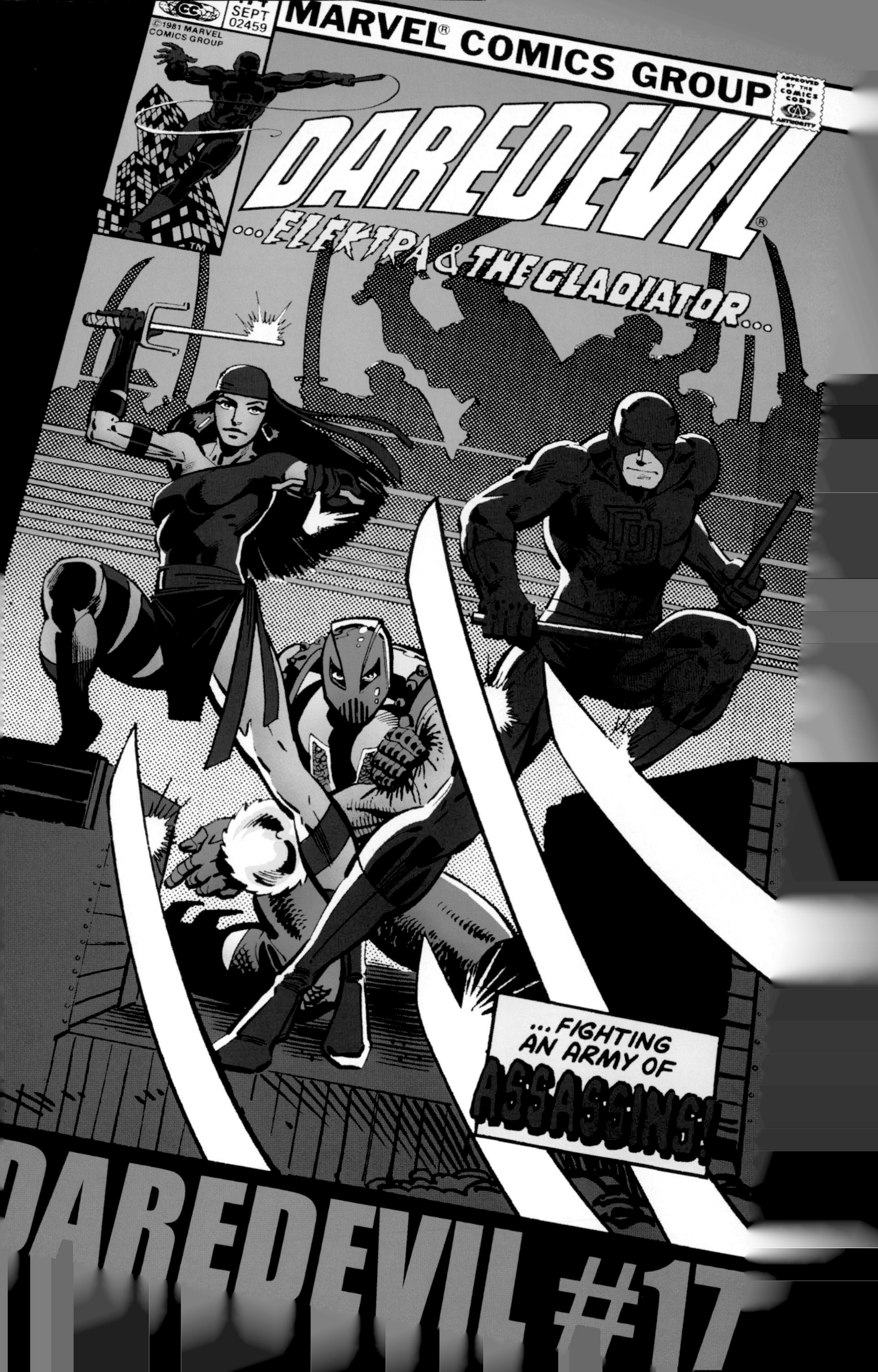

SEPT
02459
©1981 MARVEL COMICS GROUP
MARVEL® COMICS GROUP
APPROVED BY THE COMICS CODE AUTHORITY
DAREDEVIL®
...ELEKTRA & THE GLADIATOR...
...FIGHTING AN ARMY OF ASSASSINS!
DAREDEVIL #17

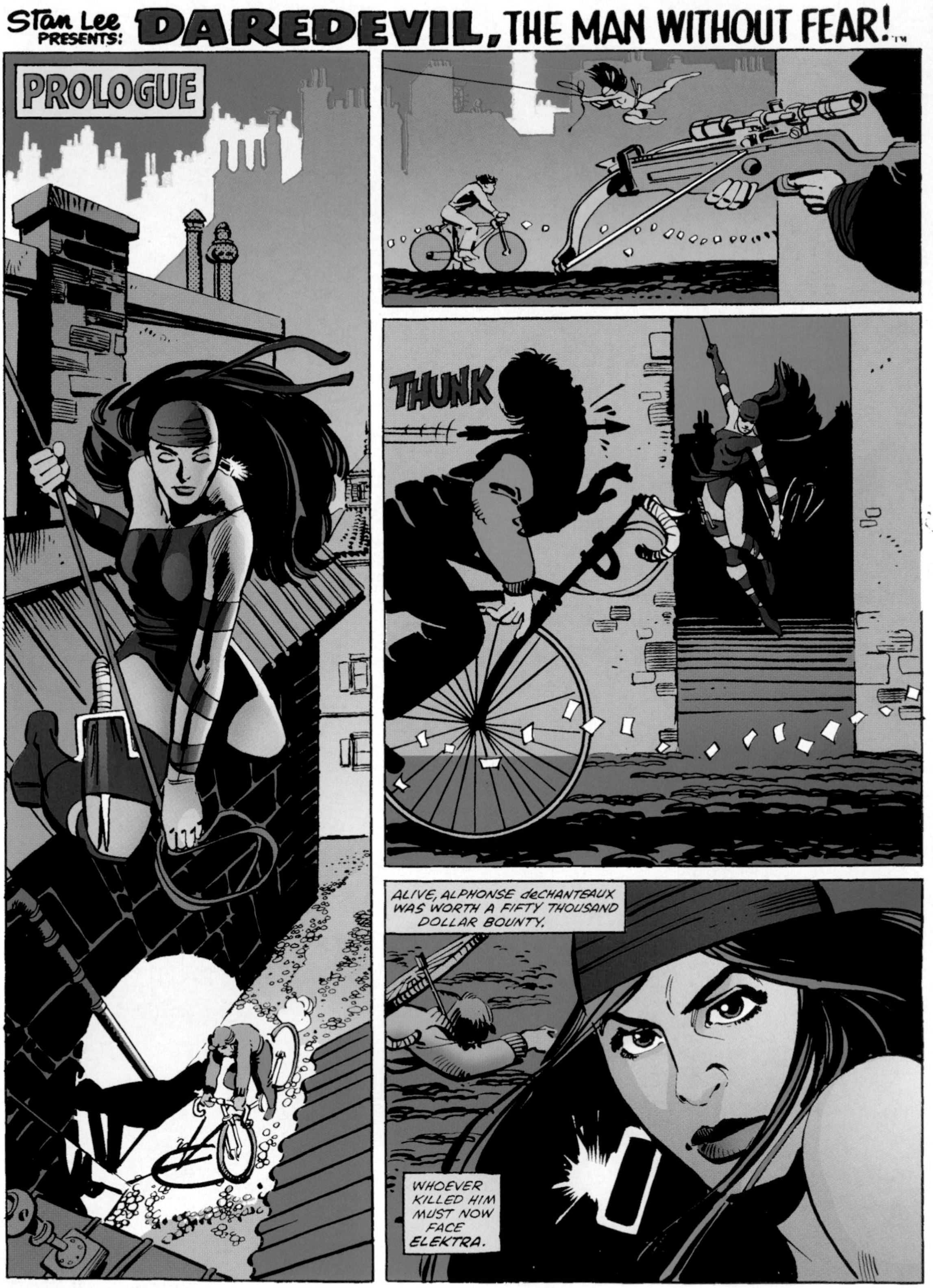
Stan Lee PRESENTS: DAREDEVIL, THE MAN WITHOUT FEAR!™
PROLOGUE
THUNK
ALIVE, ALPHONSE deCHANTEAUX WAS WORTH A FIFTY THOUSAND DOLLAR BOUNTY.
WHOEVER KILLED HIM MUST NOW FACE ELEKTRA.

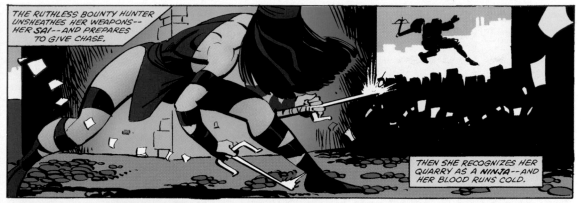

THE RUTHLESS BOUNTY HUNTER UNSHEATHES HER WEAPONS-- HER *SAI*--AND PREPARES TO GIVE CHASE.

THEN SHE RECOGNIZES HER QUARRY AS A *NINJA*--AND HER BLOOD RUNS COLD.

A CLOSER LOOK CON- FIRMS HER SUSPICION. HE IS ONE OF *THE HAND.*

THE HAND...THE SAME ORDER OF MASTER ASSASSINS THAT TAUGHT HER THE MANY WAYS OF *MURDER*--

--BEFORE SHE BROKE TRAINING, TO OPERATE ON HER OWN.

THEY ARE PLEDGED TO HER DEATH.

BUT WHAT ARE THEY DOING HERE, IN PARIS, THOUSANDS OF MILES FROM THEIR TERRITORY?

SHE SHOULD NOT WONDER. SHE SHOULD TURN AND RUN. SHE SHOULD FLEE THIS CITY, AND NEVER RETURN.

YET, SHE FOLLOWS...

...AND LISTENS...

deCHANTEAUX IS DEAD.

YOU HAVE DONE WELL, *GENIN.*

RECEIVE NOW THE IMAGE OF OUR LATEST PREY.

HE IS AN AMERICAN.

A LAWYER...

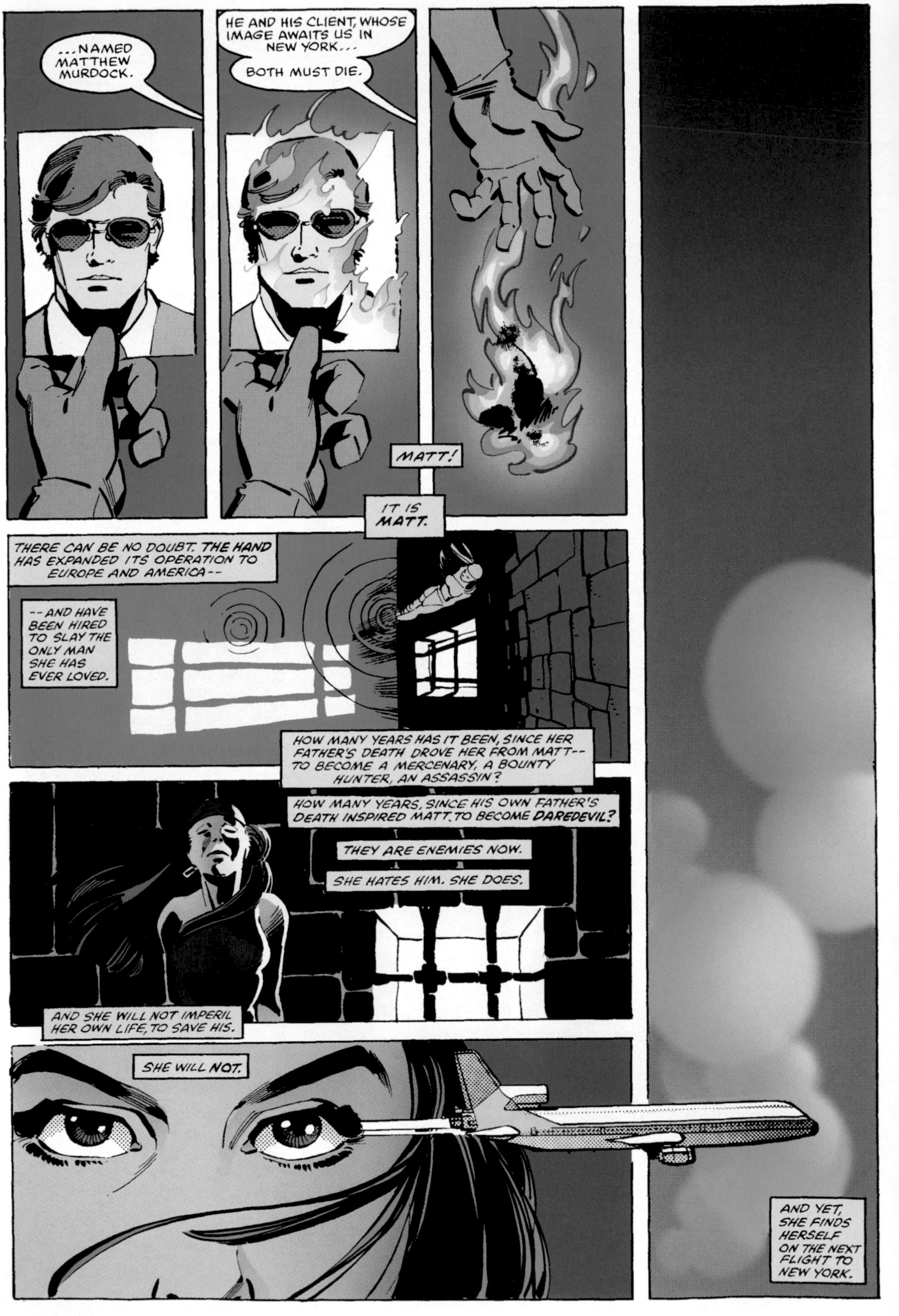

...NAMED MATTHEW MURDOCK.
HE AND HIS CLIENT, WHOSE IMAGE AWAITS US IN NEW YORK...
BOTH MUST DIE.
MATT!
IT IS MATT.
THERE CAN BE NO DOUBT. THE HAND HAS EXPANDED ITS OPERATION TO EUROPE AND AMERICA--
--AND HAVE BEEN HIRED TO SLAY THE ONLY MAN SHE HAS EVER LOVED.
HOW MANY YEARS HAS IT BEEN, SINCE HER FATHER'S DEATH DROVE HER FROM MATT-- TO BECOME A MERCENARY, A BOUNTY HUNTER, AN ASSASSIN?
HOW MANY YEARS, SINCE HIS OWN FATHER'S DEATH INSPIRED MATT TO BECOME DAREDEVIL?
THEY ARE ENEMIES NOW.
SHE HATES HIM. SHE DOES.
AND SHE WILL NOT IMPERIL HER OWN LIFE, TO SAVE HIS.
SHE WILL NOT.
AND YET, SHE FINDS HERSELF ON THE NEXT FLIGHT TO NEW YORK.

THE ASSASSINATION OF MATT MURDOCK

MILLER
STORY & ART
JANSON
FINISHED ART
WEIN AND JANSON
COLORS
ROSEN
LETTERS
O'NEIL
EDITOR
SHOOTER
ED.-IN-CHIEF

MELVIN POTTER IS *INNOCENT!*

HE HAS BEEN CHARGED WITH CRIMES COMMITTED BY THE *GLADIATOR*--

--BUT THAT MONSTER NO LONGER DWELLS IN MELVIN'S MIND.

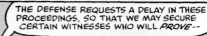

THE DEFENSE REQUESTS A DELAY IN THESE PROCEEDINGS, SO THAT WE MAY SECURE CERTAIN WITNESSES WHO WILL *PROVE*--

YOUR HONOR, THIS IS THE THIRD SUCH DELAY THAT MR. MURDOCK HAS REQUESTED.

SURELY, HE HAS EXHAUSTED THE PATIENCE OF THIS COURT.

HEY-- WHAT'S WITH MURDOCK? THE PROSECUTION IS EATING HIM ALIVE!

YOU DON'T SEE HIS PARTNER UP THERE, DO YOU?

WORD IS THEY'RE KAPUT.

YER KIDDIN' ME, BEN. *NELSON AND MURDOCK*-- THE HOTTEST LEGAL TEAM IN THE COUNTRY-- ON THE OUTS?

THAT'S WHAT I HEAR.

SHHHH!

THE PROSECUTION IS READY TO PROCEED, YOUR HONOR.

SHALL WE?

INDEED WE SHALL.

THUMP

COURT WILL CONVENE AT TEN O'CLOCK TOMORROW MORNING.

MELVIN-- DON'T WORRY. WE'LL WIN THIS CASE.

YOU JUST HAVE TO TRUST ME.

THAT'S WHAT YOU KEEP SAYIN', MURDOCK.

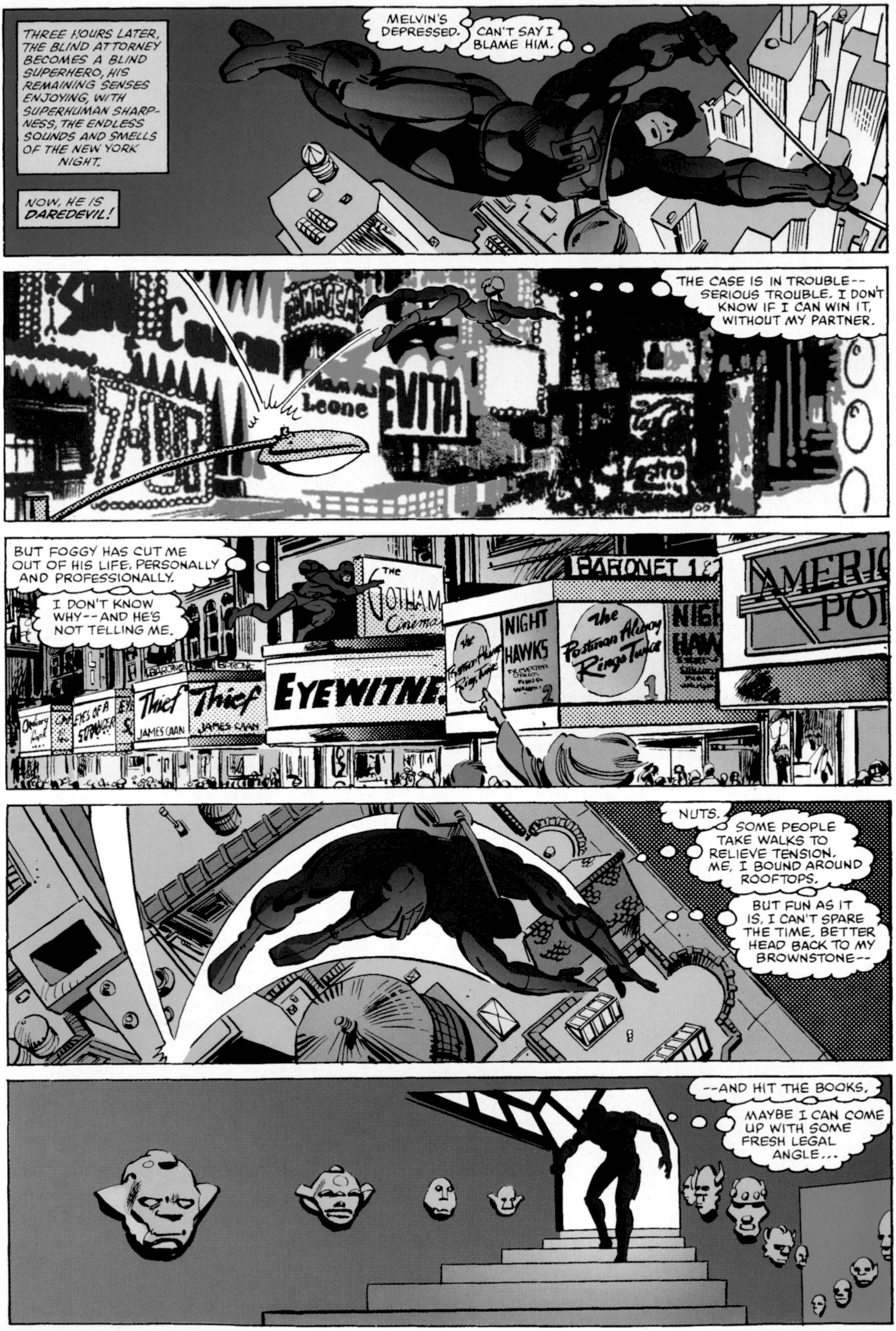
THREE HOURS LATER, THE BLIND ATTORNEY BECOMES A BLIND SUPERHERO, HIS REMAINING SENSES ENJOYING, WITH SUPERHUMAN SHARPNESS, THE ENDLESS SOUNDS AND SMELLS OF THE NEW YORK NIGHT.
NOW, HE IS DAREDEVIL!
MELVIN'S DEPRESSED.
CAN'T SAY I BLAME HIM.
THE CASE IS IN TROUBLE-- SERIOUS TROUBLE. I DON'T KNOW IF I CAN WIN IT, WITHOUT MY PARTNER.
Leone
EVITA
BUT FOGGY HAS CUT ME OUT OF HIS LIFE, PERSONALLY AND PROFESSIONALLY.
I DON'T KNOW WHY--AND HE'S NOT TELLING ME.
BARONET
THE GOTHAM Cinema
NIGHT HAWKS
the Postman Always Rings Twice
EYEWITNE
Thief
JAMES CAAN
EYES OF A STRANGER
NUTS.
SOME PEOPLE TAKE WALKS TO RELIEVE TENSION. ME, I BOUND AROUND ROOFTOPS.
BUT FUN AS IT IS, I CAN'T SPARE THE TIME. BETTER HEAD BACK TO MY BROWNSTONE--
--AND HIT THE BOOKS.
MAYBE I CAN COME UP WITH SOME FRESH LEGAL ANGLE...

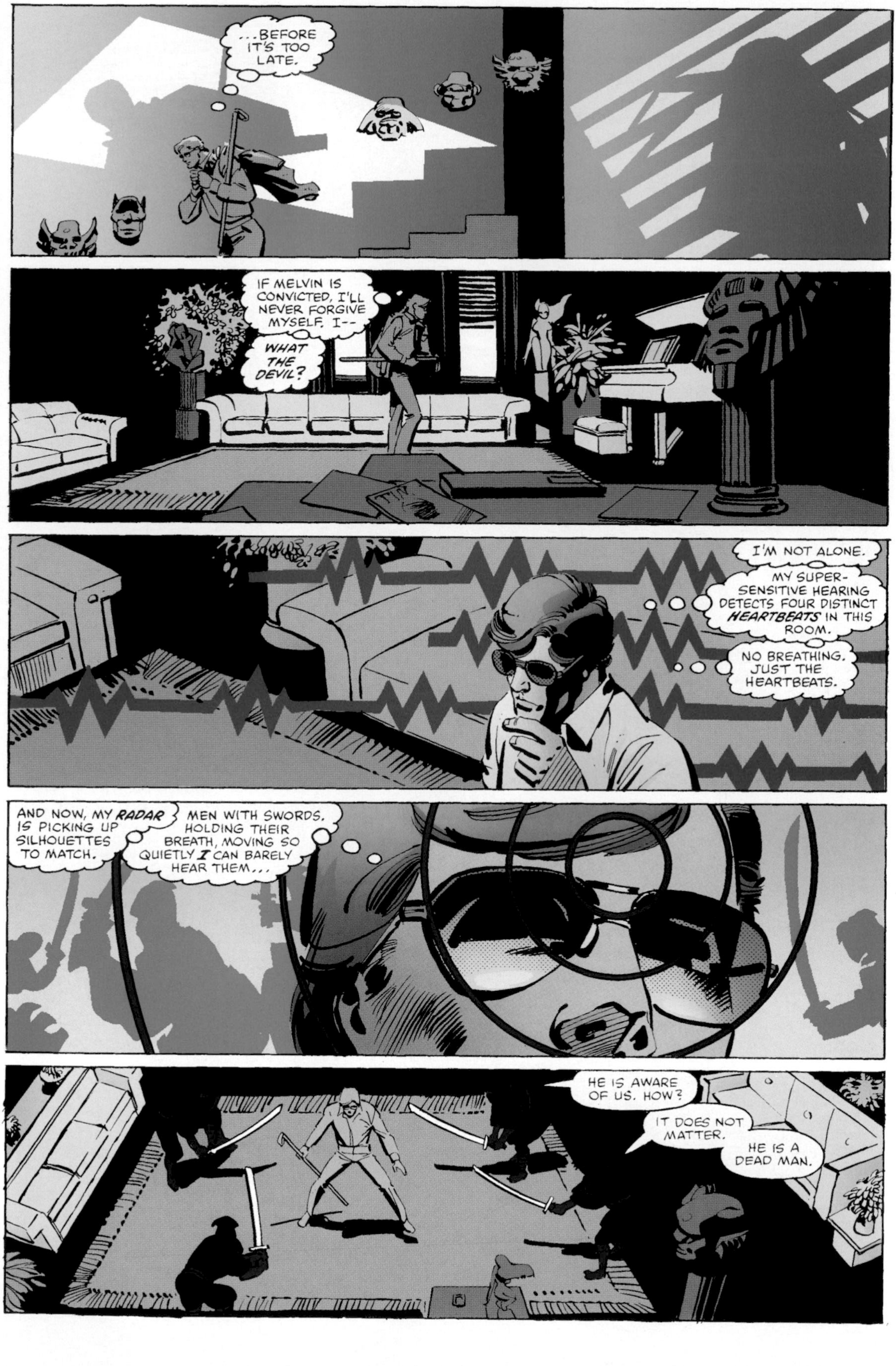
...BEFORE IT'S TOO LATE.
IF MELVIN IS CONVICTED, I'LL NEVER FORGIVE MYSELF. I--
WHAT THE DEVIL?
I'M NOT ALONE.
MY SUPER-SENSITIVE HEARING DETECTS FOUR DISTINCT HEARTBEATS IN THIS ROOM.
NO BREATHING. JUST THE HEARTBEATS.
AND NOW, MY RADAR IS PICKING UP SILHOUETTES TO MATCH.
MEN WITH SWORDS. HOLDING THEIR BREATH, MOVING SO QUIETLY I CAN BARELY HEAR THEM...
HE IS AWARE OF US. HOW?
IT DOES NOT MATTER.
HE IS A DEAD MAN.

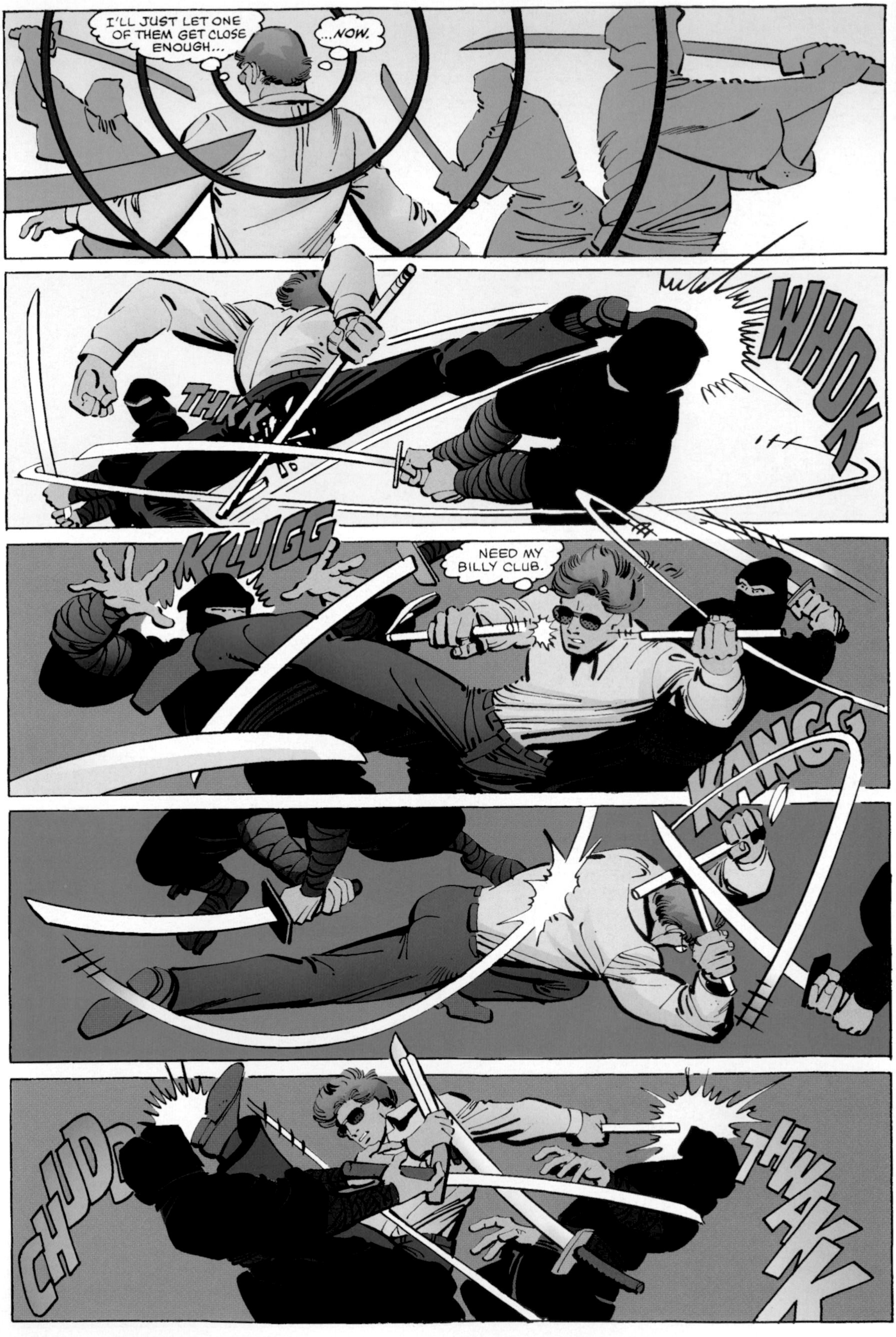
I'LL JUST LET ONE OF THEM GET CLOSE ENOUGH...
...NOW.
WHOK
THKK
KLUGG
NEED MY BILLY CLUB.
KANGG
CHUD
THWAKK

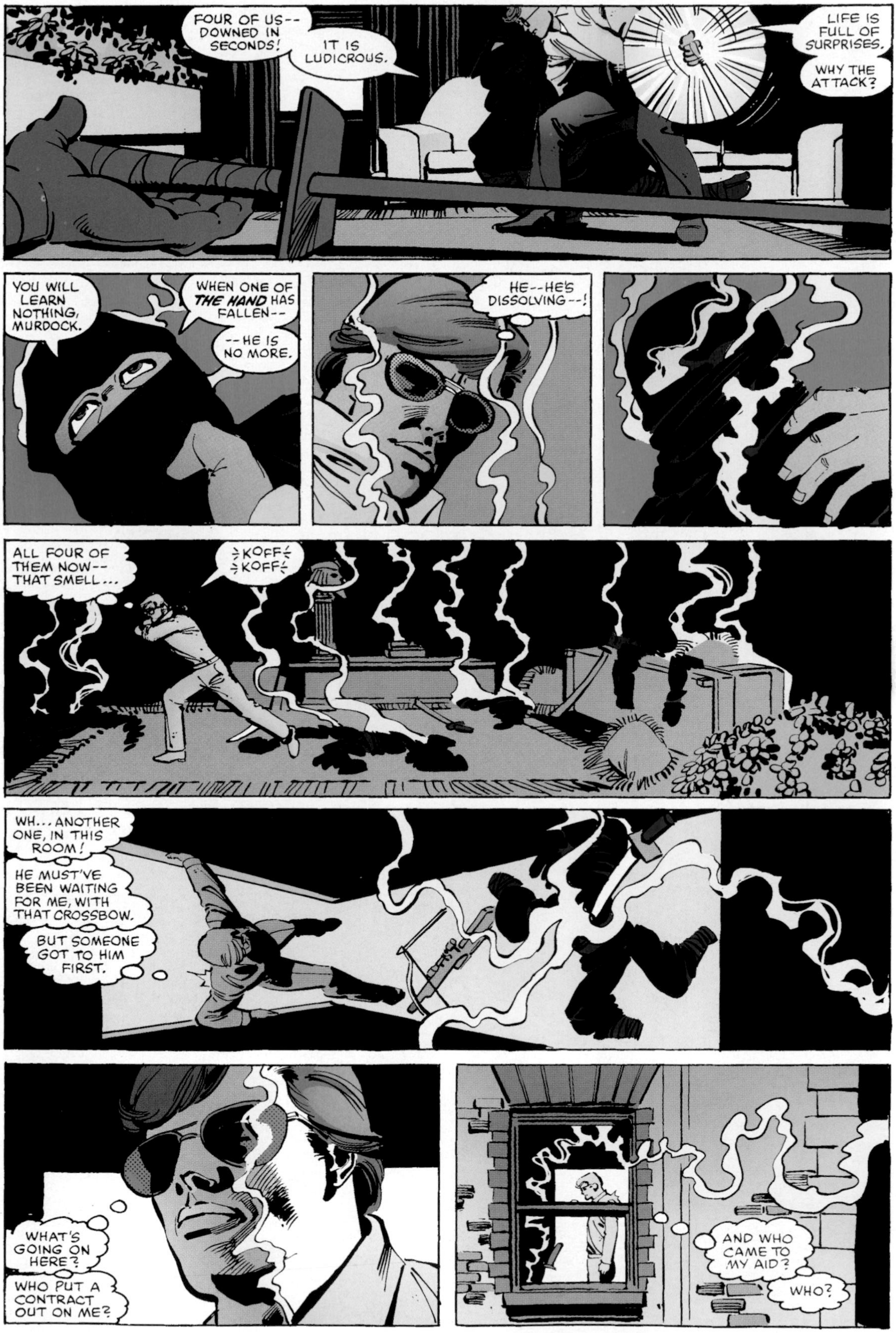
FOUR OF US-- DOWNED IN SECONDS!
IT IS LUDICROUS.
LIFE IS FULL OF SURPRISES.
WHY THE ATTACK?
YOU WILL LEARN NOTHING, MURDOCK.
WHEN ONE OF THE HAND HAS FALLEN--
--HE IS NO MORE.
HE--HE'S DISSOLVING--!
ALL FOUR OF THEM NOW-- THAT SMELL...
KOFF KOFF
WH... ANOTHER ONE, IN THIS ROOM!
HE MUST'VE BEEN WAITING FOR ME, WITH THAT CROSSBOW.
BUT SOMEONE GOT TO HIM FIRST.
WHAT'S GOING ON HERE?
WHO PUT A CONTRACT OUT ON ME?
AND WHO CAME TO MY AID?
WHO?

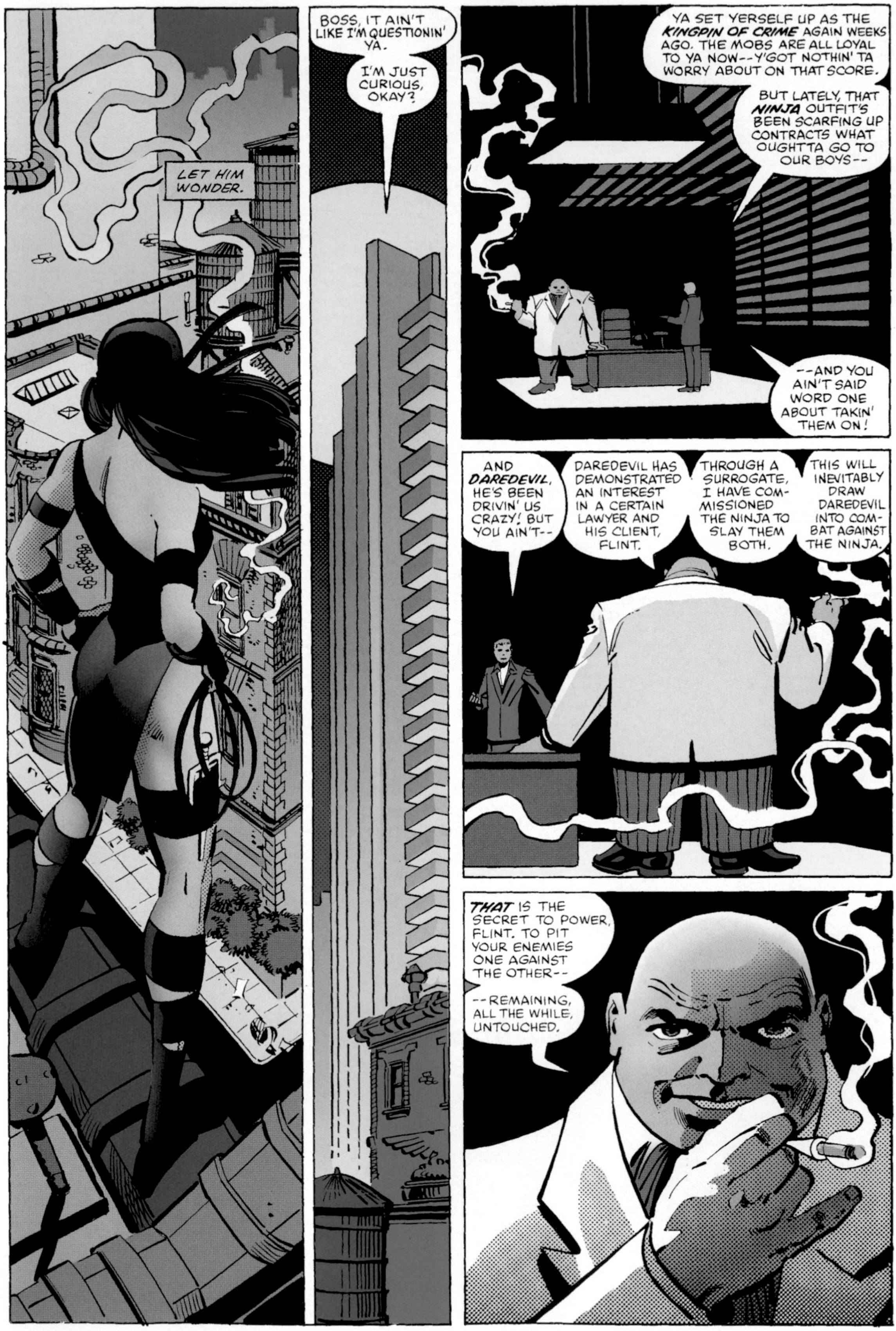
LET HIM WONDER.
BOSS, IT AIN'T LIKE I'M QUESTIONIN' YA.
I'M JUST CURIOUS, OKAY?
YA SET YERSELF UP AS THE KINGPIN OF CRIME AGAIN WEEKS AGO. THE MOBS ARE ALL LOYAL TO YA NOW--Y'GOT NOTHIN' TA WORRY ABOUT ON THAT SCORE.
BUT LATELY, THAT NINJA OUTFIT'S BEEN SCARFING UP CONTRACTS WHAT OUGHTTA GO TO OUR BOYS--
--AND YOU AIN'T SAID WORD ONE ABOUT TAKIN' THEM ON!
AND DAREDEVIL, HE'S BEEN DRIVIN' US CRAZY! BUT YOU AIN'T--
DAREDEVIL HAS DEMONSTRATED AN INTEREST IN A CERTAIN LAWYER AND HIS CLIENT, FLINT.
THROUGH A SURROGATE, I HAVE COMMISSIONED THE NINJA TO SLAY THEM BOTH.
THIS WILL INEVITABLY DRAW DAREDEVIL INTO COMBAT AGAINST THE NINJA.
THAT IS THE SECRET TO POWER, FLINT. TO PIT YOUR ENEMIES ONE AGAINST THE OTHER--
--REMAINING, ALL THE WHILE, UNTOUCHED.

LATER...

IT IS HIM, MURDOCK.

SHALL HE BE ALONE, IN HIS OFFICE?

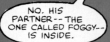

NO. HIS PARTNER-- THE ONE CALLED FOGGY-- IS INSIDE.

WE SHALL KILL THEM BOTH. PREPARE THE EXPLOSIVE.

I NEVER THOUGHT IT WOULD COME TO THIS. BUT ALL THAT'S LEFT NOW-- IS TO EMPTY MY DESK.

MATT'S ON HIS OWN NOW. HE WON'T HAVE ME AS A PARTNER ANYMORE.

BIG LOSS.

FOGGY? IS THAT YOU?

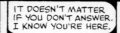

IT DOESN'T MATTER IF YOU DON'T ANSWER. I KNOW YOU'RE HERE.

AND I KNOW THAT SOMETHING IS TORTURING YOU--WRECKING YOUR MARRIAGE, OUR PARTNERSHIP, OUR FRIENDSHIP.

FOGGY--I CAN'T LET IT ALL GO WITHOUT KNOWING WHY.

OKAY, MATT.

I'LL TELL YOU.

SSSSSSSSSSSSSSSSSSSSSSS

WHAT THE...

YOU!

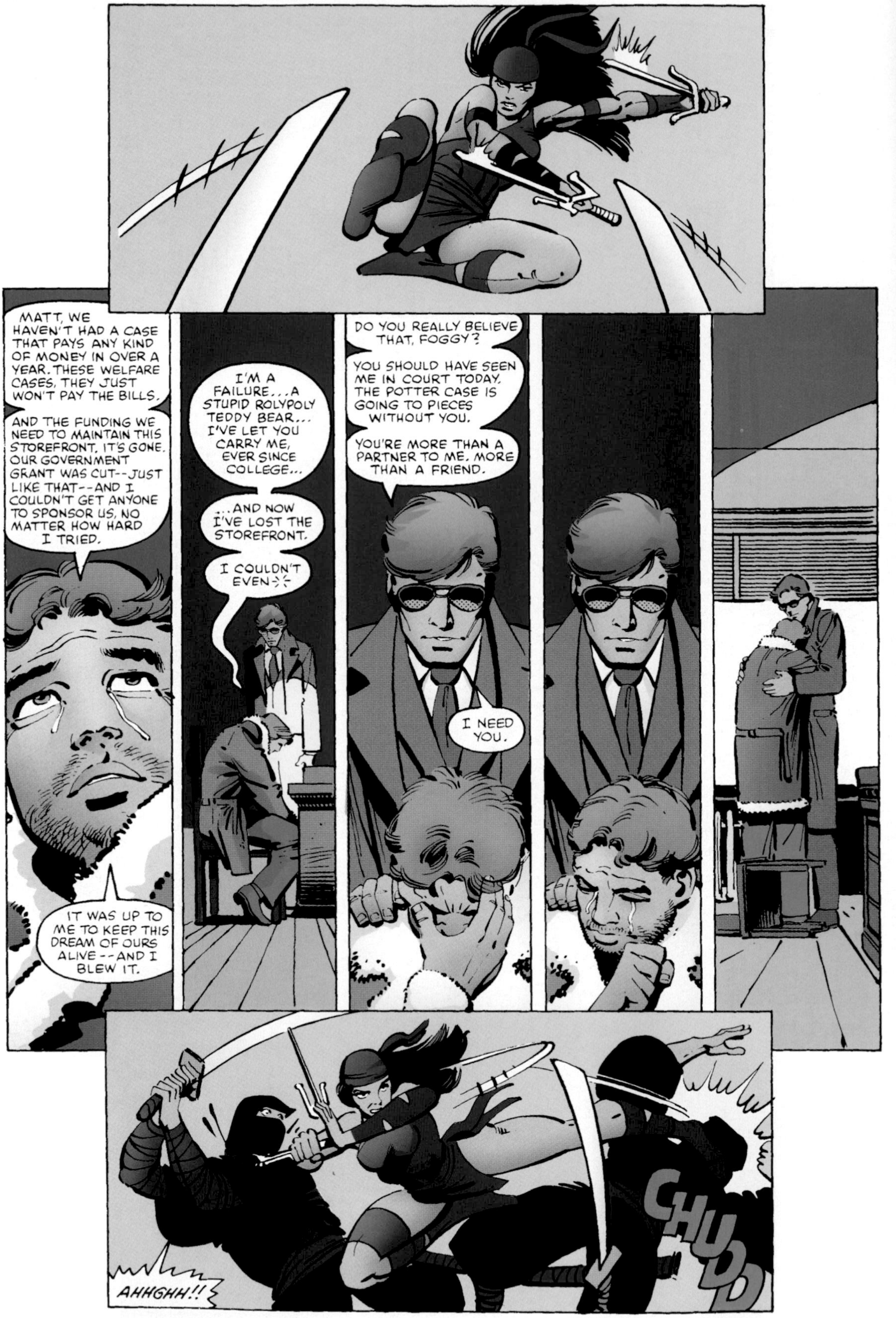

MATT, WE HAVEN'T HAD A CASE THAT PAYS ANY KIND OF MONEY IN OVER A YEAR. THESE WELFARE CASES, THEY JUST WON'T PAY THE BILLS.
AND THE FUNDING WE NEED TO MAINTAIN THIS STOREFRONT, IT'S GONE. OUR GOVERNMENT GRANT WAS CUT--JUST LIKE THAT--AND I COULDN'T GET ANYONE TO SPONSOR US, NO MATTER HOW HARD I TRIED.
IT WAS UP TO ME TO KEEP THIS DREAM OF OURS ALIVE--AND I BLEW IT.
I'M A FAILURE...A STUPID ROLYPOLY TEDDY BEAR... I'VE LET YOU CARRY ME, EVER SINCE COLLEGE...
...AND NOW I'VE LOST THE STOREFRONT.
I COULDN'T EVEN
DO YOU REALLY BELIEVE THAT, FOGGY?
YOU SHOULD HAVE SEEN ME IN COURT TODAY. THE POTTER CASE IS GOING TO PIECES WITHOUT YOU.
YOU'RE MORE THAN A PARTNER TO ME. MORE THAN A FRIEND.
I NEED YOU.
AHHGHH!!
CHUDD

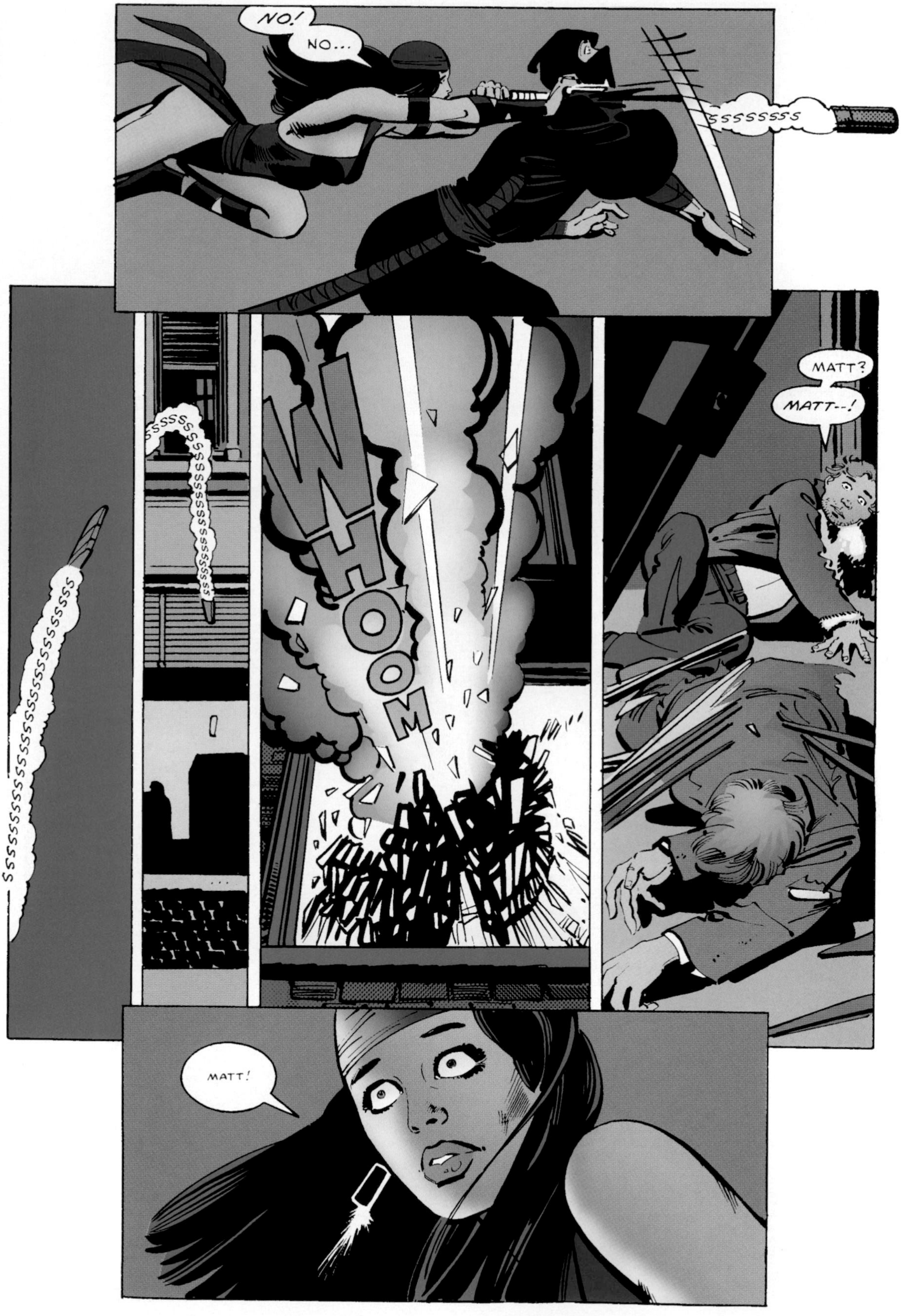
NO!
NO...
SSSSSSSS
WHOOOM
MATT?
MATT--!
MATT!

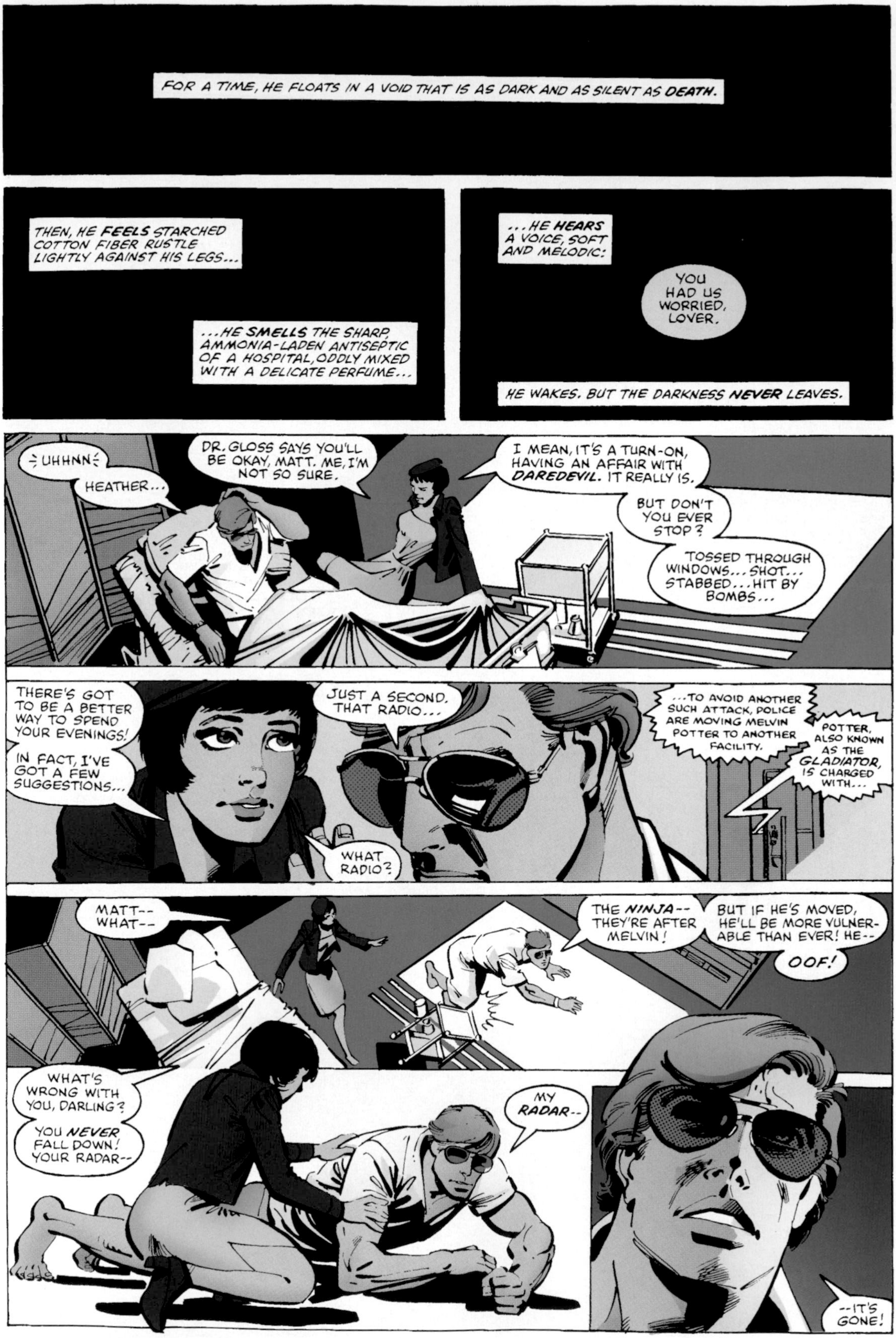
FOR A TIME, HE FLOATS IN A VOID THAT IS AS DARK AND AS SILENT AS DEATH.
THEN, HE FEELS STARCHED COTTON FIBER RUSTLE LIGHTLY AGAINST HIS LEGS...
...HE SMELLS THE SHARP, AMMONIA-LADEN ANTISEPTIC OF A HOSPITAL, ODDLY MIXED WITH A DELICATE PERFUME...
...HE HEARS A VOICE, SOFT AND MELODIC:
YOU HAD US WORRIED, LOVER.
HE WAKES. BUT THE DARKNESS NEVER LEAVES.
UHHNN
HEATHER...
DR. GLOSS SAYS YOU'LL BE OKAY, MATT. ME, I'M NOT SO SURE.
I MEAN, IT'S A TURN-ON, HAVING AN AFFAIR WITH DAREDEVIL. IT REALLY IS.
BUT DON'T YOU EVER STOP?
TOSSED THROUGH WINDOWS... SHOT... STABBED... HIT BY BOMBS...
THERE'S GOT TO BE A BETTER WAY TO SPEND YOUR EVENINGS!
IN FACT, I'VE GOT A FEW SUGGESTIONS...
JUST A SECOND. THAT RADIO...
WHAT RADIO?
...TO AVOID ANOTHER SUCH ATTACK, POLICE ARE MOVING MELVIN POTTER TO ANOTHER FACILITY.
POTTER, ALSO KNOWN AS THE GLADIATOR, IS CHARGED WITH...
MATT-- WHAT--
THE NINJA-- THEY'RE AFTER MELVIN!
BUT IF HE'S MOVED, HE'LL BE MORE VULNERABLE THAN EVER! HE--
OOF!
WHAT'S WRONG WITH YOU, DARLING?
YOU NEVER FALL DOWN! YOUR RADAR--
MY RADAR--
--IT'S GONE!

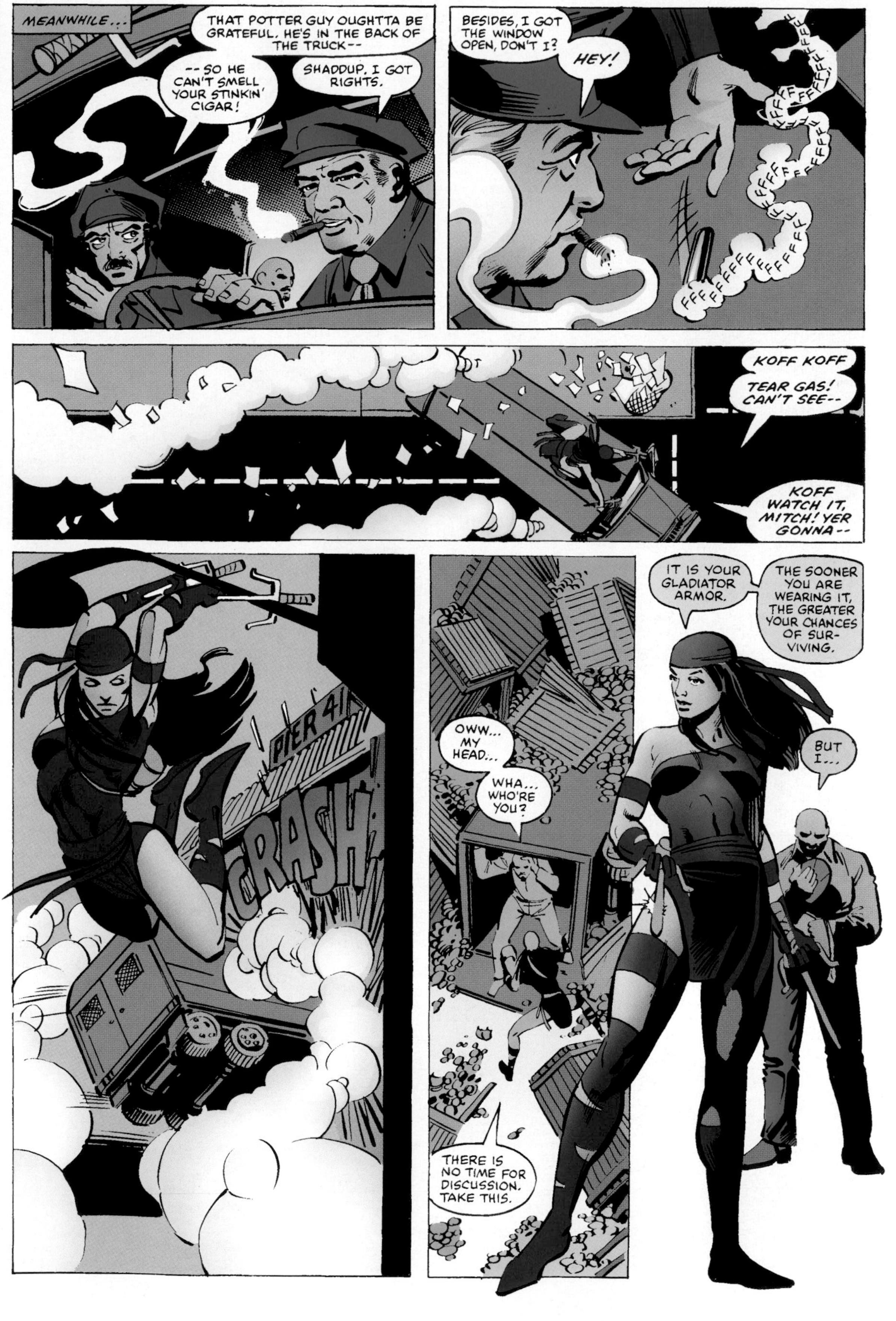

MEANWHILE...
THAT POTTER GUY OUGHTTA BE GRATEFUL. HE'S IN THE BACK OF THE TRUCK--
--SO HE CAN'T SMELL YOUR STINKIN' CIGAR!
SHADDUP. I GOT RIGHTS.
BESIDES, I GOT THE WINDOW OPEN, DON'T I?
HEY!
KOFF KOFF
TEAR GAS! CAN'T SEE--
KOFF WATCH IT, MITCH! YER GONNA--
PIER 41
CRASH
OWW... MY HEAD...
WHA... WHO'RE YOU?
THERE IS NO TIME FOR DISCUSSION. TAKE THIS.
IT IS YOUR GLADIATOR ARMOR.
THE SOONER YOU ARE WEARING IT, THE GREATER YOUR CHANCES OF SURVIVING.
BUT I...

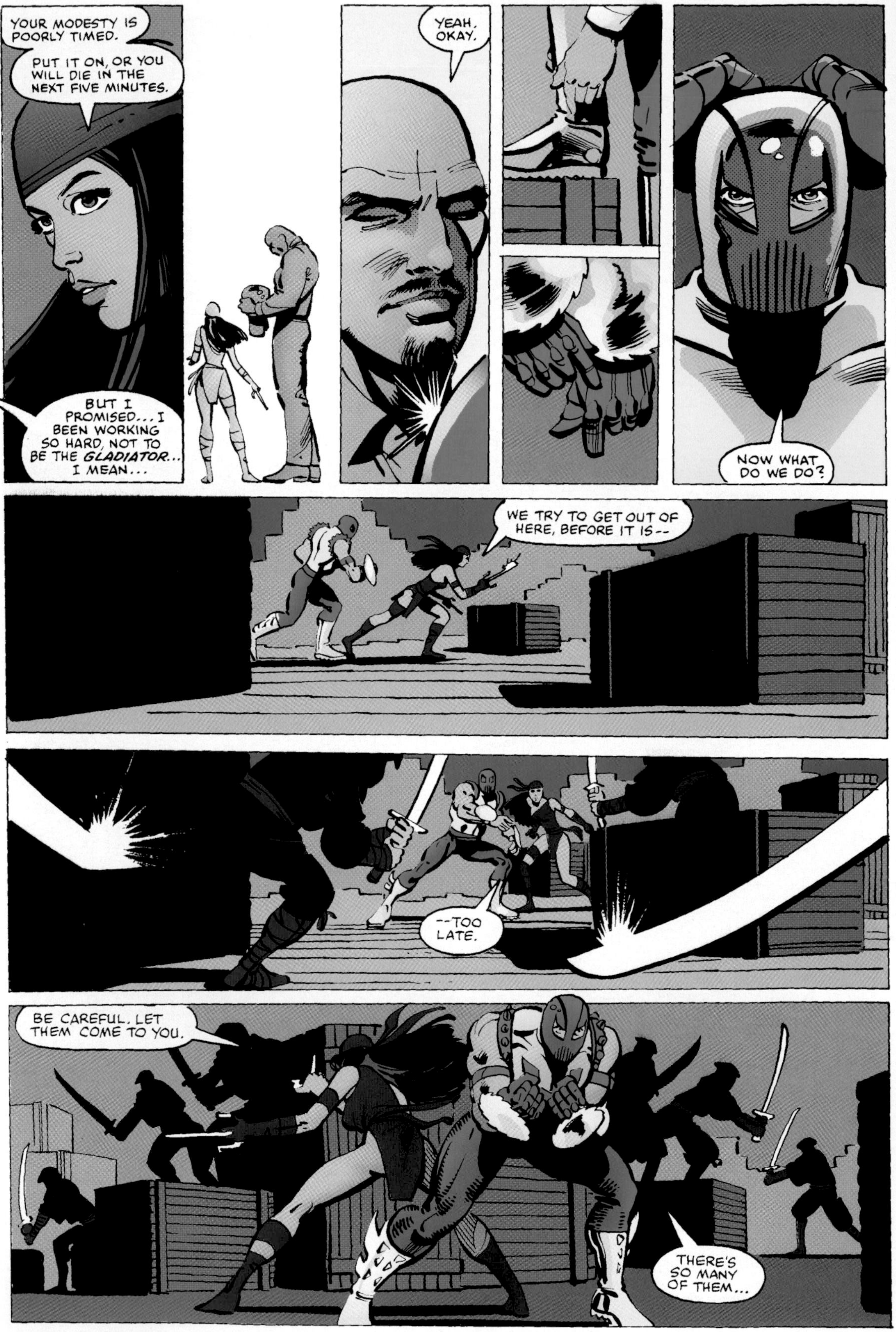
YOUR MODESTY IS POORLY TIMED.
PUT IT ON, OR YOU WILL DIE IN THE NEXT FIVE MINUTES.
BUT I PROMISED... I BEEN WORKING SO HARD, NOT TO BE THE GLADIATOR... I MEAN...
YEAH, OKAY.
NOW WHAT DO WE DO?
WE TRY TO GET OUT OF HERE, BEFORE IT IS--
--TOO LATE.
BE CAREFUL. LET THEM COME TO YOU.
THERE'S SO MANY OF THEM...

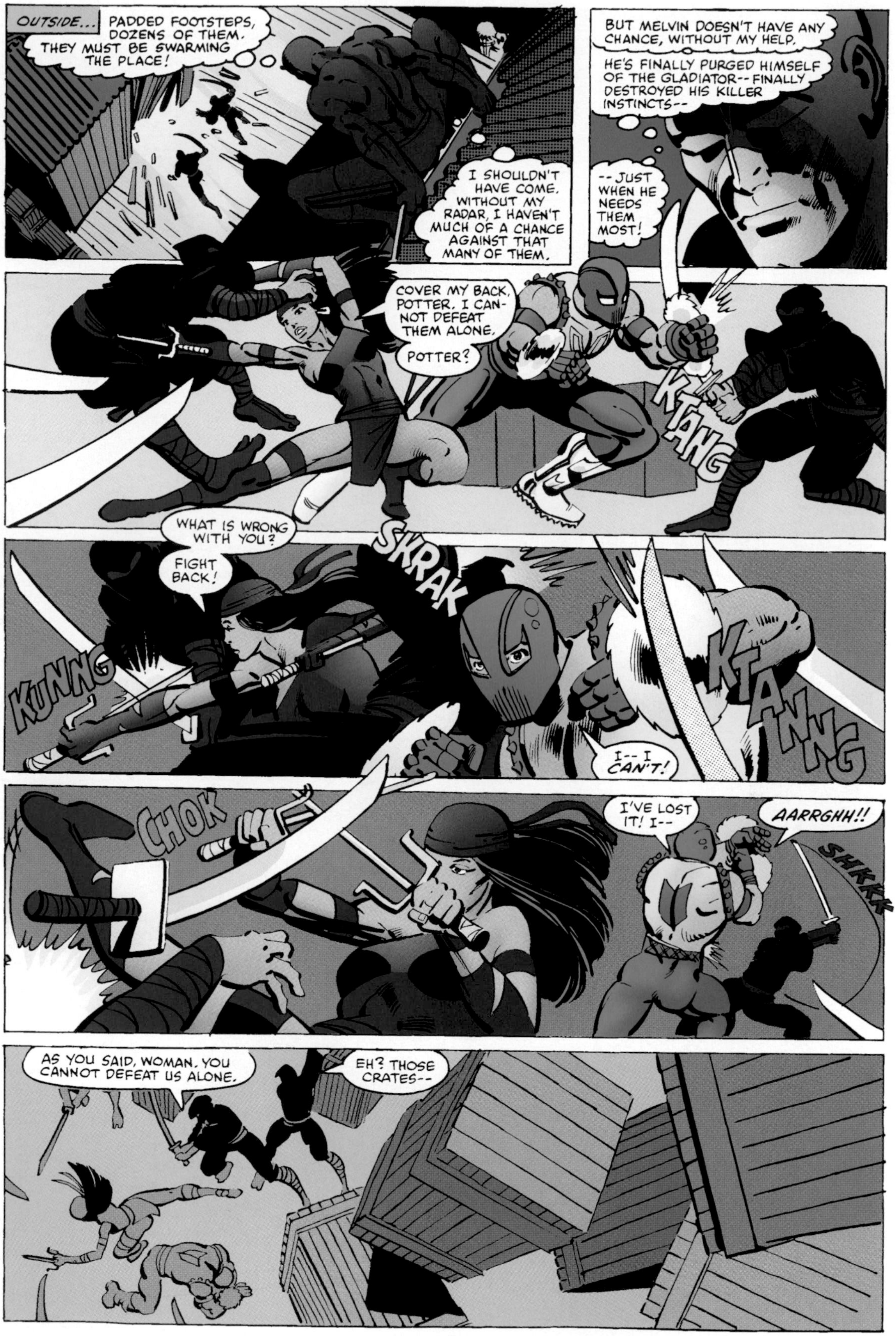
OUTSIDE...
PADDED FOOTSTEPS, DOZENS OF THEM. THEY MUST BE SWARMING THE PLACE!
I SHOULDN'T HAVE COME. WITHOUT MY RADAR, I HAVEN'T MUCH OF A CHANCE AGAINST THAT MANY OF THEM.
BUT MELVIN DOESN'T HAVE ANY CHANCE, WITHOUT MY HELP.
HE'S FINALLY PURGED HIMSELF OF THE GLADIATOR--FINALLY DESTROYED HIS KILLER INSTINCTS--
--JUST WHEN HE NEEDS THEM MOST!
COVER MY BACK, POTTER. I CANNOT DEFEAT THEM ALONE.
POTTER?
KTANG
WHAT IS WRONG WITH YOU?
FIGHT BACK!
SKRAK
KUNNG
KTANNG
I-- I CAN'T!
CHOK
I'VE LOST IT! I--
AARRGHH!!
SHIKKK
AS YOU SAID, WOMAN. YOU CANNOT DEFEAT US ALONE.
EH? THOSE CRATES--

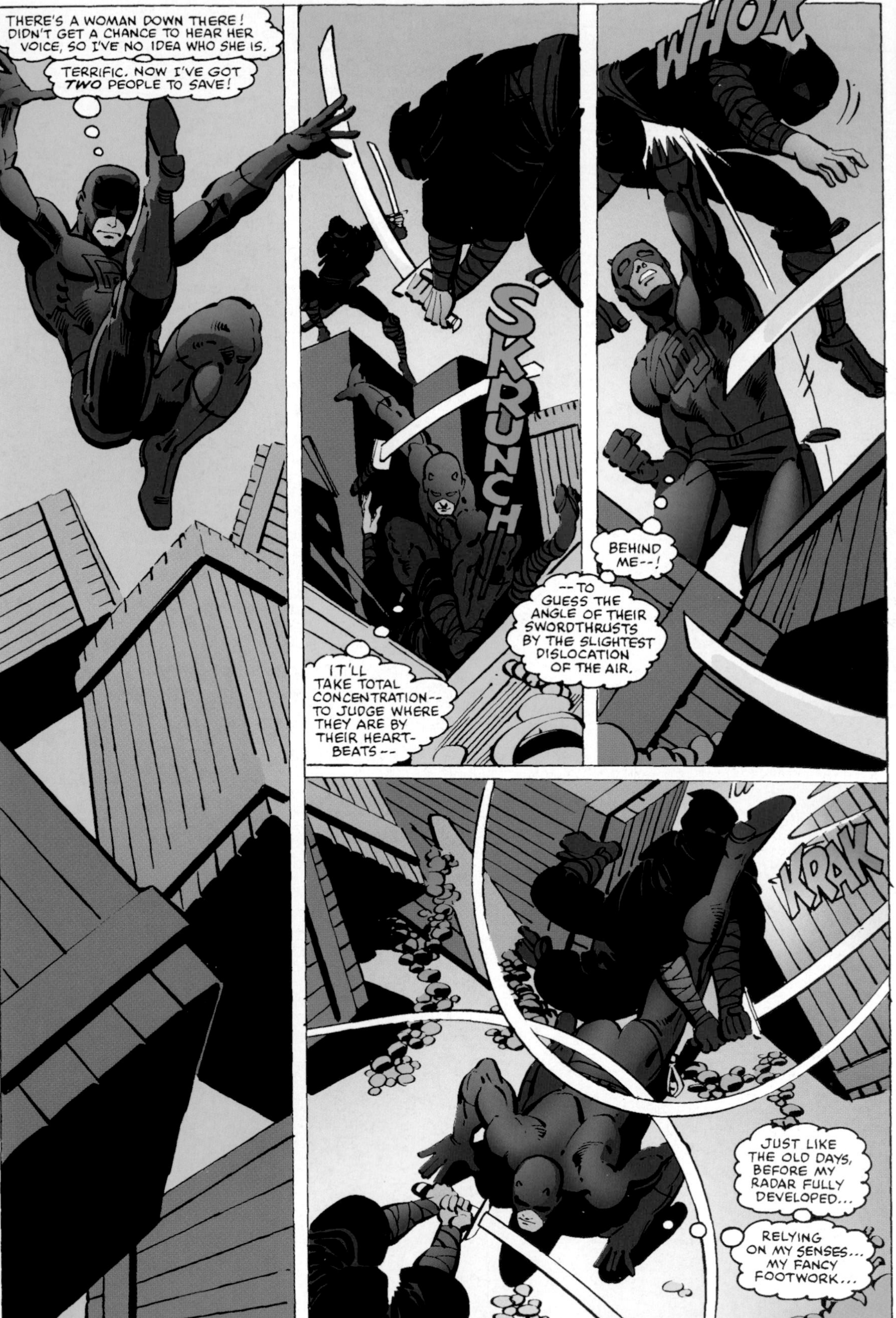
THERE'S A WOMAN DOWN THERE! DIDN'T GET A CHANCE TO HEAR HER VOICE, SO I'VE NO IDEA WHO SHE IS.
TERRIFIC. NOW I'VE GOT TWO PEOPLE TO SAVE!
SKRUNCH
IT'LL TAKE TOTAL CONCENTRATION-- TO JUDGE WHERE THEY ARE BY THEIR HEART-BEATS--
--TO GUESS THE ANGLE OF THEIR SWORDTHRUSTS BY THE SLIGHTEST DISLOCATION OF THE AIR.
WHOK
BEHIND ME--!
KRAK
JUST LIKE THE OLD DAYS, BEFORE MY RADAR FULLY DEVELOPED...
RELYING ON MY SENSES... MY FANCY FOOTWORK...

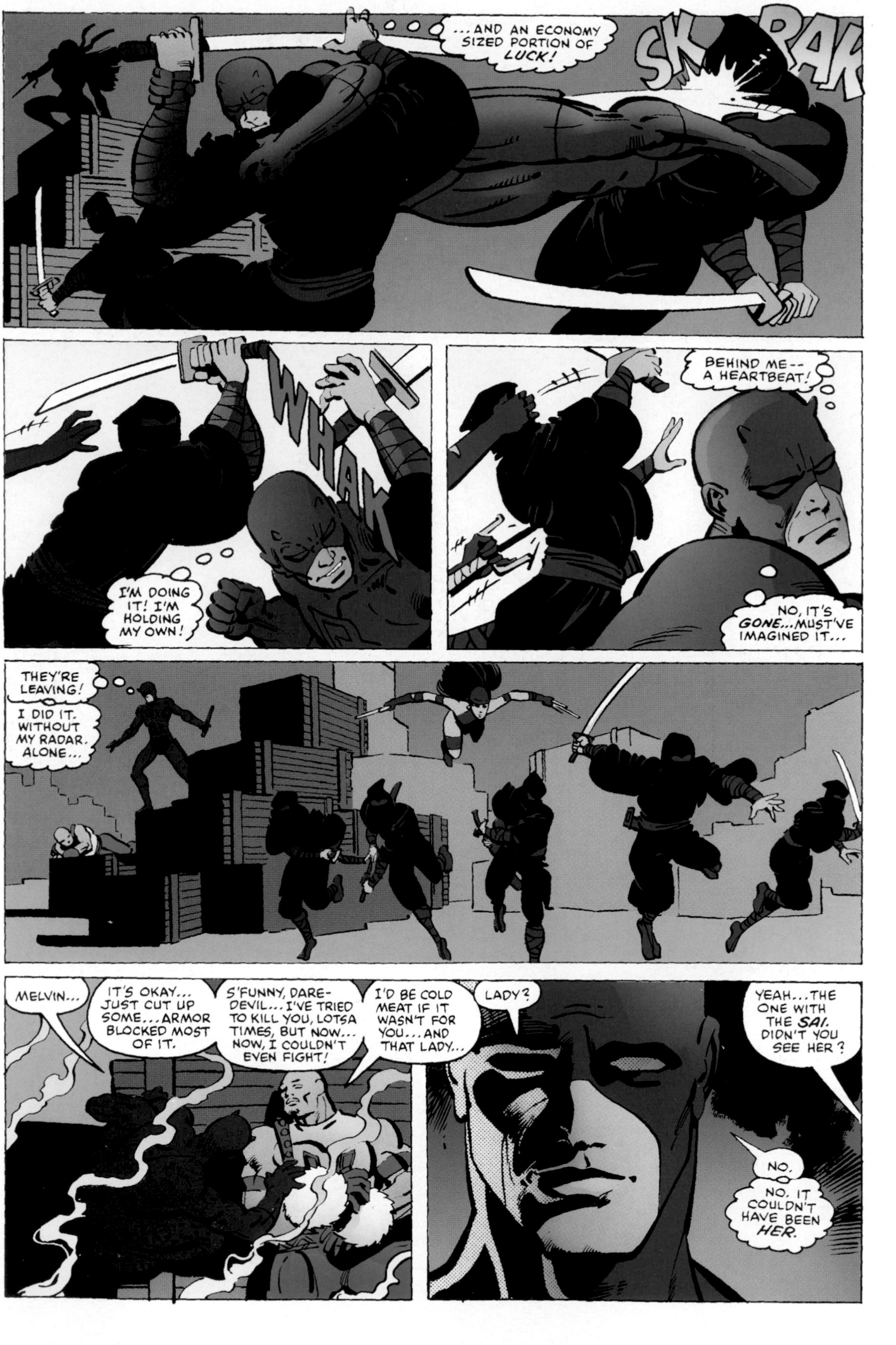
...AND AN ECONOMY SIZED PORTION OF LUCK!
SKRAK
WHAK
I'M DOING IT! I'M HOLDING MY OWN!
BEHIND ME-- A HEARTBEAT!
NO, IT'S GONE... MUST'VE IMAGINED IT...
THEY'RE LEAVING!
I DID IT. WITHOUT MY RADAR. ALONE...
MELVIN...
IT'S OKAY... JUST CUT UP SOME... ARMOR BLOCKED MOST OF IT.
S'FUNNY, DARE-DEVIL... I'VE TRIED TO KILL YOU, LOTSA TIMES, BUT NOW... NOW, I COULDN'T EVEN FIGHT!
I'D BE COLD MEAT IF IT WASN'T FOR YOU... AND THAT LADY...
LADY?
YEAH... THE ONE WITH THE SAI. DIDN'T YOU SEE HER?
NO.
NO, IT COULDN'T HAVE BEEN HER.

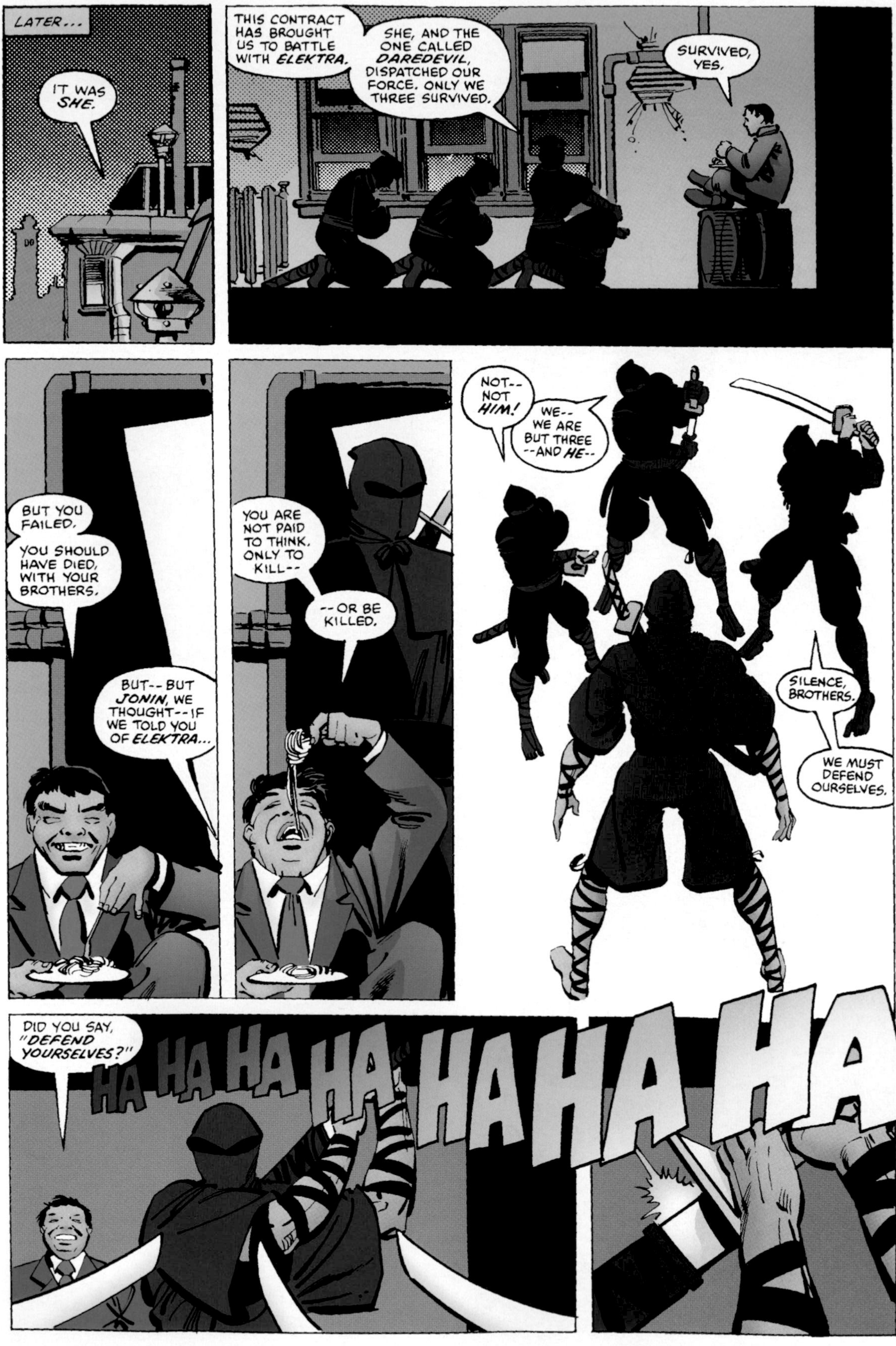
LATER...
IT WAS SHE.
THIS CONTRACT HAS BROUGHT US TO BATTLE WITH ELEKTRA.
SHE, AND THE ONE CALLED DAREDEVIL, DISPATCHED OUR FORCE. ONLY WE THREE SURVIVED.
SURVIVED, YES.
BUT YOU FAILED.
YOU SHOULD HAVE DIED, WITH YOUR BROTHERS.
BUT-- BUT JONIN, WE THOUGHT--IF WE TOLD YOU OF ELEKTRA...
YOU ARE NOT PAID TO THINK. ONLY TO KILL--
--OR BE KILLED.
NOT-- NOT HIM!
WE-- WE ARE BUT THREE --AND HE--
SILENCE, BROTHERS.
WE MUST DEFEND OURSELVES.
DID YOU SAY, "DEFEND YOURSELVES?"
HA HA HA HA HA HA HA HA

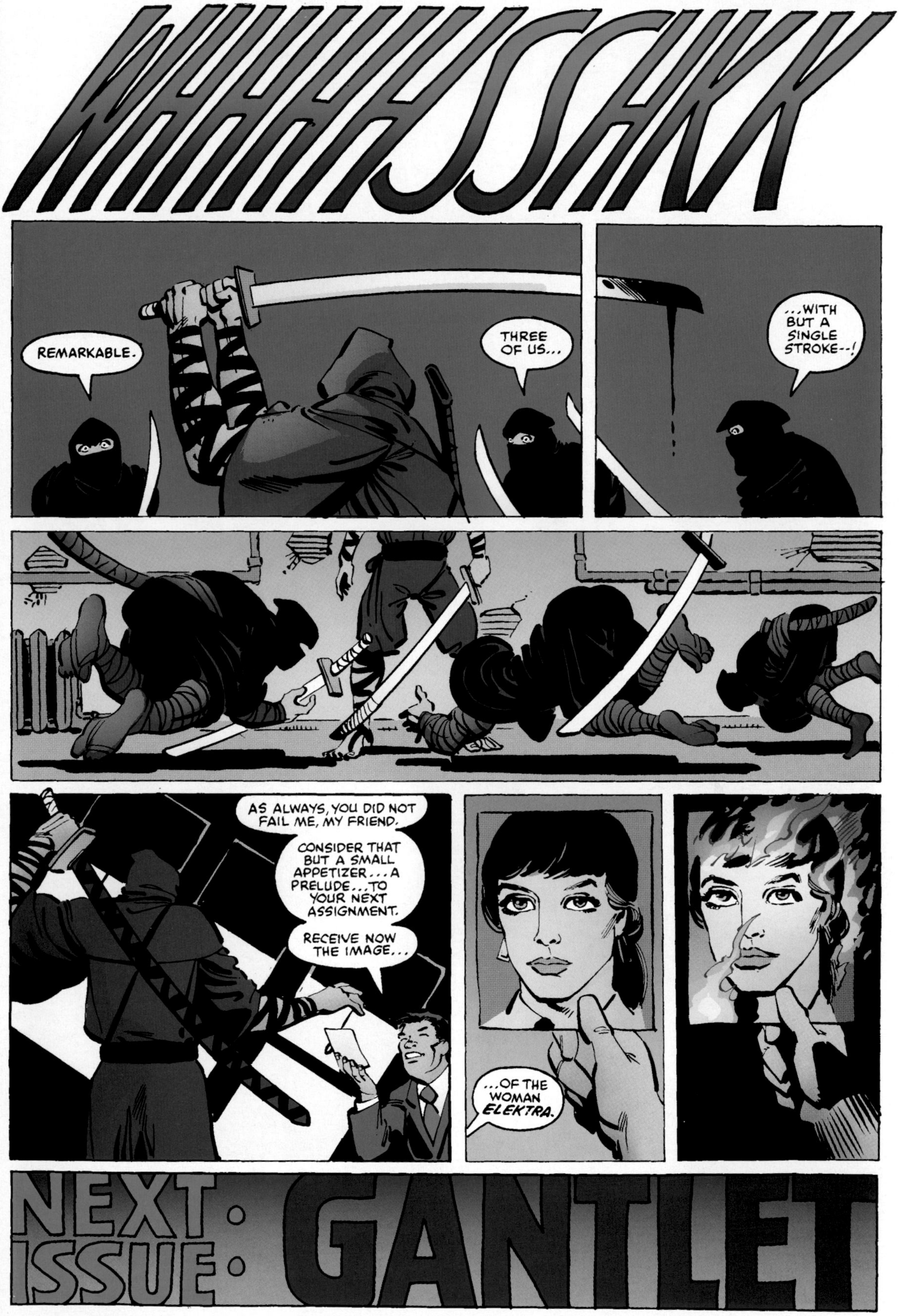
WHHHSSHKK
REMARKABLE.
THREE OF US...
...WITH BUT A SINGLE STROKE--!
AS ALWAYS, YOU DID NOT FAIL ME, MY FRIEND.
CONSIDER THAT BUT A SMALL APPETIZER... A PRELUDE... TO YOUR NEXT ASSIGNMENT.
RECEIVE NOW THE IMAGE...
...OF THE WOMAN ELEKTRA.
NEXT ISSUE: GANTLET

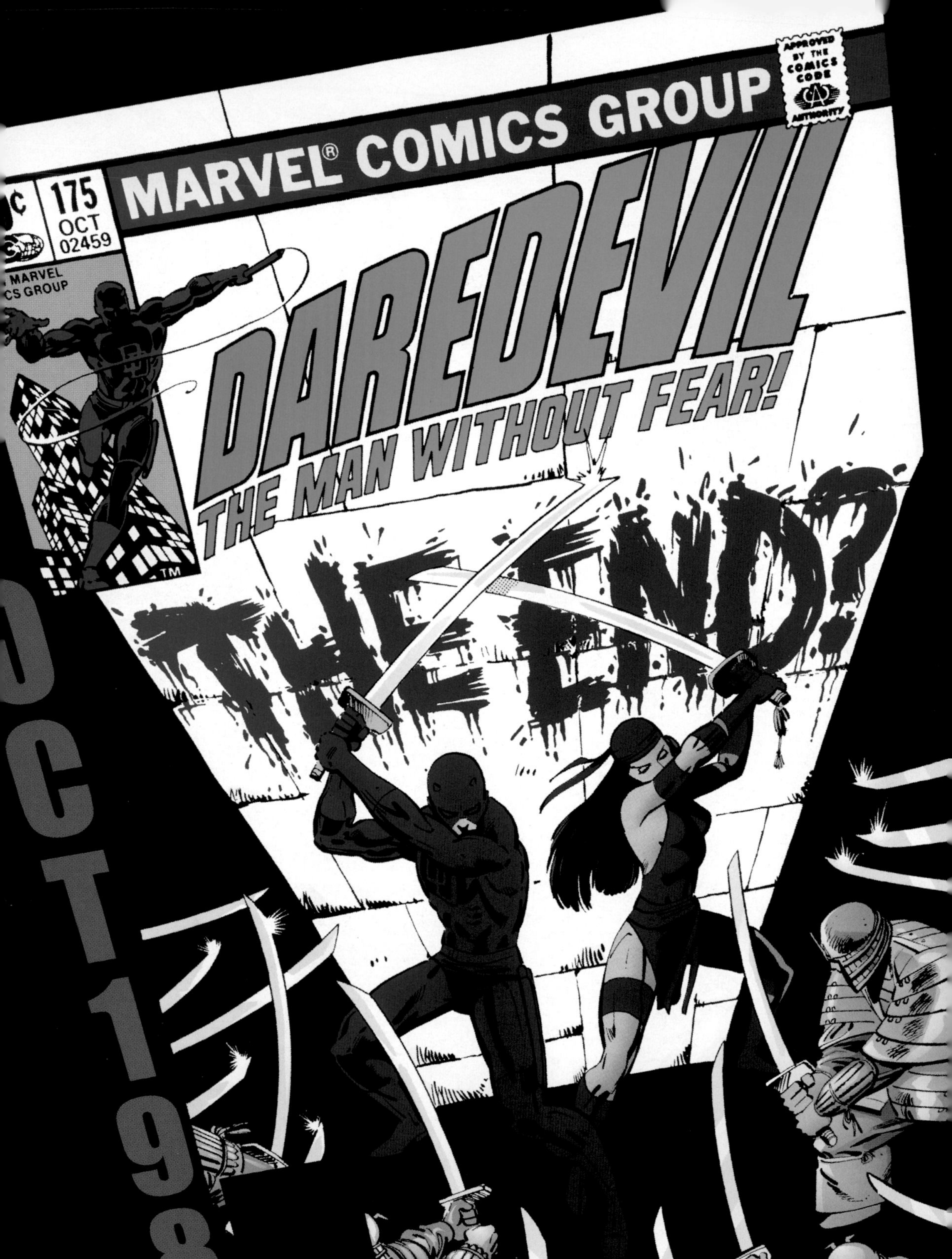
MARVEL® COMICS GROUP
APPROVED BY THE COMICS CODE AUTHORITY
175
OCT
02459
MARVEL COMICS GROUP
DAREDEVIL
THE MAN WITHOUT FEAR!
THE END?
OCT 1981
DAREDEVIL #175

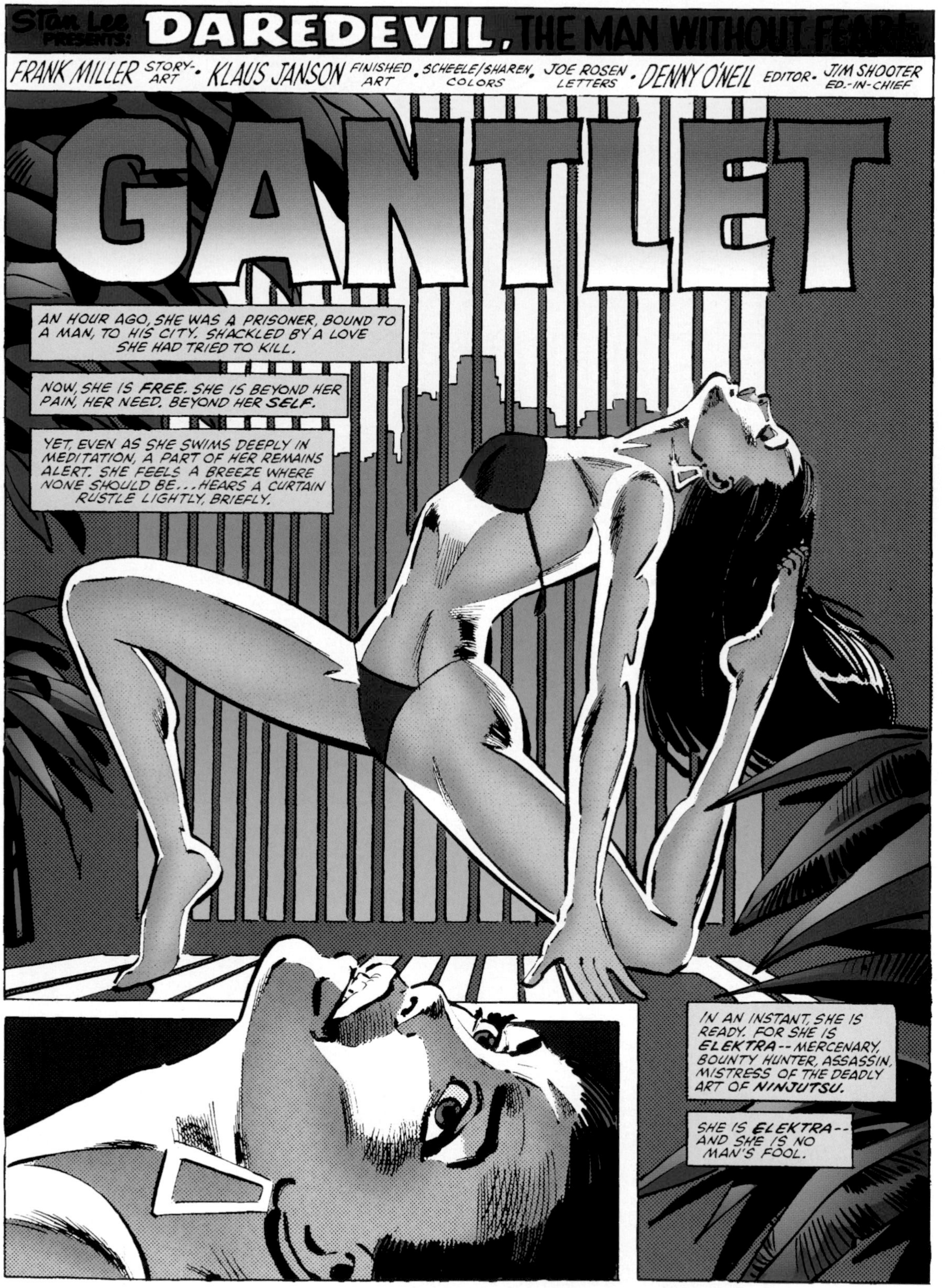

Stan Lee presents: DAREDEVIL, THE MAN WITHOUT FEAR!
FRANK MILLER STORY-ART • KLAUS JANSON FINISHED ART • SCHEELE/SHAREN COLORS • JOE ROSEN LETTERS • DENNY O'NEIL EDITOR • JIM SHOOTER ED.-IN-CHIEF
GANTLET
AN HOUR AGO, SHE WAS A PRISONER, BOUND TO A MAN, TO HIS CITY. SHACKLED BY A LOVE SHE HAD TRIED TO KILL.
NOW, SHE IS FREE. SHE IS BEYOND HER PAIN, HER NEED. BEYOND HER SELF.
YET, EVEN AS SHE SWIMS DEEPLY IN MEDITATION, A PART OF HER REMAINS ALERT. SHE FEELS A BREEZE WHERE NONE SHOULD BE... HEARS A CURTAIN RUSTLE LIGHTLY, BRIEFLY.
IN AN INSTANT, SHE IS READY. FOR SHE IS ELEKTRA-- MERCENARY, BOUNTY HUNTER, ASSASSIN, MISTRESS OF THE DEADLY ART OF NINJUTSU.
SHE IS ELEKTRA-- AND SHE IS NO MAN'S FOOL.

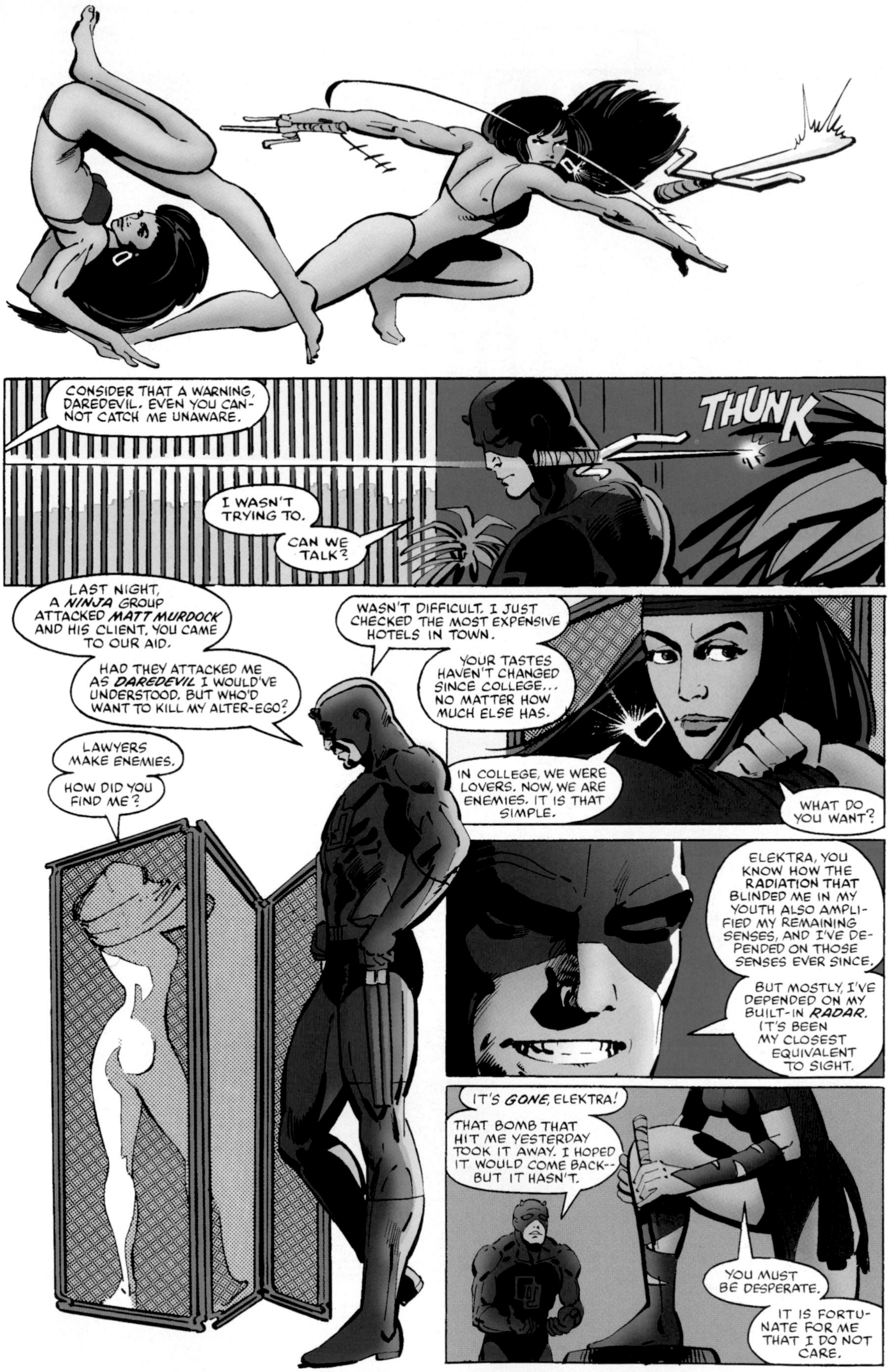
CONSIDER THAT A WARNING, DAREDEVIL. EVEN YOU CANNOT CATCH ME UNAWARE.
THUNK
I WASN'T TRYING TO.
CAN WE TALK?
LAST NIGHT, A NINJA GROUP ATTACKED MATT MURDOCK AND HIS CLIENT. YOU CAME TO OUR AID.
HAD THEY ATTACKED ME AS DAREDEVIL I WOULD'VE UNDERSTOOD. BUT WHO'D WANT TO KILL MY ALTER-EGO?
LAWYERS MAKE ENEMIES.
HOW DID YOU FIND ME?
WASN'T DIFFICULT. I JUST CHECKED THE MOST EXPENSIVE HOTELS IN TOWN.
YOUR TASTES HAVEN'T CHANGED SINCE COLLEGE... NO MATTER HOW MUCH ELSE HAS.
IN COLLEGE, WE WERE LOVERS. NOW, WE ARE ENEMIES. IT IS THAT SIMPLE.
WHAT DO YOU WANT?
ELEKTRA, YOU KNOW HOW THE RADIATION THAT BLINDED ME IN MY YOUTH ALSO AMPLIFIED MY REMAINING SENSES, AND I'VE DEPENDED ON THOSE SENSES EVER SINCE.
BUT MOSTLY, I'VE DEPENDED ON MY BUILT-IN RADAR. IT'S BEEN MY CLOSEST EQUIVALENT TO SIGHT.
IT'S GONE, ELEKTRA!
THAT BOMB THAT HIT ME YESTERDAY TOOK IT AWAY. I HOPED IT WOULD COME BACK-- BUT IT HASN'T.
YOU MUST BE DESPERATE.
IT IS FORTUNATE FOR ME THAT I DO NOT CARE.

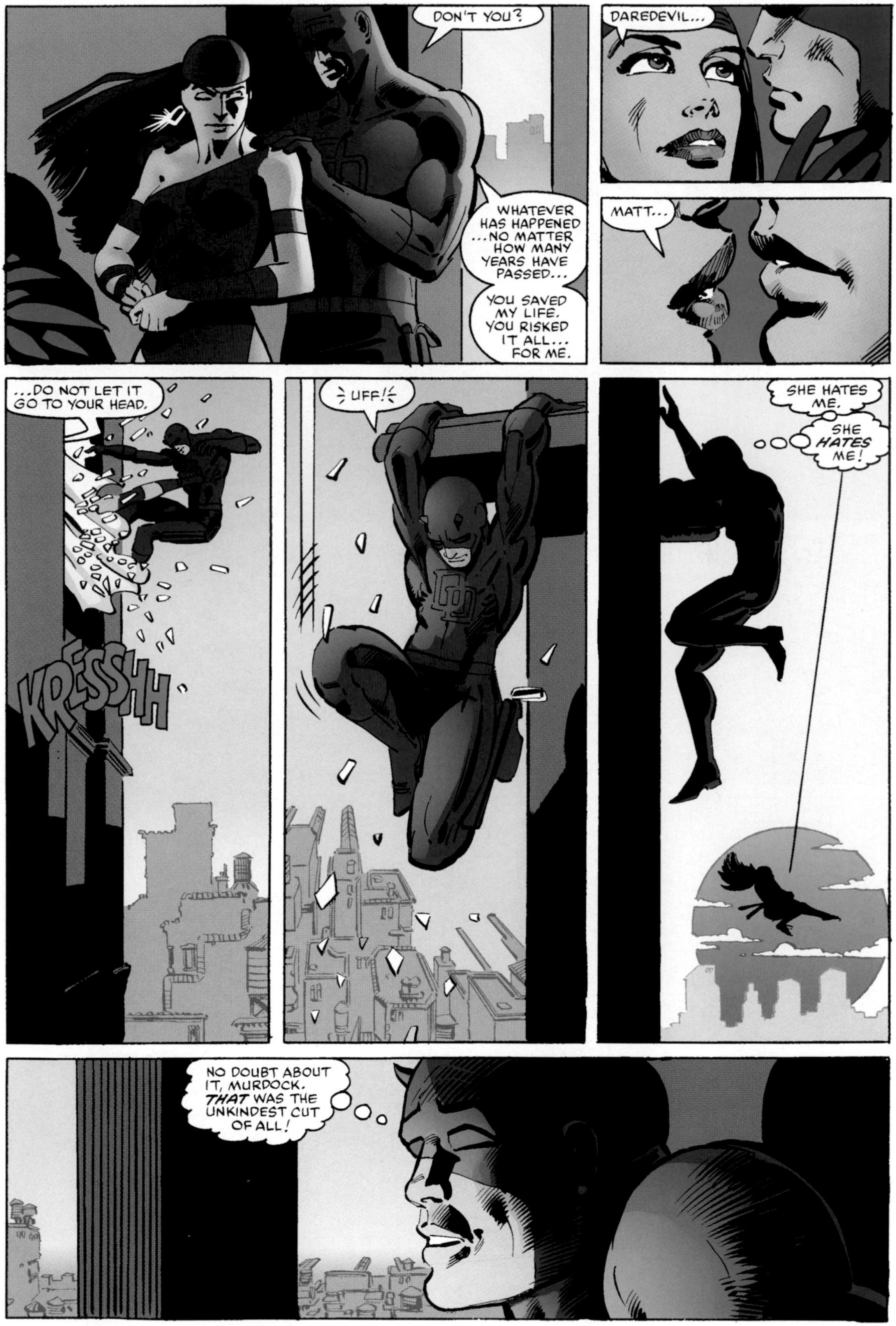
DON'T YOU?
DAREDEVIL...
WHATEVER HAS HAPPENED ...NO MATTER HOW MANY YEARS HAVE PASSED...
YOU SAVED MY LIFE. YOU RISKED IT ALL... FOR ME.
MATT...
...DO NOT LET IT GO TO YOUR HEAD.
KRESSHH
UFF!
SHE HATES ME.
SHE HATES ME!
NO DOUBT ABOUT IT, MURDOCK. THAT WAS THE UNKINDEST CUT OF ALL!

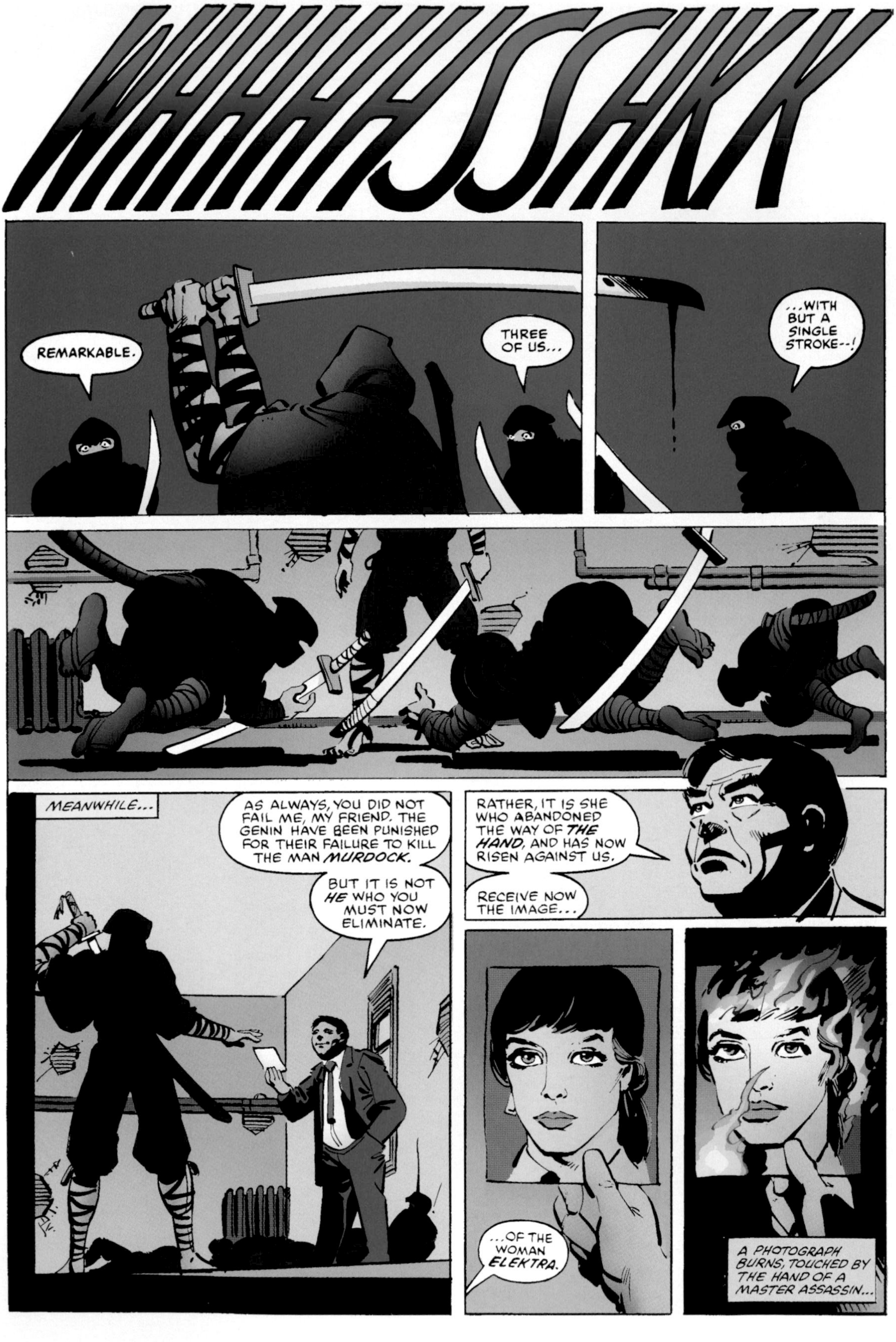
WHHHHSSHKK
REMARKABLE.
THREE OF US...
...WITH BUT A SINGLE STROKE--!
MEANWHILE...
AS ALWAYS, YOU DID NOT FAIL ME, MY FRIEND. THE GENIN HAVE BEEN PUNISHED FOR THEIR FAILURE TO KILL THE MAN MURDOCK.
BUT IT IS NOT HE WHO YOU MUST NOW ELIMINATE.
RATHER, IT IS SHE WHO ABANDONED THE WAY OF THE HAND, AND HAS NOW RISEN AGAINST US.
RECEIVE NOW THE IMAGE...
...OF THE WOMAN ELEKTRA.
A PHOTOGRAPH BURNS, TOUCHED BY THE HAND OF A MASTER ASSASSIN...

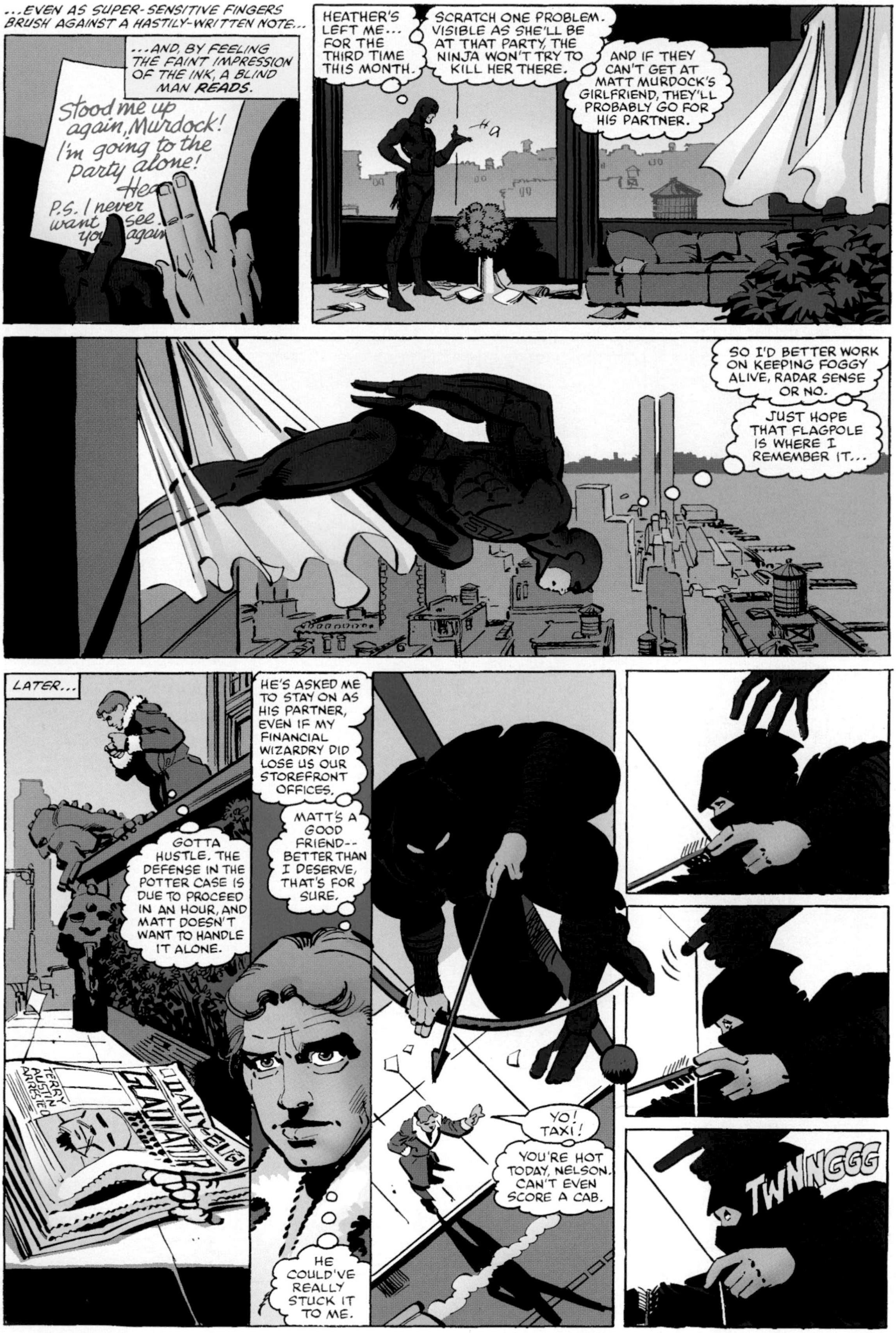
...EVEN AS SUPER-SENSITIVE FINGERS BRUSH AGAINST A HASTILY-WRITTEN NOTE...
...AND, BY FEELING THE FAINT IMPRESSION OF THE INK, A BLIND MAN READS.
Stood me up again, Murdock! I'm going to the party alone!
HEATHER'S LEFT ME... FOR THE THIRD TIME THIS MONTH.
SCRATCH ONE PROBLEM. VISIBLE AS SHE'LL BE AT THAT PARTY, THE NINJA WON'T TRY TO KILL HER THERE.
AND IF THEY CAN'T GET AT MATT MURDOCK'S GIRLFRIEND, THEY'LL PROBABLY GO FOR HIS PARTNER.
HA
SO I'D BETTER WORK ON KEEPING FOGGY ALIVE, RADAR SENSE OR NO.
JUST HOPE THAT FLAGPOLE IS WHERE I REMEMBER IT...
LATER...
GOTTA HUSTLE. THE DEFENSE IN THE POTTER CASE IS DUE TO PROCEED IN AN HOUR, AND MATT DOESN'T WANT TO HANDLE IT ALONE.
DAILY BUGLE
GLADIATOR
TERRY AUSTIN ARRESTED
HE'S ASKED ME TO STAY ON AS HIS PARTNER, EVEN IF MY FINANCIAL WIZARDRY DID LOSE US OUR STOREFRONT OFFICES.
MATT'S A GOOD FRIEND-- BETTER THAN I DESERVE, THAT'S FOR SURE.
HE COULD'VE REALLY STUCK IT TO ME.
YO! TAXI!
YOU'RE HOT TODAY, NELSON. CAN'T EVEN SCORE A CAB.
TWNNGGG

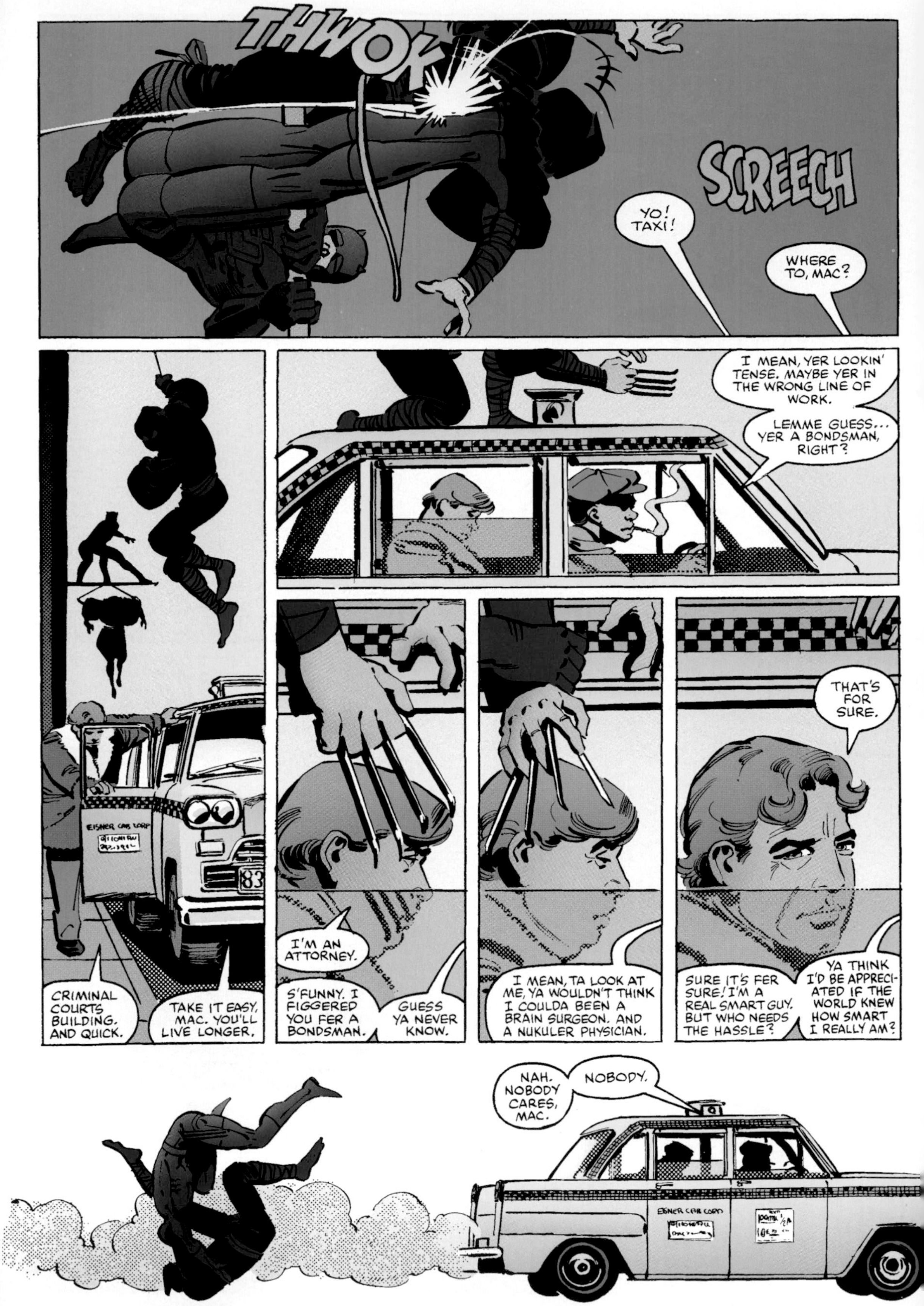
THWOK
SCREECH
YO! TAXI!
WHERE TO, MAC?
I MEAN, YER LOOKIN' TENSE. MAYBE YER IN THE WRONG LINE OF WORK.
LEMME GUESS... YER A BONDSMAN, RIGHT?
THAT'S FOR SURE.
CRIMINAL COURTS BUILDING. AND QUICK.
TAKE IT EASY, MAC. YOU'LL LIVE LONGER.
I'M AN ATTORNEY.
S'FUNNY. I FIGGERED YOU FER A BONDSMAN.
GUESS YA NEVER KNOW.
I MEAN, TA LOOK AT ME, YA WOULDN'T THINK I COULDA BEEN A BRAIN SURGEON. AND A NUKULER PHYSICIAN.
SURE IT'S FER SURE! I'M A REAL SMART GUY. BUT WHO NEEDS THE HASSLE?
YA THINK I'D BE APPRECIATED IF THE WORLD KNEW HOW SMART I REALLY AM?
NAH. NOBODY CARES, MAC.
NOBODY.
EISNER CAB CORP

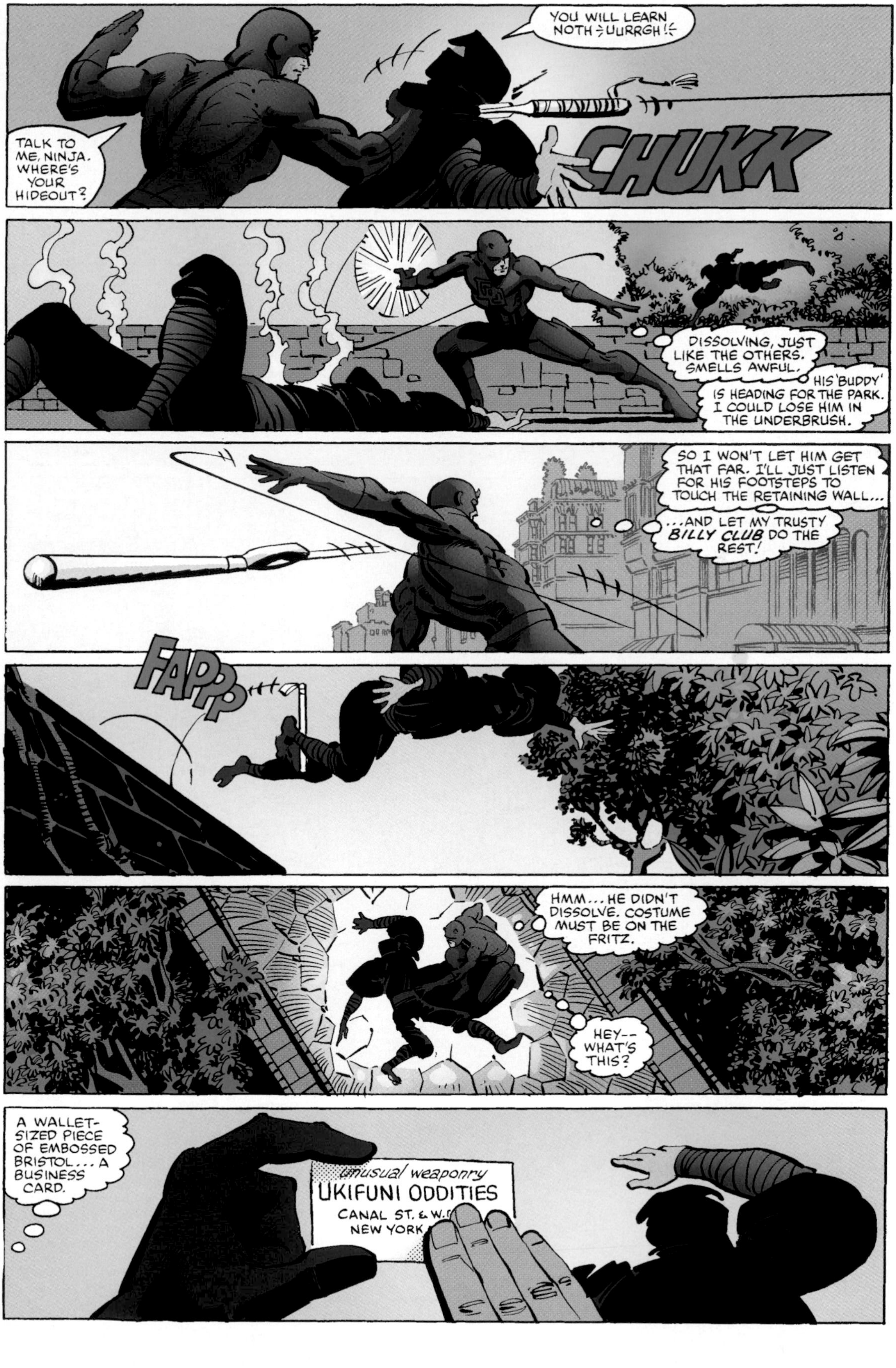

TALK TO ME, NINJA. WHERE'S YOUR HIDEOUT?
YOU WILL LEARN NOTH--UURRGH!
CHUKK
DISSOLVING, JUST LIKE THE OTHERS. SMELLS AWFUL.
HIS 'BUDDY' IS HEADING FOR THE PARK. I COULD LOSE HIM IN THE UNDERBRUSH.
SO I WON'T LET HIM GET THAT FAR. I'LL JUST LISTEN FOR HIS FOOTSTEPS TO TOUCH THE RETAINING WALL...
...AND LET MY TRUSTY BILLY CLUB DO THE REST!
FAPPP
HMM... HE DIDN'T DISSOLVE. COSTUME MUST BE ON THE FRITZ.
HEY-- WHAT'S THIS?
A WALLET-SIZED PIECE OF EMBOSSED BRISTOL... A BUSINESS CARD.
unusual weaponry
UKIFUNI ODDITIES
CANAL ST. & W.
NEW YORK

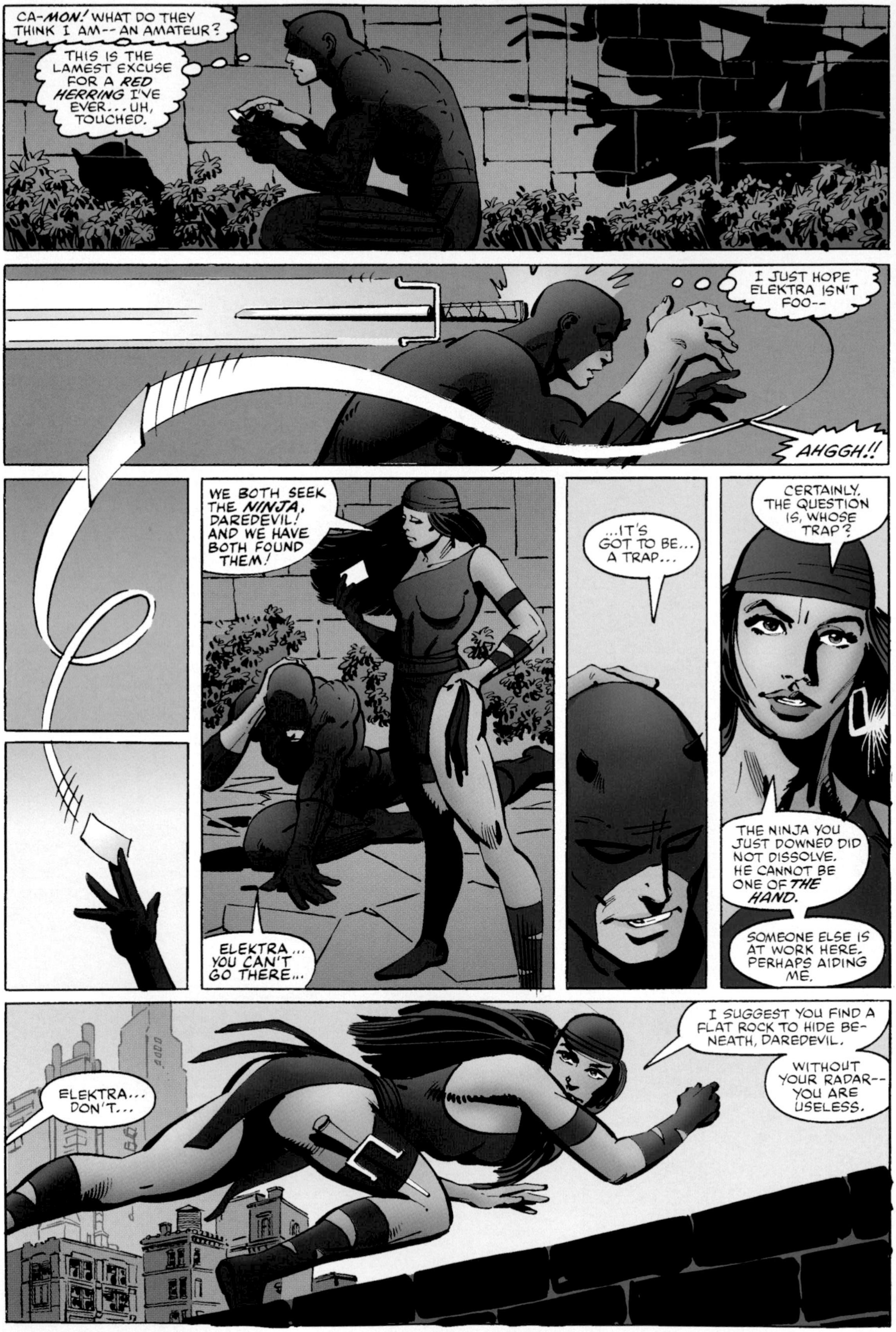
CA-MON! WHAT DO THEY THINK I AM-- AN AMATEUR?
THIS IS THE LAMEST EXCUSE FOR A RED HERRING I'VE EVER... UH, TOUCHED.
I JUST HOPE ELEKTRA ISN'T FOO--
AHGGH!!
WE BOTH SEEK THE NINJA, DAREDEVIL! AND WE HAVE BOTH FOUND THEM!
ELEKTRA... YOU CAN'T GO THERE...
...IT'S GOT TO BE... A TRAP...
CERTAINLY. THE QUESTION IS, WHOSE TRAP?
THE NINJA YOU JUST DOWNED DID NOT DISSOLVE. HE CANNOT BE ONE OF THE HAND.
SOMEONE ELSE IS AT WORK HERE. PERHAPS AIDING ME.
I SUGGEST YOU FIND A FLAT ROCK TO HIDE BE-NEATH, DAREDEVIL.
WITHOUT YOUR RADAR-- YOU ARE USELESS.
ELEKTRA... DON'T...

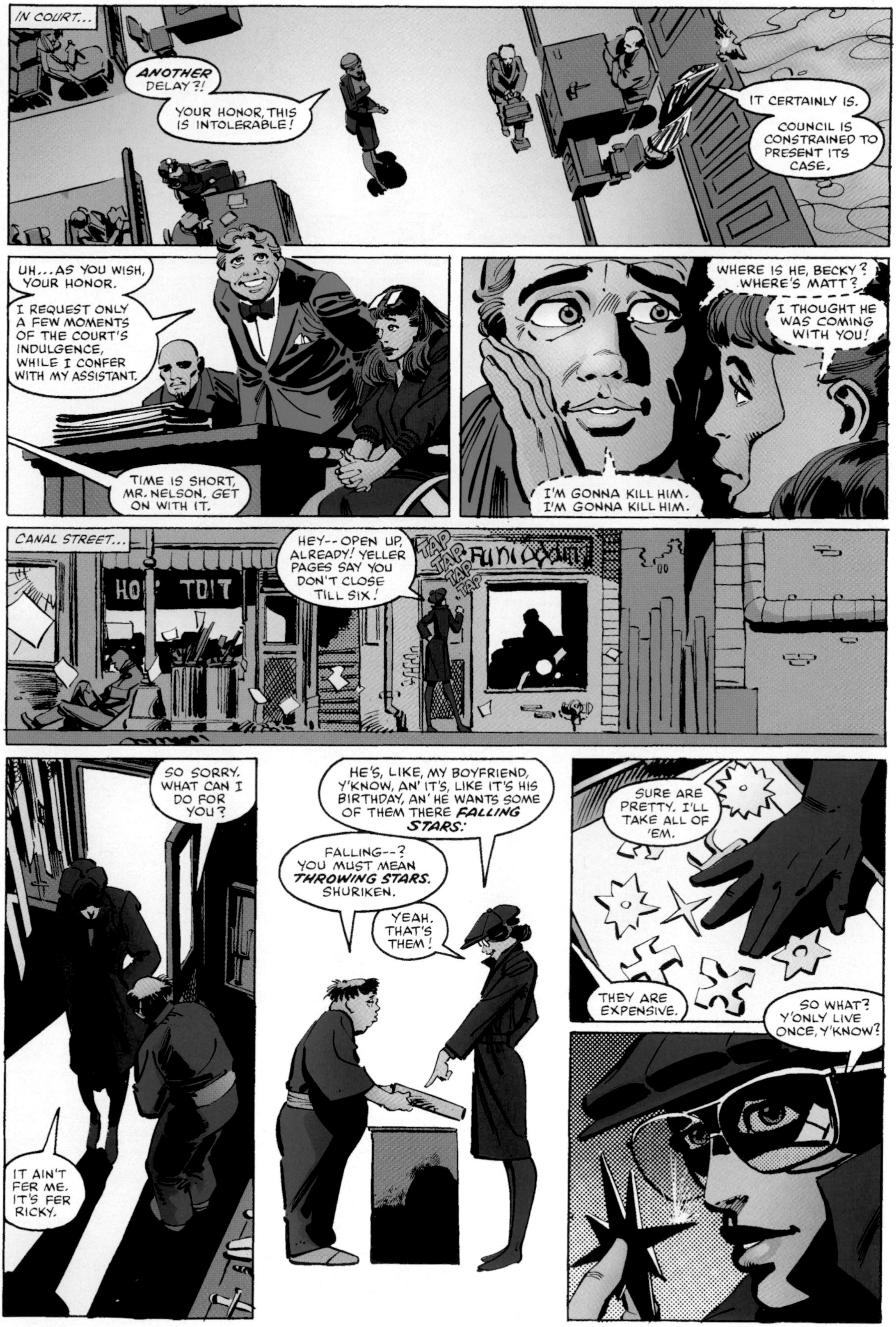
IN COURT...
ANOTHER DELAY?!
YOUR HONOR, THIS IS INTOLERABLE!
IT CERTAINLY IS.
COUNCIL IS CONSTRAINED TO PRESENT ITS CASE.
UH... AS YOU WISH, YOUR HONOR.
I REQUEST ONLY A FEW MOMENTS OF THE COURT'S INDULGENCE, WHILE I CONFER WITH MY ASSISTANT.
TIME IS SHORT, MR. NELSON. GET ON WITH IT.
WHERE IS HE, BECKY? WHERE'S MATT?
I THOUGHT HE WAS COMING WITH YOU!
I'M GONNA KILL HIM. I'M GONNA KILL HIM.
CANAL STREET...
HEY-- OPEN UP, ALREADY! YELLER PAGES SAY YOU DON'T CLOSE TILL SIX!
TAP TAP TAP TAP
SO SORRY. WHAT CAN I DO FOR YOU?
IT AIN'T FER ME. IT'S FER RICKY.
HE'S, LIKE, MY BOYFRIEND, Y'KNOW, AN' IT'S, LIKE IT'S HIS BIRTHDAY, AN' HE WANTS SOME OF THEM THERE FALLING STARS.
FALLING--? YOU MUST MEAN THROWING STARS. SHURIKEN.
YEAH. THAT'S THEM!
SURE ARE PRETTY. I'LL TAKE ALL OF 'EM.
THEY ARE EXPENSIVE.
SO WHAT? Y'ONLY LIVE ONCE, Y'KNOW?

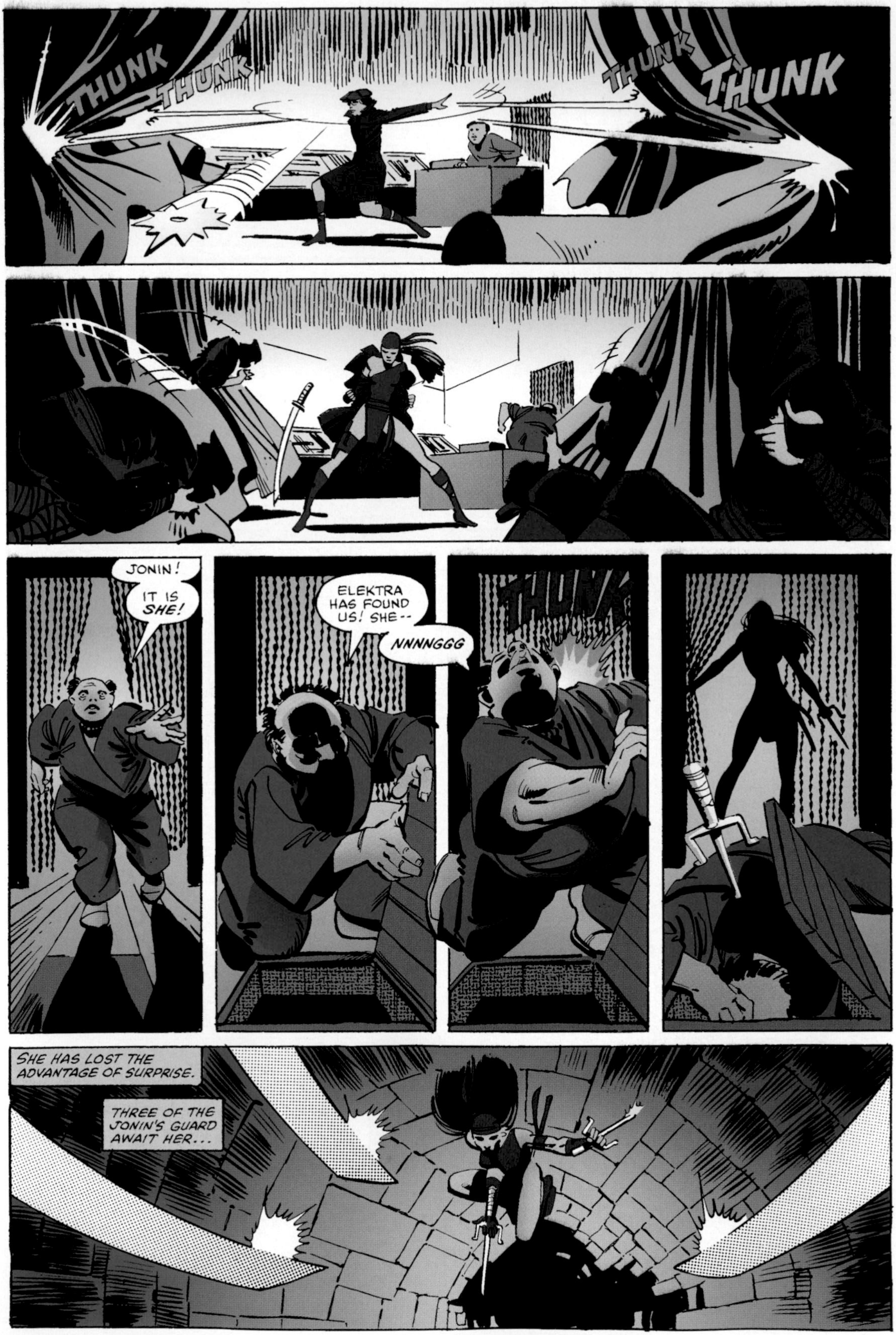
THUNK
THUNK
THUNK
THUNK
JONIN!
IT IS SHE!
ELEKTRA HAS FOUND US! SHE--
NNNNGGG
THUNK
SHE HAS LOST THE ADVANTAGE OF SURPRISE.
THREE OF THE JONIN'S GUARD AWAIT HER...

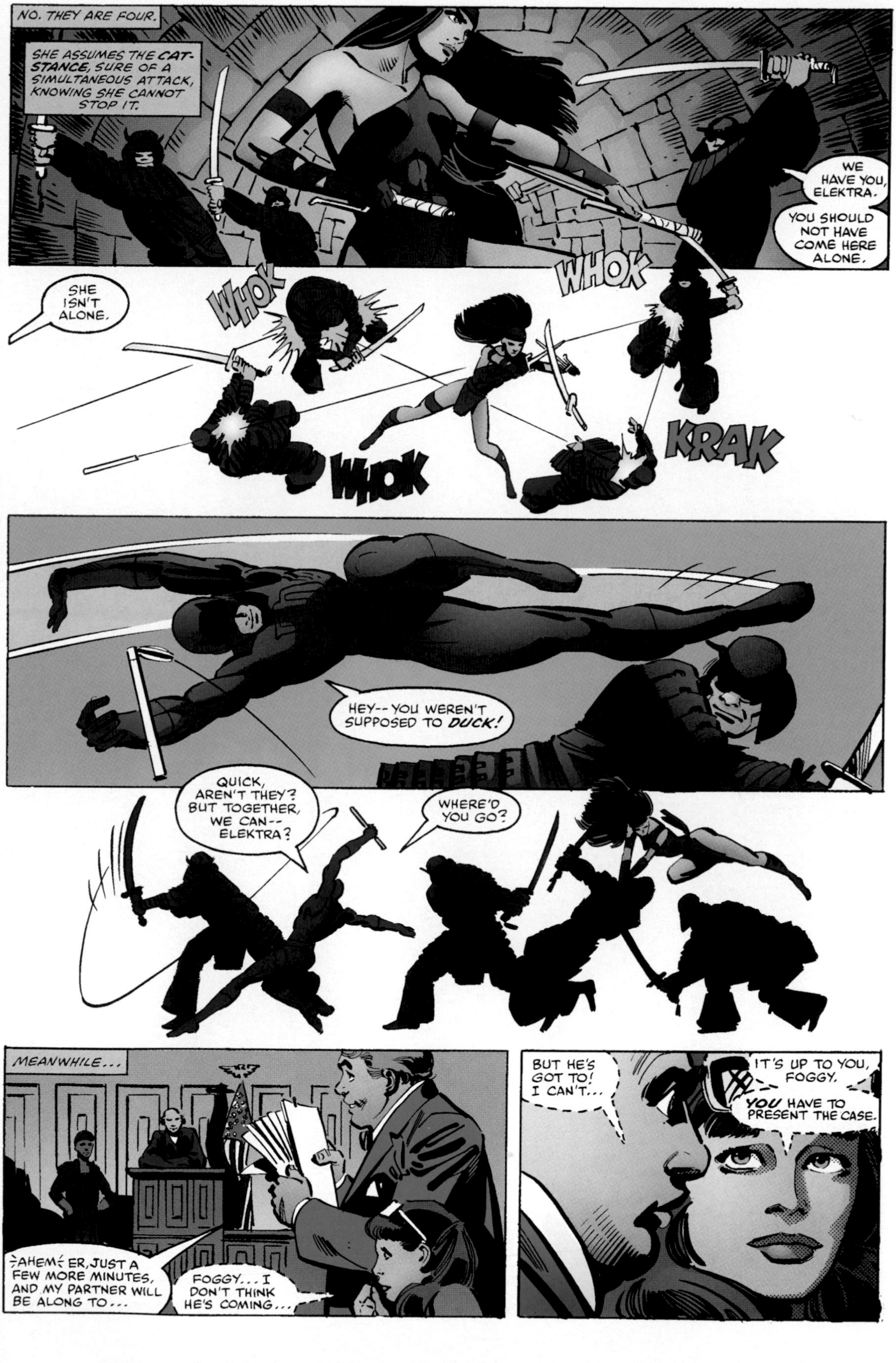

NO. THEY ARE FOUR.
SHE ASSUMES THE CAT-STANCE, SURE OF A SIMULTANEOUS ATTACK, KNOWING SHE CANNOT STOP IT.
WE HAVE YOU, ELEKTRA.
YOU SHOULD NOT HAVE COME HERE ALONE.
SHE ISN'T ALONE.
WHOK
WHOK
WHOK
KRAK
HEY-- YOU WEREN'T SUPPOSED TO DUCK!
QUICK, AREN'T THEY? BUT TOGETHER, WE CAN-- ELEKTRA?
WHERE'D YOU GO?
MEANWHILE...
AHEM ER, JUST A FEW MORE MINUTES, AND MY PARTNER WILL BE ALONG TO...
FOGGY... I DON'T THINK HE'S COMING...
BUT HE'S GOT TO! I CAN'T...
IT'S UP TO YOU, FOGGY.
YOU HAVE TO PRESENT THE CASE.

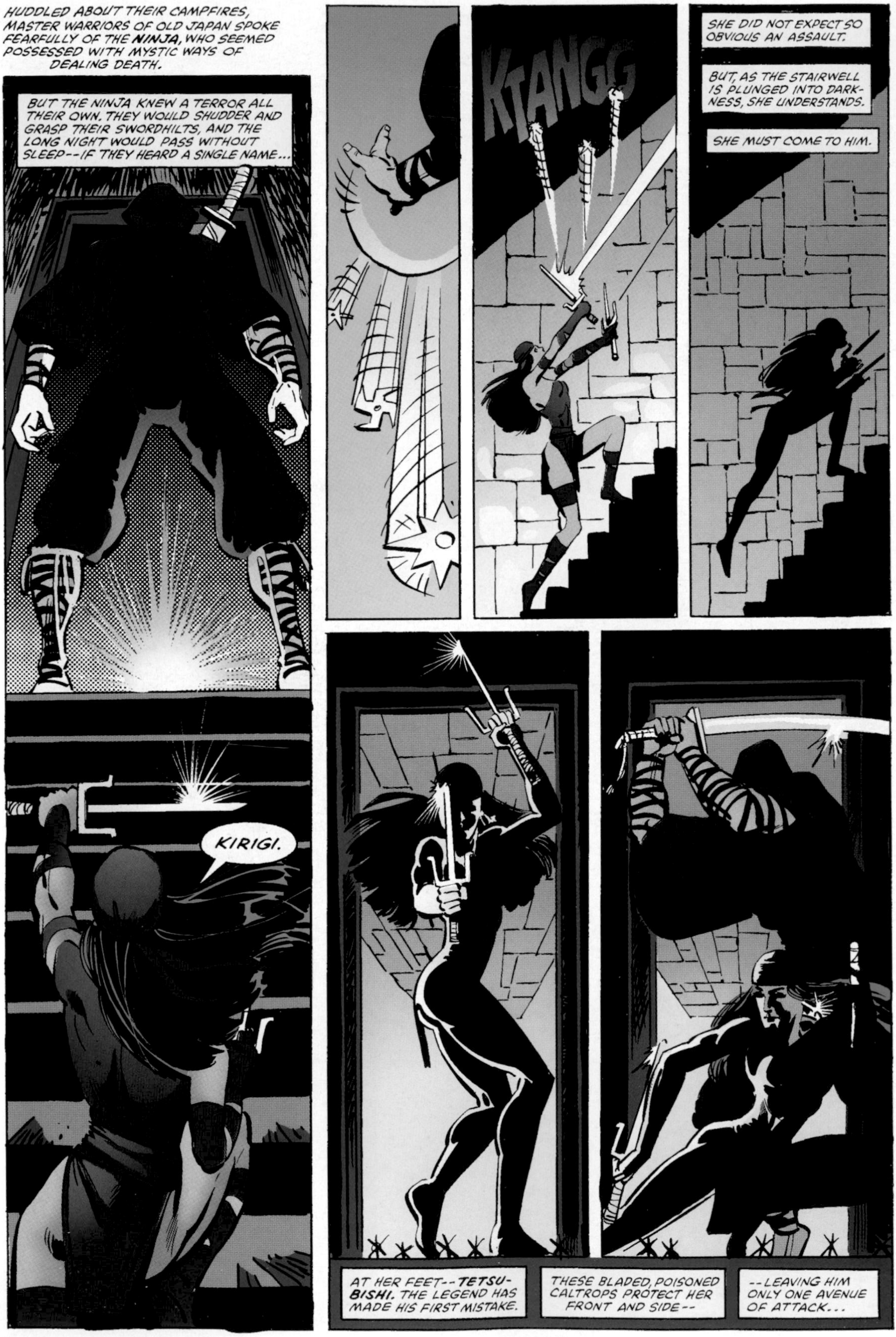
HUDDLED ABOUT THEIR CAMPFIRES, MASTER WARRIORS OF OLD JAPAN SPOKE FEARFULLY OF THE NINJA, WHO SEEMED POSSESSED WITH MYSTIC WAYS OF DEALING DEATH.
BUT THE NINJA KNEW A TERROR ALL THEIR OWN. THEY WOULD SHUDDER AND GRASP THEIR SWORDHILTS, AND THE LONG NIGHT WOULD PASS WITHOUT SLEEP--IF THEY HEARD A SINGLE NAME...
KIRIGI.
KTANGG
SHE DID NOT EXPECT SO OBVIOUS AN ASSAULT.
BUT, AS THE STAIRWELL IS PLUNGED INTO DARKNESS, SHE UNDERSTANDS.
SHE MUST COME TO HIM.
AT HER FEET--TETSU-BISHI. THE LEGEND HAS MADE HIS FIRST MISTAKE.
THESE BLADED, POISONED CALTROPS PROTECT HER FRONT AND SIDE--
--LEAVING HIM ONLY ONE AVENUE OF ATTACK...

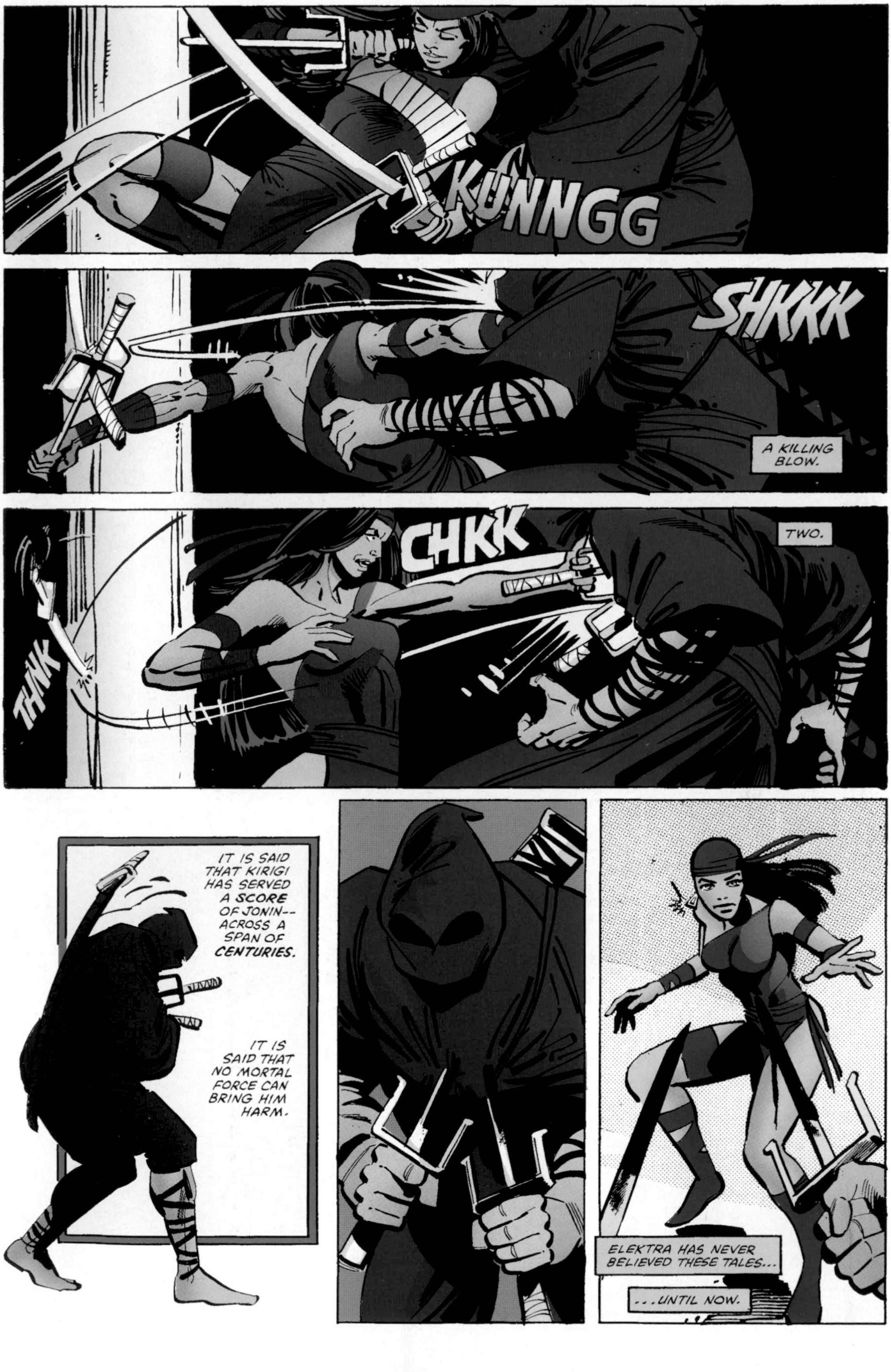
KUNNGG
SHKKK
A KILLING BLOW.
TWO.
CHKK
THNK
IT IS SAID THAT KIRIGI HAS SERVED A SCORE OF JONIN-- ACROSS A SPAN OF CENTURIES.
IT IS SAID THAT NO MORTAL FORCE CAN BRING HIM HARM.
ELEKTRA HAS NEVER BELIEVED THESE TALES...
...UNTIL NOW.

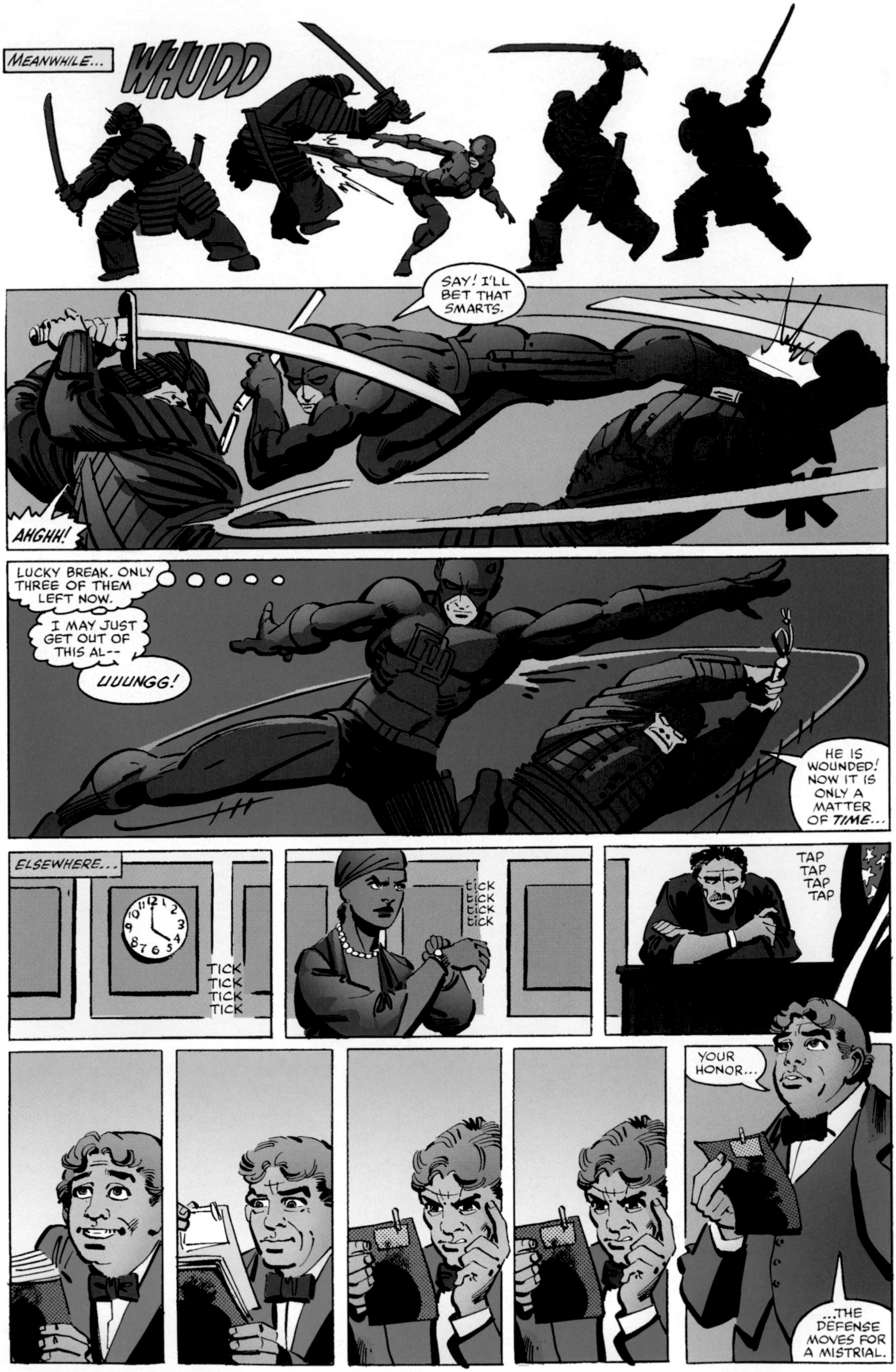
MEANWHILE...
WHUDD
SAY! I'LL BET THAT SMARTS.
AHGHH!
LUCKY BREAK. ONLY THREE OF THEM LEFT NOW.
I MAY JUST GET OUT OF THIS AL--
UUUNGG!
HE IS WOUNDED! NOW IT IS ONLY A MATTER OF TIME...
ELSEWHERE...
TICK TICK TICK TICK
tick tick tick tick
TAP TAP TAP TAP
YOUR HONOR...
...THE DEFENSE MOVES FOR A MISTRIAL.

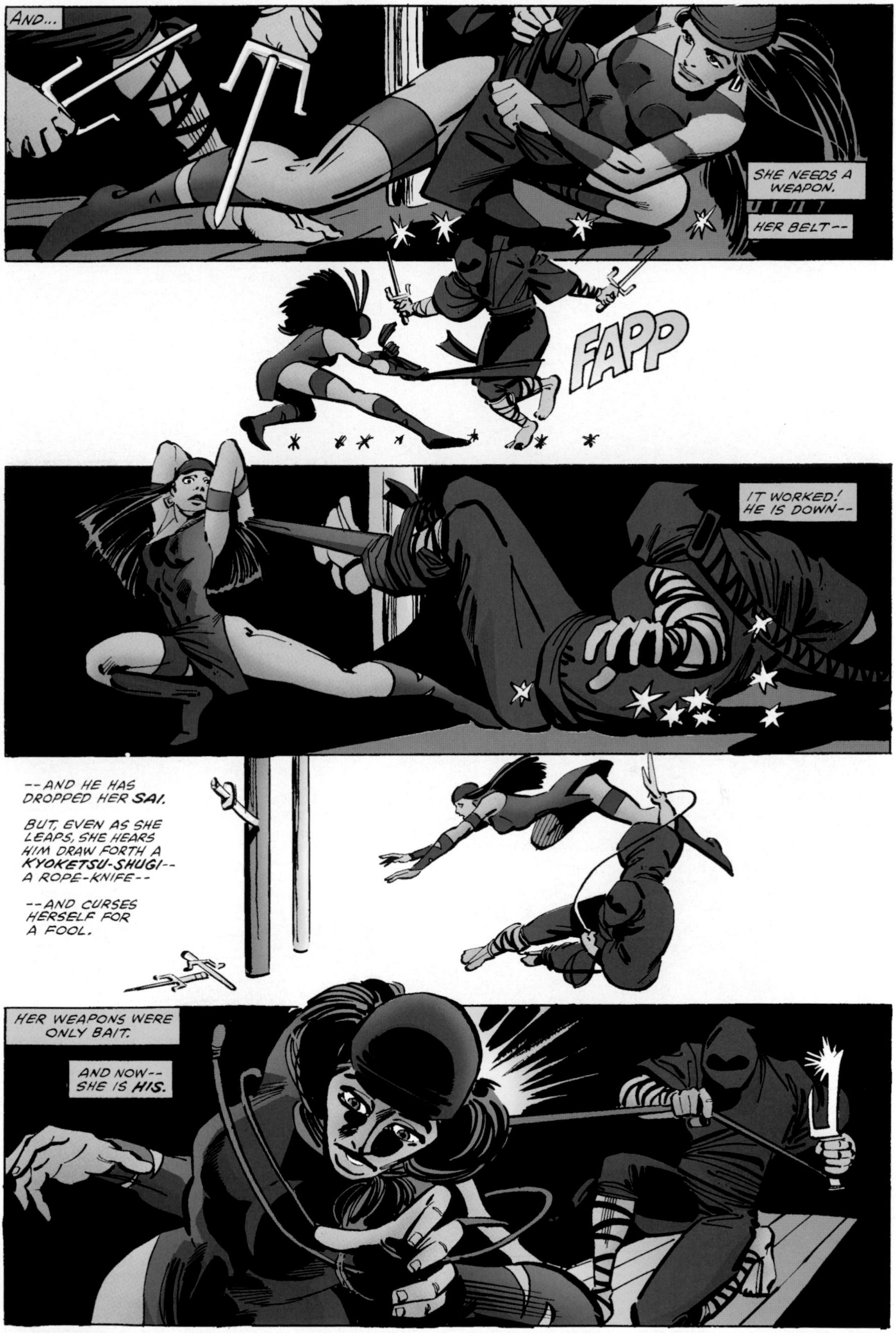
AND...
SHE NEEDS A WEAPON.
HER BELT--
FAPP
IT WORKED! HE IS DOWN--
--AND HE HAS DROPPED HER SAI.
BUT, EVEN AS SHE LEAPS, SHE HEARS HIM DRAW FORTH A KYOKETSU-SHUGI-- A ROPE-KNIFE--
--AND CURSES HERSELF FOR A FOOL.
HER WEAPONS WERE ONLY BAIT.
AND NOW-- SHE IS HIS.

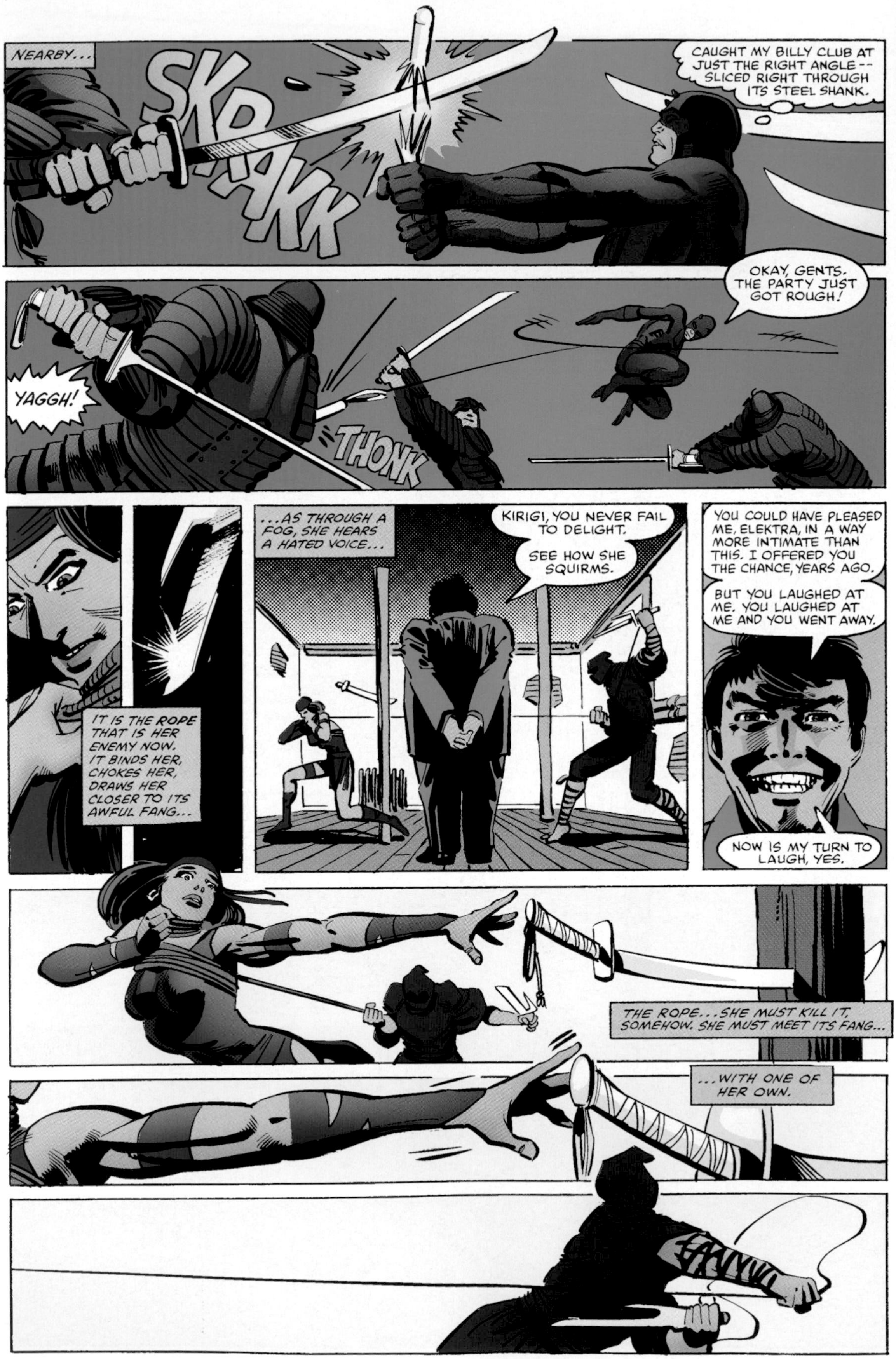
NEARBY...
SKRAKK
CAUGHT MY BILLY CLUB AT JUST THE RIGHT ANGLE -- SLICED RIGHT THROUGH ITS STEEL SHANK.
OKAY, GENTS. THE PARTY JUST GOT ROUGH!
YAGGH!
THONK
IT IS THE ROPE THAT IS HER ENEMY NOW. IT BINDS HER, CHOKES HER, DRAWS HER CLOSER TO ITS AWFUL FANG...
...AS THROUGH A FOG, SHE HEARS A HATED VOICE...
KIRIGI, YOU NEVER FAIL TO DELIGHT.
SEE HOW SHE SQUIRMS.
YOU COULD HAVE PLEASED ME, ELEKTRA, IN A WAY MORE INTIMATE THAN THIS. I OFFERED YOU THE CHANCE, YEARS AGO.
BUT YOU LAUGHED AT ME. YOU LAUGHED AT ME AND YOU WENT AWAY.
NOW IS MY TURN TO LAUGH, YES.
THE ROPE...SHE MUST KILL IT, SOMEHOW. SHE MUST MEET ITS FANG...
...WITH ONE OF HER OWN.

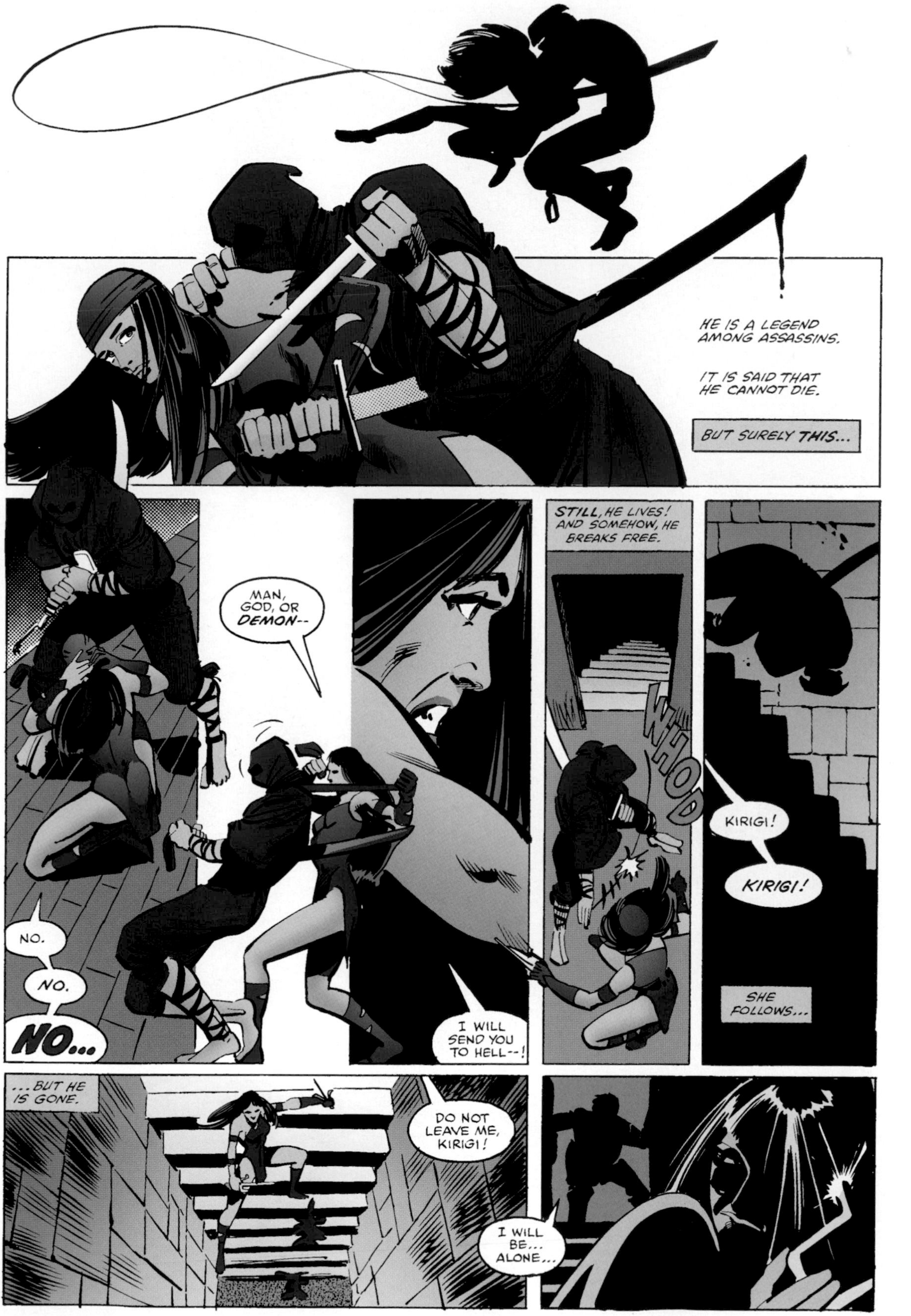
HE IS A LEGEND AMONG ASSASSINS.
IT IS SAID THAT HE CANNOT DIE.
BUT SURELY THIS...
MAN, GOD, OR DEMON--
NO.
NO.
NO...
I WILL SEND YOU TO HELL--!
STILL, HE LIVES! AND SOMEHOW, HE BREAKS FREE.
WHOD
KIRIGI!
KIRIGI!
SHE FOLLOWS...
...BUT HE IS GONE.
DO NOT LEAVE ME, KIRIGI!
I WILL BE... ALONE...

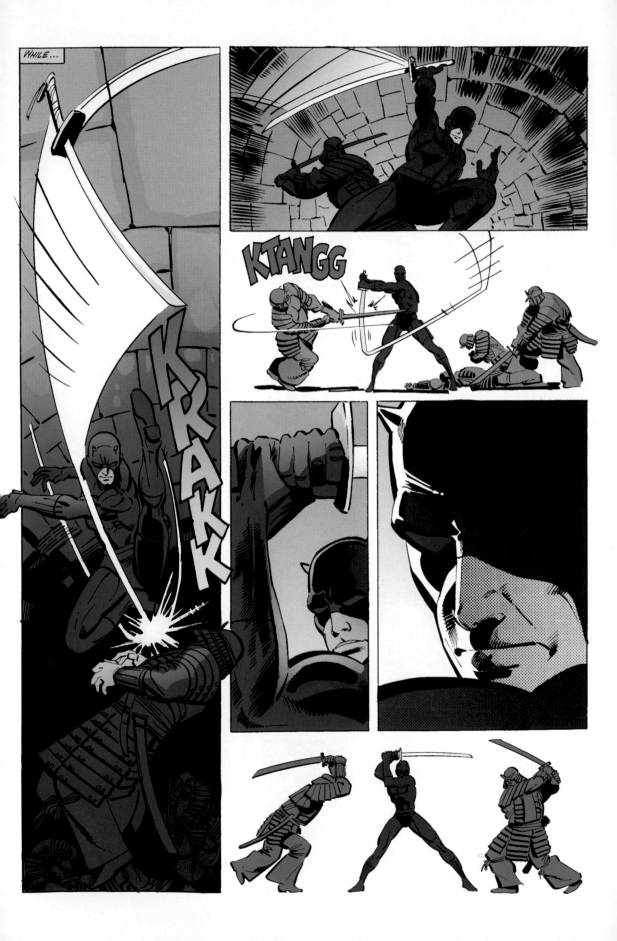

WHILE...

KTANGG

KRAKK

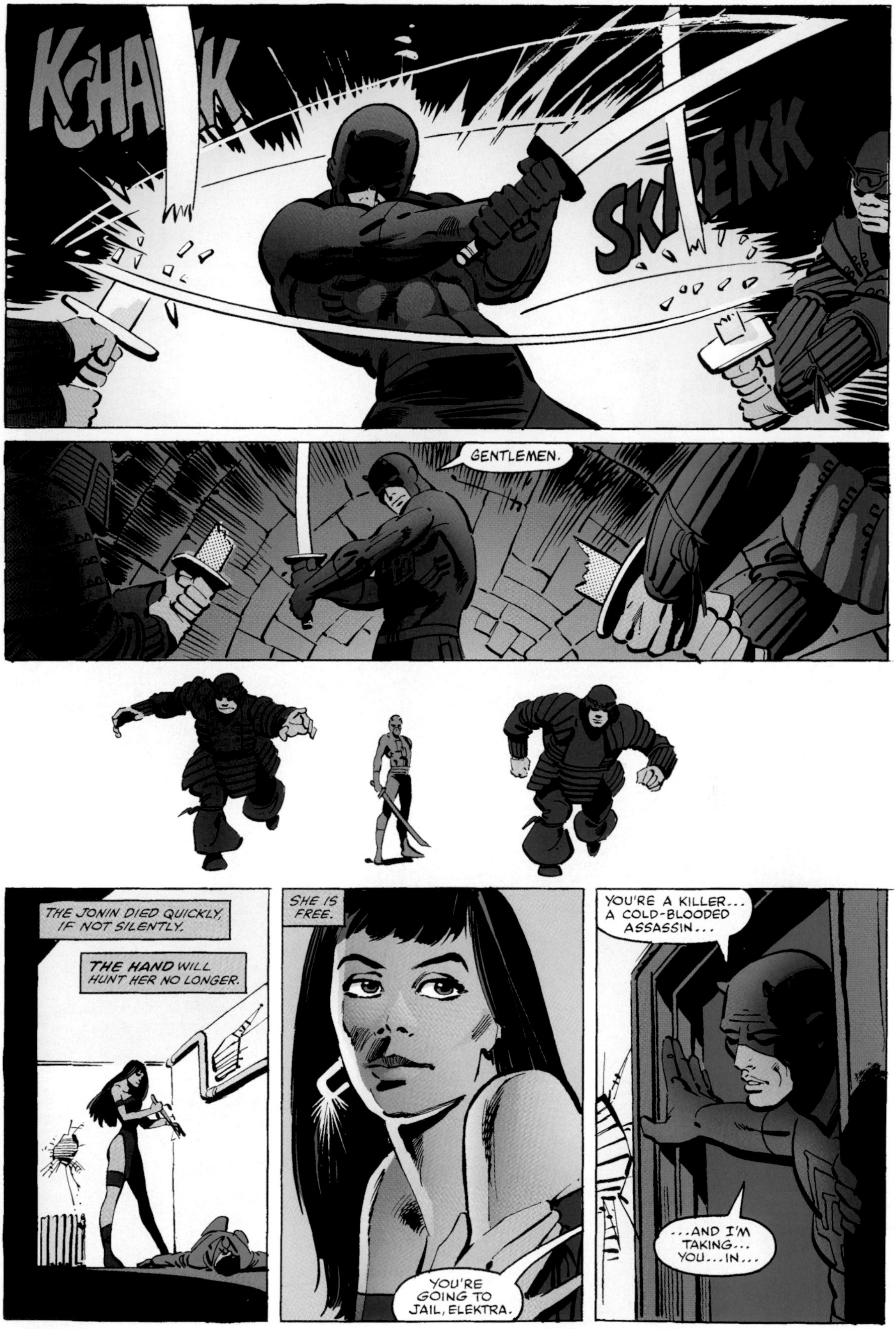
KCHAKK
SKREKK
GENTLEMEN.
THE JONIN DIED QUICKLY, IF NOT SILENTLY.
THE HAND WILL HUNT HER NO LONGER.
SHE IS FREE.
YOU'RE GOING TO JAIL, ELEKTRA.
YOU'RE A KILLER... A COLD-BLOODED ASSASSIN...
...AND I'M TAKING... YOU...IN...

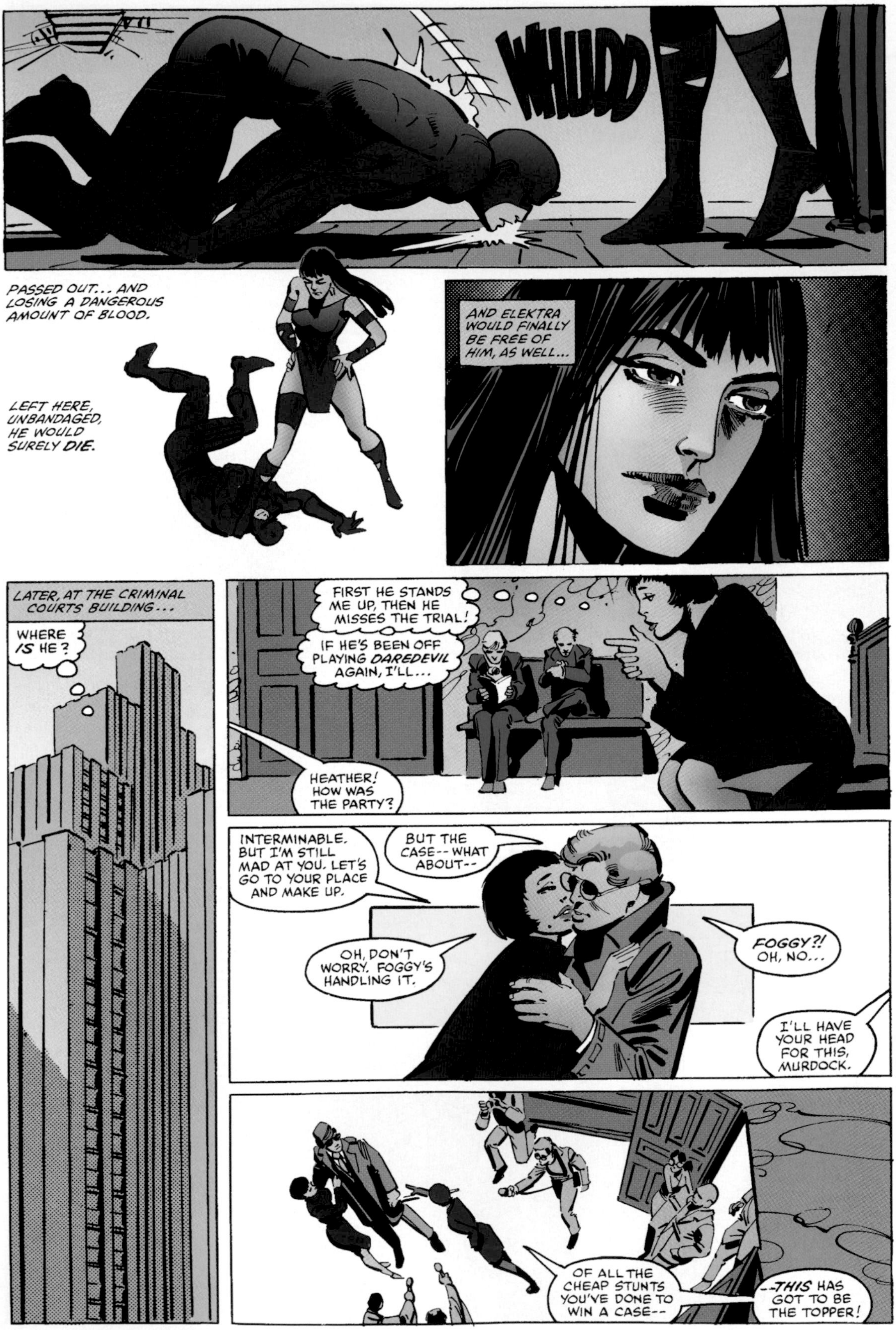
WHUDD
PASSED OUT... AND LOSING A DANGEROUS AMOUNT OF BLOOD.
LEFT HERE, UNBANDAGED, HE WOULD SURELY DIE.
AND ELEKTRA WOULD FINALLY BE FREE OF HIM, AS WELL...
LATER, AT THE CRIMINAL COURTS BUILDING...
WHERE IS HE?
FIRST HE STANDS ME UP, THEN HE MISSES THE TRIAL!
IF HE'S BEEN OFF PLAYING DAREDEVIL AGAIN, I'LL...
HEATHER! HOW WAS THE PARTY?
INTERMINABLE. BUT I'M STILL MAD AT YOU. LET'S GO TO YOUR PLACE AND MAKE UP.
BUT THE CASE-- WHAT ABOUT--
OH, DON'T WORRY. FOGGY'S HANDLING IT.
FOGGY?! OH, NO...
I'LL HAVE YOUR HEAD FOR THIS, MURDOCK.
OF ALL THE CHEAP STUNTS YOU'VE DONE TO WIN A CASE--
--THIS HAS GOT TO BE THE TOPPER!

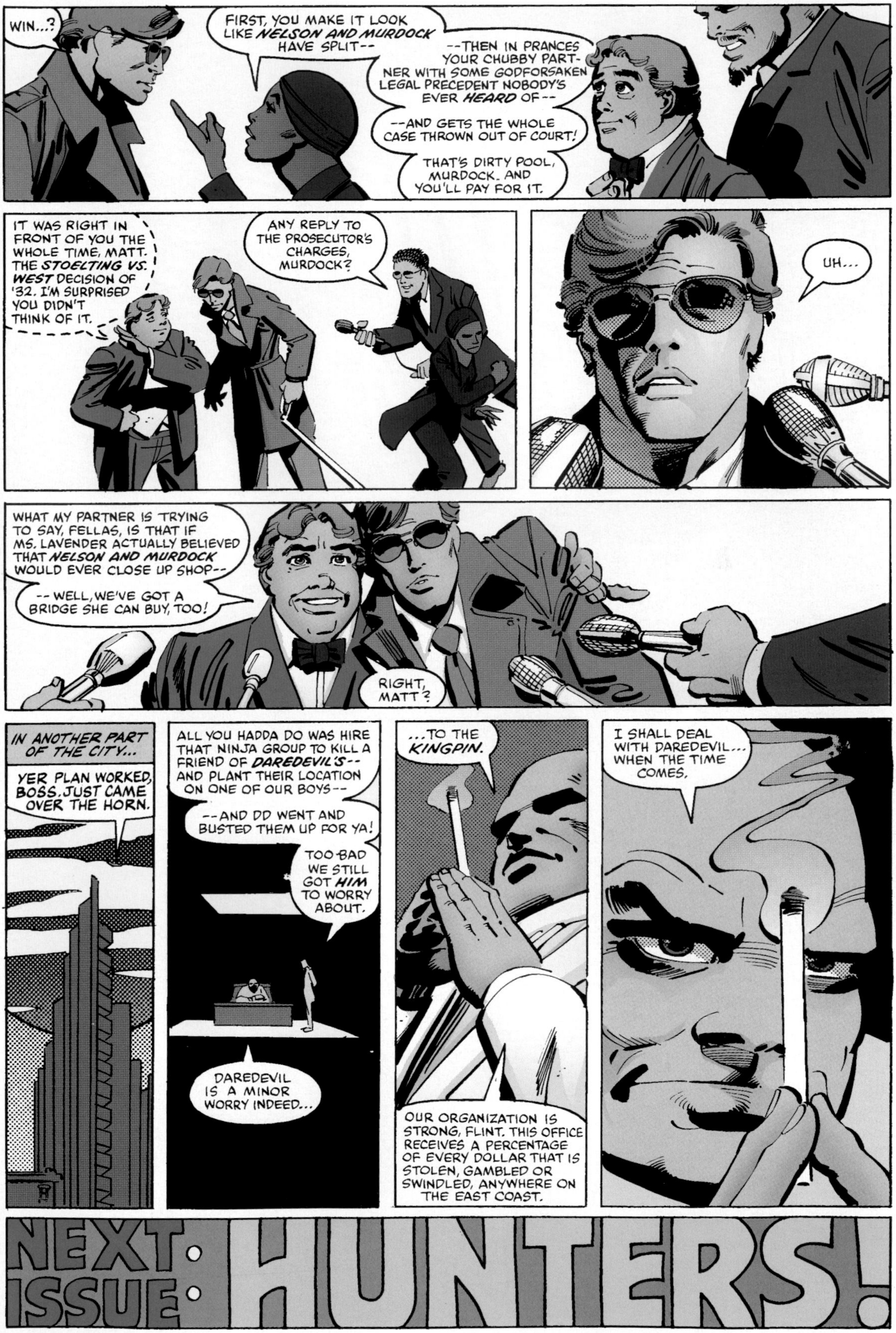
WIN...?
FIRST, YOU MAKE IT LOOK LIKE NELSON AND MURDOCK HAVE SPLIT--
--THEN IN PRANCES YOUR CHUBBY PARTNER WITH SOME GODFORSAKEN LEGAL PRECEDENT NOBODY'S EVER HEARD OF--
--AND GETS THE WHOLE CASE THROWN OUT OF COURT!
THAT'S DIRTY POOL, MURDOCK. AND YOU'LL PAY FOR IT.
IT WAS RIGHT IN FRONT OF YOU THE WHOLE TIME, MATT. THE STOELTING VS. WEST DECISION OF '32. I'M SURPRISED YOU DIDN'T THINK OF IT.
ANY REPLY TO THE PROSECUTOR'S CHARGES, MURDOCK?
UH...
WHAT MY PARTNER IS TRYING TO SAY, FELLAS, IS THAT IF MS. LAVENDER ACTUALLY BELIEVED THAT NELSON AND MURDOCK WOULD EVER CLOSE UP SHOP--
--WELL, WE'VE GOT A BRIDGE SHE CAN BUY, TOO!
RIGHT, MATT?
IN ANOTHER PART OF THE CITY...
YER PLAN WORKED, BOSS. JUST CAME OVER THE HORN.
ALL YOU HADDA DO WAS HIRE THAT NINJA GROUP TO KILL A FRIEND OF DAREDEVIL'S--AND PLANT THEIR LOCATION ON ONE OF OUR BOYS--
--AND DD WENT AND BUSTED THEM UP FOR YA!
TOO BAD WE STILL GOT HIM TO WORRY ABOUT.
DAREDEVIL IS A MINOR WORRY INDEED...
...TO THE KINGPIN.
OUR ORGANIZATION IS STRONG, FLINT. THIS OFFICE RECEIVES A PERCENTAGE OF EVERY DOLLAR THAT IS STOLEN, GAMBLED OR SWINDLED, ANYWHERE ON THE EAST COAST.
I SHALL DEAL WITH DAREDEVIL... WHEN THE TIME COMES.
NEXT ISSUE: HUNTERS!

DAREDEVIL #176

NOV 1981

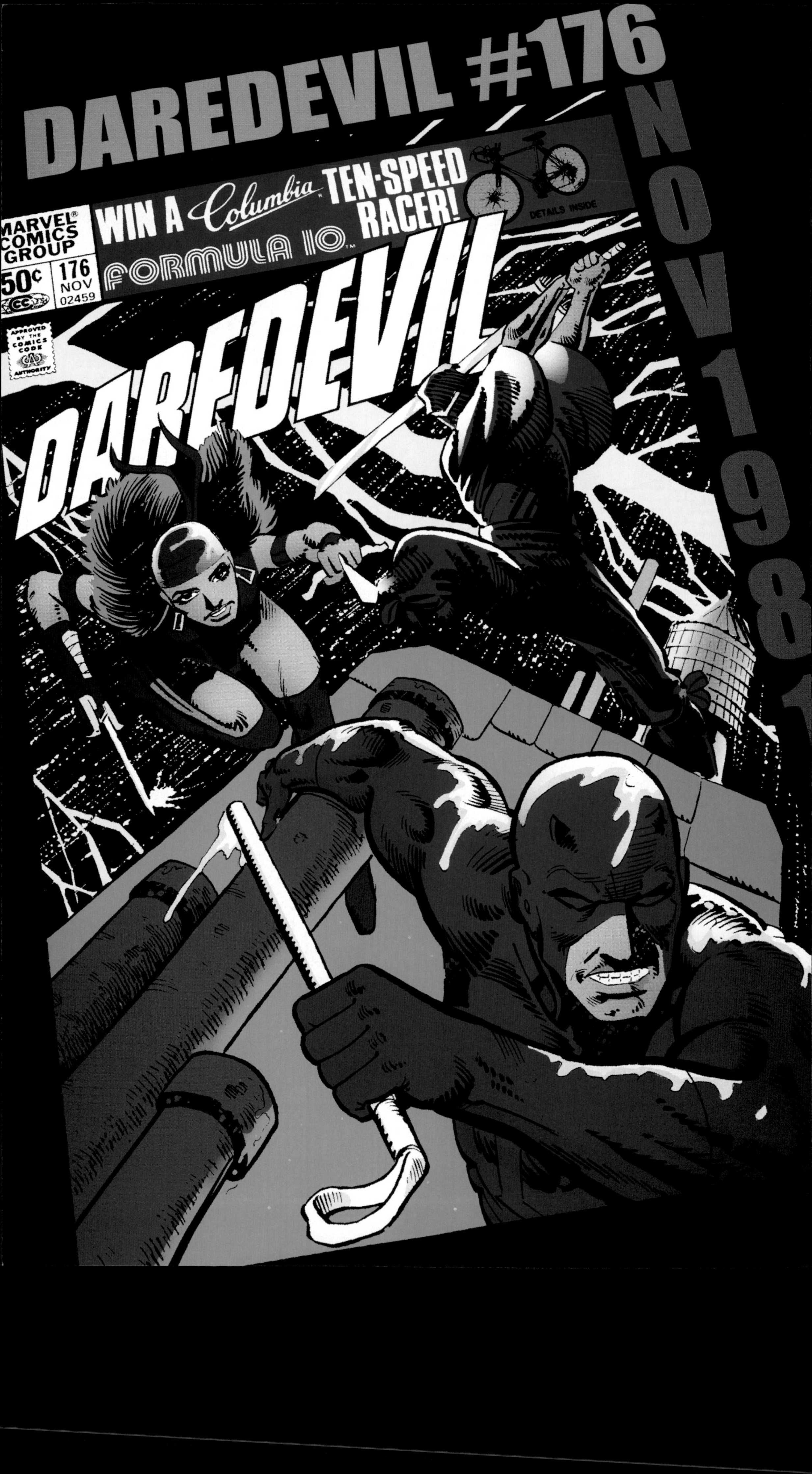
MARVEL® COMICS GROUP
50¢
176 NOV
02459
APPROVED BY THE COMICS CODE AUTHORITY
WIN A Columbia TEN-SPEED RACER!
FORMULA 10™
DETAILS INSIDE
DAREDEVIL

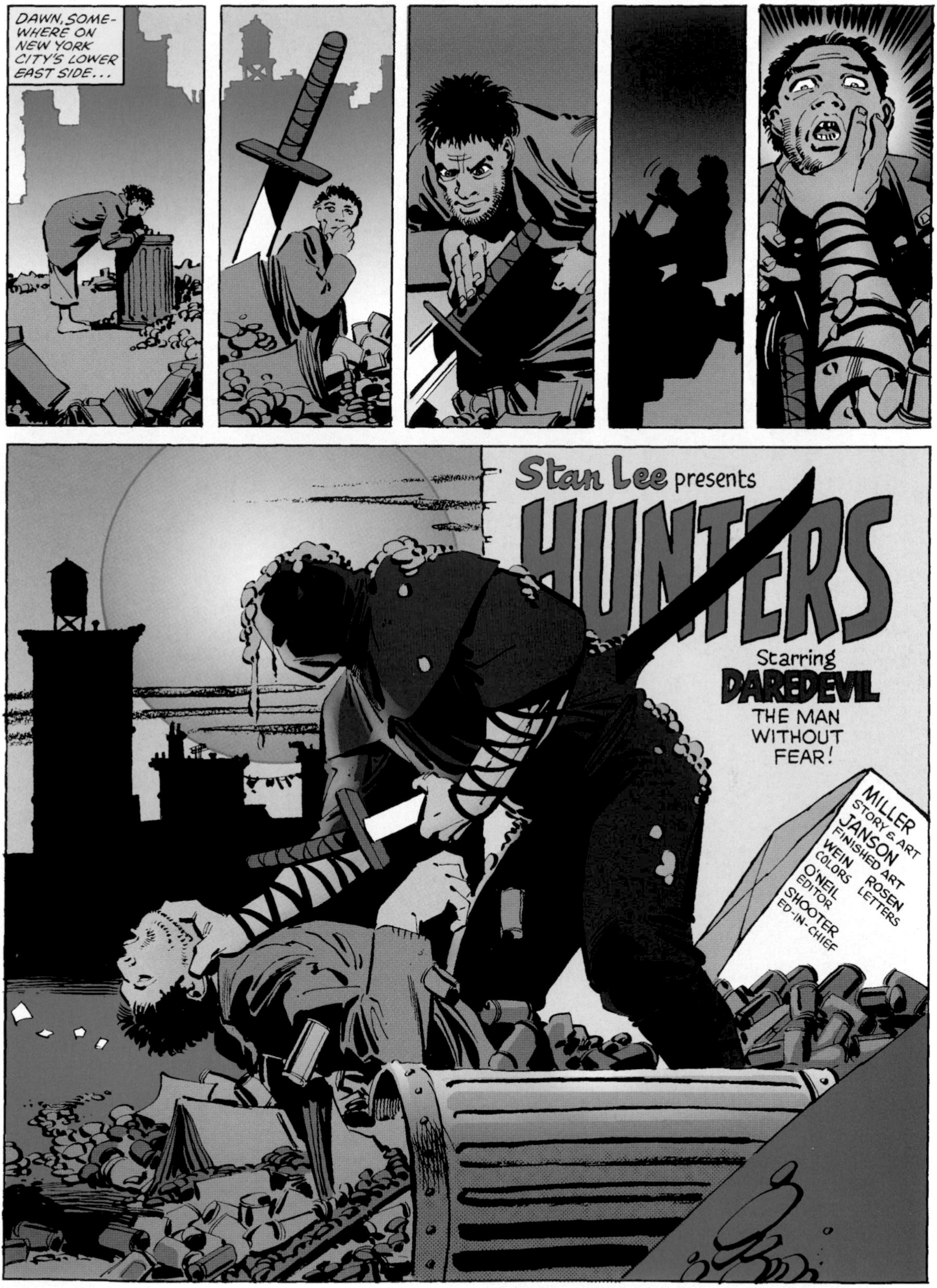
DAWN, SOME-WHERE ON NEW YORK CITY'S LOWER EAST SIDE...
Stan Lee presents
HUNTERS
Starring DAREDEVIL
THE MAN WITHOUT FEAR!
MILLER STORY & ART
JANSON FINISHED ART
ROSEN LETTERS
WEIN COLORS
O'NEIL EDITOR
SHOOTER ED-IN-CHIEF

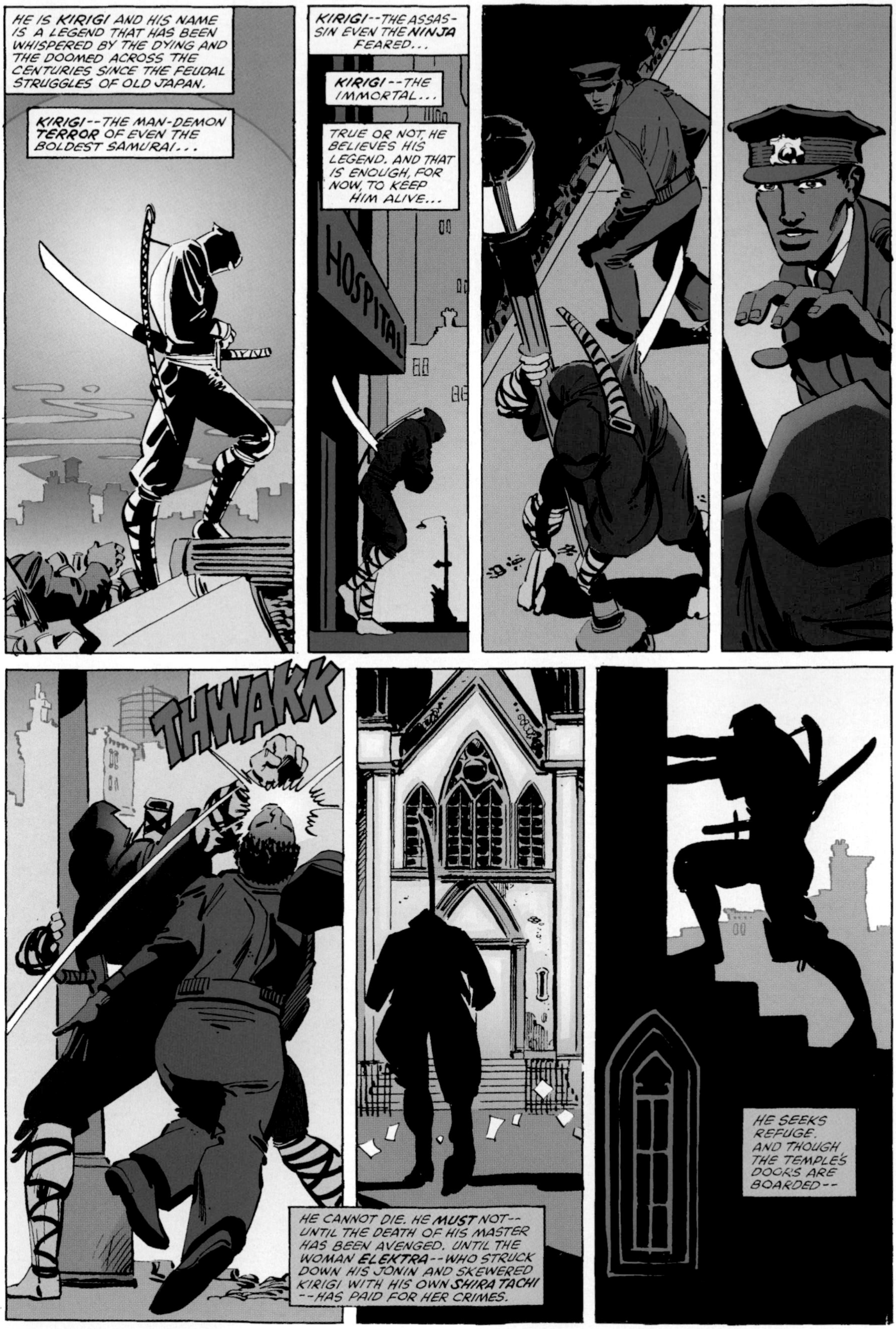
HE IS KIRIGI AND HIS NAME IS A LEGEND THAT HAS BEEN WHISPERED BY THE DYING AND THE DOOMED ACROSS THE CENTURIES SINCE THE FEUDAL STRUGGLES OF OLD JAPAN.
KIRIGI--THE MAN-DEMON TERROR OF EVEN THE BOLDEST SAMURAI...
KIRIGI--THE ASSASSIN EVEN THE NINJA FEARED...
KIRIGI--THE IMMORTAL...
TRUE OR NOT, HE BELIEVES HIS LEGEND. AND THAT IS ENOUGH, FOR NOW, TO KEEP HIM ALIVE...
HOSPITAL
THWAKK
HE CANNOT DIE. HE MUST NOT-- UNTIL THE DEATH OF HIS MASTER HAS BEEN AVENGED. UNTIL THE WOMAN ELEKTRA--WHO STRUCK DOWN HIS JONIN AND SKEWERED KIRIGI WITH HIS OWN SHIRA TACHI --HAS PAID FOR HER CRIMES.
HE SEEKS REFUGE. AND THOUGH THE TEMPLE'S DOORS ARE BOARDED--

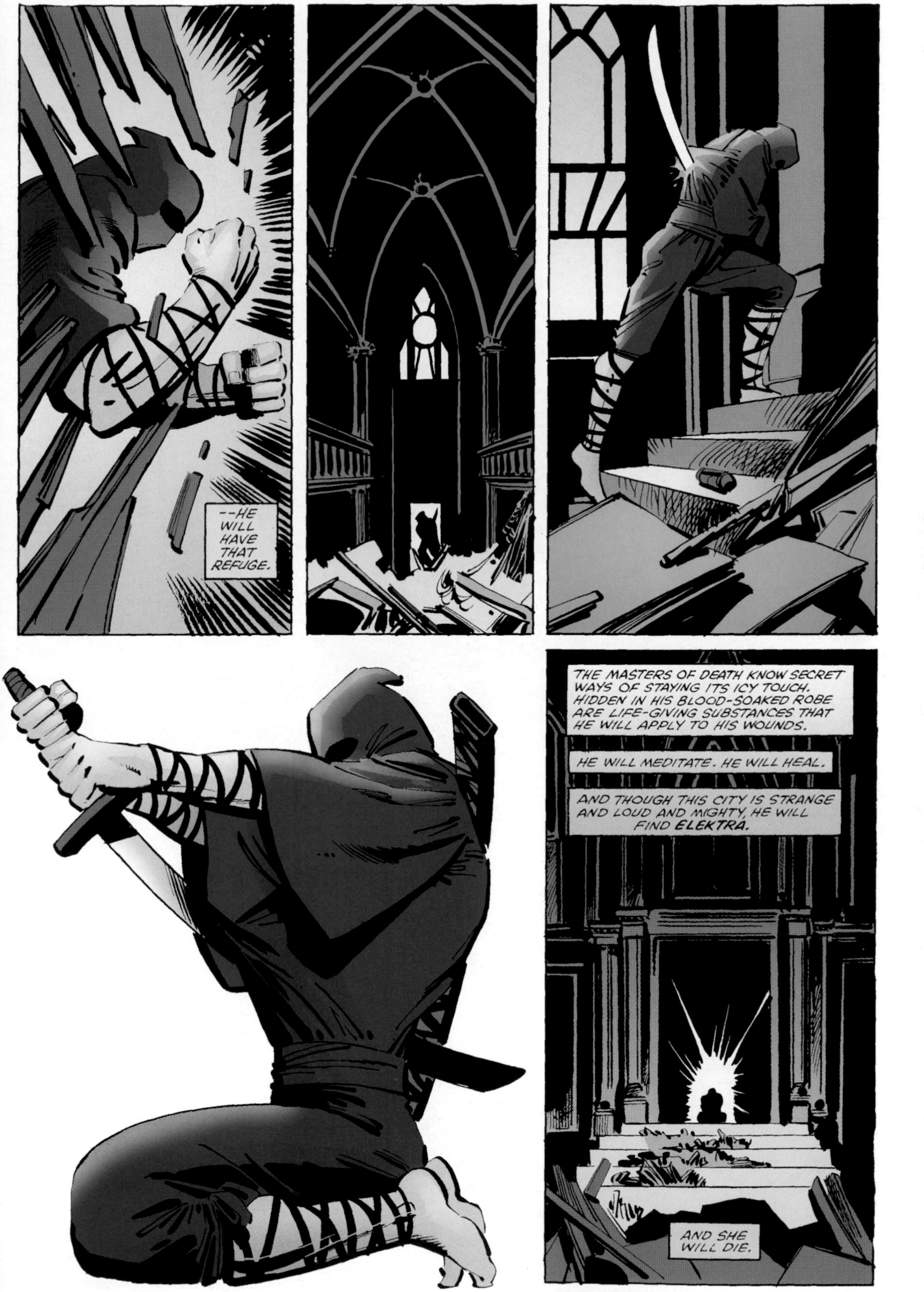
--HE WILL HAVE THAT REFUGE.
THE MASTERS OF DEATH KNOW SECRET WAYS OF STAYING ITS ICY TOUCH. HIDDEN IN HIS BLOOD-SOAKED ROBE ARE LIFE-GIVING SUBSTANCES THAT HE WILL APPLY TO HIS WOUNDS.
HE WILL MEDITATE. HE WILL HEAL.
AND THOUGH THIS CITY IS STRANGE AND LOUD AND MIGHTY, HE WILL FIND ELEKTRA.
AND SHE WILL DIE.

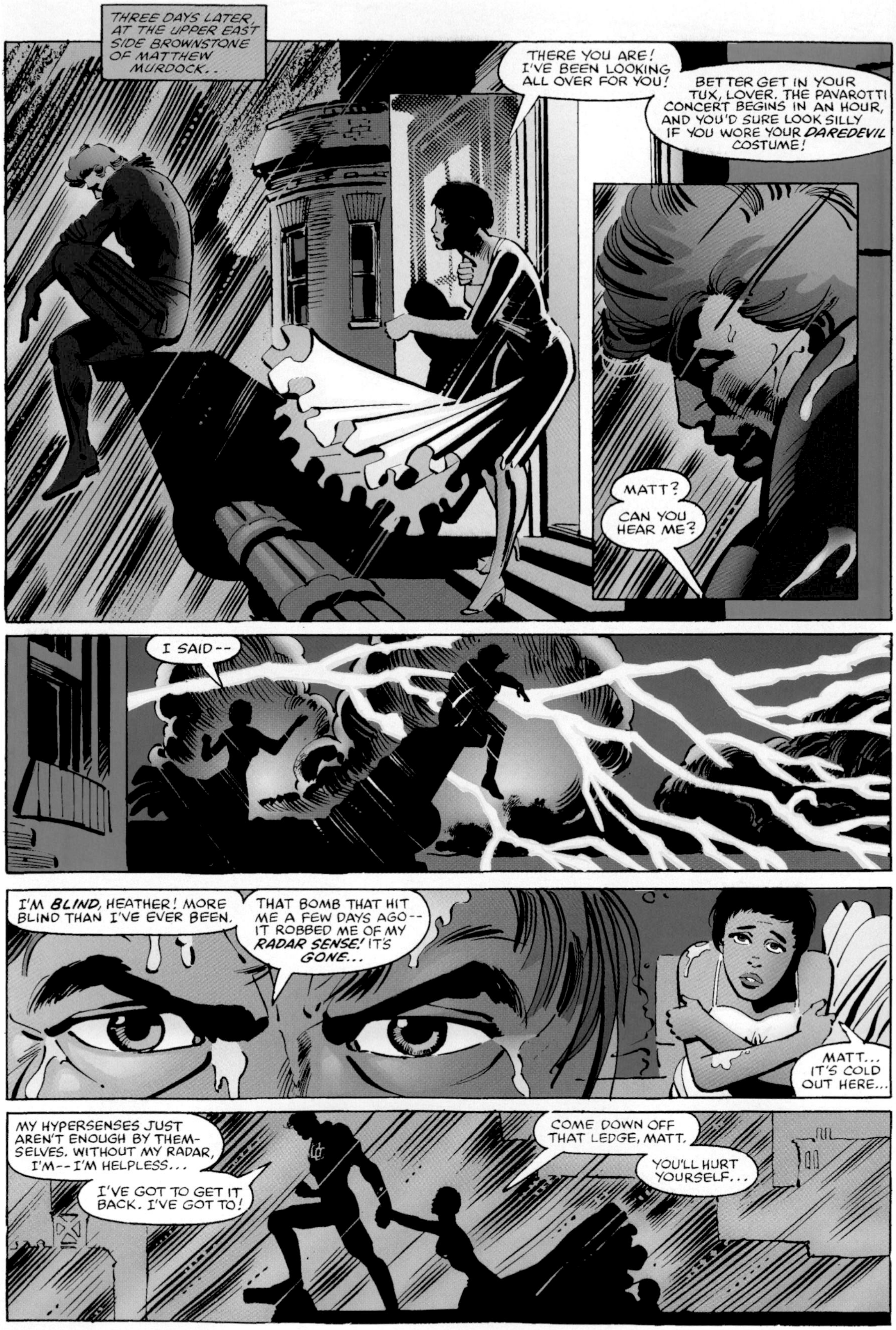
THREE DAYS LATER, AT THE UPPER EAST SIDE BROWNSTONE OF MATTHEW MURDOCK..
THERE YOU ARE! I'VE BEEN LOOKING ALL OVER FOR YOU!
BETTER GET IN YOUR TUX, LOVER. THE PAVAROTTI CONCERT BEGINS IN AN HOUR, AND YOU'D SURE LOOK SILLY IF YOU WORE YOUR DAREDEVIL COSTUME!
MATT? CAN YOU HEAR ME?
I SAID--
I'M BLIND, HEATHER! MORE BLIND THAN I'VE EVER BEEN.
THAT BOMB THAT HIT ME A FEW DAYS AGO--IT ROBBED ME OF MY RADAR SENSE! IT'S GONE...
MATT... IT'S COLD OUT HERE...
MY HYPERSENSES JUST AREN'T ENOUGH BY THEMSELVES. WITHOUT MY RADAR, I'M--I'M HELPLESS...
I'VE GOT TO GET IT BACK. I'VE GOT TO!
COME DOWN OFF THAT LEDGE, MATT.
YOU'LL HURT YOURSELF...

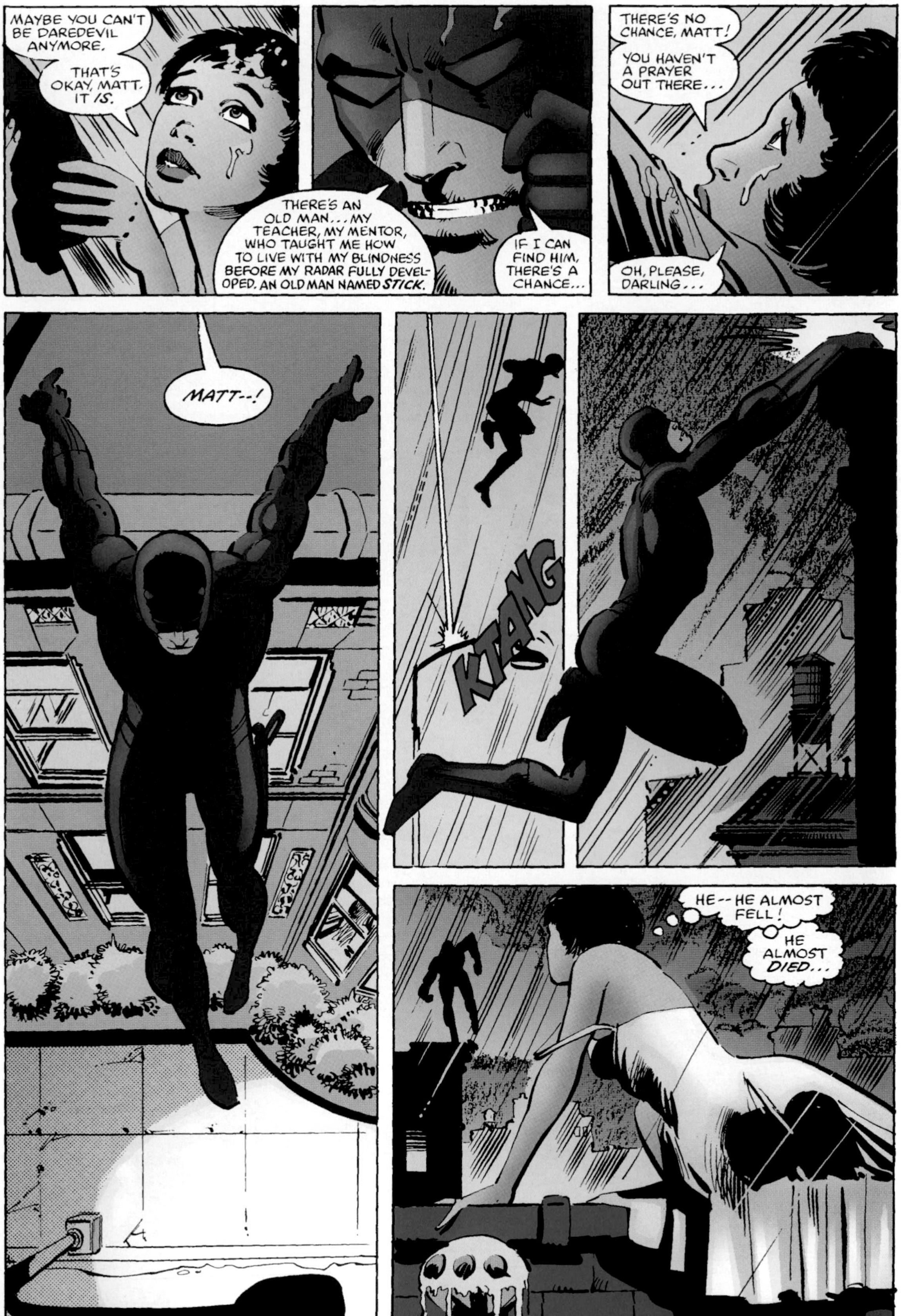
MAYBE YOU CAN'T BE DAREDEVIL ANYMORE.
THAT'S OKAY, MATT. IT IS.
THERE'S AN OLD MAN... MY TEACHER, MY MENTOR, WHO TAUGHT ME HOW TO LIVE WITH MY BLINDNESS BEFORE MY RADAR FULLY DEVELOPED. AN OLD MAN NAMED STICK.
IF I CAN FIND HIM, THERE'S A CHANCE...
THERE'S NO CHANCE, MATT!
YOU HAVEN'T A PRAYER OUT THERE...
OH, PLEASE, DARLING...
MATT--!
KTANG
HE--HE ALMOST FELL!
HE ALMOST DIED...

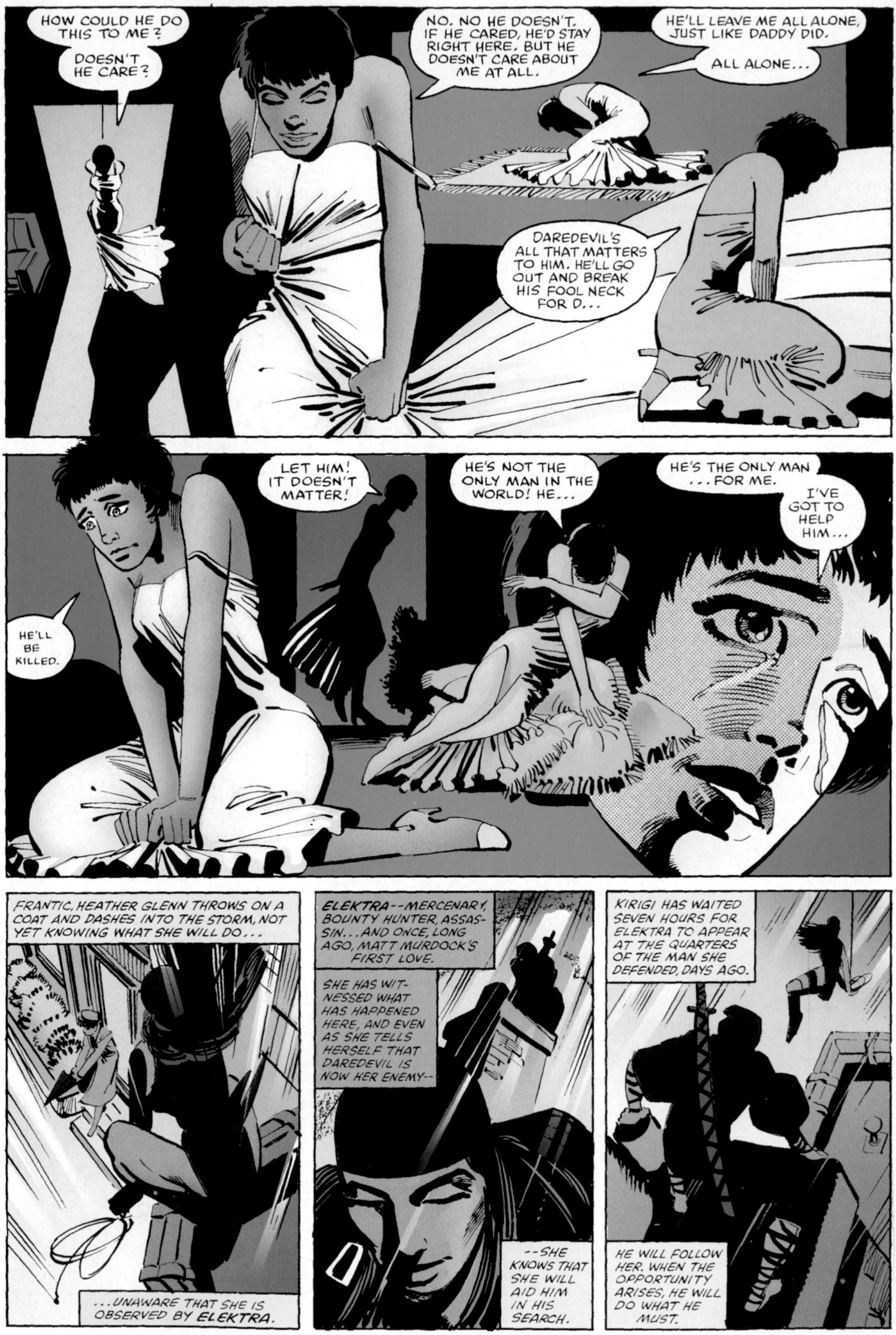
HOW COULD HE DO THIS TO ME?
DOESN'T HE CARE?
NO. NO HE DOESN'T. IF HE CARED, HE'D STAY RIGHT HERE. BUT HE DOESN'T CARE ABOUT ME AT ALL.
HE'LL LEAVE ME ALL ALONE, JUST LIKE DADDY DID.
ALL ALONE...
DAREDEVIL'S ALL THAT MATTERS TO HIM. HE'LL GO OUT AND BREAK HIS FOOL NECK FOR D...
HE'LL BE KILLED.
LET HIM! IT DOESN'T MATTER!
HE'S NOT THE ONLY MAN IN THE WORLD! HE...
HE'S THE ONLY MAN ...FOR ME.
I'VE GOT TO HELP HIM...
FRANTIC, HEATHER GLENN THROWS ON A COAT AND DASHES INTO THE STORM, NOT YET KNOWING WHAT SHE WILL DO...
...UNAWARE THAT SHE IS OBSERVED BY ELEKTRA.
ELEKTRA--MERCENARY, BOUNTY HUNTER, ASSAS-SIN...AND ONCE, LONG AGO, MATT MURDOCK'S FIRST LOVE.
SHE HAS WIT-NESSED WHAT HAS HAPPENED HERE, AND EVEN AS SHE TELLS HERSELF THAT DAREDEVIL IS NOW HER ENEMY--
--SHE KNOWS THAT SHE WILL AID HIM IN HIS SEARCH.
KIRIGI HAS WAITED SEVEN HOURS FOR ELEKTRA TO APPEAR AT THE QUARTERS OF THE MAN SHE DEFENDED, DAYS AGO.
HE WILL FOLLOW HER. WHEN THE OPPORTUNITY ARISES, HE WILL DO WHAT HE MUST.

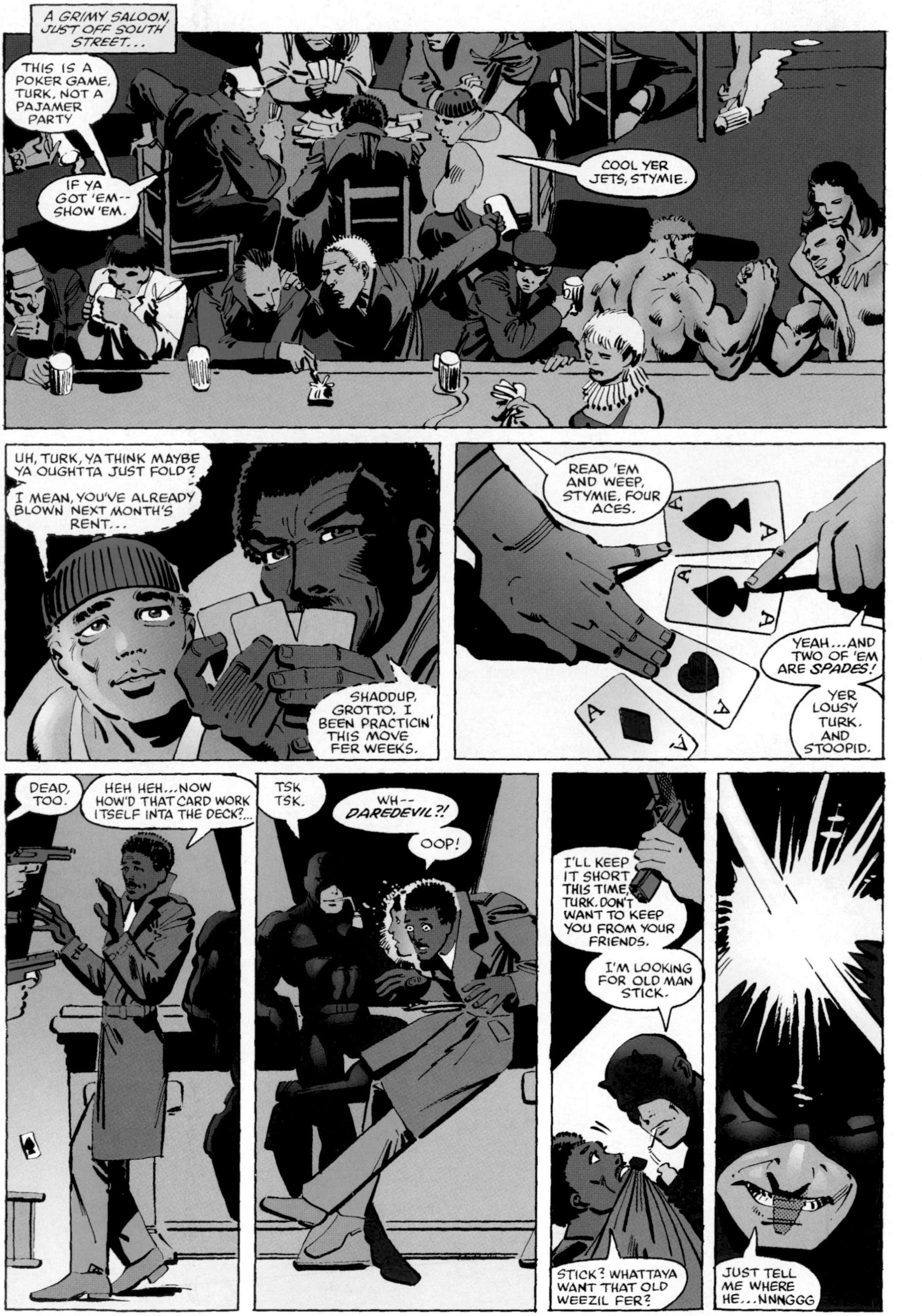
A GRIMY SALOON, JUST OFF SOUTH STREET...
THIS IS A POKER GAME, TURK, NOT A PAJAMER PARTY
IF YA GOT 'EM-- SHOW 'EM.
COOL YER JETS, STYMIE.
UH, TURK, YA THINK MAYBE YA OUGHTTA JUST FOLD?
I MEAN, YOU'VE ALREADY BLOWN NEXT MONTH'S RENT...
SHADDUP, GROTTO. I BEEN PRACTICIN' THIS MOVE FER WEEKS.
READ 'EM AND WEEP, STYMIE. FOUR ACES.
YEAH...AND TWO OF 'EM ARE SPADES!
YER LOUSY TURK. AND STOOPID.
DEAD, TOO.
HEH HEH...NOW HOW'D THAT CARD WORK ITSELF INTA THE DECK?...
TSK TSK.
WH-- DAREDEVIL?!
OOP!
I'LL KEEP IT SHORT THIS TIME, TURK. DON'T WANT TO KEEP YOU FROM YOUR FRIENDS.
I'M LOOKING FOR OLD MAN STICK.
STICK? WHATTAYA WANT THAT OLD WEEZIL FER?
JUST TELL ME WHERE HE...NNNGGG

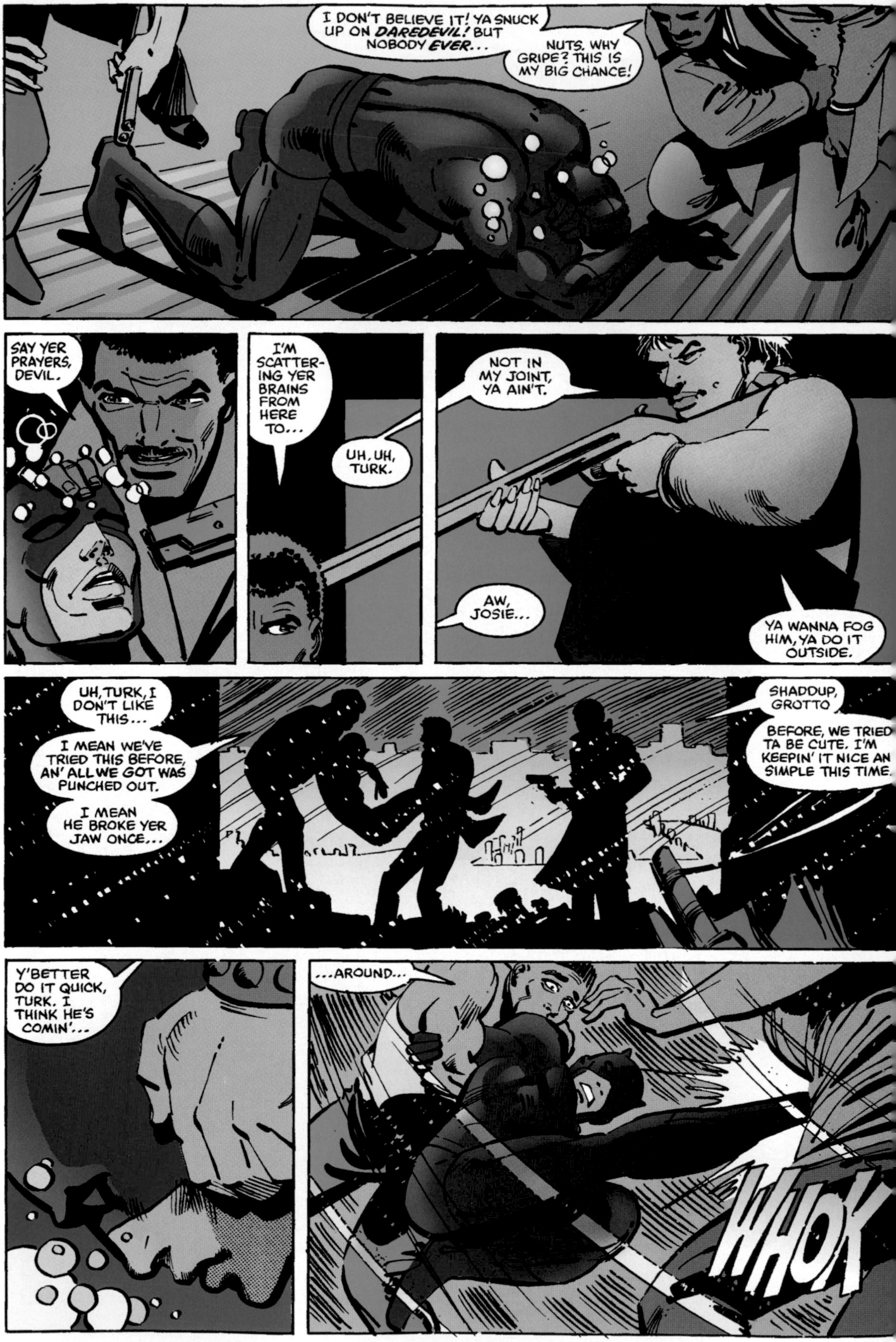
I DON'T BELIEVE IT! YA SNUCK UP ON DAREDEVIL! BUT NOBODY EVER...
NUTS. WHY GRIPE? THIS IS MY BIG CHANCE!
SAY YER PRAYERS, DEVIL.
I'M SCATTERING YER BRAINS FROM HERE TO...
UH, UH, TURK.
NOT IN MY JOINT, YA AIN'T.
AW, JOSIE...
YA WANNA FOG HIM, YA DO IT OUTSIDE.
UH, TURK, I DON'T LIKE THIS...
I MEAN WE'VE TRIED THIS BEFORE, AN' ALL WE GOT WAS PUNCHED OUT.
I MEAN HE BROKE YER JAW ONCE...
SHADDUP, GROTTO
BEFORE, WE TRIED TA BE CUTE. I'M KEEPIN' IT NICE AN SIMPLE THIS TIME.
Y'BETTER DO IT QUICK, TURK. I THINK HE'S COMIN'...
...AROUND...
WHOK

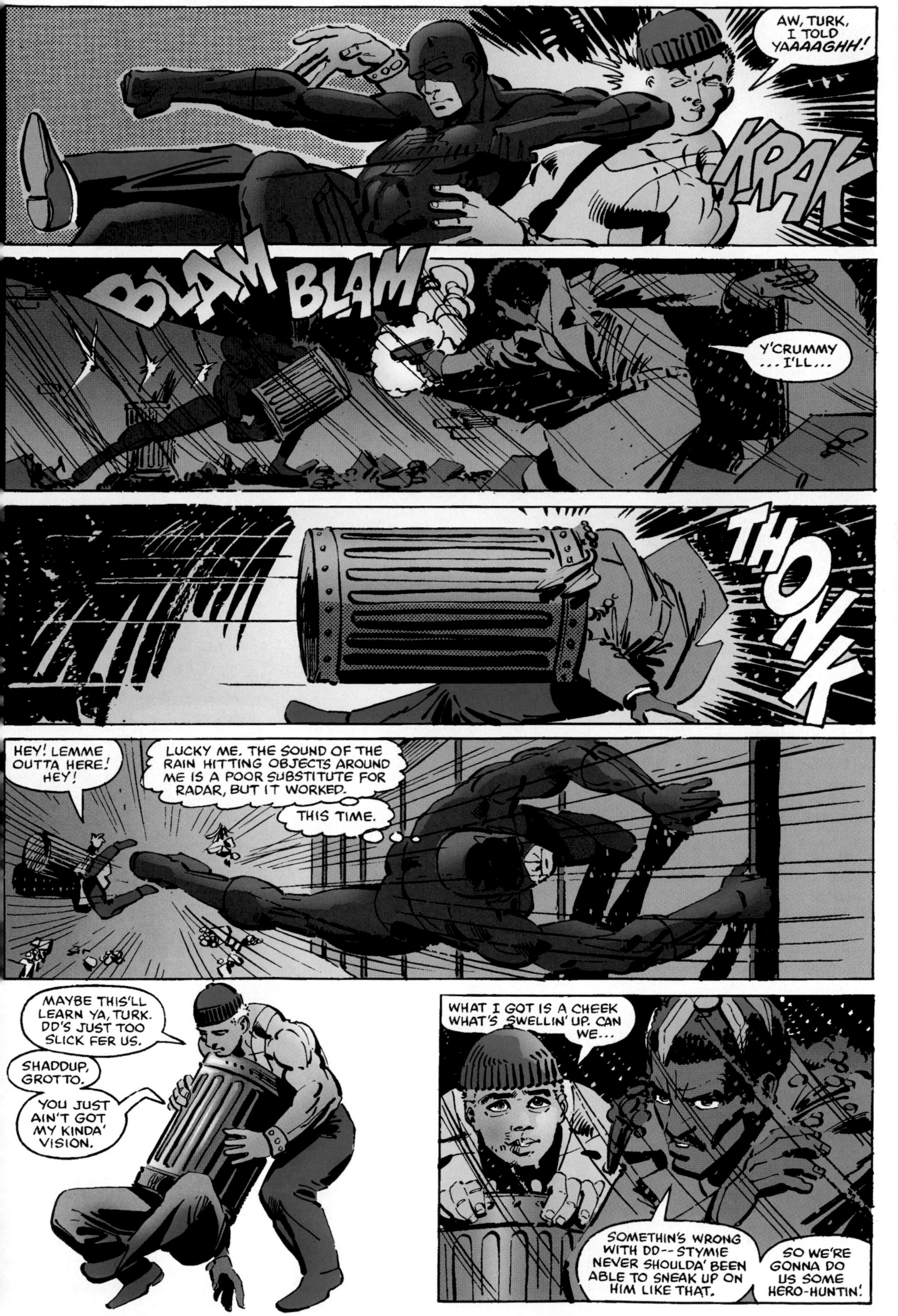
AW, TURK, I TOLD YAAAAGHH!
KRAK
BLAM BLAM
Y'CRUMMY ...I'LL...
THONK
HEY! LEMME OUTTA HERE! HEY!
LUCKY ME. THE SOUND OF THE RAIN HITTING OBJECTS AROUND ME IS A POOR SUBSTITUTE FOR RADAR, BUT IT WORKED.
THIS TIME.
MAYBE THIS'LL LEARN YA, TURK. DD'S JUST TOO SLICK FER US.
SHADDUP, GROTTO.
YOU JUST AIN'T GOT MY KINDA' VISION.
WHAT I GOT IS A CHEEK WHAT'S SWELLIN' UP. CAN WE...
SOMETHIN'S WRONG WITH DD-- STYMIE NEVER SHOULDA' BEEN ABLE TO SNEAK UP ON HIM LIKE THAT.
SO WE'RE GONNA DO US SOME HERO-HUNTIN'.

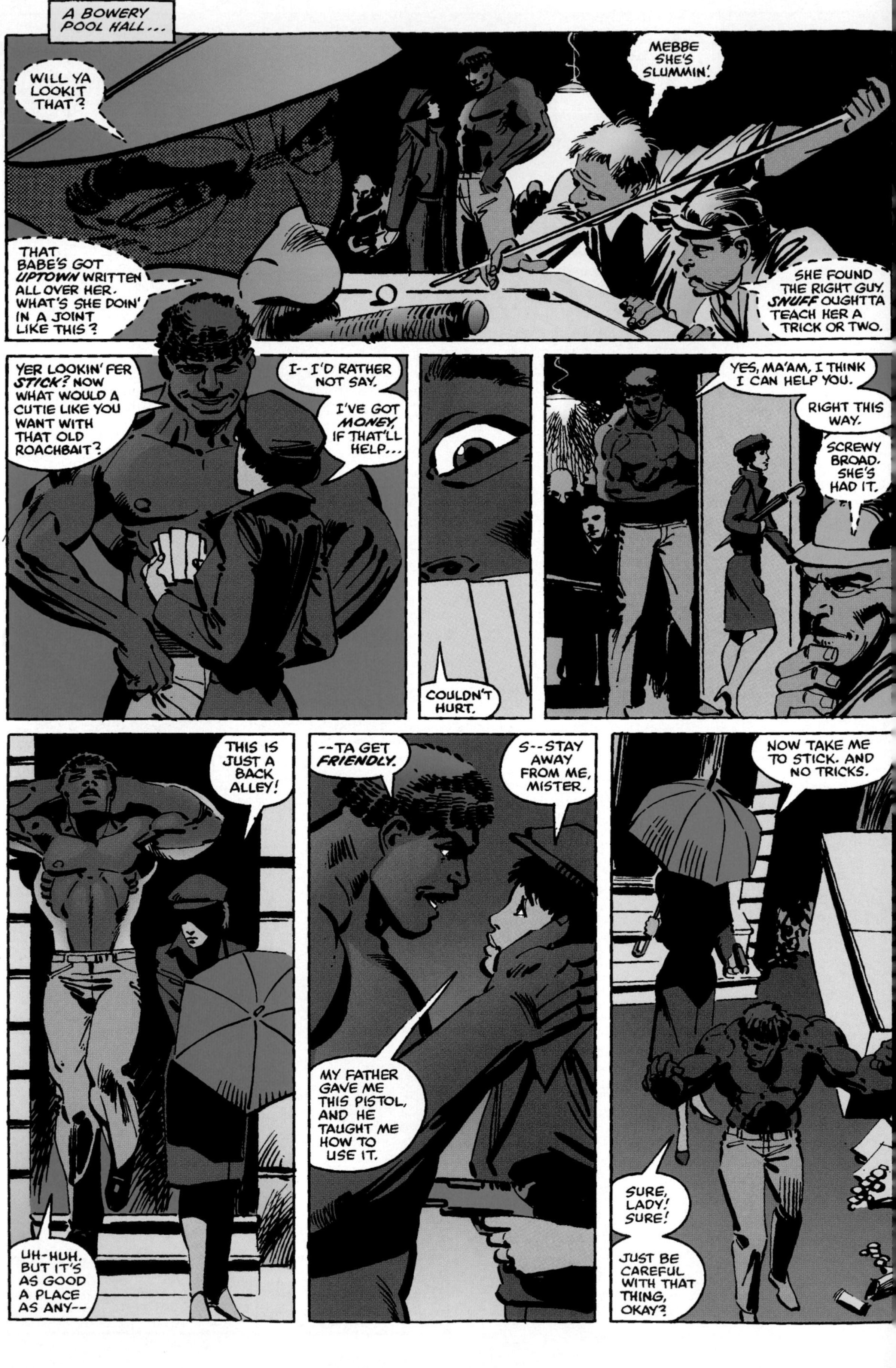
A BOWERY POOL HALL...
WILL YA LOOKIT THAT?
MEBBE SHE'S SLUMMIN'.
THAT BABE'S GOT UPTOWN WRITTEN ALL OVER HER. WHAT'S SHE DOIN' IN A JOINT LIKE THIS?
SHE FOUND THE RIGHT GUY. SNUFF OUGHTTA TEACH HER A TRICK OR TWO.
YER LOOKIN' FER STICK? NOW WHAT WOULD A CUTIE LIKE YOU WANT WITH THAT OLD ROACHBAIT?
I-- I'D RATHER NOT SAY.
I'VE GOT MONEY, IF THAT'LL HELP...
COULDN'T HURT.
YES, MA'AM, I THINK I CAN HELP YOU.
RIGHT THIS WAY.
SCREWY BROAD. SHE'S HAD IT.
THIS IS JUST A BACK ALLEY!
UH-HUH. BUT IT'S AS GOOD A PLACE AS ANY--
--TA GET FRIENDLY.
S--STAY AWAY FROM ME, MISTER.
MY FATHER GAVE ME THIS PISTOL, AND HE TAUGHT ME HOW TO USE IT.
NOW TAKE ME TO STICK. AND NO TRICKS.
SURE, LADY! SURE!
JUST BE CAREFUL WITH THAT THING, OKAY?

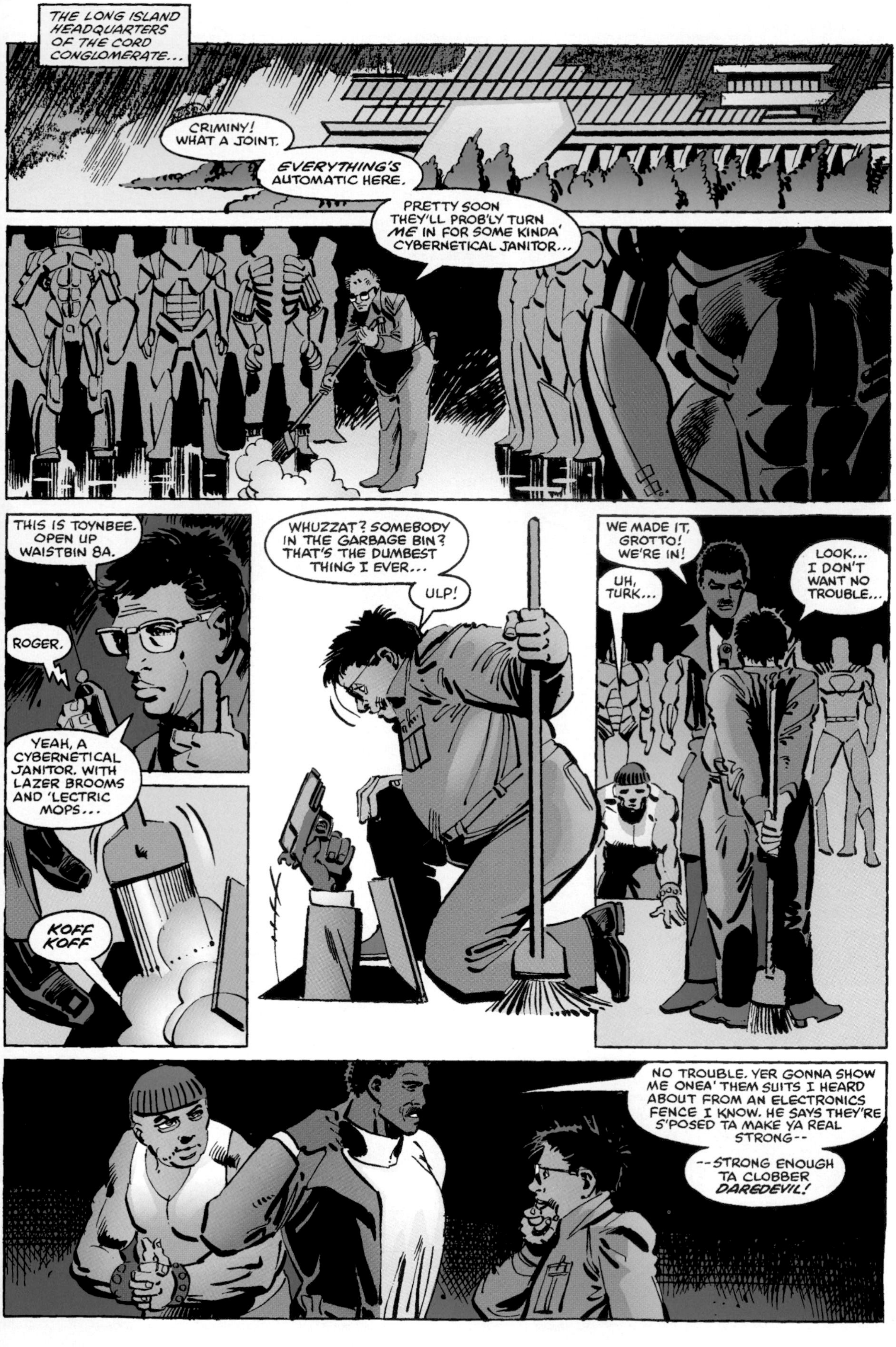
THE LONG ISLAND HEADQUARTERS OF THE CORD CONGLOMERATE...
CRIMINY! WHAT A JOINT.
EVERYTHING'S AUTOMATIC HERE.
PRETTY SOON THEY'LL PROB'LY TURN ME IN FOR SOME KINDA' CYBERNETICAL JANITOR...
THIS IS TOYNBEE. OPEN UP WAISTBIN 8A.
ROGER.
YEAH, A CYBERNETICAL JANITOR. WITH LAZER BROOMS AND 'LECTRIC MOPS...
KOFF KOFF
WHUZZAT? SOMEBODY IN THE GARBAGE BIN? THAT'S THE DUMBEST THING I EVER...
ULP!
WE MADE IT, GROTTO! WE'RE IN!
UH, TURK...
LOOK... I DON'T WANT NO TROUBLE...
NO TROUBLE. YER GONNA SHOW ME ONEA' THEM SUITS I HEARD ABOUT FROM AN ELECTRONICS FENCE I KNOW. HE SAYS THEY'RE S'POSED TA MAKE YA REAL STRONG--
--STRONG ENOUGH TA CLOBBER DAREDEVIL!

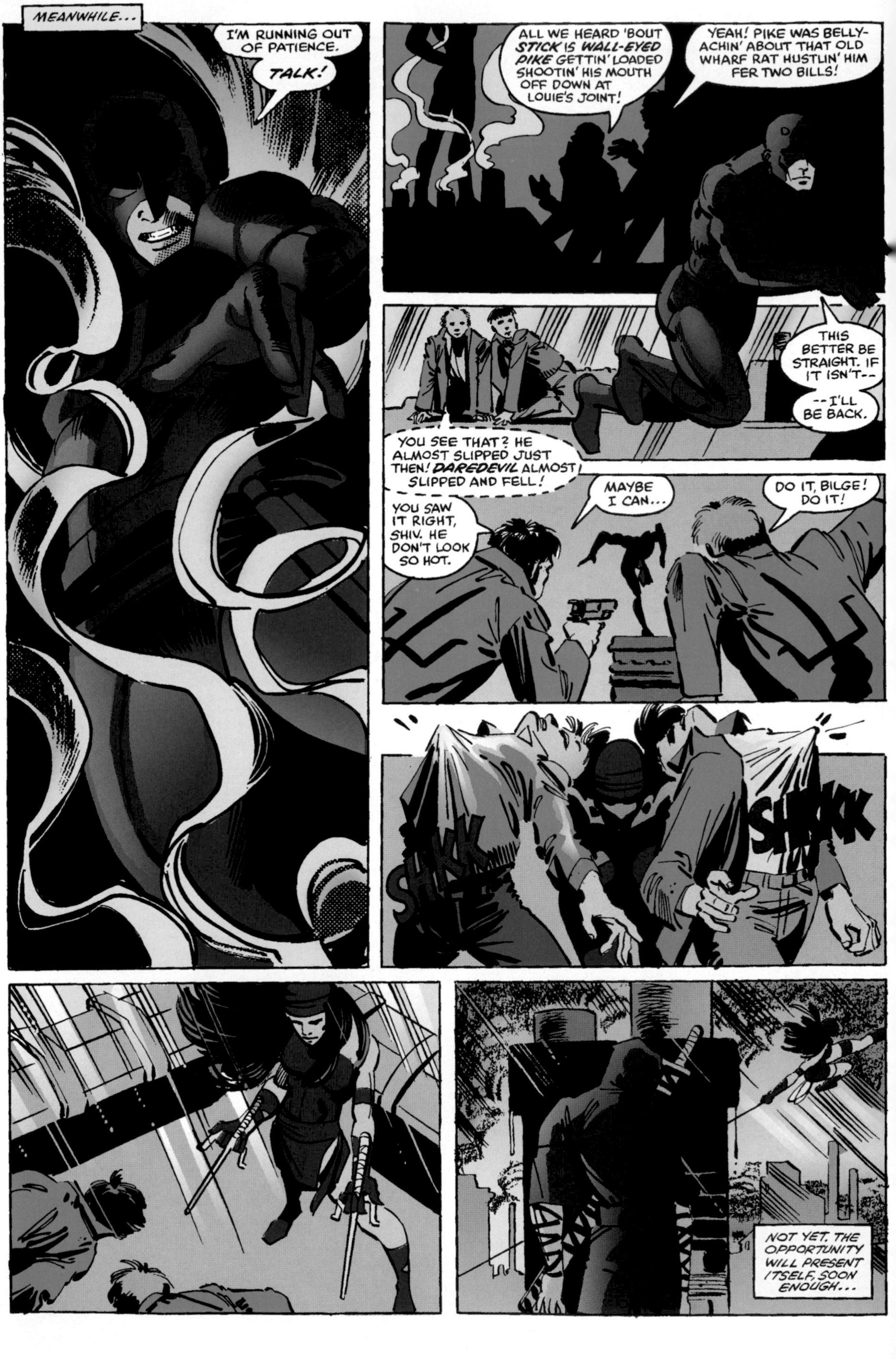
MEANWHILE...
I'M RUNNING OUT OF PATIENCE.
TALK!
ALL WE HEARD 'BOUT STICK IS WALL-EYED PIKE GETTIN' LOADED SHOOTIN' HIS MOUTH OFF DOWN AT LOUIE'S JOINT!
YEAH! PIKE WAS BELLY-ACHIN' ABOUT THAT OLD WHARF RAT HUSTLIN' HIM FER TWO BILLS!
THIS BETTER BE STRAIGHT. IF IT ISN'T--
--I'LL BE BACK.
YOU SEE THAT? HE ALMOST SLIPPED JUST THEN! DAREDEVIL ALMOST SLIPPED AND FELL!
YOU SAW IT RIGHT, SHIV. HE DON'T LOOK SO HOT.
MAYBE I CAN...
DO IT, BILGE! DO IT!
SHKK
SHKK
NOT YET. THE OPPORTUNITY WILL PRESENT ITSELF, SOON ENOUGH...

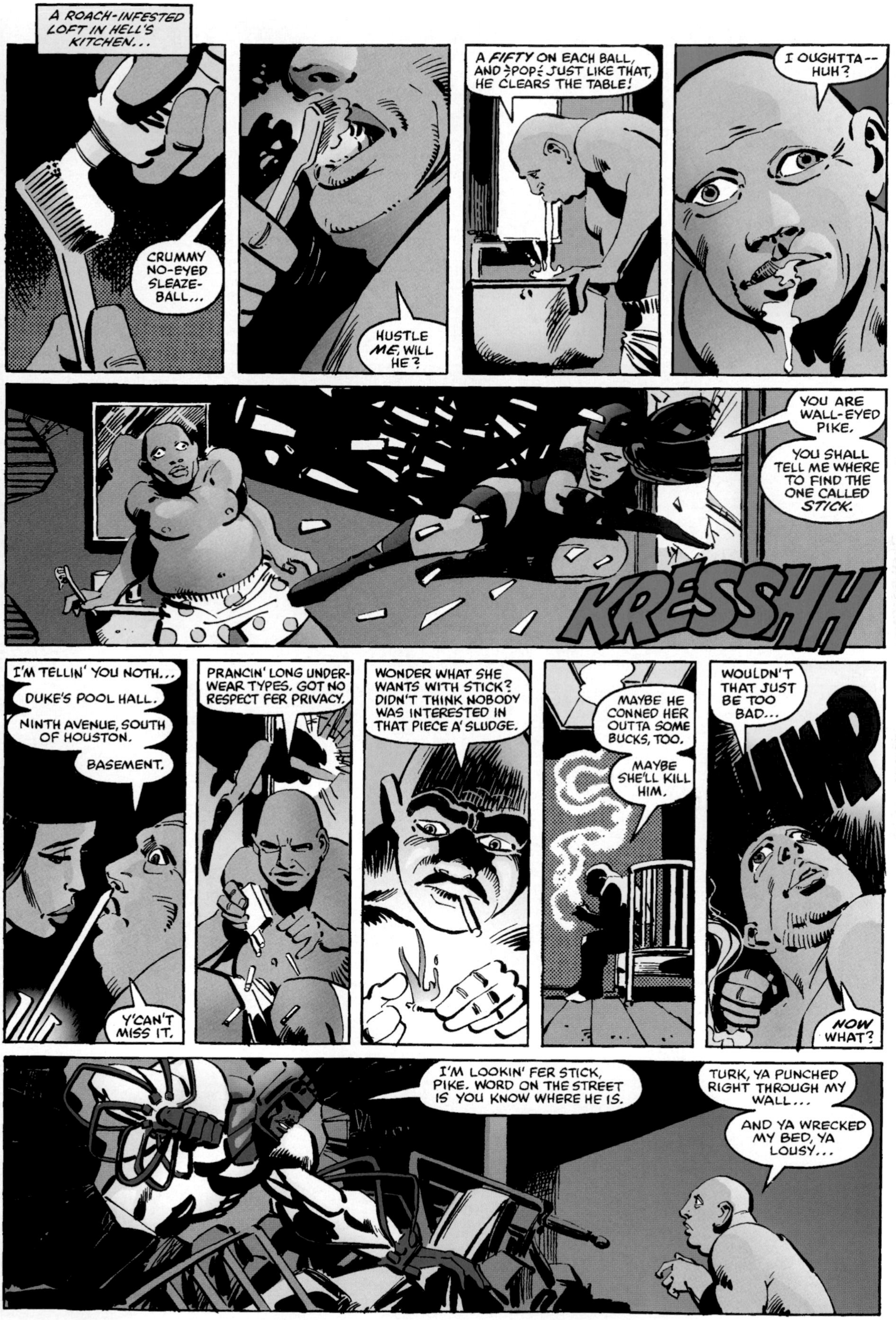
A ROACH-INFESTED LOFT IN HELL'S KITCHEN...
CRUMMY NO-EYED SLEAZE-BALL...
HUSTLE ME, WILL HE?
A FIFTY ON EACH BALL, AND POP JUST LIKE THAT, HE CLEARS THE TABLE!
I OUGHTTA-- HUH?
YOU ARE WALL-EYED PIKE.
YOU SHALL TELL ME WHERE TO FIND THE ONE CALLED STICK.
KRESSHH
I'M TELLIN' YOU NOTH...
DUKE'S POOL HALL.
NINTH AVENUE, SOUTH OF HOUSTON.
BASEMENT.
Y'CAN'T MISS IT.
PRANCIN' LONG UNDER-WEAR TYPES, GOT NO RESPECT FER PRIVACY.
WONDER WHAT SHE WANTS WITH STICK? DIDN'T THINK NOBODY WAS INTERESTED IN THAT PIECE A' SLUDGE.
MAYBE HE CONNED HER OUTTA SOME BUCKS, TOO.
MAYBE SHE'LL KILL HIM.
WOULDN'T THAT JUST BE TOO BAD...
NOW WHAT?
I'M LOOKIN' FER STICK, PIKE. WORD ON THE STREET IS YOU KNOW WHERE HE IS.
TURK, YA PUNCHED RIGHT THROUGH MY WALL...
AND YA WRECKED MY BED, YA LOUSY...

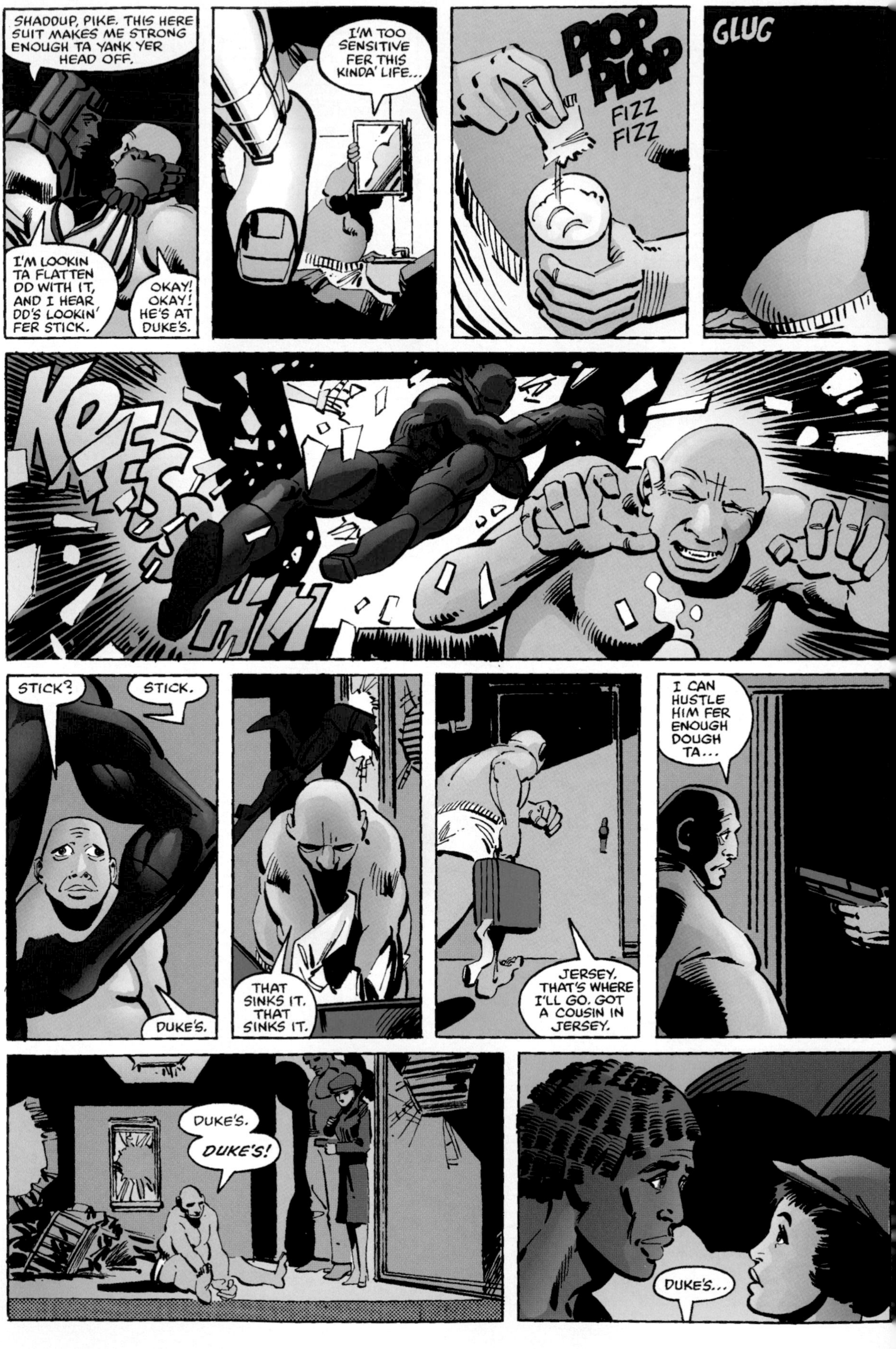
SHADDUP, PIKE. THIS HERE SUIT MAKES ME STRONG ENOUGH TA YANK YER HEAD OFF.
I'M LOOKIN TA FLATTEN DD WITH IT, AND I HEAR DD'S LOOKIN' FER STICK.
OKAY! OKAY! HE'S AT DUKE'S.
I'M TOO SENSITIVE FER THIS KINDA' LIFE...
PLOP PLOP
FIZZ FIZZ
GLUG
KEESSH
STICK?
STICK.
DUKE'S.
THAT SINKS IT. THAT SINKS IT.
JERSEY. THAT'S WHERE I'LL GO. GOT A COUSIN IN JERSEY.
I CAN HUSTLE HIM FER ENOUGH DOUGH TA...
DUKE'S.
DUKE'S!
DUKE'S...

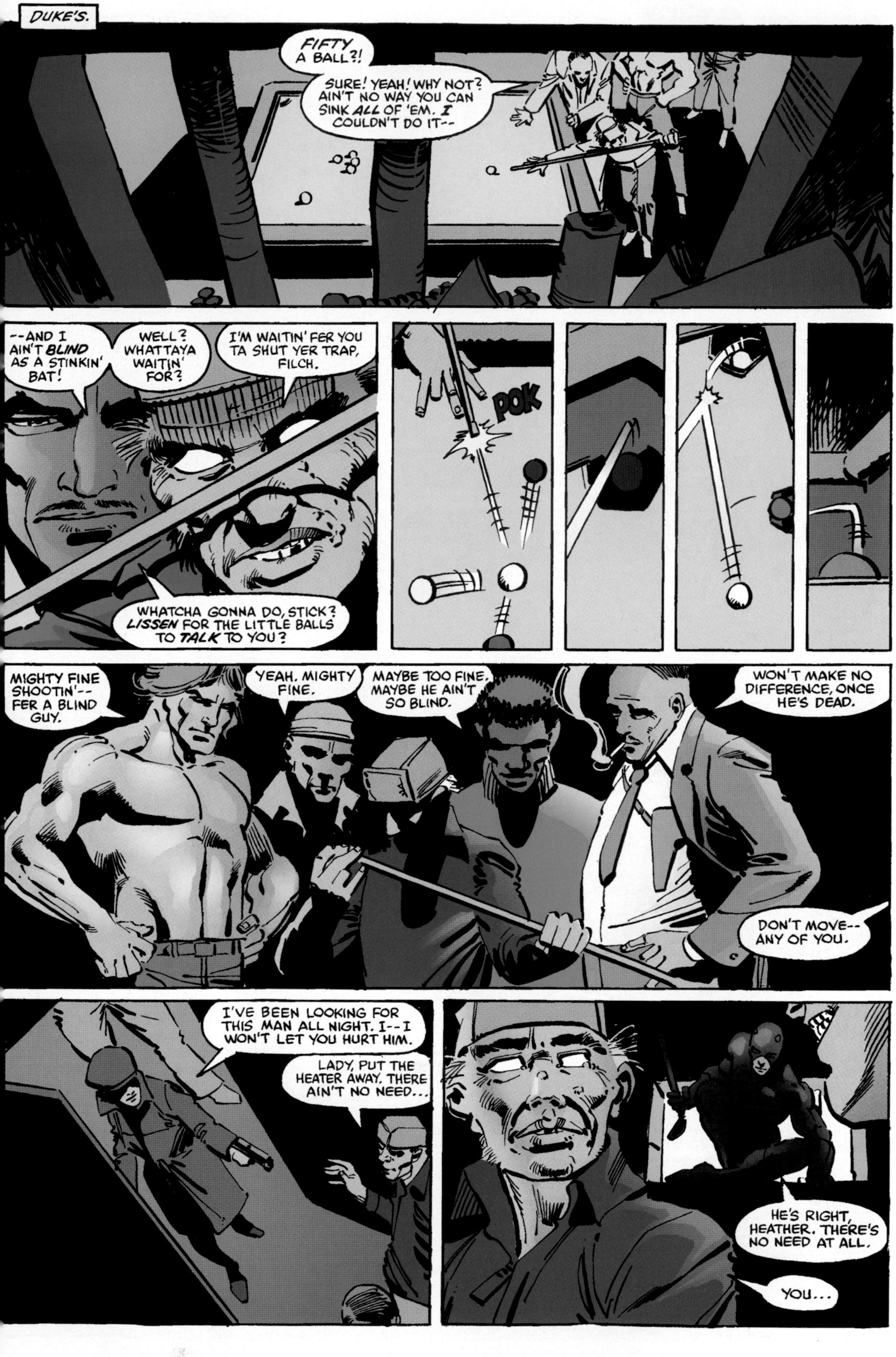
DUKE'S.
FIFTY A BALL?!
SURE! YEAH! WHY NOT? AIN'T NO WAY YOU CAN SINK ALL OF 'EM. I COULDN'T DO IT--
--AND I AIN'T BLIND AS A STINKIN' BAT!
WELL? WHATTAYA WAITIN' FOR?
I'M WAITIN' FER YOU TA SHUT YER TRAP, FILCH.
WHATCHA GONNA DO, STICK? LISSEN FOR THE LITTLE BALLS TO TALK TO YOU?
POK
MIGHTY FINE SHOOTIN'-- FER A BLIND GUY.
YEAH. MIGHTY FINE.
MAYBE TOO FINE. MAYBE HE AIN'T SO BLIND.
WON'T MAKE NO DIFFERENCE, ONCE HE'S DEAD.
DON'T MOVE-- ANY OF YOU.
I'VE BEEN LOOKING FOR THIS MAN ALL NIGHT. I--I WON'T LET YOU HURT HIM.
LADY, PUT THE HEATER AWAY. THERE AIN'T NO NEED...
HE'S RIGHT, HEATHER. THERE'S NO NEED AT ALL.
YOU...

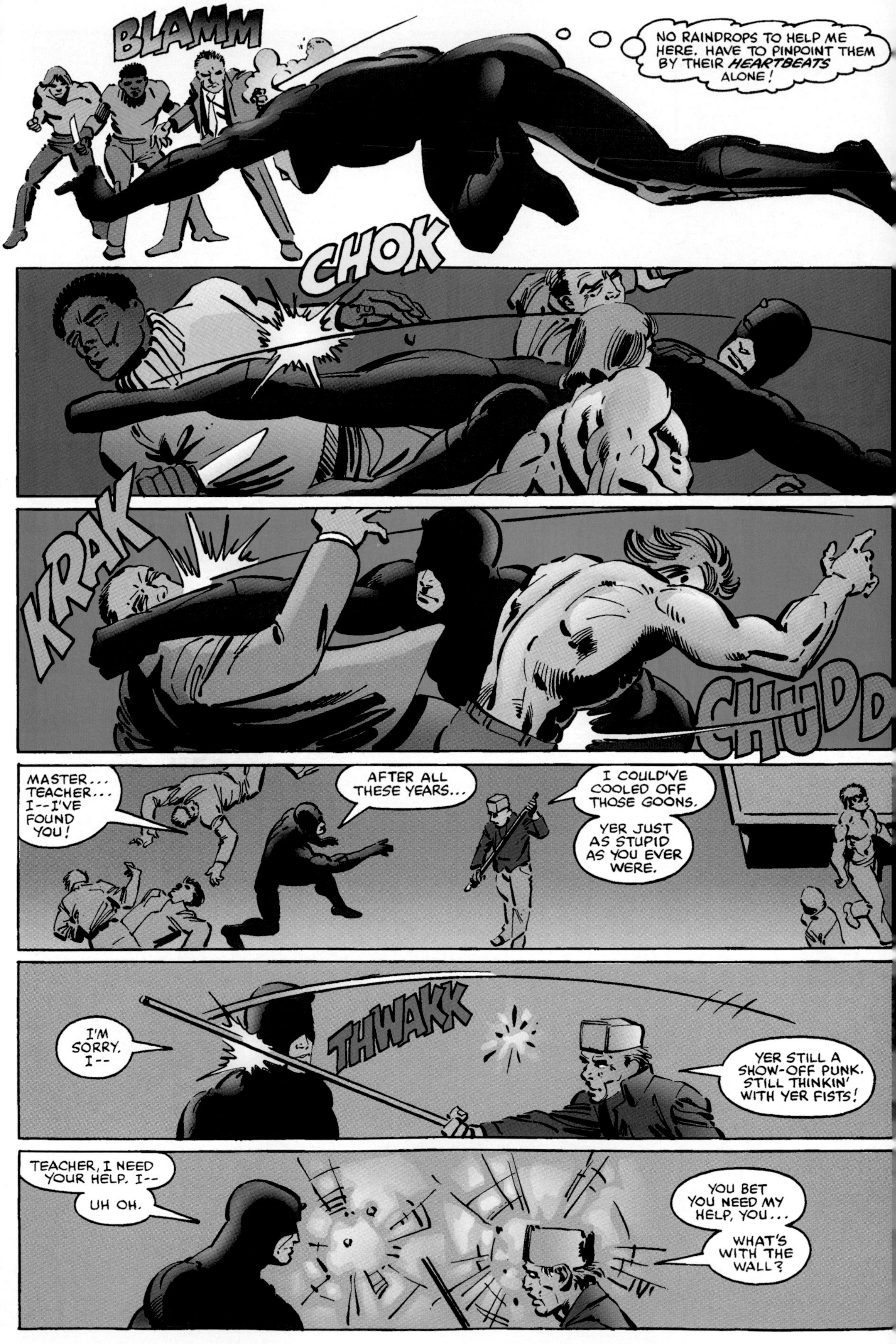
BLAMM
NO RAINDROPS TO HELP ME HERE. HAVE TO PINPOINT THEM BY THEIR HEARTBEATS ALONE!
CHOK
KRAK
CHUDD
MASTER... TEACHER... I--I'VE FOUND YOU!
AFTER ALL THESE YEARS...
I COULD'VE COOLED OFF THOSE GOONS.
YER JUST AS STUPID AS YOU EVER WERE.
I'M SORRY. I--
THWAKK
YER STILL A SHOW-OFF PUNK. STILL THINKIN' WITH YER FISTS!
TEACHER, I NEED YOUR HELP. I--
UH OH.
YOU BET YOU NEED MY HELP, YOU...
WHAT'S WITH THE WALL?

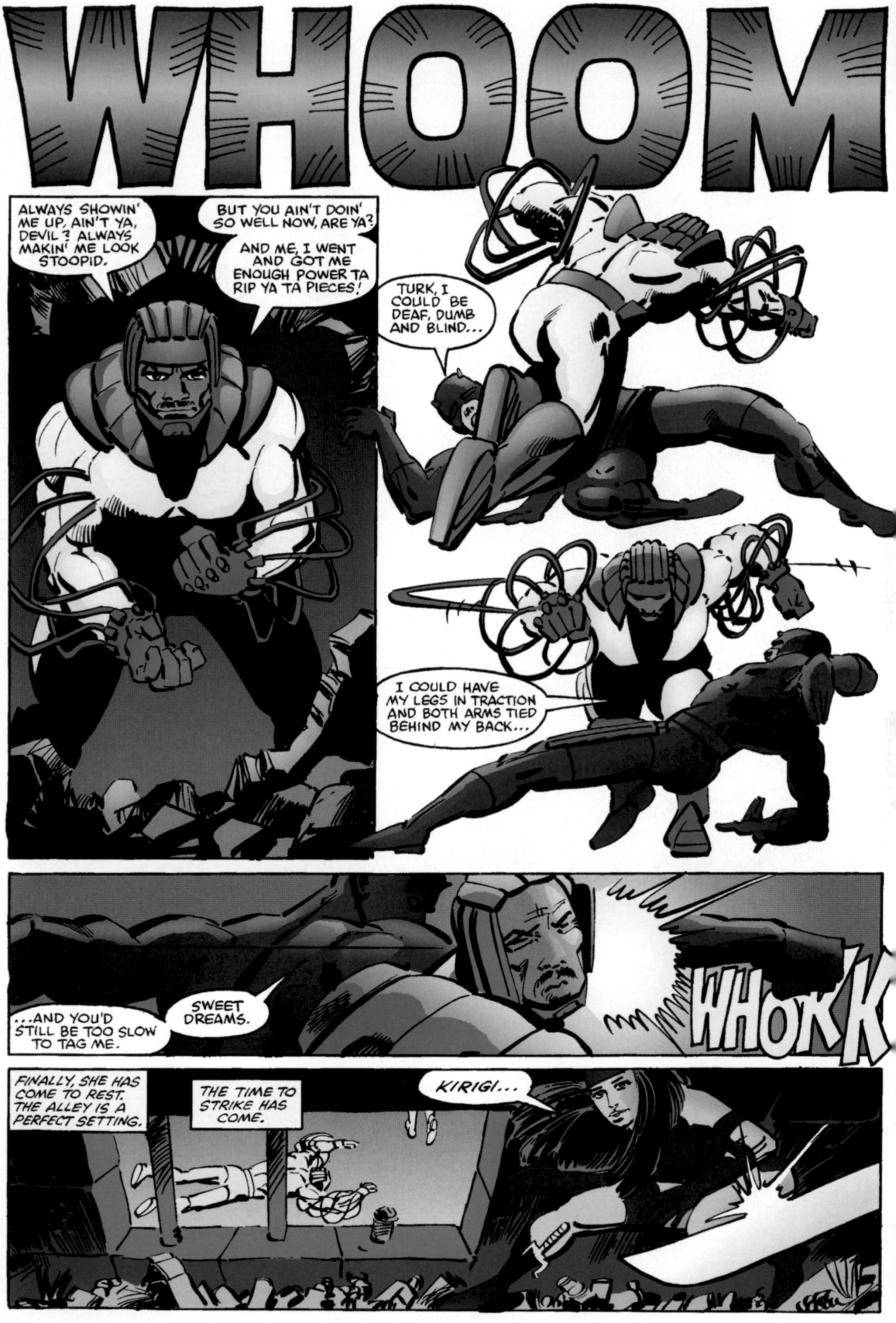
WHOOM
ALWAYS SHOWIN' ME UP, AIN'T YA, DEVIL? ALWAYS MAKIN' ME LOOK STOOPID.
BUT YOU AIN'T DOIN' SO WELL NOW, ARE YA?
AND ME, I WENT AND GOT ME ENOUGH POWER TA RIP YA TA PIECES!
TURK, I COULD BE DEAF, DUMB AND BLIND...
I COULD HAVE MY LEGS IN TRACTION AND BOTH ARMS TIED BEHIND MY BACK...
...AND YOU'D STILL BE TOO SLOW TO TAG ME.
SWEET DREAMS.
WHOKK
FINALLY, SHE HAS COME TO REST. THE ALLEY IS A PERFECT SETTING.
THE TIME TO STRIKE HAS COME.
KIRIGI...

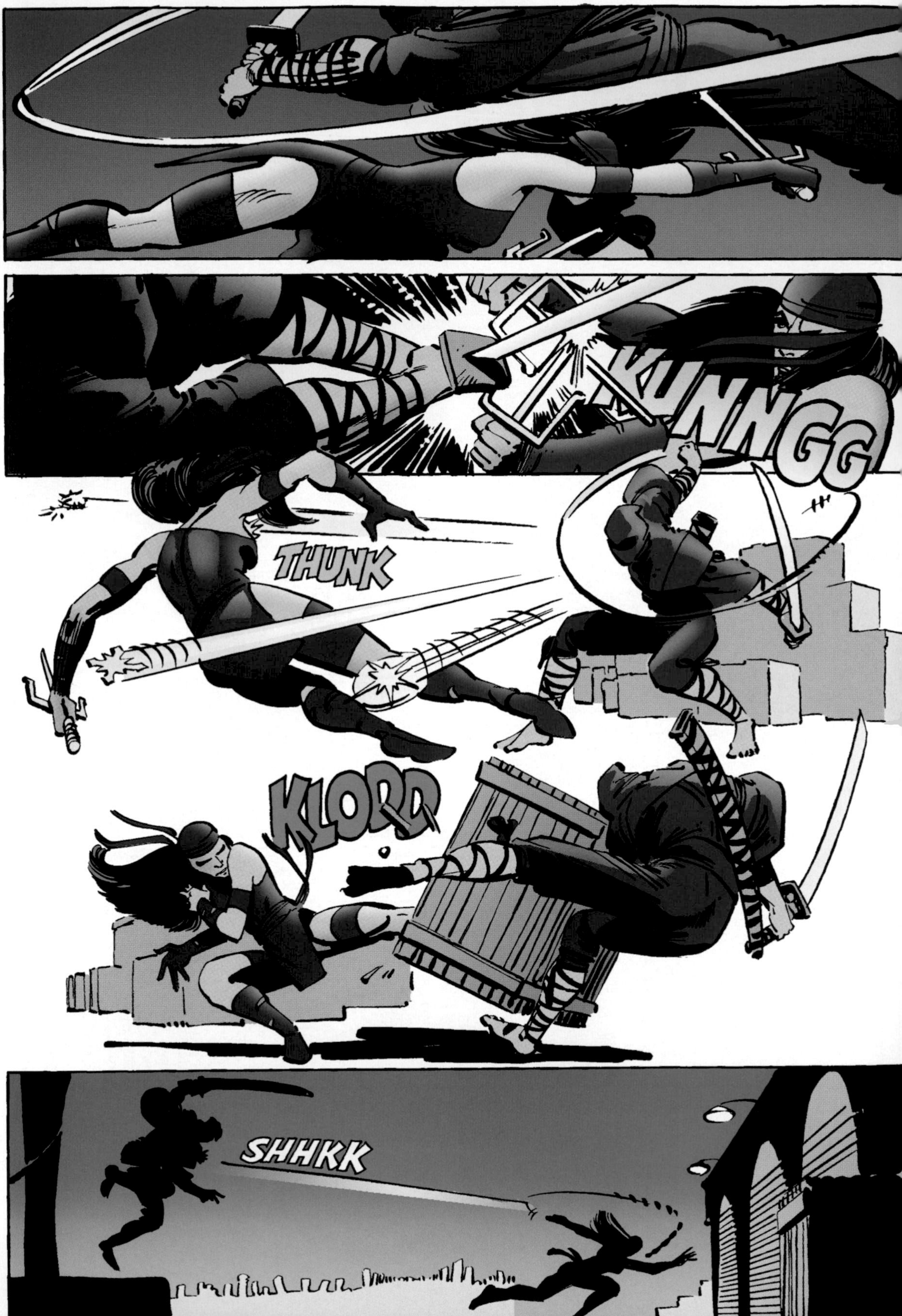

KUNNGG
THUNK
KLORD
SHHKK

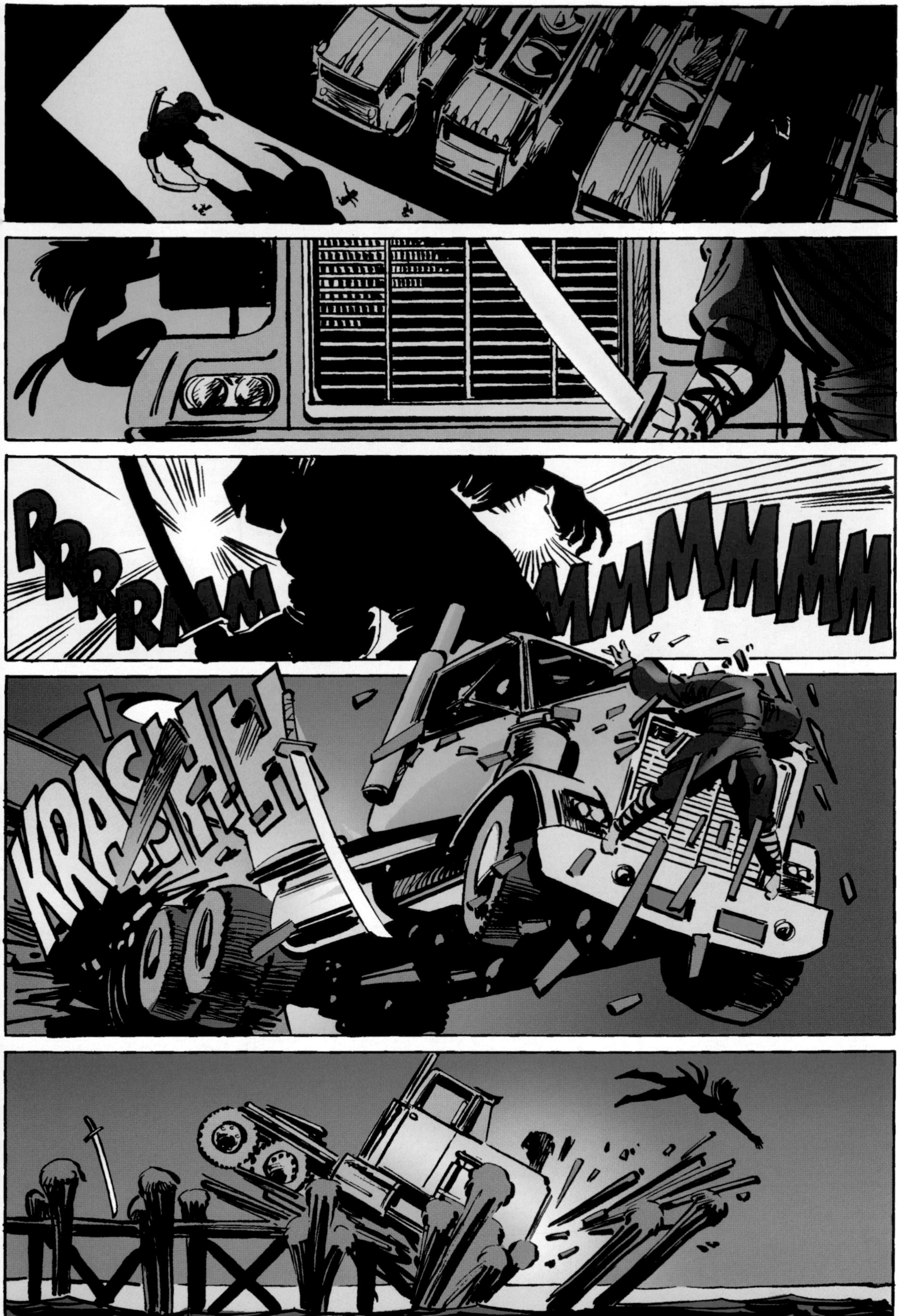
RRRRRAAM
MMMMMMMM
KRASHH!

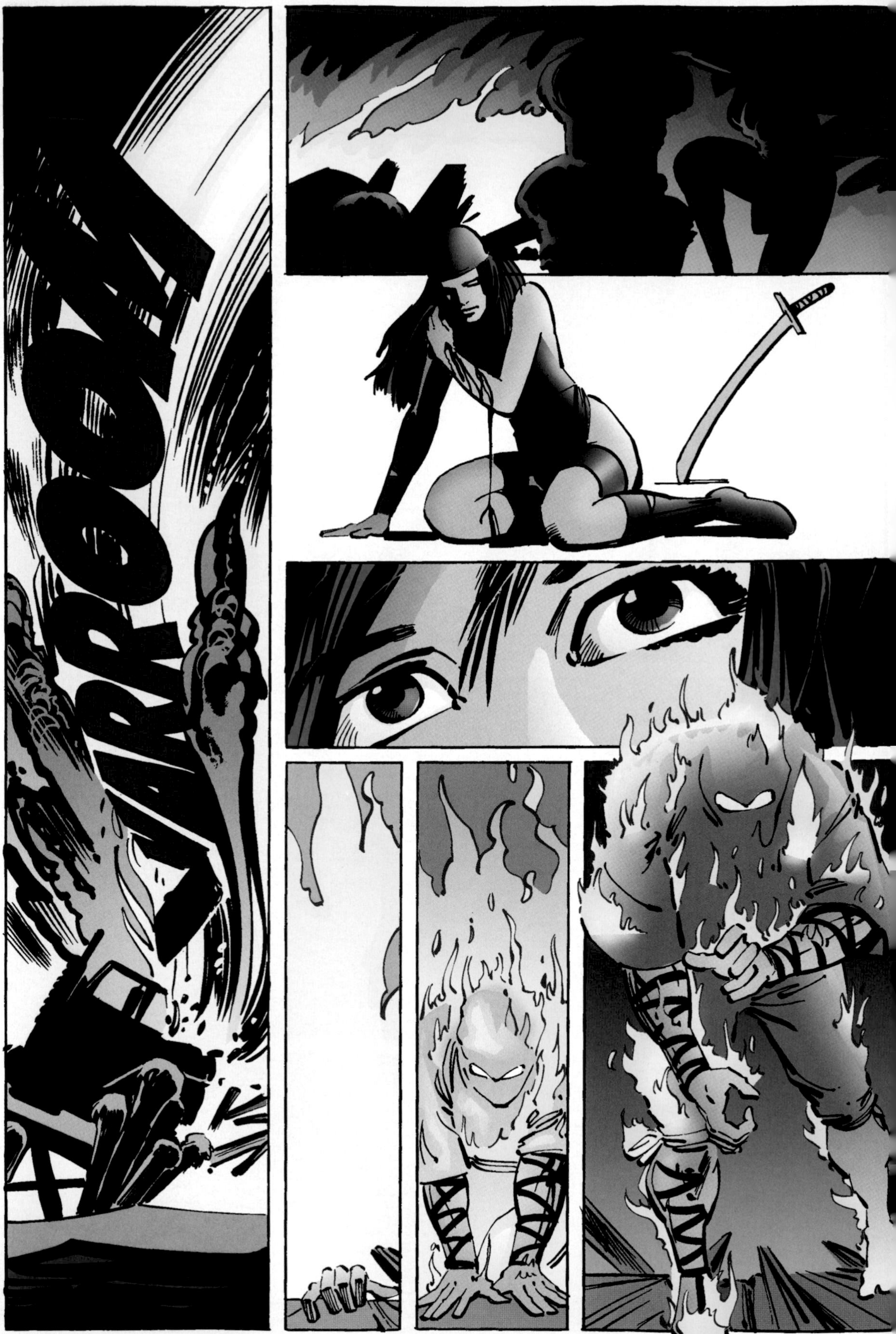

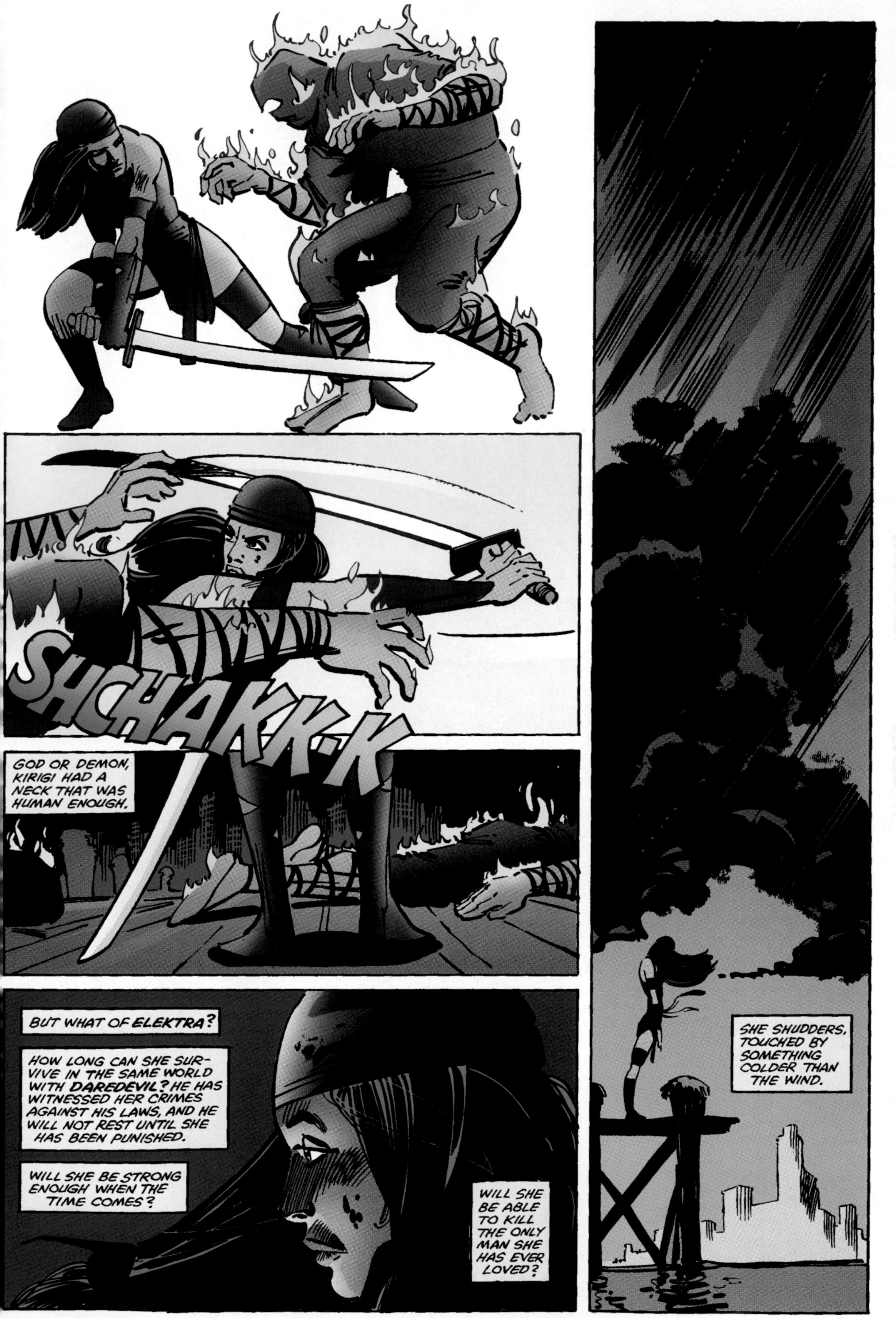
SHCHAKK-K
GOD OR DEMON, KIRIGI HAD A NECK THAT WAS HUMAN ENOUGH.
BUT WHAT OF ELEKTRA?
HOW LONG CAN SHE SURVIVE IN THE SAME WORLD WITH DAREDEVIL? HE HAS WITNESSED HER CRIMES AGAINST HIS LAWS, AND HE WILL NOT REST UNTIL SHE HAS BEEN PUNISHED.
WILL SHE BE STRONG ENOUGH WHEN THE TIME COMES?
WILL SHE BE ABLE TO KILL THE ONLY MAN SHE HAS EVER LOVED?
SHE SHUDDERS, TOUCHED BY SOMETHING COLDER THAN THE WIND.

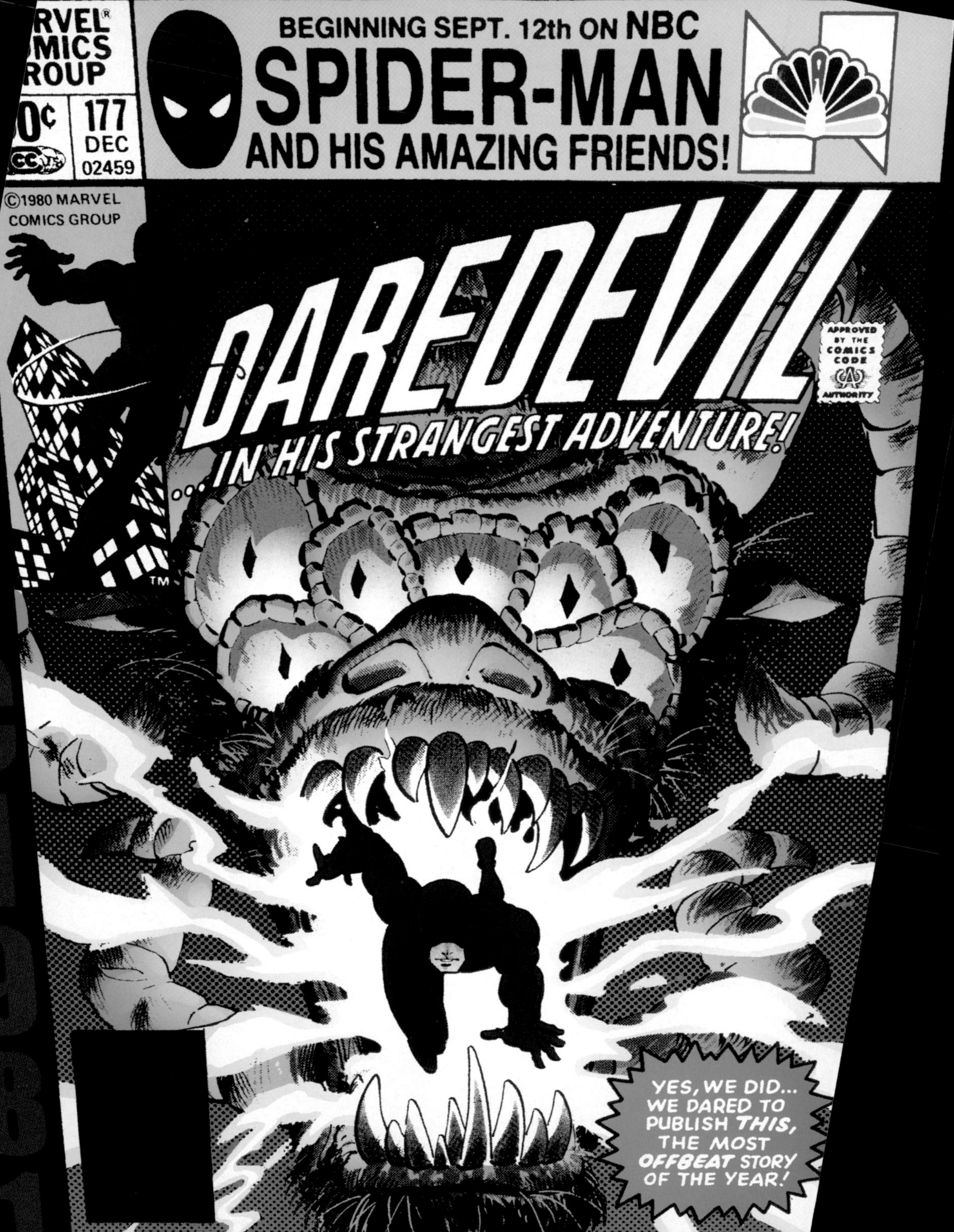
MARVEL® COMICS GROUP
50¢
177
DEC
02459
BEGINNING SEPT. 12th ON NBC
SPIDER-MAN
AND HIS AMAZING FRIENDS!
©1980 MARVEL COMICS GROUP
DAREDEVIL
...IN HIS STRANGEST ADVENTURE!
APPROVED BY THE COMICS CODE AUTHORITY
YES, WE DID... WE DARED TO PUBLISH THIS, THE MOST OFFBEAT STORY OF THE YEAR!

DEC 1981

DAREDEVIL #177

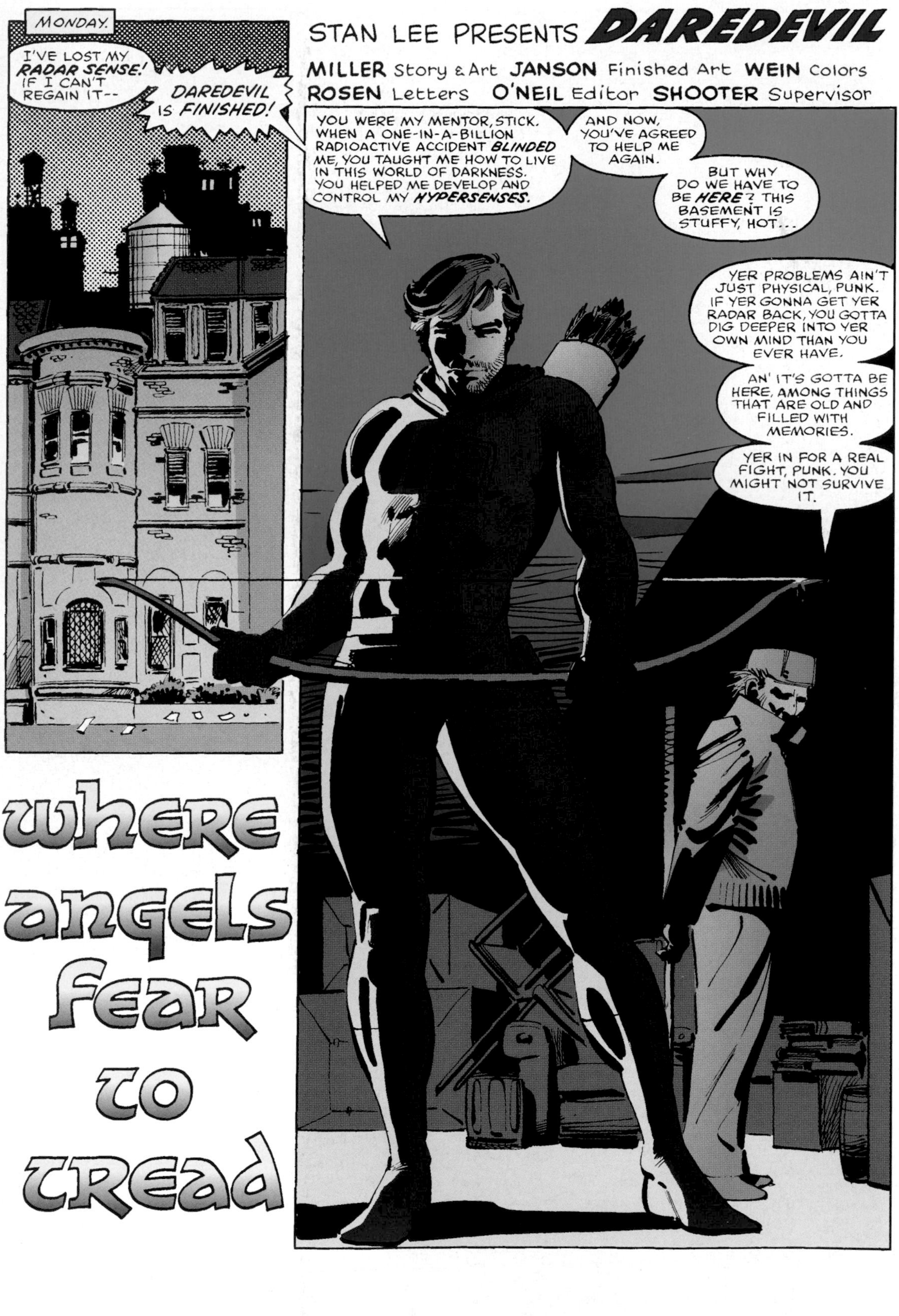

MONDAY.
I'VE LOST MY RADAR SENSE! IF I CAN'T REGAIN IT--
DAREDEVIL IS FINISHED!
STAN LEE PRESENTS DAREDEVIL
MILLER Story & Art JANSON Finished Art WEIN Colors
ROSEN Letters O'NEIL Editor SHOOTER Supervisor
YOU WERE MY MENTOR, STICK. WHEN A ONE-IN-A-BILLION RADIOACTIVE ACCIDENT BLINDED ME, YOU TAUGHT ME HOW TO LIVE IN THIS WORLD OF DARKNESS. YOU HELPED ME DEVELOP AND CONTROL MY HYPERSENSES.
AND NOW, YOU'VE AGREED TO HELP ME AGAIN.
BUT WHY DO WE HAVE TO BE HERE? THIS BASEMENT IS STUFFY, HOT...
YER PROBLEMS AIN'T JUST PHYSICAL, PUNK. IF YER GONNA GET YER RADAR BACK, YOU GOTTA DIG DEEPER INTO YER OWN MIND THAN YOU EVER HAVE.
AN' IT'S GOTTA BE HERE, AMONG THINGS THAT ARE OLD AND FILLED WITH MEMORIES.
YER IN FOR A REAL FIGHT, PUNK. YOU MIGHT NOT SURVIVE IT.
where angels fear to tread

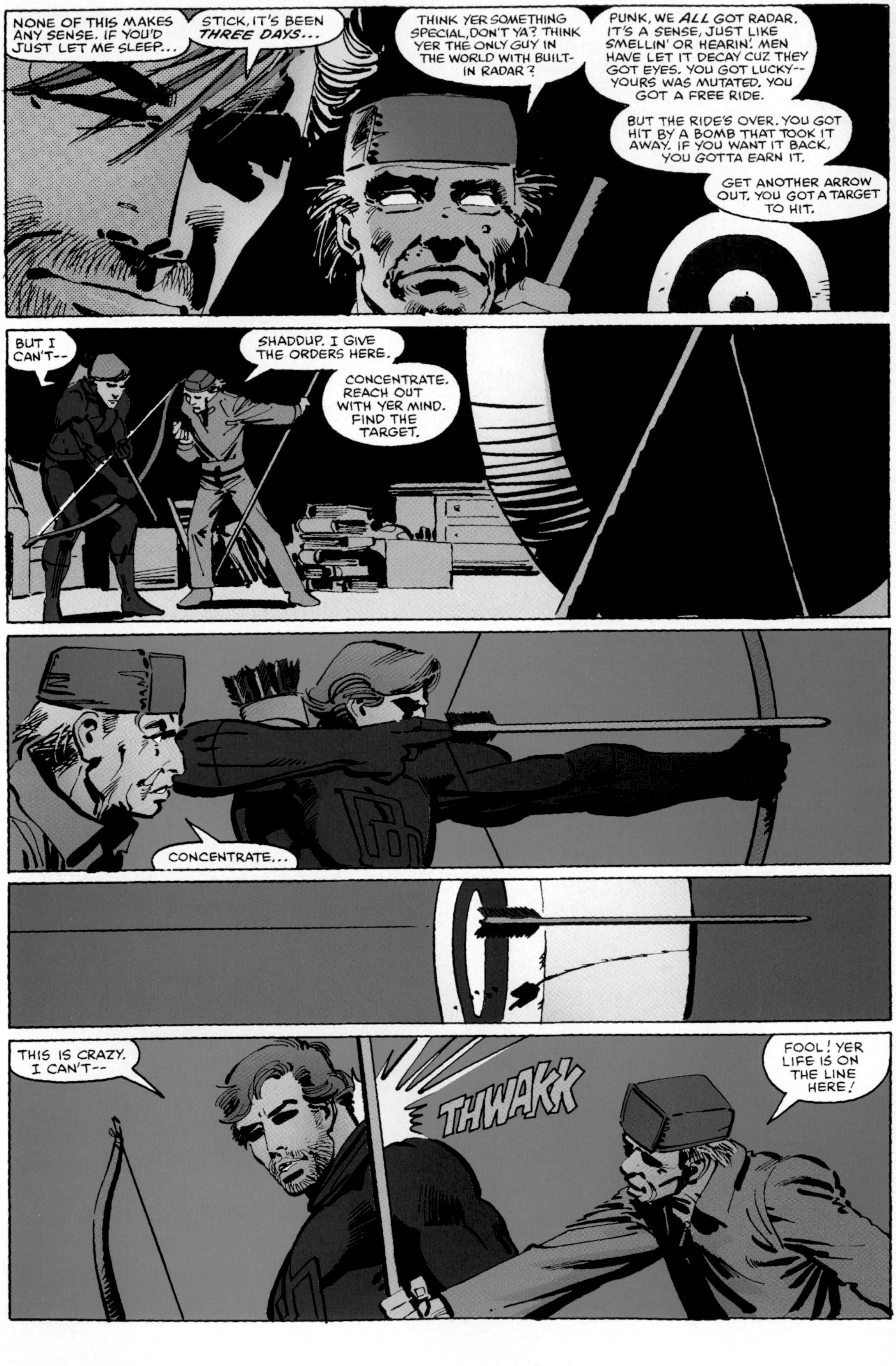
NONE OF THIS MAKES ANY SENSE. IF YOU'D JUST LET ME SLEEP...
STICK, IT'S BEEN *THREE DAYS*...
THINK YER SOMETHING SPECIAL, DON'T YA? THINK YER THE ONLY GUY IN THE WORLD WITH BUILT-IN RADAR?
PUNK, WE *ALL* GOT RADAR. IT'S A SENSE, JUST LIKE SMELLIN' OR HEARIN'. MEN HAVE LET IT DECAY CUZ THEY GOT EYES. YOU GOT LUCKY-- YOURS WAS MUTATED. YOU GOT A FREE RIDE.
BUT THE RIDE'S OVER. YOU GOT HIT BY A BOMB THAT TOOK IT AWAY. IF YOU WANT IT BACK, YOU GOTTA EARN IT.
GET ANOTHER ARROW OUT. YOU GOT A TARGET TO HIT.
BUT I CAN'T--
SHADDUP. I GIVE THE ORDERS HERE.
CONCENTRATE. REACH OUT WITH YER MIND. FIND THE TARGET.
CONCENTRATE...
THIS IS CRAZY. I CAN'T--
THWAKK
FOOL! YER LIFE IS ON THE LINE HERE!

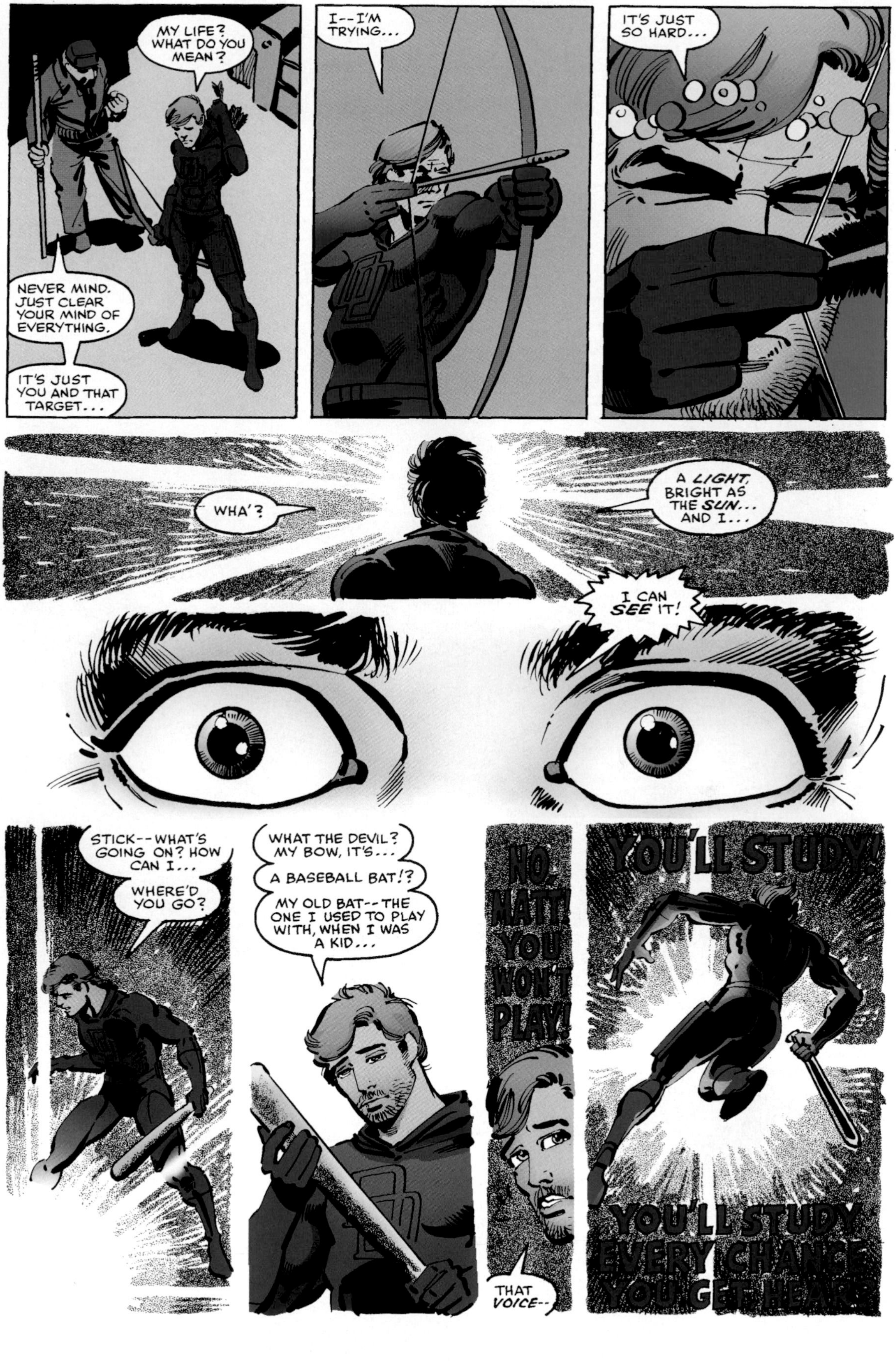
MY LIFE? WHAT DO YOU MEAN?
NEVER MIND. JUST CLEAR YOUR MIND OF EVERYTHING.
IT'S JUST YOU AND THAT TARGET...
I--I'M TRYING...
IT'S JUST SO HARD...
WHA'?
A LIGHT, BRIGHT AS THE SUN... AND I...
I CAN SEE IT!
STICK--WHAT'S GOING ON? HOW CAN I...
WHERE'D YOU GO?
WHAT THE DEVIL? MY BOW, IT'S...
A BASEBALL BAT!?
MY OLD BAT--THE ONE I USED TO PLAY WITH, WHEN I WAS A KID...
NO, MATT! YOU WON'T PLAY!
THAT VOICE--
YOU'LL STUDY!
YOU'LL STUDY EVERY CHANCE YOU GET, HEAR?

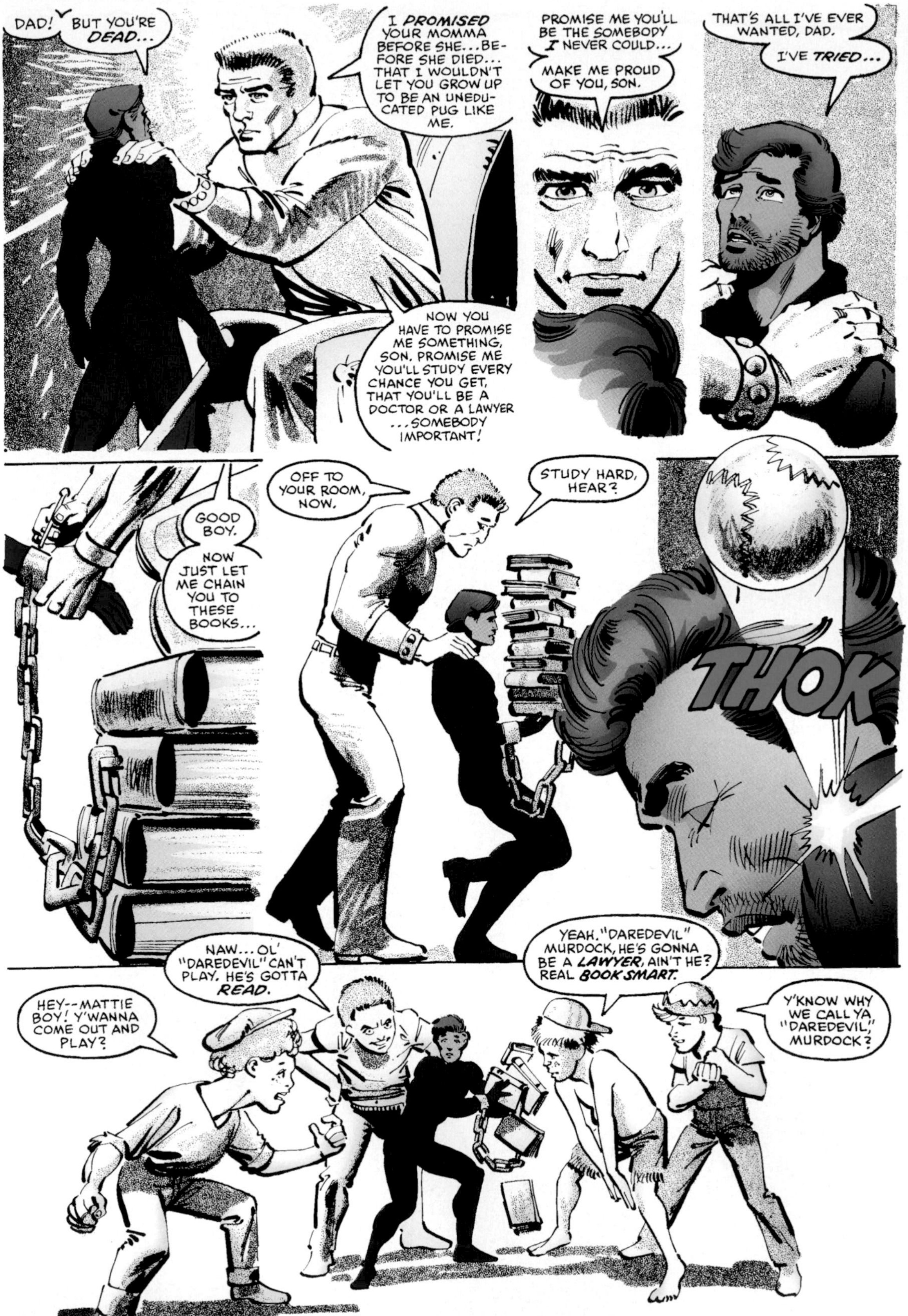
DAD!
BUT YOU'RE DEAD...
I PROMISED YOUR MOMMA BEFORE SHE... BEFORE SHE DIED... THAT I WOULDN'T LET YOU GROW UP TO BE AN UNEDUCATED PUG LIKE ME.
NOW YOU HAVE TO PROMISE ME SOMETHING, SON. PROMISE ME YOU'LL STUDY EVERY CHANCE YOU GET, THAT YOU'LL BE A DOCTOR OR A LAWYER ...SOMEBODY IMPORTANT!
PROMISE ME YOU'LL BE THE SOMEBODY I NEVER COULD...
MAKE ME PROUD OF YOU, SON.
THAT'S ALL I'VE EVER WANTED, DAD.
I'VE TRIED...
GOOD BOY.
NOW JUST LET ME CHAIN YOU TO THESE BOOKS...
OFF TO YOUR ROOM, NOW.
STUDY HARD, HEAR?
THOK
HEY--MATTIE BOY! Y'WANNA COME OUT AND PLAY?
NAW... OL' "DAREDEVIL" CAN'T PLAY. HE'S GOTTA READ.
YEAH. "DAREDEVIL" MURDOCK, HE'S GONNA BE A LAWYER, AIN'T HE? REAL BOOK SMART.
Y'KNOW WHY WE CALL YA "DAREDEVIL," MURDOCK?

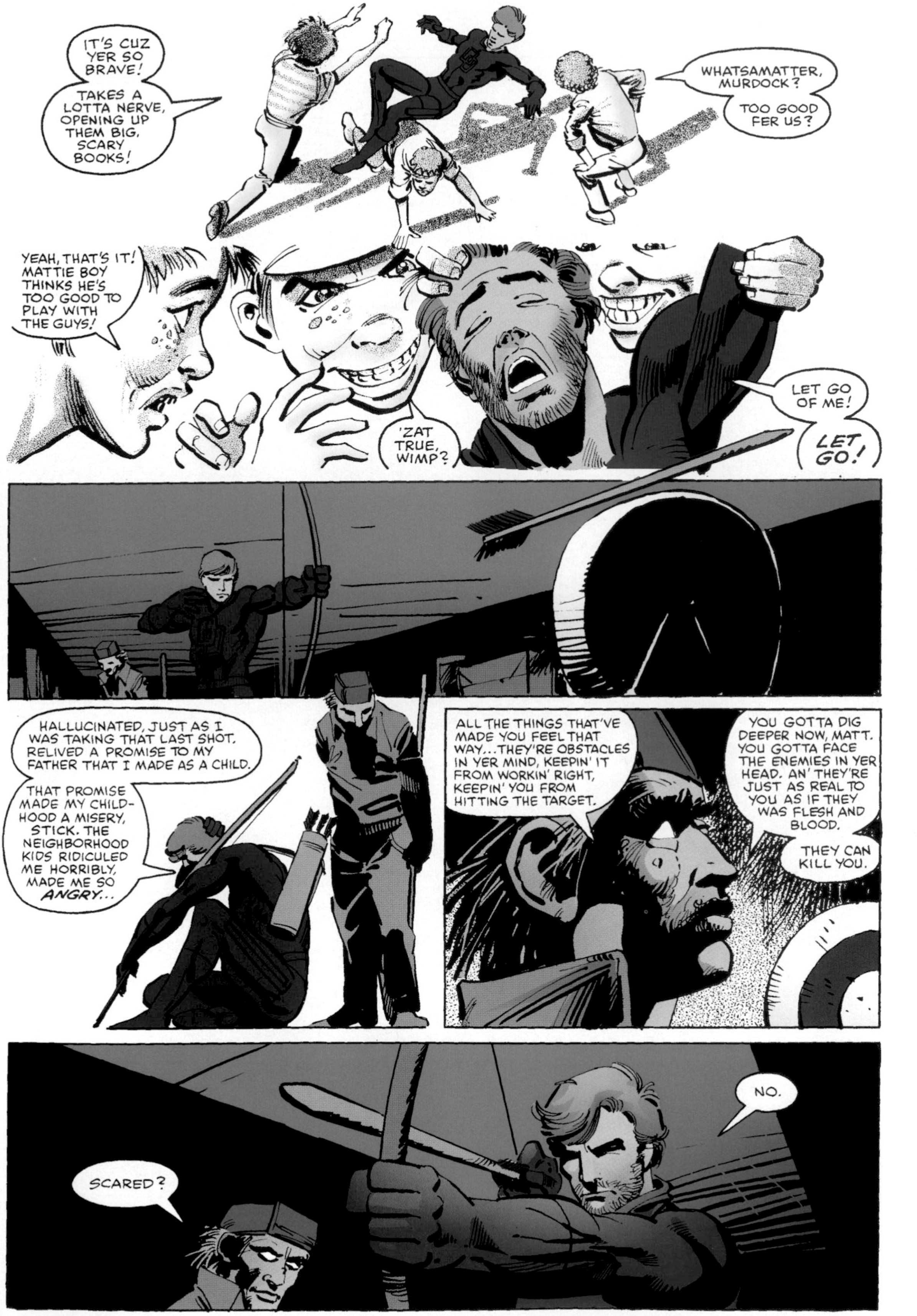
IT'S CUZ YER SO BRAVE!
TAKES A LOTTA NERVE, OPENING UP THEM BIG, SCARY BOOKS!
WHATSAMATTER, MURDOCK?
TOO GOOD FER US?
YEAH, THAT'S IT! MATTIE BOY THINKS HE'S TOO GOOD TO PLAY WITH THE GUYS!
'ZAT TRUE, WIMP?
LET GO OF ME!
LET GO!
HALLUCINATED, JUST AS I WAS TAKING THAT LAST SHOT. RELIVED A PROMISE TO MY FATHER THAT I MADE AS A CHILD.
THAT PROMISE MADE MY CHILDHOOD A MISERY, STICK. THE NEIGHBORHOOD KIDS RIDICULED ME HORRIBLY, MADE ME SO ANGRY...
ALL THE THINGS THAT'VE MADE YOU FEEL THAT WAY... THEY'RE OBSTACLES IN YER MIND, KEEPIN' IT FROM WORKIN' RIGHT, KEEPIN' YOU FROM HITTING THE TARGET.
YOU GOTTA DIG DEEPER NOW, MATT. YOU GOTTA FACE THE ENEMIES IN YER HEAD. AN' THEY'RE JUST AS REAL TO YOU AS IF THEY WAS FLESH AND BLOOD.
THEY CAN KILL YOU.
SCARED?
NO.

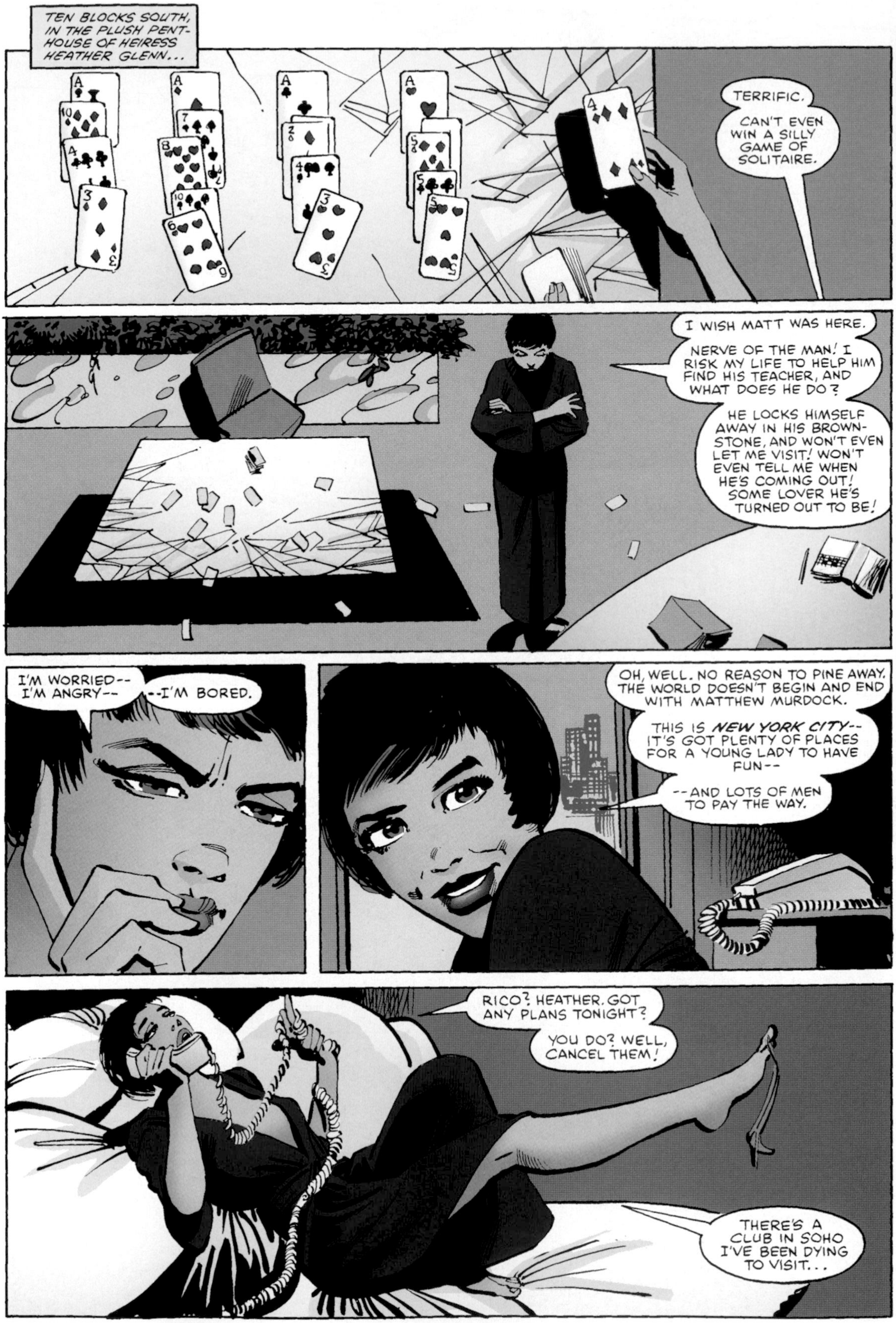
TEN BLOCKS SOUTH, IN THE PLUSH PENTHOUSE OF HEIRESS HEATHER GLENN...
TERRIFIC.
CAN'T EVEN WIN A SILLY GAME OF SOLITAIRE.
I WISH MATT WAS HERE.
NERVE OF THE MAN! I RISK MY LIFE TO HELP HIM FIND HIS TEACHER, AND WHAT DOES HE DO?
HE LOCKS HIMSELF AWAY IN HIS BROWNSTONE, AND WON'T EVEN LET ME VISIT! WON'T EVEN TELL ME WHEN HE'S COMING OUT! SOME LOVER HE'S TURNED OUT TO BE!
I'M WORRIED-- I'M ANGRY--
--I'M BORED.
OH, WELL. NO REASON TO PINE AWAY. THE WORLD DOESN'T BEGIN AND END WITH MATTHEW MURDOCK.
THIS IS NEW YORK CITY-- IT'S GOT PLENTY OF PLACES FOR A YOUNG LADY TO HAVE FUN--
--AND LOTS OF MEN TO PAY THE WAY.
RICO? HEATHER. GOT ANY PLANS TONIGHT?
YOU DO? WELL, CANCEL THEM!
THERE'S A CLUB IN SOHO I'VE BEEN DYING TO VISIT...

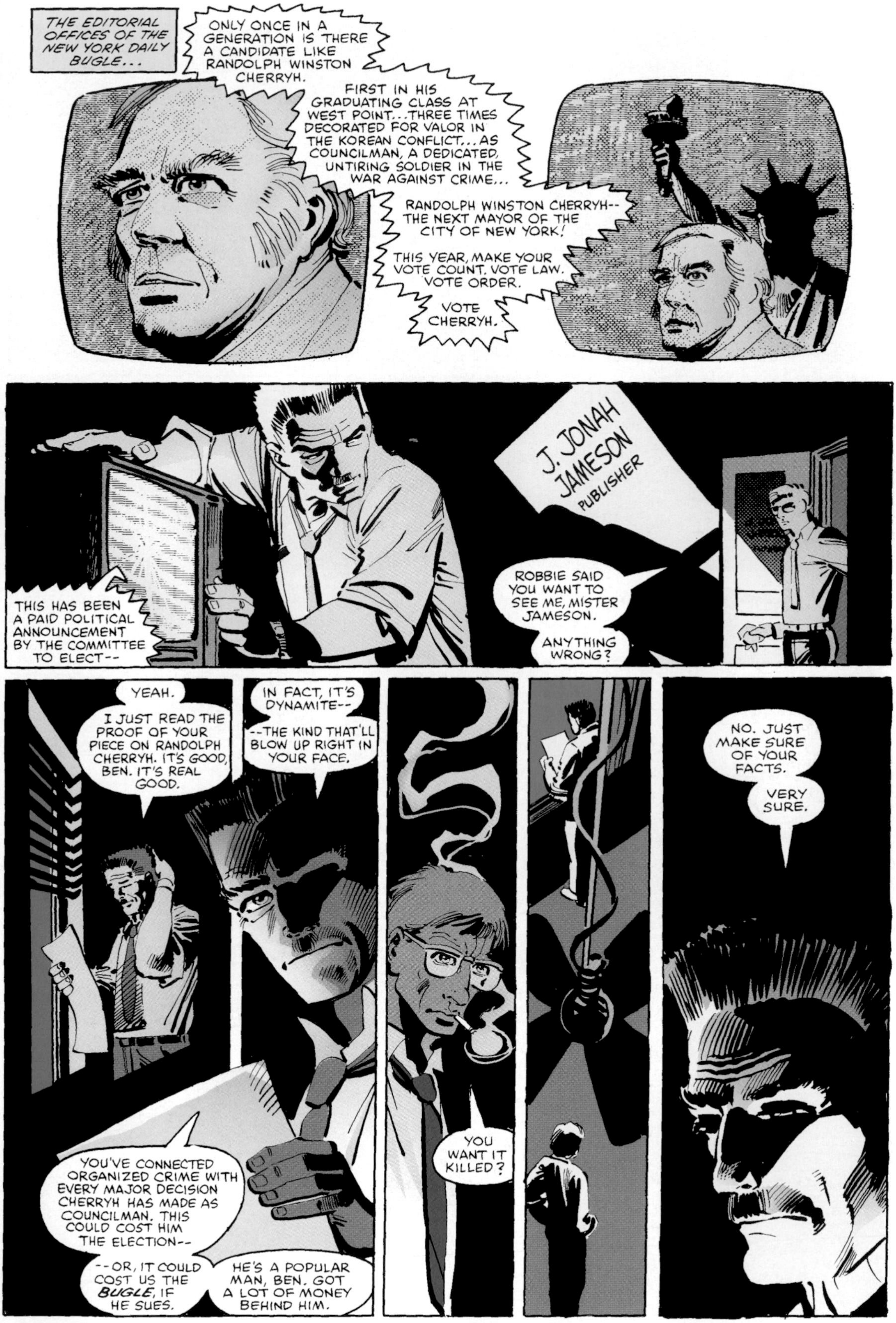
THE EDITORIAL OFFICES OF THE NEW YORK DAILY BUGLE...
ONLY ONCE IN A GENERATION IS THERE A CANDIDATE LIKE RANDOLPH WINSTON CHERRYH.
FIRST IN HIS GRADUATING CLASS AT WEST POINT...THREE TIMES DECORATED FOR VALOR IN THE KOREAN CONFLICT...AS COUNCILMAN, A DEDICATED, UNTIRING SOLDIER IN THE WAR AGAINST CRIME...
RANDOLPH WINSTON CHERRYH-- THE NEXT MAYOR OF THE CITY OF NEW YORK!
THIS YEAR, MAKE YOUR VOTE COUNT. VOTE LAW. VOTE ORDER.
VOTE CHERRYH.
J. JONAH JAMESON PUBLISHER
THIS HAS BEEN A PAID POLITICAL ANNOUNCEMENT BY THE COMMITTEE TO ELECT--
ROBBIE SAID YOU WANT TO SEE ME, MISTER JAMESON.
ANYTHING WRONG?
YEAH.
I JUST READ THE PROOF OF YOUR PIECE ON RANDOLPH CHERRYH. IT'S GOOD, BEN. IT'S REAL GOOD.
YOU'VE CONNECTED ORGANIZED CRIME WITH EVERY MAJOR DECISION CHERRYH HAS MADE AS COUNCILMAN. THIS COULD COST HIM THE ELECTION--
--OR, IT COULD COST US THE *BUGLE*, IF HE SUES.
IN FACT, IT'S DYNAMITE--
--THE KIND THAT'LL BLOW UP RIGHT IN YOUR FACE.
HE'S A POPULAR MAN, BEN. GOT A LOT OF MONEY BEHIND HIM.
YOU WANT IT KILLED?
NO. JUST MAKE SURE OF YOUR FACTS.
VERY SURE.

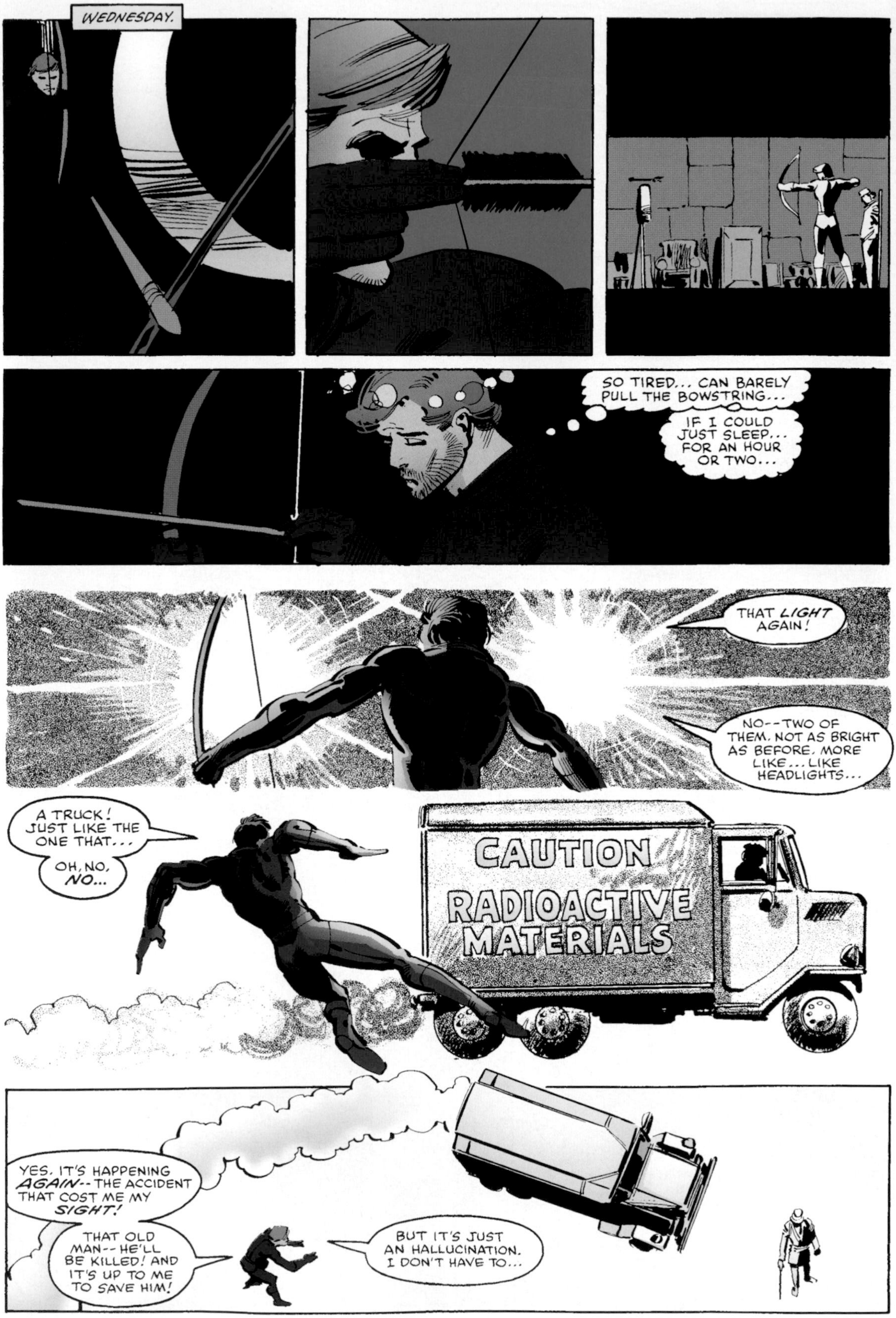
WEDNESDAY.
SO TIRED... CAN BARELY PULL THE BOWSTRING...
IF I COULD JUST SLEEP... FOR AN HOUR OR TWO...
THAT LIGHT AGAIN!
NO--TWO OF THEM. NOT AS BRIGHT AS BEFORE. MORE LIKE... LIKE HEADLIGHTS...
A TRUCK! JUST LIKE THE ONE THAT...
OH, NO, NO...
CAUTION
RADIOACTIVE MATERIALS
YES. IT'S HAPPENING AGAIN-- THE ACCIDENT THAT COST ME MY SIGHT!
THAT OLD MAN-- HE'LL BE KILLED! AND IT'S UP TO ME TO SAVE HIM!
BUT IT'S JUST AN HALLUCINATION. I DON'T HAVE TO...

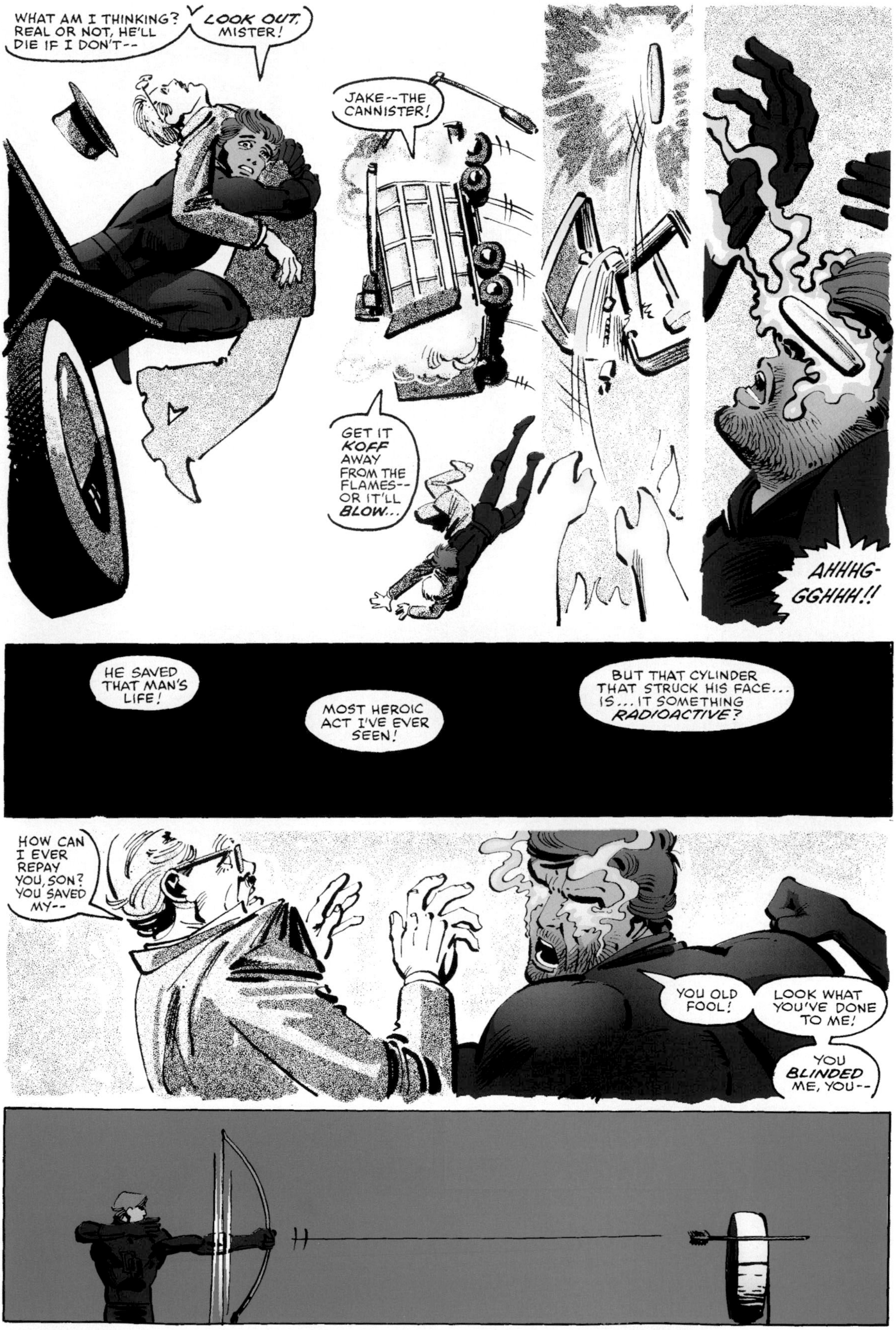
WHAT AM I THINKING? REAL OR NOT, HE'LL DIE IF I DON'T--
LOOK OUT, MISTER!
JAKE--THE CANNISTER!
GET IT KOFF AWAY FROM THE FLAMES-- OR IT'LL BLOW...
AHHHG-GGHHH!!
HE SAVED THAT MAN'S LIFE!
MOST HEROIC ACT I'VE EVER SEEN!
BUT THAT CYLINDER THAT STRUCK HIS FACE... IS... IT SOMETHING RADIOACTIVE?
HOW CAN I EVER REPAY YOU, SON? YOU SAVED MY--
YOU OLD FOOL!
LOOK WHAT YOU'VE DONE TO ME!
YOU BLINDED ME, YOU--

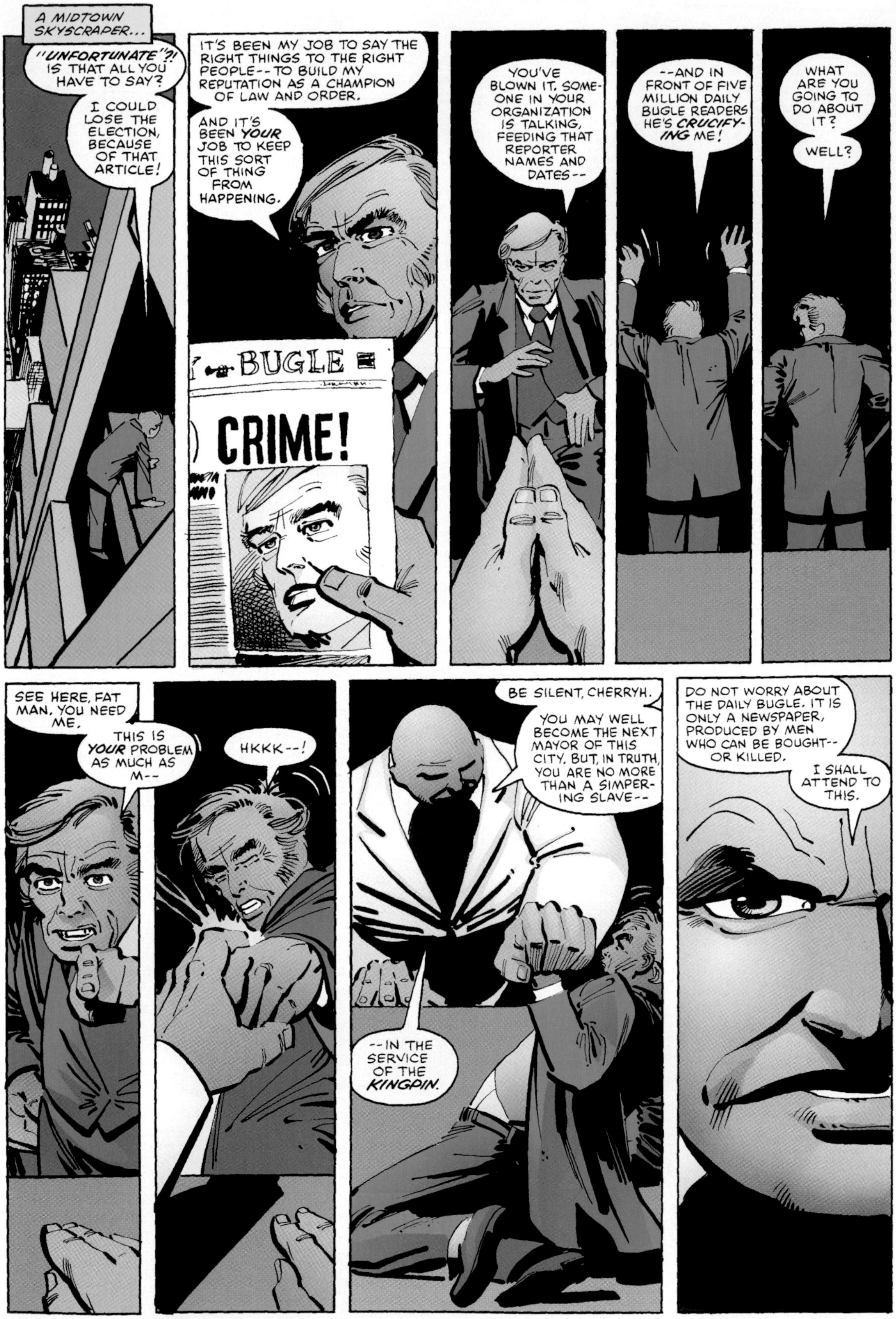
A MIDTOWN SKYSCRAPER...
"UNFORTUNATE"?! IS THAT ALL YOU HAVE TO SAY?
I COULD LOSE THE ELECTION, BECAUSE OF THAT ARTICLE!
IT'S BEEN MY JOB TO SAY THE RIGHT THINGS TO THE RIGHT PEOPLE--TO BUILD MY REPUTATION AS A CHAMPION OF LAW AND ORDER.
AND IT'S BEEN YOUR JOB TO KEEP THIS SORT OF THING FROM HAPPENING.
BUGLE
CRIME!
YOU'VE BLOWN IT. SOMEONE IN YOUR ORGANIZATION IS TALKING, FEEDING THAT REPORTER NAMES AND DATES--
--AND IN FRONT OF FIVE MILLION DAILY BUGLE READERS HE'S CRUCIFYING ME!
WHAT ARE YOU GOING TO DO ABOUT IT?
WELL?
SEE HERE, FAT MAN. YOU NEED ME.
THIS IS YOUR PROBLEM AS MUCH AS M--
HKKK--!
BE SILENT, CHERRYH.
YOU MAY WELL BECOME THE NEXT MAYOR OF THIS CITY. BUT, IN TRUTH, YOU ARE NO MORE THAN A SIMPERING SLAVE--
--IN THE SERVICE OF THE KINGPIN.
DO NOT WORRY ABOUT THE DAILY BUGLE. IT IS ONLY A NEWSPAPER, PRODUCED BY MEN WHO CAN BE BOUGHT--OR KILLED.
I SHALL ATTEND TO THIS.

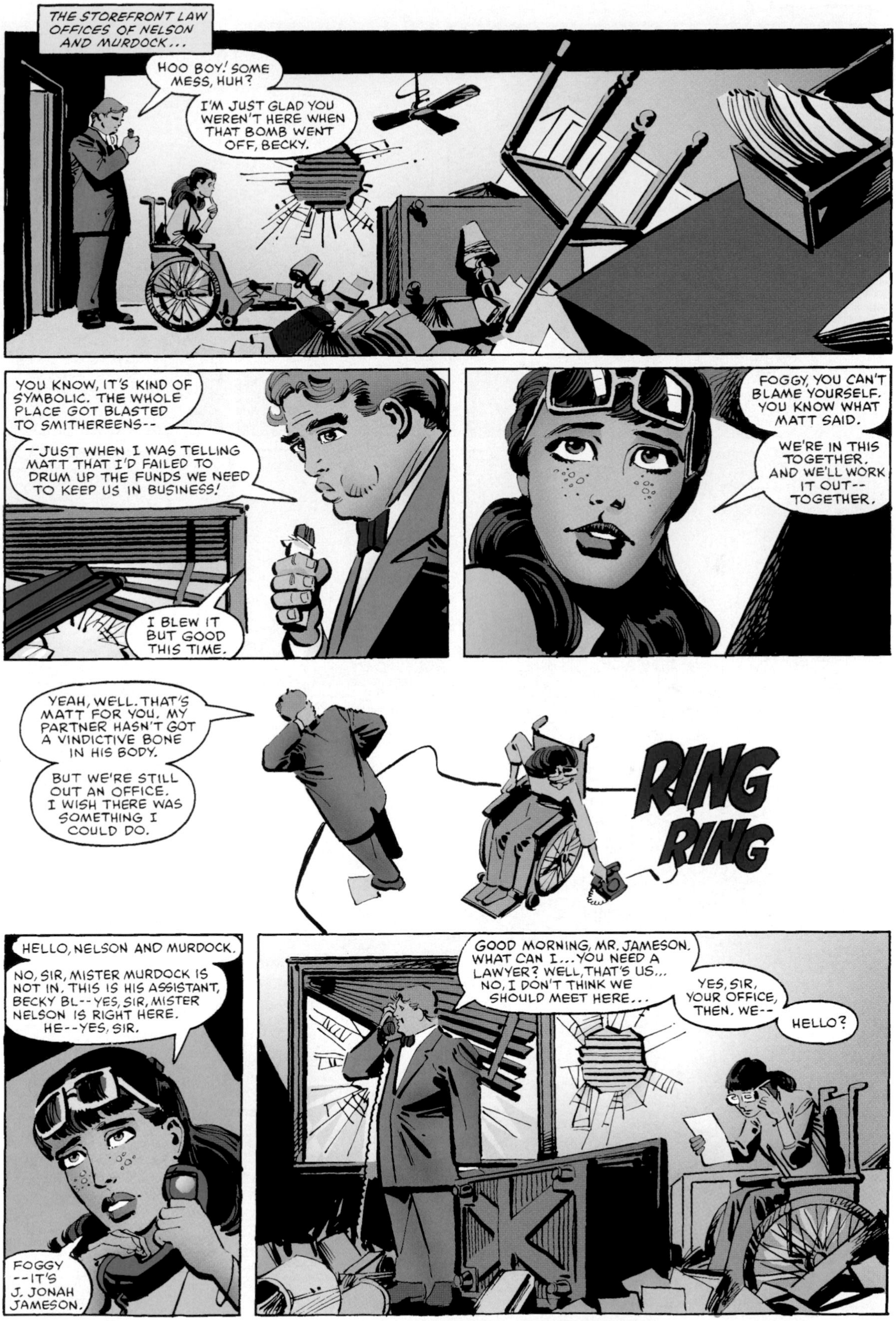
THE STOREFRONT LAW OFFICES OF NELSON AND MURDOCK...
HOO BOY! SOME MESS, HUH?
I'M JUST GLAD YOU WEREN'T HERE WHEN THAT BOMB WENT OFF, BECKY.
YOU KNOW, IT'S KIND OF SYMBOLIC. THE WHOLE PLACE GOT BLASTED TO SMITHEREENS--
--JUST WHEN I WAS TELLING MATT THAT I'D FAILED TO DRUM UP THE FUNDS WE NEED TO KEEP US IN BUSINESS!
I BLEW IT BUT GOOD THIS TIME.
FOGGY, YOU CAN'T BLAME YOURSELF. YOU KNOW WHAT MATT SAID.
WE'RE IN THIS TOGETHER, AND WE'LL WORK IT OUT--TOGETHER.
YEAH, WELL. THAT'S MATT FOR YOU. MY PARTNER HASN'T GOT A VINDICTIVE BONE IN HIS BODY.
BUT WE'RE STILL OUT AN OFFICE. I WISH THERE WAS SOMETHING I COULD DO.
RING RING
HELLO, NELSON AND MURDOCK.
NO, SIR, MISTER MURDOCK IS NOT IN. THIS IS HIS ASSISTANT, BECKY BL--YES, SIR, MISTER NELSON IS RIGHT HERE. HE--YES, SIR.
FOGGY--IT'S J. JONAH JAMESON.
GOOD MORNING, MR. JAMESON. WHAT CAN I... YOU NEED A LAWYER? WELL, THAT'S US... NO, I DON'T THINK WE SHOULD MEET HERE...
YES, SIR, YOUR OFFICE, THEN. WE--
HELLO?

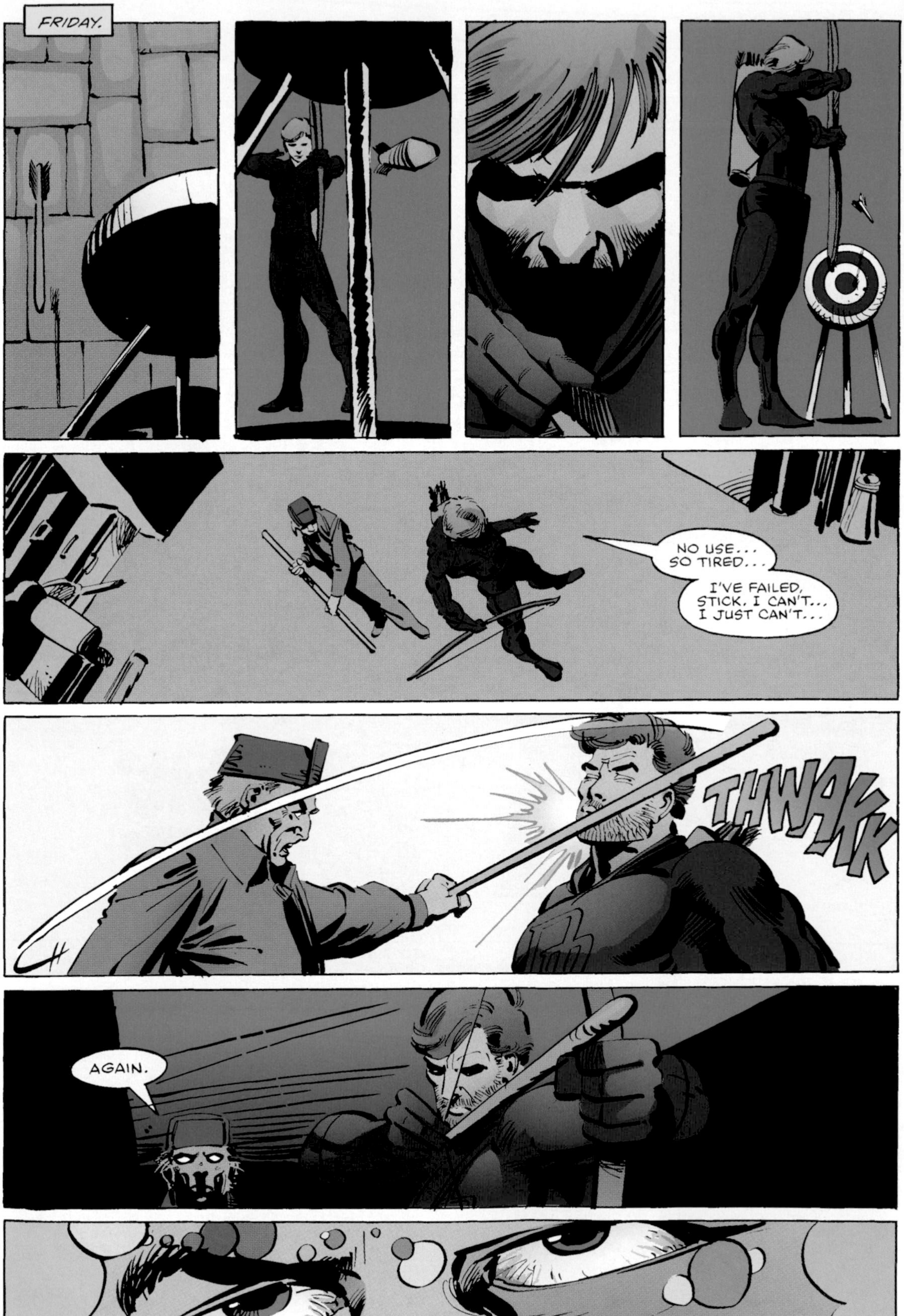
FRIDAY.
NO USE... SO TIRED...
I'VE FAILED, STICK. I CAN'T... I JUST CAN'T...
THWAKK
AGAIN.

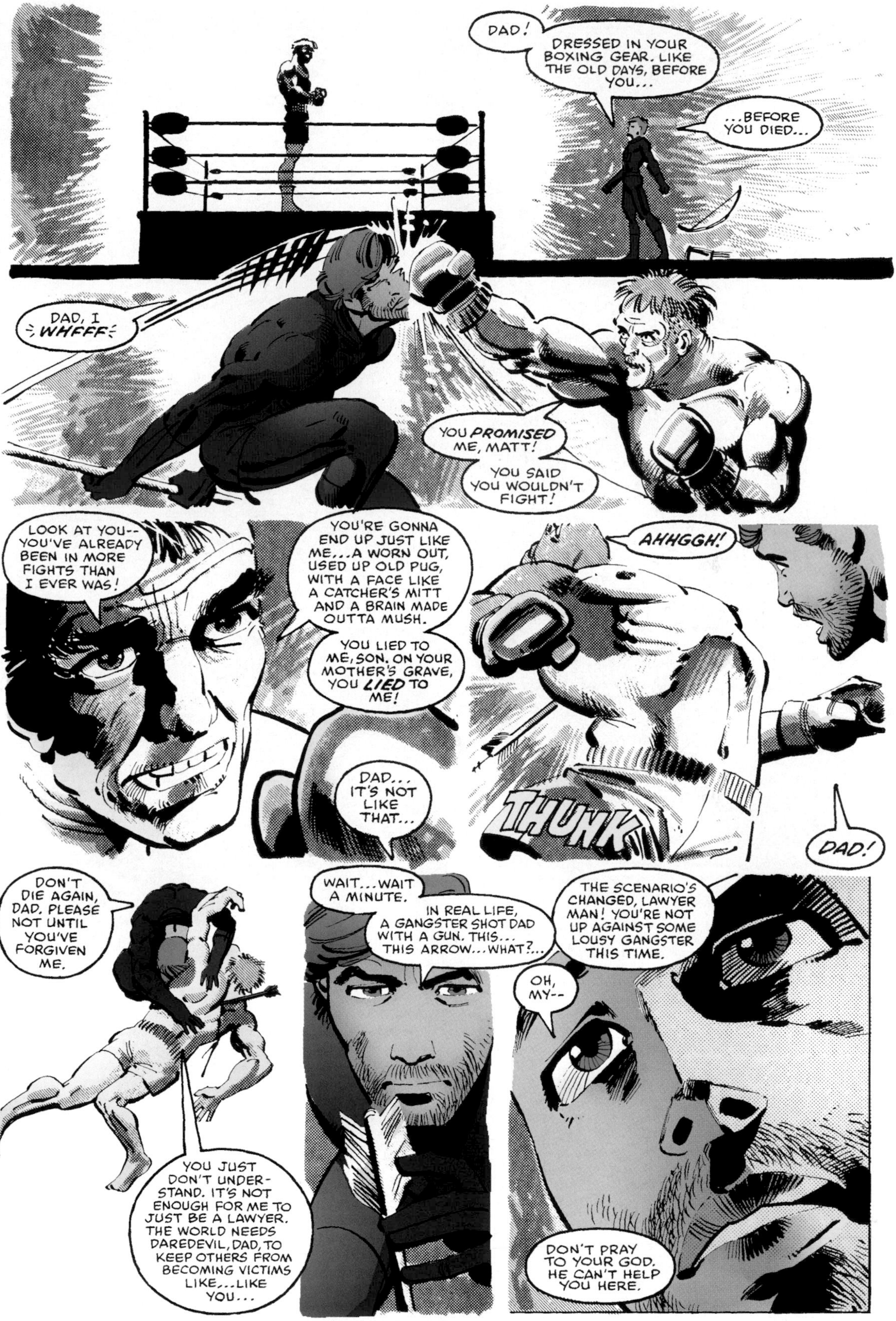
DAD!
DRESSED IN YOUR BOXING GEAR. LIKE THE OLD DAYS, BEFORE YOU...
...BEFORE YOU DIED...
DAD, I WHFFF
YOU PROMISED ME, MATT!
YOU SAID YOU WOULDN'T FIGHT!
LOOK AT YOU-- YOU'VE ALREADY BEEN IN MORE FIGHTS THAN I EVER WAS!
YOU'RE GONNA END UP JUST LIKE ME... A WORN OUT, USED UP OLD PUG, WITH A FACE LIKE A CATCHER'S MITT AND A BRAIN MADE OUTTA MUSH.
YOU LIED TO ME, SON. ON YOUR MOTHER'S GRAVE, YOU LIED TO ME!
DAD... IT'S NOT LIKE THAT...
AHHGGH!
THUNK
DAD!
DON'T DIE AGAIN, DAD. PLEASE NOT UNTIL YOU'VE FORGIVEN ME.
YOU JUST DON'T UNDERSTAND. IT'S NOT ENOUGH FOR ME TO JUST BE A LAWYER. THE WORLD NEEDS DAREDEVIL, DAD, TO KEEP OTHERS FROM BECOMING VICTIMS LIKE... LIKE YOU...
WAIT... WAIT A MINUTE.
IN REAL LIFE, A GANGSTER SHOT DAD WITH A GUN. THIS... THIS ARROW... WHAT?...
THE SCENARIO'S CHANGED, LAWYER MAN! YOU'RE NOT UP AGAINST SOME LOUSY GANGSTER THIS TIME.
OH, MY--
DON'T PRAY TO YOUR GOD. HE CAN'T HELP YOU HERE.

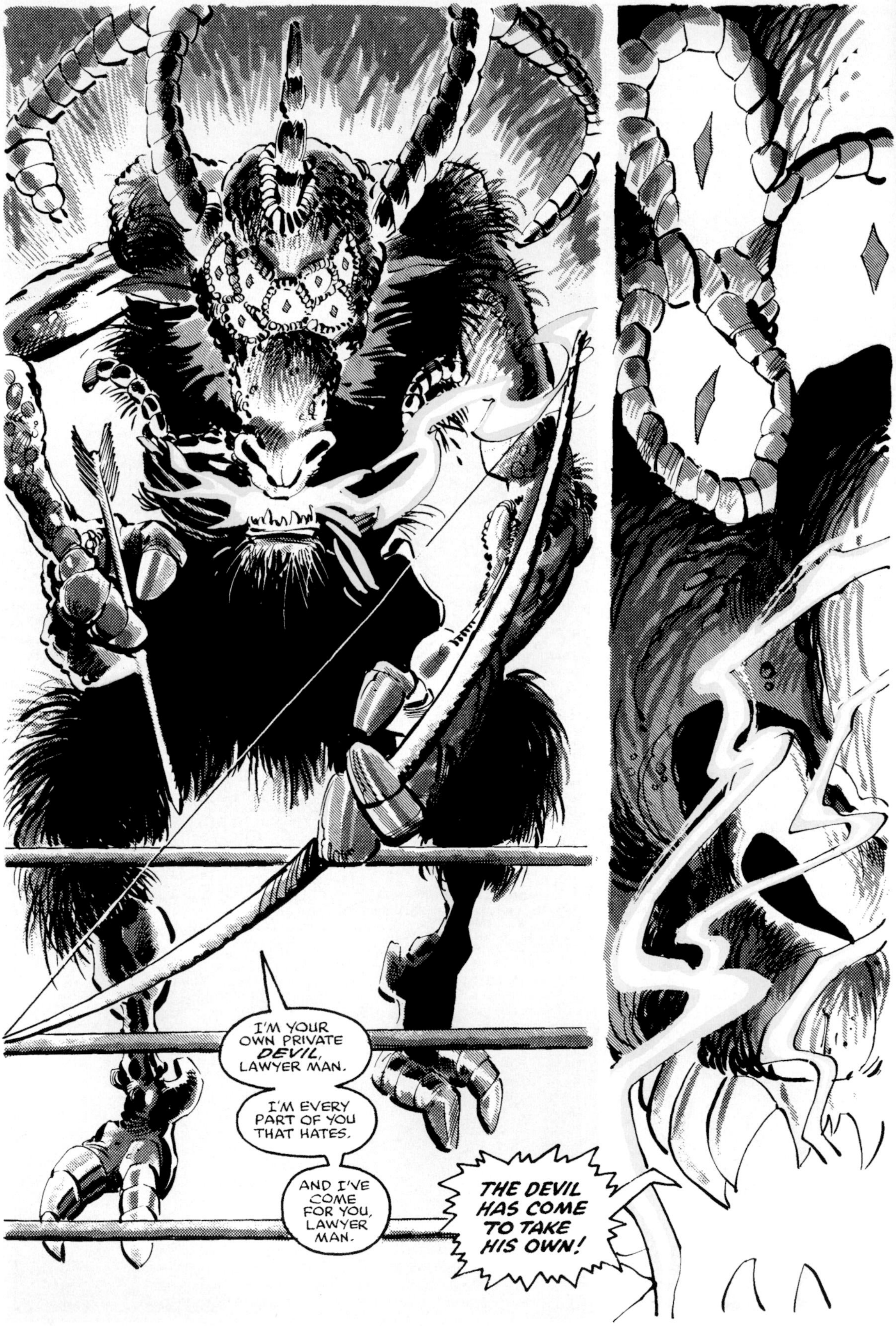
I'M YOUR OWN PRIVATE DEVIL, LAWYER MAN.
I'M EVERY PART OF YOU THAT HATES.
AND I'VE COME FOR YOU, LAWYER MAN.
THE DEVIL HAS COME TO TAKE HIS OWN!

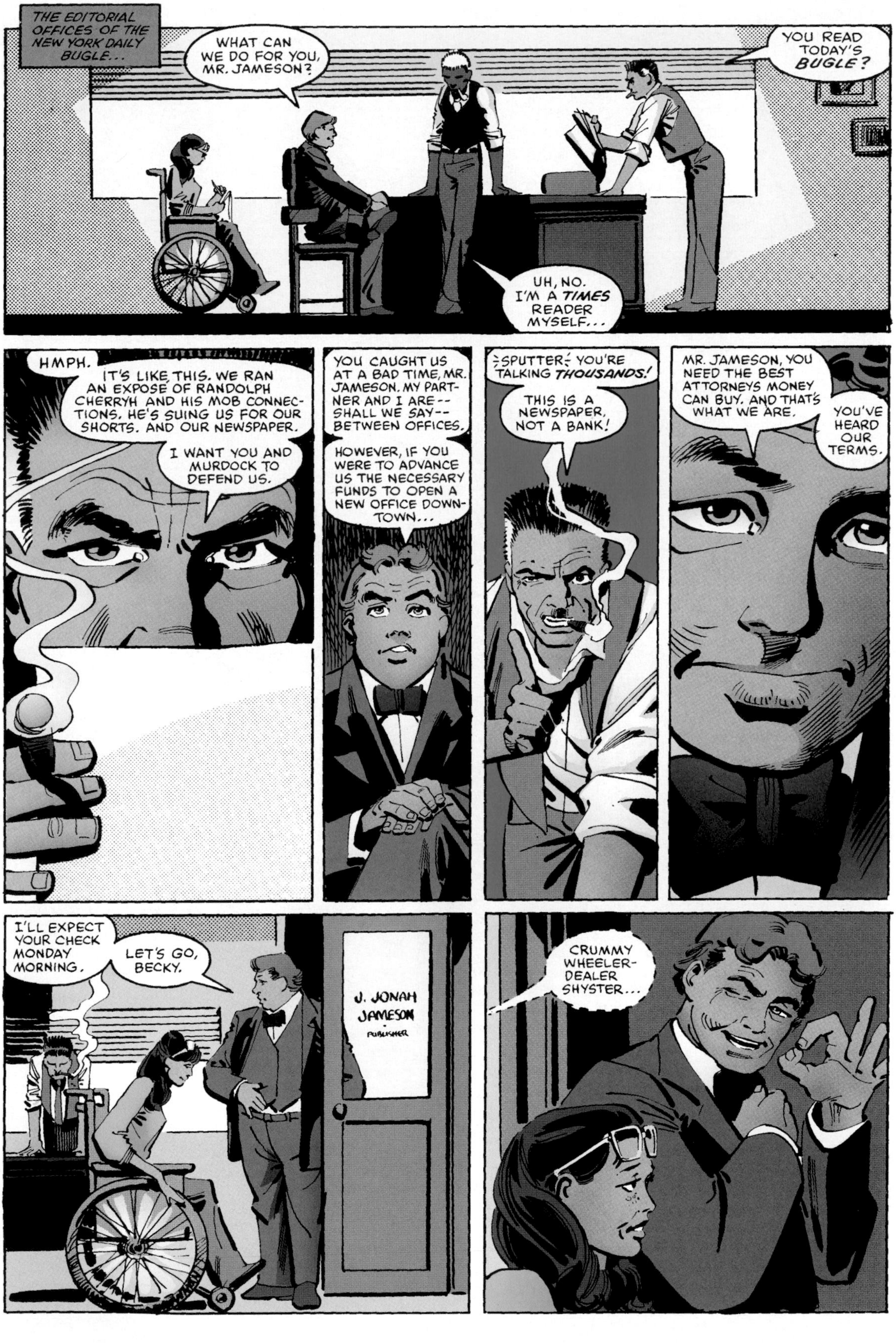
THE EDITORIAL OFFICES OF THE NEW YORK DAILY BUGLE...
WHAT CAN WE DO FOR YOU, MR. JAMESON?
YOU READ TODAY'S BUGLE?
UH, NO. I'M A TIMES READER MYSELF...
HMPH.
IT'S LIKE THIS. WE RAN AN EXPOSÉ OF RANDOLPH CHERRYH AND HIS MOB CONNECTIONS. HE'S SUING US FOR OUR SHORTS. AND OUR NEWSPAPER.
I WANT YOU AND MURDOCK TO DEFEND US.
YOU CAUGHT US AT A BAD TIME, MR. JAMESON. MY PARTNER AND I ARE-- SHALL WE SAY-- BETWEEN OFFICES.
HOWEVER, IF YOU WERE TO ADVANCE US THE NECESSARY FUNDS TO OPEN A NEW OFFICE DOWNTOWN...
-SPUTTER- YOU'RE TALKING THOUSANDS!
THIS IS A NEWSPAPER, NOT A BANK!
MR. JAMESON, YOU NEED THE BEST ATTORNEYS MONEY CAN BUY. AND THAT'S WHAT WE ARE.
YOU'VE HEARD OUR TERMS.
I'LL EXPECT YOUR CHECK MONDAY MORNING.
LET'S GO, BECKY.
J. JONAH JAMESON
PUBLISHER
CRUMMY WHEELER-DEALER SHYSTER...

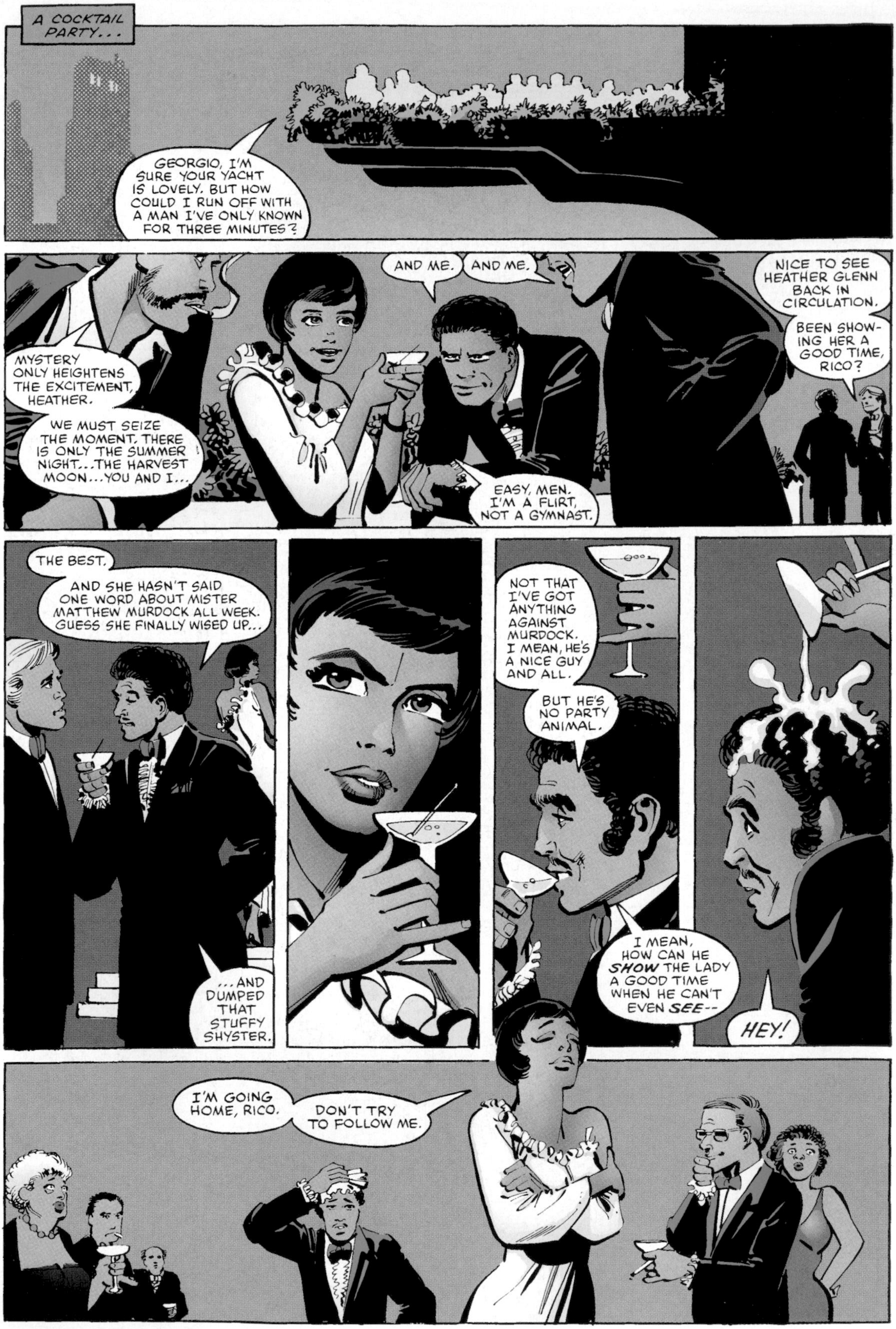
A COCKTAIL PARTY...
GEORGIO, I'M SURE YOUR YACHT IS LOVELY. BUT HOW COULD I RUN OFF WITH A MAN I'VE ONLY KNOWN FOR THREE MINUTES?
MYSTERY ONLY HEIGHTENS THE EXCITEMENT, HEATHER.
WE MUST SEIZE THE MOMENT. THERE IS ONLY THE SUMMER NIGHT... THE HARVEST MOON... YOU AND I...
AND ME.
AND ME.
EASY, MEN. I'M A FLIRT, NOT A GYMNAST.
NICE TO SEE HEATHER GLENN BACK IN CIRCULATION.
BEEN SHOWING HER A GOOD TIME, RICO?
THE BEST.
AND SHE HASN'T SAID ONE WORD ABOUT MISTER MATTHEW MURDOCK ALL WEEK. GUESS SHE FINALLY WISED UP...
...AND DUMPED THAT STUFFY SHYSTER.
NOT THAT I'VE GOT ANYTHING AGAINST MURDOCK. I MEAN, HE'S A NICE GUY AND ALL.
BUT HE'S NO PARTY ANIMAL.
I MEAN, HOW CAN HE SHOW THE LADY A GOOD TIME WHEN HE CAN'T EVEN SEE--
HEY!
I'M GOING HOME, RICO.
DON'T TRY TO FOLLOW ME.

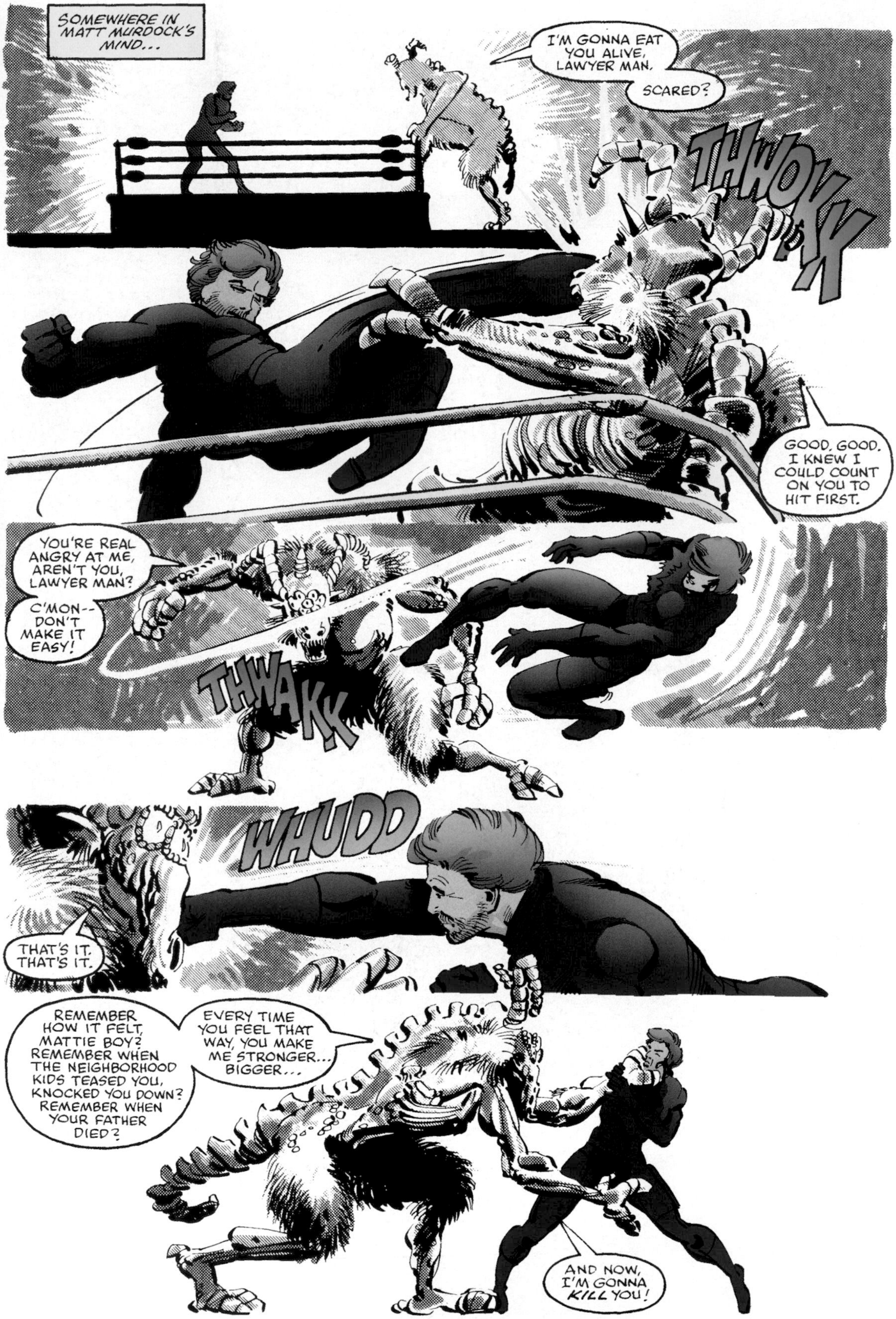
SOMEWHERE IN MATT MURDOCK'S MIND...
I'M GONNA EAT YOU ALIVE, LAWYER MAN.
SCARED?
THWOKK
GOOD, GOOD. I KNEW I COULD COUNT ON YOU TO HIT FIRST.
YOU'RE REAL ANGRY AT ME, AREN'T YOU, LAWYER MAN?
C'MON-- DON'T MAKE IT EASY!
THWAKK
WHUDD
THAT'S IT. THAT'S IT.
REMEMBER HOW IT FELT, MATTIE BOY? REMEMBER WHEN THE NEIGHBORHOOD KIDS TEASED YOU, KNOCKED YOU DOWN? REMEMBER WHEN YOUR FATHER DIED?
EVERY TIME YOU FEEL THAT WAY, YOU MAKE ME STRONGER... BIGGER...
AND NOW, I'M GONNA KILL YOU!

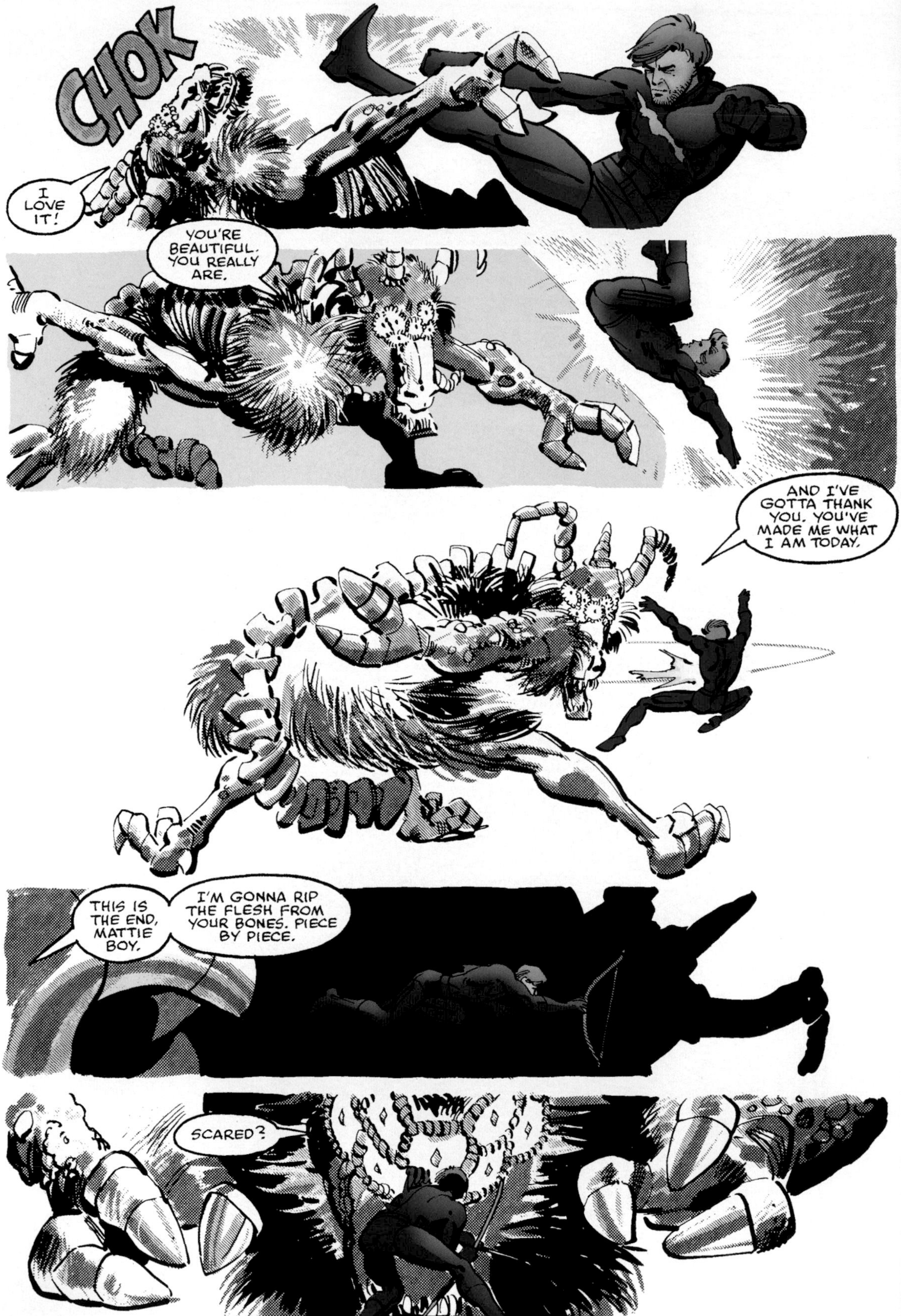
CHOK
I LOVE IT!
YOU'RE BEAUTIFUL. YOU REALLY ARE.
AND I'VE GOTTA THANK YOU. YOU'VE MADE ME WHAT I AM TODAY.
THIS IS THE END, MATTIE BOY.
I'M GONNA RIP THE FLESH FROM YOUR BONES. PIECE BY PIECE.
SCARED?

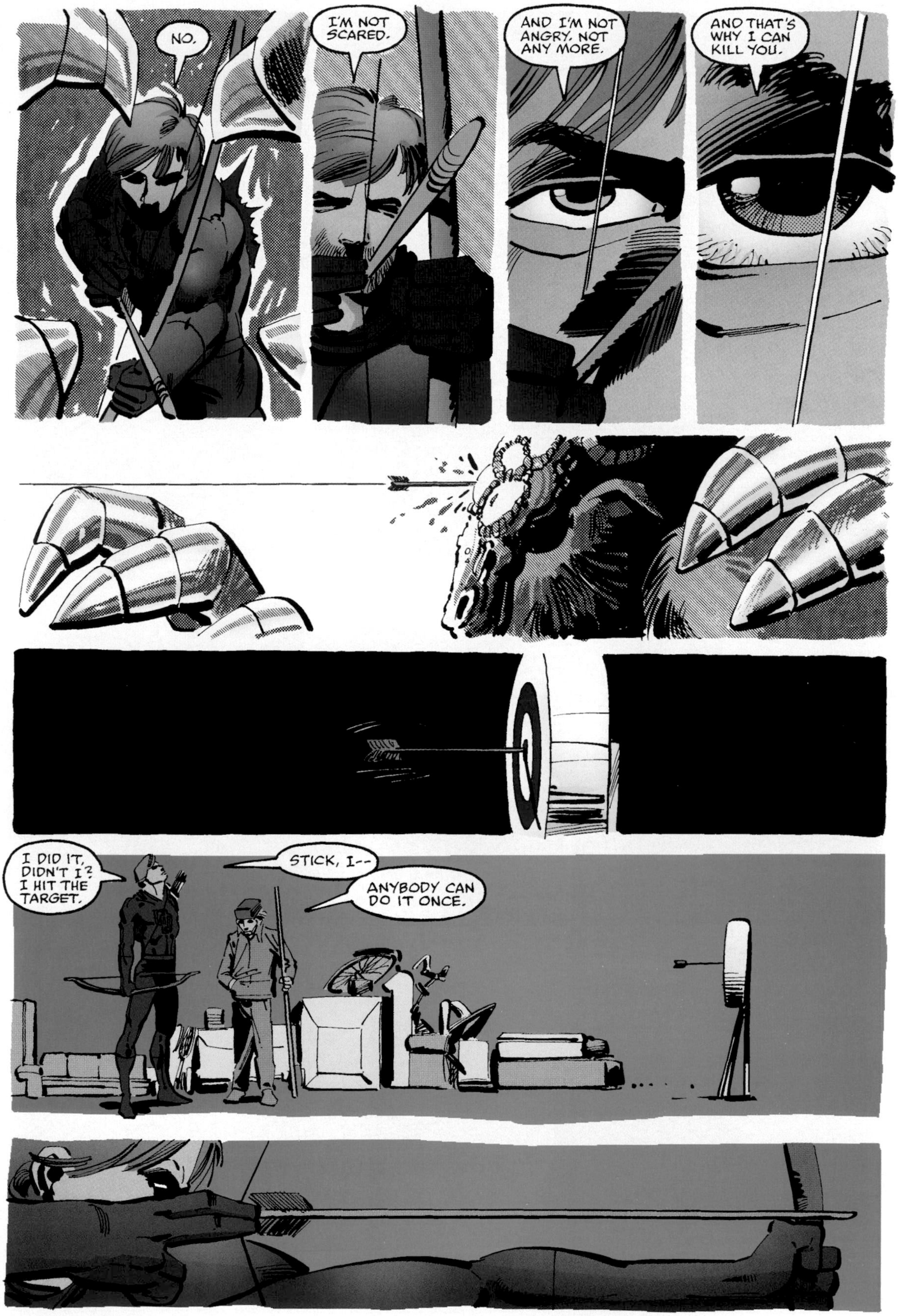
NO.
I'M NOT SCARED.
AND I'M NOT ANGRY. NOT ANY MORE.
AND THAT'S WHY I CAN KILL YOU.
I DID IT, DIDN'T I? I HIT THE TARGET.
STICK, I--
ANYBODY CAN DO IT ONCE.

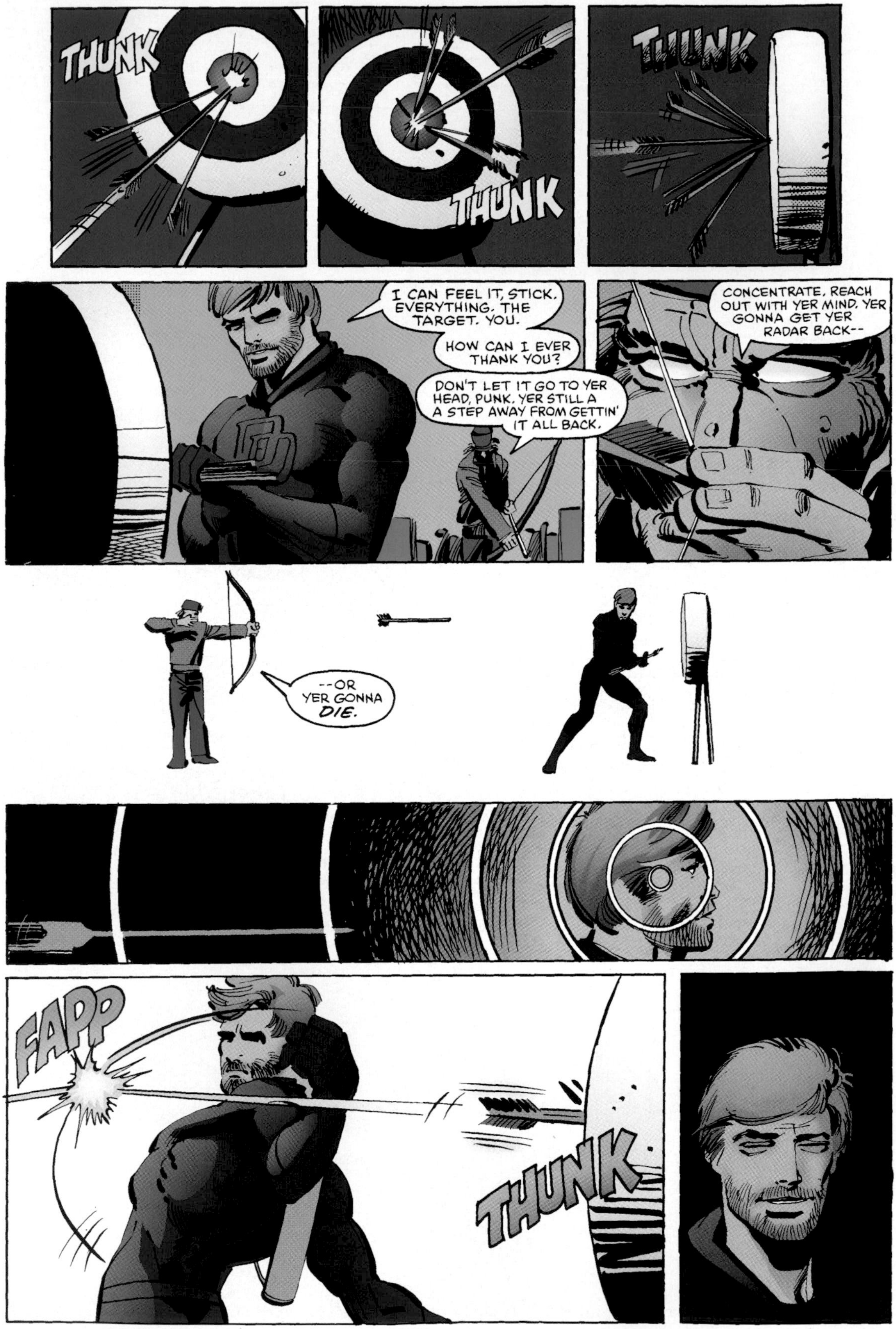
THUNK
THUNK
THUNK
I CAN FEEL IT, STICK. EVERYTHING. THE TARGET. YOU.
HOW CAN I EVER THANK YOU?
DON'T LET IT GO TO YER HEAD, PUNK. YER STILL A A STEP AWAY FROM GETTIN' IT ALL BACK.
CONCENTRATE, REACH OUT WITH YER MIND. YER GONNA GET YER RADAR BACK--
--OR YER GONNA DIE.
FAPP
THUNK

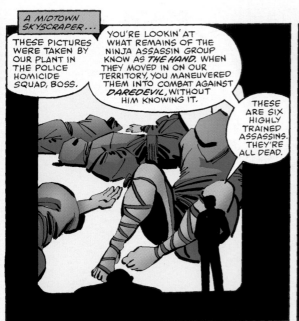

A MIDTOWN SKYSCRAPER...

THESE PICTURES WERE TAKEN BY OUR PLANT IN THE POLICE HOMICIDE SQUAD, BOSS.

YOU'RE LOOKIN' AT WHAT REMAINS OF THE NINJA ASSASSIN GROUP KNOW AS *THE HAND*. WHEN THEY MOVED IN ON OUR TERRITORY, YOU MANEUVERED THEM INTO COMBAT AGAINST *DAREDEVIL*, WITHOUT HIM KNOWING IT.

THESE ARE SIX HIGHLY TRAINED ASSASSINS. THEY'RE ALL DEAD.

SO ARE THE LEADER OF THE HAND AND THESE MEN, HIS PERSONAL GUARD.

ELEVEN STIFFS, TOTAL.

DAREDEVIL DID NOT DO THIS. HE IS NOT A KILLER.

RIGHT. AND THAT'S WHERE IT ALL GETS REAL INTERESTING.

IT WAS A LADY--A FORMER NINJA HERSELF--THAT DID THEM IN. LOUIE TOOK THESE SHOTS OF HER WHEN SHE HUNTED THE LAST OF THEM DOWN OUTSIDE OF DUKE'S POOL HALL.

SO WE CHECKED HER OUT. HER NAME'S *ELEKTRA*. SHE'S A MERCENARY, A BOUNTY HUNTER, AND A KILLER-FOR-HIRE. AS YOU CAN SEE, SHE'S THE BEST AT IT SINCE *BULLSEYE*. AND HE'S DOING TIME.

ANY INSTRUCTIONS?

YES. FIND HER.

NEXT ISSUE: *PAPER CHASE!*

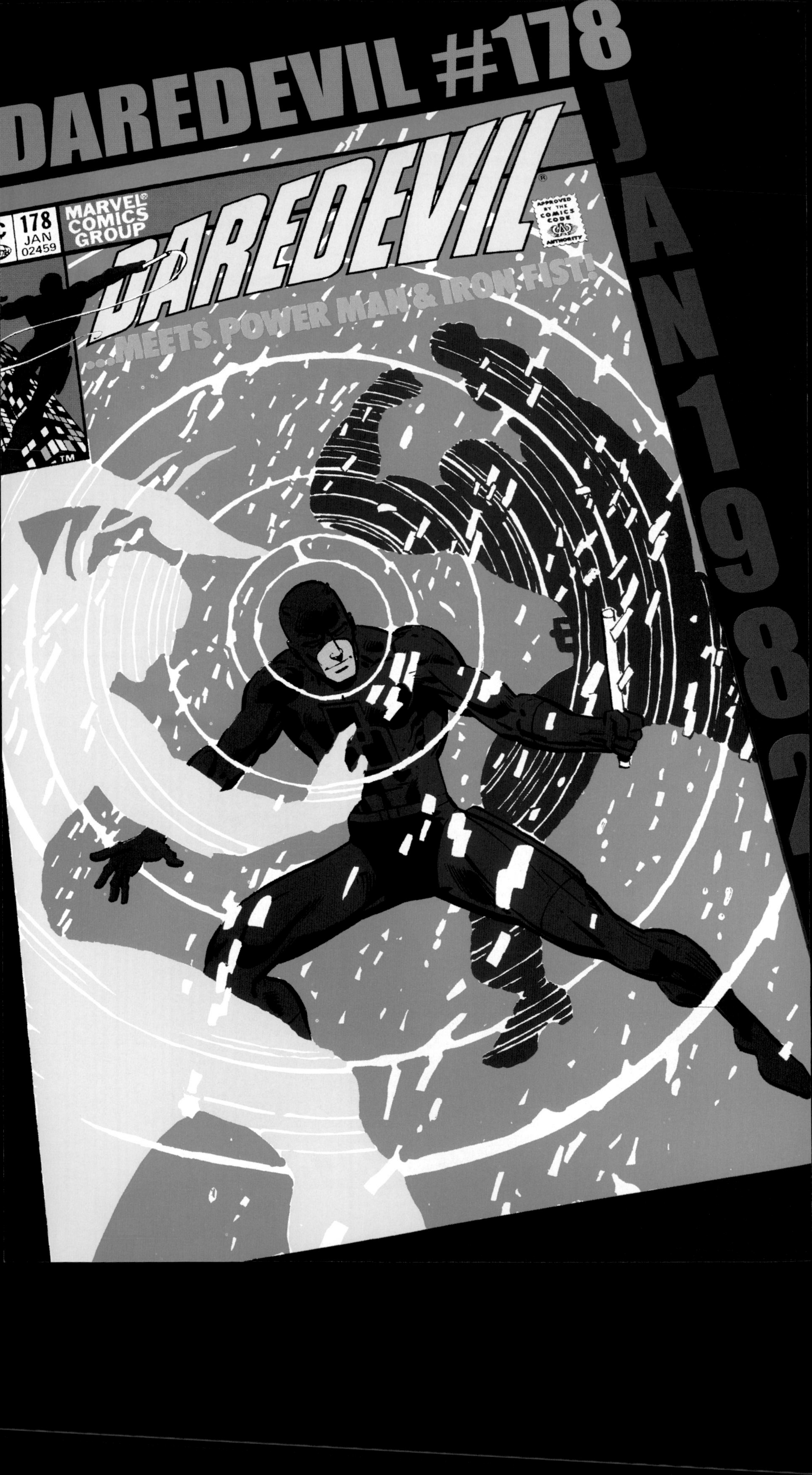
DAREDEVIL #178
JAN 1982
178
JAN
02459
MARVEL
COMICS
GROUP
DAREDEVIL
APPROVED BY THE COMICS CODE AUTHORITY
...MEETS POWER MAN & IRON FIST!

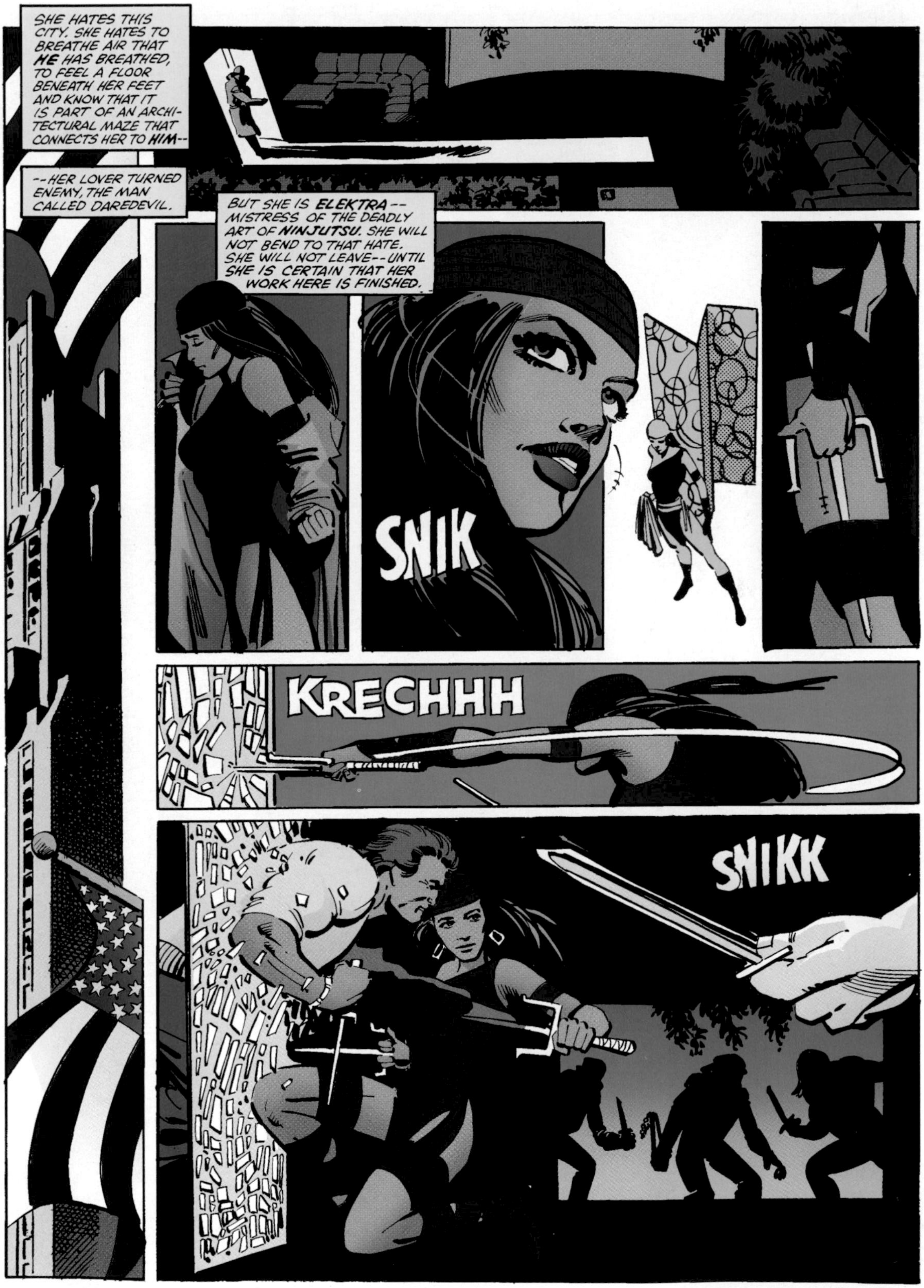
SHE HATES THIS CITY. SHE HATES TO BREATHE AIR THAT HE HAS BREATHED, TO FEEL A FLOOR BENEATH HER FEET AND KNOW THAT IT IS PART OF AN ARCHITECTURAL MAZE THAT CONNECTS HER TO HIM--
--HER LOVER TURNED ENEMY, THE MAN CALLED DAREDEVIL.
BUT SHE IS ELEKTRA-- MISTRESS OF THE DEADLY ART OF NINJUTSU. SHE WILL NOT BEND TO THAT HATE. SHE WILL NOT LEAVE--UNTIL SHE IS CERTAIN THAT HER WORK HERE IS FINISHED.
SNIK
KRECHHH
SNIKK

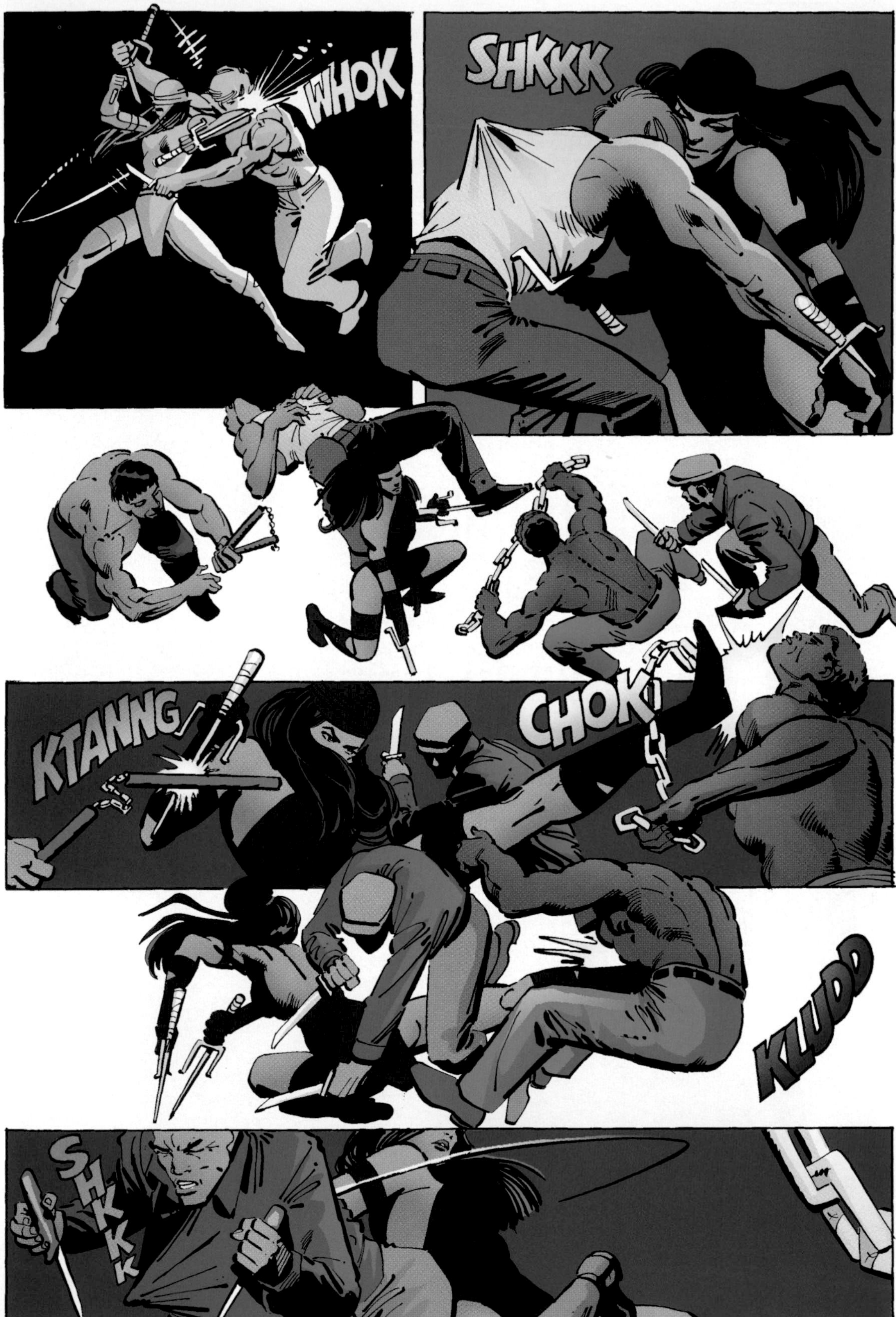
WHOK
SHKKK
KTANNG
CHOK
KLUDD
SHKKK

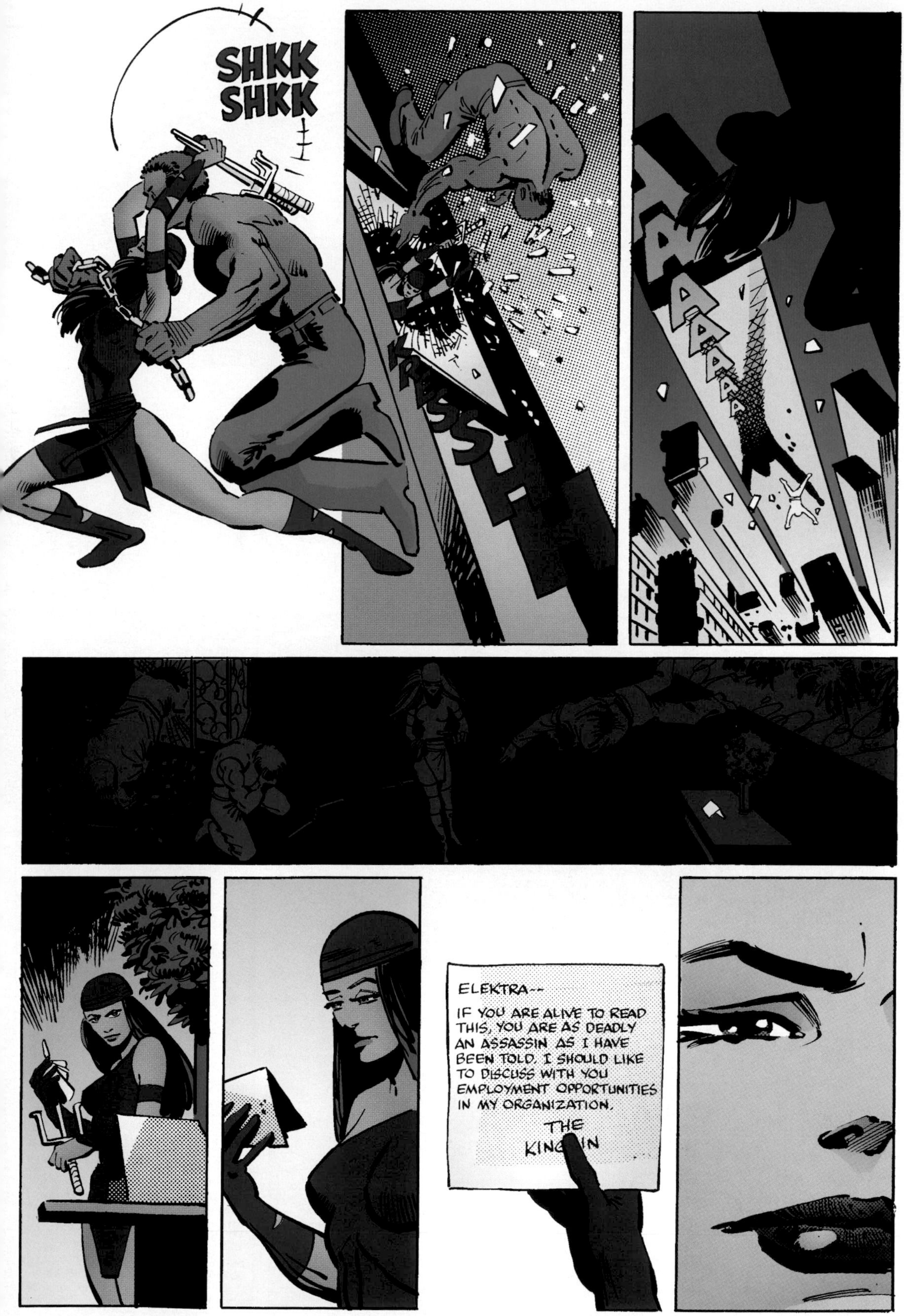
SHKK
SHKK
KRESSH
AAAAAAAA
ELEKTRA--
IF YOU ARE ALIVE TO READ THIS, YOU ARE AS DEADLY AN ASSASSIN AS I HAVE BEEN TOLD. I SHOULD LIKE TO DISCUSS WITH YOU EMPLOYMENT OPPORTUNITIES IN MY ORGANIZATION.
THE KING

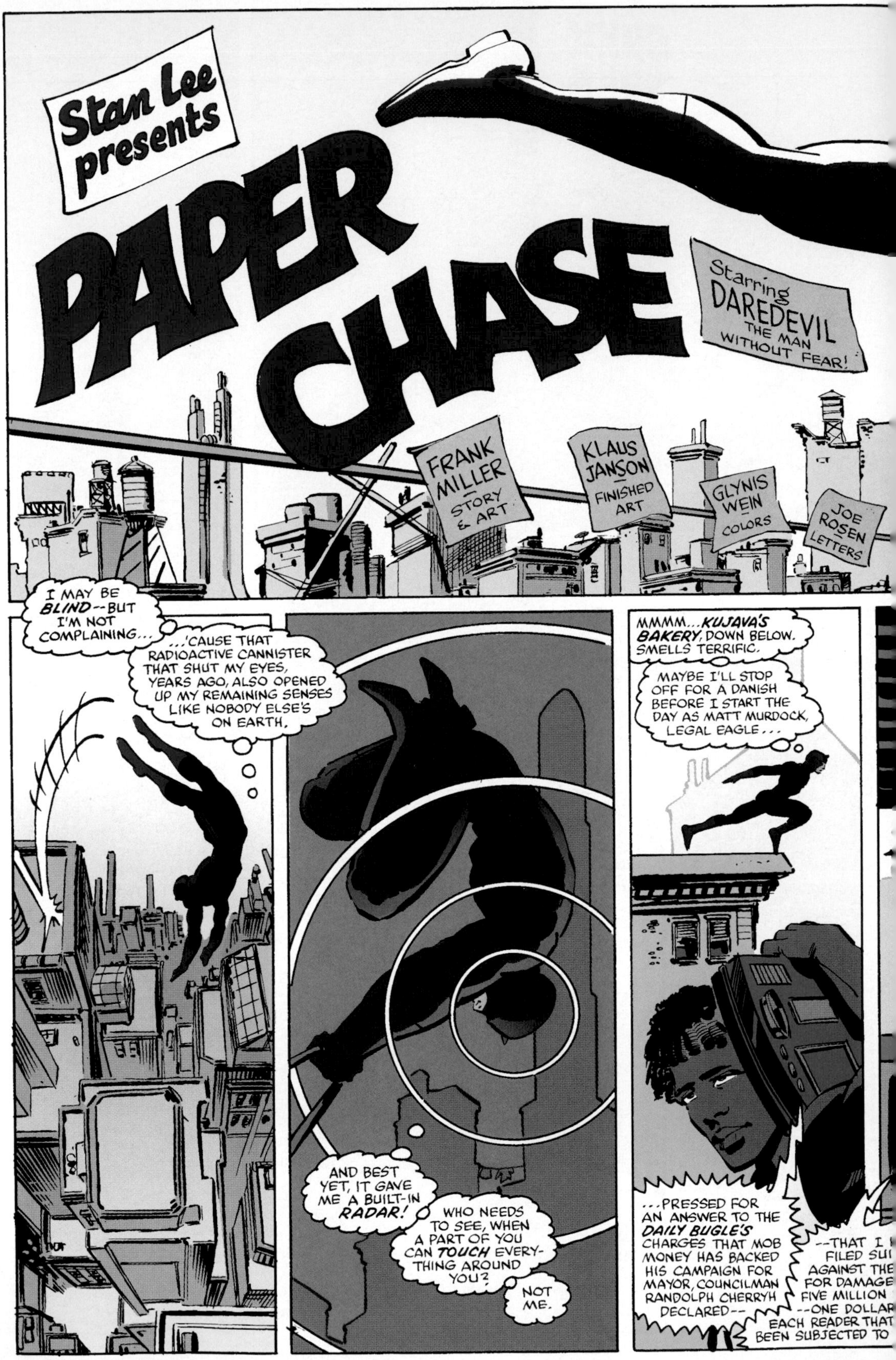
Stan Lee presents
PAPER CHASE
Starring DAREDEVIL THE MAN WITHOUT FEAR!
FRANK MILLER STORY & ART
KLAUS JANSON FINISHED ART
GLYNIS WEIN COLORS
JOE ROSEN LETTERS
I MAY BE BLIND--BUT I'M NOT COMPLAINING...
...'CAUSE THAT RADIOACTIVE CANNISTER THAT SHUT MY EYES, YEARS AGO, ALSO OPENED UP MY REMAINING SENSES LIKE NOBODY ELSE'S ON EARTH.
AND BEST YET, IT GAVE ME A BUILT-IN RADAR!
WHO NEEDS TO SEE, WHEN A PART OF YOU CAN TOUCH EVERYTHING AROUND YOU?
NOT ME.
MMMM...KUJAVA'S BAKERY, DOWN BELOW. SMELLS TERRIFIC.
MAYBE I'LL STOP OFF FOR A DANISH BEFORE I START THE DAY AS MATT MURDOCK, LEGAL EAGLE...
...PRESSED FOR AN ANSWER TO THE DAILY BUGLE'S CHARGES THAT MOB MONEY HAS BACKED HIS CAMPAIGN FOR MAYOR, COUNCILMAN RANDOLPH CHERRYH DECLARED--

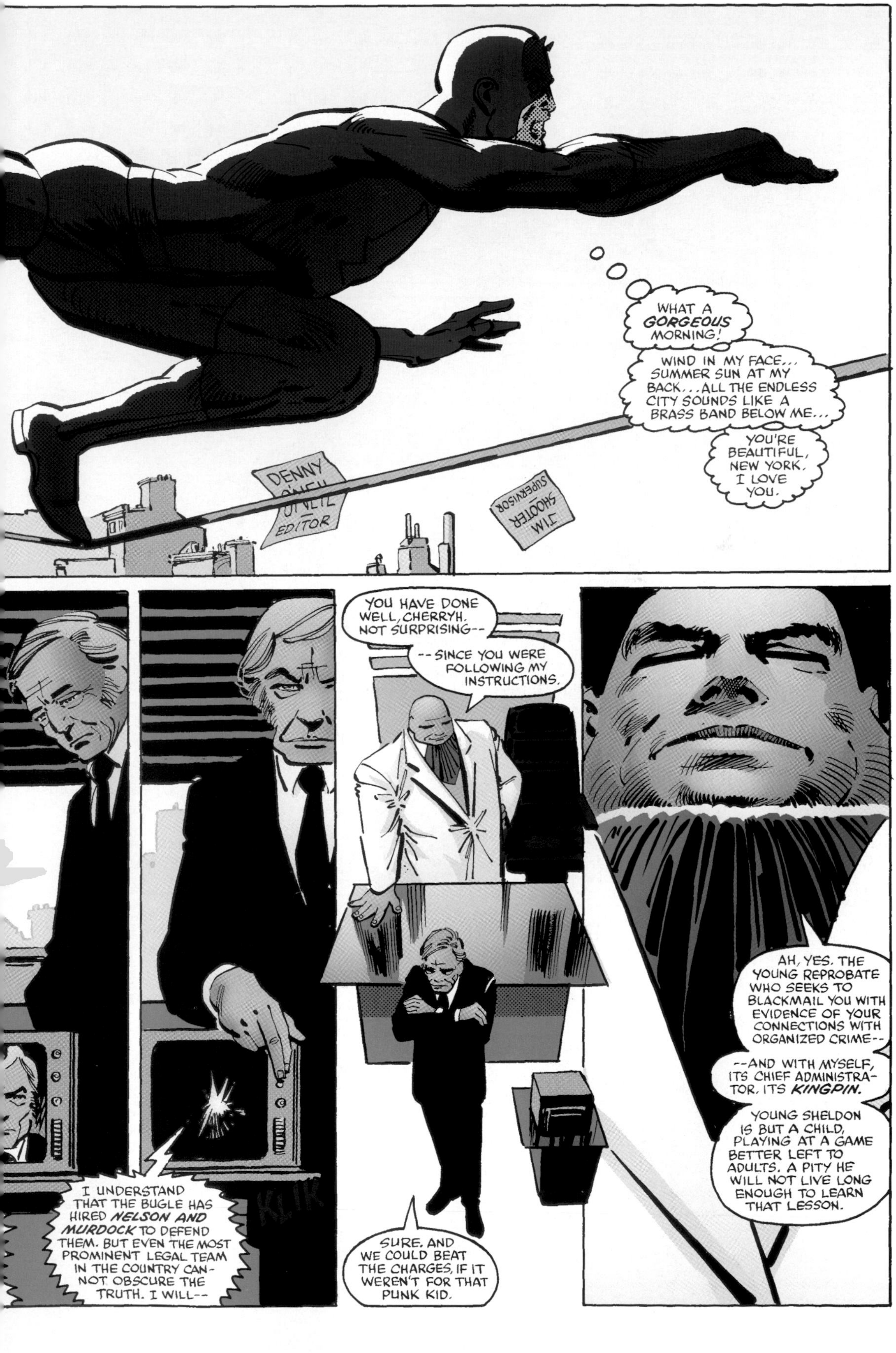
WHAT A GORGEOUS MORNING!
WIND IN MY FACE... SUMMER SUN AT MY BACK... ALL THE ENDLESS CITY SOUNDS LIKE A BRASS BAND BELOW ME...
YOU'RE BEAUTIFUL, NEW YORK. I LOVE YOU.
DENNY O'NEIL EDITOR
JIM SHOOTER SUPERVISOR
I UNDERSTAND THAT THE BUGLE HAS HIRED NELSON AND MURDOCK TO DEFEND THEM. BUT EVEN THE MOST PROMINENT LEGAL TEAM IN THE COUNTRY CAN-NOT OBSCURE THE TRUTH. I WILL--
KLIK
YOU HAVE DONE WELL, CHERRYH. NOT SURPRISING--
--SINCE YOU WERE FOLLOWING MY INSTRUCTIONS.
SURE. AND WE COULD BEAT THE CHARGES, IF IT WEREN'T FOR THAT PUNK KID.
AH, YES. THE YOUNG REPROBATE WHO SEEKS TO BLACKMAIL YOU WITH EVIDENCE OF YOUR CONNECTIONS WITH ORGANIZED CRIME--
--AND WITH MYSELF, ITS CHIEF ADMINISTRA-TOR. ITS KINGPIN.
YOUNG SHELDON IS BUT A CHILD, PLAYING AT A GAME BETTER LEFT TO ADULTS. A PITY HE WILL NOT LIVE LONG ENOUGH TO LEARN THAT LESSON.

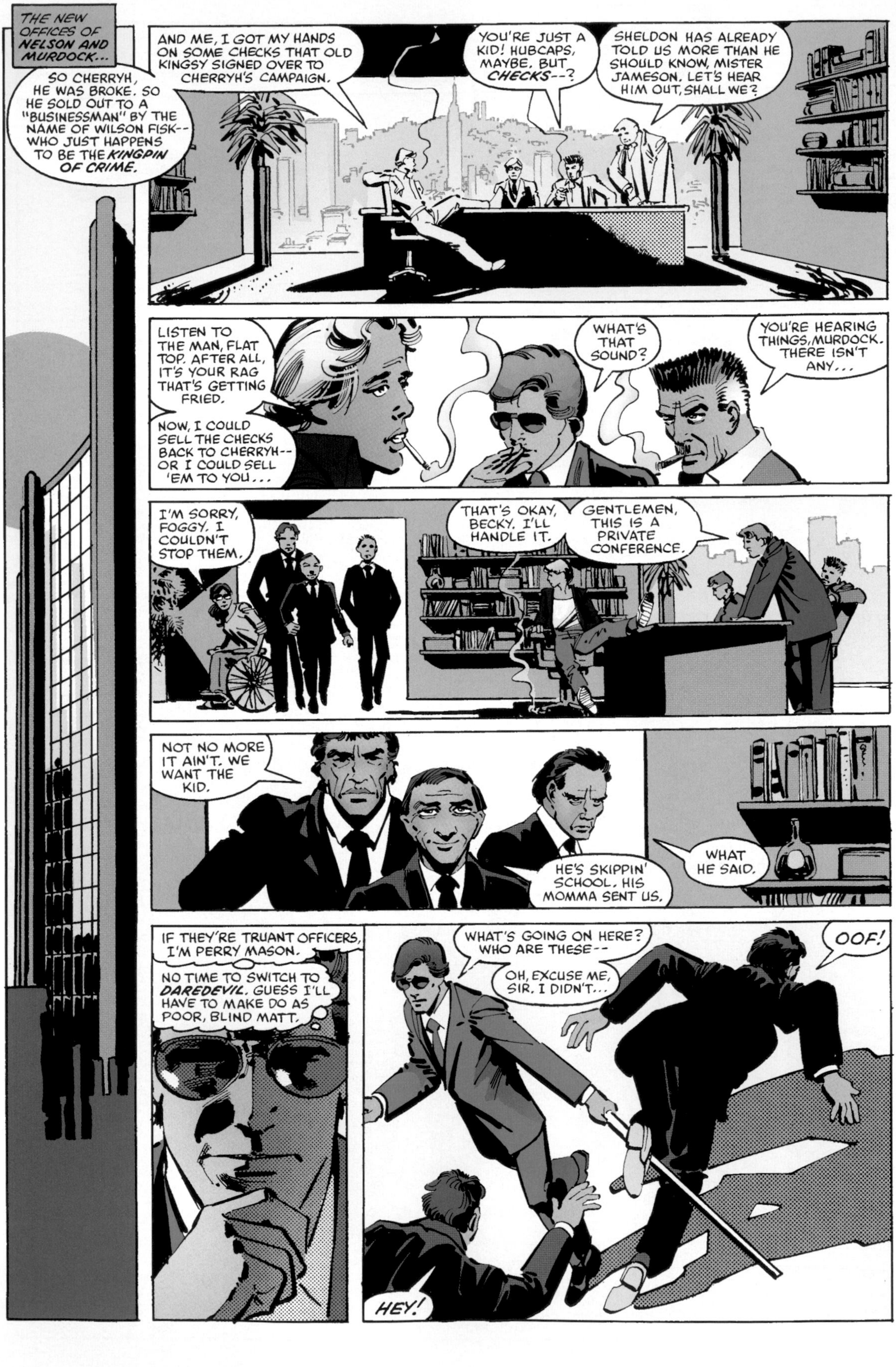
THE NEW OFFICES OF NELSON AND MURDOCK...
SO CHERRYH, HE WAS BROKE. SO HE SOLD OUT TO A "BUSINESSMAN" BY THE NAME OF WILSON FISK-- WHO JUST HAPPENS TO BE THE KINGPIN OF CRIME.
AND ME, I GOT MY HANDS ON SOME CHECKS THAT OLD KINGSY SIGNED OVER TO CHERRYH'S CAMPAIGN.
YOU'RE JUST A KID! HUBCAPS, MAYBE. BUT CHECKS--?
SHELDON HAS ALREADY TOLD US MORE THAN HE SHOULD KNOW, MISTER JAMESON. LET'S HEAR HIM OUT, SHALL WE?
LISTEN TO THE MAN, FLAT TOP. AFTER ALL, IT'S YOUR RAG THAT'S GETTING FRIED.
NOW, I COULD SELL THE CHECKS BACK TO CHERRYH-- OR I COULD SELL 'EM TO YOU...
WHAT'S THAT SOUND?
YOU'RE HEARING THINGS, MURDOCK. THERE ISN'T ANY...
I'M SORRY, FOGGY. I COULDN'T STOP THEM.
THAT'S OKAY, BECKY. I'LL HANDLE IT.
GENTLEMEN, THIS IS A PRIVATE CONFERENCE.
NOT NO MORE IT AIN'T. WE WANT THE KID.
HE'S SKIPPIN' SCHOOL. HIS MOMMA SENT US.
WHAT HE SAID.
IF THEY'RE TRUANT OFFICERS, I'M PERRY MASON.
NO TIME TO SWITCH TO DAREDEVIL. GUESS I'LL HAVE TO MAKE DO AS POOR, BLIND MATT.
WHAT'S GOING ON HERE? WHO ARE THESE--
OH, EXCUSE ME, SIR. I DIDN'T...
OOF!
HEY!

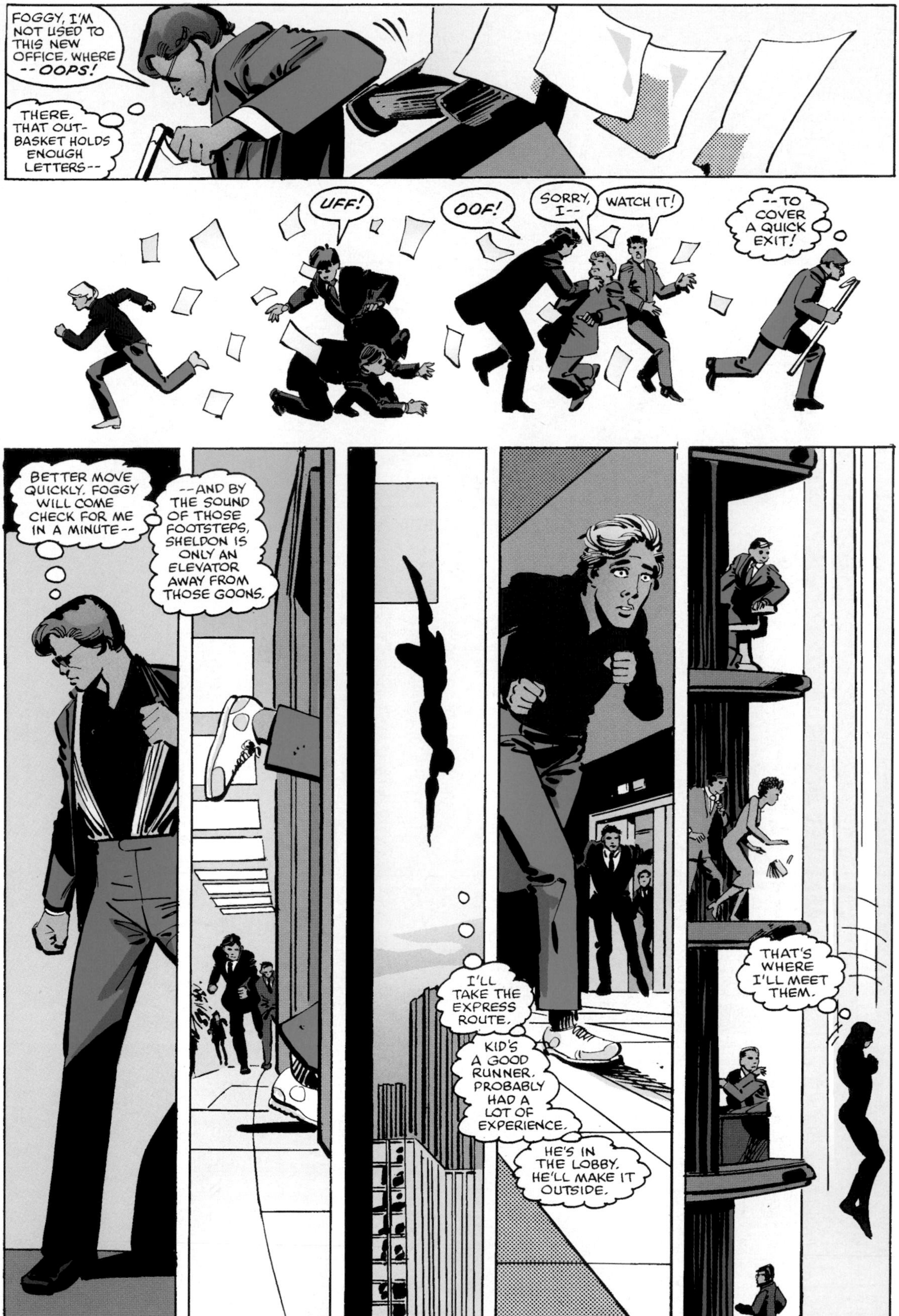

FOGGY, I'M NOT USED TO THIS NEW OFFICE, WHERE --OOPS!
THERE, THAT OUT-BASKET HOLDS ENOUGH LETTERS--
UFF!
OOF!
SORRY, I--
WATCH IT!
--TO COVER A QUICK EXIT!
BETTER MOVE QUICKLY. FOGGY WILL COME CHECK FOR ME IN A MINUTE--
--AND BY THE SOUND OF THOSE FOOTSTEPS, SHELDON IS ONLY AN ELEVATOR AWAY FROM THOSE GOONS.
I'LL TAKE THE EXPRESS ROUTE.
KID'S A GOOD RUNNER. PROBABLY HAD A LOT OF EXPERIENCE.
HE'S IN THE LOBBY. HE'LL MAKE IT OUTSIDE.
THAT'S WHERE I'LL MEET THEM.

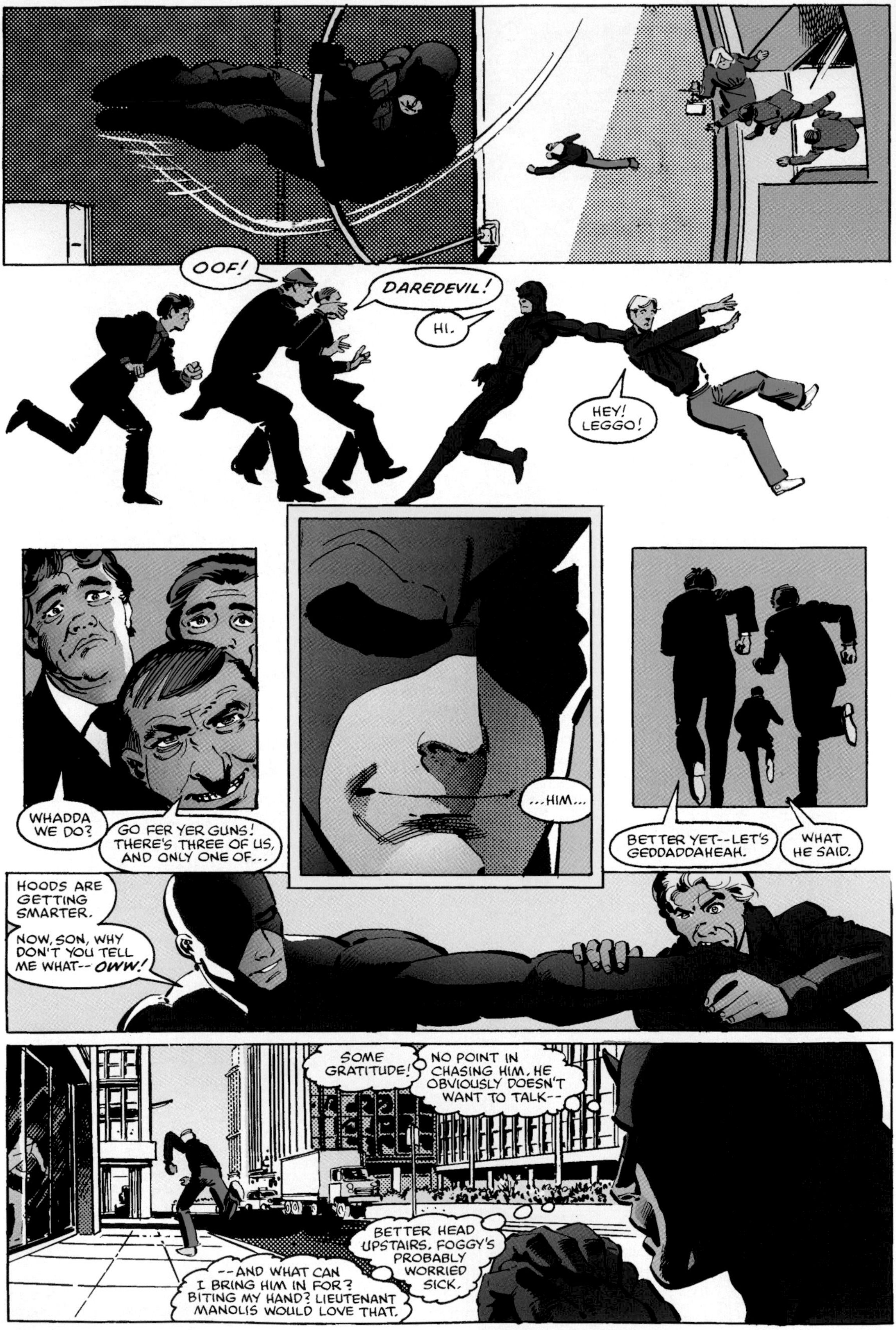
OOF!
DAREDEVIL!
HI.
HEY! LEGGO!
WHADDA WE DO?
GO FER YER GUNS! THERE'S THREE OF US, AND ONLY ONE OF...
...HIM...
BETTER YET--LET'S GEDDADDAHEAH.
WHAT HE SAID.
HOODS ARE GETTING SMARTER.
NOW, SON, WHY DON'T YOU TELL ME WHAT-- OWW!
SOME GRATITUDE!
NO POINT IN CHASING HIM. HE OBVIOUSLY DOESN'T WANT TO TALK--
--AND WHAT CAN I BRING HIM IN FOR? BITING MY HAND? LIEUTENANT MANOLIS WOULD LOVE THAT.
BETTER HEAD UPSTAIRS. FOGGY'S PROBABLY WORRIED SICK.

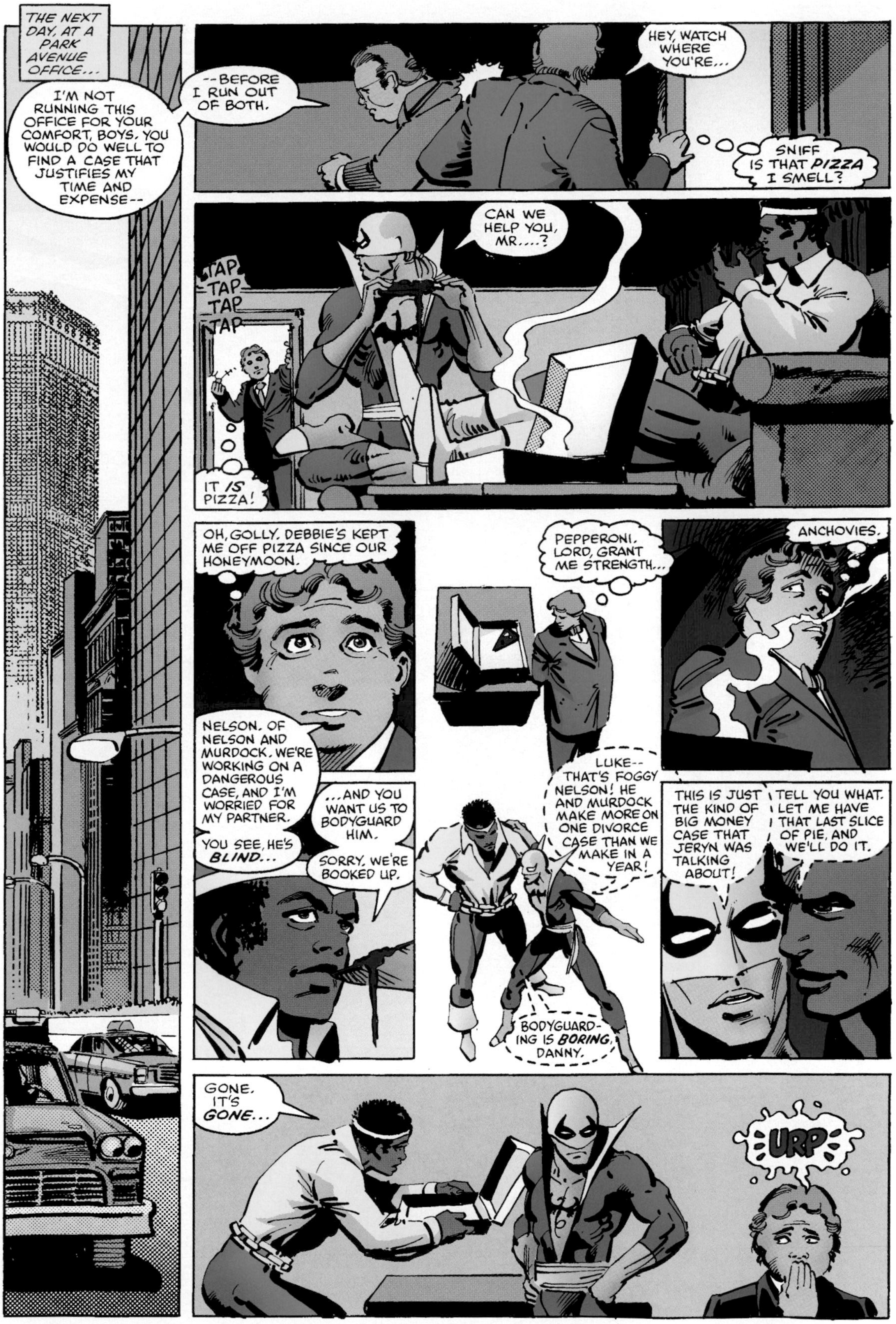

THE NEXT DAY, AT A PARK AVENUE OFFICE...
I'M NOT RUNNING THIS OFFICE FOR YOUR COMFORT, BOYS. YOU WOULD DO WELL TO FIND A CASE THAT JUSTIFIES MY TIME AND EXPENSE--
--BEFORE I RUN OUT OF BOTH.
HEY, WATCH WHERE YOU'RE...
SNIFF IS THAT PIZZA I SMELL?
TAP TAP TAP TAP
CAN WE HELP YOU, MR....?
IT IS PIZZA!
OH, GOLLY. DEBBIE'S KEPT ME OFF PIZZA SINCE OUR HONEYMOON.
PEPPERONI. LORD, GRANT ME STRENGTH...
ANCHOVIES.
NELSON. OF NELSON AND MURDOCK. WE'RE WORKING ON A DANGEROUS CASE, AND I'M WORRIED FOR MY PARTNER.
YOU SEE, HE'S BLIND...
...AND YOU WANT US TO BODYGUARD HIM.
SORRY. WE'RE BOOKED UP.
LUKE-- THAT'S FOGGY NELSON! HE AND MURDOCK MAKE MORE ON ONE DIVORCE CASE THAN WE MAKE IN A YEAR!
BODYGUARDING IS BORING, DANNY.
THIS IS JUST THE KIND OF BIG MONEY CASE THAT JERYN WAS TALKING ABOUT!
TELL YOU WHAT. LET ME HAVE THAT LAST SLICE OF PIE, AND WE'LL DO IT.
GONE. IT'S GONE...
URP

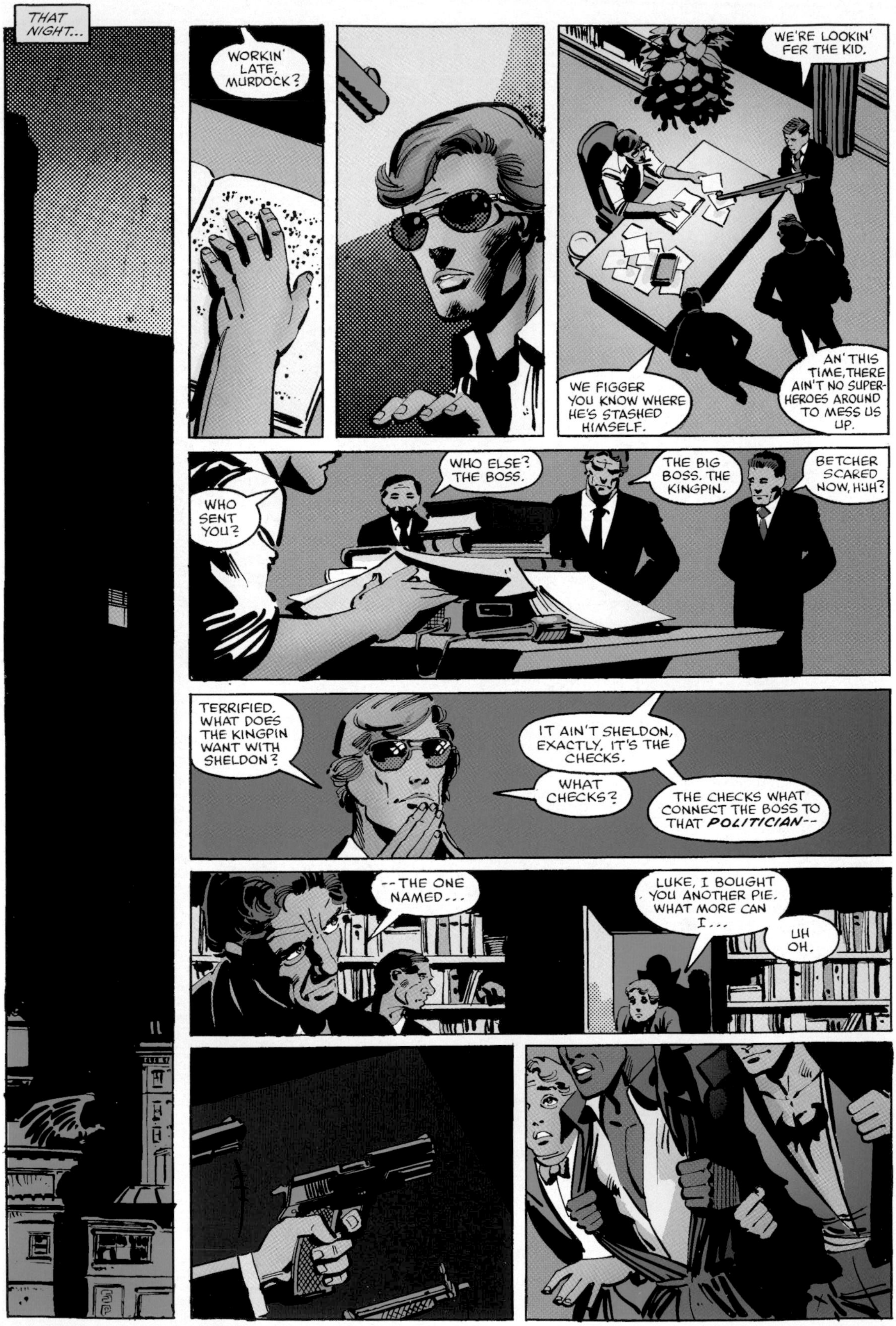
THAT NIGHT...
WORKIN' LATE, MURDOCK?
WE'RE LOOKIN' FER THE KID.
WE FIGGER YOU KNOW WHERE HE'S STASHED HIMSELF.
AN' THIS TIME, THERE AIN'T NO SUPER-HEROES AROUND TO MESS US UP.
WHO SENT YOU?
WHO ELSE? THE BOSS.
THE BIG BOSS. THE KINGPIN.
BETCHER SCARED NOW, HUH?
TERRIFIED. WHAT DOES THE KINGPIN WANT WITH SHELDON?
IT AIN'T SHELDON, EXACTLY. IT'S THE CHECKS.
WHAT CHECKS?
THE CHECKS WHAT CONNECT THE BOSS TO THAT POLITICIAN--
--THE ONE NAMED...
LUKE, I BOUGHT YOU ANOTHER PIE. WHAT MORE CAN I...
UH OH.

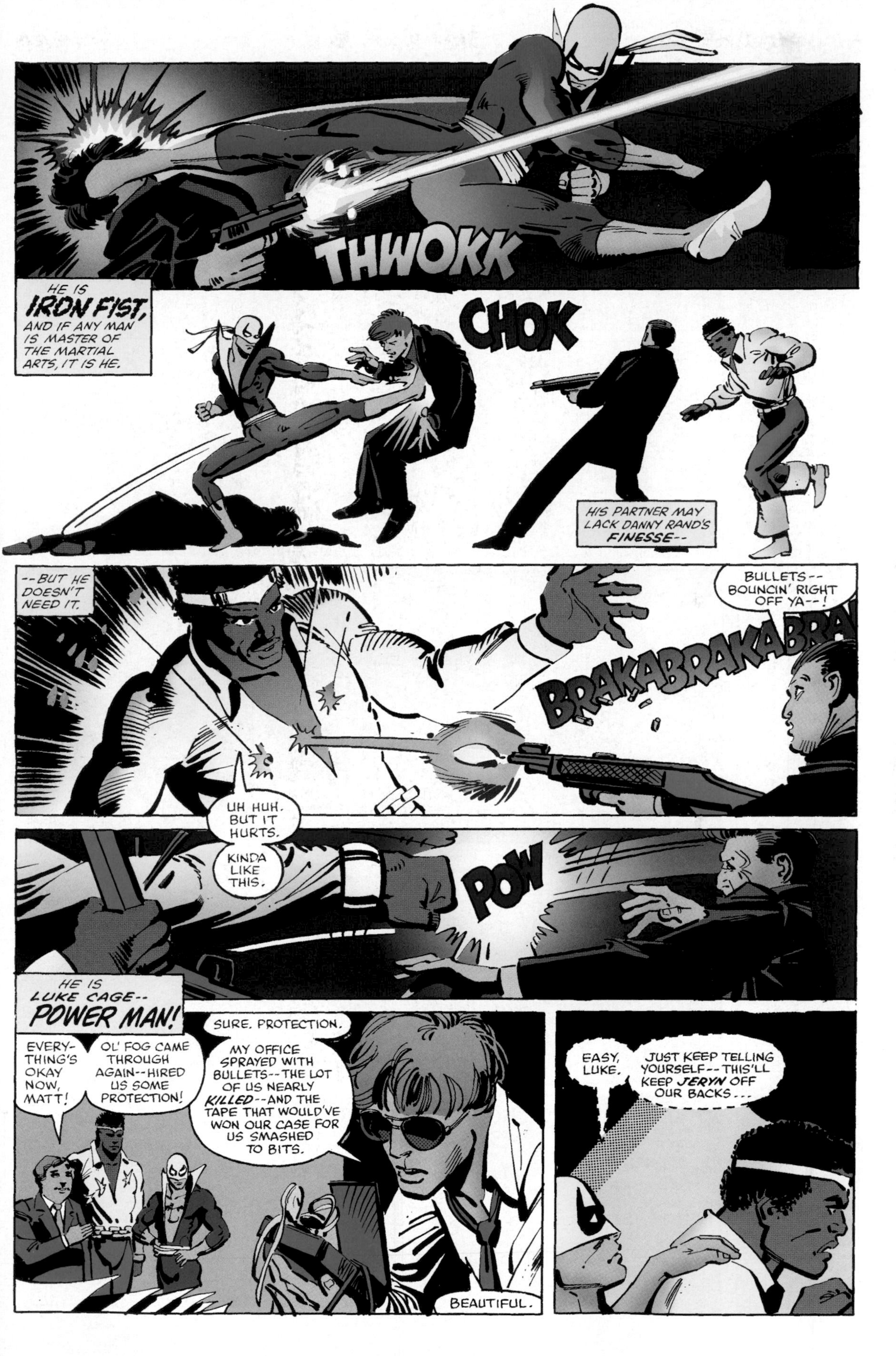
THWOKK
HE IS IRON FIST, AND IF ANY MAN IS MASTER OF THE MARTIAL ARTS, IT IS HE.
CHOK
HIS PARTNER MAY LACK DANNY RAND'S FINESSE--
--BUT HE DOESN'T NEED IT.
BULLETS--BOUNCIN' RIGHT OFF YA--!
BRAKABRAKABRA
UH HUH. BUT IT HURTS.
KINDA LIKE THIS.
POW
HE IS LUKE CAGE--POWER MAN!
EVERY-THING'S OKAY NOW, MATT!
OL' FOG CAME THROUGH AGAIN--HIRED US SOME PROTECTION!
SURE. PROTECTION.
MY OFFICE SPRAYED WITH BULLETS--THE LOT OF US NEARLY KILLED--AND THE TAPE THAT WOULD'VE WON OUR CASE FOR US SMASHED TO BITS.
BEAUTIFUL.
EASY, LUKE.
JUST KEEP TELLING YOURSELF--THIS'LL KEEP JERYN OFF OUR BACKS...

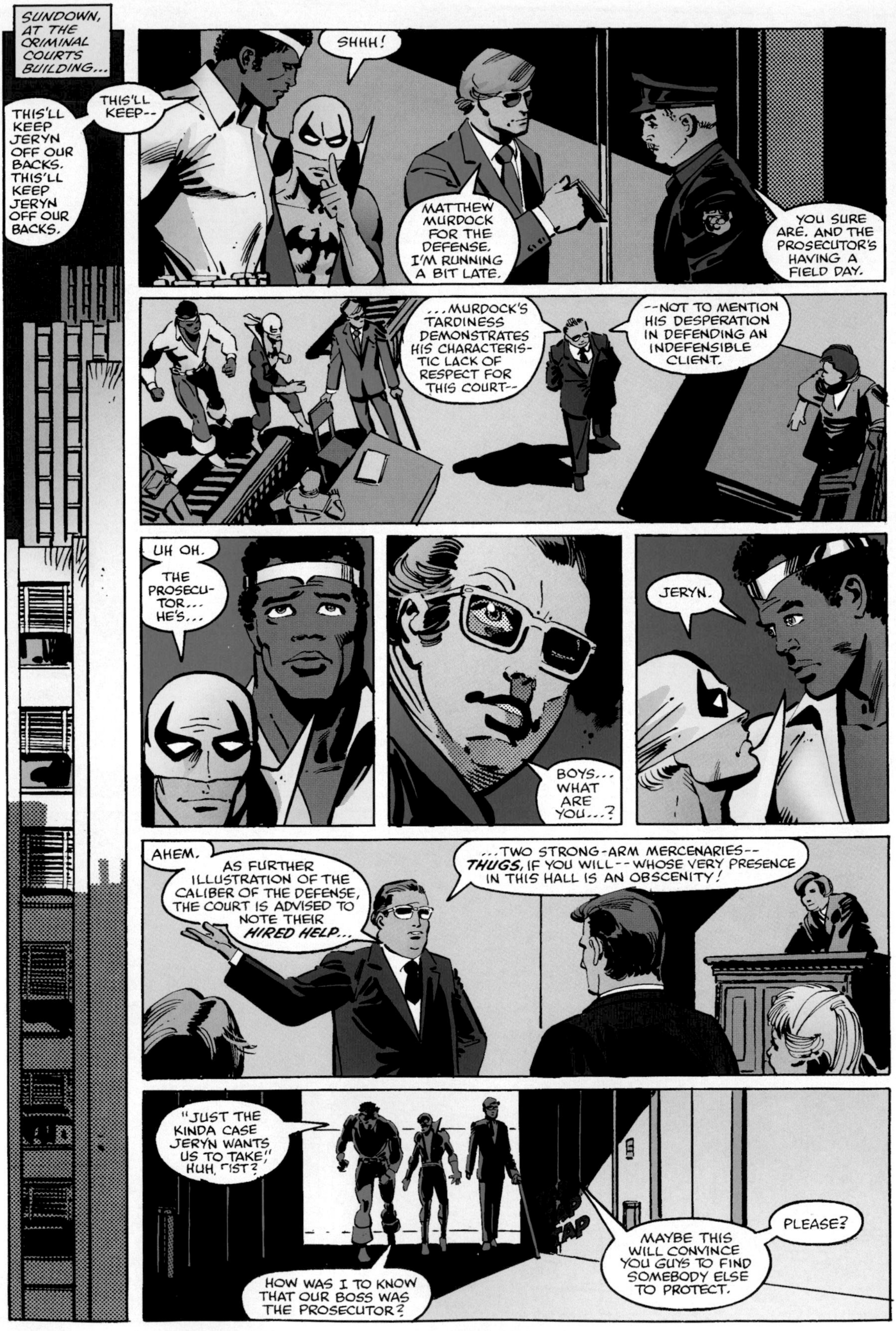

SUNDOWN, AT THE CRIMINAL COURTS BUILDING...
THIS'LL KEEP JERYN OFF OUR BACKS. THIS'LL KEEP JERYN OFF OUR BACKS.
THIS'LL KEEP--
SHHH!
MATTHEW MURDOCK FOR THE DEFENSE. I'M RUNNING A BIT LATE.
YOU SURE ARE. AND THE PROSECUTOR'S HAVING A FIELD DAY.
...MURDOCK'S TARDINESS DEMONSTRATES HIS CHARACTERISTIC LACK OF RESPECT FOR THIS COURT--
--NOT TO MENTION HIS DESPERATION IN DEFENDING AN INDEFENSIBLE CLIENT.
UH OH.
THE PROSECUTOR... HE'S...
BOYS... WHAT ARE YOU...?
JERYN.
AHEM.
AS FURTHER ILLUSTRATION OF THE CALIBER OF THE DEFENSE, THE COURT IS ADVISED TO NOTE THEIR HIRED HELP...
...TWO STRONG-ARM MERCENARIES-- THUGS, IF YOU WILL-- WHOSE VERY PRESENCE IN THIS HALL IS AN OBSCENITY!
"JUST THE KINDA CASE JERYN WANTS US TO TAKE," HUH, FIST?
HOW WAS I TO KNOW THAT OUR BOSS WAS THE PROSECUTOR?
TAP TAP
MAYBE THIS WILL CONVINCE YOU GUYS TO FIND SOMEBODY ELSE TO PROTECT.
PLEASE?

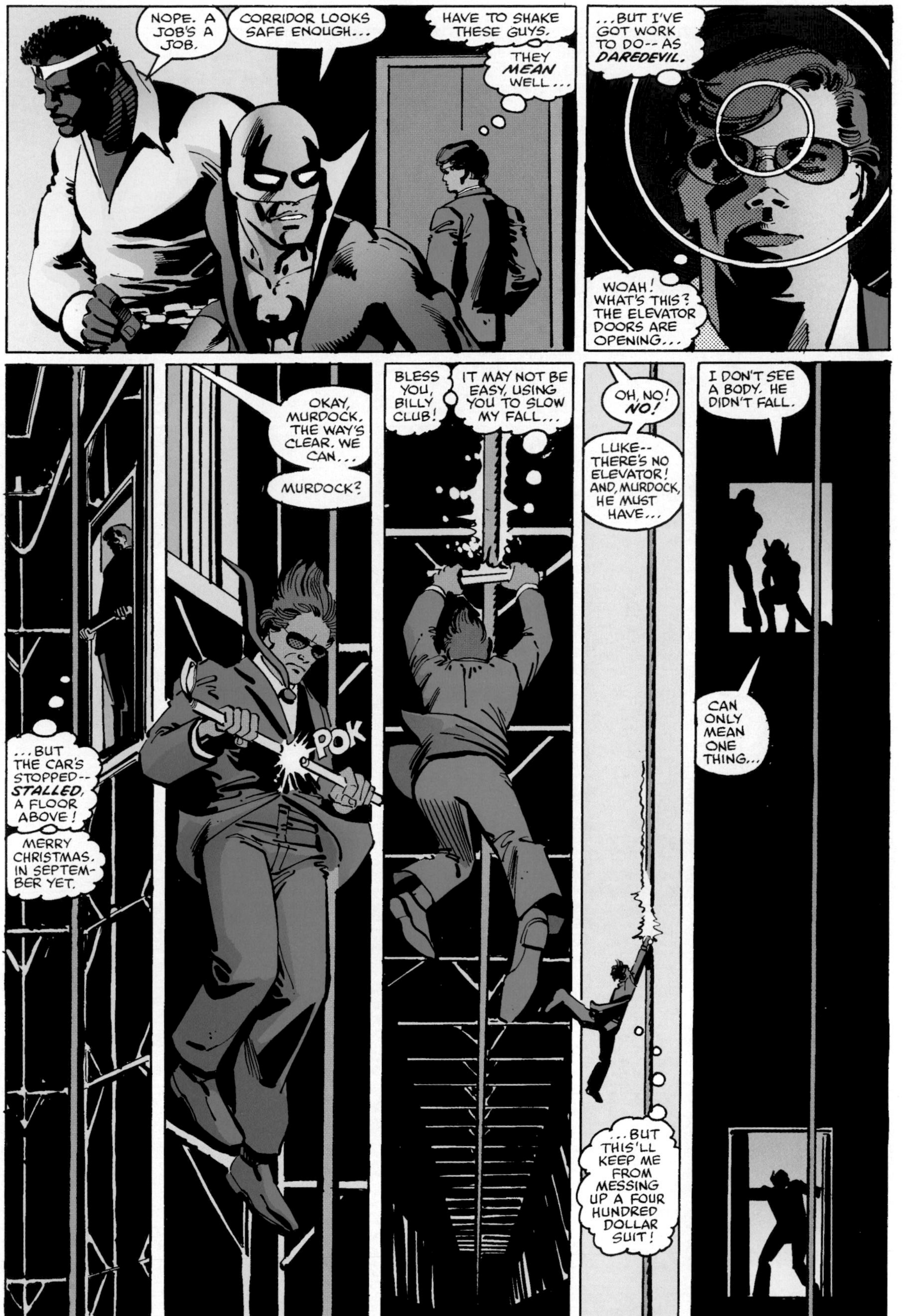
NOPE. A JOB'S A JOB.
CORRIDOR LOOKS SAFE ENOUGH...
HAVE TO SHAKE THESE GUYS.
THEY MEAN WELL...
...BUT I'VE GOT WORK TO DO-- AS DAREDEVIL.
WOAH! WHAT'S THIS? THE ELEVATOR DOORS ARE OPENING...
...BUT THE CAR'S STOPPED-- STALLED, A FLOOR ABOVE!
MERRY CHRISTMAS. IN SEPTEMBER YET.
OKAY, MURDOCK. THE WAY'S CLEAR. WE CAN...
MURDOCK?
POK
BLESS YOU, BILLY CLUB!
IT MAY NOT BE EASY, USING YOU TO SLOW MY FALL...
OH, NO! NO!
LUKE-- THERE'S NO ELEVATOR! AND, MURDOCK, HE MUST HAVE...
...BUT THIS'LL KEEP ME FROM MESSING UP A FOUR HUNDRED DOLLAR SUIT!
I DON'T SEE A BODY. HE DIDN'T FALL.
CAN ONLY MEAN ONE THING...

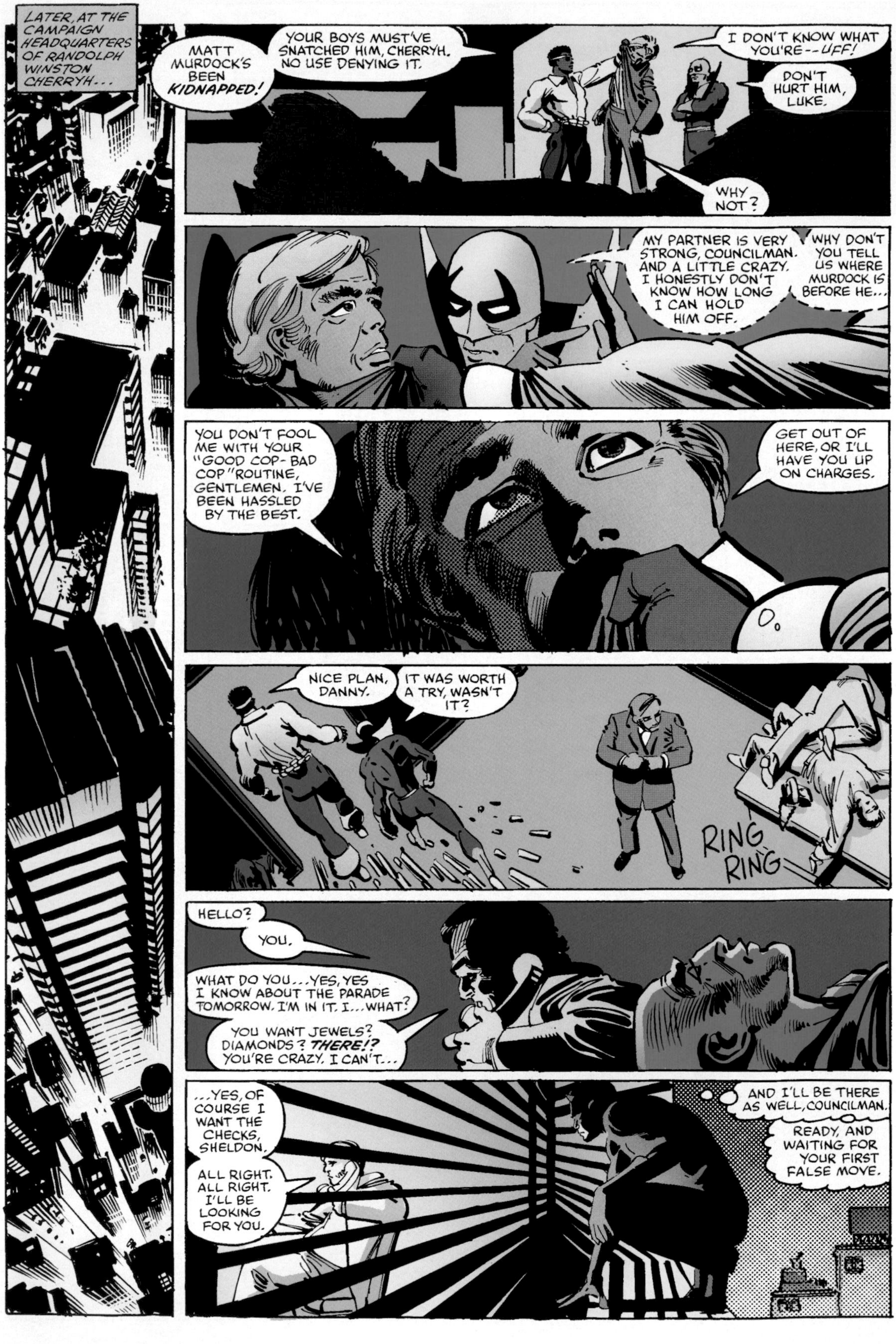
LATER, AT THE CAMPAIGN HEADQUARTERS OF RANDOLPH WINSTON CHERRYH...
MATT MURDOCK'S BEEN *KIDNAPPED!*
YOUR BOYS MUST'VE SNATCHED HIM, CHERRYH. NO USE DENYING IT.
I DON'T KNOW WHAT YOU'RE--*UFF!*
DON'T HURT HIM, LUKE.
WHY NOT?
MY PARTNER IS VERY STRONG, COUNCILMAN. AND A LITTLE CRAZY. I HONESTLY DON'T KNOW HOW LONG I CAN HOLD HIM OFF.
WHY DON'T YOU TELL US WHERE MURDOCK IS BEFORE HE...
YOU DON'T FOOL ME WITH YOUR "GOOD COP- BAD COP" ROUTINE, GENTLEMEN. I'VE BEEN HASSLED BY THE BEST.
GET OUT OF HERE, OR I'LL HAVE YOU UP ON CHARGES.
NICE PLAN, DANNY.
IT WAS WORTH A TRY, WASN'T IT?
RING RING
HELLO?
YOU.
WHAT DO YOU... YES, YES I KNOW ABOUT THE PARADE TOMORROW. I'M IN IT. I... WHAT?
YOU WANT JEWELS? DIAMONDS? *THERE!?* YOU'RE CRAZY. I CAN'T...
...YES, OF COURSE I WANT THE CHECKS, SHELDON.
ALL RIGHT. ALL RIGHT. I'LL BE LOOKING FOR YOU.
AND I'LL BE THERE AS WELL, COUNCILMAN.
READY, AND WAITING FOR YOUR FIRST FALSE MOVE.

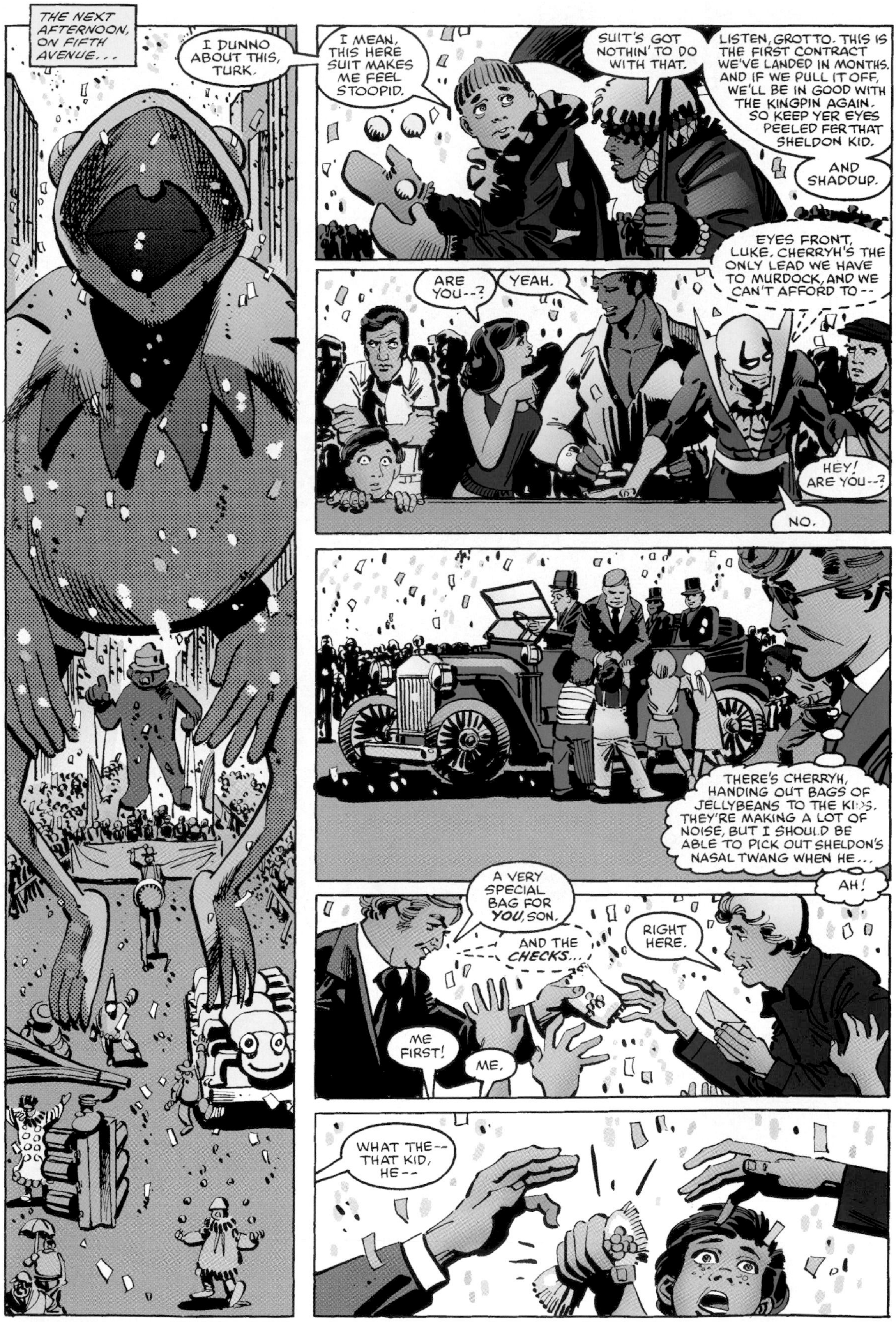
THE NEXT AFTERNOON, ON FIFTH AVENUE...
I DUNNO ABOUT THIS, TURK.
I MEAN, THIS HERE SUIT MAKES ME FEEL STOOPID.
SUIT'S GOT NOTHIN' TO DO WITH THAT.
LISTEN, GROTTO. THIS IS THE FIRST CONTRACT WE'VE LANDED IN MONTHS. AND IF WE PULL IT OFF, WE'LL BE IN GOOD WITH THE KINGPIN AGAIN. SO KEEP YER EYES PEELED FER THAT SHELDON KID.
AND SHADDUP.
ARE YOU--?
YEAH.
EYES FRONT, LUKE. CHERRYH'S THE ONLY LEAD WE HAVE TO MURDOCK, AND WE CAN'T AFFORD TO--
HEY! ARE YOU--?
NO.
THERE'S CHERRYH, HANDING OUT BAGS OF JELLYBEANS TO THE KIDS. THEY'RE MAKING A LOT OF NOISE, BUT I SHOULD BE ABLE TO PICK OUT SHELDON'S NASAL TWANG WHEN HE...
AH!
A VERY SPECIAL BAG FOR YOU, SON.
AND THE CHECKS...
RIGHT HERE.
ME FIRST!
ME.
WHAT THE-- THAT KID, HE--

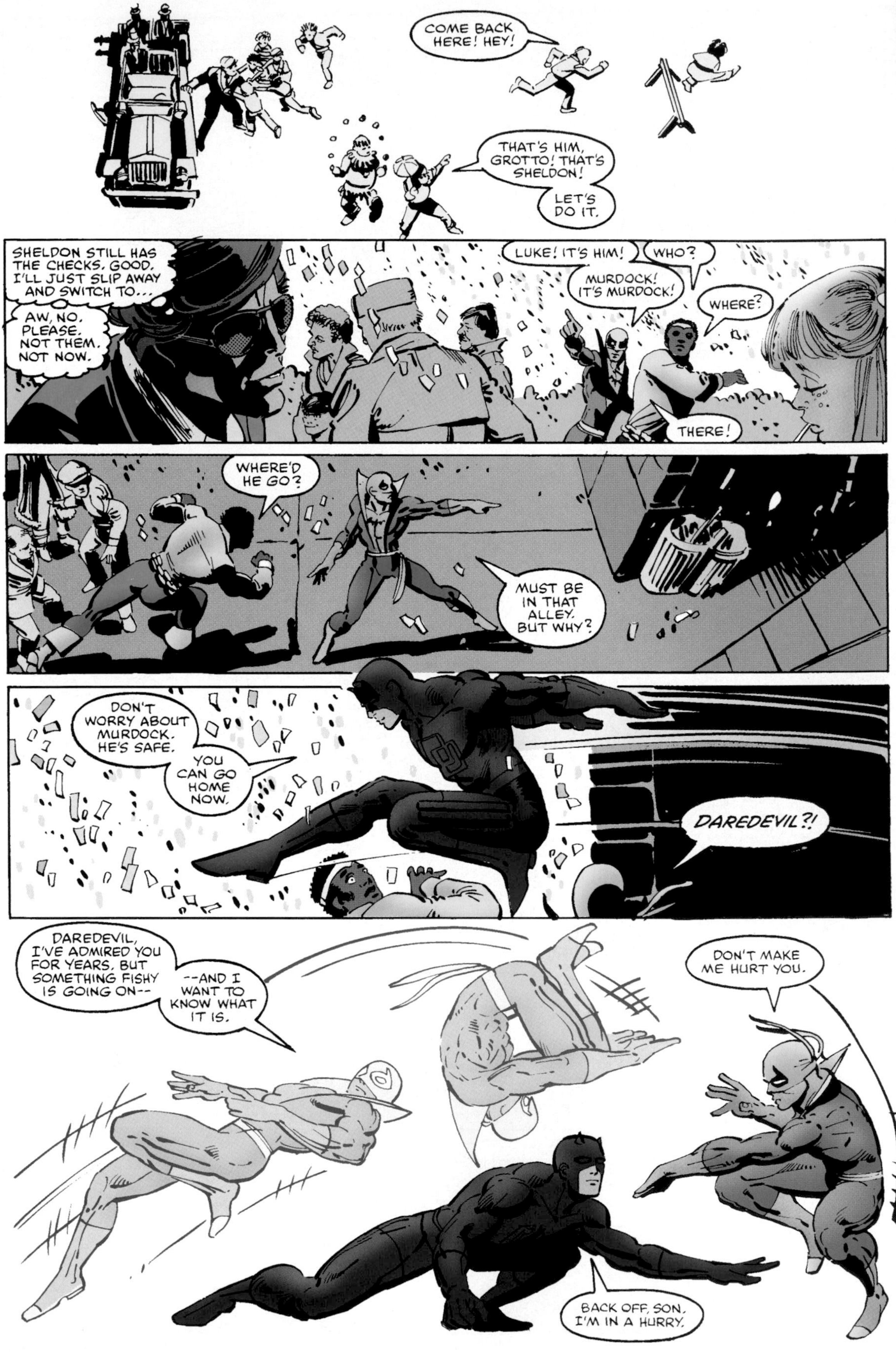
COME BACK HERE! HEY!
THAT'S HIM, GROTTO! THAT'S SHELDON!
LET'S DO IT.
SHELDON STILL HAS THE CHECKS. GOOD. I'LL JUST SLIP AWAY AND SWITCH TO...
AW, NO. PLEASE. NOT THEM. NOT NOW.
LUKE! IT'S HIM!
WHO?
MURDOCK! IT'S MURDOCK!
WHERE?
THERE!
WHERE'D HE GO?
MUST BE IN THAT ALLEY. BUT WHY?
DON'T WORRY ABOUT MURDOCK. HE'S SAFE.
YOU CAN GO HOME NOW.
DAREDEVIL?!
DAREDEVIL, I'VE ADMIRED YOU FOR YEARS, BUT SOMETHING FISHY IS GOING ON--
--AND I WANT TO KNOW WHAT IT IS.
DON'T MAKE ME HURT YOU.
BACK OFF, SON. I'M IN A HURRY.

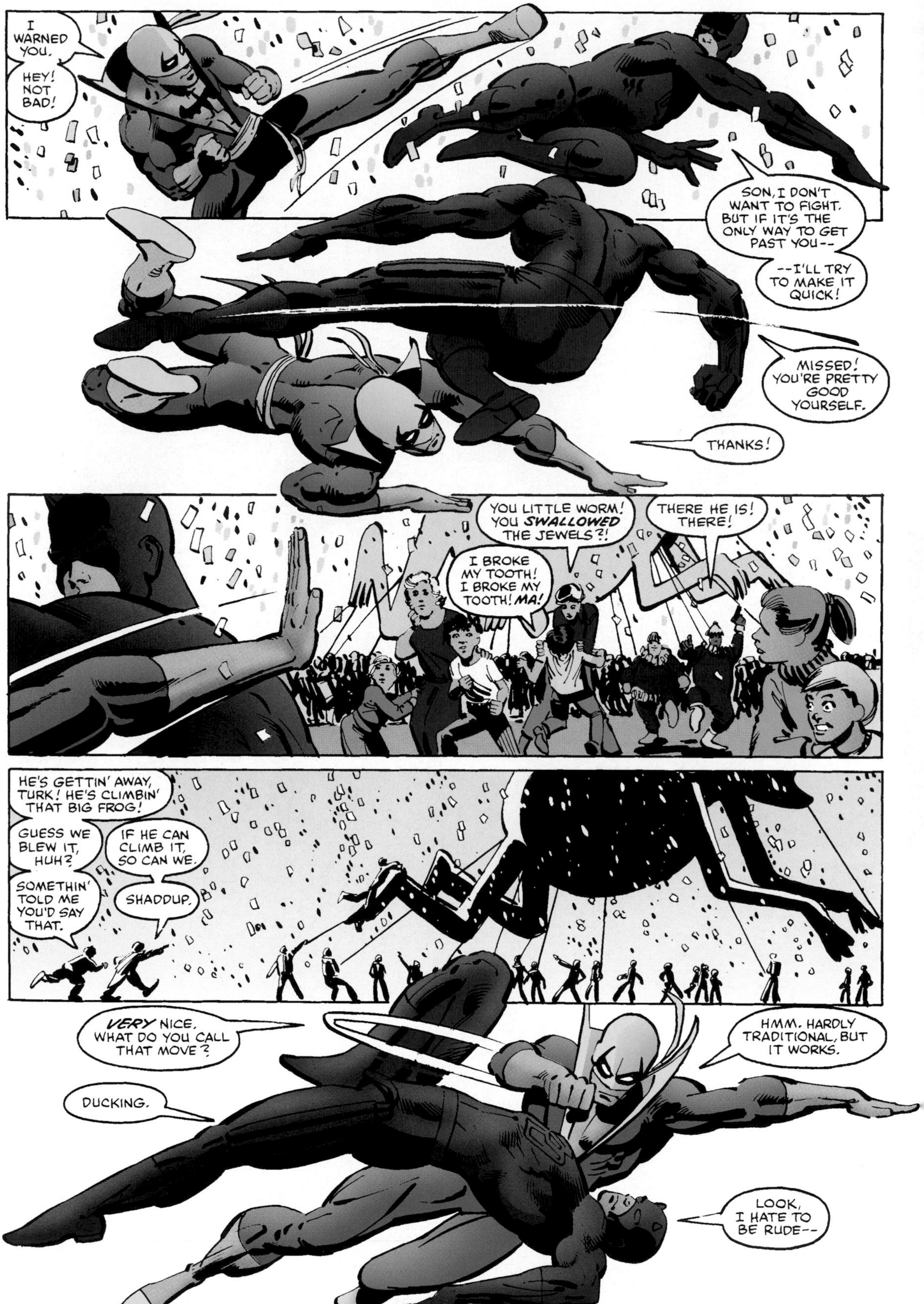
I WARNED YOU.
HEY! NOT BAD!
SON, I DON'T WANT TO FIGHT. BUT IF IT'S THE ONLY WAY TO GET PAST YOU--
--I'LL TRY TO MAKE IT QUICK!
MISSED! YOU'RE PRETTY GOOD YOURSELF.
THANKS!
YOU LITTLE WORM! YOU SWALLOWED THE JEWELS?!
THERE HE IS! THERE!
I BROKE MY TOOTH! I BROKE MY TOOTH! MA!
HE'S GETTIN' AWAY, TURK! HE'S CLIMBIN' THAT BIG FROG!
GUESS WE BLEW IT, HUH?
IF HE CAN CLIMB IT, SO CAN WE.
SOMETHIN' TOLD ME YOU'D SAY THAT.
SHADDUP.
VERY NICE. WHAT DO YOU CALL THAT MOVE?
HMM. HARDLY TRADITIONAL, BUT IT WORKS.
DUCKING.
LOOK, I HATE TO BE RUDE--

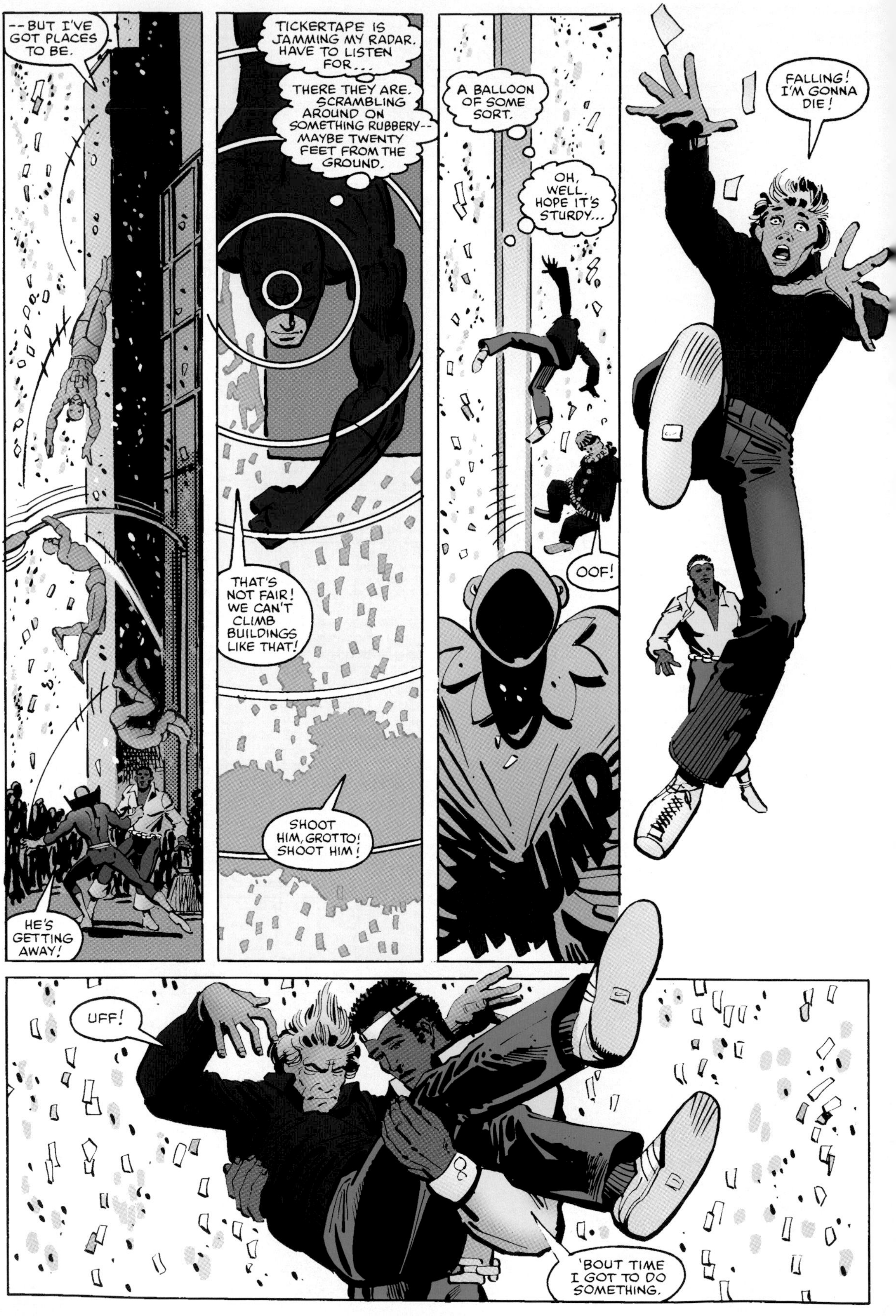
--BUT I'VE GOT PLACES TO BE.
HE'S GETTING AWAY!
TICKERTAPE IS JAMMING MY RADAR. HAVE TO LISTEN FOR...
THERE THEY ARE. SCRAMBLING AROUND ON SOMETHING RUBBERY-- MAYBE TWENTY FEET FROM THE GROUND.
THAT'S NOT FAIR! WE CAN'T CLIMB BUILDINGS LIKE THAT!
SHOOT HIM, GROTTO! SHOOT HIM!
A BALLOON OF SOME SORT.
OH, WELL. HOPE IT'S STURDY...
OOF!
FALLING! I'M GONNA DIE!
UFF!
'BOUT TIME I GOT TO DO SOMETHING.

TAMMI LU! I DONE IT FOR TAMMI LU!

I HATE TO ASK, DD -- BUT WHAT IS GOING ON HERE? WHO IS THIS GUY?

HE'S A BLACKMAILER.

WHO'S TAMMI LU?

SHE'S MY *SISTER*. MY SWEET, BEAUTIFUL SISTER WHO'S NEVER DONE NOTHING TO NOBODY IN HER LIFE!

ALL SHE'S EVER CARED ABOUT IS HER *DANCING*, AND SHE LANDED A PART IN A SHOW-- A BIG SHOW-- THAT WOULDA MADE HER FAMOUS.

BUT HER LEGS-- SOMETHING'S WRONG WITH THEM AND SHE NEEDS AN OPERATION, AND THAT BOSS OF HERS, HE FINKED OUT ON PAYING HER INSURANCE, JUST UP AND REPLACED HER WITH SOME RUSSIAN CHICK. JUST LIKE THAT.

SO I THOUGHT I COULD RAISE THE BUCKS TO GET HER LEGS FIXED, BUT I *FAILED*-- AND NOW TAMMI LU WILL NEVER... DANCE...AGAIN...

WHAT DO YOU SAY, FIST?

I SAY WE HELP, AFTER WE FIND MURDOCK, THAT IS.

MURDOCK IS ALL RIGHT. HE ASKED ME TO 'KIDNAP' HIM, JUST TO GET HIM AWAY FROM YOU TWO.

SHELDON-- THE CHECKS.

SURE. HERE THEY...

UH OH.

MUST'VE SLIPPED OUT WHEN I FELL. OH, GEE. WITH THE WIND LIKE IT IS, AND ALL THAT TICKERTAPE, YOU'LL NEVER FIND...

OH, GEE...

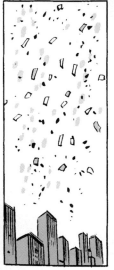

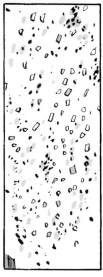

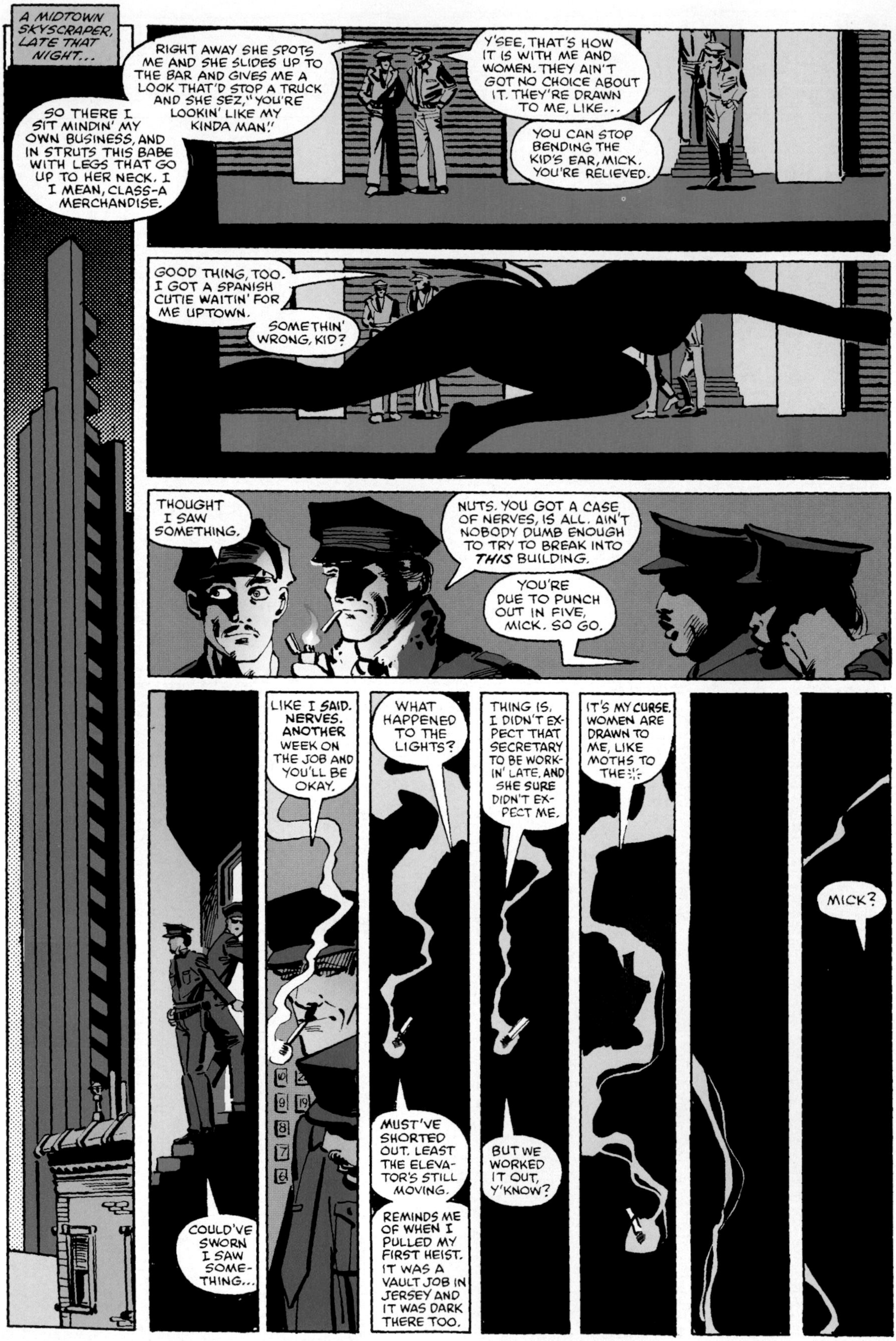
A MIDTOWN SKYSCRAPER, LATE THAT NIGHT...
SO THERE I SIT MINDIN' MY OWN BUSINESS, AND IN STRUTS THIS BABE WITH LEGS THAT GO UP TO HER NECK. I I MEAN, CLASS-A MERCHANDISE.
RIGHT AWAY SHE SPOTS ME AND SHE SLIDES UP TO THE BAR AND GIVES ME A LOOK THAT'D STOP A TRUCK AND SHE SEZ, "YOU'RE LOOKIN' LIKE MY KINDA MAN."
Y'SEE, THAT'S HOW IT IS WITH ME AND WOMEN. THEY AIN'T GOT NO CHOICE ABOUT IT. THEY'RE DRAWN TO ME, LIKE...
YOU CAN STOP BENDING THE KID'S EAR, MICK. YOU'RE RELIEVED.
GOOD THING, TOO. I GOT A SPANISH CUTIE WAITIN' FOR ME UPTOWN.
SOMETHIN' WRONG, KID?
THOUGHT I SAW SOMETHING.
NUTS. YOU GOT A CASE OF NERVES, IS ALL. AIN'T NOBODY DUMB ENOUGH TO TRY TO BREAK INTO THIS BUILDING.
YOU'RE DUE TO PUNCH OUT IN FIVE, MICK. SO GO.
COULD'VE SWORN I SAW SOME-THING...
LIKE I SAID. NERVES. ANOTHER WEEK ON THE JOB AND YOU'LL BE OKAY.
WHAT HAPPENED TO THE LIGHTS?
MUST'VE SHORTED OUT. LEAST THE ELEVA-TOR'S STILL MOVING.
REMINDS ME OF WHEN I PULLED MY FIRST HEIST. IT WAS A VAULT JOB IN JERSEY AND IT WAS DARK THERE TOO.
THING IS, I DIDN'T EX-PECT THAT SECRETARY TO BE WORK-IN' LATE, AND SHE SURE DIDN'T EX-PECT ME.
BUT WE WORKED IT OUT, Y'KNOW?
IT'S MY CURSE. WOMEN ARE DRAWN TO ME, LIKE MOTHS TO THE
MICK?

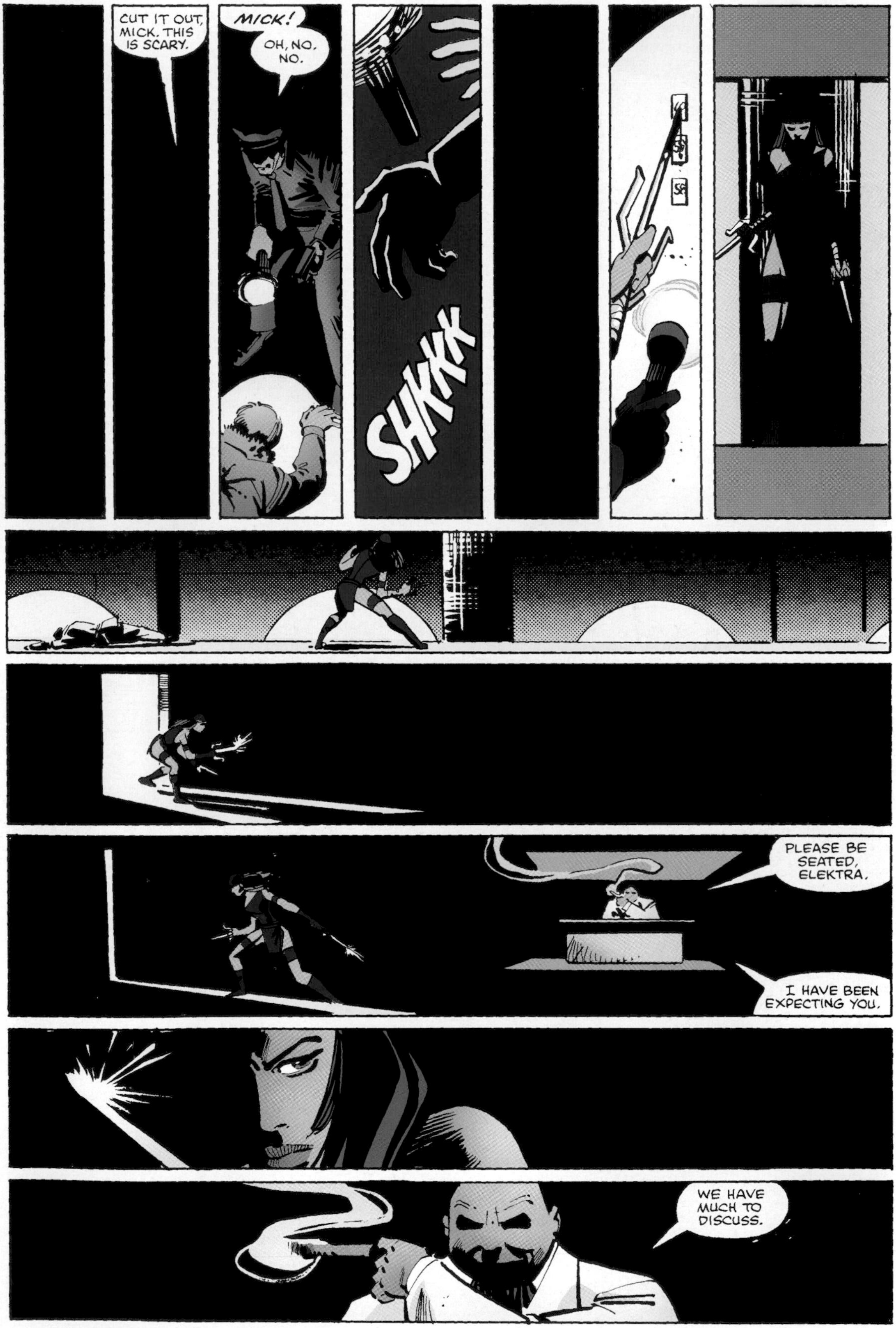
CUT IT OUT, MICK. THIS IS SCARY.
MICK!
OH, NO. NO.
SHKKK
PLEASE BE SEATED, ELEKTRA.
I HAVE BEEN EXPECTING YOU.
WE HAVE MUCH TO DISCUSS.

FEB 1982
DAREDEVIL #179

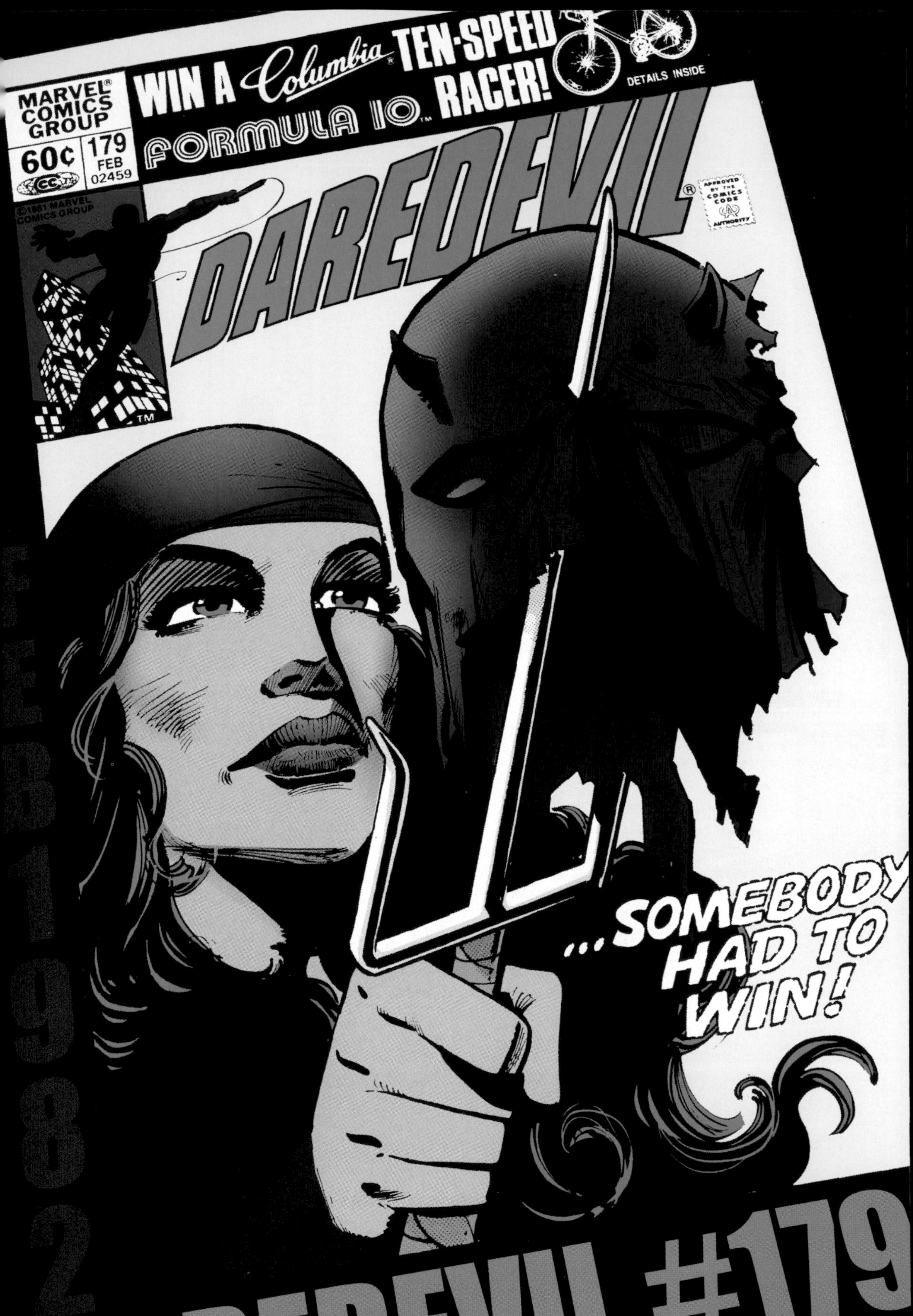

MARVEL® COMICS GROUP
60¢ 179 FEB 02459
©1981 MARVEL COMICS GROUP
WIN A Columbia® TEN-SPEED FORMULA 10™ RACER!
DETAILS INSIDE
DAREDEVIL®
APPROVED BY THE COMICS CODE AUTHORITY
...SOMEBODY HAD TO WIN!

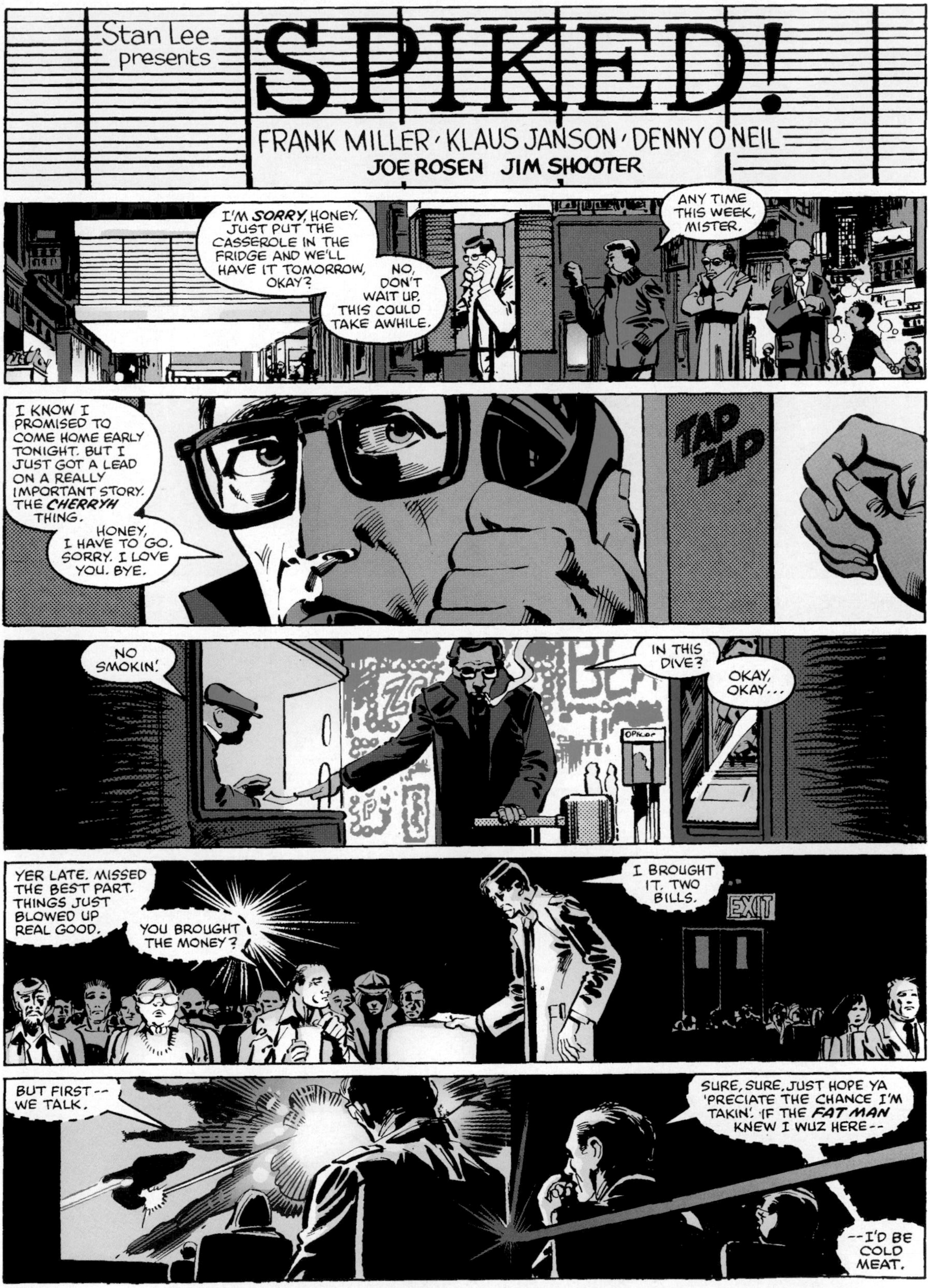
Stan Lee presents
SPIKED!
FRANK MILLER · KLAUS JANSON · DENNY O'NEIL
JOE ROSEN JIM SHOOTER
I'M SORRY, HONEY. JUST PUT THE CASSEROLE IN THE FRIDGE AND WE'LL HAVE IT TOMORROW, OKAY?
NO, DON'T WAIT UP. THIS COULD TAKE AWHILE.
ANY TIME THIS WEEK, MISTER.
I KNOW I PROMISED TO COME HOME EARLY TONIGHT. BUT I JUST GOT A LEAD ON A REALLY IMPORTANT STORY. THE CHERRYH THING.
HONEY, I HAVE TO GO. SORRY. I LOVE YOU. BYE.
TAP TAP
NO SMOKIN'.
IN THIS DIVE?
OKAY, OKAY...
YER LATE. MISSED THE BEST PART. THINGS JUST BLOWED UP REAL GOOD.
YOU BROUGHT THE MONEY?
I BROUGHT IT. TWO BILLS.
EXIT
BUT FIRST -- WE TALK.
SURE, SURE, JUST HOPE YA 'PRECIATE THE CHANCE I'M TAKIN'. IF THE FAT MAN KNEW I WUZ HERE --
-- I'D BE COLD MEAT.

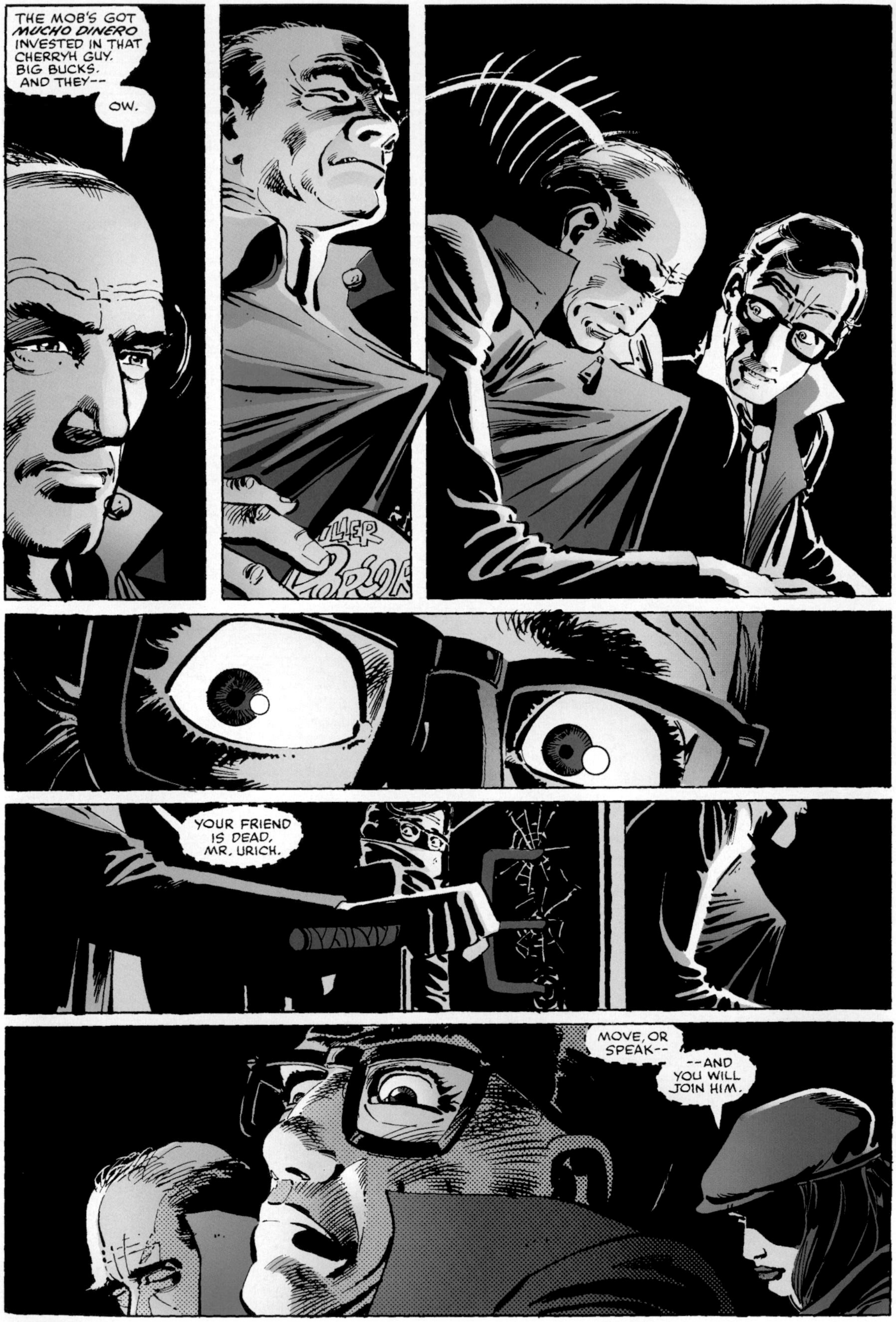
THE MOB'S GOT *MUCHO DINERO* INVESTED IN THAT CHERRYH GUY. BIG BUCKS. AND THEY--
OW.
YOUR FRIEND IS DEAD, MR. URICH.
MOVE, OR SPEAK--
--AND YOU WILL JOIN HIM.

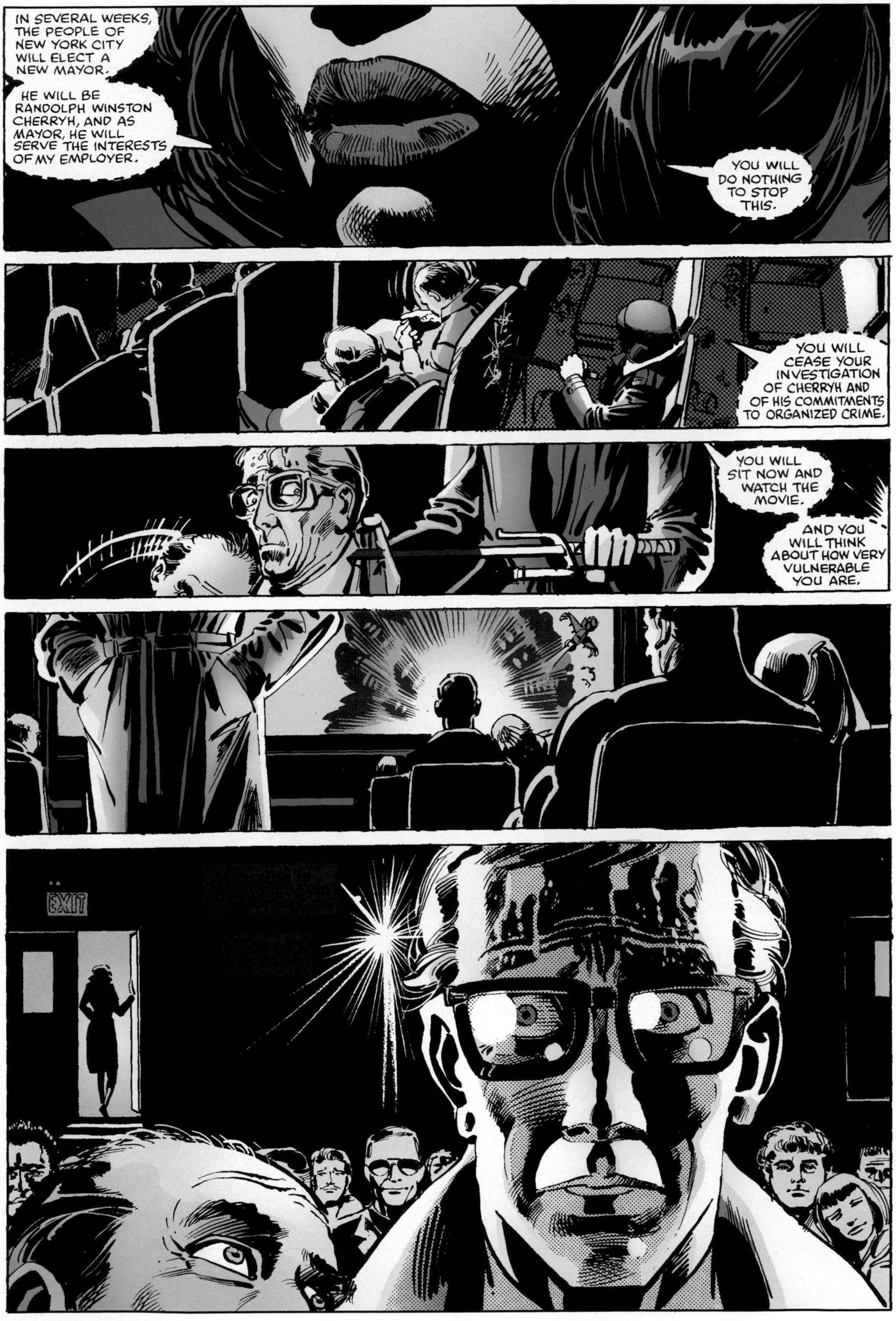
IN SEVERAL WEEKS, THE PEOPLE OF NEW YORK CITY WILL ELECT A NEW MAYOR.
HE WILL BE RANDOLPH WINSTON CHERRYH, AND AS MAYOR, HE WILL SERVE THE INTERESTS OF MY EMPLOYER.
YOU WILL DO NOTHING TO STOP THIS.
YOU WILL CEASE YOUR INVESTIGATION OF CHERRYH AND OF HIS COMMITMENTS TO ORGANIZED CRIME.
YOU WILL SIT NOW AND WATCH THE MOVIE.
AND YOU WILL THINK ABOUT HOW VERY VULNERABLE YOU ARE.
EXIT

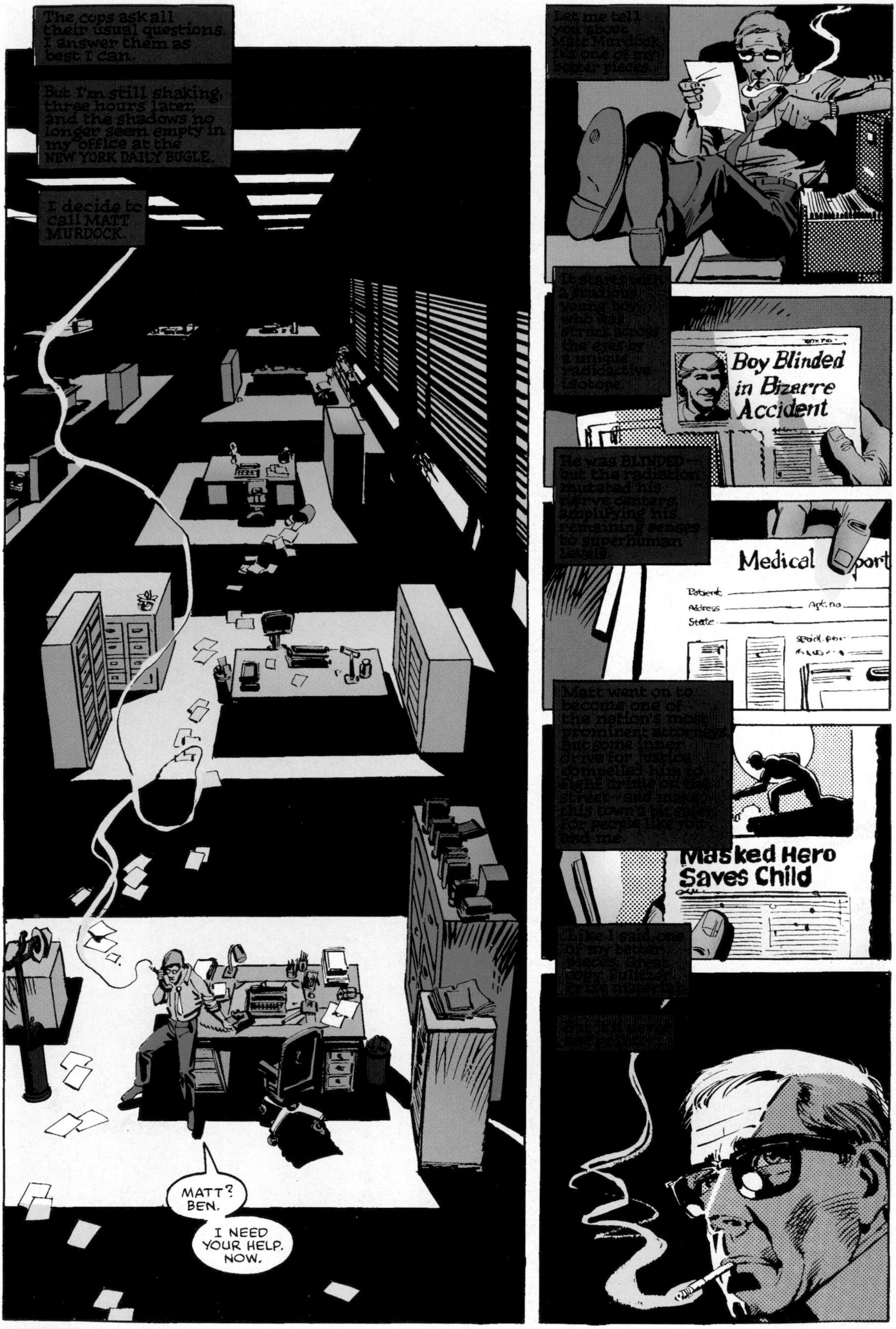
The cops ask all their usual questions. I answer them as best I can.
But I'm still shaking three hours later, and the shadows no longer seem empty in my office at the NEW YORK DAILY BUGLE.
I decide to call MATT MURDOCK.
MATT? BEN.
I NEED YOUR HELP. NOW.
Let me tell you about Matt Murdock. It's one of my better pieces.
It starts with a studious young boy who was struck across the eyes by a unique radioactive isotope.
Boy Blinded in Bizarre Accident
He was BLINDED— but the radiation mutated his nerve centers, amplifying his remaining senses to superhuman levels.
Medical
Patient
Address
Apt. no
State
Matt went on to become one of the nation's most prominent attorneys.
Masked Hero Saves Child
Like I said, one of my better

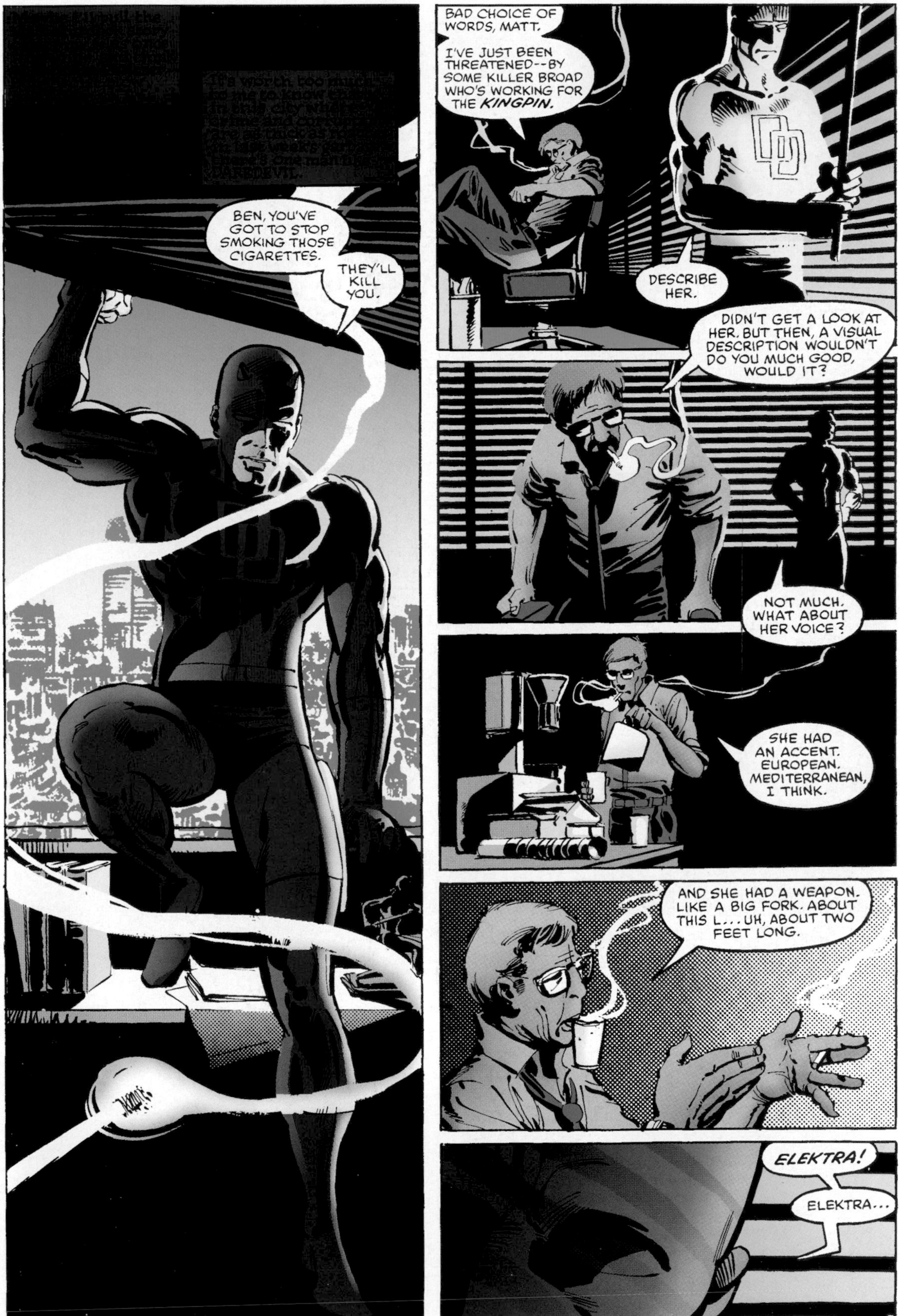
BEN, YOU'VE GOT TO STOP SMOKING THOSE CIGARETTES.
THEY'LL KILL YOU.
BAD CHOICE OF WORDS, MATT.
I'VE JUST BEEN THREATENED--BY SOME KILLER BROAD WHO'S WORKING FOR THE KINGPIN.
DESCRIBE HER.
DIDN'T GET A LOOK AT HER. BUT THEN, A VISUAL DESCRIPTION WOULDN'T DO YOU MUCH GOOD, WOULD IT?
NOT MUCH. WHAT ABOUT HER VOICE?
SHE HAD AN ACCENT. EUROPEAN. MEDITERRANEAN, I THINK.
AND SHE HAD A WEAPON. LIKE A BIG FORK. ABOUT THIS L... UH, ABOUT TWO FEET LONG.
ELEKTRA!
ELEKTRA...

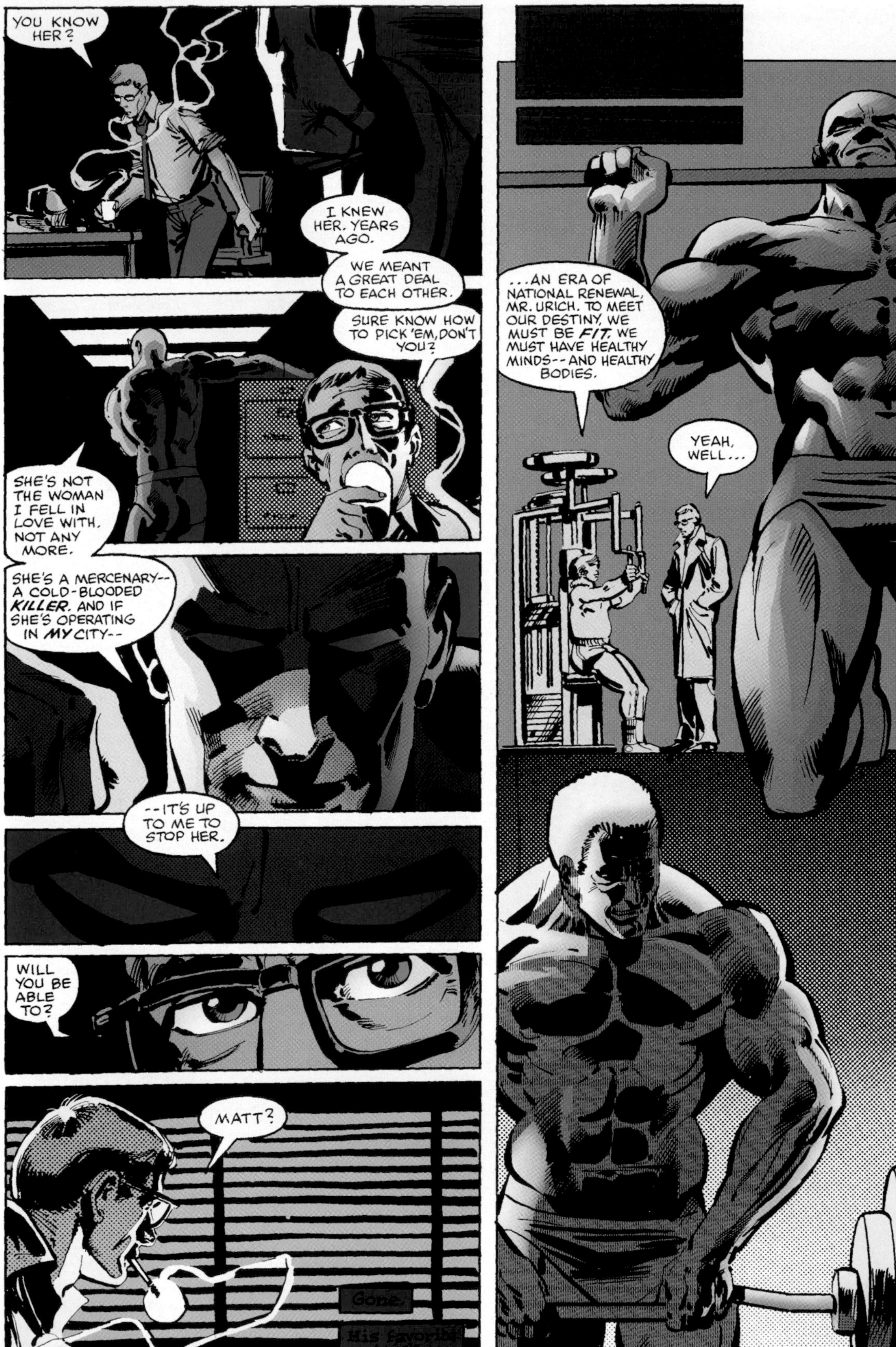
YOU KNOW HER?
I KNEW HER. YEARS AGO.
WE MEANT A GREAT DEAL TO EACH OTHER.
SURE KNOW HOW TO PICK 'EM, DON'T YOU?
SHE'S NOT THE WOMAN I FELL IN LOVE WITH, NOT ANY MORE.
SHE'S A MERCENARY-- A COLD-BLOODED KILLER. AND IF SHE'S OPERATING IN MY CITY--
--IT'S UP TO ME TO STOP HER.
WILL YOU BE ABLE TO?
MATT?
Gone.
His favorite trick.
...AN ERA OF NATIONAL RENEWAL, MR. URICH. TO MEET OUR DESTINY, WE MUST BE FIT. WE MUST HAVE HEALTHY MINDS--AND HEALTHY BODIES.
YEAH, WELL...

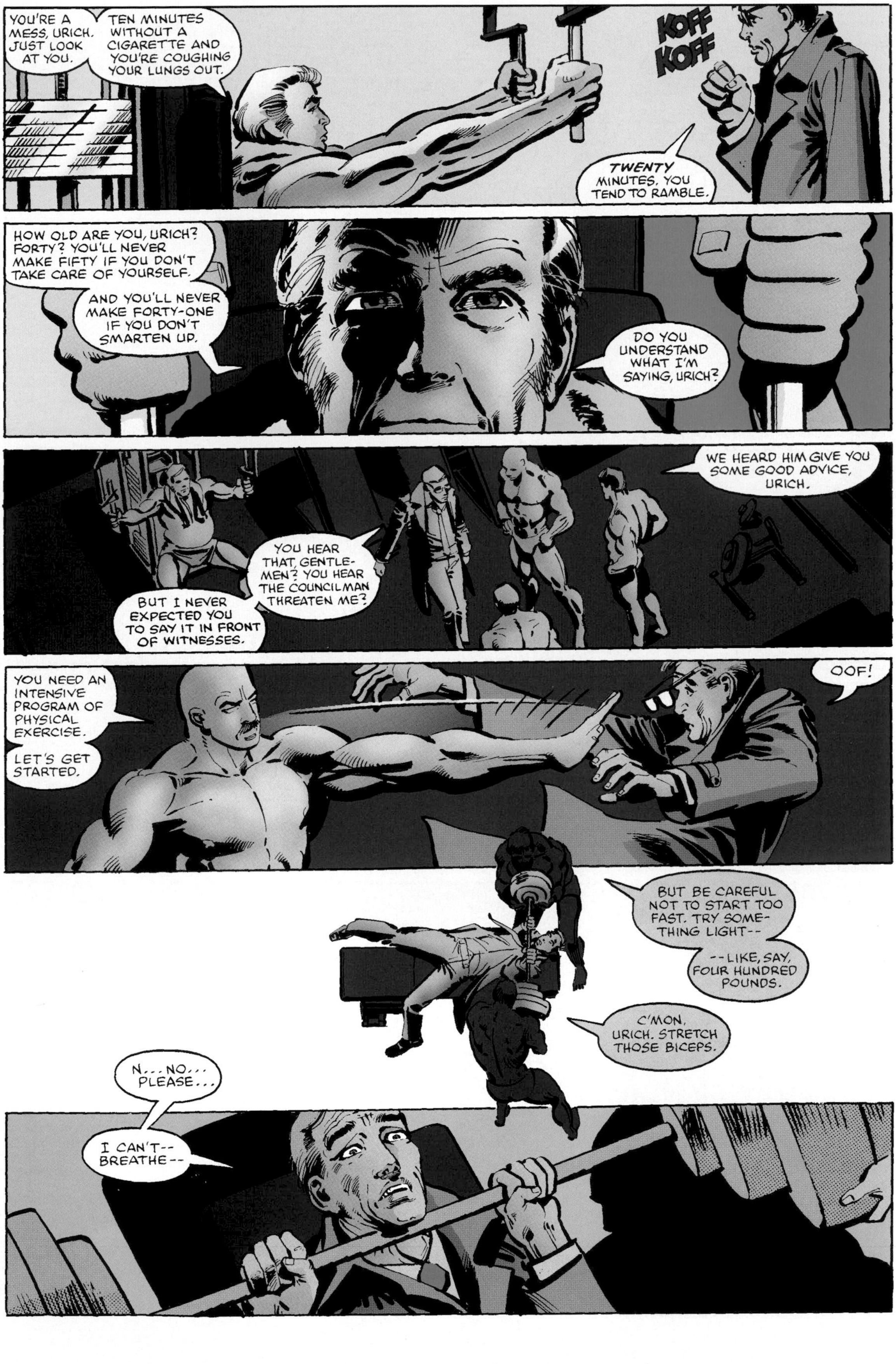

YOU'RE A MESS, URICH. JUST LOOK AT YOU.
TEN MINUTES WITHOUT A CIGARETTE AND YOU'RE COUGHING YOUR LUNGS OUT.
KOFF KOFF
TWENTY MINUTES. YOU TEND TO RAMBLE.
HOW OLD ARE YOU, URICH? FORTY? YOU'LL NEVER MAKE FIFTY IF YOU DON'T TAKE CARE OF YOURSELF.
AND YOU'LL NEVER MAKE FORTY-ONE IF YOU DON'T SMARTEN UP.
DO YOU UNDERSTAND WHAT I'M SAYING, URICH?
WE HEARD HIM GIVE YOU SOME GOOD ADVICE, URICH.
YOU HEAR THAT, GENTLE-MEN? YOU HEAR THE COUNCILMAN THREATEN ME?
BUT I NEVER EXPECTED YOU TO SAY IT IN FRONT OF WITNESSES.
YOU NEED AN INTENSIVE PROGRAM OF PHYSICAL EXERCISE.
LET'S GET STARTED.
OOF!
BUT BE CAREFUL NOT TO START TOO FAST. TRY SOME-THING LIGHT--
--LIKE, SAY, FOUR HUNDRED POUNDS.
C'MON, URICH. STRETCH THOSE BICEPS.
N... NO... PLEASE...
I CAN'T-- BREATHE--

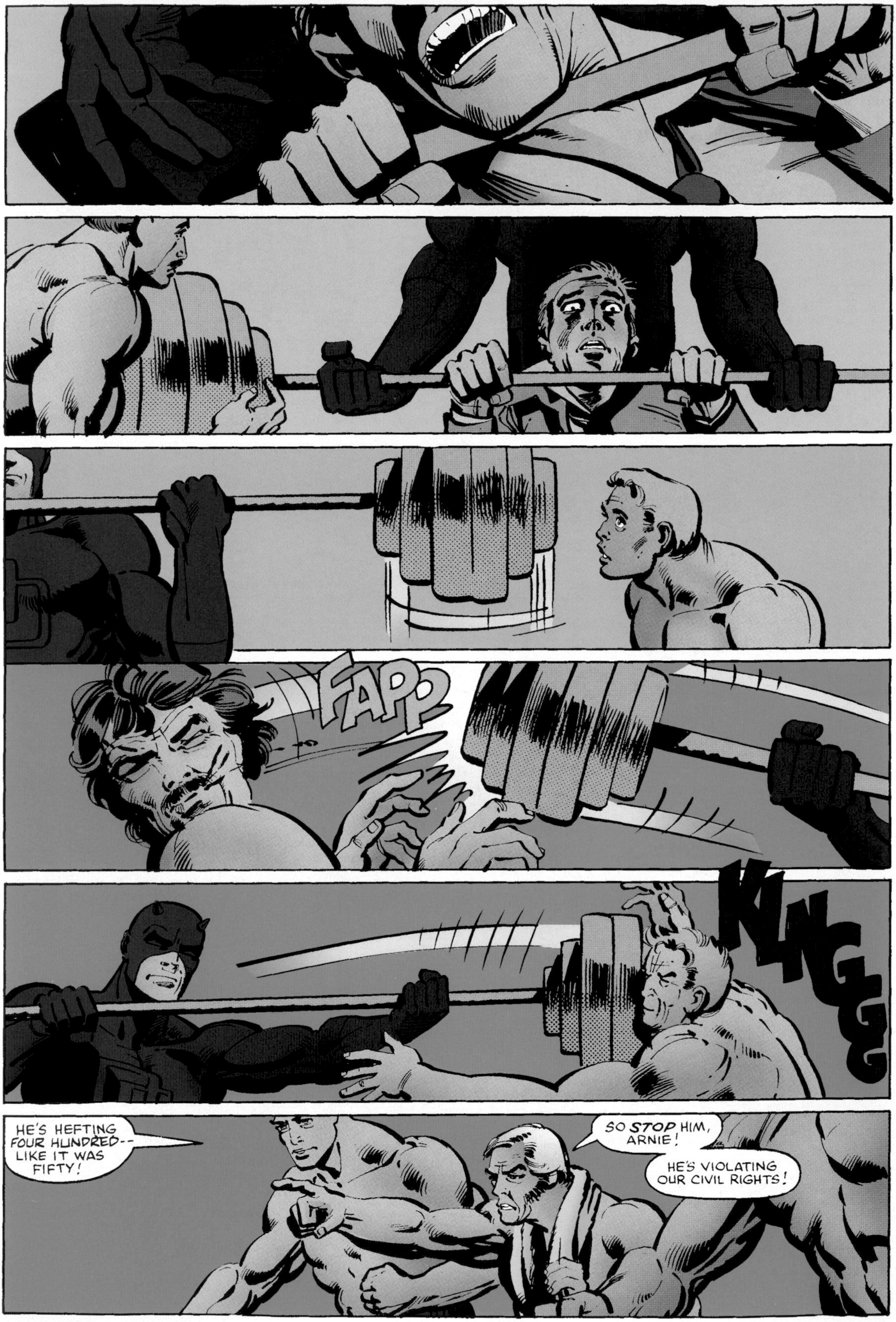
FAPP
KLANGGG
HE'S HEFTING FOUR HUNDRED-- LIKE IT WAS FIFTY!
SO STOP HIM, ARNIE!
HE'S VIOLATING OUR CIVIL RIGHTS!

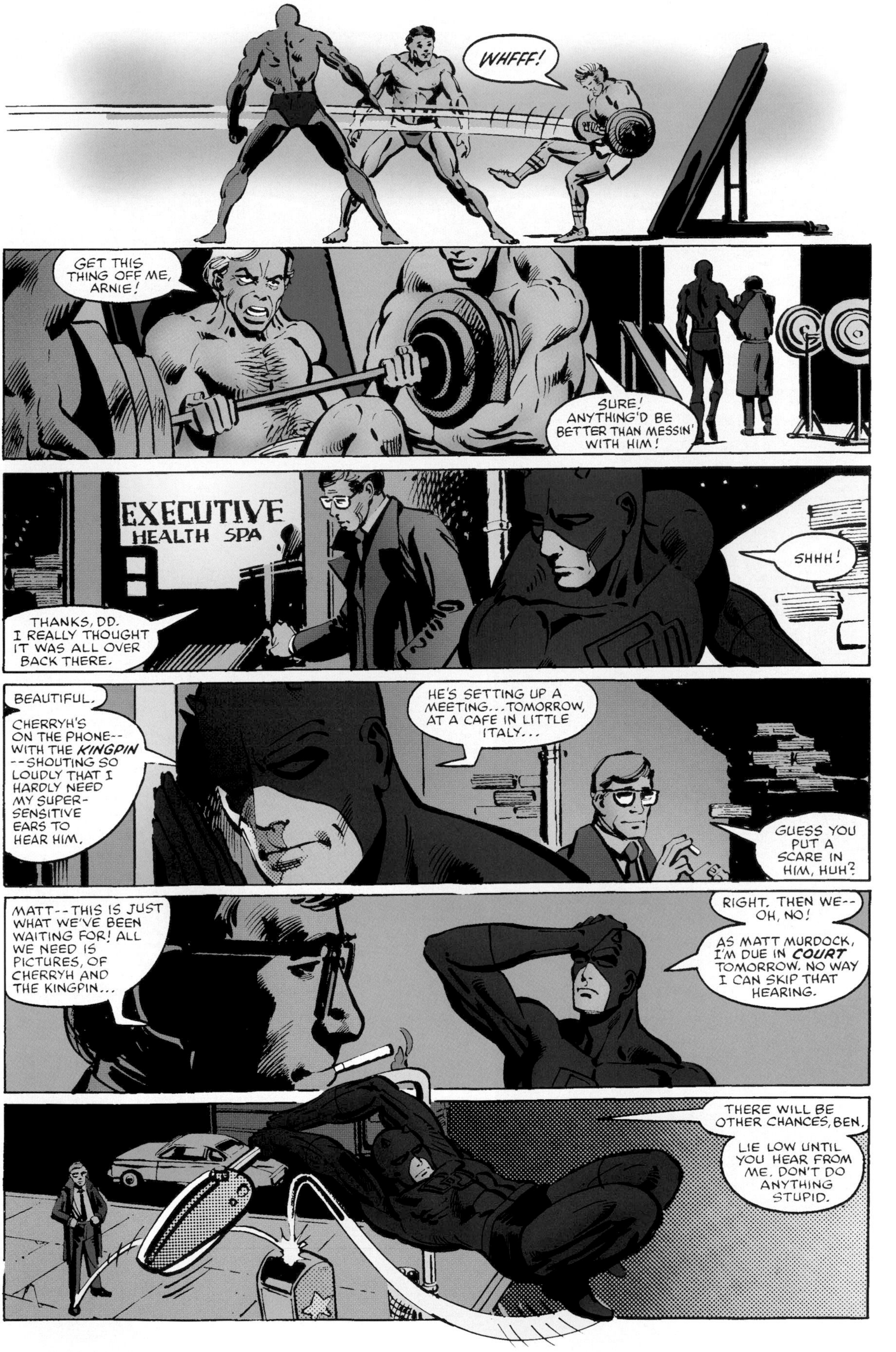
WHFFF!
GET THIS THING OFF ME, ARNIE!
SURE! ANYTHING'D BE BETTER THAN MESSIN' WITH HIM!
EXECUTIVE HEALTH SPA
THANKS, DD. I REALLY THOUGHT IT WAS ALL OVER BACK THERE.
SHHH!
BEAUTIFUL.
CHERRYH'S ON THE PHONE-- WITH THE KINGPIN --SHOUTING SO LOUDLY THAT I HARDLY NEED MY SUPER-SENSITIVE EARS TO HEAR HIM.
HE'S SETTING UP A MEETING... TOMORROW, AT A CAFE IN LITTLE ITALY...
GUESS YOU PUT A SCARE IN HIM, HUH?
MATT--THIS IS JUST WHAT WE'VE BEEN WAITING FOR! ALL WE NEED IS PICTURES, OF CHERRYH AND THE KINGPIN...
RIGHT. THEN WE-- OH, NO!
AS MATT MURDOCK, I'M DUE IN COURT TOMORROW. NO WAY I CAN SKIP THAT HEARING.
THERE WILL BE OTHER CHANCES, BEN.
LIE LOW UNTIL YOU HEAR FROM ME. DON'T DO ANYTHING STUPID.

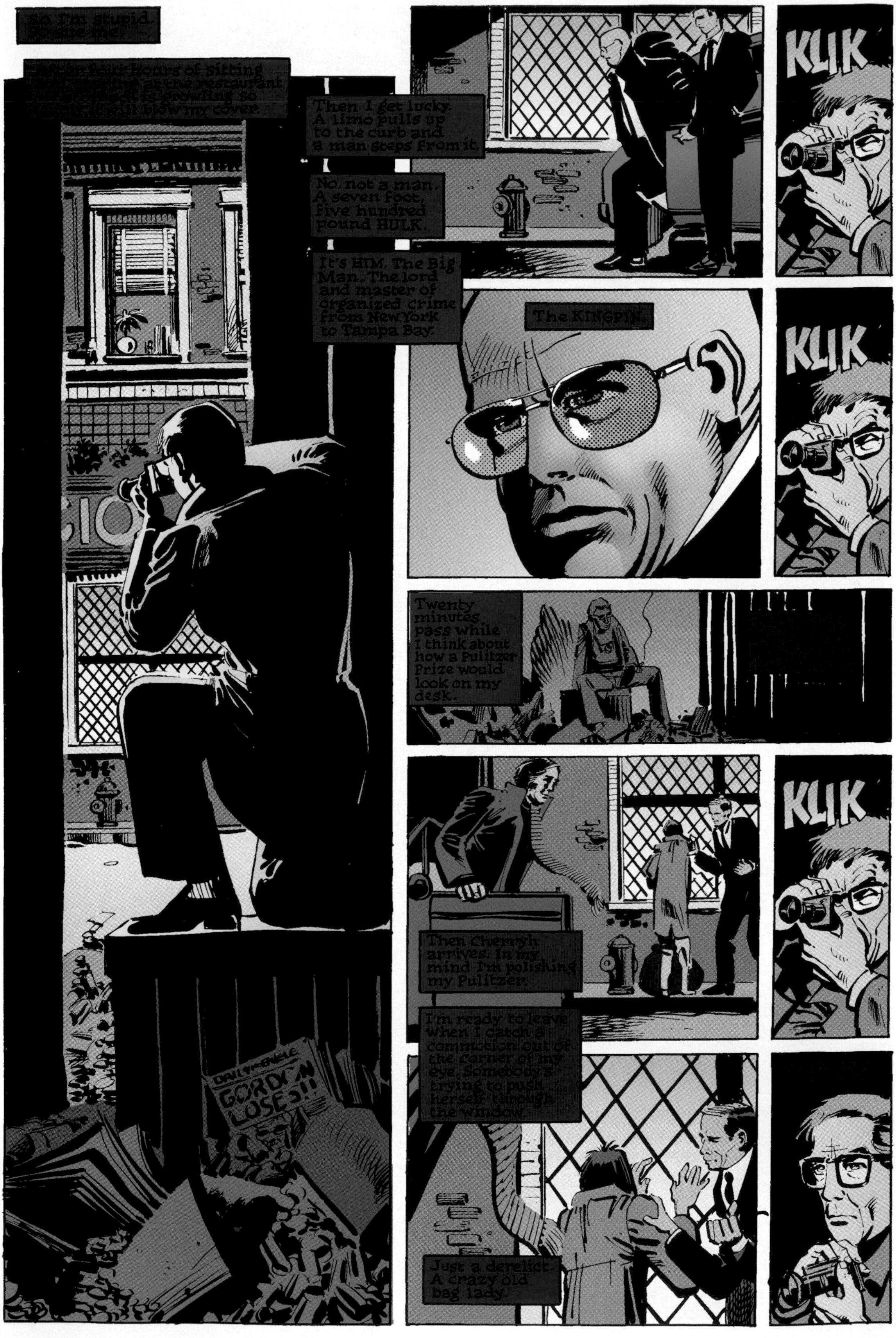
So I'm stupid.
Then I get lucky. A limo pulls up to the curb and a man steps from it.
KLIK
No, not a man. A seven foot, five hundred pound HULK.
It's HIM. The Big Man. The lord and master of organized crime from New York to Tampa Bay.
The KINGPIN.
KLIK
Twenty minutes pass while I think about how a Pulitzer Prize would look on my desk.
Then Cherryh arrives. In my mind I'm polishing my Pulitzer.
KLIK
I'm ready to leave when I catch a commotion out of the corner of my eye. Somebody's trying to push herself through the window.
Just a derelict. A crazy old bag lady.
GORDON LOSES!!

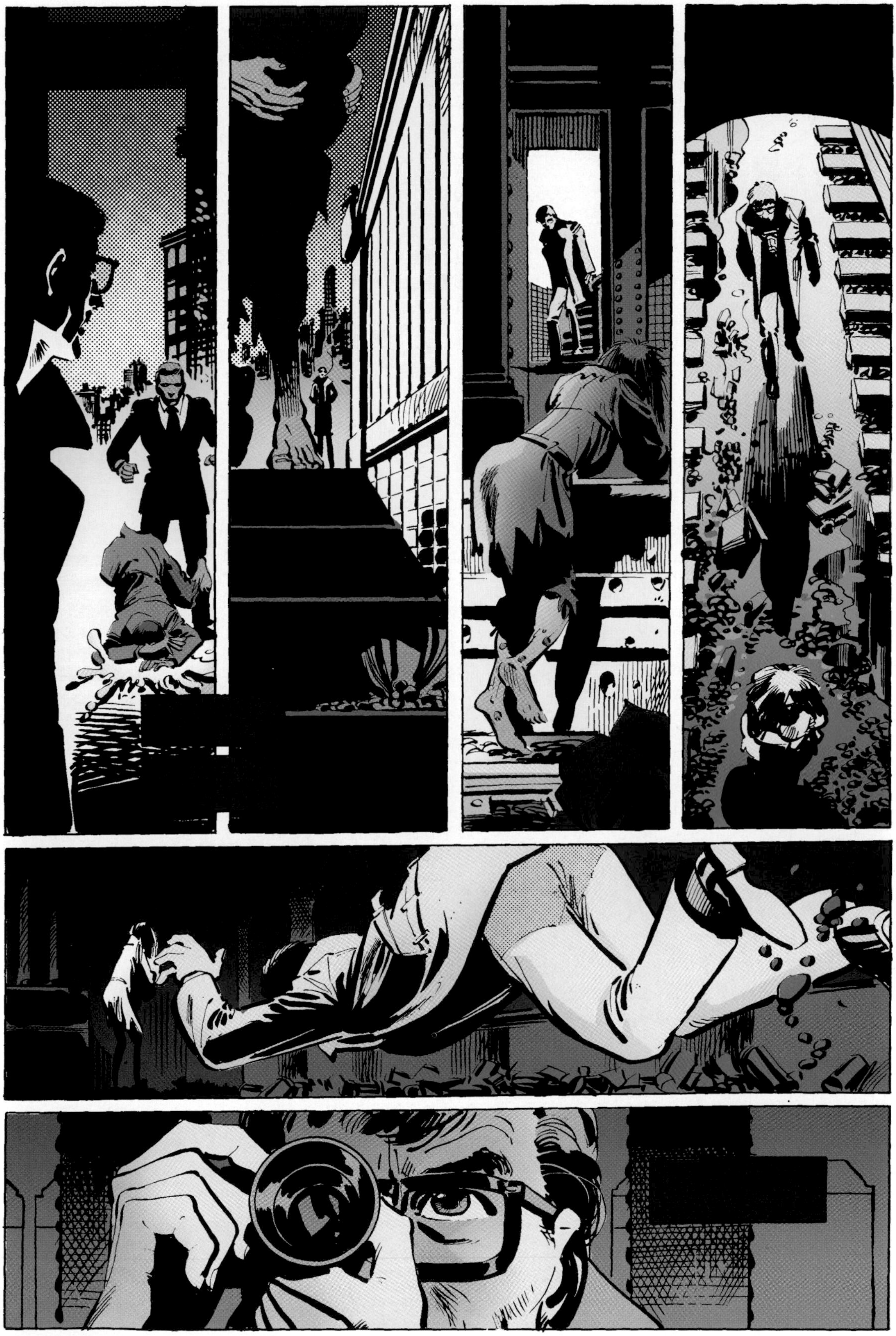

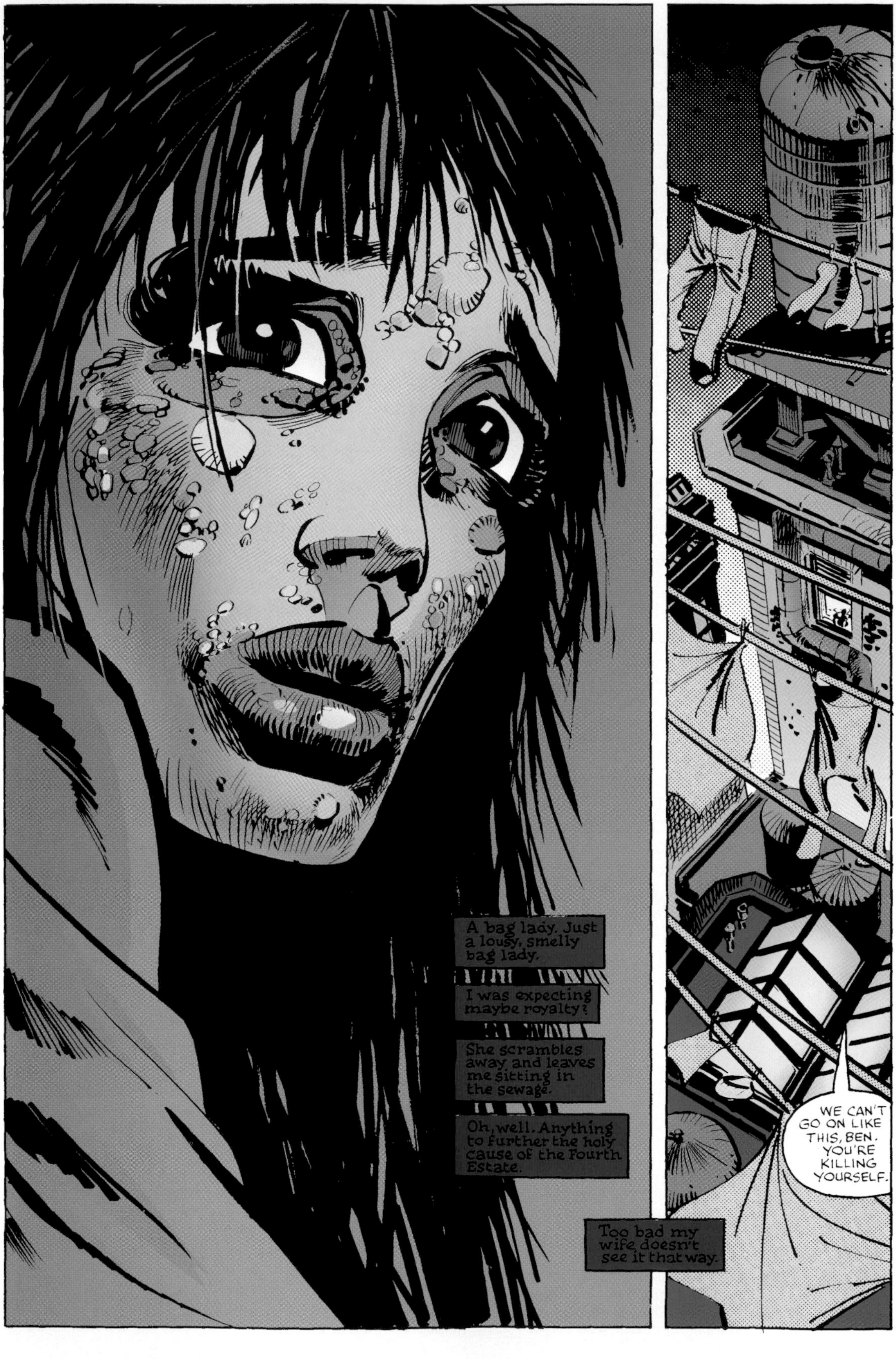
A bag lady. Just a lousy, smelly bag lady.
I was expecting maybe royalty?
She scrambles away and leaves me sitting in the sewage.
Oh, well. Anything to further the holy cause of the Fourth Estate.
Too bad my wife doesn't see it that way.
WE CAN'T GO ON LIKE THIS, BEN. YOU'RE KILLING YOURSELF.

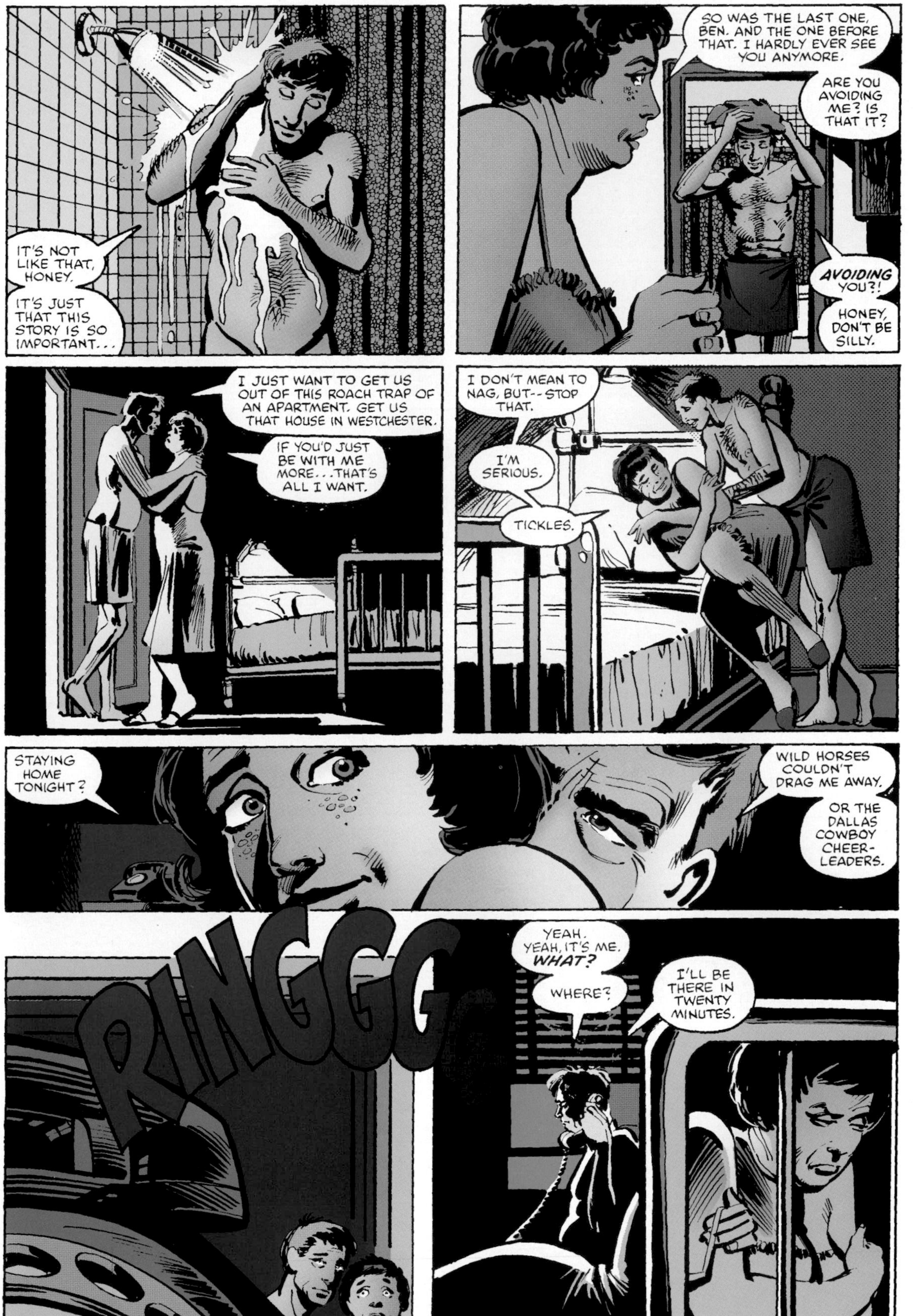
IT'S NOT LIKE THAT, HONEY.
IT'S JUST THAT THIS STORY IS SO IMPORTANT...
SO WAS THE LAST ONE, BEN. AND THE ONE BEFORE THAT. I HARDLY EVER SEE YOU ANYMORE.
ARE YOU AVOIDING ME? IS THAT IT?
AVOIDING YOU?!
HONEY, DON'T BE SILLY.
I JUST WANT TO GET US OUT OF THIS ROACH TRAP OF AN APARTMENT. GET US THAT HOUSE IN WESTCHESTER.
IF YOU'D JUST BE WITH ME MORE...THAT'S ALL I WANT.
I DON'T MEAN TO NAG, BUT--STOP THAT.
I'M SERIOUS.
TICKLES.
STAYING HOME TONIGHT?
WILD HORSES COULDN'T DRAG ME AWAY.
OR THE DALLAS COWBOY CHEER-LEADERS.
RINGGG
YEAH. YEAH, IT'S ME. WHAT?
WHERE?
I'LL BE THERE IN TWENTY MINUTES.

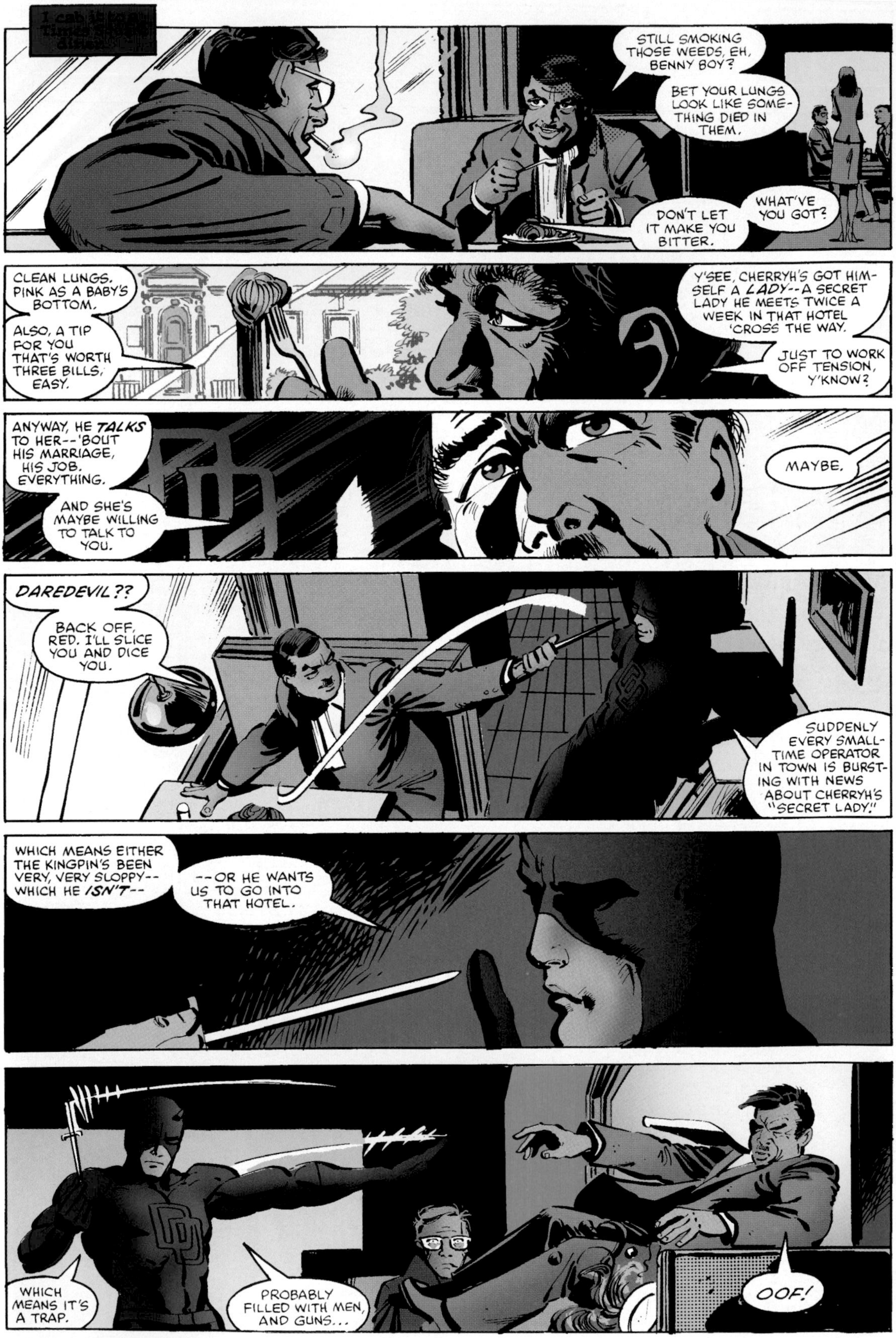
STILL SMOKING THOSE WEEDS, EH, BENNY BOY?
BET YOUR LUNGS LOOK LIKE SOME-THING DIED IN THEM.
DON'T LET IT MAKE YOU BITTER.
WHAT'VE YOU GOT?
CLEAN LUNGS. PINK AS A BABY'S BOTTOM.
ALSO, A TIP FOR YOU THAT'S WORTH THREE BILLS, EASY.
Y'SEE, CHERRYH'S GOT HIM-SELF A LADY--A SECRET LADY HE MEETS TWICE A WEEK IN THAT HOTEL 'CROSS THE WAY.
JUST TO WORK OFF TENSION, Y'KNOW?
ANYWAY, HE TALKS TO HER--'BOUT HIS MARRIAGE, HIS JOB. EVERYTHING.
AND SHE'S MAYBE WILLING TO TALK TO YOU.
MAYBE.
DAREDEVIL??
BACK OFF, RED. I'LL SLICE YOU AND DICE YOU.
SUDDENLY EVERY SMALL-TIME OPERATOR IN TOWN IS BURST-ING WITH NEWS ABOUT CHERRYH'S "SECRET LADY."
WHICH MEANS EITHER THE KINGPIN'S BEEN VERY, VERY SLOPPY-- WHICH HE ISN'T--
--OR HE WANTS US TO GO INTO THAT HOTEL.
WHICH MEANS IT'S A TRAP.
PROBABLY FILLED WITH MEN, AND GUNS...
OOF!

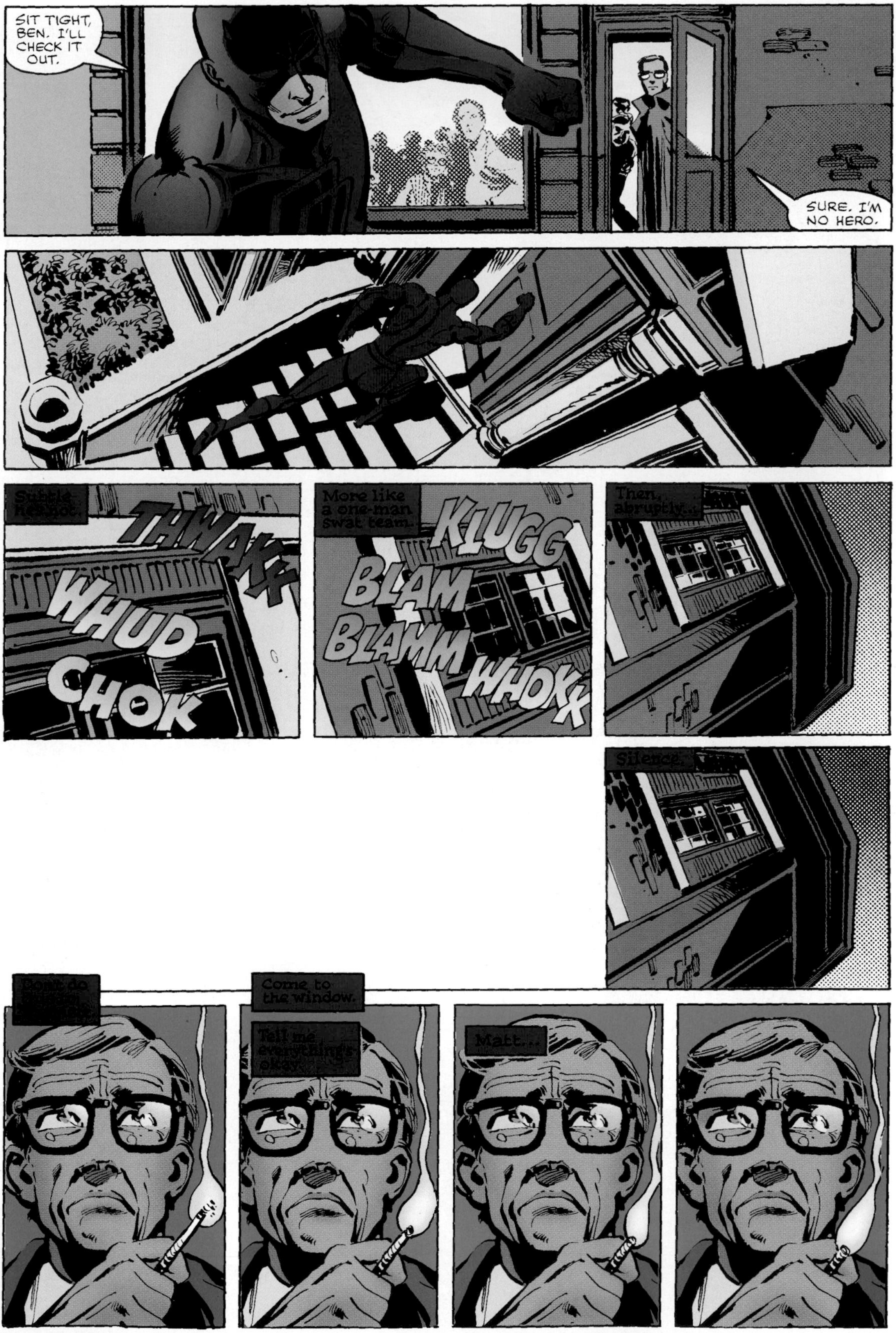
SIT TIGHT, BEN. I'LL CHECK IT OUT.
SURE. I'M NO HERO.
Subtle he's not.
THWAKK
WHUD
CHOK
More like a one-man swat team.
KLUGG
BLAM
BLAMM
WHOKK
Then, abruptly...
Silence.
Don't do
Come to the window.
Tell me everything's okay.
Matt...

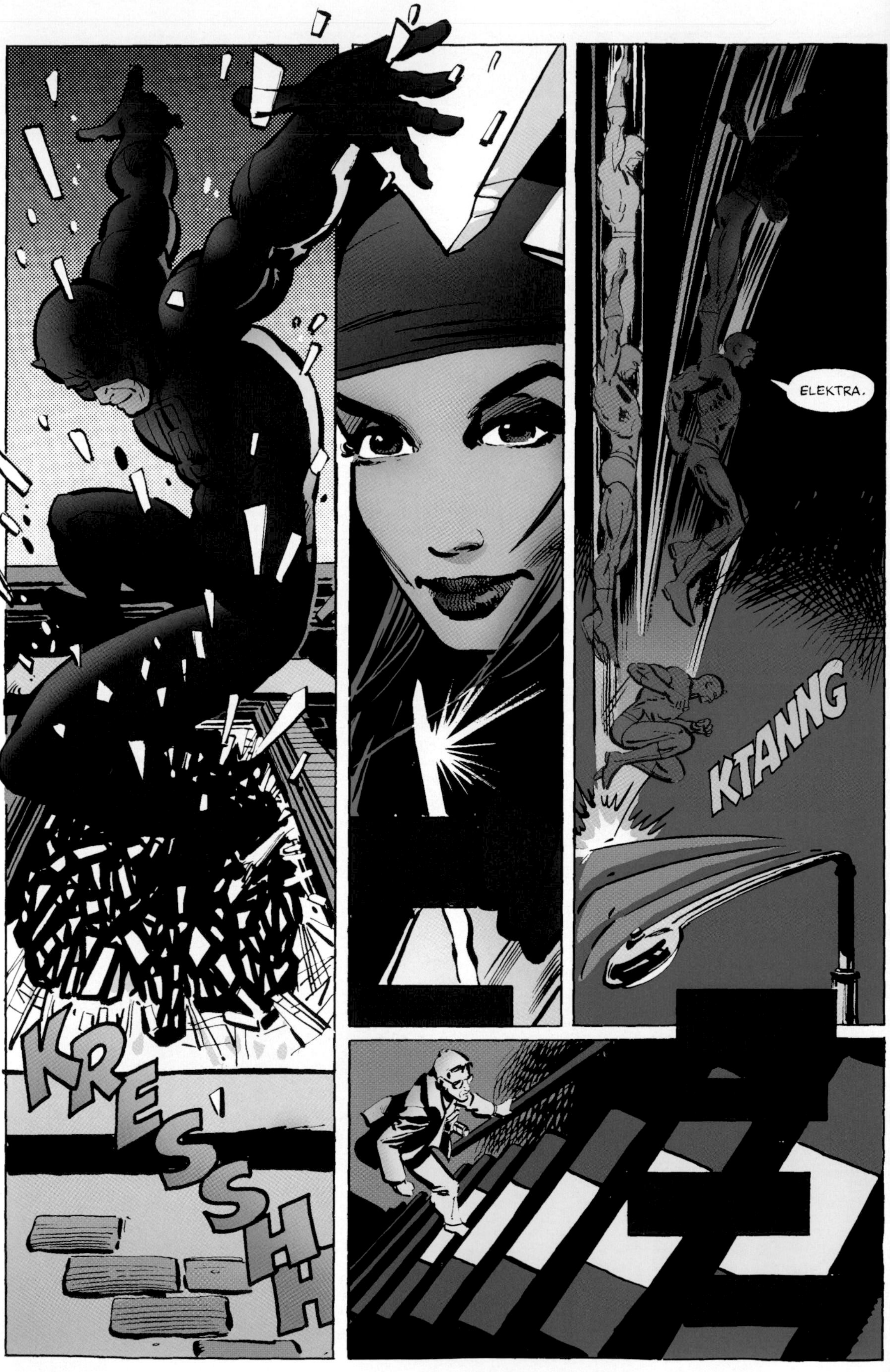
KRESSHH
ELEKTRA.
KTANNG

You'd never know what they were to each other unless you saw their faces--

--and glimpsed pain and anger far more personal than it should be.

He doesn't want this, I can tell.

He wants to hold her, to kiss her, to caress her-- to make every part of her part of his loving.

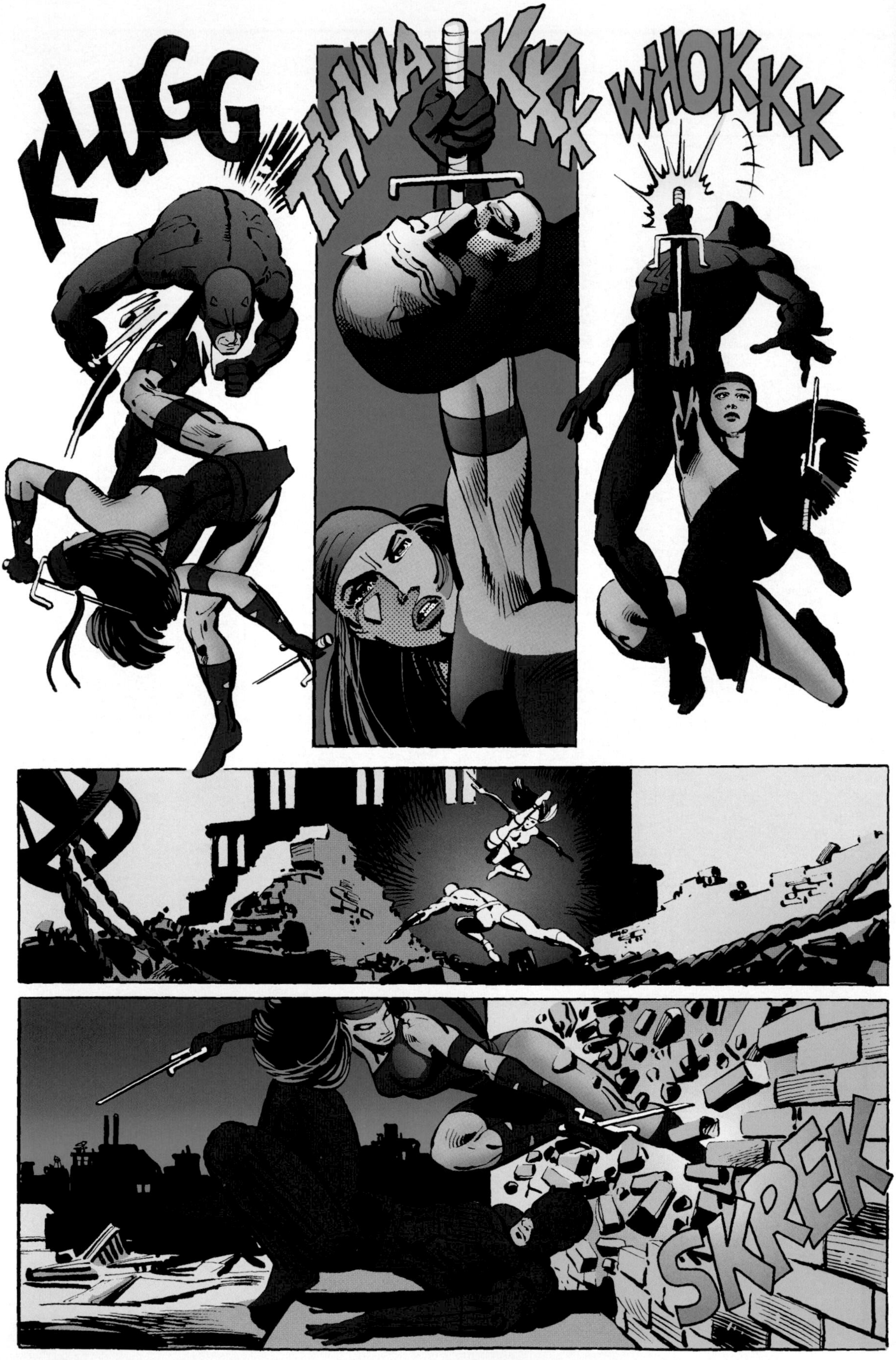
KLUGG
THWAKK
WHOKKK
SKREK

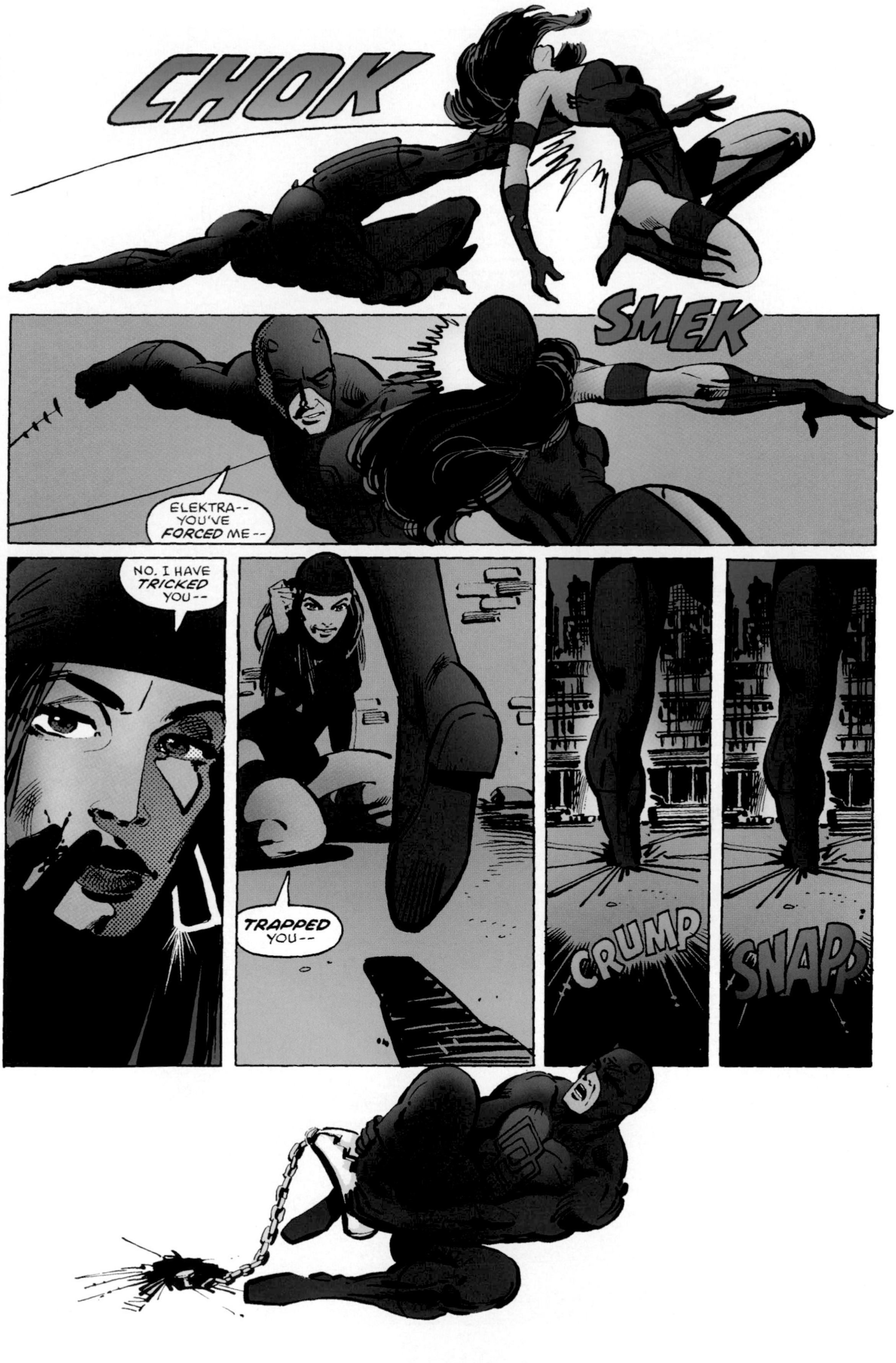
CHOK
SMEK
ELEKTRA-- YOU'VE FORCED ME--
NO. I HAVE TRICKED YOU--
TRAPPED YOU--
CRUMP
SNAPP

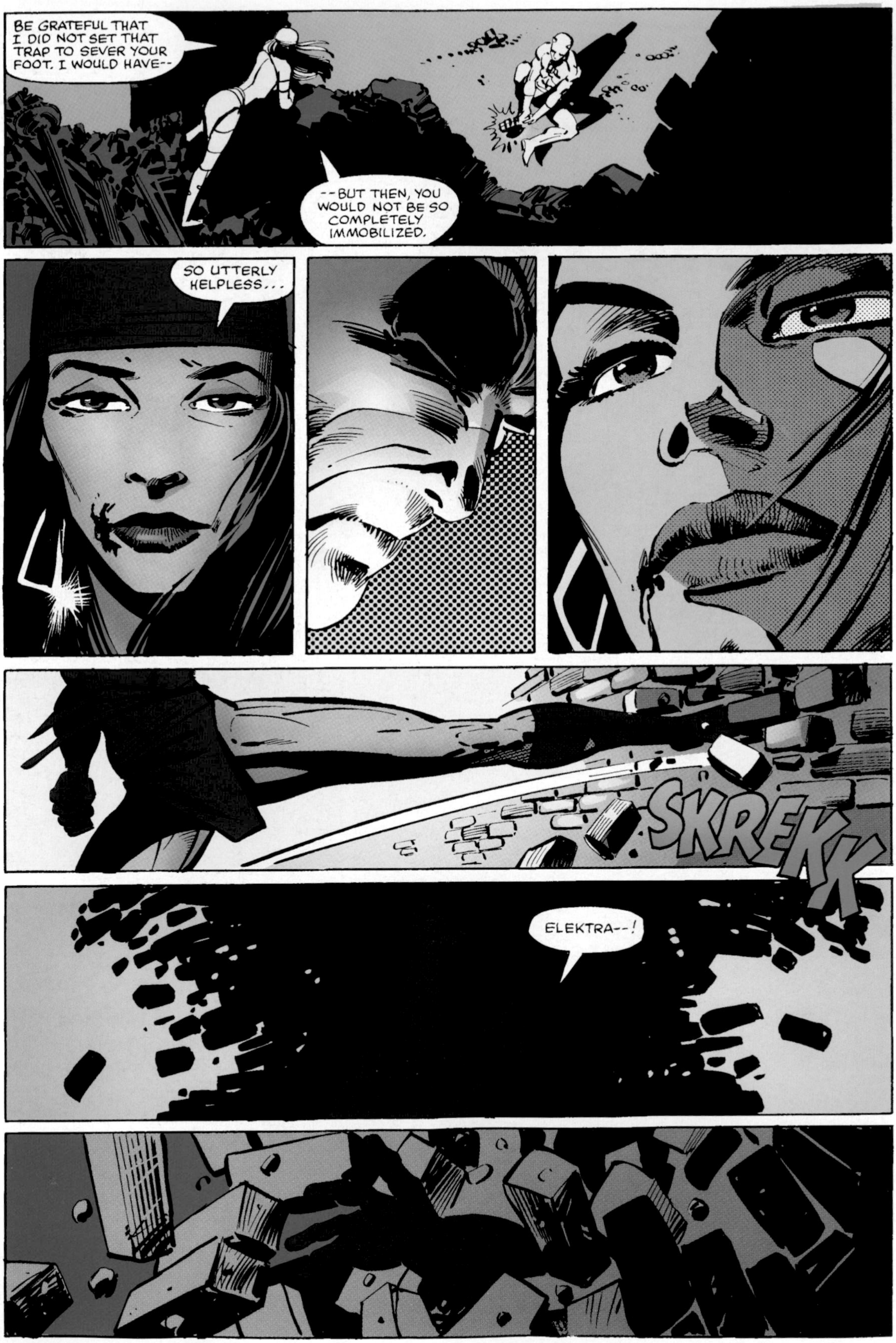
BE GRATEFUL THAT I DID NOT SET THAT TRAP TO SEVER YOUR FOOT. I WOULD HAVE--
--BUT THEN, YOU WOULD NOT BE SO COMPLETELY IMMOBILIZED.
SO UTTERLY HELPLESS...
SKREKK
ELEKTRA--!

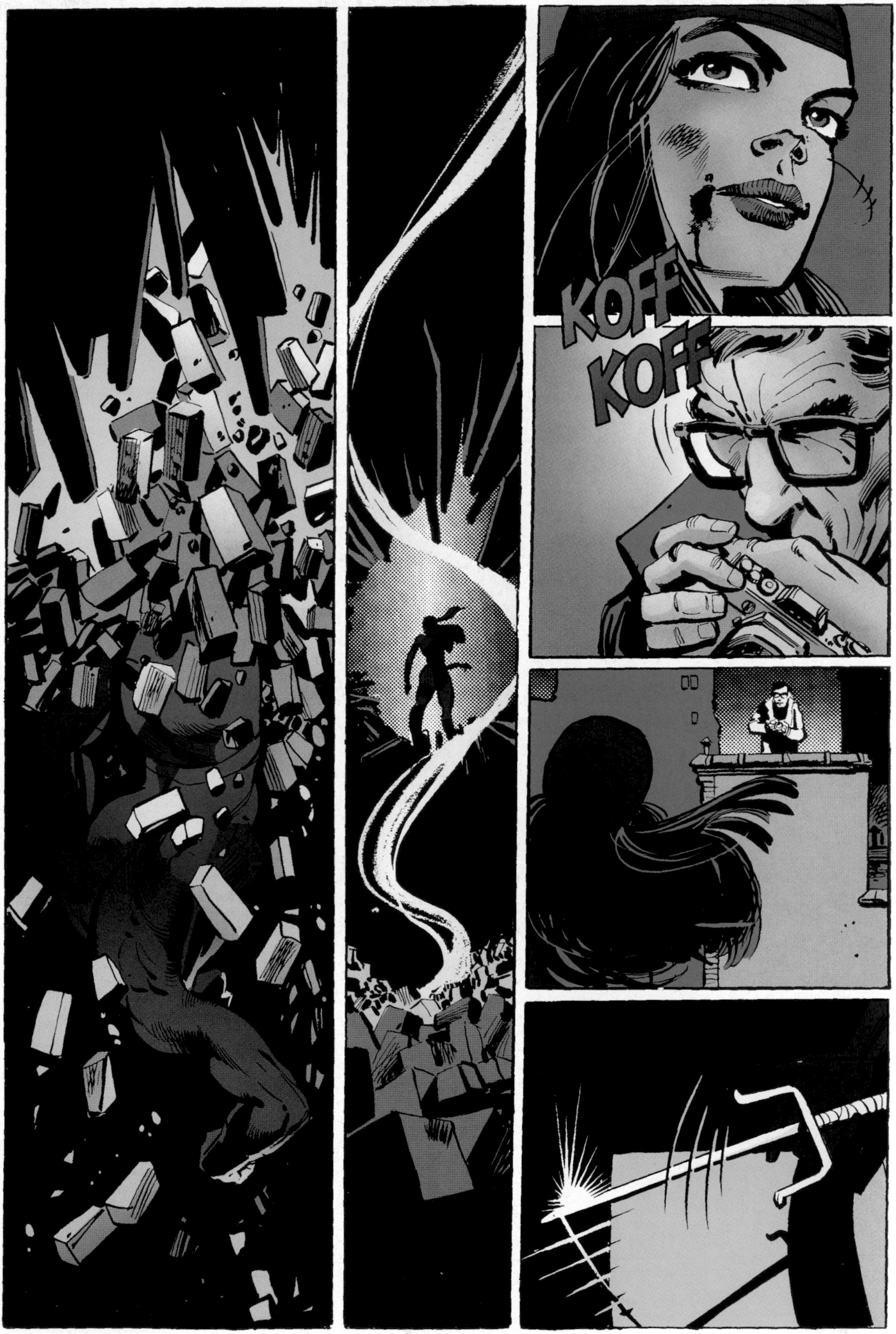
KOFF
KOFF

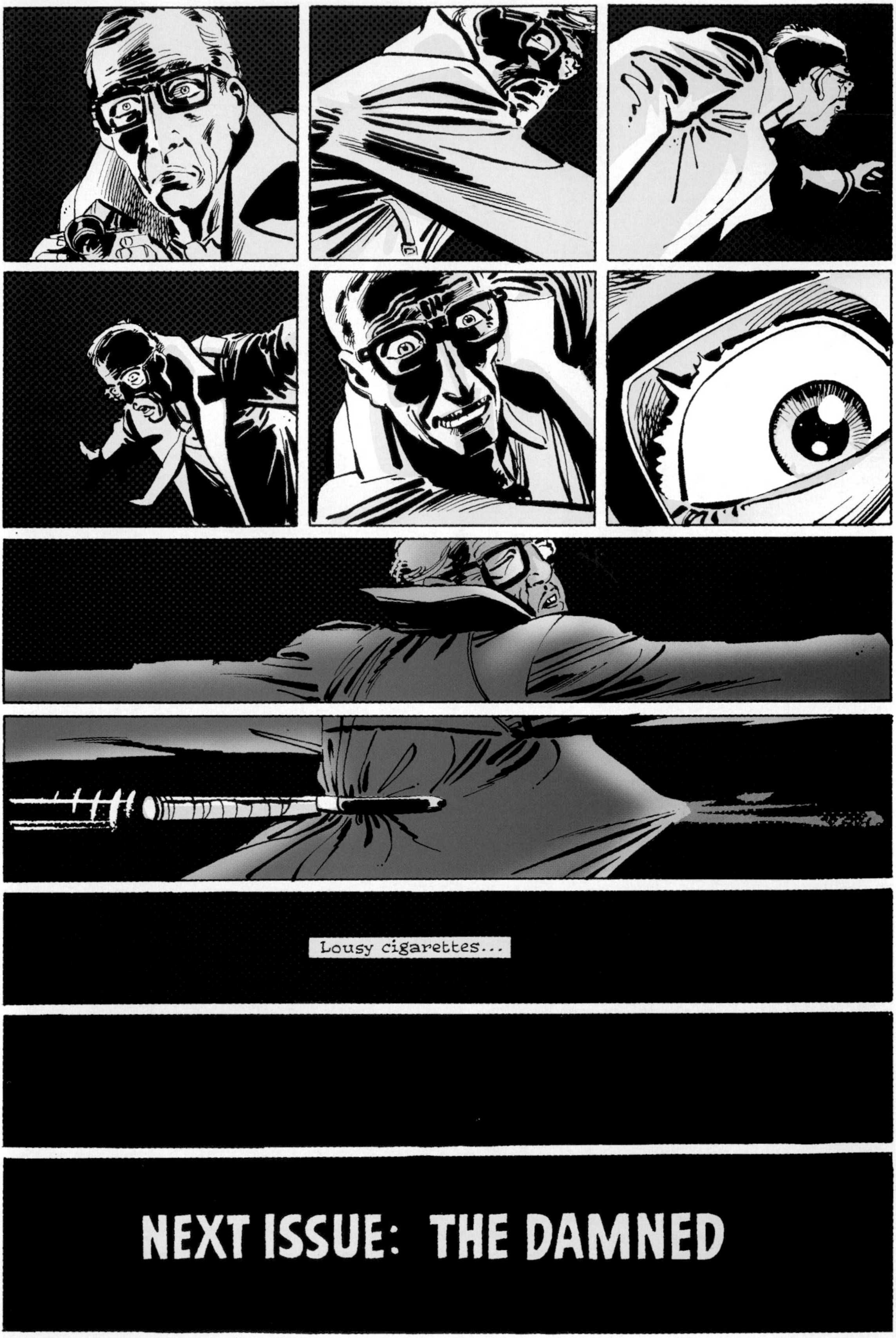
Lousy cigarettes...
NEXT ISSUE: THE DAMNED

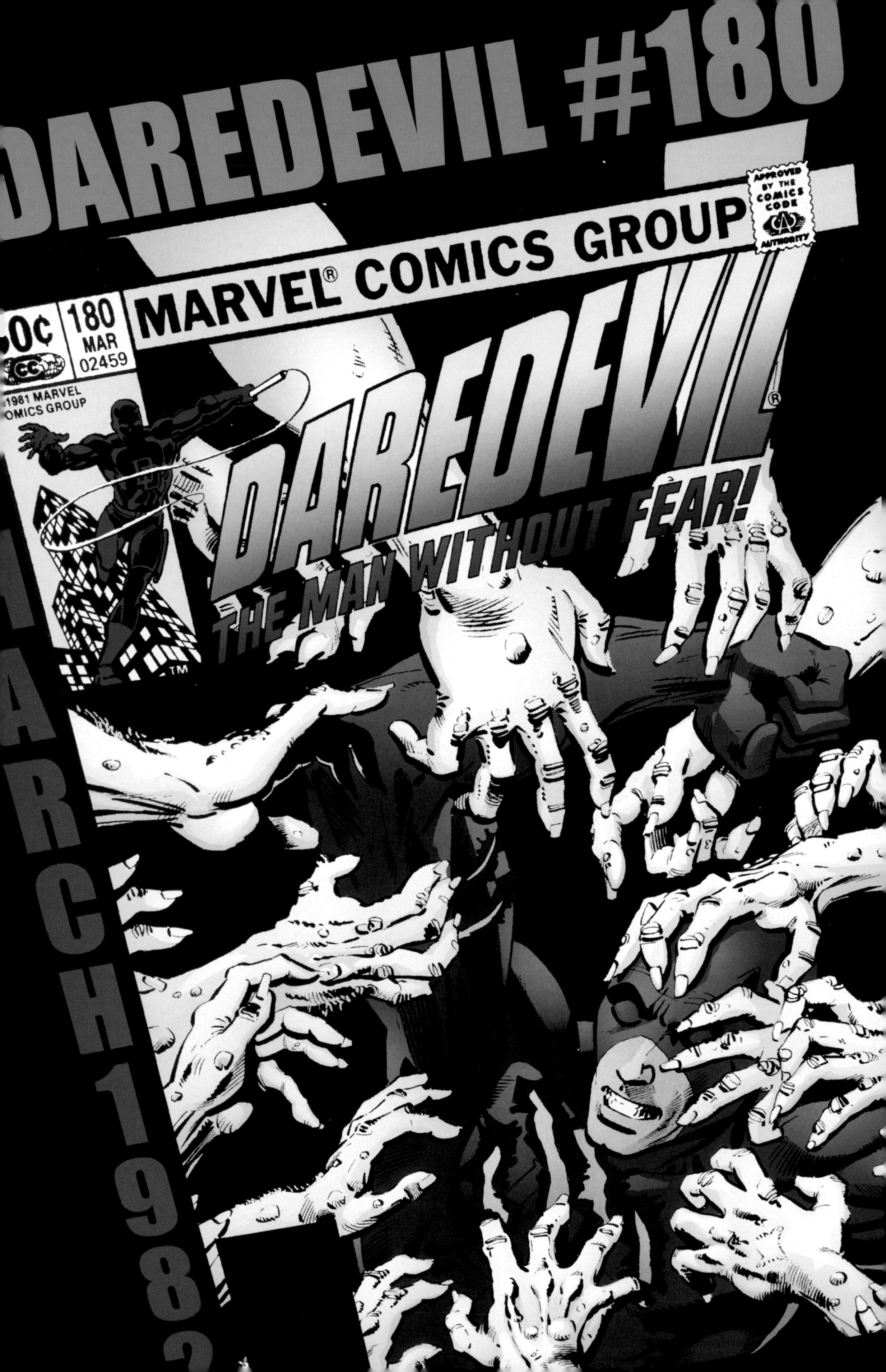

DAREDEVIL #180
MARCH 1982
MARVEL® COMICS GROUP
APPROVED BY THE COMICS CODE AUTHORITY
60¢
180
MAR
02459
©1981 MARVEL COMICS GROUP
DAREDEVIL®
THE MAN WITHOUT FEAR!
TM

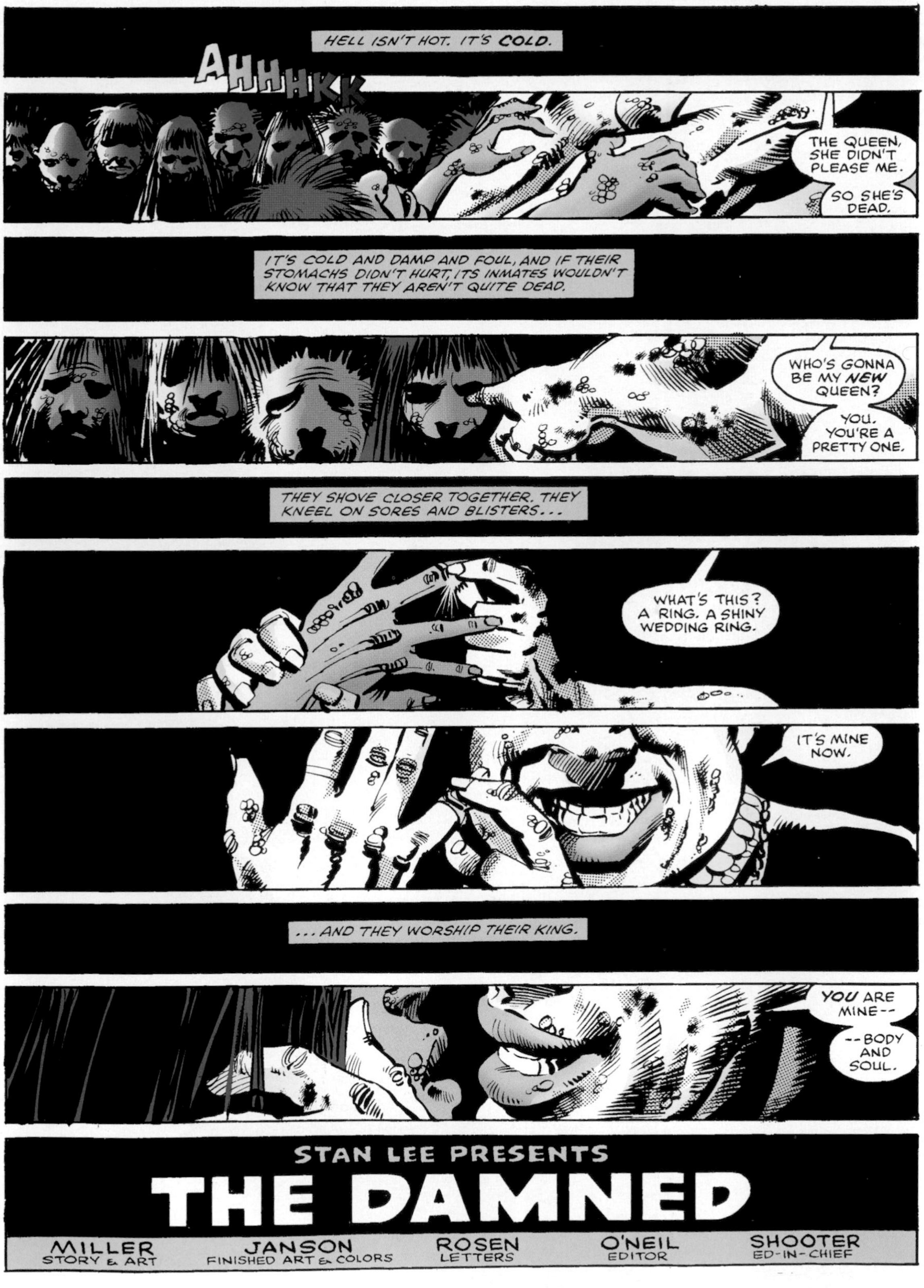

HELL ISN'T HOT. IT'S COLD.
AHHHHKK
THE QUEEN, SHE DIDN'T PLEASE ME.
SO SHE'S DEAD.
IT'S COLD AND DAMP AND FOUL, AND IF THEIR STOMACHS DIDN'T HURT, ITS INMATES WOULDN'T KNOW THAT THEY AREN'T QUITE DEAD.
WHO'S GONNA BE MY NEW QUEEN?
YOU. YOU'RE A PRETTY ONE.
THEY SHOVE CLOSER TOGETHER. THEY KNEEL ON SORES AND BLISTERS...
WHAT'S THIS? A RING. A SHINY WEDDING RING.
IT'S MINE NOW.
...AND THEY WORSHIP THEIR KING.
YOU ARE MINE--
--BODY AND SOUL.
STAN LEE PRESENTS
THE DAMNED
MILLER STORY & ART
JANSON FINISHED ART & COLORS
ROSEN LETTERS
O'NEIL EDITOR
SHOOTER ED-IN-CHIEF

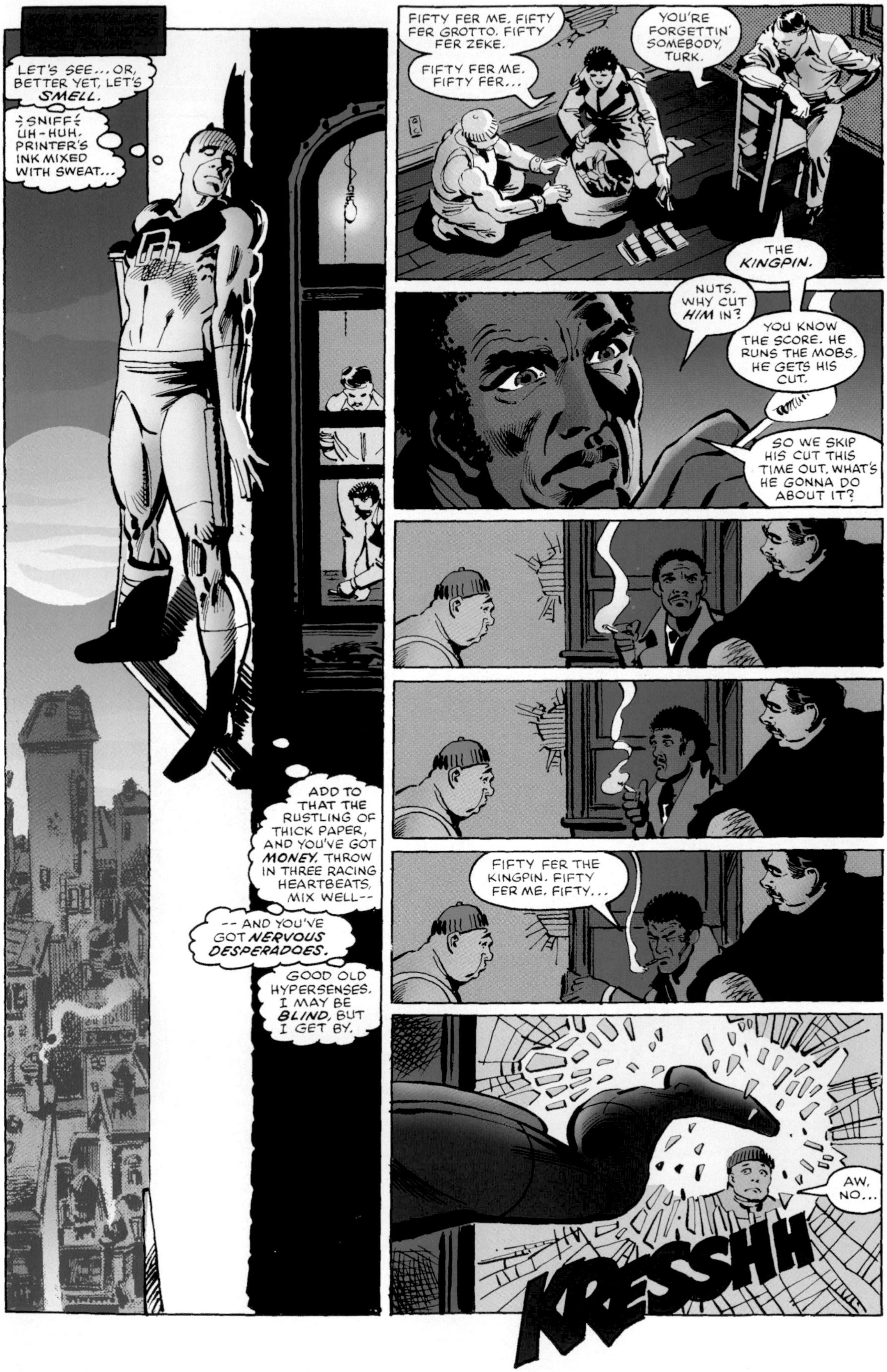
LET'S SEE... OR, BETTER YET, LET'S SMELL.
-SNIFF- UH-HUH. PRINTER'S INK MIXED WITH SWEAT...
ADD TO THAT THE RUSTLING OF THICK PAPER, AND YOU'VE GOT MONEY. THROW IN THREE RACING HEARTBEATS, MIX WELL--
-- AND YOU'VE GOT NERVOUS DESPERADOES.
GOOD OLD HYPERSENSES. I MAY BE BLIND, BUT I GET BY.
FIFTY FER ME. FIFTY FER GROTTO. FIFTY FER ZEKE.
FIFTY FER ME. FIFTY FER...
YOU'RE FORGETTIN' SOMEBODY, TURK.
THE KINGPIN.
NUTS. WHY CUT HIM IN?
YOU KNOW THE SCORE. HE RUNS THE MOBS. HE GETS HIS CUT.
SO WE SKIP HIS CUT THIS TIME OUT. WHAT'S HE GONNA DO ABOUT IT?
FIFTY FER THE KINGPIN. FIFTY FER ME. FIFTY...
AW, NO...
KRESSHH

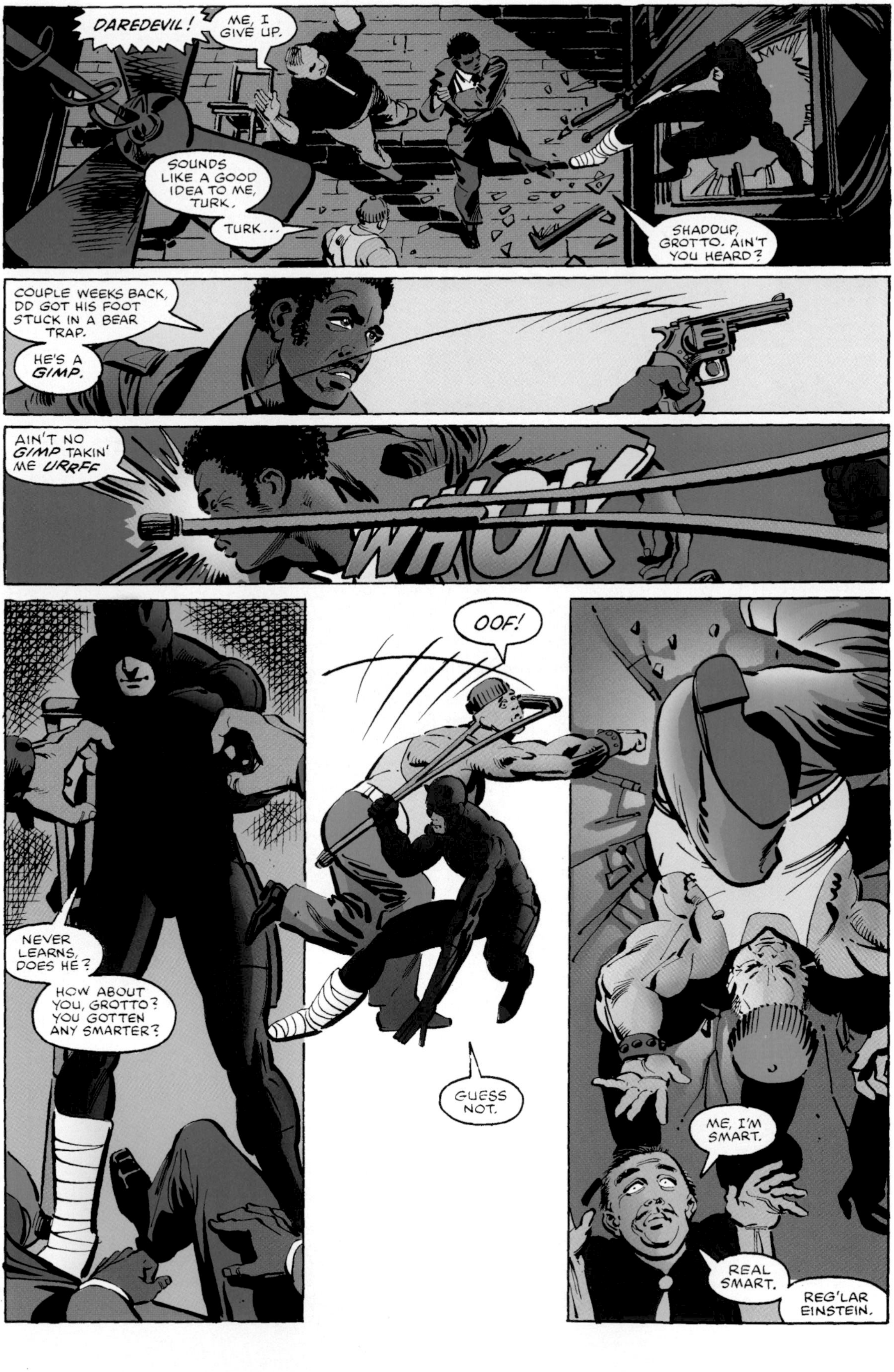
DAREDEVIL!
ME, I GIVE UP.
SOUNDS LIKE A GOOD IDEA TO ME, TURK.
TURK...
SHADDUP, GROTTO. AIN'T YOU HEARD?
COUPLE WEEKS BACK, DD GOT HIS FOOT STUCK IN A BEAR TRAP.
HE'S A GIMP.
AIN'T NO GIMP TAKIN' ME URRFF
WHOK
NEVER LEARNS, DOES HE?
HOW ABOUT YOU, GROTTO? YOU GOTTEN ANY SMARTER?
OOF!
GUESS NOT.
ME, I'M SMART.
REAL SMART.
REG'LAR EINSTEIN.

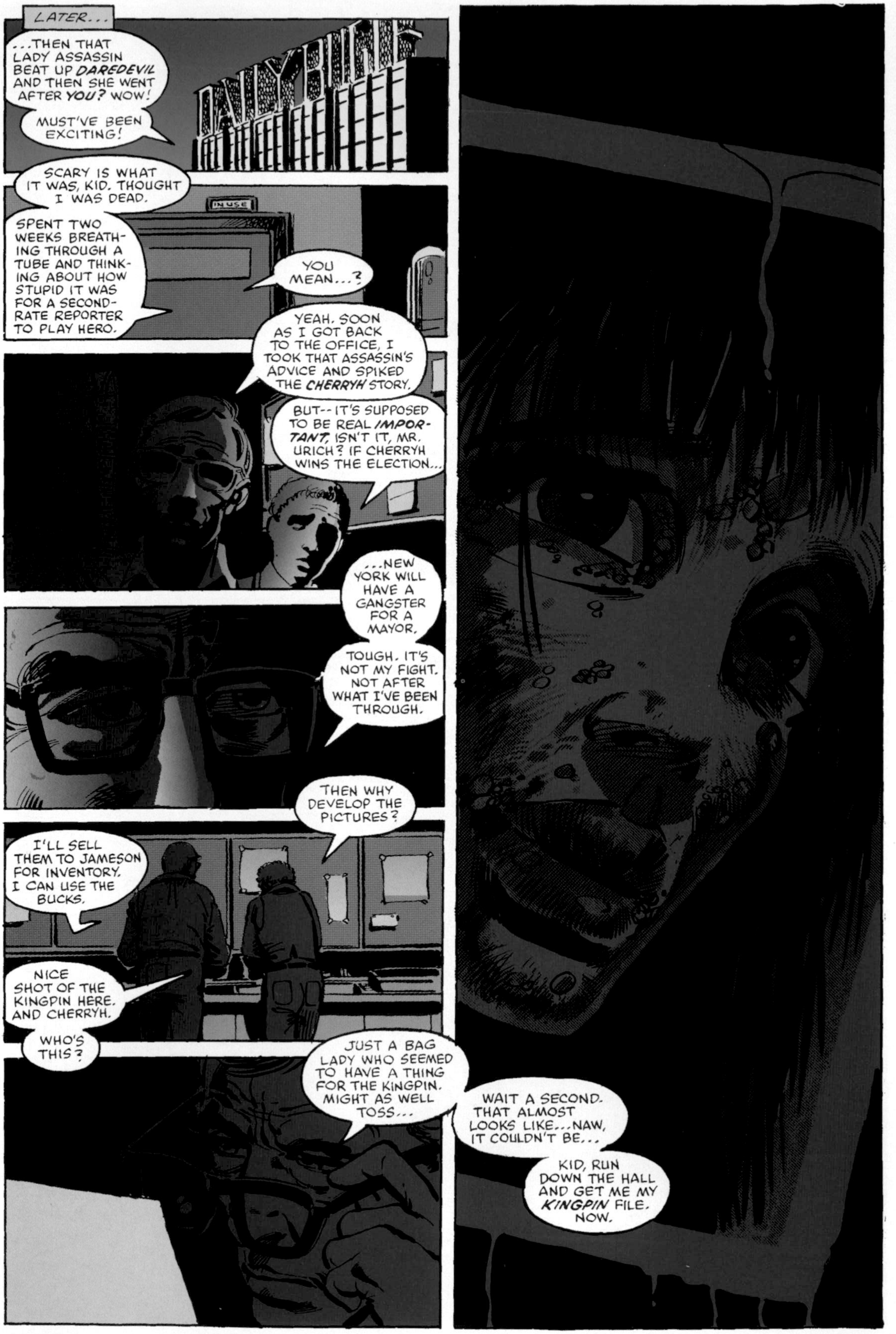

LATER...
...THEN THAT LADY ASSASSIN BEAT UP DAREDEVIL AND THEN SHE WENT AFTER YOU? WOW!
MUST'VE BEEN EXCITING!
SCARY IS WHAT IT WAS, KID. THOUGHT I WAS DEAD.
IN USE
SPENT TWO WEEKS BREATHING THROUGH A TUBE AND THINKING ABOUT HOW STUPID IT WAS FOR A SECOND-RATE REPORTER TO PLAY HERO.
YOU MEAN...?
YEAH. SOON AS I GOT BACK TO THE OFFICE, I TOOK THAT ASSASSIN'S ADVICE AND SPIKED THE CHERRYH STORY.
BUT-- IT'S SUPPOSED TO BE REAL IMPORTANT, ISN'T IT, MR. URICH? IF CHERRYH WINS THE ELECTION...
...NEW YORK WILL HAVE A GANGSTER FOR A MAYOR.
TOUGH. IT'S NOT MY FIGHT. NOT AFTER WHAT I'VE BEEN THROUGH.
THEN WHY DEVELOP THE PICTURES?
I'LL SELL THEM TO JAMESON FOR INVENTORY. I CAN USE THE BUCKS.
NICE SHOT OF THE KINGPIN HERE. AND CHERRYH.
WHO'S THIS?
JUST A BAG LADY WHO SEEMED TO HAVE A THING FOR THE KINGPIN. MIGHT AS WELL TOSS...
WAIT A SECOND. THAT ALMOST LOOKS LIKE...NAW, IT COULDN'T BE...
KID, RUN DOWN THE HALL AND GET ME MY KINGPIN FILE. NOW.

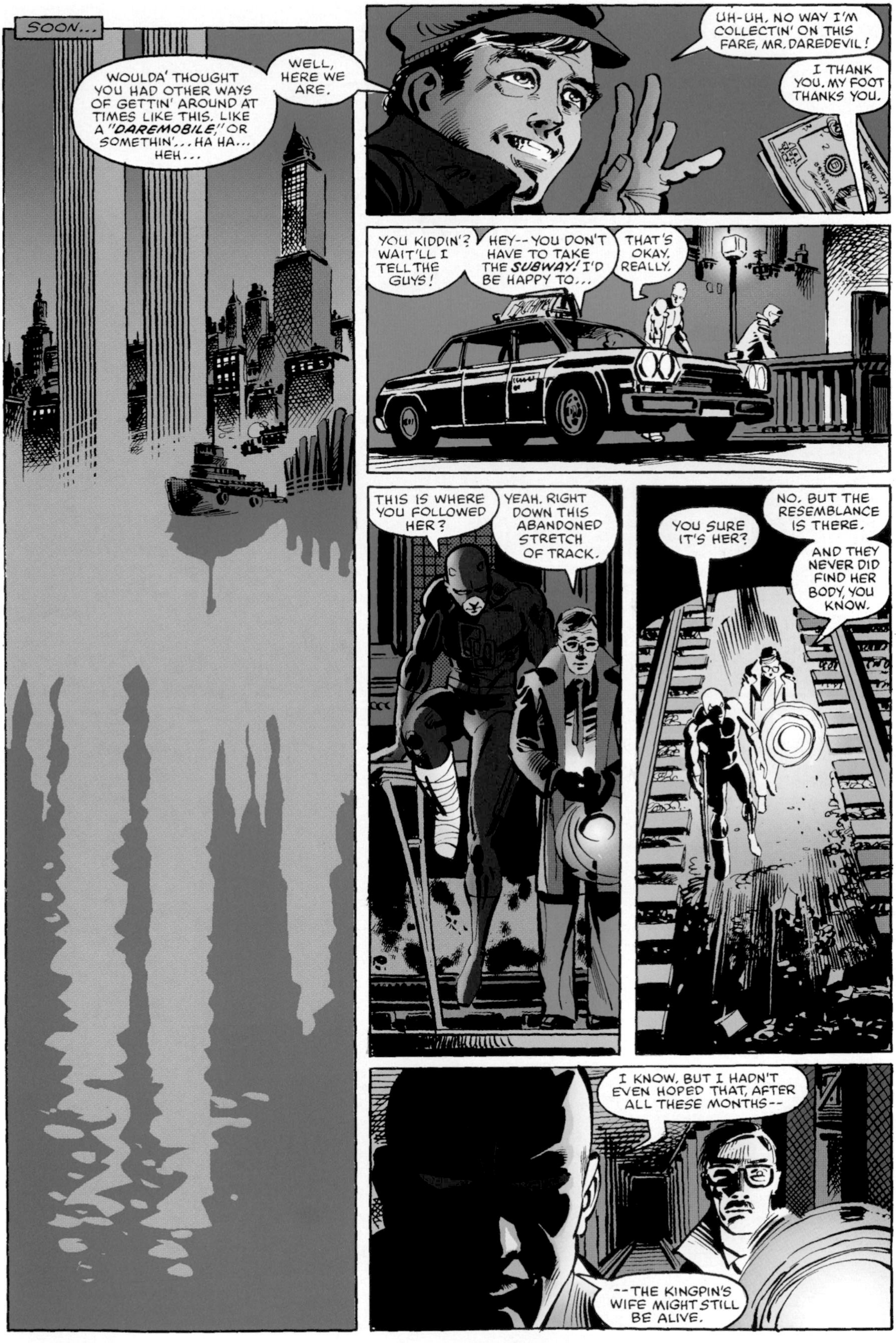
SOON...
WOULDA' THOUGHT YOU HAD OTHER WAYS OF GETTIN' AROUND AT TIMES LIKE THIS. LIKE A "DAREMOBILE," OR SOMETHIN'... HA HA... HEH...
WELL, HERE WE ARE.
UH-UH, NO WAY I'M COLLECTIN' ON THIS FARE, MR. DAREDEVIL!
I THANK YOU. MY FOOT THANKS YOU.
YOU KIDDIN'? WAIT'LL I TELL THE GUYS!
HEY--YOU DON'T HAVE TO TAKE THE SUBWAY! I'D BE HAPPY TO...
THAT'S OKAY. REALLY.
THIS IS WHERE YOU FOLLOWED HER?
YEAH. RIGHT DOWN THIS ABANDONED STRETCH OF TRACK.
YOU SURE IT'S HER?
NO. BUT THE RESEMBLANCE IS THERE.
AND THEY NEVER DID FIND HER BODY, YOU KNOW.
I KNOW. BUT I HADN'T EVEN HOPED THAT, AFTER ALL THESE MONTHS--
--THE KINGPIN'S WIFE MIGHT STILL BE ALIVE.

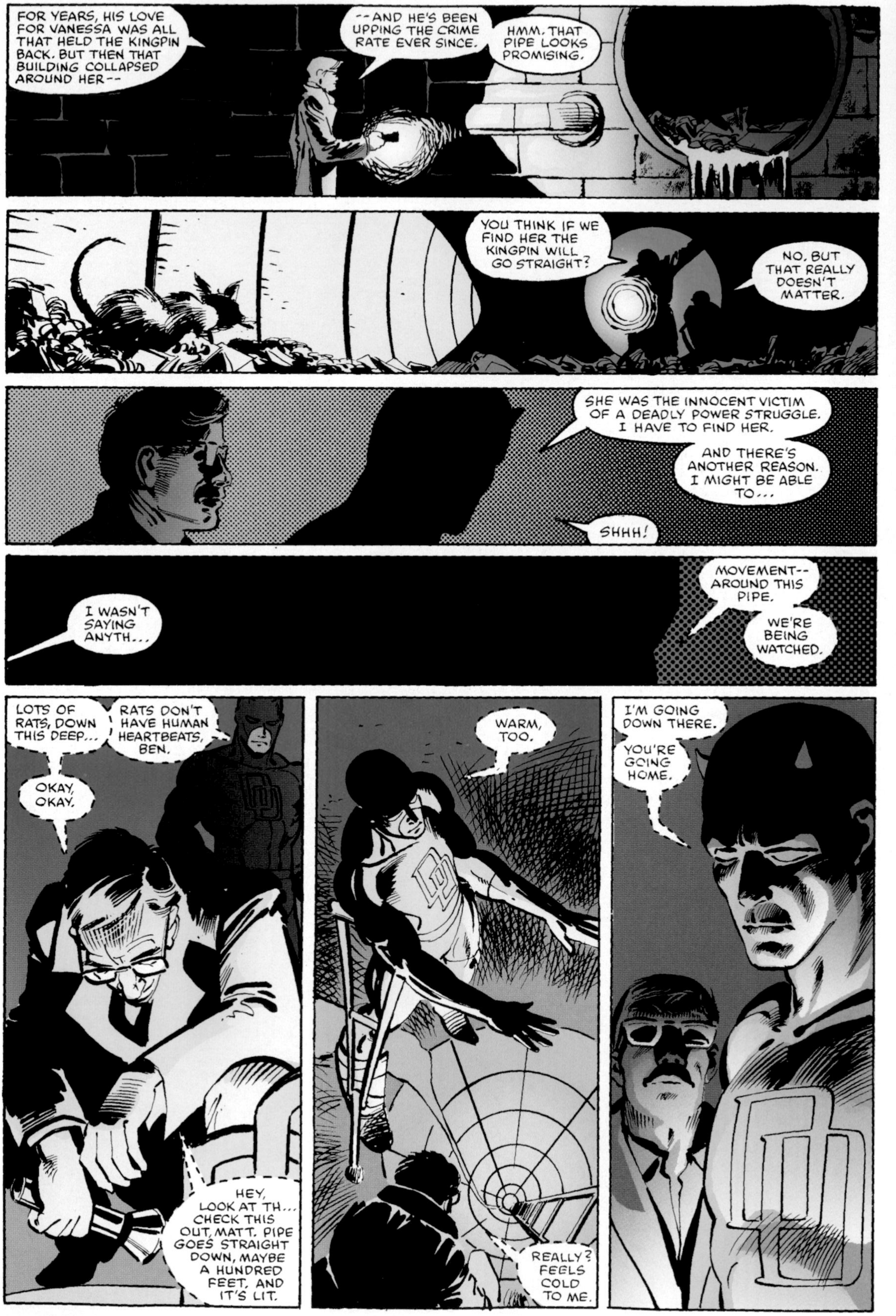
FOR YEARS, HIS LOVE FOR VANESSA WAS ALL THAT HELD THE KINGPIN BACK. BUT THEN THAT BUILDING COLLAPSED AROUND HER--
--AND HE'S BEEN UPPING THE CRIME RATE EVER SINCE.
HMM. THAT PIPE LOOKS PROMISING.
YOU THINK IF WE FIND HER THE KINGPIN WILL GO STRAIGHT?
NO, BUT THAT REALLY DOESN'T MATTER.
SHE WAS THE INNOCENT VICTIM OF A DEADLY POWER STRUGGLE. I HAVE TO FIND HER.
AND THERE'S ANOTHER REASON. I MIGHT BE ABLE TO...
SHHH!
I WASN'T SAYING ANYTH...
MOVEMENT-- AROUND THIS PIPE.
WE'RE BEING WATCHED.
LOTS OF RATS, DOWN THIS DEEP...
RATS DON'T HAVE HUMAN HEARTBEATS, BEN.
OKAY, OKAY.
HEY, LOOK AT TH... CHECK THIS OUT, MATT. PIPE GOES STRAIGHT DOWN, MAYBE A HUNDRED FEET, AND IT'S LIT.
WARM, TOO.
REALLY? FEELS COLD TO ME.
I'M GOING DOWN THERE.
YOU'RE GOING HOME.

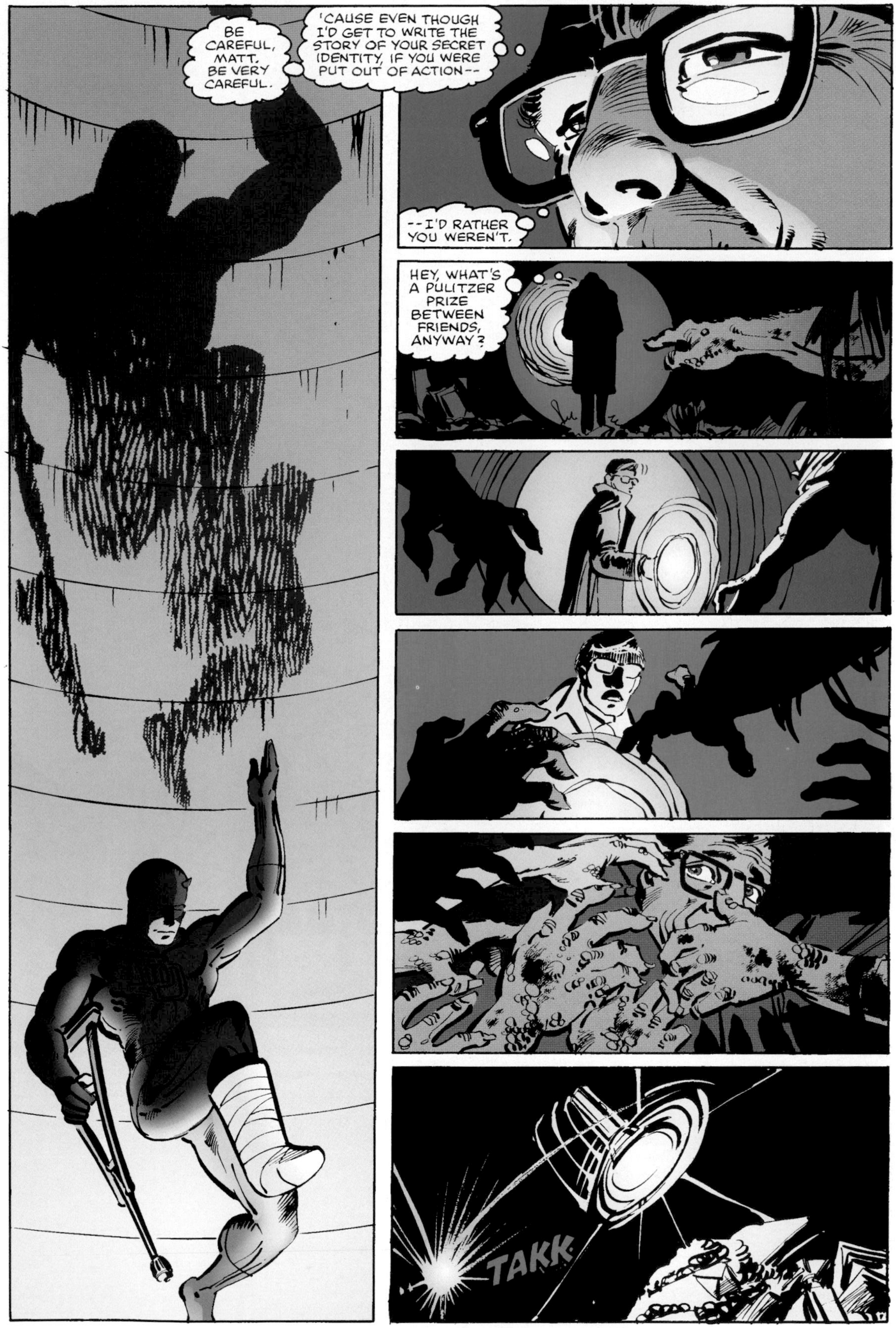
BE CAREFUL, MATT. BE VERY CAREFUL.
'CAUSE EVEN THOUGH I'D GET TO WRITE THE STORY OF YOUR SECRET IDENTITY, IF YOU WERE PUT OUT OF ACTION--
--I'D RATHER YOU WEREN'T.
HEY, WHAT'S A PULITZER PRIZE BETWEEN FRIENDS, ANYWAY?
TAKK

THE MIDTOWN
OFFICES OF
NELSON AND
MURDOCK...

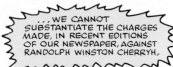

...WE CANNOT SUBSTANTIATE THE CHARGES MADE, IN RECENT EDITIONS OF OUR NEWSPAPER, AGAINST RANDOLPH WINSTON CHERRYH,

WITH THESE WORDS, J. JONAH JAMESON, PUBLISHER OF THE *NEW YORK DAILY BUGLE*, TODAY RETRACTED HIS CLAIMS THAT COUNCILMAN CHERRYH'S CAMPAIGN WAS SPONSORED BY ORGANIZED CRIME.

WITH FIVE PERCENT OF THE ELECTION RETURNS IN, CHERRYH IS NOW LEADING IN EVERY DISTRICT...

THEN-- I GUESS IT'S ALL OVER.

I'M SORRY, FOGGY, YOU AND MATT, YOU WORKED SO HARD AT DEFENDING THE *BUGLE*...

SURE WE DID, AND WE MIGHT HAVE WON IT, BECKY, WE'RE GOOD LAWYERS-- THE *BEST*--

--BUT YOU CAN'T DEFEND A CLIENT WHO FOLDS ON YOU.

THING IS, THERE'S MORE AT STAKE THAN THE REPUTATION OF *NELSON AND MURDOCK*. IF THE PEOPLE ELECT CHERRYH TONIGHT, THEY'LL BE HANDING THIS TOWN TO THE MOBS, AND THEY WON'T EVEN KNOW IT.

WHERE IS MATT, ANYWAY?

I DON'T KNOW, I TRIED HIM AT HOME.

FUNNY HOW HE DOES THAT, JUST UPS AND DISAPPEARS, FOR DAYS AT A TIME.

SOMETIMES I WONDER...

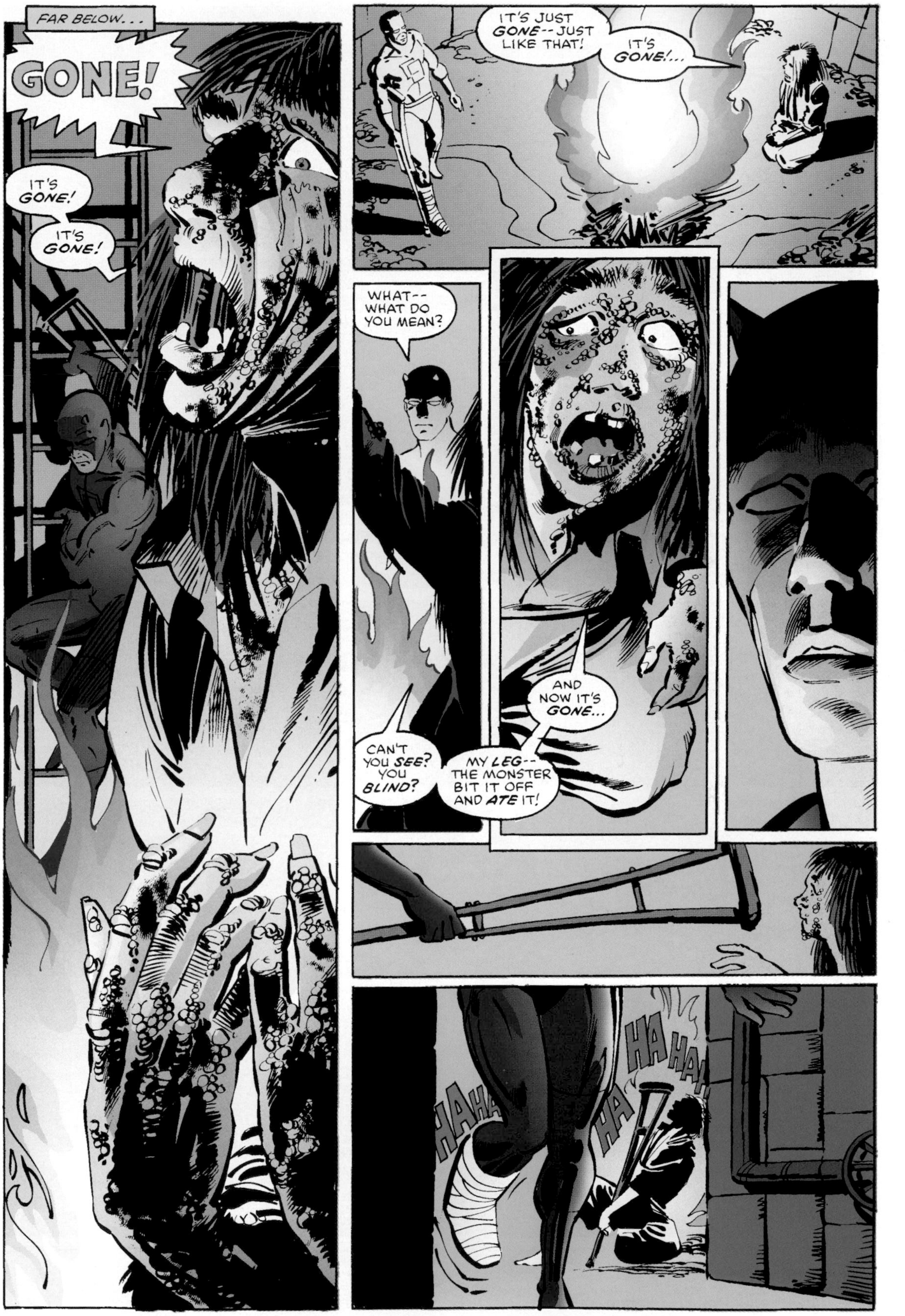

FAR BELOW...
GONE!
IT'S GONE!
IT'S GONE!
IT'S JUST GONE-- JUST LIKE THAT!
IT'S GONE!...
WHAT-- WHAT DO YOU MEAN?
AND NOW IT'S GONE...
CAN'T YOU SEE? YOU BLIND?
MY LEG-- THE MONSTER BIT IT OFF AND ATE IT!
HAHA
HA HA HA
HA

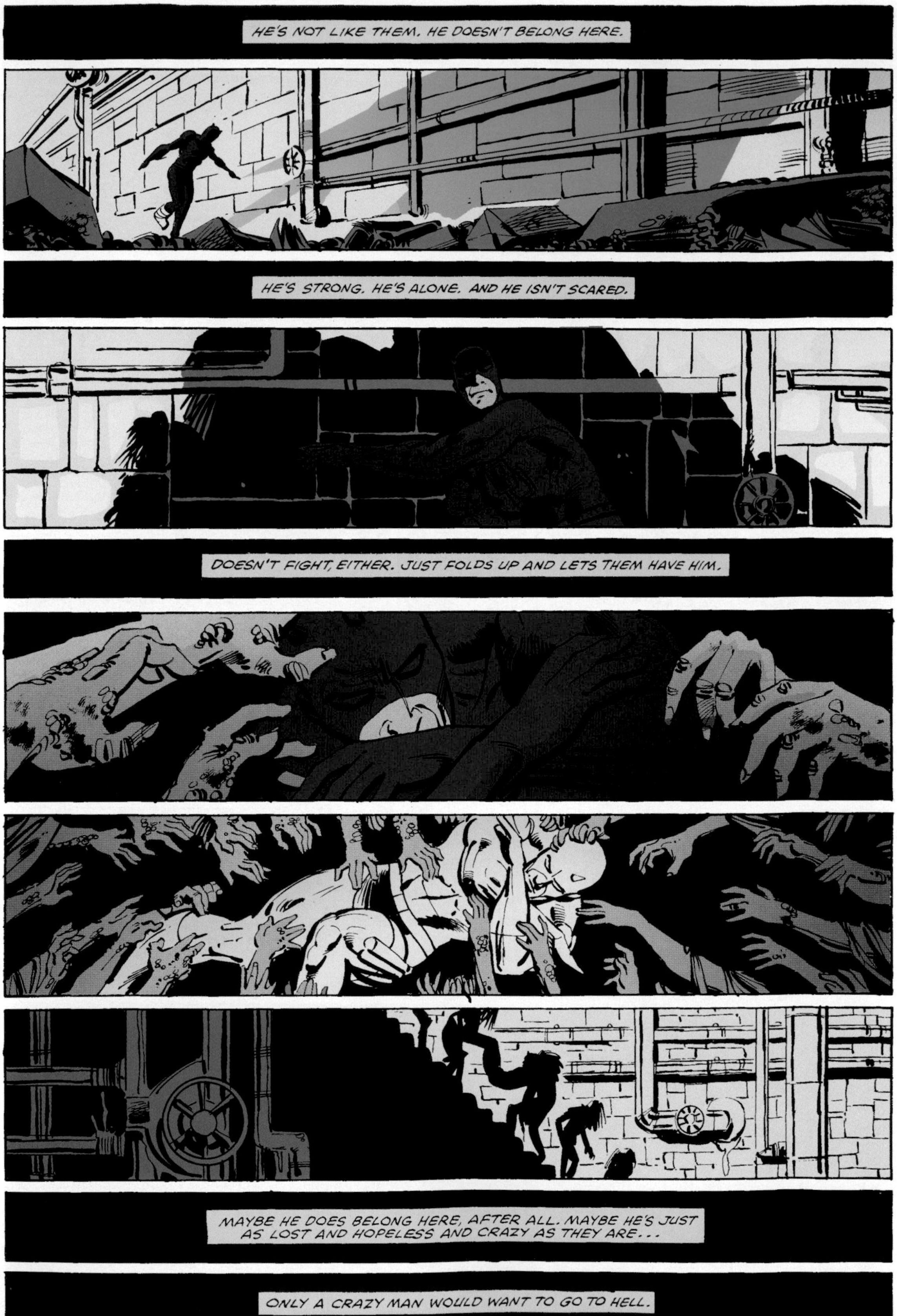
HE'S NOT LIKE THEM. HE DOESN'T BELONG HERE.
HE'S STRONG. HE'S ALONE. AND HE ISN'T SCARED.
DOESN'T FIGHT, EITHER. JUST FOLDS UP AND LETS THEM HAVE HIM.
MAYBE HE DOES BELONG HERE, AFTER ALL. MAYBE HE'S JUST AS LOST AND HOPELESS AND CRAZY AS THEY ARE...
ONLY A CRAZY MAN WOULD WANT TO GO TO HELL.

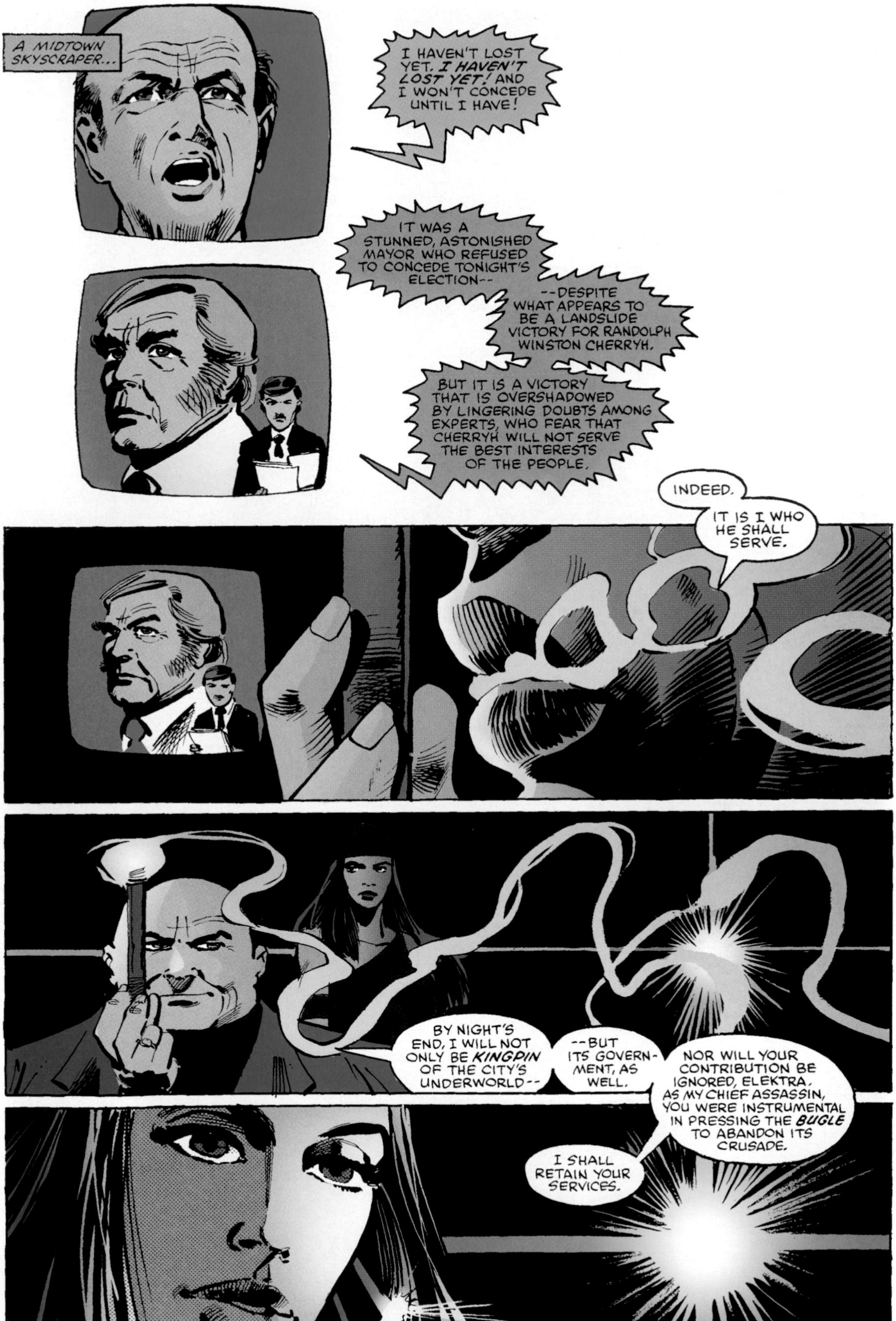

A MIDTOWN SKYSCRAPER...
I HAVEN'T LOST YET. I HAVEN'T LOST YET! AND I WON'T CONCEDE UNTIL I HAVE!
IT WAS A STUNNED, ASTONISHED MAYOR WHO REFUSED TO CONCEDE TONIGHT'S ELECTION--
--DESPITE WHAT APPEARS TO BE A LANDSLIDE VICTORY FOR RANDOLPH WINSTON CHERRYH.
BUT IT IS A VICTORY THAT IS OVERSHADOWED BY LINGERING DOUBTS AMONG EXPERTS, WHO FEAR THAT CHERRYH WILL NOT SERVE THE BEST INTERESTS OF THE PEOPLE.
INDEED.
IT IS I WHO HE SHALL SERVE.
BY NIGHT'S END, I WILL NOT ONLY BE KINGPIN OF THE CITY'S UNDERWORLD--
--BUT ITS GOVERNMENT, AS WELL.
NOR WILL YOUR CONTRIBUTION BE IGNORED, ELEKTRA. AS MY CHIEF ASSASSIN, YOU WERE INSTRUMENTAL IN PRESSING THE BUGLE TO ABANDON ITS CRUSADE.
I SHALL RETAIN YOUR SERVICES.

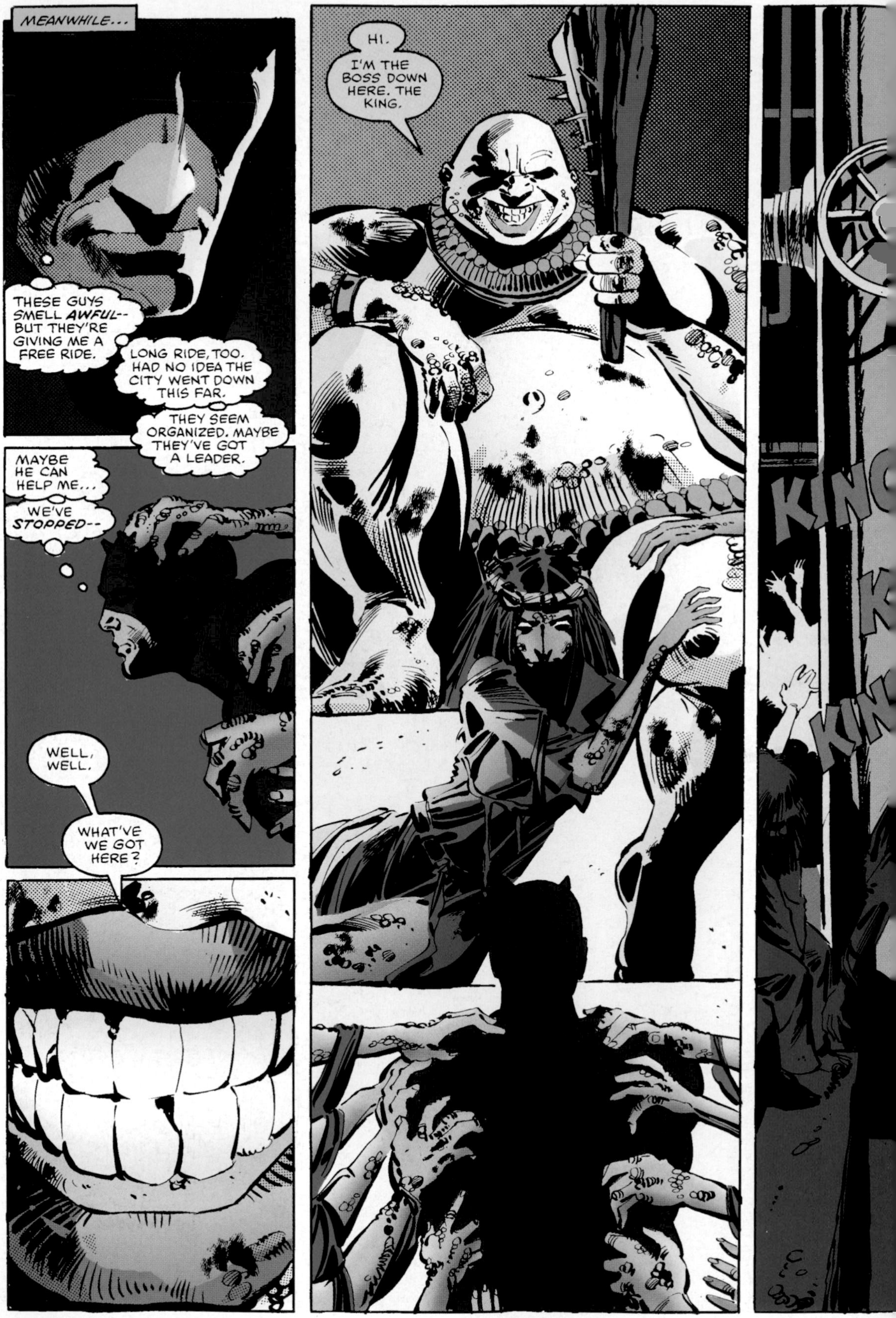
MEANWHILE...
THESE GUYS SMELL AWFUL-- BUT THEY'RE GIVING ME A FREE RIDE.
LONG RIDE, TOO. HAD NO IDEA THE CITY WENT DOWN THIS FAR.
THEY SEEM ORGANIZED. MAYBE THEY'VE GOT A LEADER.
MAYBE HE CAN HELP ME...
WE'VE STOPPED--
WELL, WELL.
WHAT'VE WE GOT HERE?
HI.
I'M THE BOSS DOWN HERE. THE KING.

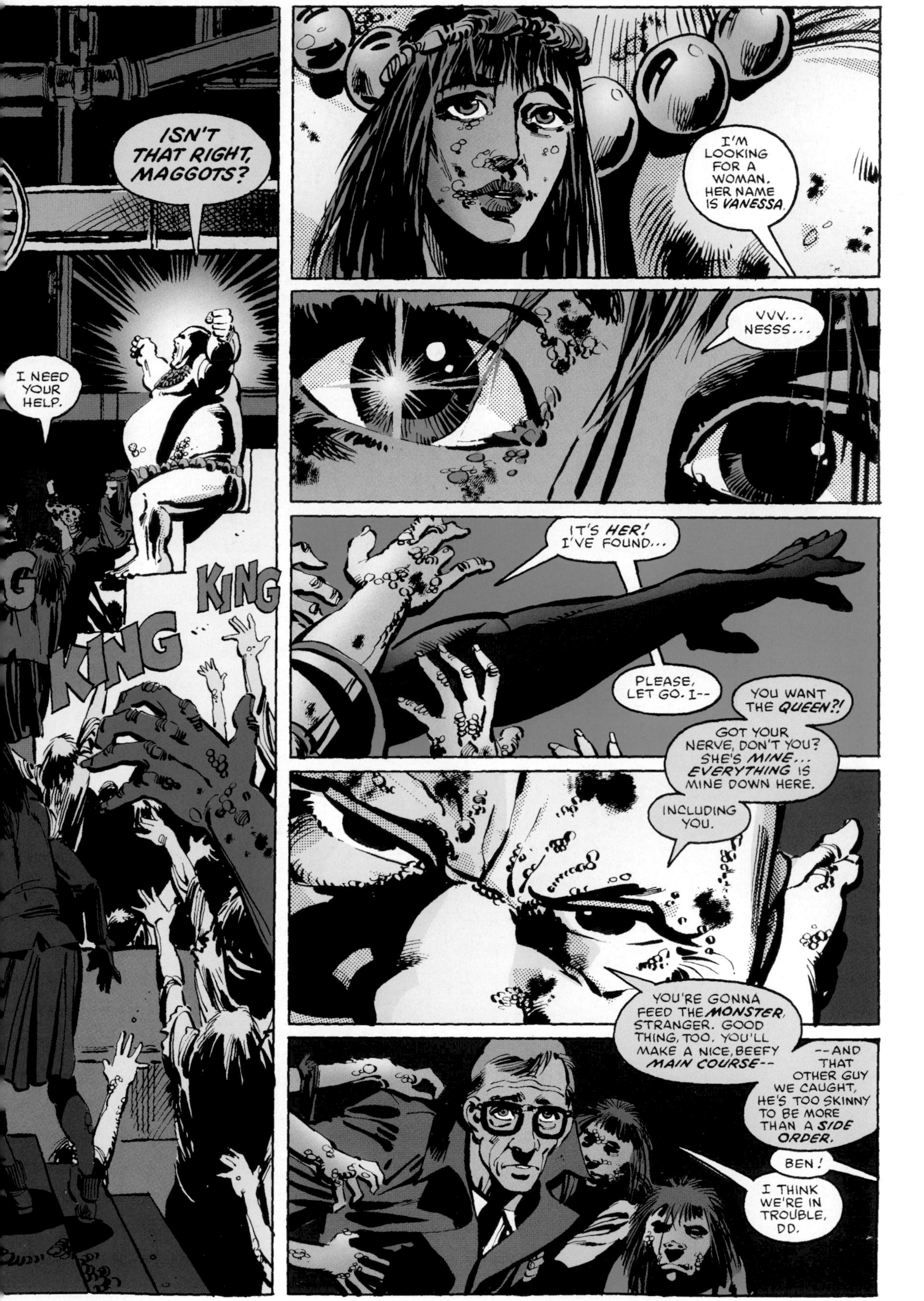

ISN'T THAT RIGHT, MAGGOTS?
I NEED YOUR HELP.
KING
KING
KING
I'M LOOKING FOR A WOMAN. HER NAME IS VANESSA.
VVV... NESSS...
IT'S HER! I'VE FOUND...
PLEASE, LET GO. I--
YOU WANT THE QUEEN?!
GOT YOUR NERVE, DON'T YOU? SHE'S MINE... EVERYTHING IS MINE DOWN HERE.
INCLUDING YOU.
YOU'RE GONNA FEED THE MONSTER, STRANGER. GOOD THING, TOO. YOU'LL MAKE A NICE, BEEFY MAIN COURSE--
--AND THAT OTHER GUY WE CAUGHT, HE'S TOO SKINNY TO BE MORE THAN A SIDE ORDER.
BEN!
I THINK WE'RE IN TROUBLE, DD.

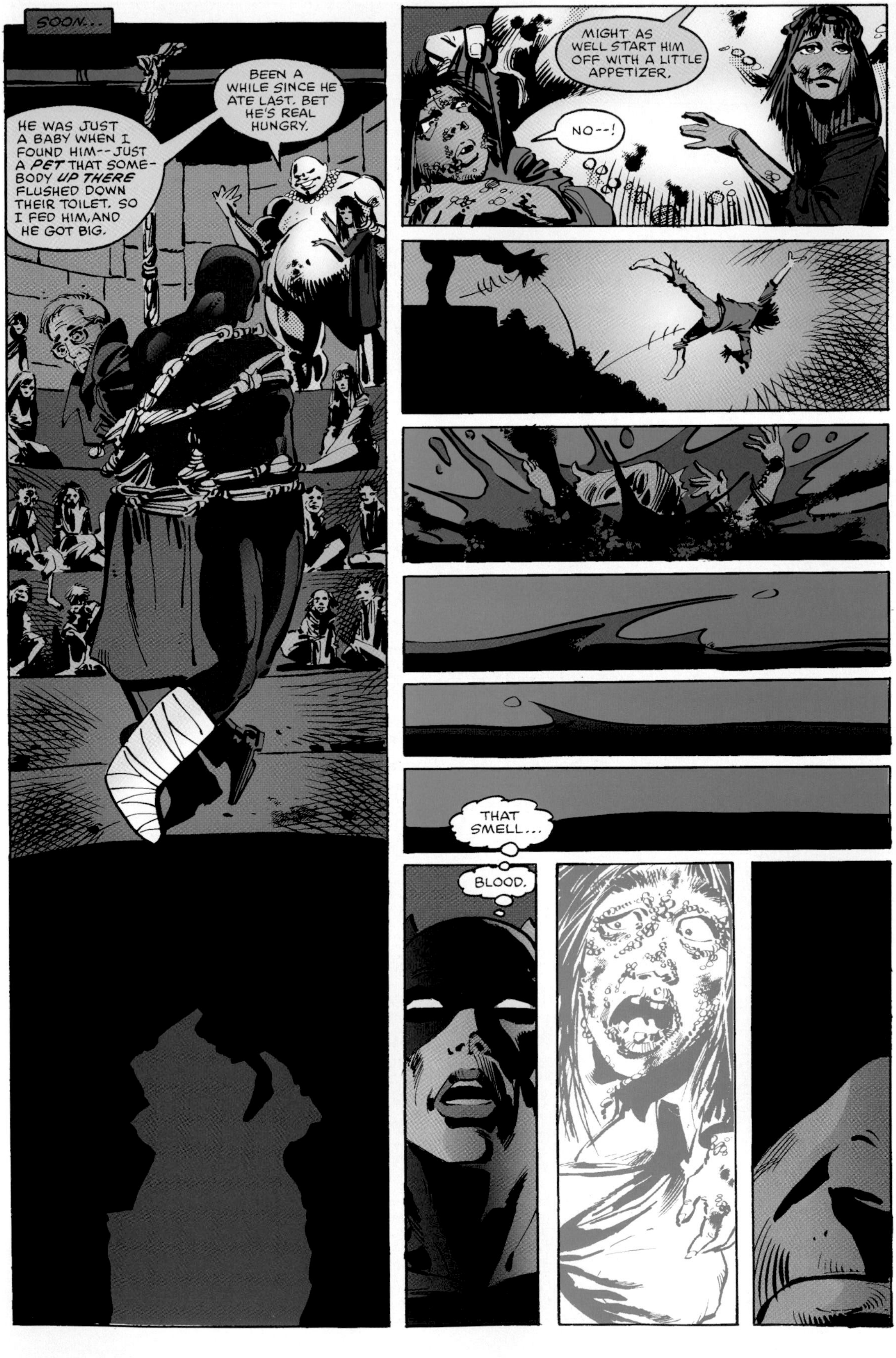
SOON...
HE WAS JUST A BABY WHEN I FOUND HIM--JUST A PET THAT SOME-BODY UP THERE FLUSHED DOWN THEIR TOILET. SO I FED HIM, AND HE GOT BIG.
BEEN A WHILE SINCE HE ATE LAST. BET HE'S REAL HUNGRY.
MIGHT AS WELL START HIM OFF WITH A LITTLE APPETIZER.
NO--!
THAT SMELL...
BLOOD.

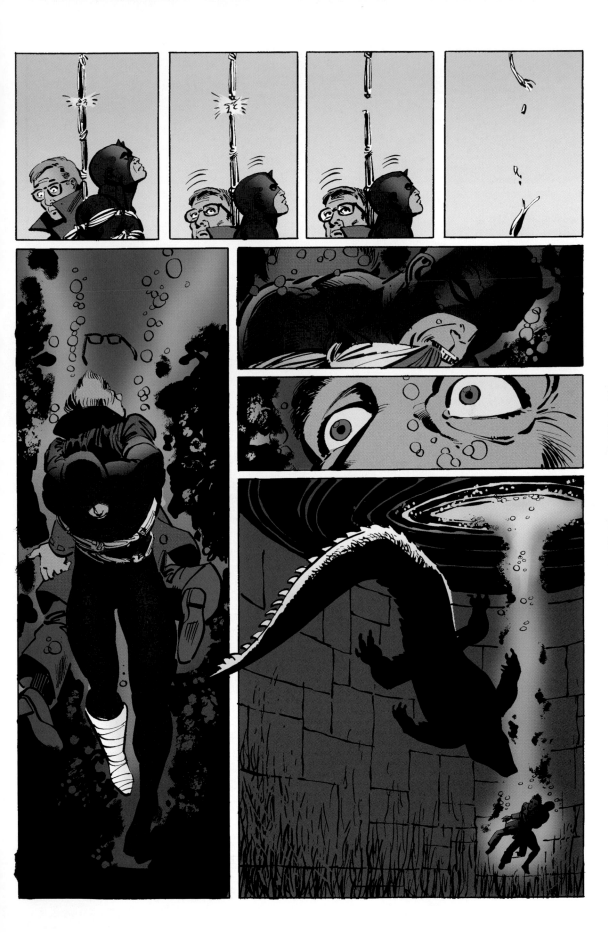

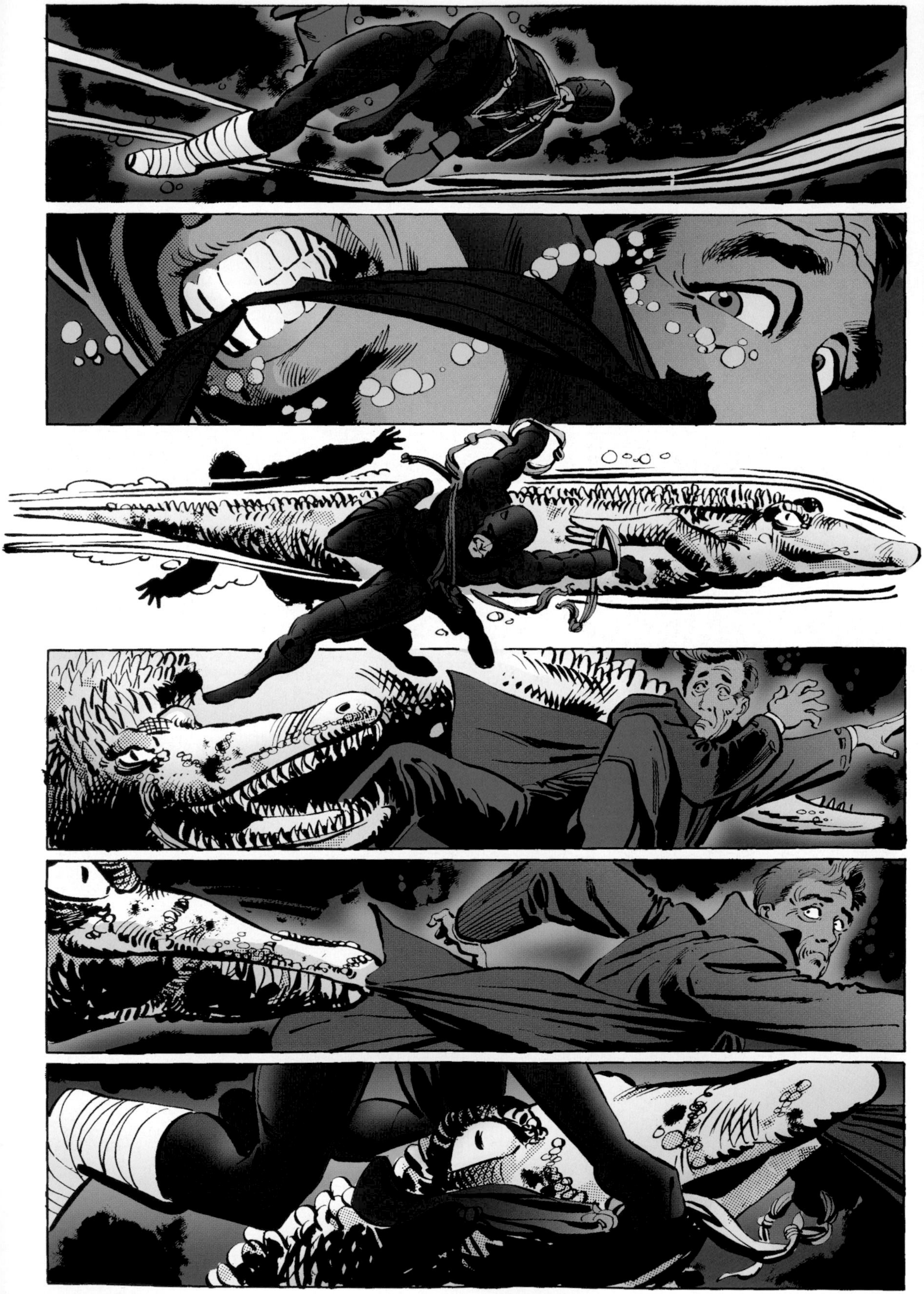

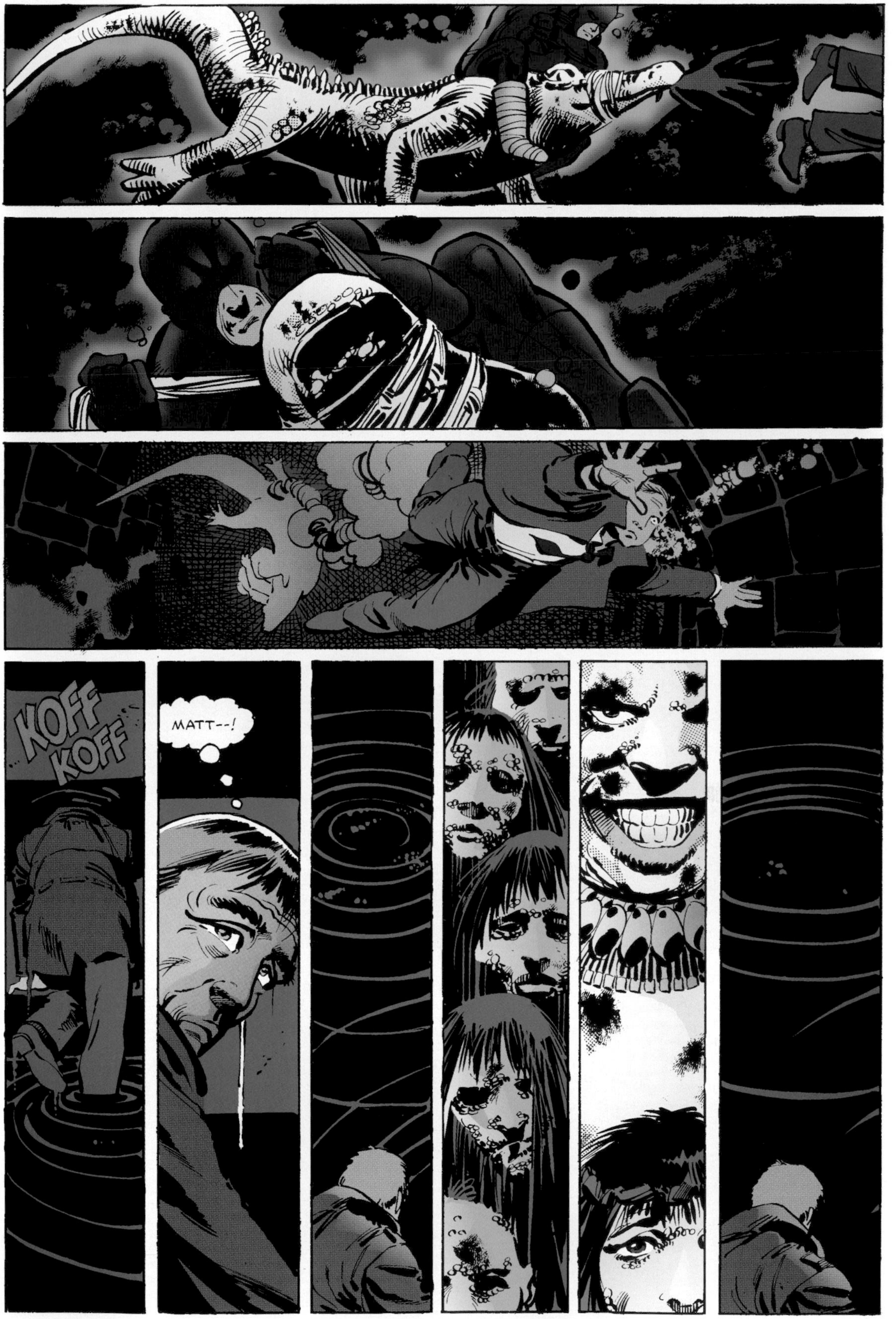

KOFF KOFF
MATT--!

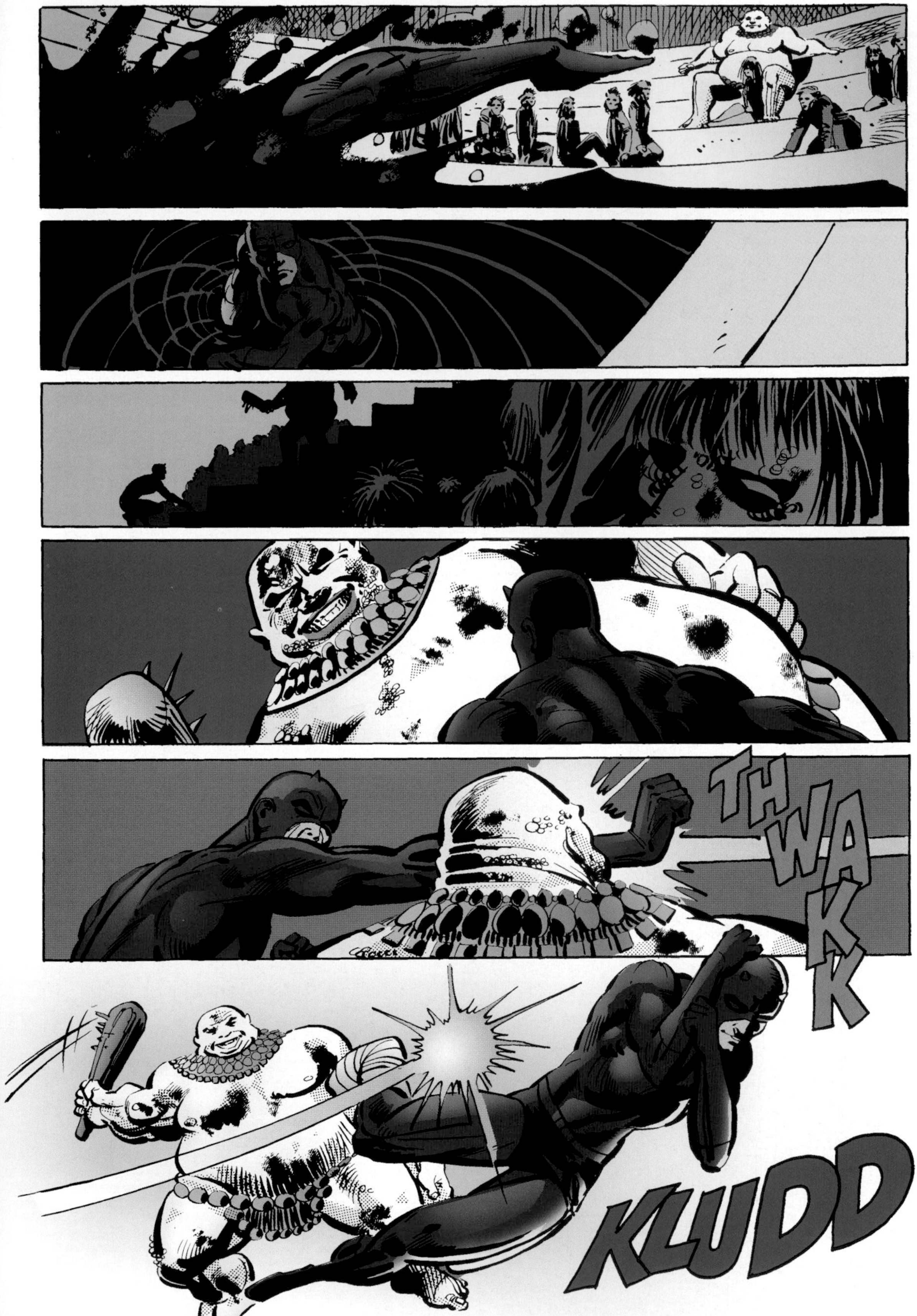
THWAKK
KLUDD

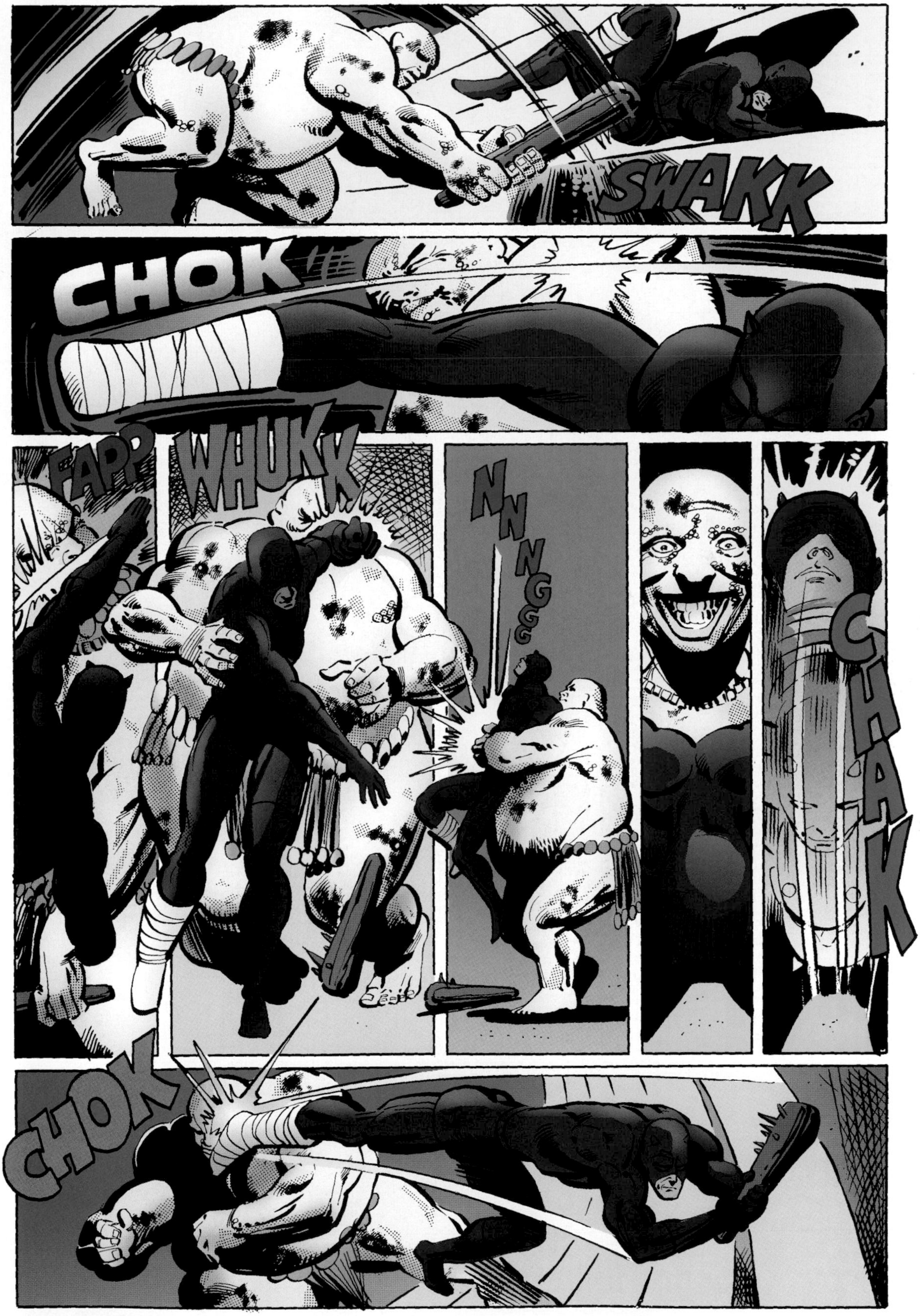

SWAKK
CHOK
FAPP
WHUKK
NNNGGG
CHAK
CHOK

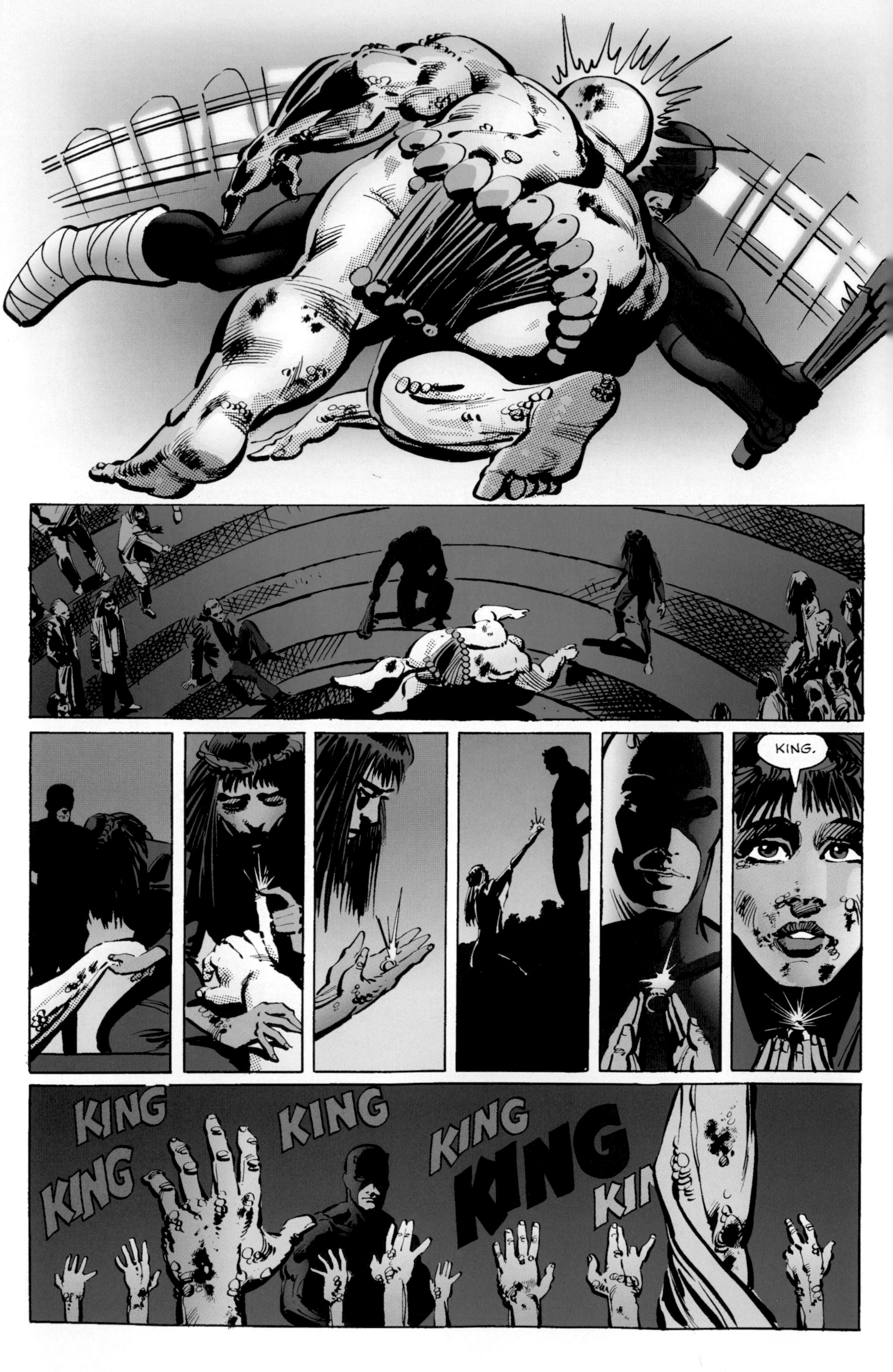

KING.
KING
KING
KING
KING
KING
KING
KI

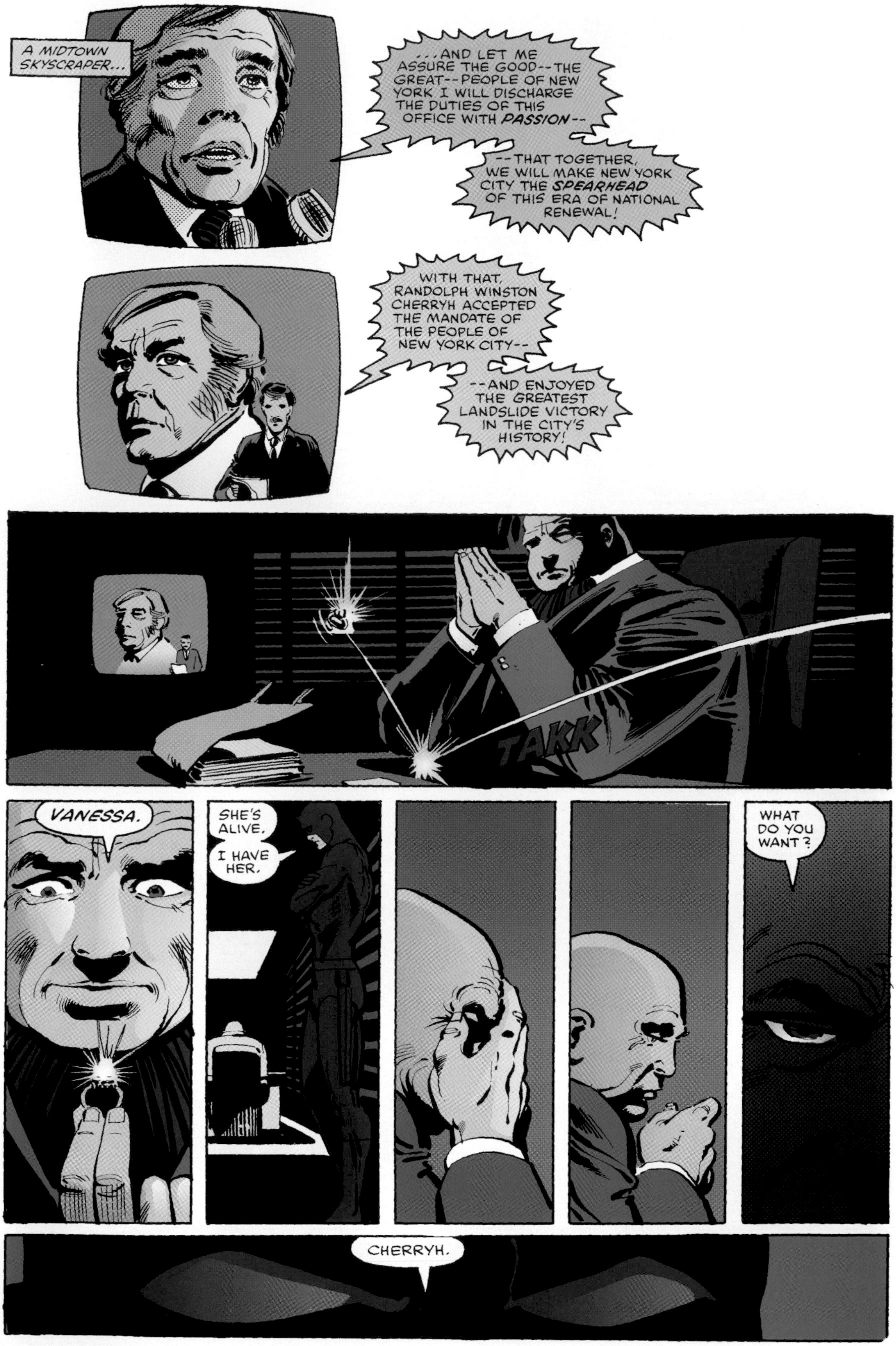
A MIDTOWN SKYSCRAPER...
...AND LET ME ASSURE THE GOOD--THE GREAT--PEOPLE OF NEW YORK I WILL DISCHARGE THE DUTIES OF THIS OFFICE WITH PASSION--
--THAT TOGETHER, WE WILL MAKE NEW YORK CITY THE SPEARHEAD OF THIS ERA OF NATIONAL RENEWAL!
WITH THAT, RANDOLPH WINSTON CHERRYH ACCEPTED THE MANDATE OF THE PEOPLE OF NEW YORK CITY--
--AND ENJOYED THE GREATEST LANDSLIDE VICTORY IN THE CITY'S HISTORY!
TAKK
VANESSA.
SHE'S ALIVE.
I HAVE HER.
WHAT DO YOU WANT?
CHERRYH.

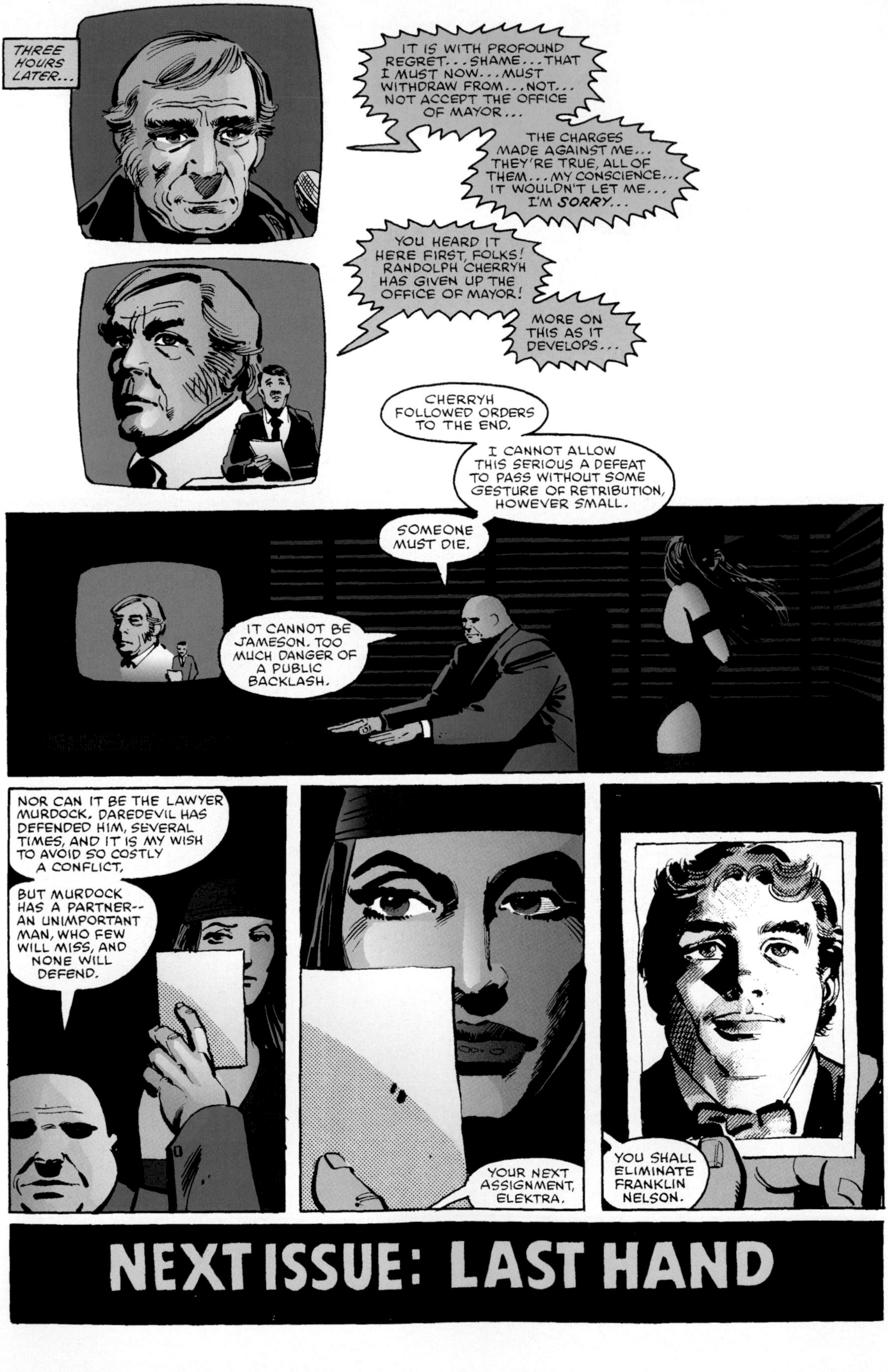
THREE HOURS LATER...
IT IS WITH PROFOUND REGRET... SHAME... THAT I MUST NOW... MUST WITHDRAW FROM... NOT... NOT ACCEPT THE OFFICE OF MAYOR...
THE CHARGES MADE AGAINST ME... THEY'RE TRUE, ALL OF THEM... MY CONSCIENCE... IT WOULDN'T LET ME... I'M SORRY...
YOU HEARD IT HERE FIRST, FOLKS! RANDOLPH CHERRYH HAS GIVEN UP THE OFFICE OF MAYOR!
MORE ON THIS AS IT DEVELOPS...
CHERRYH FOLLOWED ORDERS TO THE END.
I CANNOT ALLOW THIS SERIOUS A DEFEAT TO PASS WITHOUT SOME GESTURE OF RETRIBUTION, HOWEVER SMALL.
SOMEONE MUST DIE.
IT CANNOT BE JAMESON. TOO MUCH DANGER OF A PUBLIC BACKLASH.
NOR CAN IT BE THE LAWYER MURDOCK. DAREDEVIL HAS DEFENDED HIM, SEVERAL TIMES, AND IT IS MY WISH TO AVOID SO COSTLY A CONFLICT,
BUT MURDOCK HAS A PARTNER-- AN UNIMPORTANT MAN, WHO FEW WILL MISS, AND NONE WILL DEFEND.
YOUR NEXT ASSIGNMENT, ELEKTRA.
YOU SHALL ELIMINATE FRANKLIN NELSON.
NEXT ISSUE: LAST HAND

DAREDEVIL #181

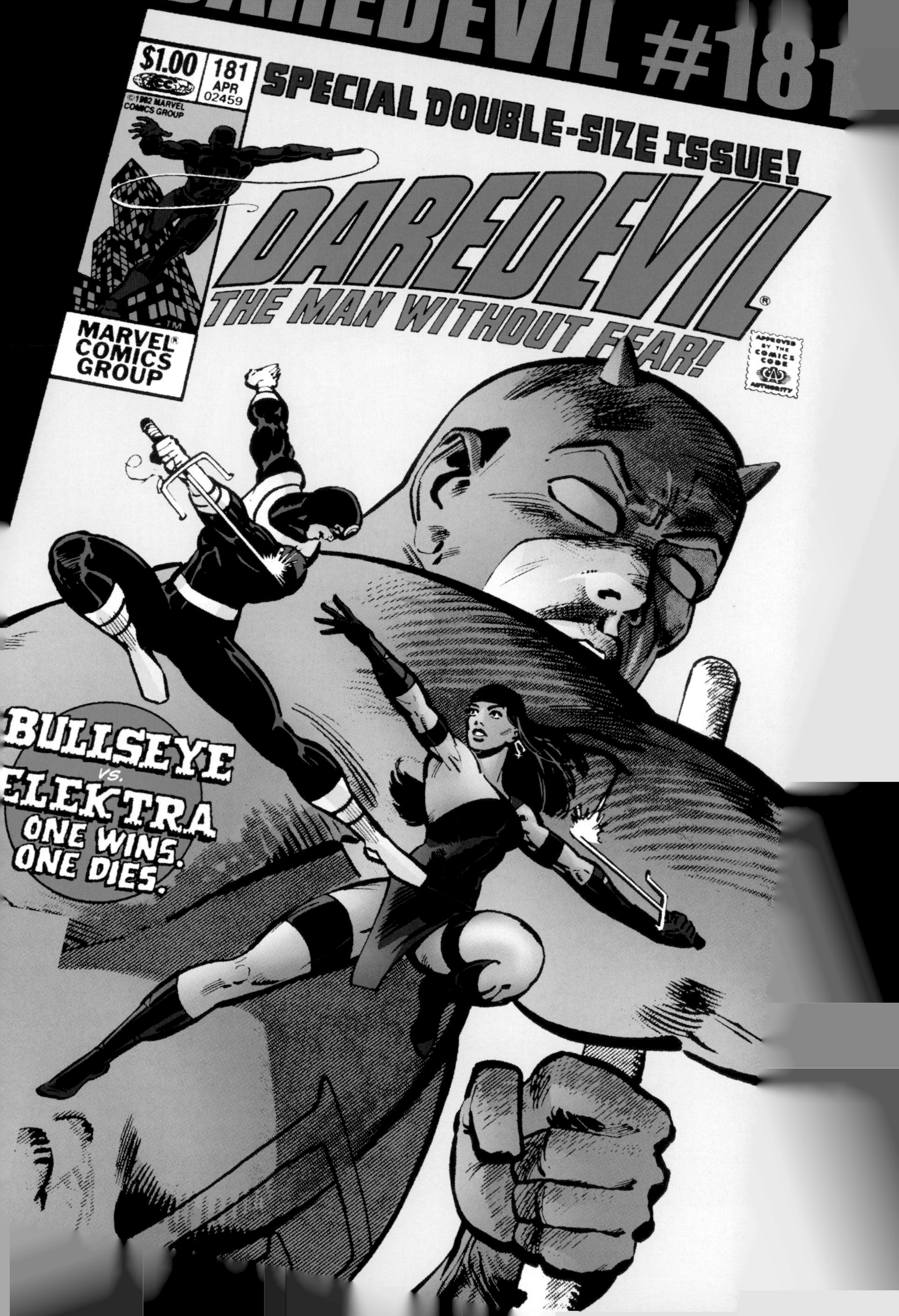

$1.00
181
APR
02459
©1982 MARVEL COMICS GROUP
SPECIAL DOUBLE-SIZE ISSUE!
DAREDEVIL
THE MAN WITHOUT FEAR!
MARVEL COMICS GROUP
APPROVED BY THE COMICS CODE AUTHORITY
BULLSEYE
VS.
ELEKTRA
ONE WINS.
ONE DIES.

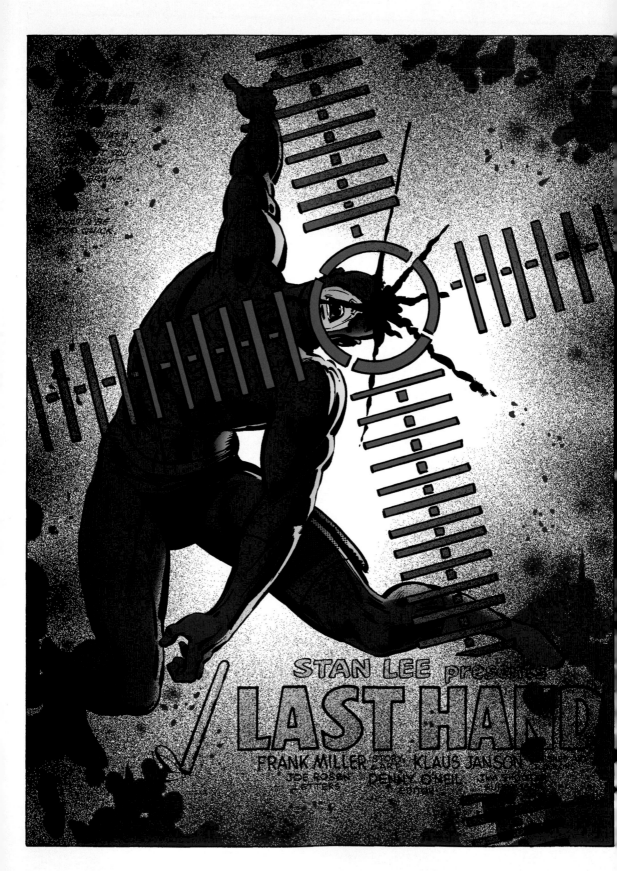

STAN LEE presents

/. LAST HAND

FRANK MILLER STORY KLAUS JANSON ART
JOE ROSEN LETTERS DENNY O'NEIL EDITOR

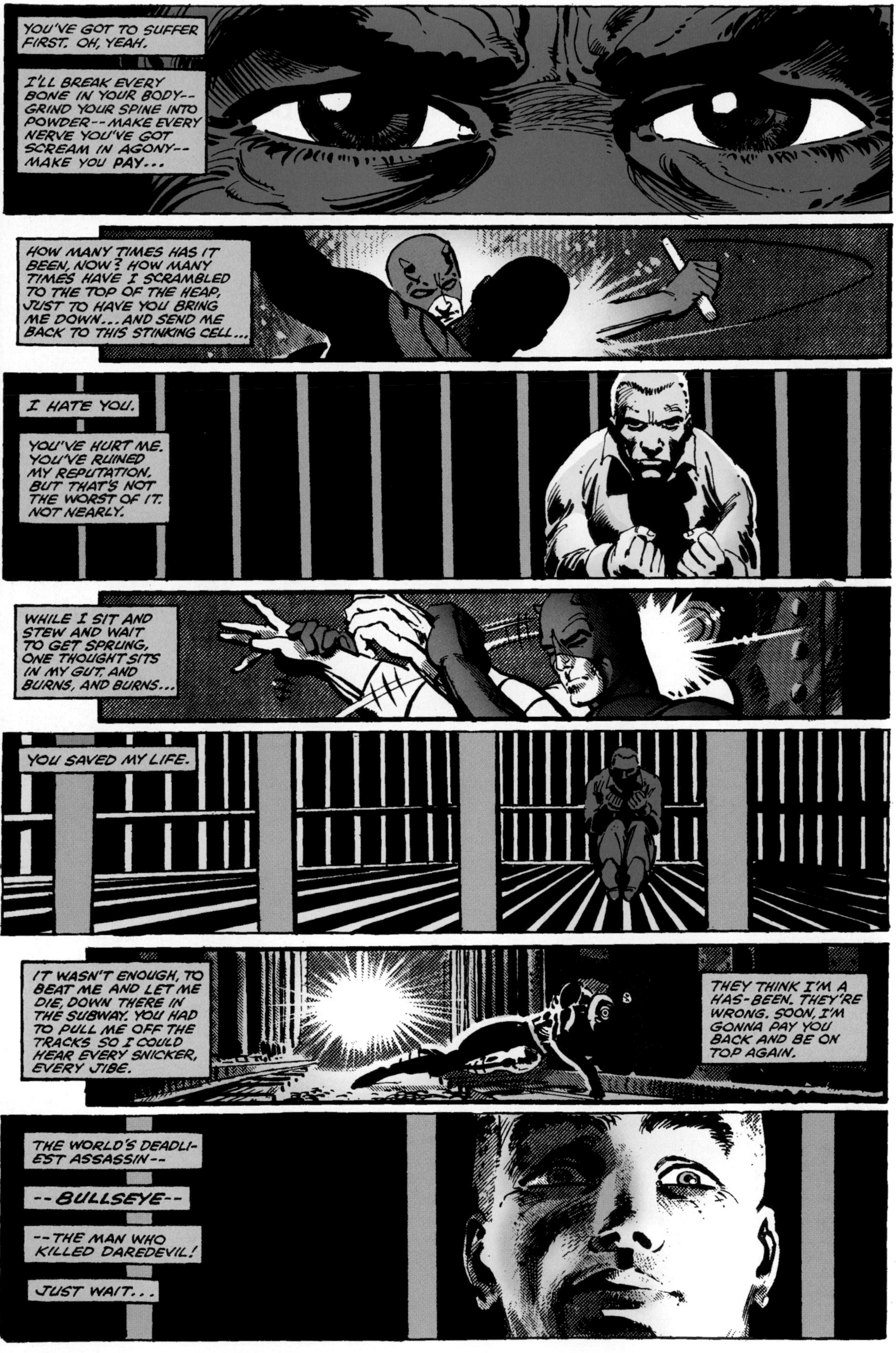
YOU'VE GOT TO SUFFER FIRST. OH, YEAH.
I'LL BREAK EVERY BONE IN YOUR BODY-- GRIND YOUR SPINE INTO POWDER--MAKE EVERY NERVE YOU'VE GOT SCREAM IN AGONY-- MAKE YOU PAY...
HOW MANY TIMES HAS IT BEEN, NOW? HOW MANY TIMES HAVE I SCRAMBLED TO THE TOP OF THE HEAP, JUST TO HAVE YOU BRING ME DOWN... AND SEND ME BACK TO THIS STINKING CELL...
I HATE YOU.
YOU'VE HURT ME. YOU'VE RUINED MY REPUTATION. BUT THAT'S NOT THE WORST OF IT. NOT NEARLY.
WHILE I SIT AND STEW AND WAIT TO GET SPRUNG, ONE THOUGHT SITS IN MY GUT, AND BURNS, AND BURNS...
YOU SAVED MY LIFE.
IT WASN'T ENOUGH, TO BEAT ME AND LET ME DIE, DOWN THERE IN THE SUBWAY. YOU HAD TO PULL ME OFF THE TRACKS SO I COULD HEAR EVERY SNICKER, EVERY JIBE.
THEY THINK I'M A HAS-BEEN. THEY'RE WRONG. SOON, I'M GONNA PAY YOU BACK AND BE ON TOP AGAIN.
THE WORLD'S DEADLIEST ASSASSIN--
--BULLSEYE--
--THE MAN WHO KILLED DAREDEVIL!
JUST WAIT...

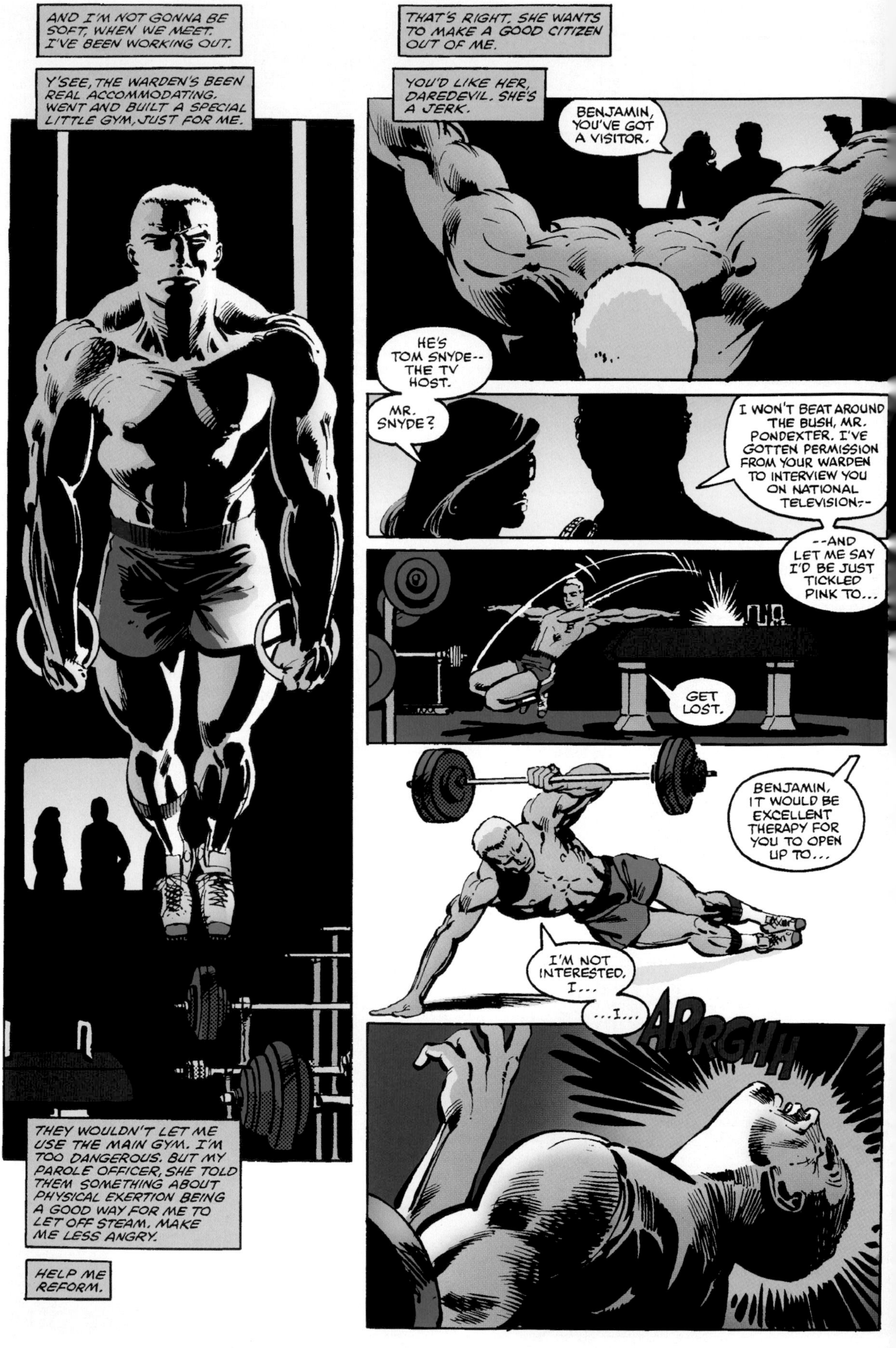
AND I'M NOT GONNA BE SOFT, WHEN WE MEET. I'VE BEEN WORKING OUT.
Y'SEE, THE WARDEN'S BEEN REAL ACCOMMODATING. WENT AND BUILT A SPECIAL LITTLE GYM, JUST FOR ME.
THEY WOULDN'T LET ME USE THE MAIN GYM. I'M TOO DANGEROUS. BUT MY PAROLE OFFICER, SHE TOLD THEM SOMETHING ABOUT PHYSICAL EXERTION BEING A GOOD WAY FOR ME TO LET OFF STEAM. MAKE ME LESS ANGRY.
HELP ME REFORM.
THAT'S RIGHT. SHE WANTS TO MAKE A GOOD CITIZEN OUT OF ME.
YOU'D LIKE HER, DAREDEVIL. SHE'S A JERK.
BENJAMIN, YOU'VE GOT A VISITOR.
HE'S TOM SNYDE-- THE TV HOST.
MR. SNYDE?
I WON'T BEAT AROUND THE BUSH, MR. PONDEXTER. I'VE GOTTEN PERMISSION FROM YOUR WARDEN TO INTERVIEW YOU ON NATIONAL TELEVISION--
--AND LET ME SAY I'D BE JUST TICKLED PINK TO...
GET LOST.
BENJAMIN, IT WOULD BE EXCELLENT THERAPY FOR YOU TO OPEN UP TO...
I'M NOT INTERESTED. I...
...I...
ARRGHH

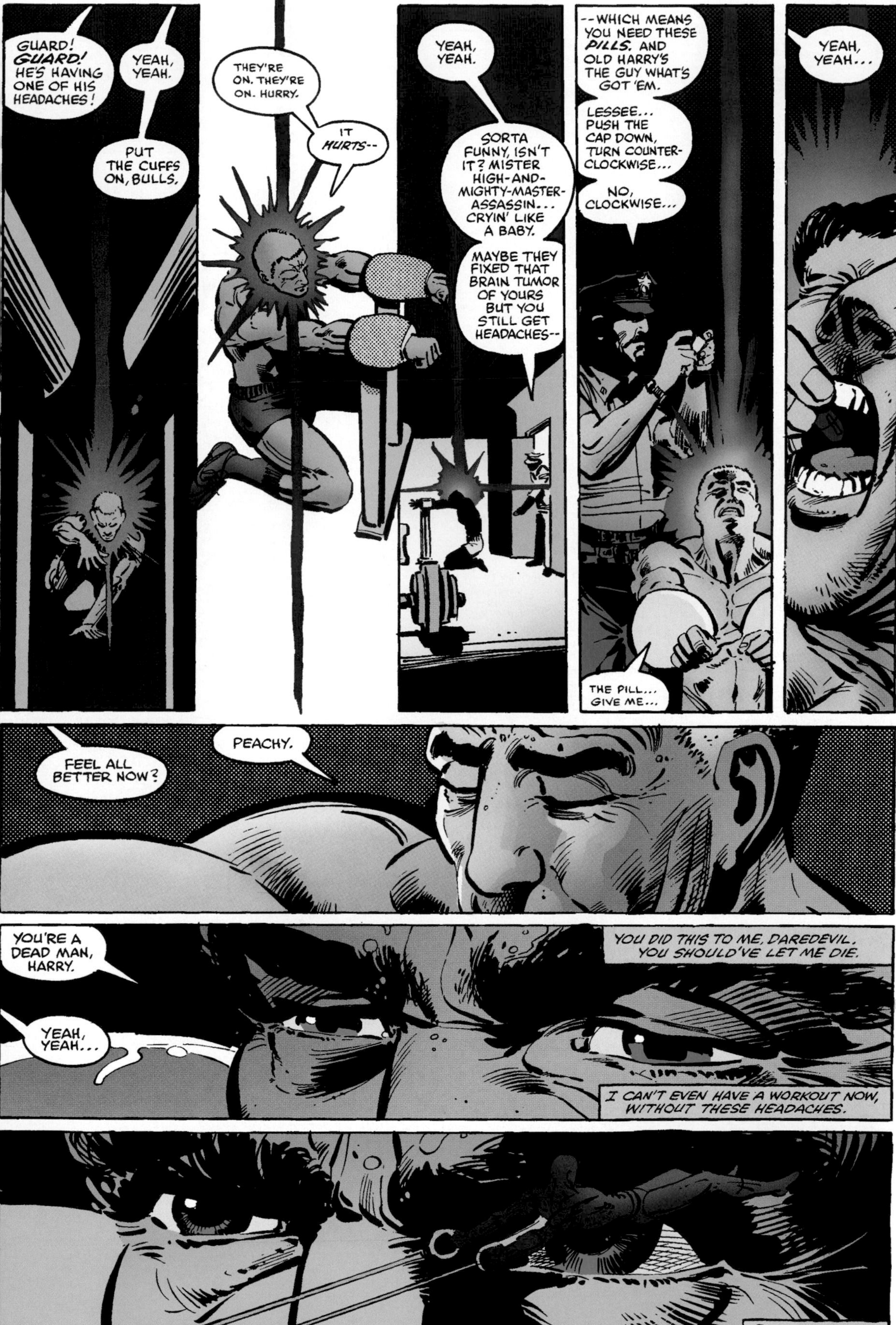
GUARD! GUARD! HE'S HAVING ONE OF HIS HEADACHES!
YEAH, YEAH.
PUT THE CUFFS ON, BULLS.
THEY'RE ON. THEY'RE ON. HURRY.
IT HURTS--
YEAH, YEAH.
SORTA FUNNY, ISN'T IT? MISTER HIGH-AND-MIGHTY-MASTER-ASSASSIN... CRYIN' LIKE A BABY.
MAYBE THEY FIXED THAT BRAIN TUMOR OF YOURS BUT YOU STILL GET HEADACHES--
--WHICH MEANS YOU NEED THESE PILLS. AND OLD HARRY'S THE GUY WHAT'S GOT 'EM.
LESSEE... PUSH THE CAP DOWN, TURN COUNTER-CLOCKWISE...
NO, CLOCKWISE...
THE PILL... GIVE ME...
YEAH, YEAH...
FEEL ALL BETTER NOW?
PEACHY.
YOU'RE A DEAD MAN, HARRY.
YEAH, YEAH...
YOU DID THIS TO ME, DAREDEVIL. YOU SHOULD'VE LET ME DIE.
I CAN'T EVEN HAVE A WORKOUT NOW, WITHOUT THESE HEADACHES.
BUT YOU CAN...

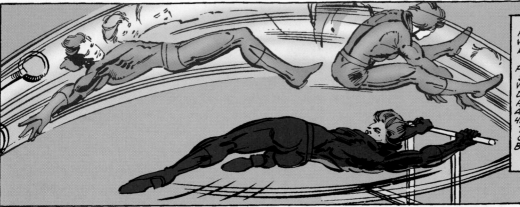

YOU'RE PROBABLY WORKING OUT RIGHT NOW, IN SOME PRIVATE GYM, SOMEWHERE WHERE YOU DON'T HAVE HEADACHES AND YOU DON'T HAVE TO LISTEN TO SNOTTY GUARDS OR BLEEDING HEART PAROLE OFFICERS.

PROBABLY PRACTICING THAT CRAZY, ECLECTIC FIGHTING STYLE OF YOURS... POLISHING UP EVERY KARATE BLOW YOU'VE USED ON ME.

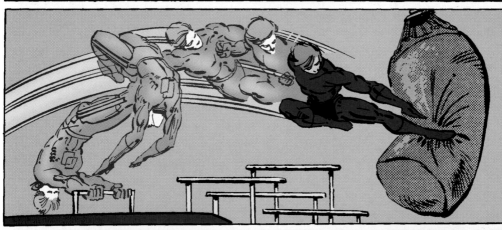

YOU JUST KEEP ON PRACTICING, DAREDEVIL. YOU PRACTICE LONG AND HARD AND MAYBE YOU'LL LAST AN EXTRA TEN MINUTES WHEN I CATCH UP WITH YOU.

BUT YOU'LL DIE JUST THE SAME.

JUST WAIT...

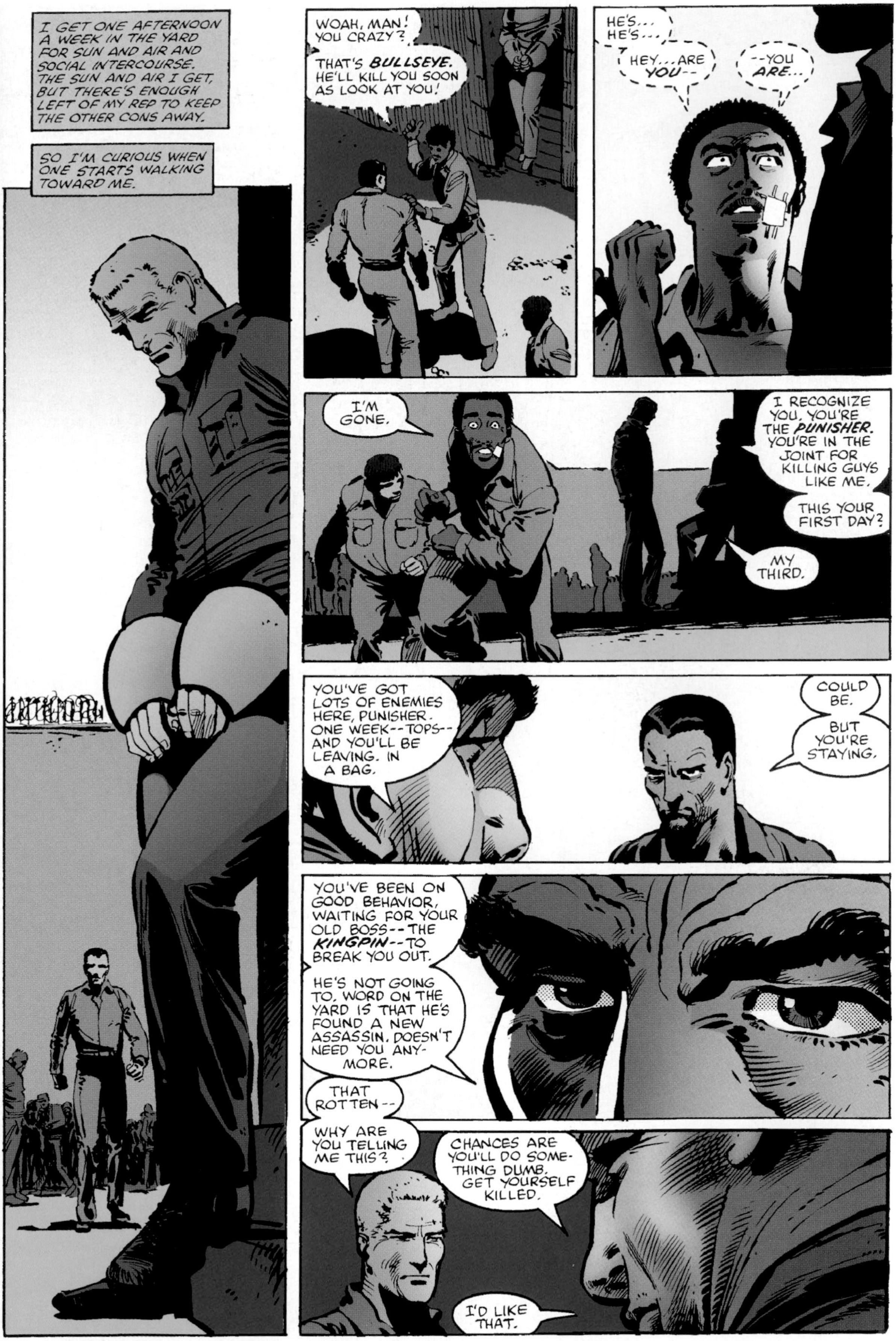

I GET ONE AFTERNOON A WEEK IN THE YARD FOR SUN AND AIR AND SOCIAL INTERCOURSE. THE SUN AND AIR I GET, BUT THERE'S ENOUGH LEFT OF MY REP TO KEEP THE OTHER CONS AWAY.
SO I'M CURIOUS WHEN ONE STARTS WALKING TOWARD ME.
WOAH, MAN! YOU CRAZY?
THAT'S BULLSEYE. HE'LL KILL YOU SOON AS LOOK AT YOU!
HE'S... HE'S...
HEY...ARE YOU--
--YOU ARE...
I'M GONE.
I RECOGNIZE YOU, YOU'RE THE PUNISHER. YOU'RE IN THE JOINT FOR KILLING GUYS LIKE ME.
THIS YOUR FIRST DAY?
MY THIRD.
YOU'VE GOT LOTS OF ENEMIES HERE, PUNISHER. ONE WEEK--TOPS--AND YOU'LL BE LEAVING. IN A BAG.
COULD BE.
BUT YOU'RE STAYING.
YOU'VE BEEN ON GOOD BEHAVIOR, WAITING FOR YOUR OLD BOSS--THE KINGPIN--TO BREAK YOU OUT.
HE'S NOT GOING TO. WORD ON THE YARD IS THAT HE'S FOUND A NEW ASSASSIN. DOESN'T NEED YOU ANY-MORE.
THAT ROTTEN--
WHY ARE YOU TELLING ME THIS?
CHANCES ARE YOU'LL DO SOME-THING DUMB. GET YOURSELF KILLED.
I'D LIKE THAT.

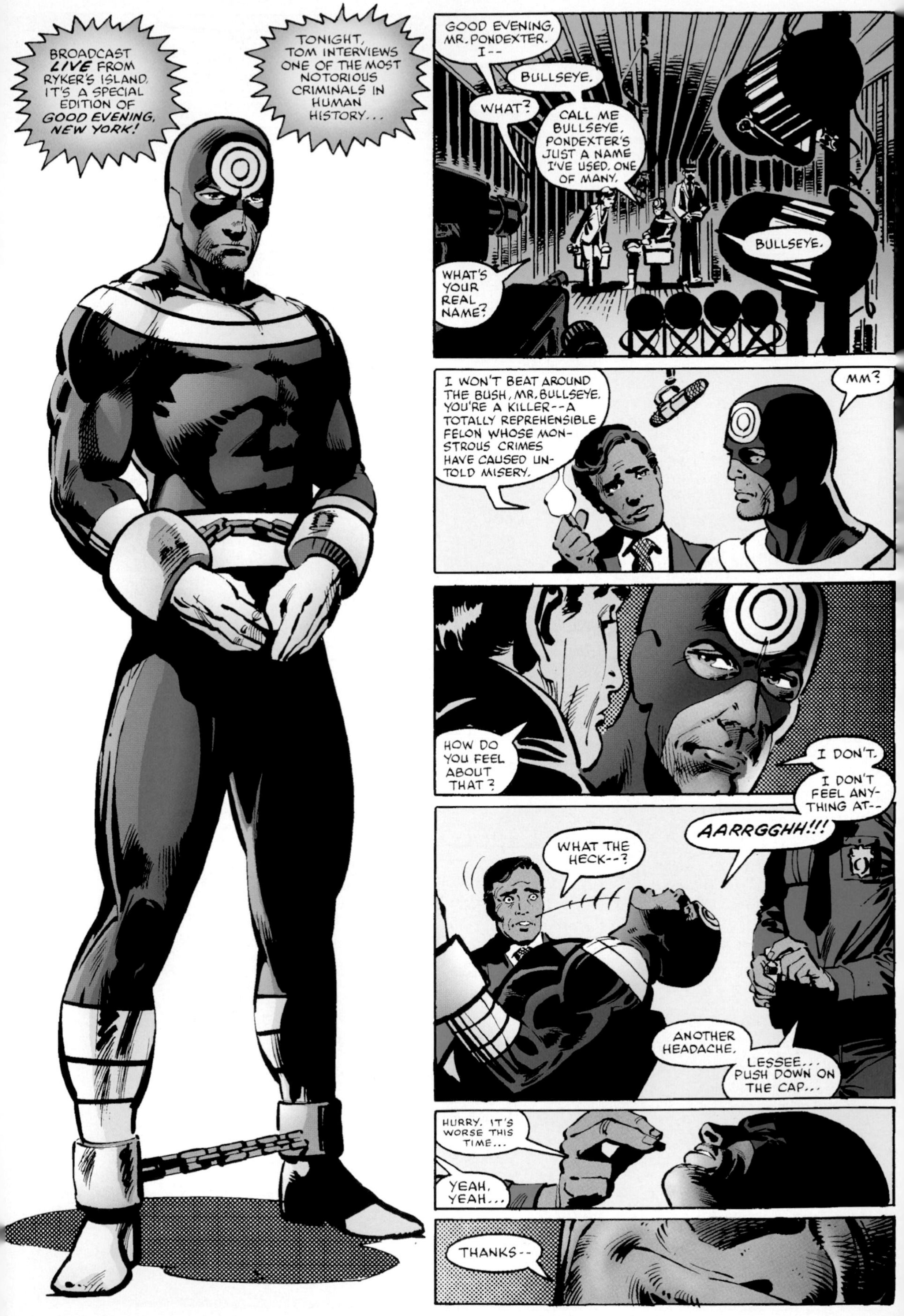
BROADCAST LIVE FROM RYKER'S ISLAND, IT'S A SPECIAL EDITION OF GOOD EVENING, NEW YORK!
TONIGHT, TOM INTERVIEWS ONE OF THE MOST NOTORIOUS CRIMINALS IN HUMAN HISTORY...
GOOD EVENING, MR. PONDEXTER. I--
BULLSEYE.
WHAT?
CALL ME BULLSEYE. PONDEXTER'S JUST A NAME I'VE USED. ONE OF MANY.
WHAT'S YOUR REAL NAME?
BULLSEYE.
I WON'T BEAT AROUND THE BUSH, MR. BULLSEYE. YOU'RE A KILLER--A TOTALLY REPREHENSIBLE FELON WHOSE MONSTROUS CRIMES HAVE CAUSED UNTOLD MISERY.
MM?
HOW DO YOU FEEL ABOUT THAT?
I DON'T.
I DON'T FEEL ANYTHING AT--
AARRGGHH!!!
WHAT THE HECK--?
ANOTHER HEADACHE.
LESSEE... PUSH DOWN ON THE CAP...
HURRY. IT'S WORSE THIS TIME...
YEAH, YEAH...
THANKS--

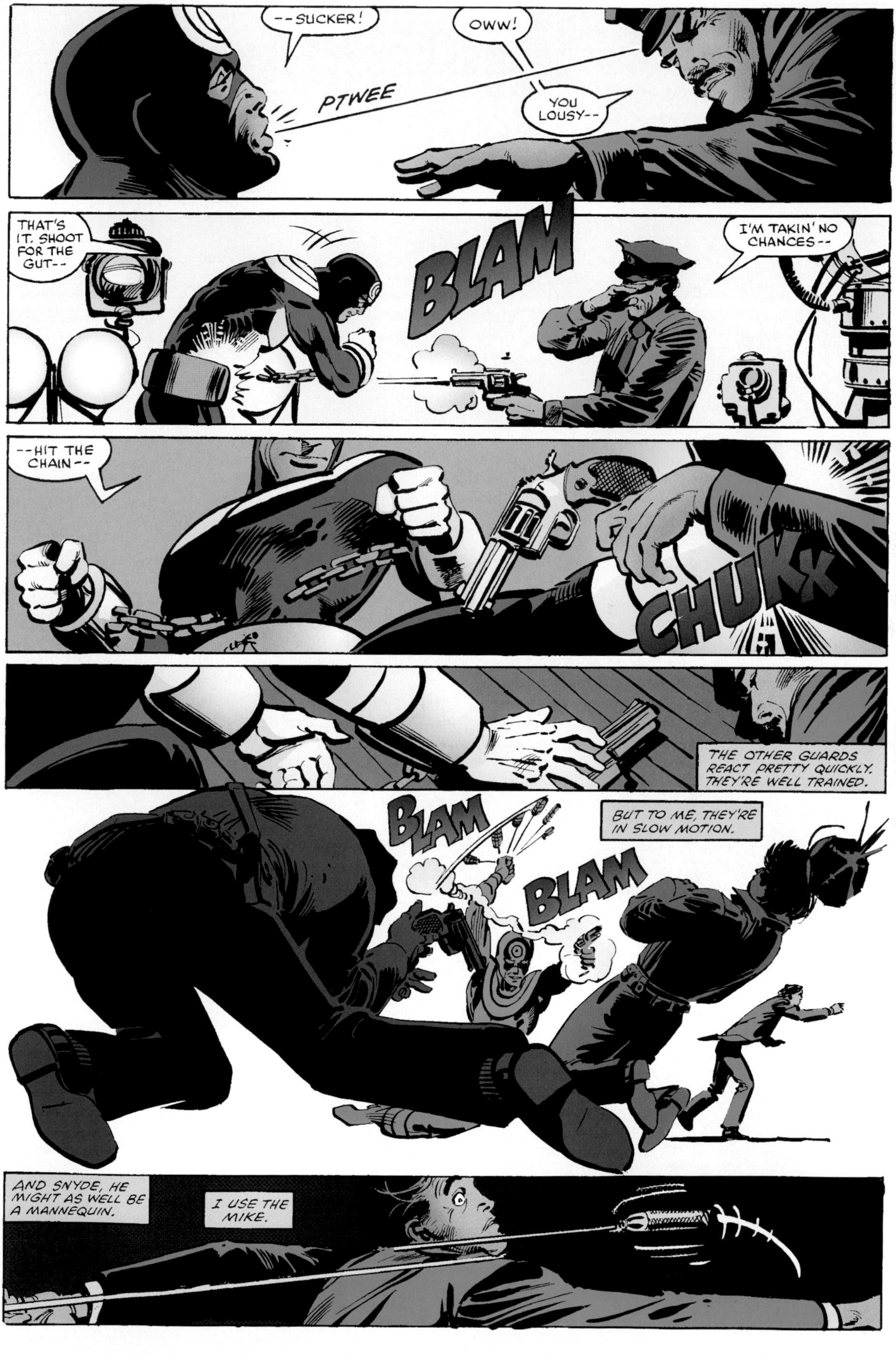
--SUCKER!
OWW!
PTWEE
YOU LOUSY--
THAT'S IT. SHOOT FOR THE GUT--
BLAM
I'M TAKIN' NO CHANCES--
--HIT THE CHAIN--
CHUKK
THE OTHER GUARDS REACT PRETTY QUICKLY. THEY'RE WELL TRAINED.
BLAM
BUT TO ME, THEY'RE IN SLOW MOTION.
BLAM
AND SNYDE, HE MIGHT AS WELL BE A MANNEQUIN.
I USE THE MIKE.

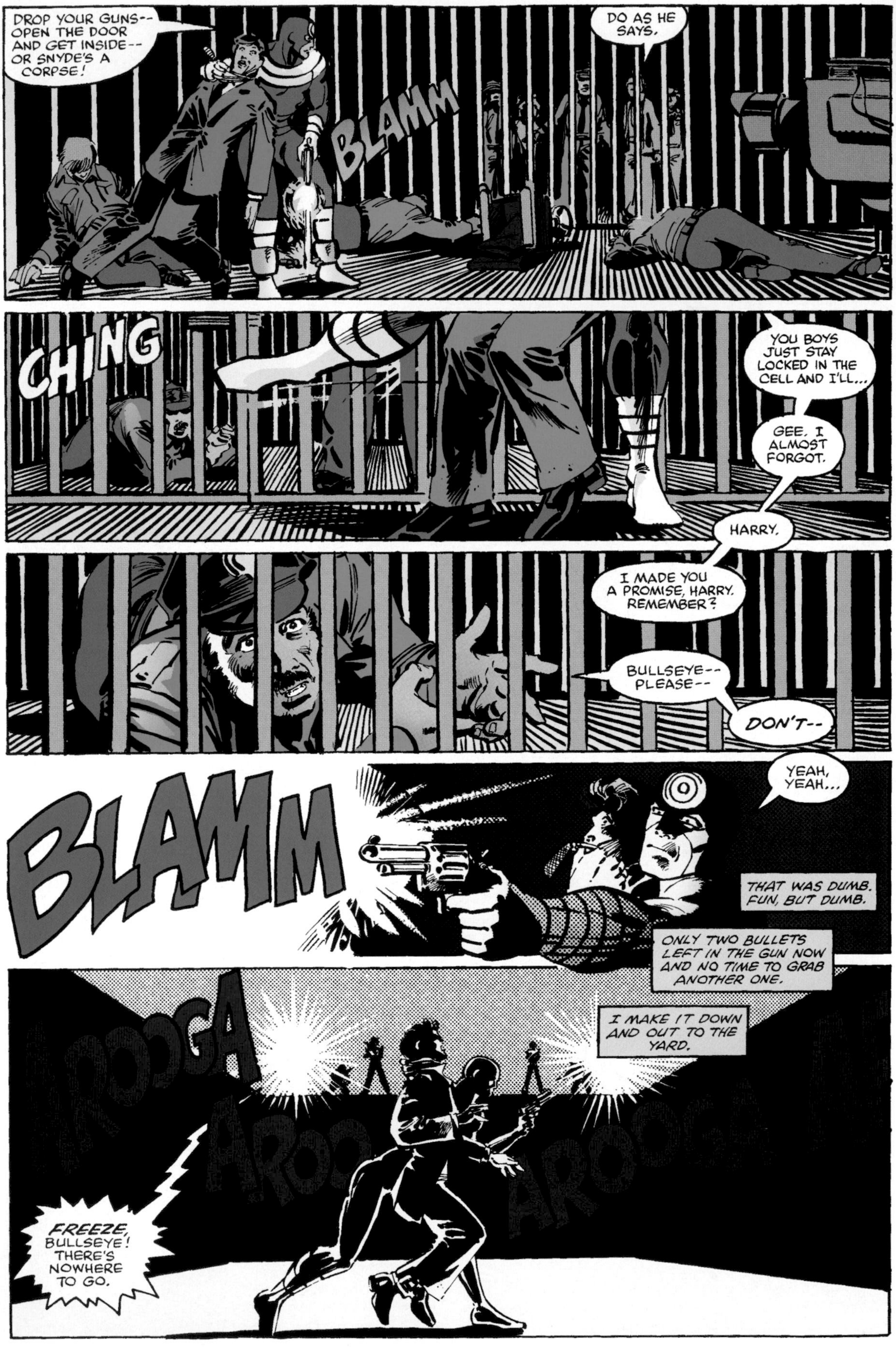
DROP YOUR GUNS-- OPEN THE DOOR AND GET INSIDE-- OR SNYDE'S A CORPSE!
DO AS HE SAYS.
BLAMM
CHING
YOU BOYS JUST STAY LOCKED IN THE CELL AND I'LL...
GEE. I ALMOST FORGOT.
HARRY.
I MADE YOU A PROMISE, HARRY. REMEMBER?
BULLSEYE-- PLEASE--
DON'T--
BLAMM
YEAH, YEAH...
THAT WAS DUMB. FUN, BUT DUMB.
ONLY TWO BULLETS LEFT IN THE GUN NOW AND NO TIME TO GRAB ANOTHER ONE.
I MAKE IT DOWN AND OUT TO THE YARD.
AROOGA
AROOGA
AROOGA
FREEZE, BULLSEYE! THERE'S NOWHERE TO GO.

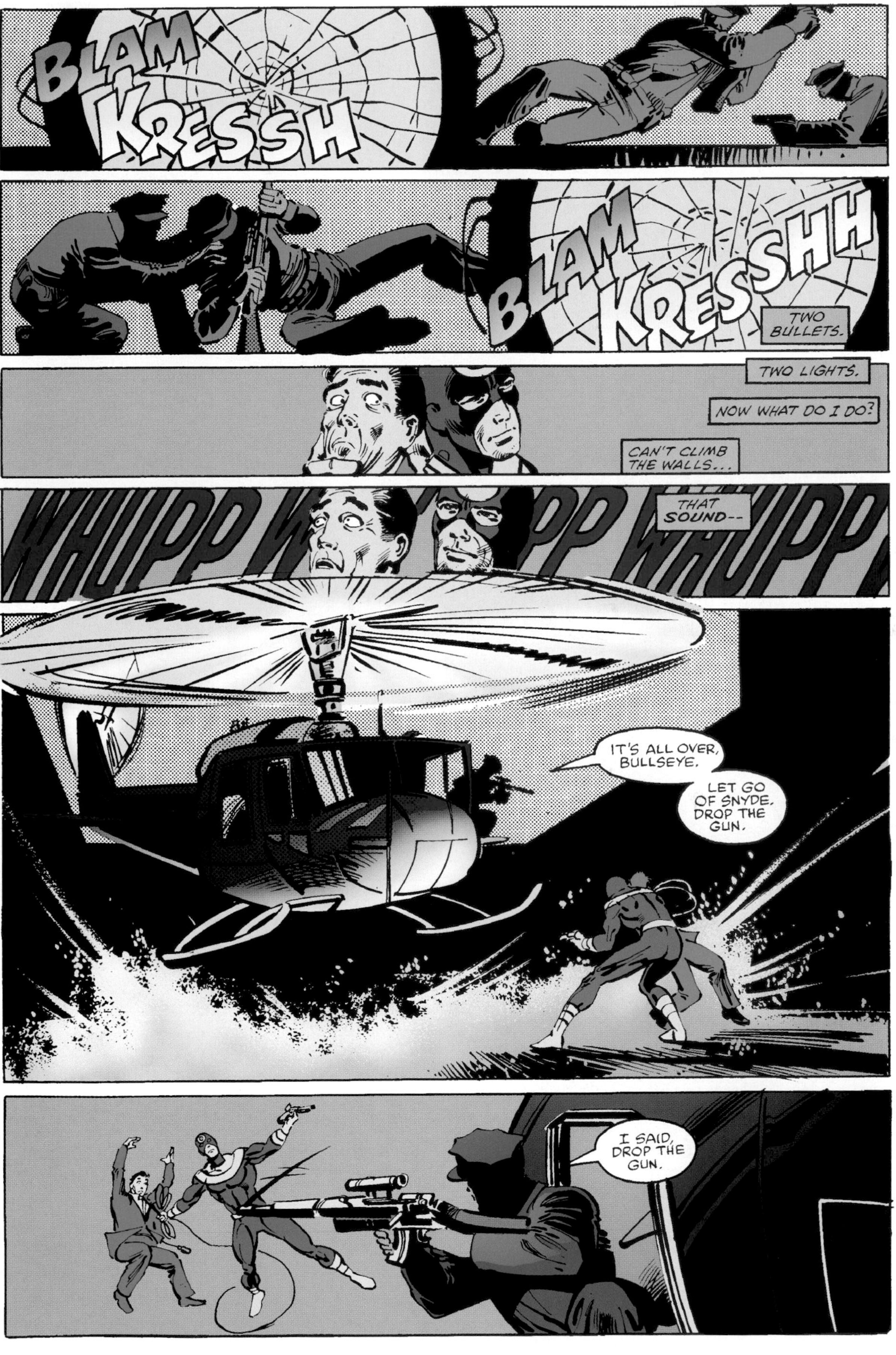
BLAM
KRESSH
BLAM
KRESSHH
TWO BULLETS.
TWO LIGHTS.
NOW WHAT DO I DO?
CAN'T CLIMB THE WALLS...
WHUPP
THAT SOUND--
PP WHUPP
IT'S ALL OVER, BULLSEYE.
LET GO OF SNYDE. DROP THE GUN.
I SAID, DROP THE GUN.

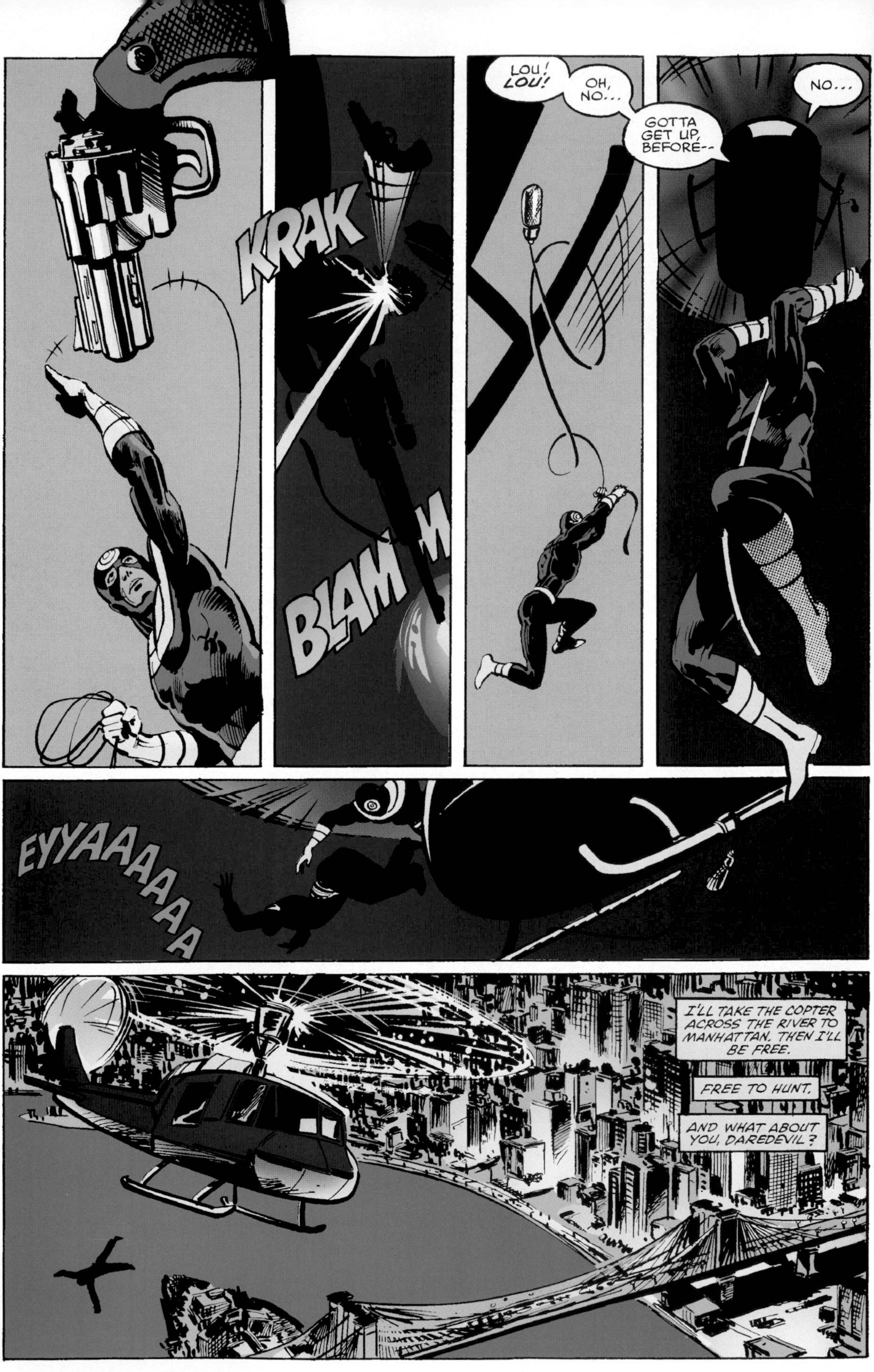
KRAK
BLAM
LOU! LOU!
OH, NO...
GOTTA GET UP, BEFORE--
NO...
EYYAAAAAAA
I'LL TAKE THE COPTER ACROSS THE RIVER TO MANHATTAN. THEN I'LL BE FREE.
FREE TO HUNT.
AND WHAT ABOUT YOU, DAREDEVIL?

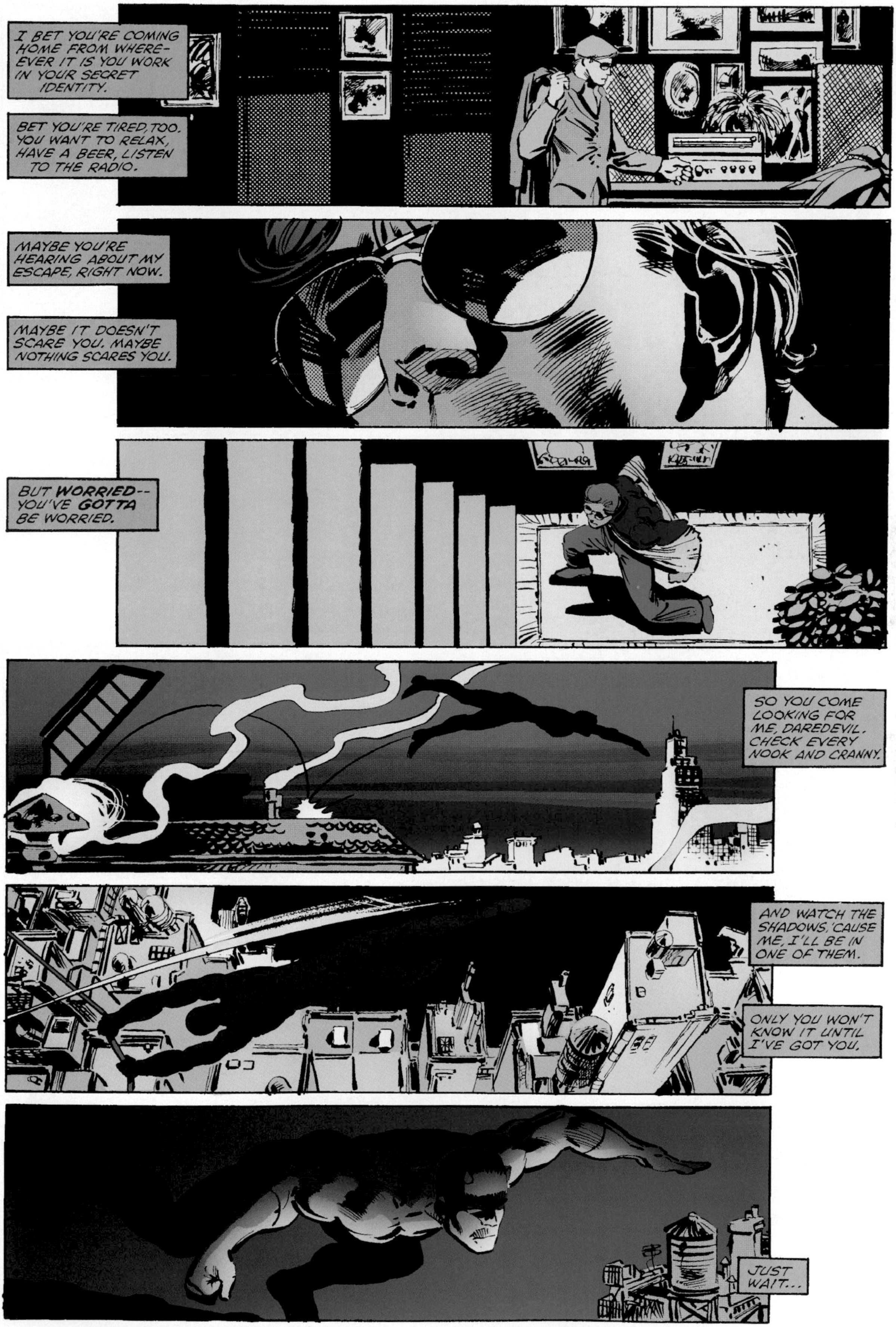
I BET YOU'RE COMING HOME FROM WHERE-EVER IT IS YOU WORK IN YOUR SECRET IDENTITY.
BET YOU'RE TIRED, TOO. YOU WANT TO RELAX, HAVE A BEER, LISTEN TO THE RADIO.
MAYBE YOU'RE HEARING ABOUT MY ESCAPE, RIGHT NOW.
MAYBE IT DOESN'T SCARE YOU. MAYBE NOTHING SCARES YOU.
BUT **WORRIED**-- YOU'VE **GOTTA** BE WORRIED.
SO YOU COME LOOKING FOR ME, DAREDEVIL. CHECK EVERY NOOK AND CRANNY.
AND WATCH THE SHADOWS. 'CAUSE ME, I'LL BE IN ONE OF THEM.
ONLY YOU WON'T KNOW IT UNTIL I'VE GOT YOU.
JUST WAIT...

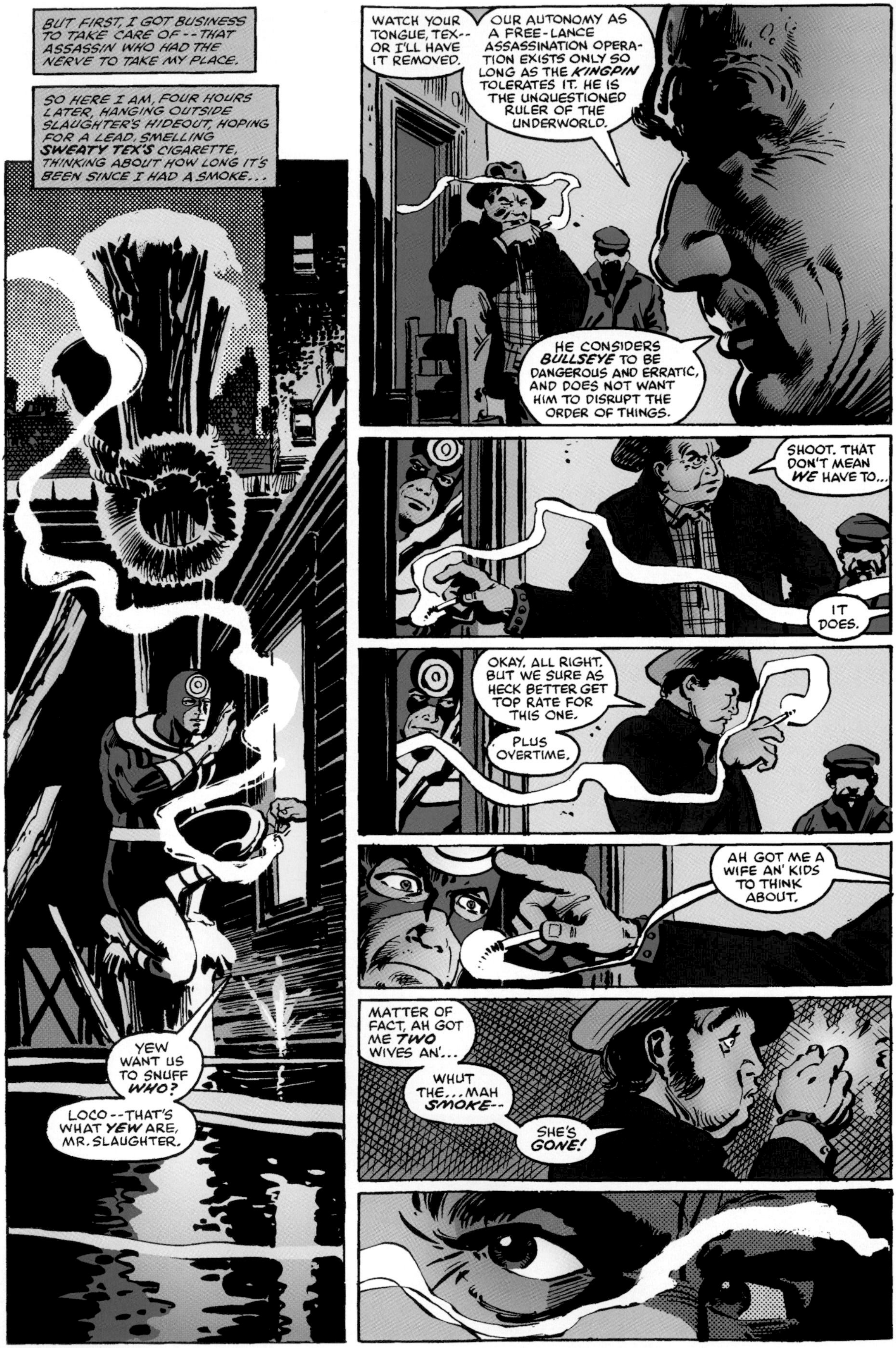
BUT FIRST, I GOT BUSINESS TO TAKE CARE OF--THAT ASSASSIN WHO HAD THE NERVE TO TAKE MY PLACE.
SO HERE I AM, FOUR HOURS LATER, HANGING OUTSIDE SLAUGHTER'S HIDEOUT, HOPING FOR A LEAD, SMELLING SWEATY TEX'S CIGARETTE, THINKING ABOUT HOW LONG IT'S BEEN SINCE I HAD A SMOKE...
YEW WANT US TO SNUFF WHO?
LOCO--THAT'S WHAT YEW ARE, MR. SLAUGHTER.
WATCH YOUR TONGUE, TEX--OR I'LL HAVE IT REMOVED.
OUR AUTONOMY AS A FREE-LANCE ASSASSINATION OPERATION EXISTS ONLY SO LONG AS THE KINGPIN TOLERATES IT. HE IS THE UNQUESTIONED RULER OF THE UNDERWORLD.
HE CONSIDERS BULLSEYE TO BE DANGEROUS AND ERRATIC, AND DOES NOT WANT HIM TO DISRUPT THE ORDER OF THINGS.
SHOOT. THAT DON'T MEAN WE HAVE TO...
IT DOES.
OKAY, ALL RIGHT. BUT WE SURE AS HECK BETTER GET TOP RATE FOR THIS ONE.
PLUS OVERTIME.
AH GOT ME A WIFE AN' KIDS TO THINK ABOUT.
MATTER OF FACT, AH GOT ME TWO WIVES AN'...
WHUT THE...MAH SMOKE--
SHE'S GONE!

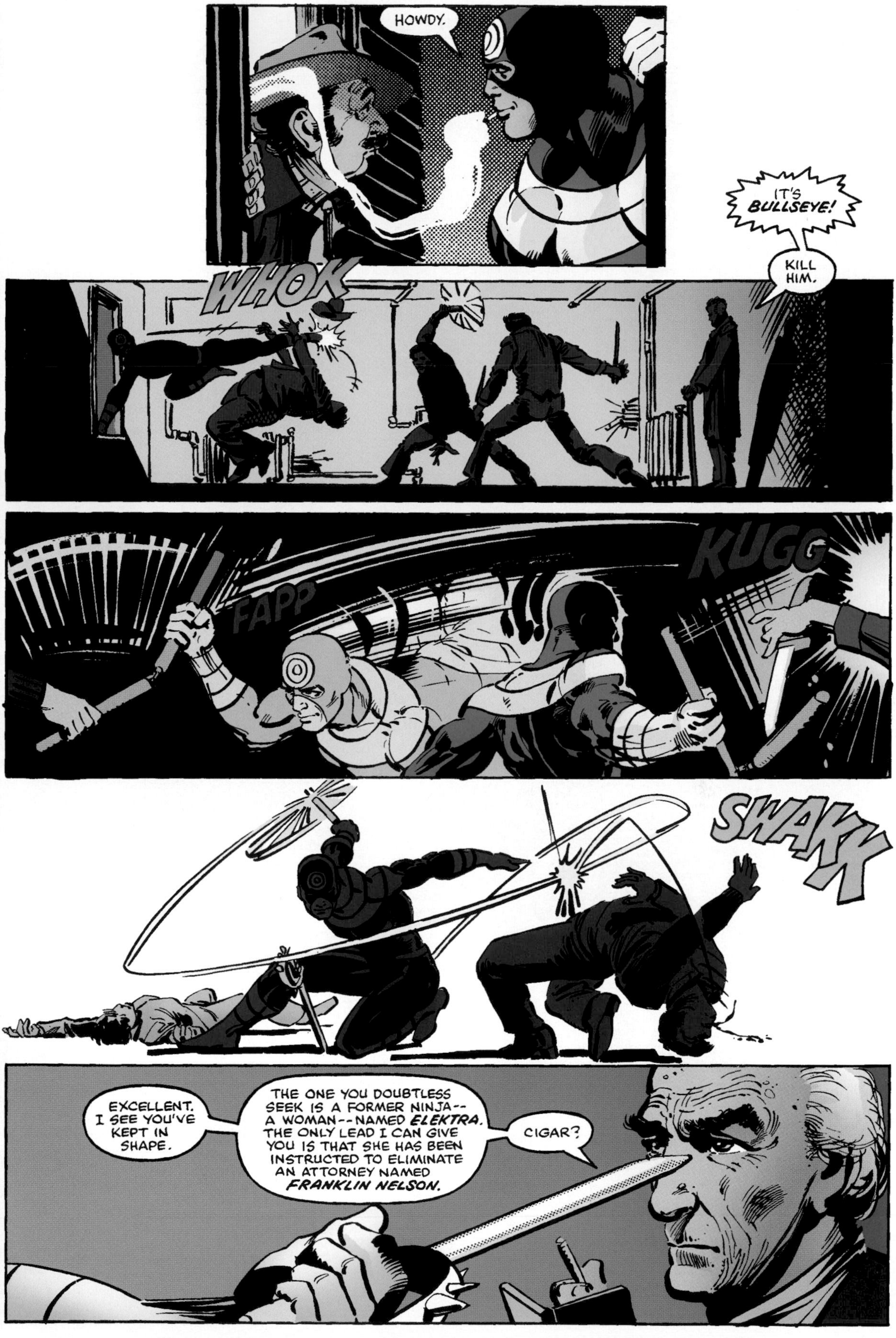
HOWDY.
IT'S BULLSEYE!
KILL HIM.
WHOK
KUGG
FAPP
SWAKK
EXCELLENT. I SEE YOU'VE KEPT IN SHAPE.
THE ONE YOU DOUBTLESS SEEK IS A FORMER NINJA-- A WOMAN--NAMED ELEKTRA. THE ONLY LEAD I CAN GIVE YOU IS THAT SHE HAS BEEN INSTRUCTED TO ELIMINATE AN ATTORNEY NAMED FRANKLIN NELSON.
CIGAR?

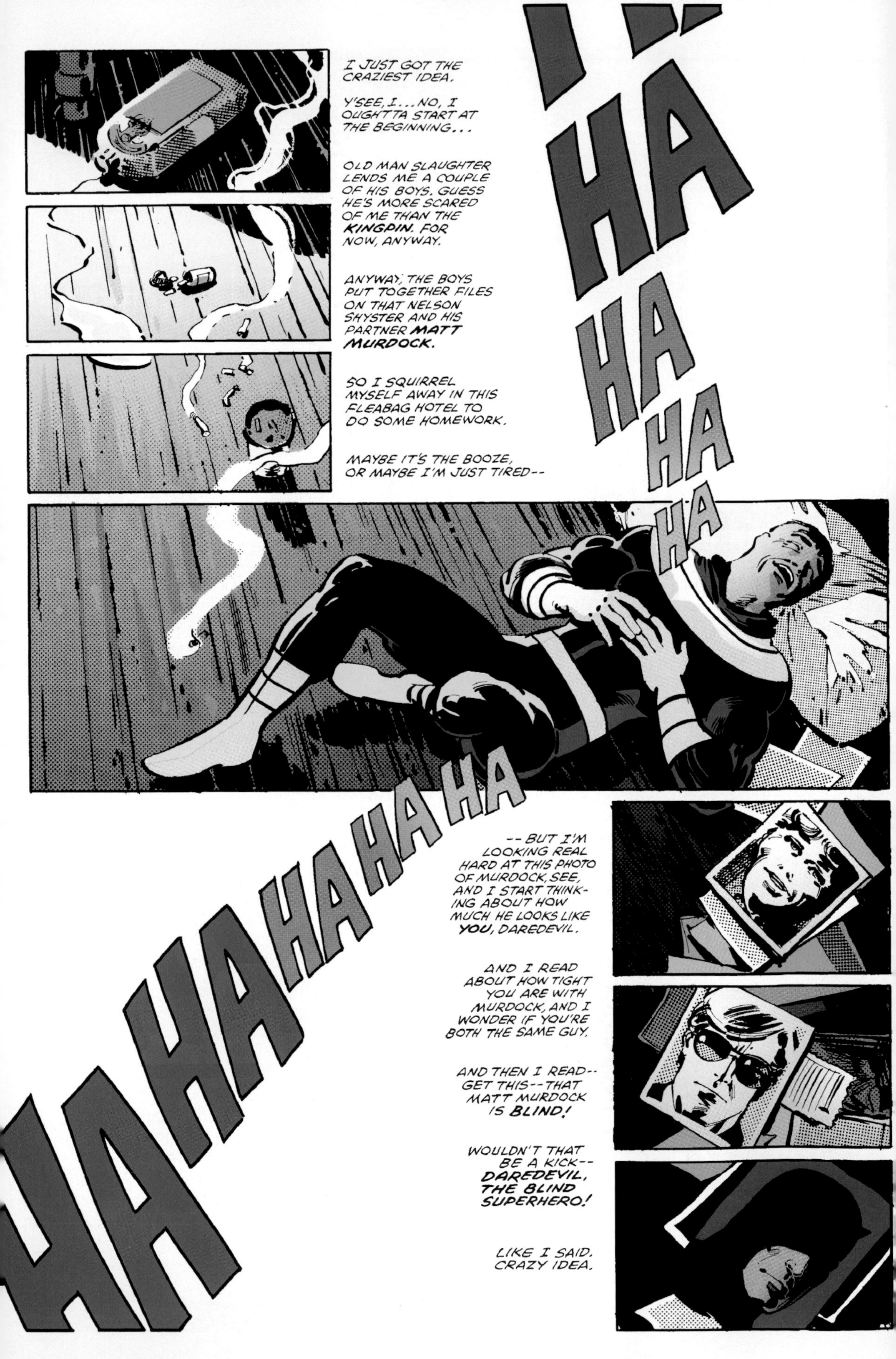
I JUST GOT THE CRAZIEST IDEA.
Y'SEE, I... NO, I OUGHTTA START AT THE BEGINNING...
OLD MAN SLAUGHTER LENDS ME A COUPLE OF HIS BOYS. GUESS HE'S MORE SCARED OF ME THAN THE KINGPIN. FOR NOW, ANYWAY.
ANYWAY, THE BOYS PUT TOGETHER FILES ON THAT NELSON SHYSTER AND HIS PARTNER MATT MURDOCK.
SO I SQUIRREL MYSELF AWAY IN THIS FLEABAG HOTEL TO DO SOME HOMEWORK.
MAYBE IT'S THE BOOZE, OR MAYBE I'M JUST TIRED--
HA HA HA HA HA HA
HA HA HA HA HA HA HA HA
--BUT I'M LOOKING REAL HARD AT THIS PHOTO OF MURDOCK, SEE, AND I START THINKING ABOUT HOW MUCH HE LOOKS LIKE YOU, DAREDEVIL.
AND I READ ABOUT HOW TIGHT YOU ARE WITH MURDOCK, AND I WONDER IF YOU'RE BOTH THE SAME GUY.
AND THEN I READ-- GET THIS--THAT MATT MURDOCK IS BLIND!
WOULDN'T THAT BE A KICK-- DAREDEVIL, THE BLIND SUPERHERO!
LIKE I SAID. CRAZY IDEA.

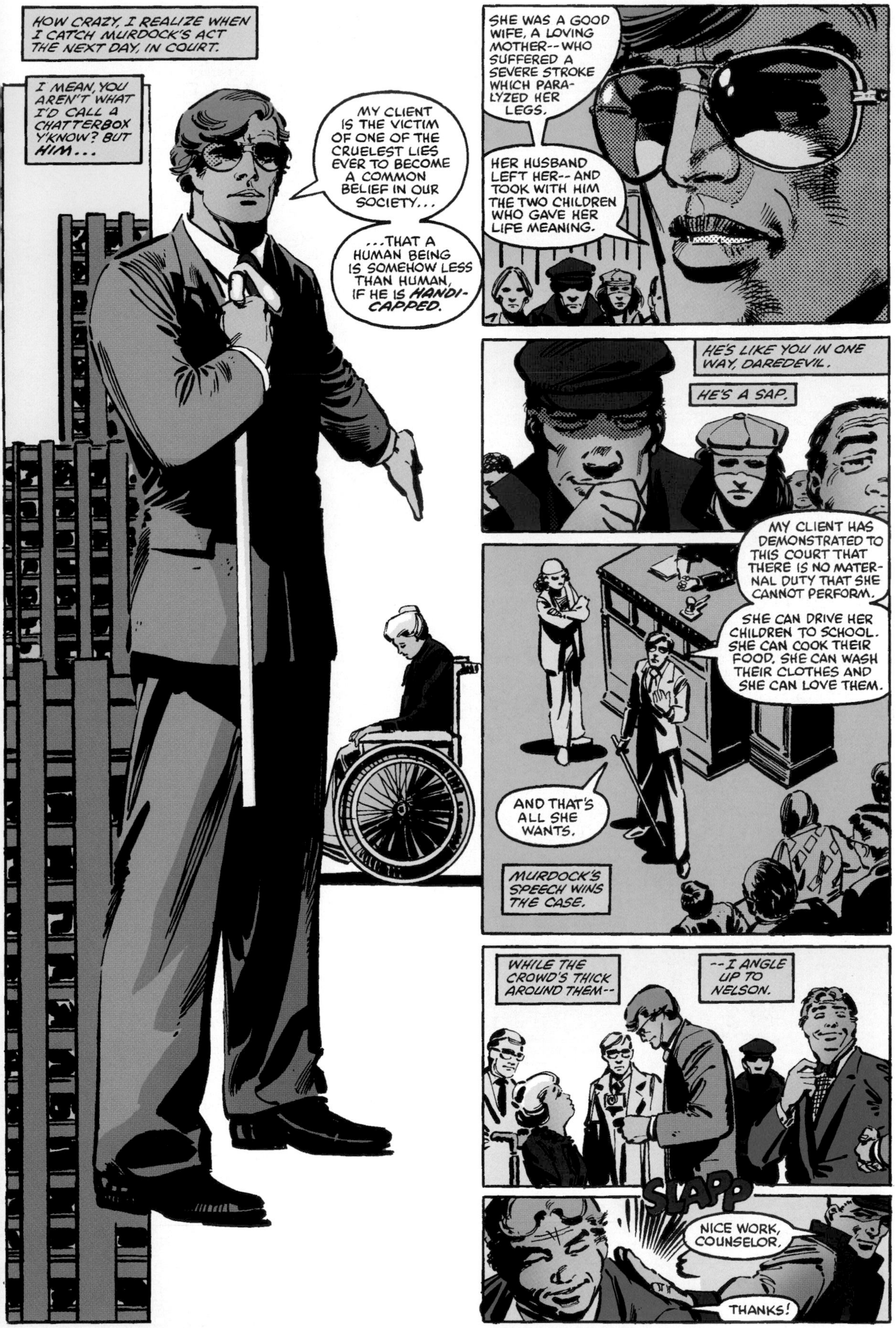
HOW CRAZY, I REALIZE WHEN I CATCH MURDOCK'S ACT THE NEXT DAY, IN COURT.
I MEAN, YOU AREN'T WHAT I'D CALL A CHATTERBOX Y'KNOW? BUT HIM...
MY CLIENT IS THE VICTIM OF ONE OF THE CRUELEST LIES EVER TO BECOME A COMMON BELIEF IN OUR SOCIETY...
...THAT A HUMAN BEING IS SOMEHOW LESS THAN HUMAN, IF HE IS HANDI-CAPPED.
SHE WAS A GOOD WIFE, A LOVING MOTHER--WHO SUFFERED A SEVERE STROKE WHICH PARA-LYZED HER LEGS.
HER HUSBAND LEFT HER--AND TOOK WITH HIM THE TWO CHILDREN WHO GAVE HER LIFE MEANING.
HE'S LIKE YOU IN ONE WAY, DAREDEVIL.
HE'S A SAP.
MY CLIENT HAS DEMONSTRATED TO THIS COURT THAT THERE IS NO MATER-NAL DUTY THAT SHE CANNOT PERFORM.
SHE CAN DRIVE HER CHILDREN TO SCHOOL. SHE CAN COOK THEIR FOOD, SHE CAN WASH THEIR CLOTHES AND SHE CAN LOVE THEM.
AND THAT'S ALL SHE WANTS.
MURDOCK'S SPEECH WINS THE CASE.
WHILE THE CROWD'S THICK AROUND THEM--
--I ANGLE UP TO NELSON.
SLAPP
NICE WORK, COUNSELOR.
THANKS!

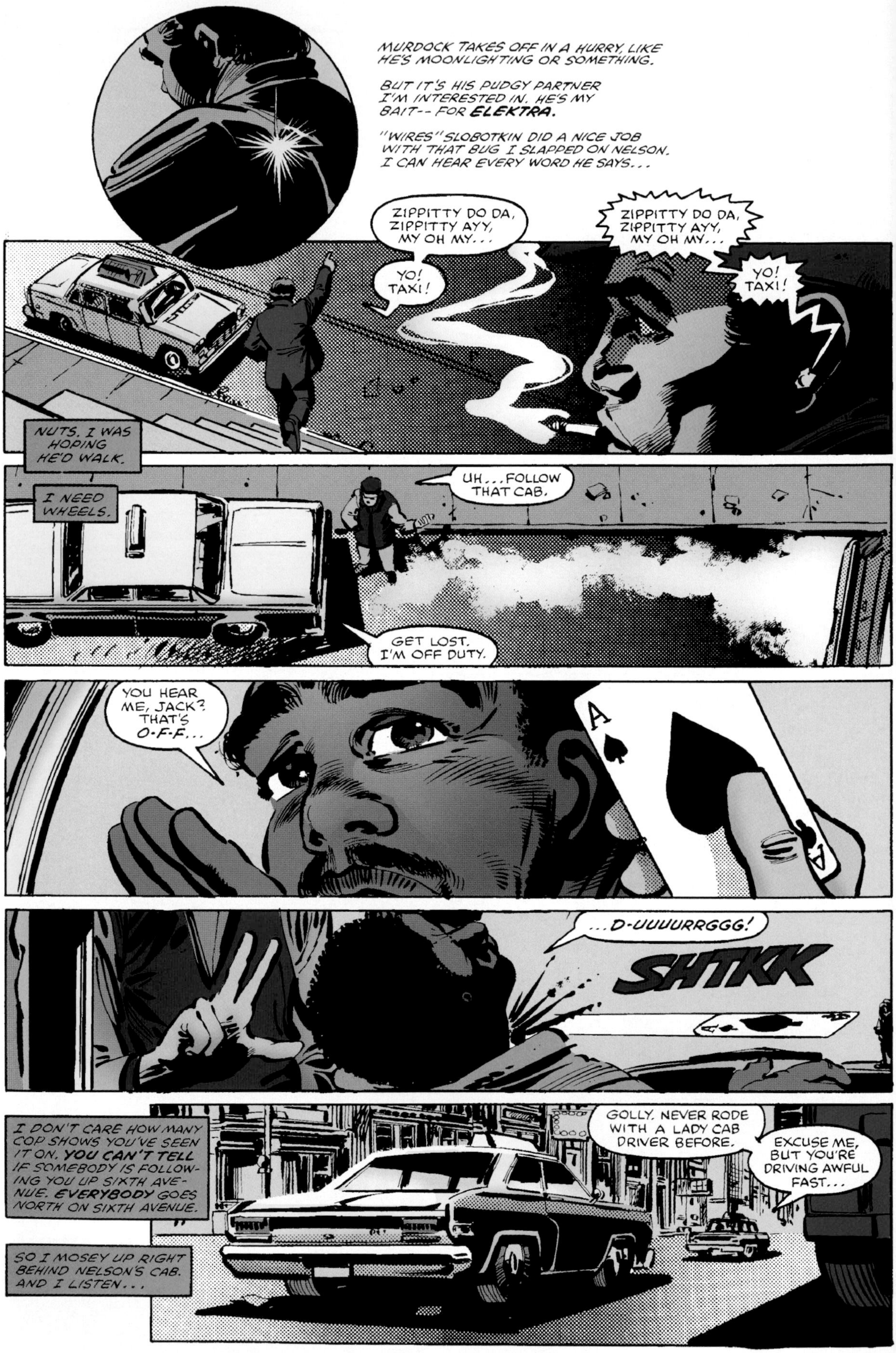
MURDOCK TAKES OFF IN A HURRY, LIKE HE'S MOONLIGHTING OR SOMETHING.
BUT IT'S HIS PUDGY PARTNER I'M INTERESTED IN. HE'S MY BAIT-- FOR ELEKTRA.
"WIRES" SLOBOTKIN DID A NICE JOB WITH THAT BUG I SLAPPED ON NELSON. I CAN HEAR EVERY WORD HE SAYS...
ZIPPITTY DO DA, ZIPPITTY AYY, MY OH MY...
YO! TAXI!
ZIPPITTY DO DA, ZIPPITTY AYY, MY OH MY...
YO! TAXI!
NUTS. I WAS HOPING HE'D WALK.
I NEED WHEELS.
UH...FOLLOW THAT CAB.
GET LOST. I'M OFF DUTY.
YOU HEAR ME, JACK? THAT'S O-F-F...
...D-UUUURRGGG!
SHTKK
I DON'T CARE HOW MANY COP SHOWS YOU'VE SEEN IT ON. YOU CAN'T TELL IF SOMEBODY IS FOLLOWING YOU UP SIXTH AVENUE. EVERYBODY GOES NORTH ON SIXTH AVENUE.
SO I MOSEY UP RIGHT BEHIND NELSON'S CAB. AND I LISTEN...
GOLLY. NEVER RODE WITH A LADY CAB DRIVER BEFORE.
EXCUSE ME, BUT YOU'RE DRIVING AWFUL FAST...

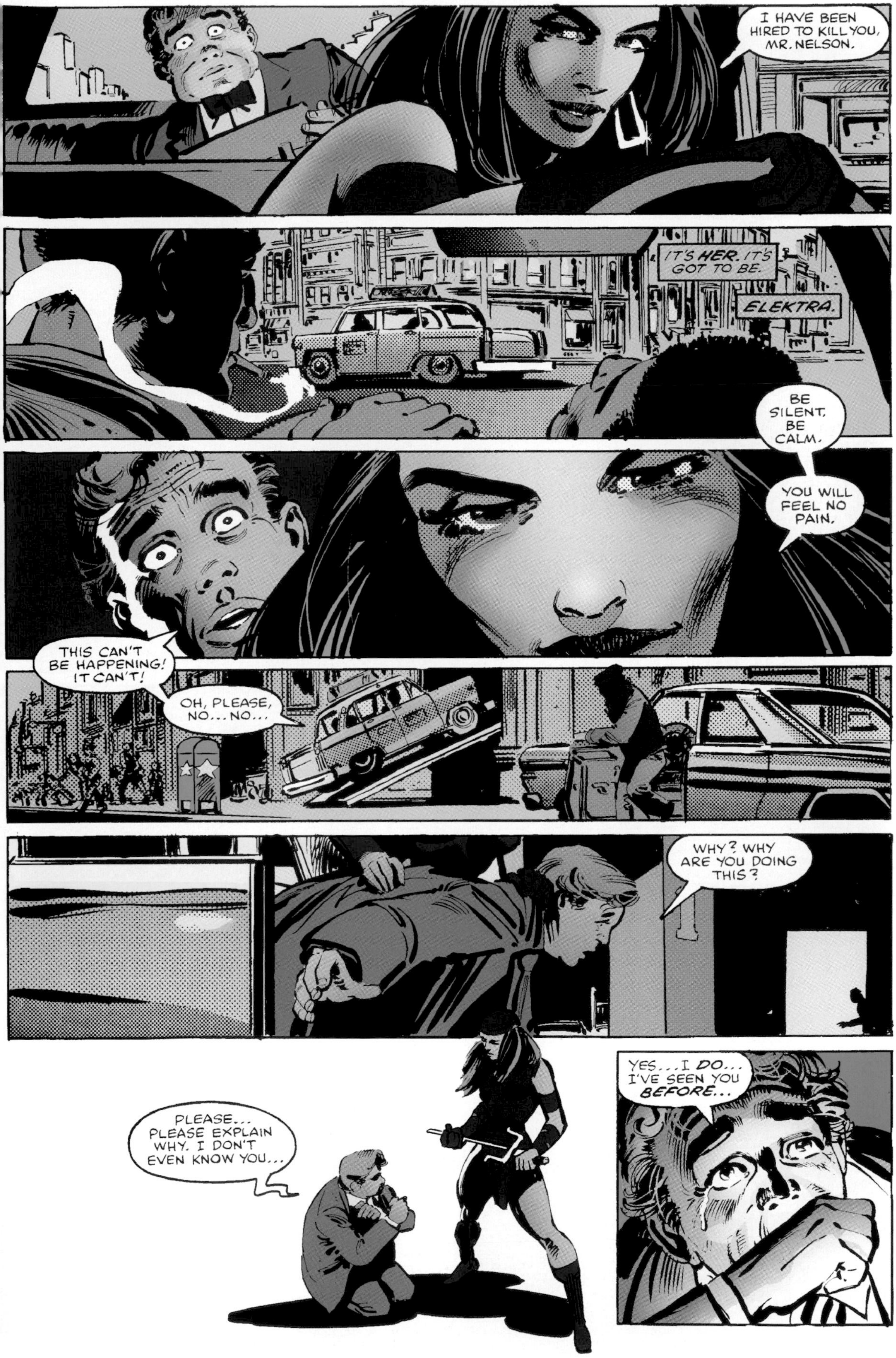
I HAVE BEEN HIRED TO KILL YOU, MR. NELSON.
IT'S HER. IT'S GOT TO BE.
ELEKTRA.
BE SILENT. BE CALM.
YOU WILL FEEL NO PAIN.
THIS CAN'T BE HAPPENING! IT CAN'T!
OH, PLEASE, NO... NO...
WHY? WHY ARE YOU DOING THIS?
PLEASE... PLEASE EXPLAIN WHY. I DON'T EVEN KNOW YOU...
YES... I DO... I'VE SEEN YOU BEFORE...

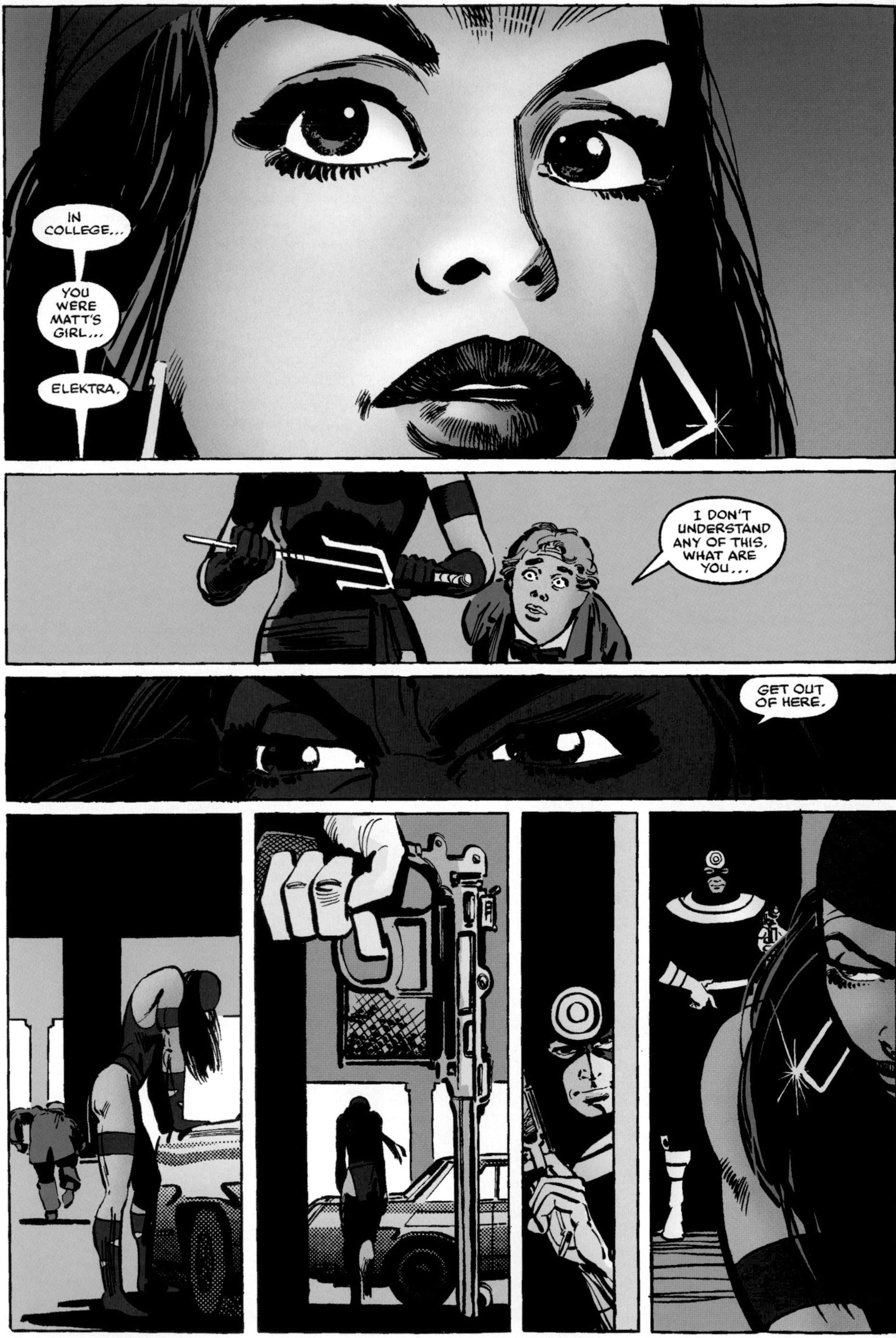
IN COLLEGE...
YOU WERE MATT'S GIRL...
ELEKTRA.
I DON'T UNDERSTAND ANY OF THIS. WHAT ARE YOU...
GET OUT OF HERE.

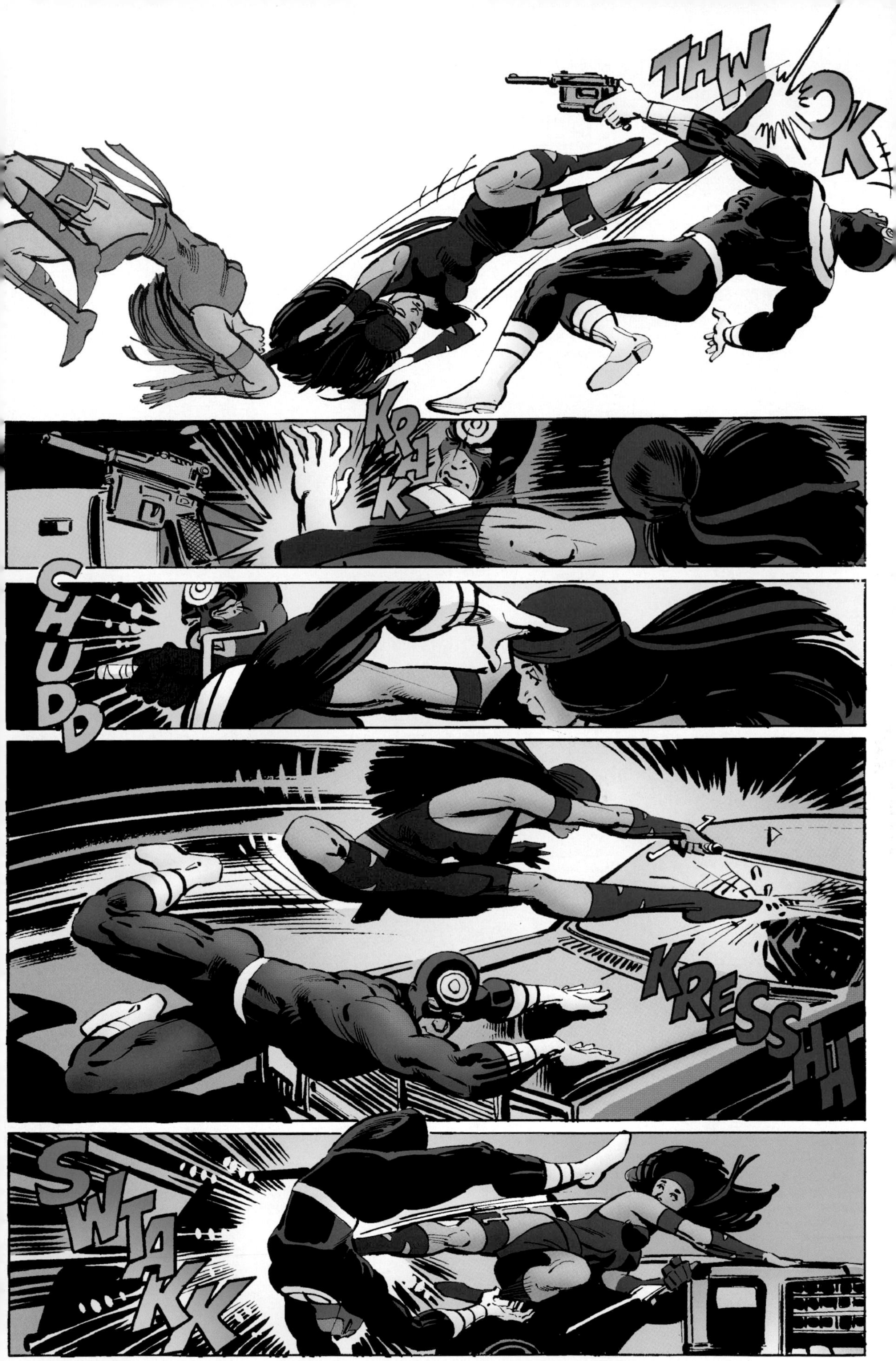
THWOK
KRAK
CHUDD
KRESSHH
SWTAKK

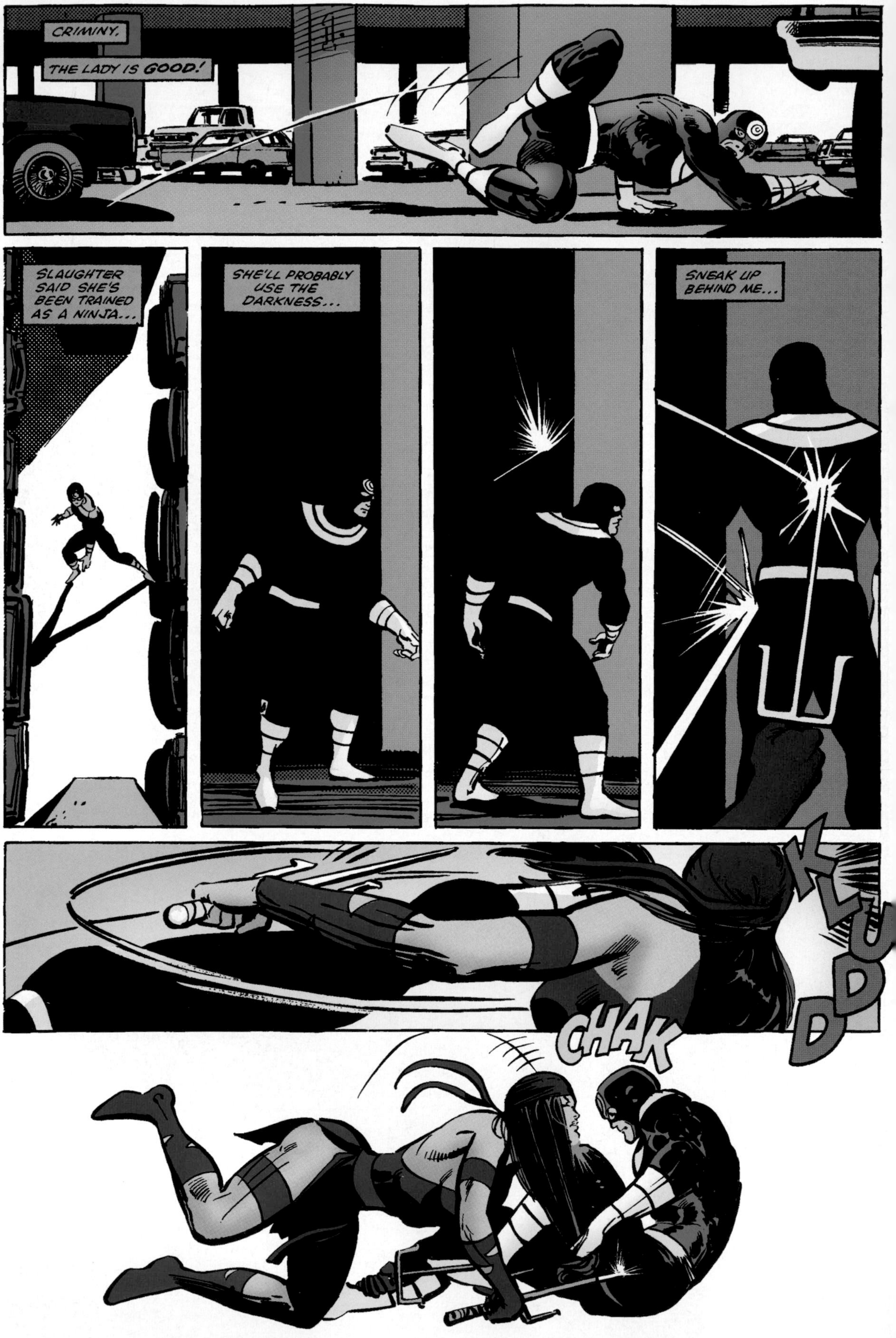
CRIMINY.
THE LADY IS GOOD!
SLAUGHTER SAID SHE'S BEEN TRAINED AS A NINJA...
SHE'LL PROBABLY USE THE DARKNESS...
SNEAK UP BEHIND ME...
KLUDD
CHAK

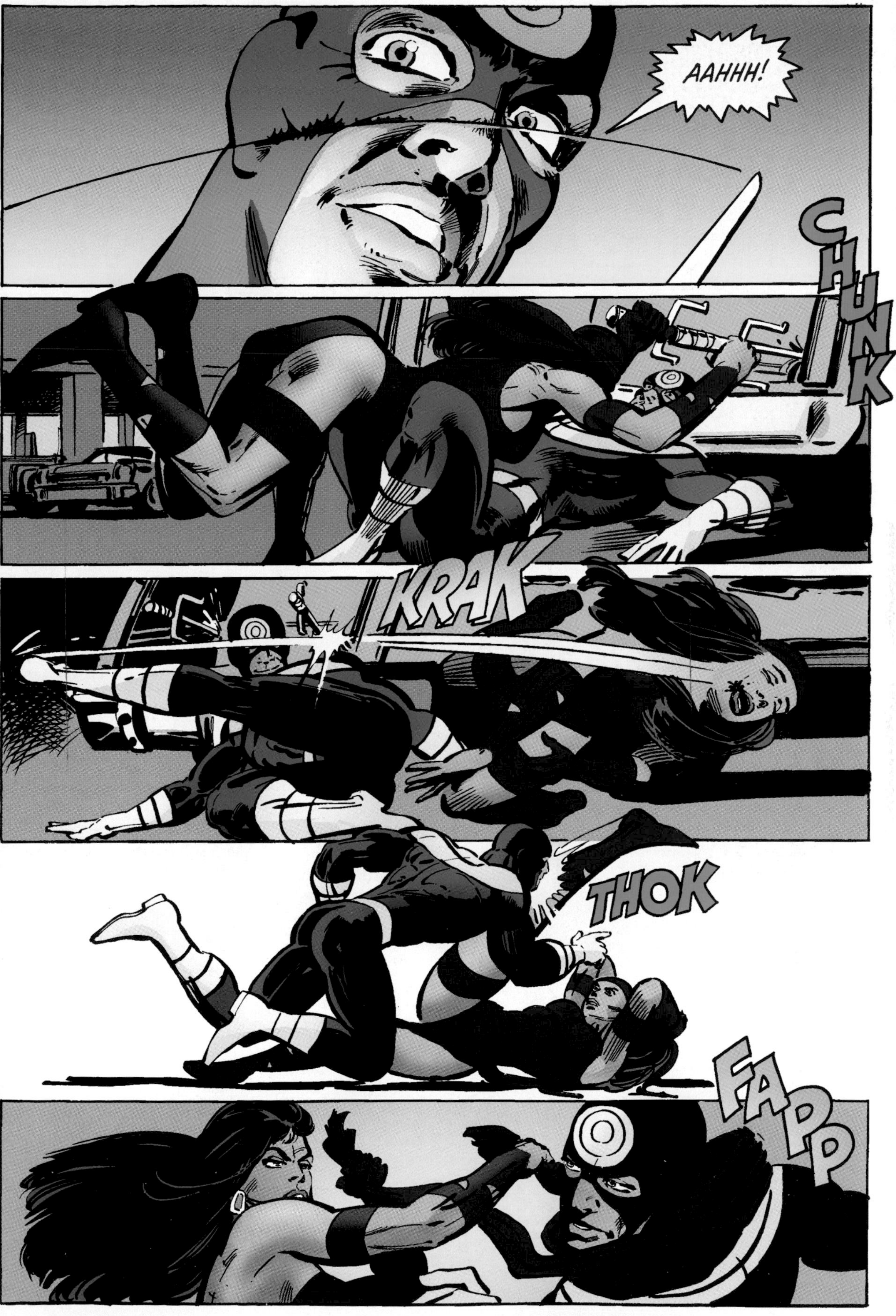

AAHHH!
CHUNK
KRAK
THOK
FAPP

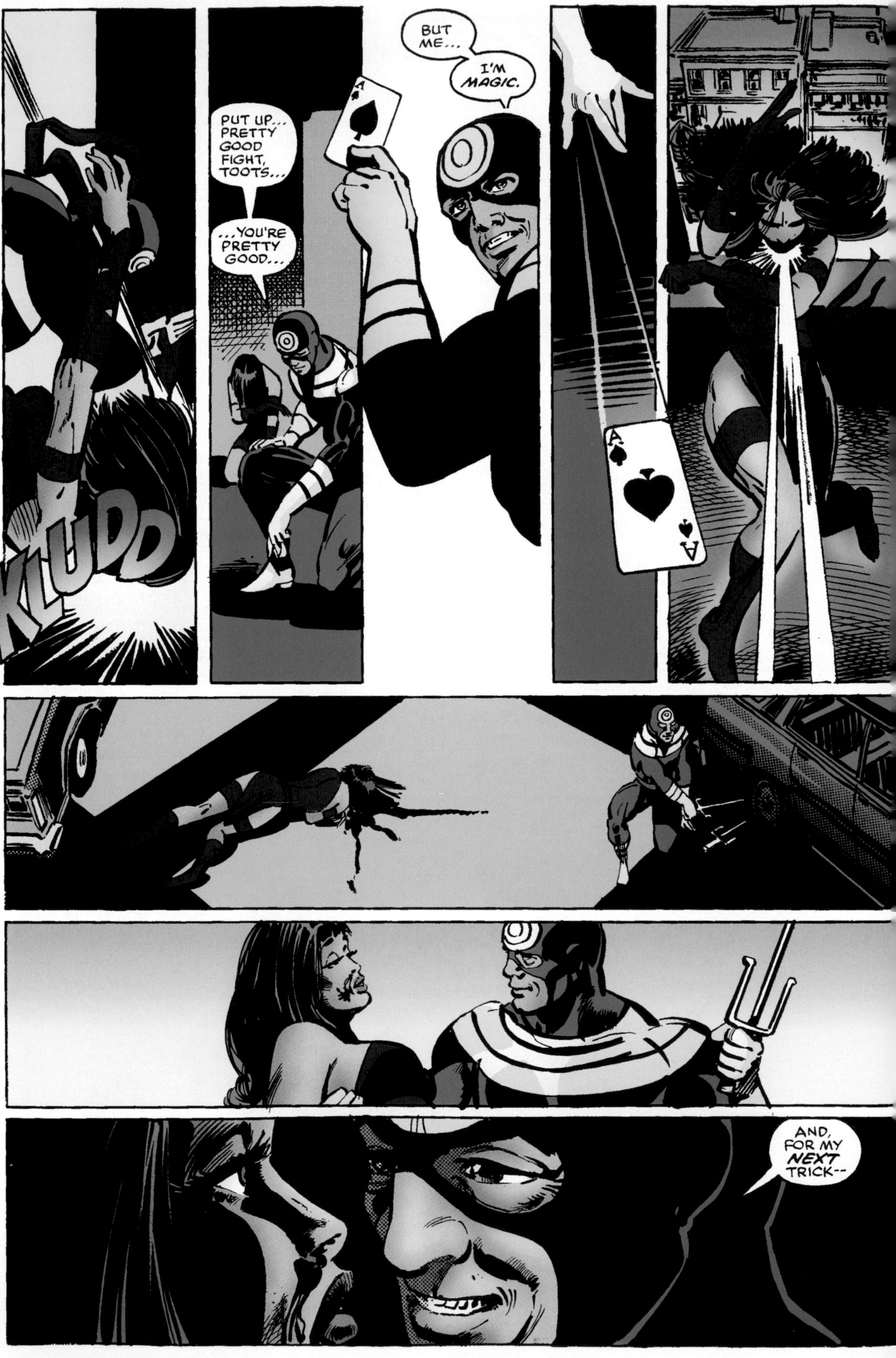
KLUDD
PUT UP... PRETTY GOOD FIGHT, TOOTS...
...YOU'RE PRETTY GOOD...
BUT ME...
I'M MAGIC.
AND, FOR MY NEXT TRICK--

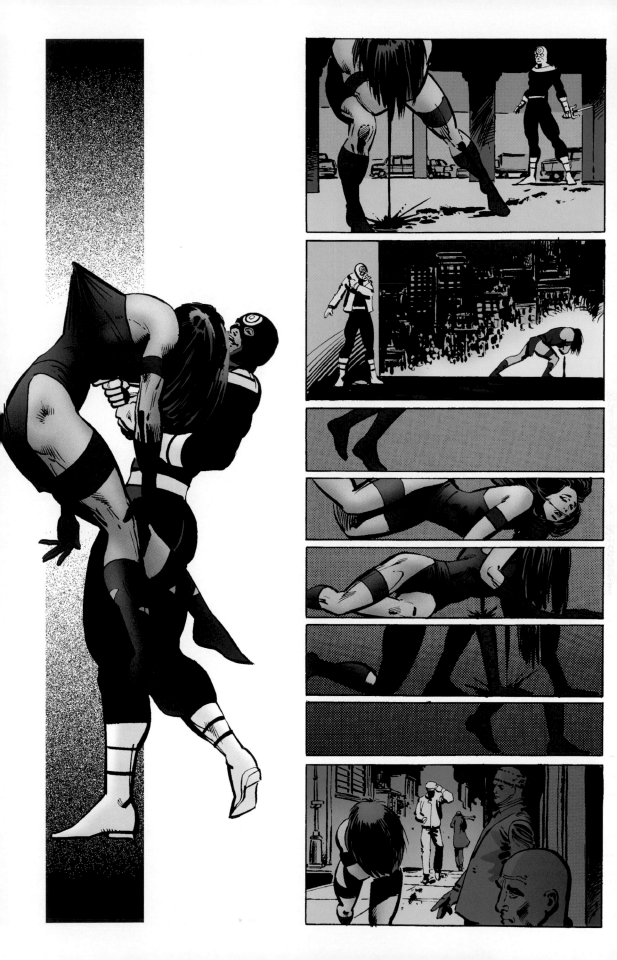

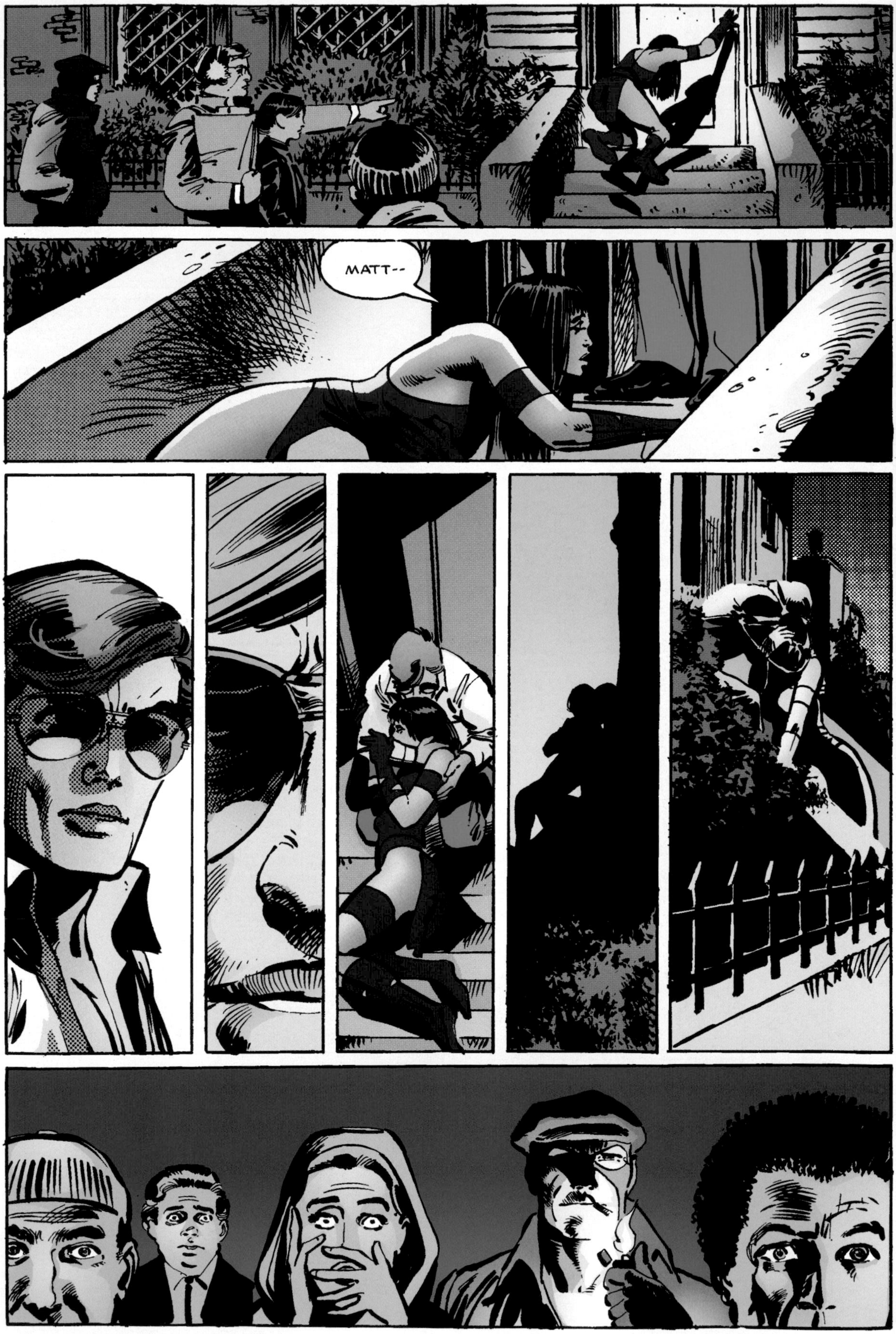
MATT--

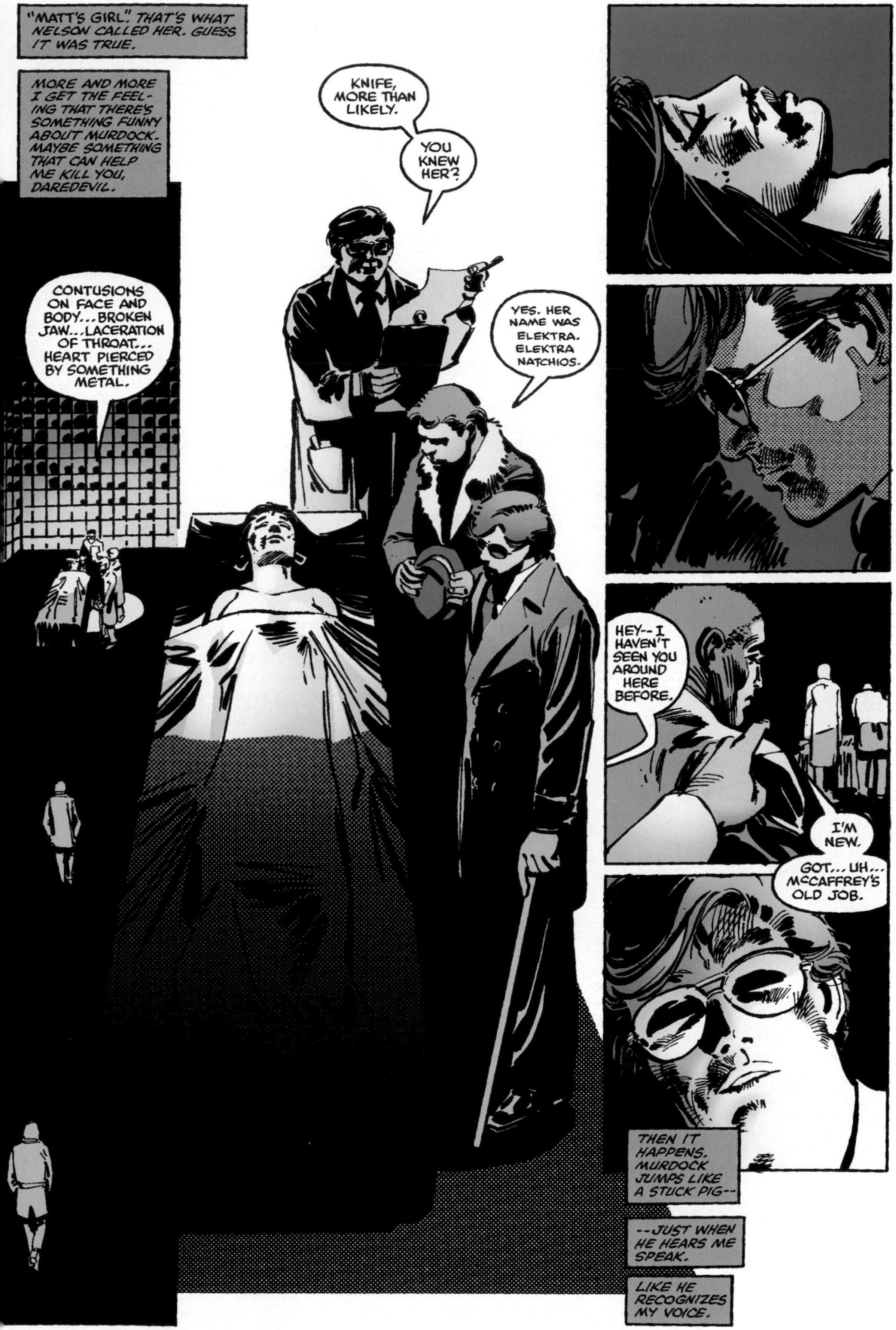
"MATT'S GIRL." THAT'S WHAT NELSON CALLED HER. GUESS IT WAS TRUE.
MORE AND MORE I GET THE FEEL-ING THAT THERE'S SOMETHING FUNNY ABOUT MURDOCK. MAYBE SOMETHING THAT CAN HELP ME KILL YOU, DAREDEVIL.
CONTUSIONS ON FACE AND BODY... BROKEN JAW... LACERATION OF THROAT... HEART PIERCED BY SOMETHING METAL.
KNIFE, MORE THAN LIKELY.
YOU KNEW HER?
YES. HER NAME WAS ELEKTRA. ELEKTRA NATCHIOS.
HEY-- I HAVEN'T SEEN YOU AROUND HERE BEFORE.
I'M NEW.
GOT... UH... McCAFFREY'S OLD JOB.
THEN IT HAPPENS. MURDOCK JUMPS LIKE A STUCK PIG--
--JUST WHEN HE HEARS ME SPEAK.
LIKE HE RECOGNIZES MY VOICE.

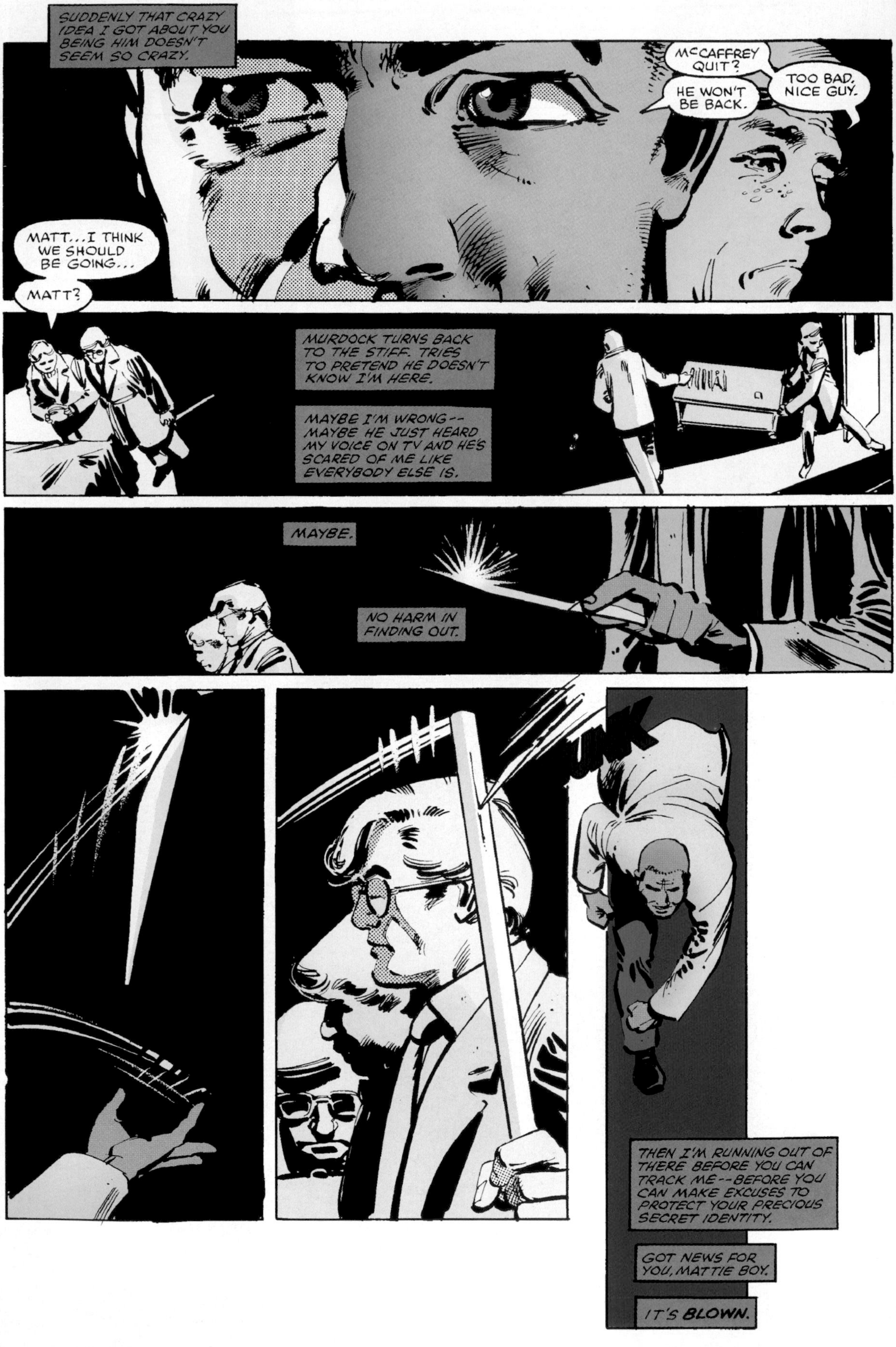
SUDDENLY THAT CRAZY IDEA I GOT ABOUT YOU BEING HIM DOESN'T SEEM SO CRAZY.
McCAFFREY QUIT?
HE WON'T BE BACK.
TOO BAD. NICE GUY.
MATT... I THINK WE SHOULD BE GOING...
MATT?
MURDOCK TURNS BACK TO THE STIFF. TRIES TO PRETEND HE DOESN'T KNOW I'M HERE.
MAYBE I'M WRONG-- MAYBE HE JUST HEARD MY VOICE ON TV AND HE'S SCARED OF ME LIKE EVERYBODY ELSE IS.
MAYBE.
NO HARM IN FINDING OUT.
THEN I'M RUNNING OUT OF THERE BEFORE YOU CAN TRACK ME--BEFORE YOU CAN MAKE EXCUSES TO PROTECT YOUR PRECIOUS SECRET IDENTITY.
GOT NEWS FOR YOU, MATTIE BOY.
IT'S BLOWN.

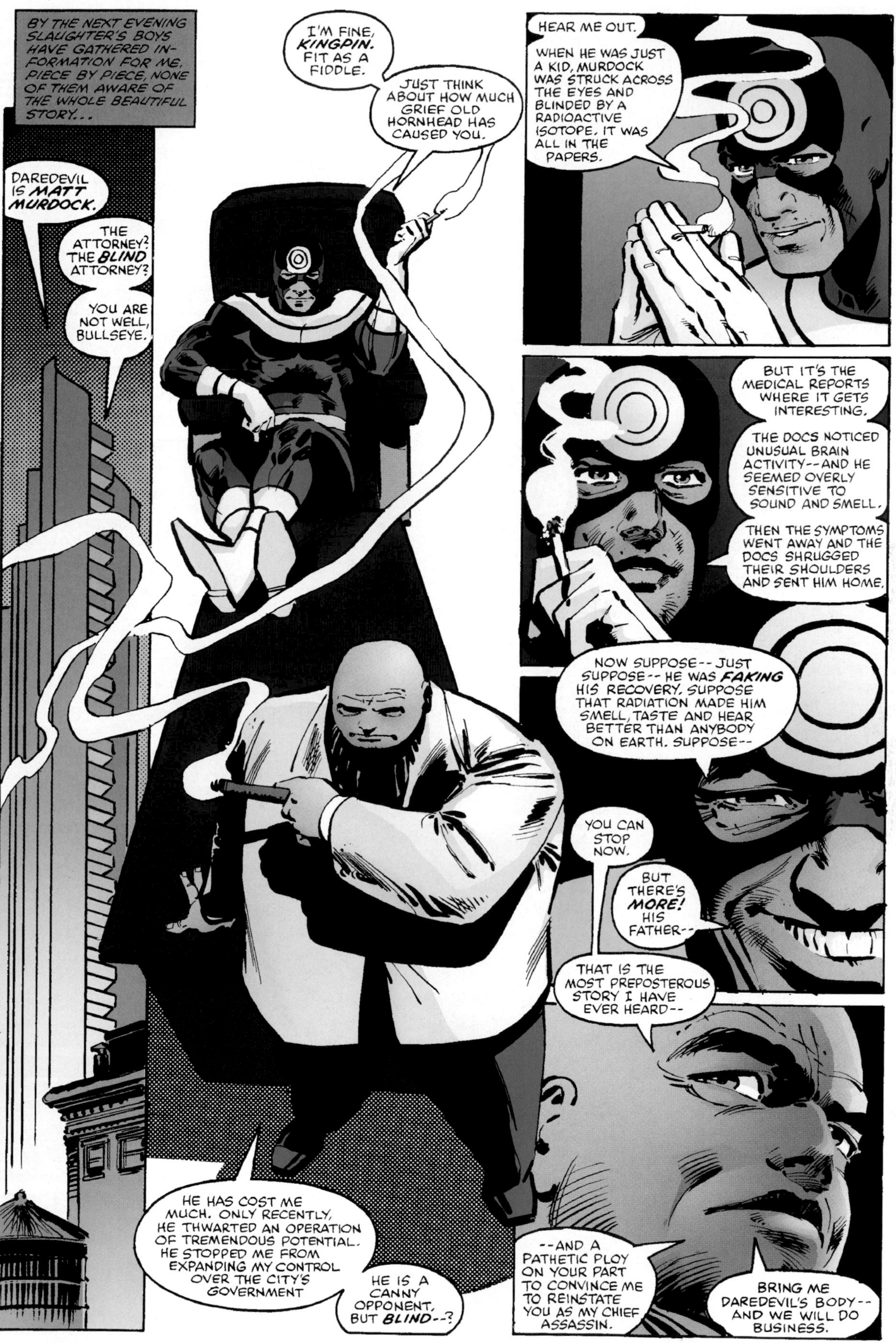

BY THE NEXT EVENING SLAUGHTER'S BOYS HAVE GATHERED INFORMATION FOR ME, PIECE BY PIECE, NONE OF THEM AWARE OF THE WHOLE BEAUTIFUL STORY...
DAREDEVIL IS MATT MURDOCK.
THE ATTORNEY? THE BLIND ATTORNEY?
YOU ARE NOT WELL, BULLSEYE.
I'M FINE, KINGPIN. FIT AS A FIDDLE.
JUST THINK ABOUT HOW MUCH GRIEF OLD HORNHEAD HAS CAUSED YOU.
HE HAS COST ME MUCH. ONLY RECENTLY, HE THWARTED AN OPERATION OF TREMENDOUS POTENTIAL. HE STOPPED ME FROM EXPANDING MY CONTROL OVER THE CITY'S GOVERNMENT
HE IS A CANNY OPPONENT, BUT BLIND--?
HEAR ME OUT.
WHEN HE WAS JUST A KID, MURDOCK WAS STRUCK ACROSS THE EYES AND BLINDED BY A RADIOACTIVE ISOTOPE. IT WAS ALL IN THE PAPERS.
BUT IT'S THE MEDICAL REPORTS WHERE IT GETS INTERESTING.
THE DOCS NOTICED UNUSUAL BRAIN ACTIVITY--AND HE SEEMED OVERLY SENSITIVE TO SOUND AND SMELL.
THEN THE SYMPTOMS WENT AWAY AND THE DOCS SHRUGGED THEIR SHOULDERS AND SENT HIM HOME.
NOW SUPPOSE-- JUST SUPPOSE-- HE WAS FAKING HIS RECOVERY. SUPPOSE THAT RADIATION MADE HIM SMELL, TASTE AND HEAR BETTER THAN ANYBODY ON EARTH. SUPPOSE--
YOU CAN STOP NOW.
BUT THERE'S MORE! HIS FATHER--
THAT IS THE MOST PREPOSTEROUS STORY I HAVE EVER HEARD--
--AND A PATHETIC PLOY ON YOUR PART TO CONVINCE ME TO REINSTATE YOU AS MY CHIEF ASSASSIN.
BRING ME DAREDEVIL'S BODY-- AND WE WILL DO BUSINESS.

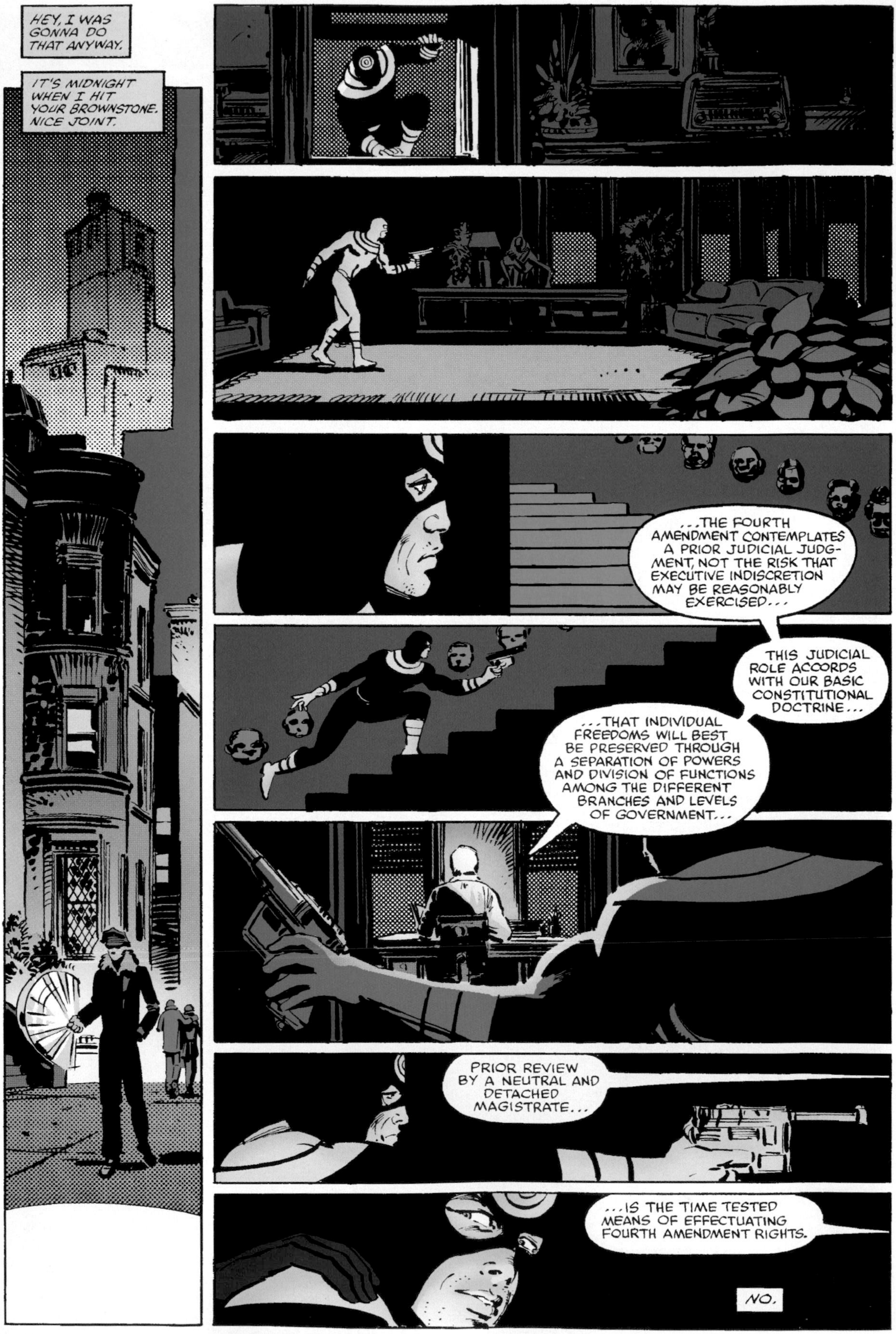
HEY, I WAS GONNA DO THAT ANYWAY.
IT'S MIDNIGHT WHEN I HIT YOUR BROWNSTONE. NICE JOINT.
...THE FOURTH AMENDMENT CONTEMPLATES A PRIOR JUDICIAL JUDGMENT, NOT THE RISK THAT EXECUTIVE INDISCRETION MAY BE REASONABLY EXERCISED...
THIS JUDICIAL ROLE ACCORDS WITH OUR BASIC CONSTITUTIONAL DOCTRINE...
...THAT INDIVIDUAL FREEDOMS WILL BEST BE PRESERVED THROUGH A SEPARATION OF POWERS AND DIVISION OF FUNCTIONS AMONG THE DIFFERENT BRANCHES AND LEVELS OF GOVERNMENT...
PRIOR REVIEW BY A NEUTRAL AND DETACHED MAGISTRATE...
...IS THE TIME TESTED MEANS OF EFFECTUATING FOURTH AMENDMENT RIGHTS.
NO.

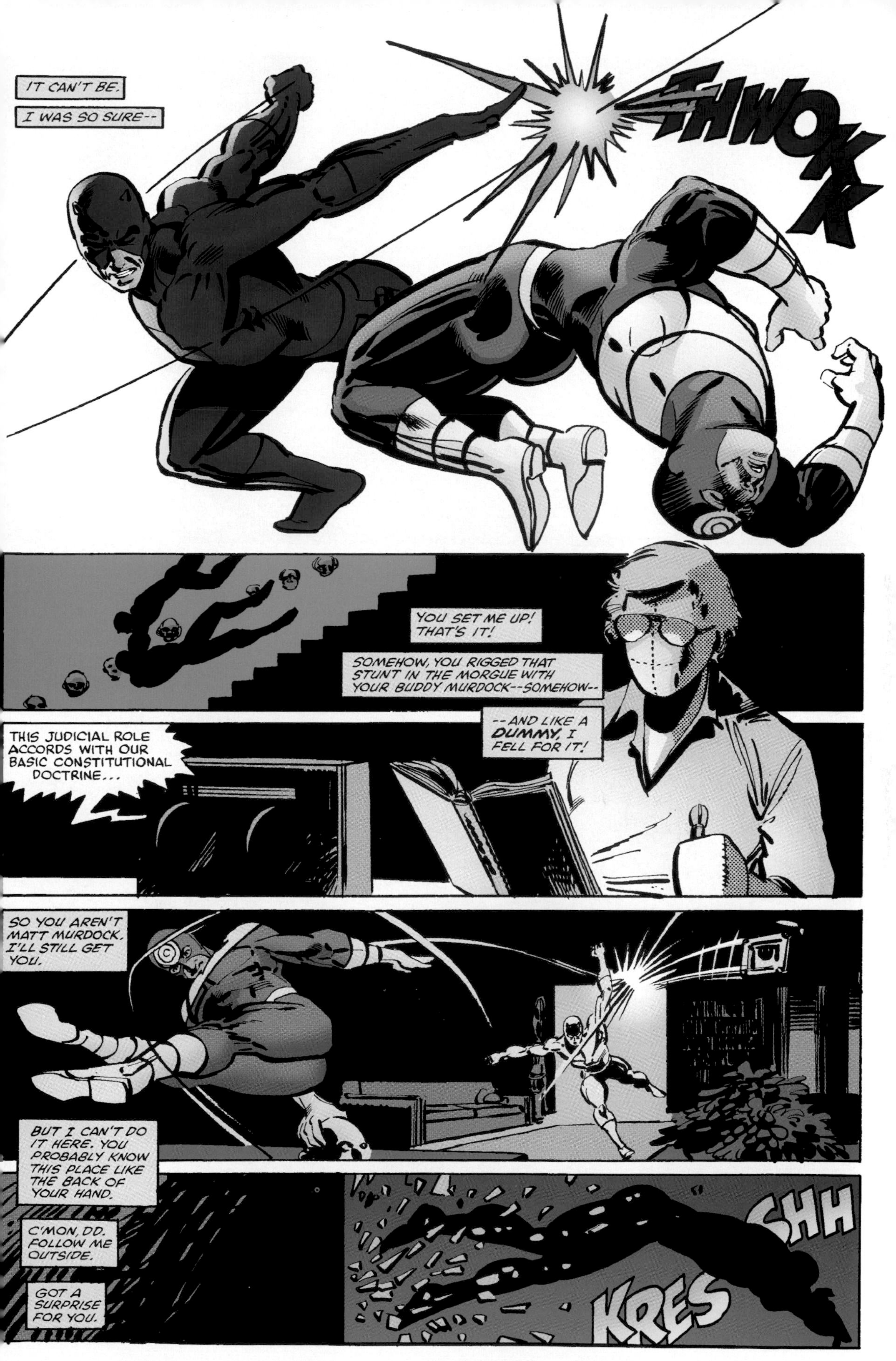
IT CAN'T BE.
I WAS SO SURE--
THWOKK
YOU SET ME UP! THAT'S IT!
SOMEHOW, YOU RIGGED THAT STUNT IN THE MORGUE WITH YOUR BUDDY MURDOCK--SOMEHOW--
--AND LIKE A DUMMY, I FELL FOR IT!
THIS JUDICIAL ROLE ACCORDS WITH OUR BASIC CONSTITUTIONAL DOCTRINE...
SO YOU AREN'T MATT MURDOCK. I'LL STILL GET YOU.
BUT I CAN'T DO IT HERE. YOU PROBABLY KNOW THIS PLACE LIKE THE BACK OF YOUR HAND.
C'MON, DD. FOLLOW ME OUTSIDE.
GOT A SURPRISE FOR YOU.
KRESHH

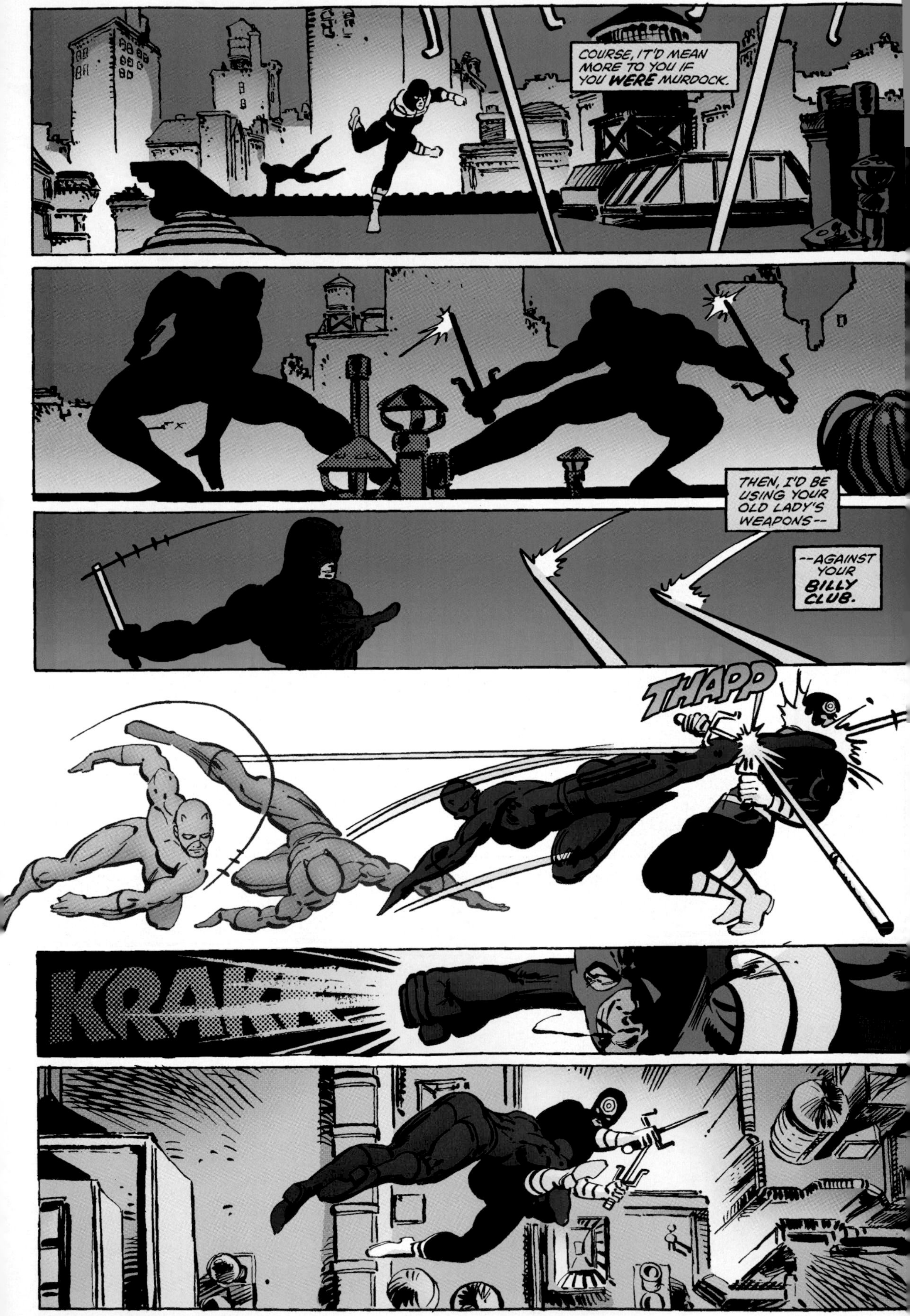
COURSE, IT'D MEAN MORE TO YOU IF YOU WERE MURDOCK.
THEN, I'D BE USING YOUR OLD LADY'S WEAPONS--
--AGAINST YOUR BILLY CLUB.
THAPP
KRAK

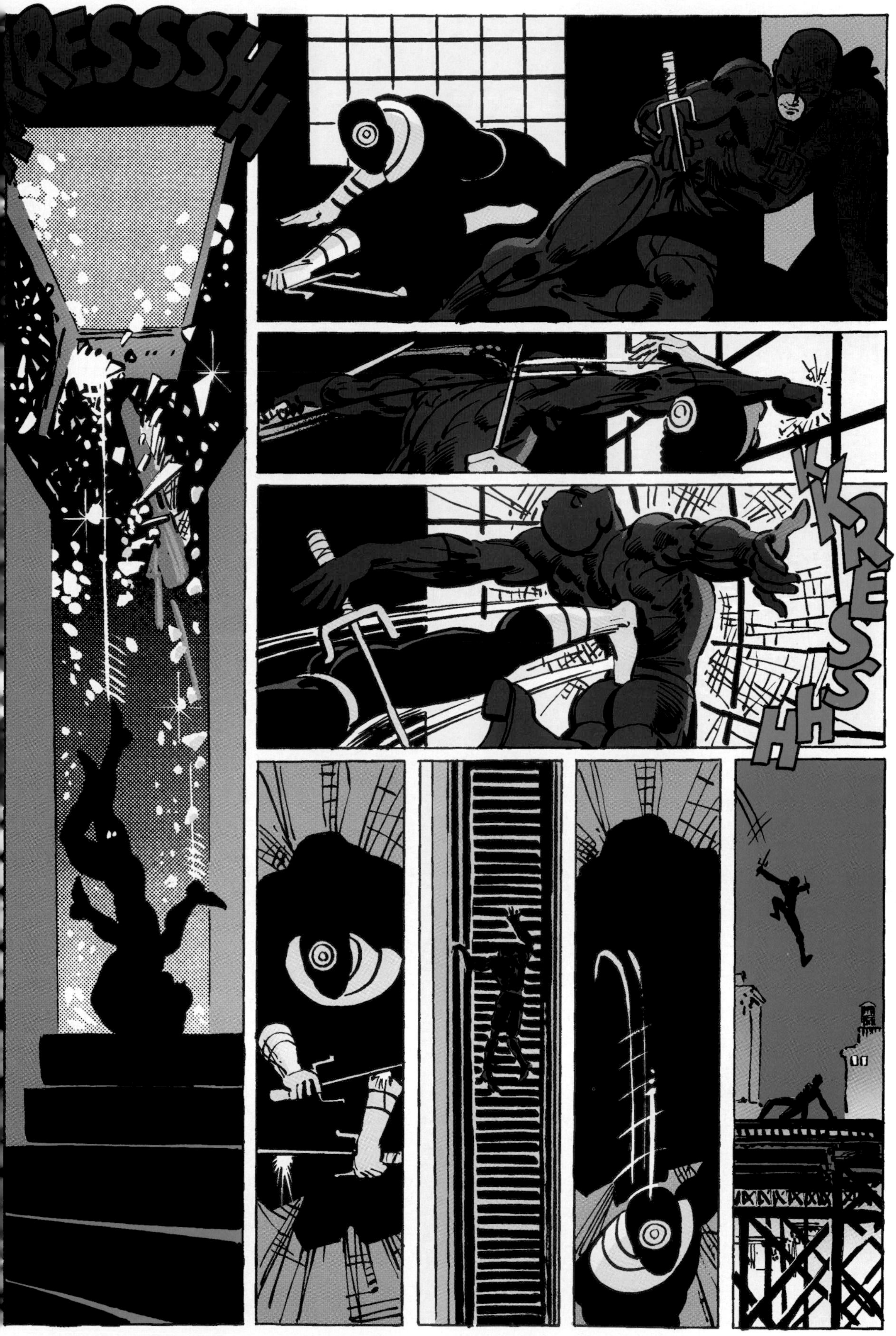
RESSSHH
KKRESSHH

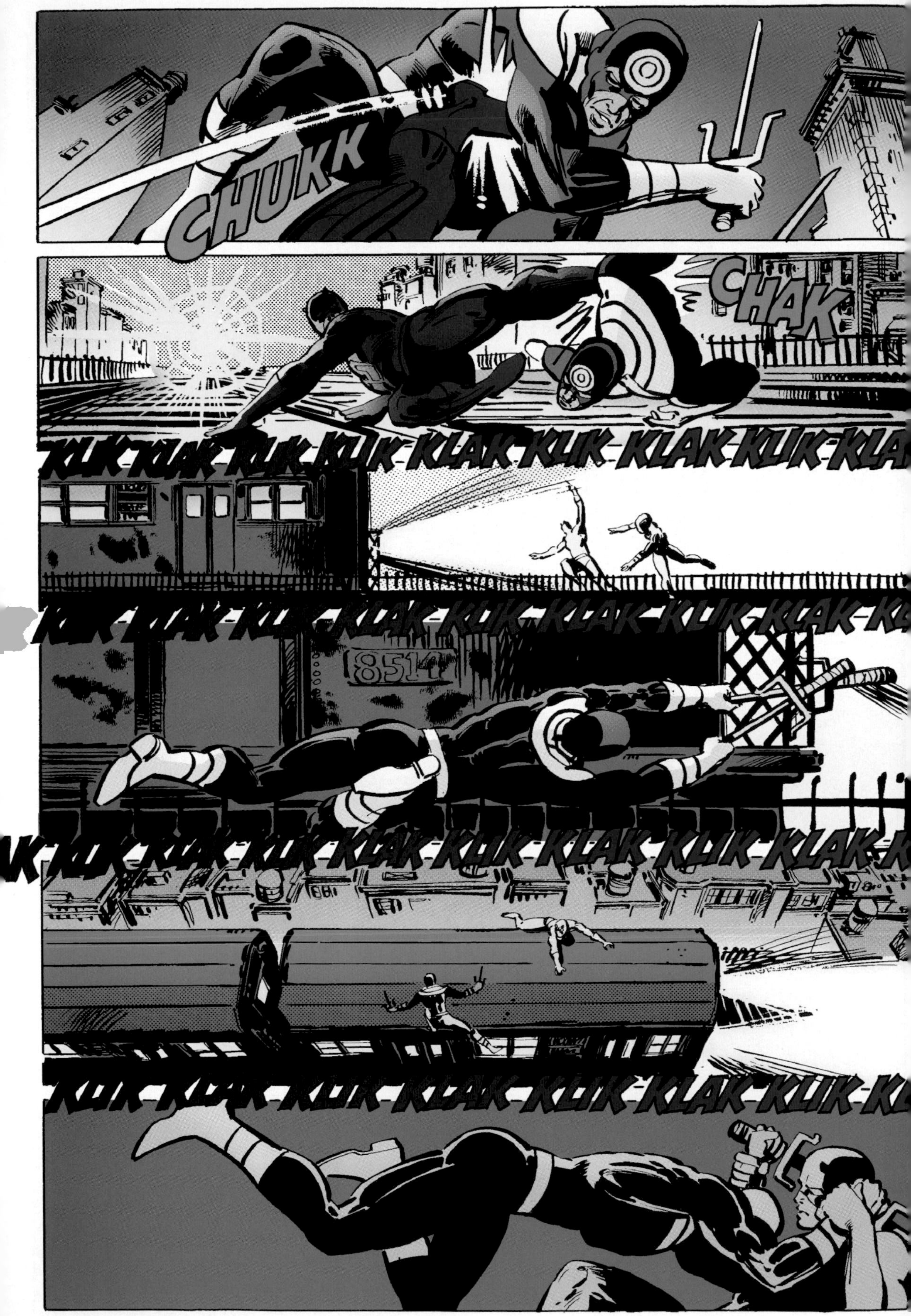
CHUKK
CHAK
KLIK KLAK KLIK KLIK KLAK KLIK KLAK KLIK KLA
KLIK KLAK KLIK KLAK KLIK KLAK KLIK KLAK KL
8514
K KLIK KLAK KLIK KLAK KLIK KLAK KLIK KLAK K
KLIK KLAK KLIK KLAK KLIK KLAK KLIK KL

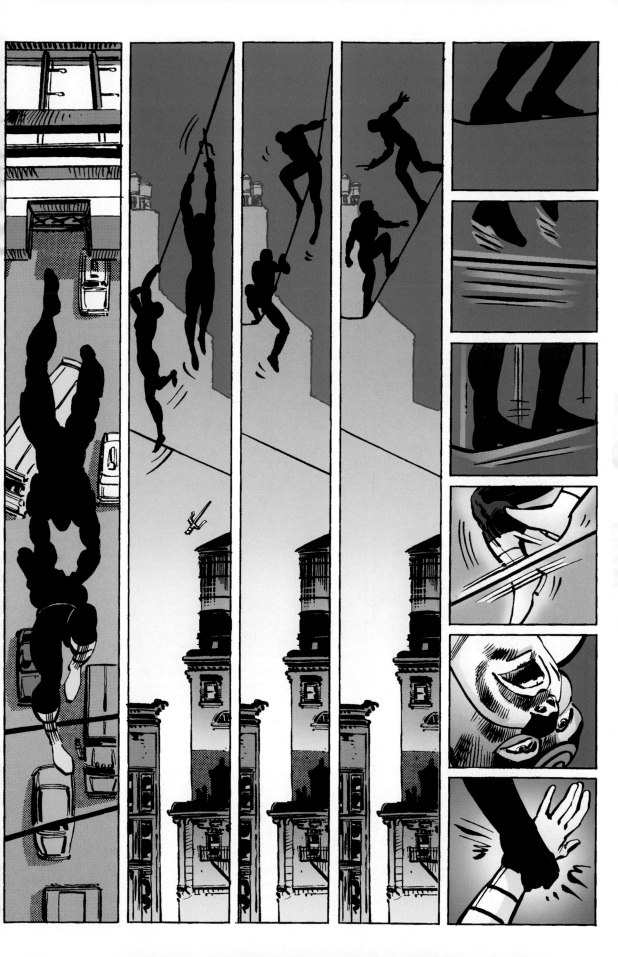

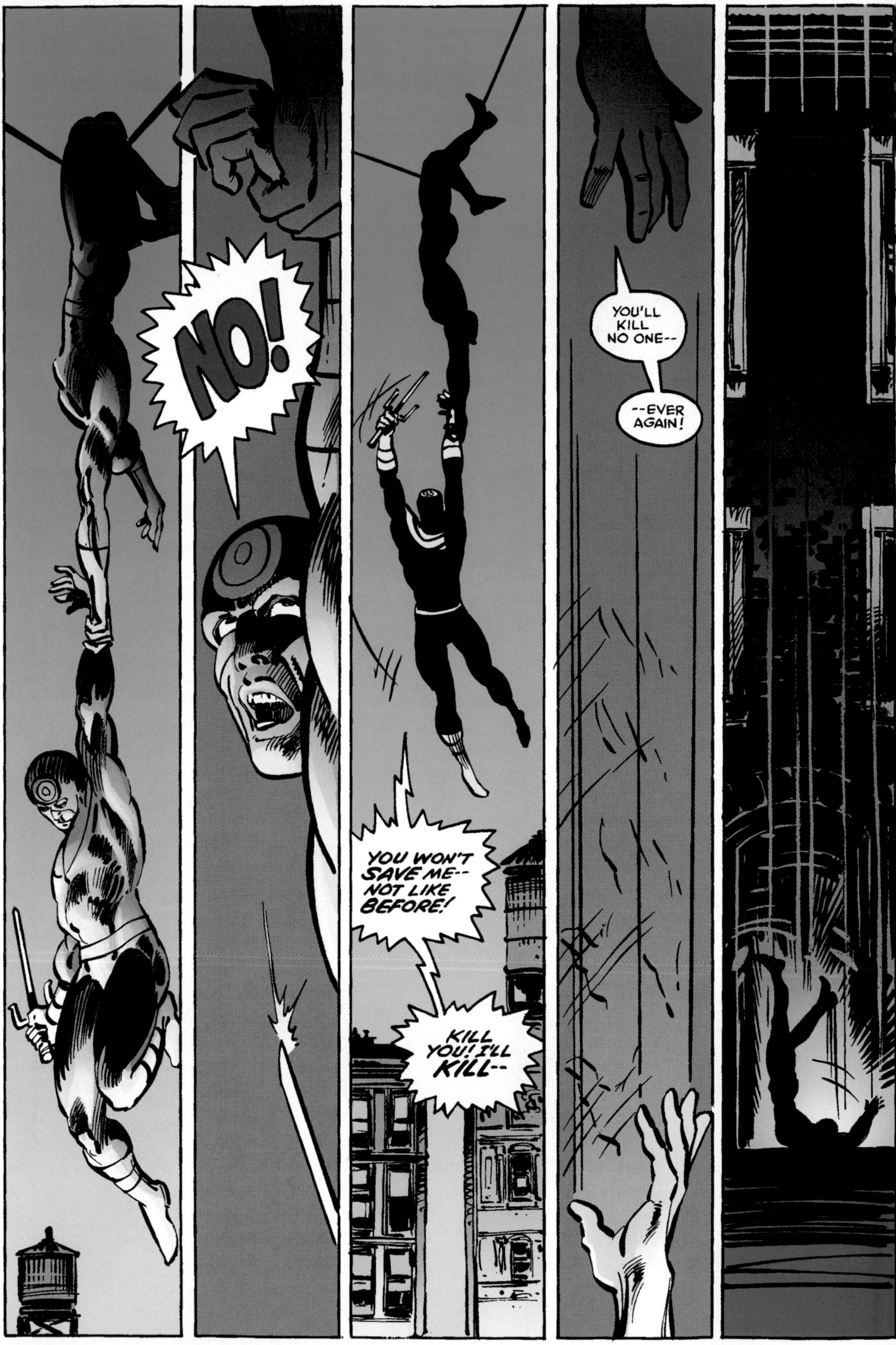
NO!
YOU WON'T SAVE ME-- NOT LIKE BEFORE!
KILL YOU! I'LL KILL--
YOU'LL KILL NO ONE--
--EVER AGAIN!

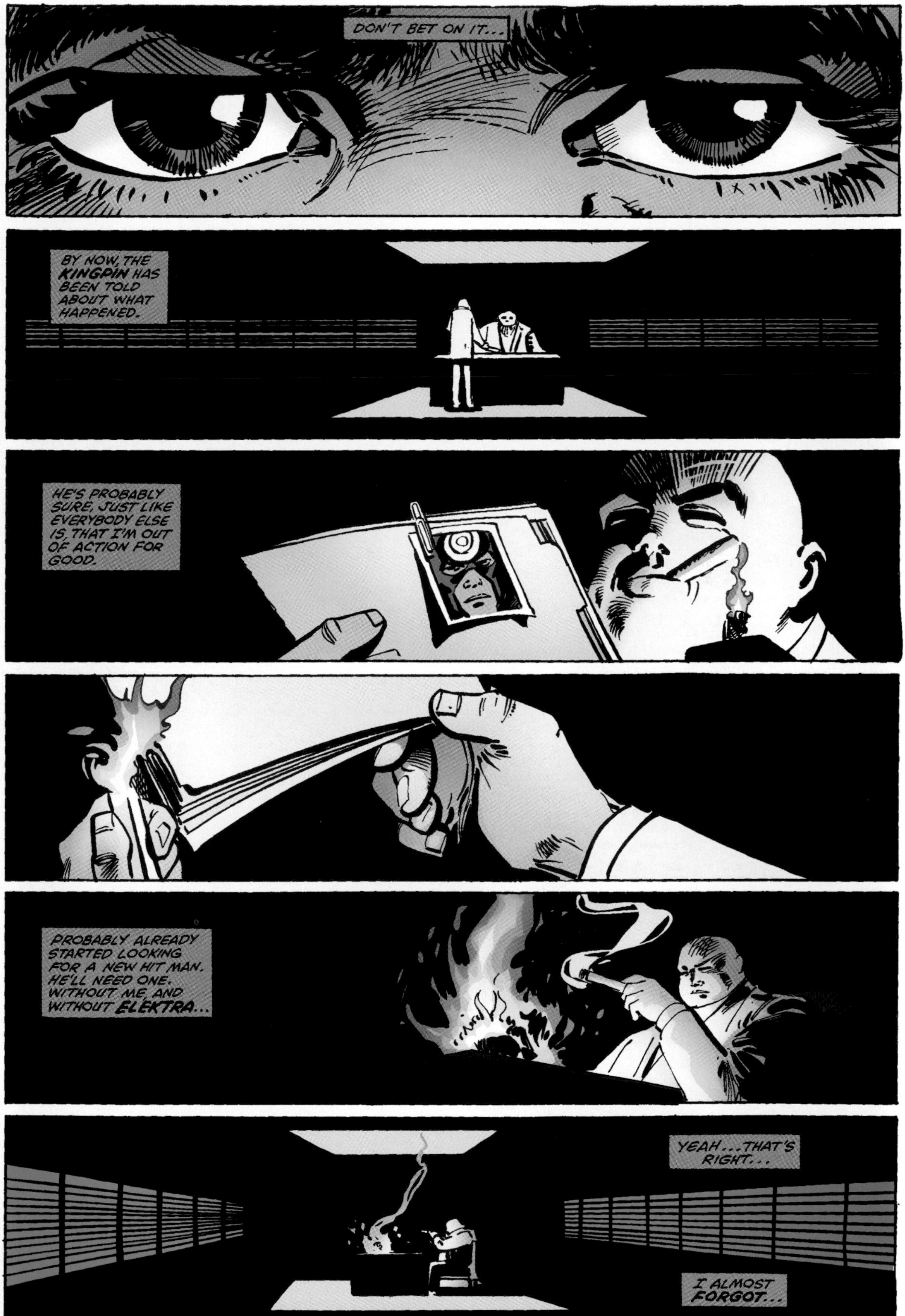
DON'T BET ON IT...
BY NOW, THE KINGPIN HAS BEEN TOLD ABOUT WHAT HAPPENED.
HE'S PROBABLY SURE, JUST LIKE EVERYBODY ELSE IS, THAT I'M OUT OF ACTION FOR GOOD.
PROBABLY ALREADY STARTED LOOKING FOR A NEW HIT MAN. HE'LL NEED ONE. WITHOUT ME, AND WITHOUT ELEKTRA...
YEAH...THAT'S RIGHT...
I ALMOST FORGOT...

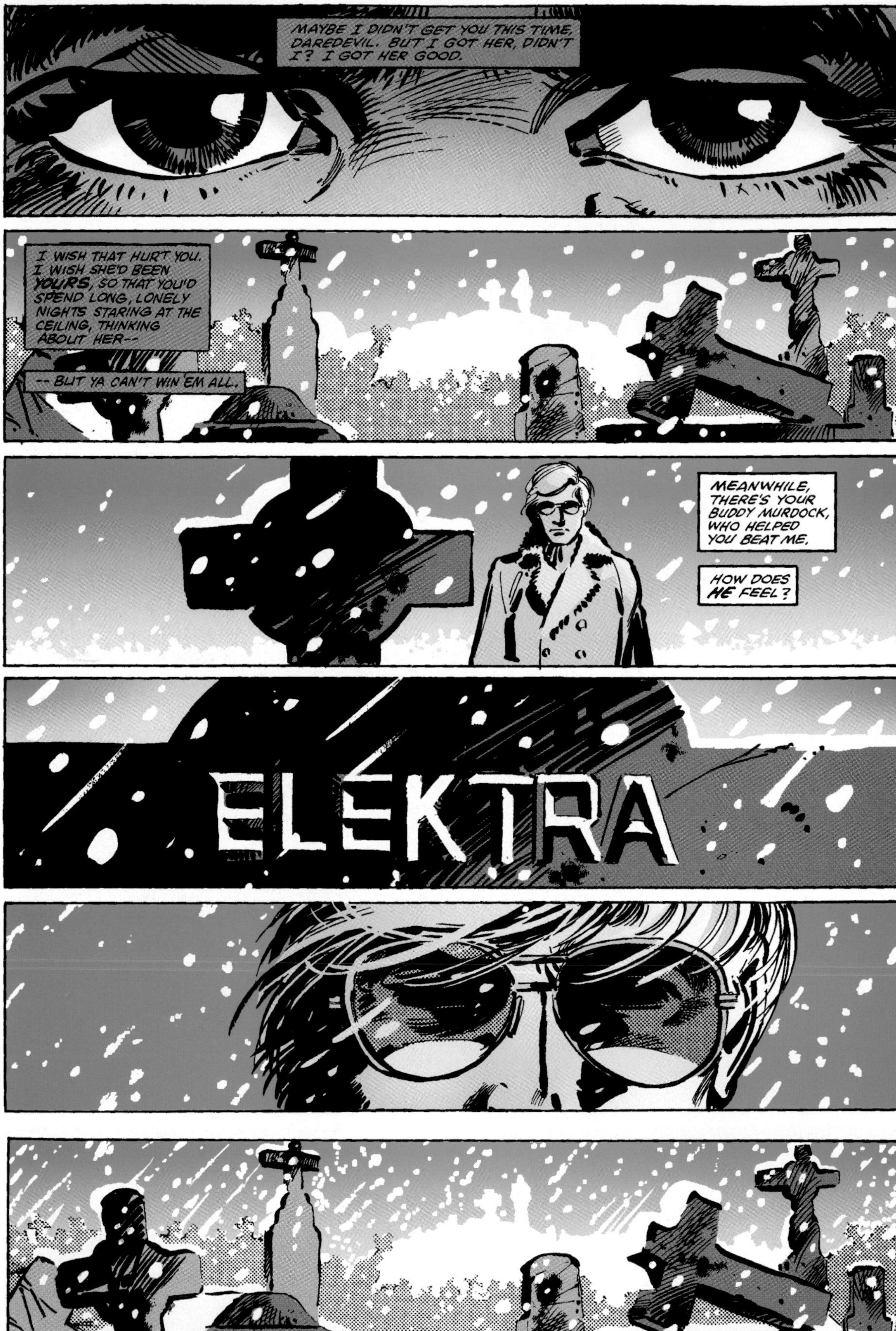
MAYBE I DIDN'T GET YOU THIS TIME, DAREDEVIL. BUT I GOT HER, DIDN'T I? I GOT HER GOOD.
I WISH THAT HURT YOU. I WISH SHE'D BEEN YOURS, SO THAT YOU'D SPEND LONG, LONELY NIGHTS STARING AT THE CEILING, THINKING ABOUT HER--
-- BUT YA CAN'T WIN 'EM ALL.
MEANWHILE, THERE'S YOUR BUDDY MURDOCK, WHO HELPED YOU BEAT ME.
HOW DOES HE FEEL?
ELEKTRA

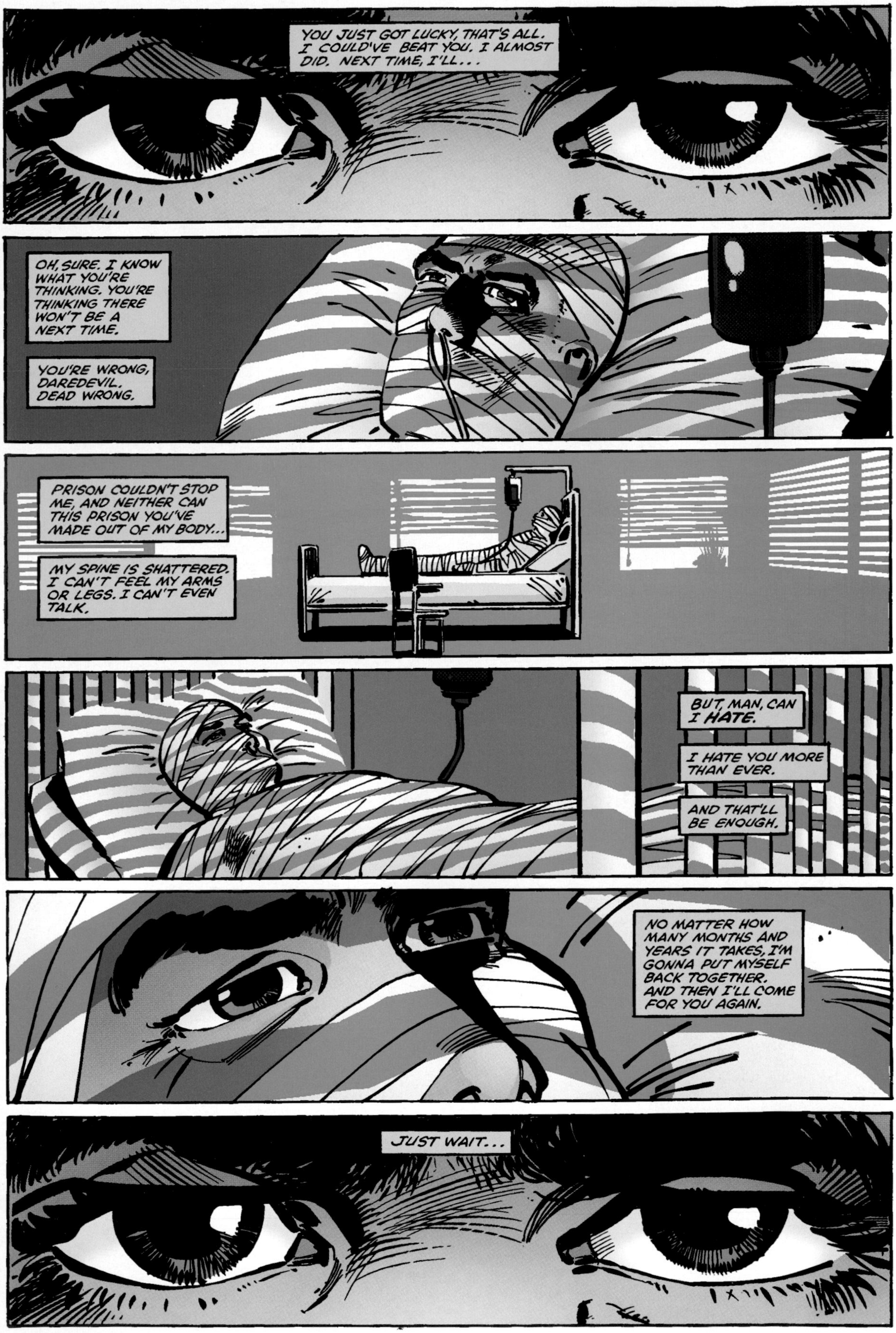
YOU JUST GOT LUCKY, THAT'S ALL. I COULD'VE BEAT YOU. I ALMOST DID. NEXT TIME, I'LL...
OH, SURE. I KNOW WHAT YOU'RE THINKING. YOU'RE THINKING THERE WON'T BE A NEXT TIME.
YOU'RE WRONG, DAREDEVIL. DEAD WRONG.
PRISON COULDN'T STOP ME, AND NEITHER CAN THIS PRISON YOU'VE MADE OUT OF MY BODY...
MY SPINE IS SHATTERED. I CAN'T FEEL MY ARMS OR LEGS. I CAN'T EVEN TALK.
BUT, MAN, CAN I HATE.
I HATE YOU MORE THAN EVER.
AND THAT'LL BE ENOUGH.
NO MATTER HOW MANY MONTHS AND YEARS IT TAKES, I'M GONNA PUT MYSELF BACK TOGETHER. AND THEN I'LL COME FOR YOU AGAIN.
JUST WAIT...

DAREDEVIL #182

MAY 1982

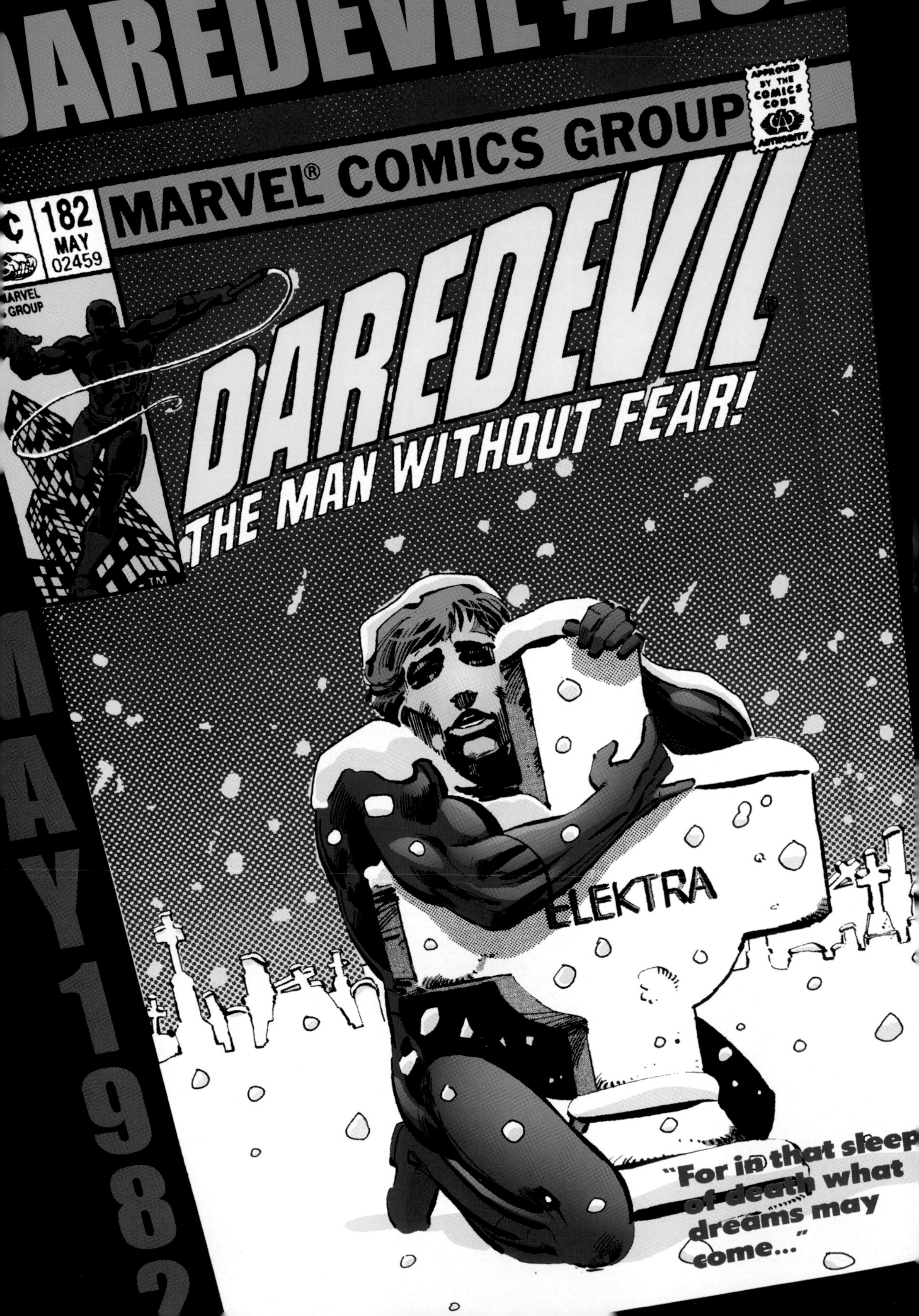

MARVEL® COMICS GROUP
APPROVED BY THE COMICS CODE AUTHORITY
182
MAY
02459
DAREDEVIL®
THE MAN WITHOUT FEAR!
ELEKTRA
"For in that sleep of death what dreams may come..."

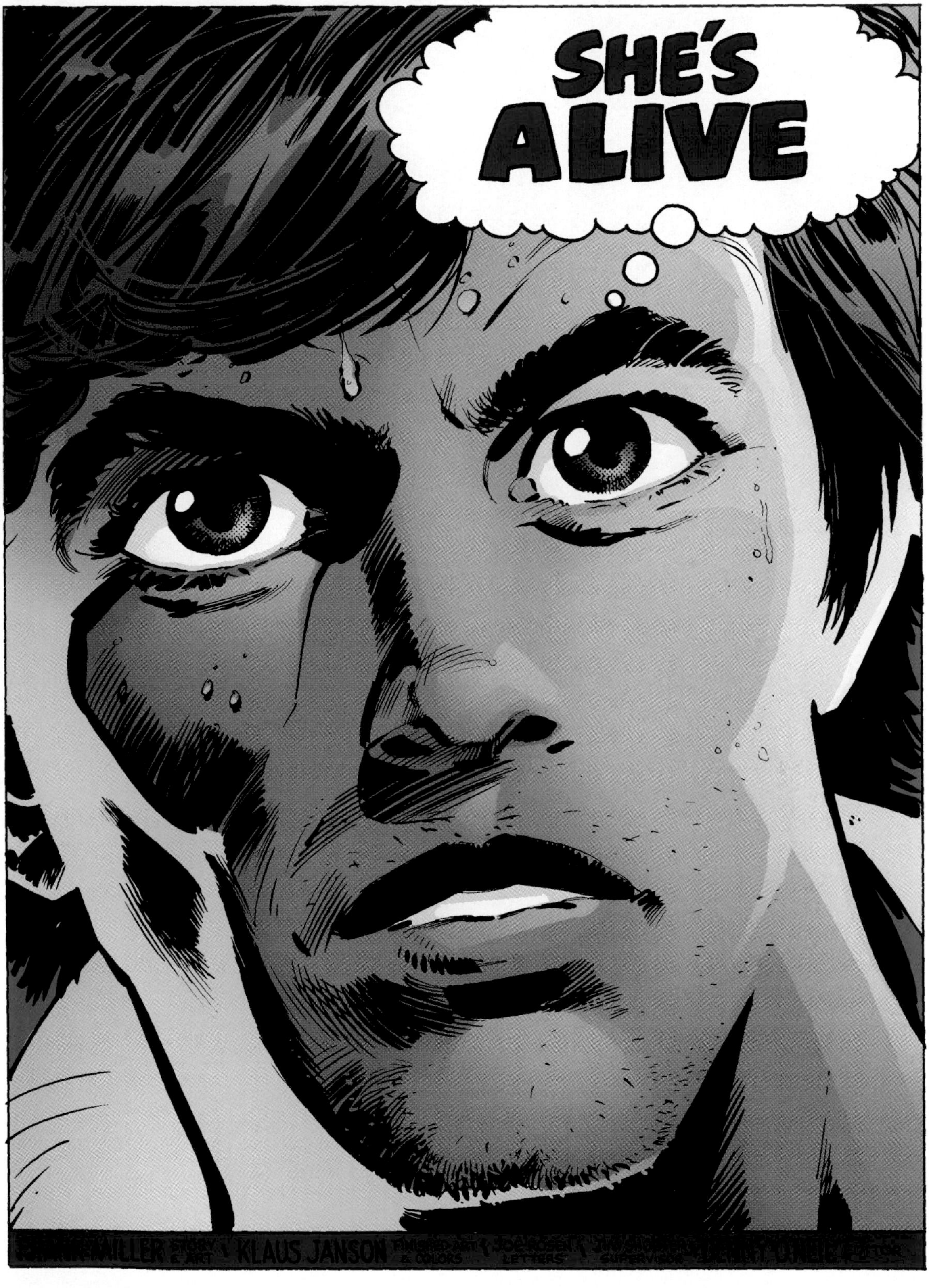
SHE'S ALIVE
MILLER STORY & ART
KLAUS JANSON
& COLORS
LETTERS
SUPERVISION

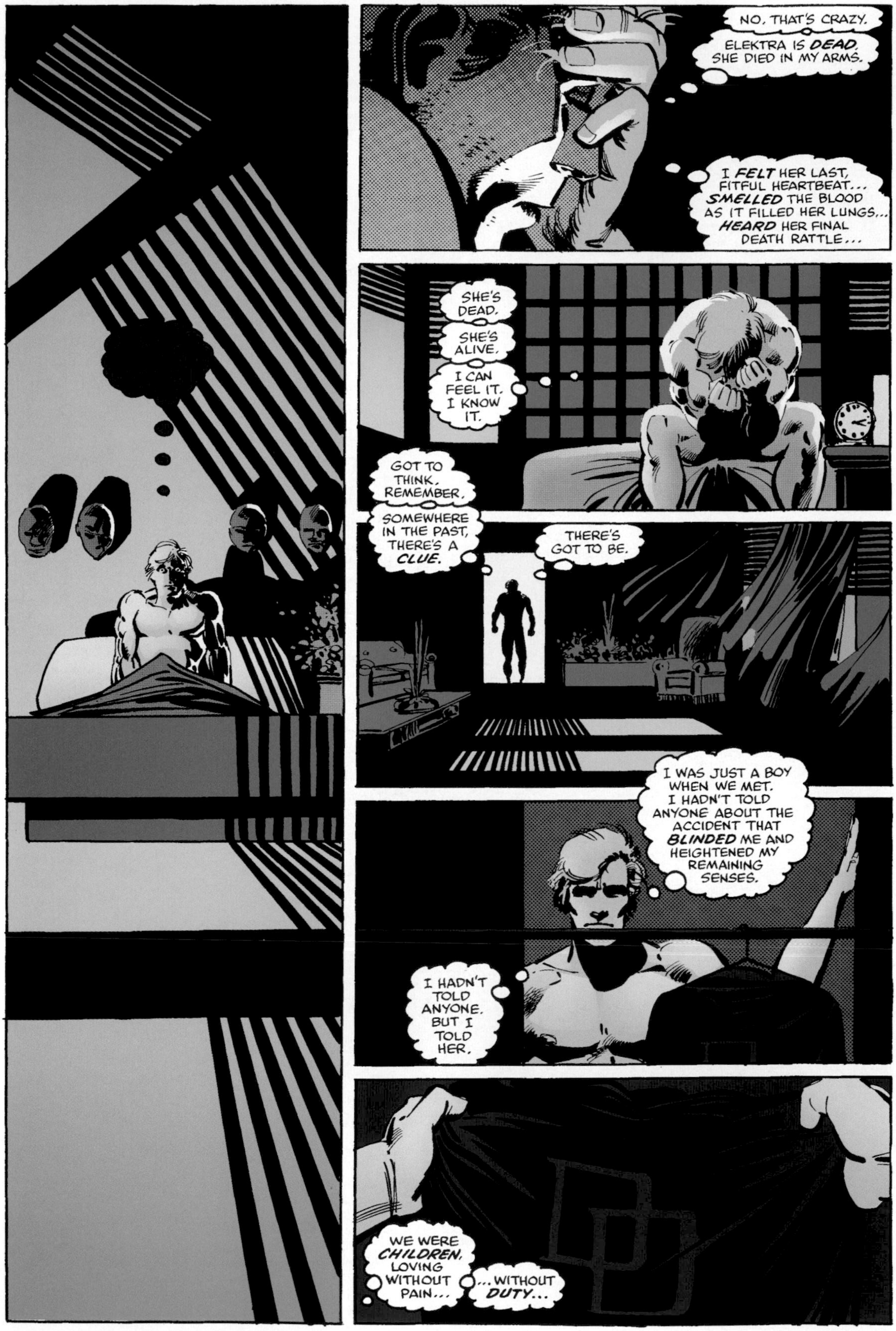
NO, THAT'S CRAZY.
ELEKTRA IS DEAD. SHE DIED IN MY ARMS.
I FELT HER LAST, FITFUL HEARTBEAT... SMELLED THE BLOOD AS IT FILLED HER LUNGS... HEARD HER FINAL DEATH RATTLE...
SHE'S DEAD.
SHE'S ALIVE.
I CAN FEEL IT. I KNOW IT.
GOT TO THINK. REMEMBER.
SOMEWHERE IN THE PAST, THERE'S A CLUE.
THERE'S GOT TO BE.
I WAS JUST A BOY WHEN WE MET. I HADN'T TOLD ANYONE ABOUT THE ACCIDENT THAT BLINDED ME AND HEIGHTENED MY REMAINING SENSES.
I HADN'T TOLD ANYONE. BUT I TOLD HER.
WE WERE CHILDREN. LOVING WITHOUT PAIN...
...WITHOUT DUTY...

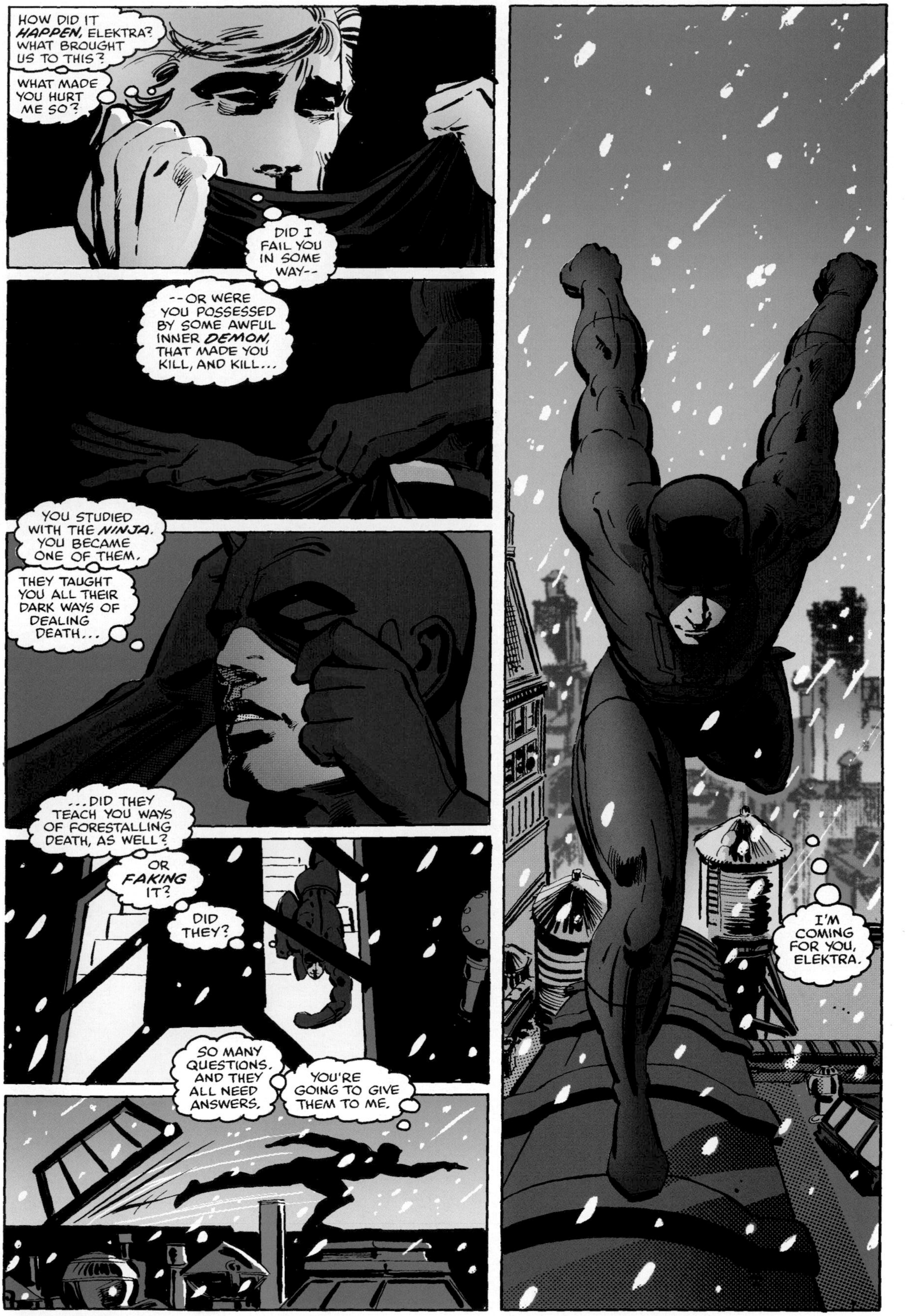
HOW DID IT HAPPEN, ELEKTRA? WHAT BROUGHT US TO THIS?
WHAT MADE YOU HURT ME SO?
DID I FAIL YOU IN SOME WAY--
--OR WERE YOU POSSESSED BY SOME AWFUL INNER DEMON, THAT MADE YOU KILL, AND KILL...
YOU STUDIED WITH THE NINJA. YOU BECAME ONE OF THEM.
THEY TAUGHT YOU ALL THEIR DARK WAYS OF DEALING DEATH...
...DID THEY TEACH YOU WAYS OF FORESTALLING DEATH, AS WELL?
OR FAKING IT?
DID THEY?
SO MANY QUESTIONS. AND THEY ALL NEED ANSWERS.
YOU'RE GOING TO GIVE THEM TO ME.
I'M COMING FOR YOU, ELEKTRA.
...

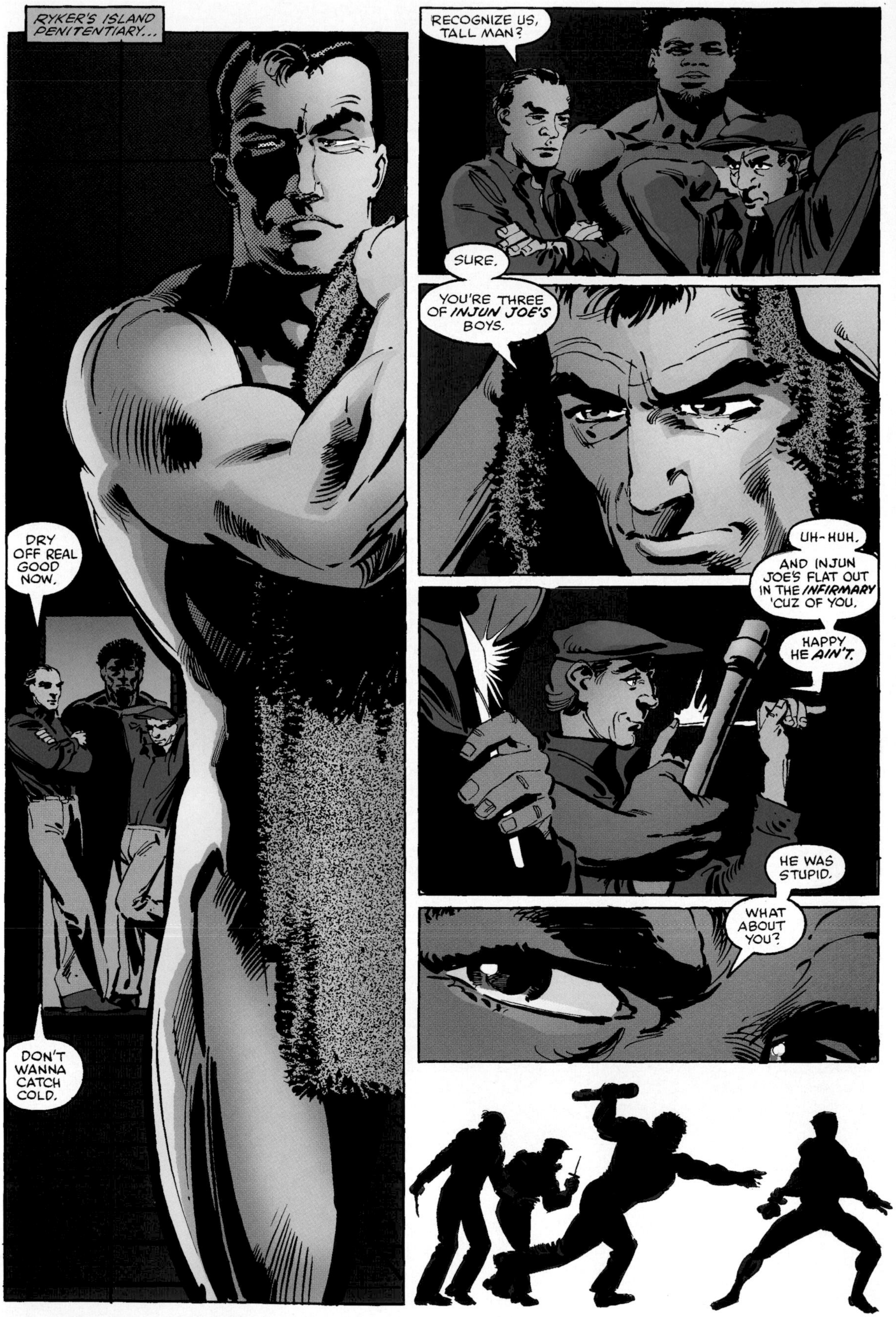
RYKER'S ISLAND PENITENTIARY...
DRY OFF REAL GOOD NOW.
DON'T WANNA CATCH COLD.
RECOGNIZE US, TALL MAN?
SURE.
YOU'RE THREE OF INJUN JOE'S BOYS.
UH-HUH.
AND INJUN JOE'S FLAT OUT IN THE INFIRMARY 'CUZ OF YOU.
HAPPY HE AIN'T.
HE WAS STUPID.
WHAT ABOUT YOU?

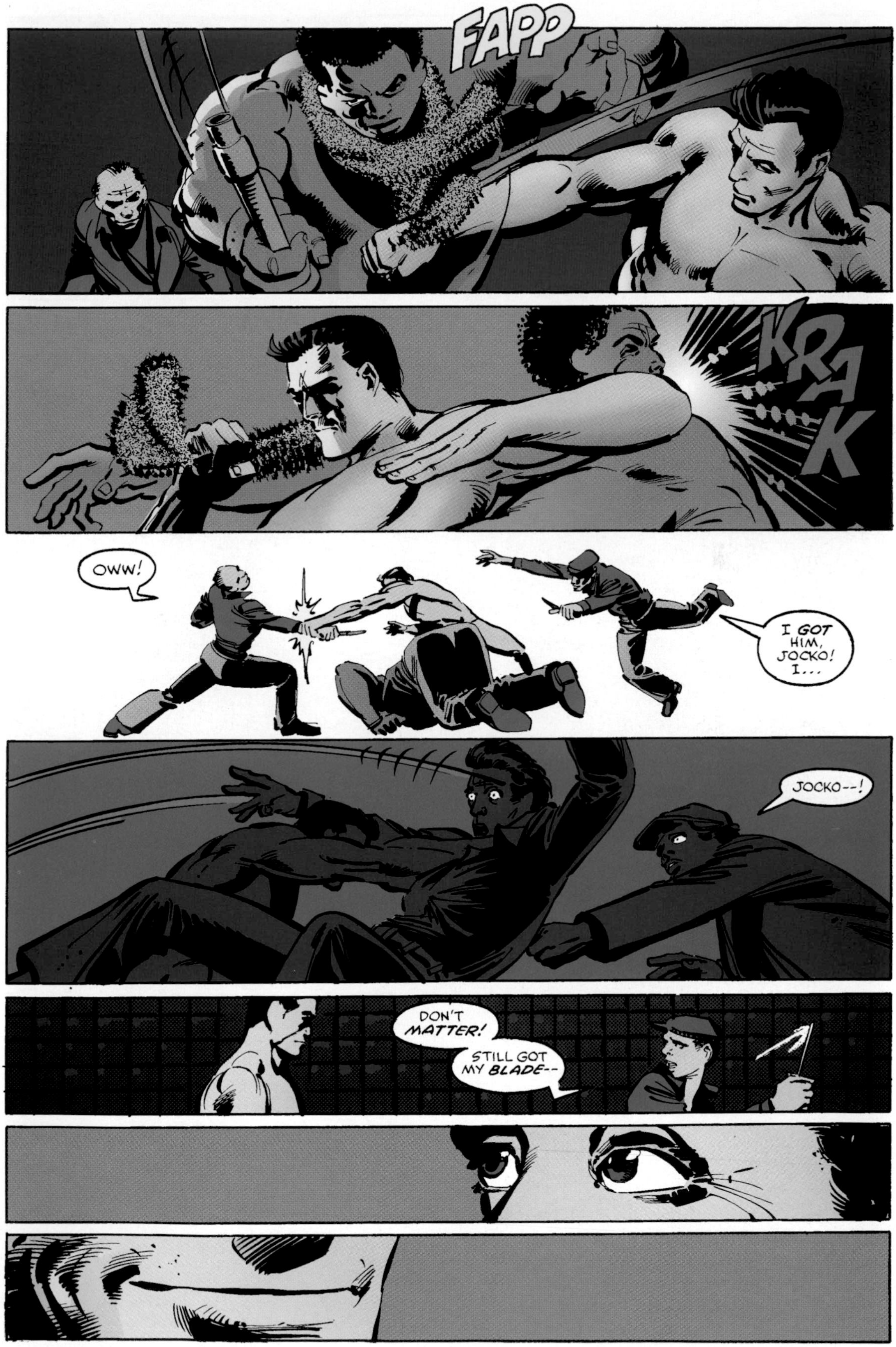
FAPP
KRAK
OWW!
I GOT HIM, JOCKO! I...
JOCKO--!
DON'T MATTER!
STILL GOT MY BLADE--

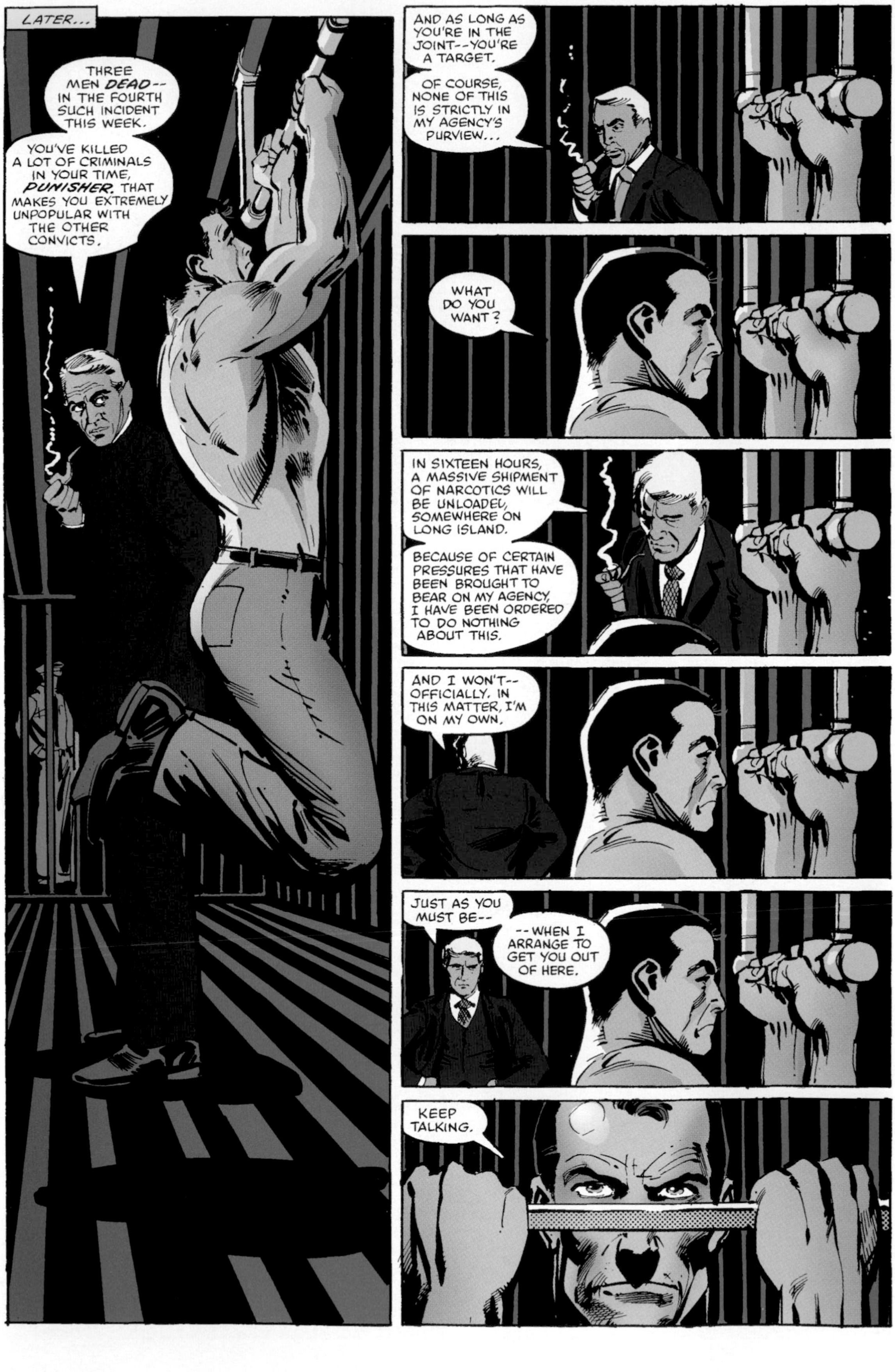
LATER...
THREE MEN DEAD-- IN THE FOURTH SUCH INCIDENT THIS WEEK.
YOU'VE KILLED A LOT OF CRIMINALS IN YOUR TIME, PUNISHER. THAT MAKES YOU EXTREMELY UNPOPULAR WITH THE OTHER CONVICTS.
AND AS LONG AS YOU'RE IN THE JOINT--YOU'RE A TARGET.
OF COURSE, NONE OF THIS IS STRICTLY IN MY AGENCY'S PURVIEW...
WHAT DO YOU WANT?
IN SIXTEEN HOURS, A MASSIVE SHIPMENT OF NARCOTICS WILL BE UNLOADED, SOMEWHERE ON LONG ISLAND.
BECAUSE OF CERTAIN PRESSURES THAT HAVE BEEN BROUGHT TO BEAR ON MY AGENCY, I HAVE BEEN ORDERED TO DO NOTHING ABOUT THIS.
AND I WON'T-- OFFICIALLY. IN THIS MATTER, I'M ON MY OWN.
JUST AS YOU MUST BE--
--WHEN I ARRANGE TO GET YOU OUT OF HERE.
KEEP TALKING.

THE MANHATTAN OFFICE OF *GLENN INDUSTRIES*...

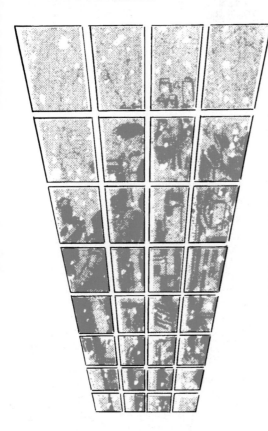

...STRICTLY A FORMALITY, MS. GLENN. HARDLY WORTH YOUR TIME.

JUST ANOTHER ATTEMPT BY OUR LEGAL DEPARTMENT TO KEEP ITSELF ON THE BUDGET.

I CAN'T MAKE HEAD NOR TAIL OF THIS. WHAT DOES IT MEAN?

SIMPLY A REORGANIZATION OF ADMINISTRATIVE SEQUENCE TO ALLOW FOR INCREASED EFFICIENCY IN THE SUPERVISION OF DUTIES.

THAT'S ALL.

SOUNDS LIKE *MATT* WROTE IT.

MATT?

YOU KNOW, *MATT MURDOCK*. MY *ATTORNEY*.

SPEAKING OF WHOM, HE MADE ME PROMISE TO SHOW HIM ANYTHING LIKE THIS BEFORE I SIGN IT.

AND, SINCE I JUST *HAPPEN* TO BE SEEING HIM TONIGHT...

YOU DON'T MIND, DO YOU?

CERTAINLY NOT, MY DEAR.

SHALL I CALL YOU TOMORROW ...SAY, AT NOON?

A WAKE UP CALL I *DON'T* NEED, MR. SPINDLE!

FLAKEY BROAD.

YES, YES...BUT INCREASINGLY TRACTABLE.

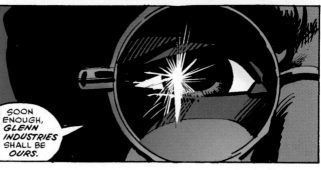

SOON ENOUGH, *GLENN INDUSTRIES* SHALL BE *OURS*.

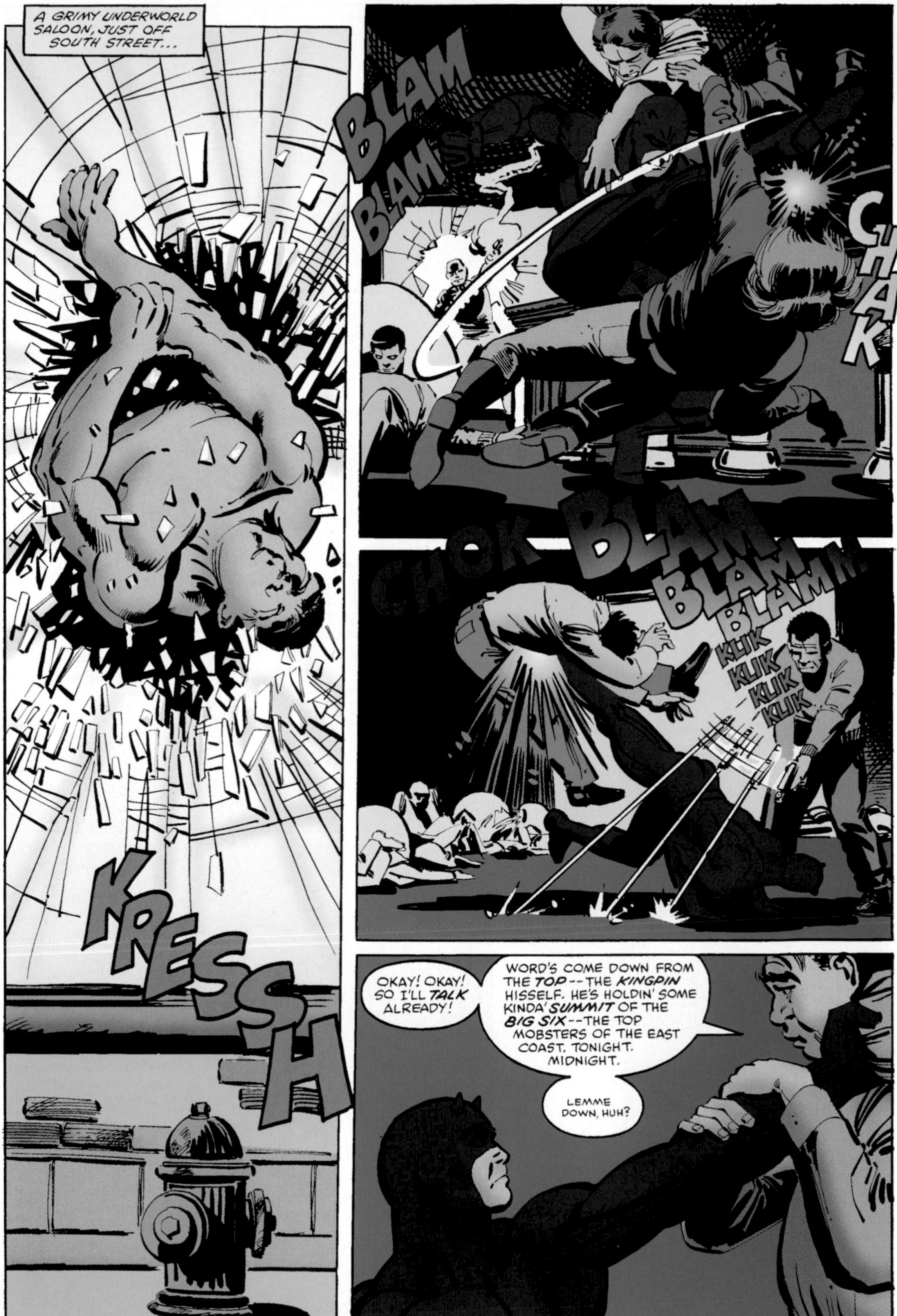
A GRIMY UNDERWORLD SALOON, JUST OFF SOUTH STREET...
KRESSSH
BLAM
BLAM
CHAK
CHOK
BLAM
BLAMM
BLAMM
KLIK
KLIK
KLIK
KLIK
OKAY! OKAY! SO I'LL TALK ALREADY!
WORD'S COME DOWN FROM THE TOP -- THE KINGPIN HISSELF. HE'S HOLDIN' SOME KINDA' SUMMIT OF THE BIG SIX -- THE TOP MOBSTERS OF THE EAST COAST. TONIGHT. MIDNIGHT.
LEMME DOWN, HUH?

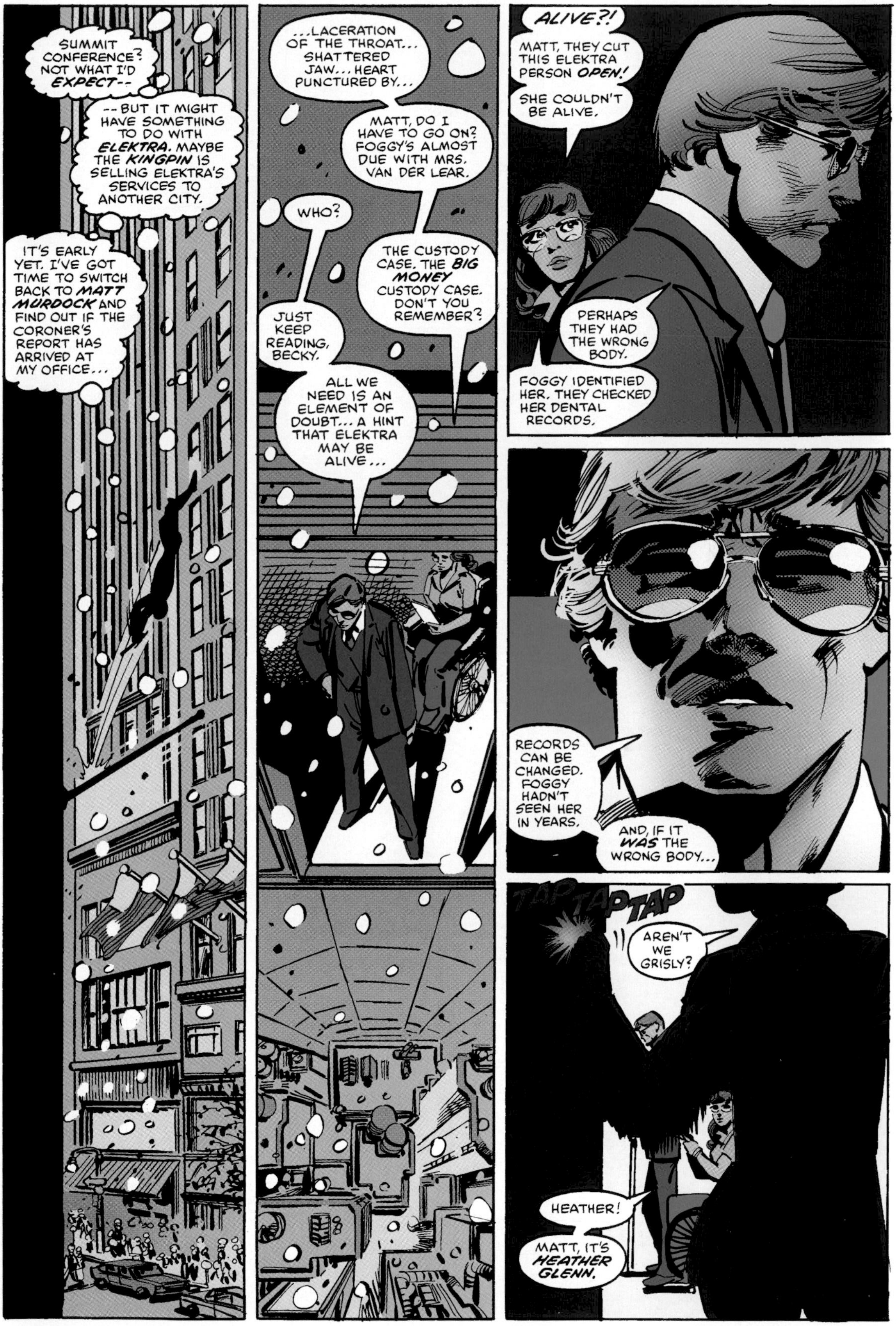
SUMMIT CONFERENCE? NOT WHAT I'D EXPECT--
--BUT IT MIGHT HAVE SOMETHING TO DO WITH ELEKTRA. MAYBE THE KINGPIN IS SELLING ELEKTRA'S SERVICES TO ANOTHER CITY.
IT'S EARLY YET. I'VE GOT TIME TO SWITCH BACK TO MATT MURDOCK AND FIND OUT IF THE CORONER'S REPORT HAS ARRIVED AT MY OFFICE...
...LACERATION OF THE THROAT... SHATTERED JAW... HEART PUNCTURED BY...
MATT, DO I HAVE TO GO ON? FOGGY'S ALMOST DUE WITH MRS. VAN DER LEAR.
WHO?
THE CUSTODY CASE. THE BIG MONEY CUSTODY CASE. DON'T YOU REMEMBER?
JUST KEEP READING, BECKY.
ALL WE NEED IS AN ELEMENT OF DOUBT... A HINT THAT ELEKTRA MAY BE ALIVE...
ALIVE?!
MATT, THEY CUT THIS ELEKTRA PERSON OPEN!
SHE COULDN'T BE ALIVE.
PERHAPS THEY HAD THE WRONG BODY.
FOGGY IDENTIFIED HER. THEY CHECKED HER DENTAL RECORDS.
RECORDS CAN BE CHANGED. FOGGY HADN'T SEEN HER IN YEARS.
AND, IF IT WAS THE WRONG BODY...
TAP TAP TAP
AREN'T WE GRISLY?
HEATHER!
MATT, IT'S HEATHER GLENN.

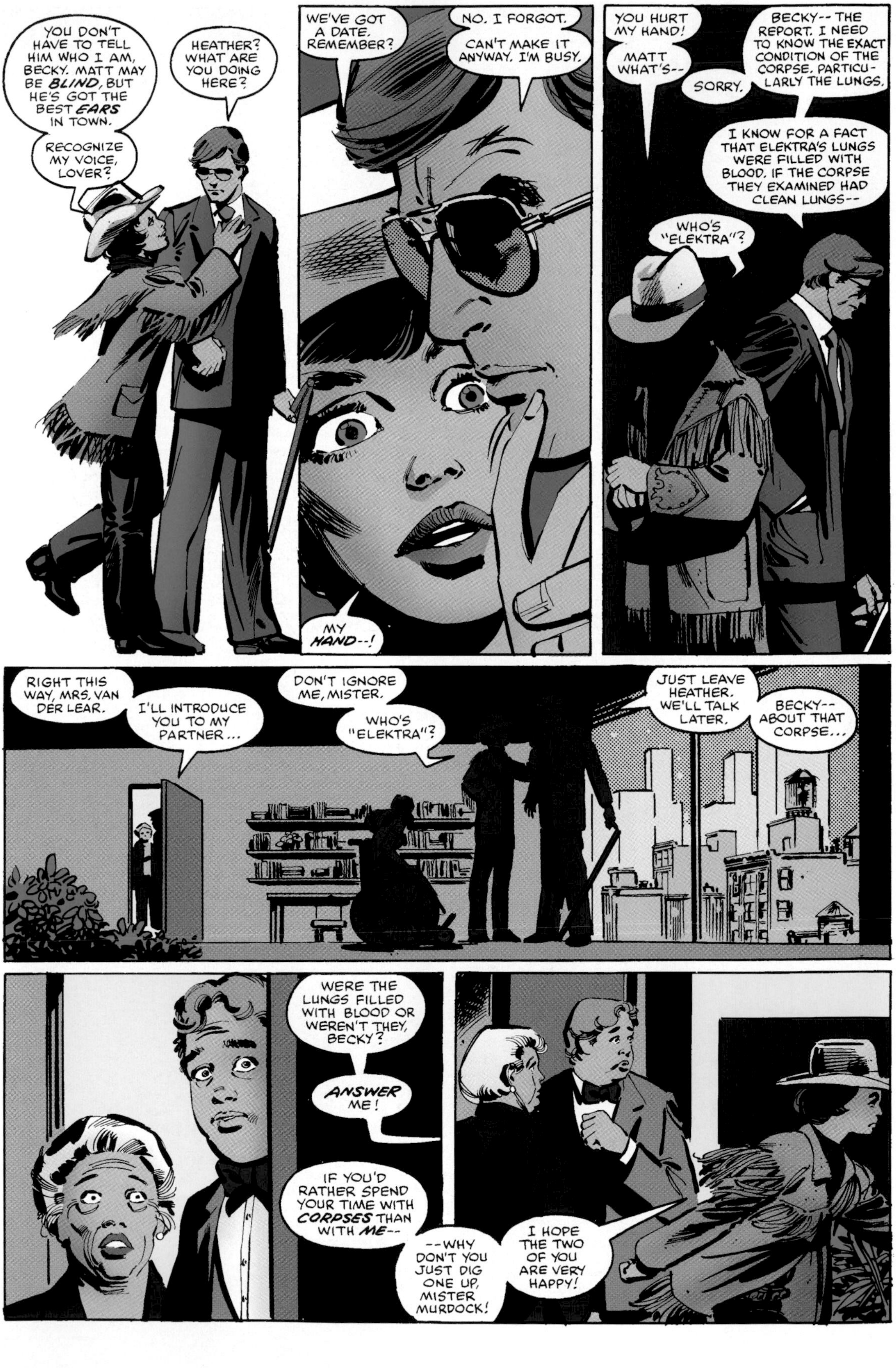
YOU DON'T HAVE TO TELL HIM WHO I AM, BECKY. MATT MAY BE BLIND, BUT HE'S GOT THE BEST EARS IN TOWN.
RECOGNIZE MY VOICE, LOVER?
HEATHER? WHAT ARE YOU DOING HERE?
WE'VE GOT A DATE. REMEMBER?
NO. I FORGOT.
CAN'T MAKE IT ANYWAY. I'M BUSY.
MY HAND--!
YOU HURT MY HAND!
MATT WHAT'S--
BECKY-- THE REPORT. I NEED TO KNOW THE EXACT CONDITION OF THE CORPSE. PARTICU-LARLY THE LUNGS.
SORRY.
I KNOW FOR A FACT THAT ELEKTRA'S LUNGS WERE FILLED WITH BLOOD. IF THE CORPSE THEY EXAMINED HAD CLEAN LUNGS--
WHO'S "ELEKTRA"?
RIGHT THIS WAY, MRS. VAN DER LEAR.
I'LL INTRODUCE YOU TO MY PARTNER...
DON'T IGNORE ME, MISTER.
WHO'S "ELEKTRA"?
JUST LEAVE HEATHER. WE'LL TALK LATER.
BECKY-- ABOUT THAT CORPSE...
WERE THE LUNGS FILLED WITH BLOOD OR WEREN'T THEY, BECKY?
ANSWER ME!
IF YOU'D RATHER SPEND YOUR TIME WITH CORPSES THAN WITH ME--
--WHY DON'T YOU JUST DIG ONE UP, MISTER MURDOCK!
I HOPE THE TWO OF YOU ARE VERY HAPPY!

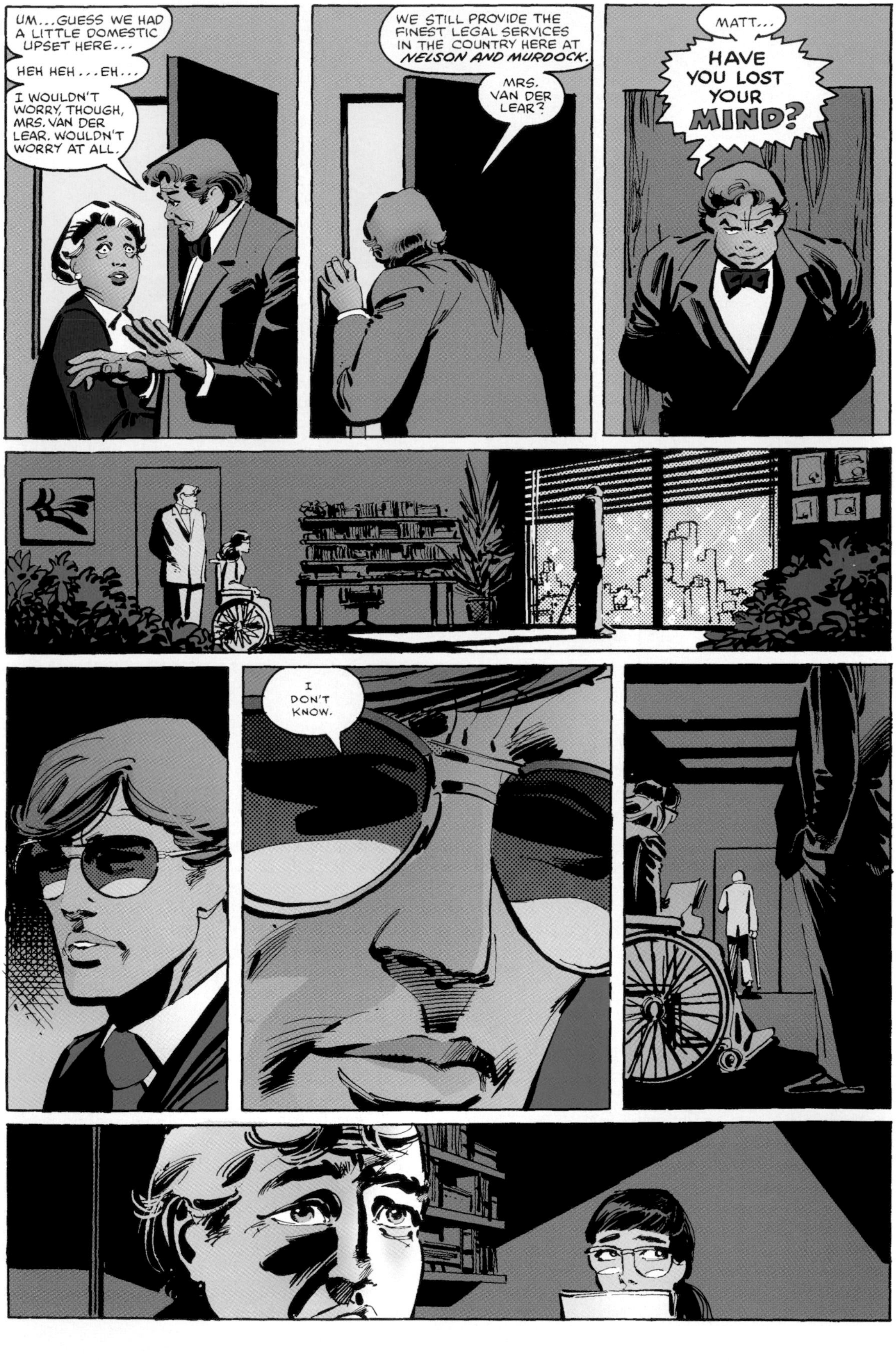

UM...GUESS WE HAD A LITTLE DOMESTIC UPSET HERE...
HEH HEH...EH...
I WOULDN'T WORRY, THOUGH, MRS. VAN DER LEAR. WOULDN'T WORRY AT ALL.
WE STILL PROVIDE THE FINEST LEGAL SERVICES IN THE COUNTRY HERE AT NELSON AND MURDOCK.
MRS. VAN DER LEAR?
MATT...
HAVE YOU LOST YOUR MIND?
I DON'T KNOW.

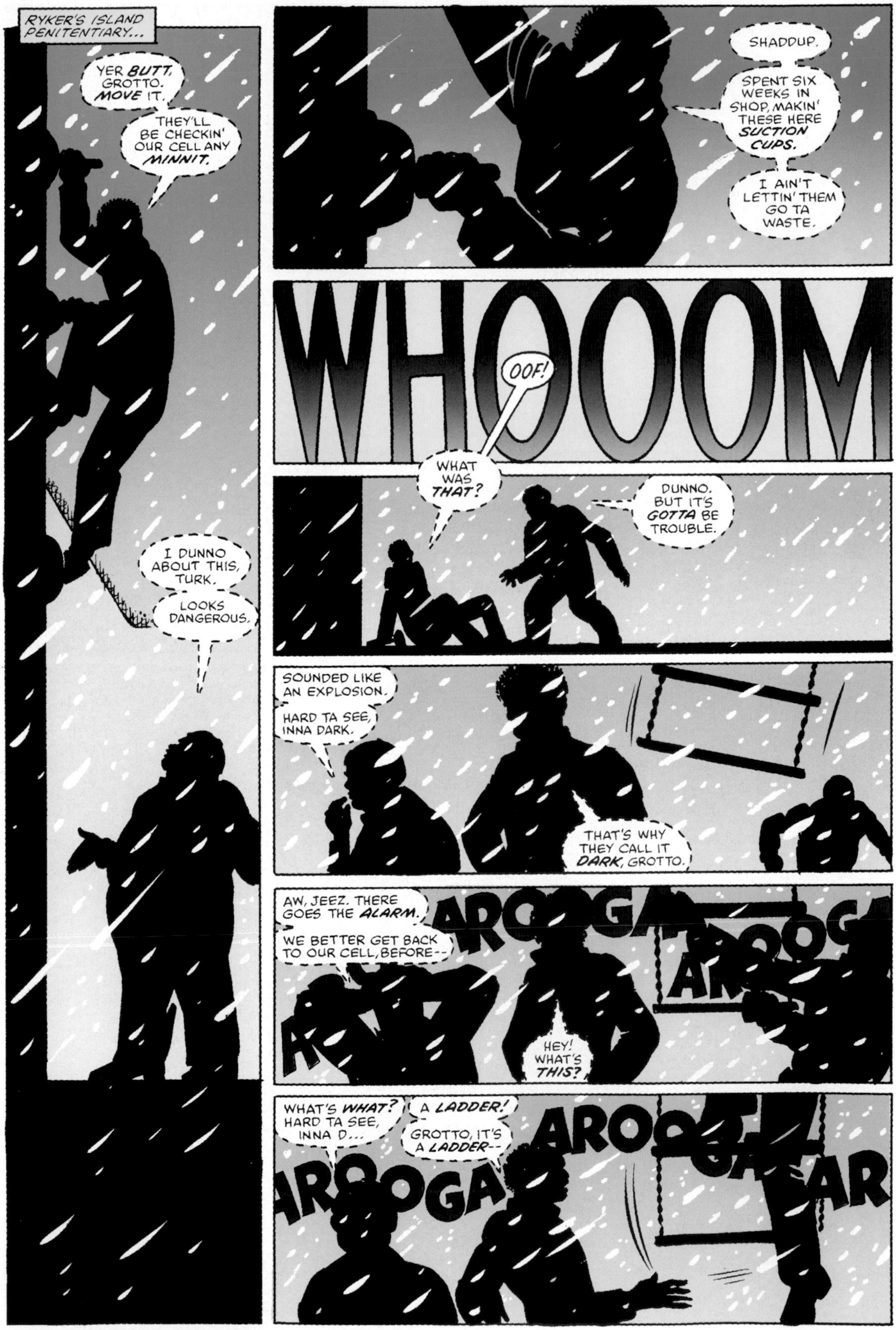
RYKER'S ISLAND PENITENTIARY...
YER BUTT, GROTTO. MOVE IT.
THEY'LL BE CHECKIN' OUR CELL ANY MINNIT.
I DUNNO ABOUT THIS, TURK.
LOOKS DANGEROUS.
SHADDUP.
SPENT SIX WEEKS IN SHOP, MAKIN' THESE HERE SUCTION CUPS.
I AIN'T LETTIN' THEM GO TA WASTE.
WHOOOM
OOF!
WHAT WAS THAT?
DUNNO. BUT IT'S GOTTA BE TROUBLE.
SOUNDED LIKE AN EXPLOSION.
HARD TA SEE, INNA DARK.
THAT'S WHY THEY CALL IT DARK, GROTTO.
AW, JEEZ. THERE GOES THE ALARM.
WE BETTER GET BACK TO OUR CELL, BEFORE--
AROOGA
HEY! WHAT'S THIS?
WHAT'S WHAT? HARD TA SEE, INNA D...
A LADDER!
GROTTO, IT'S A LADDER--
AROOGA

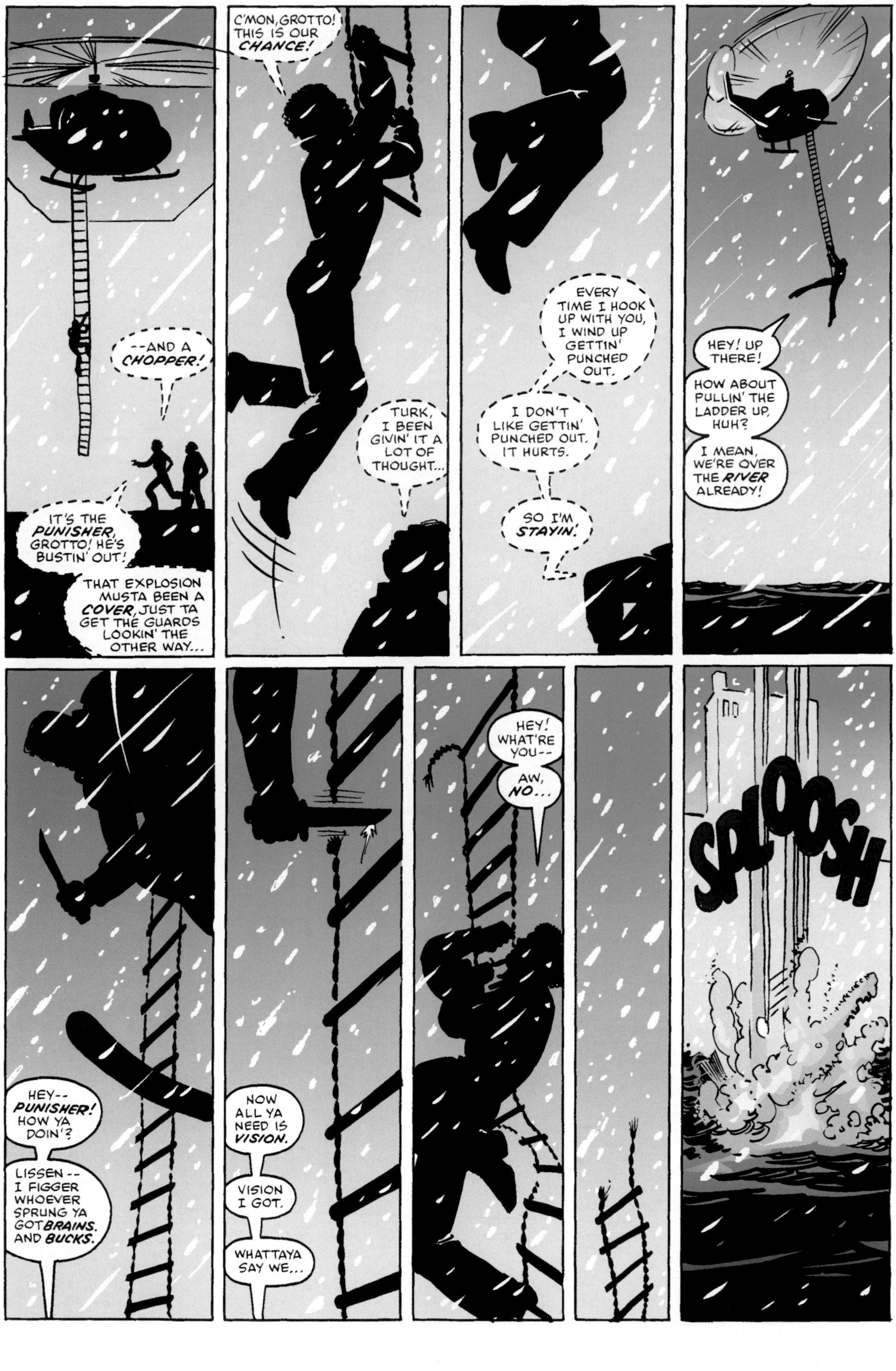
--AND A CHOPPER!
IT'S THE PUNISHER, GROTTO! HE'S BUSTIN' OUT!
THAT EXPLOSION MUSTA BEEN A COVER, JUST TA GET THE GUARDS LOOKIN' THE OTHER WAY...
C'MON, GROTTO! THIS IS OUR CHANCE!
TURK, I BEEN GIVIN' IT A LOT OF THOUGHT...
EVERY TIME I HOOK UP WITH YOU, I WIND UP GETTIN' PUNCHED OUT.
I DON'T LIKE GETTIN' PUNCHED OUT. IT HURTS.
SO I'M STAYIN'.
HEY! UP THERE!
HOW ABOUT PULLIN' THE LADDER UP, HUH?
I MEAN, WE'RE OVER THE RIVER ALREADY!
HEY-- PUNISHER! HOW YA DOIN'?
LISSEN -- I FIGGER WHOEVER SPRUNG YA GOT BRAINS. AND BUCKS.
NOW ALL YA NEED IS VISION.
VISION I GOT.
WHATTAYA SAY WE...
HEY! WHAT'RE YOU--
AW, NO...
SPLOOSH

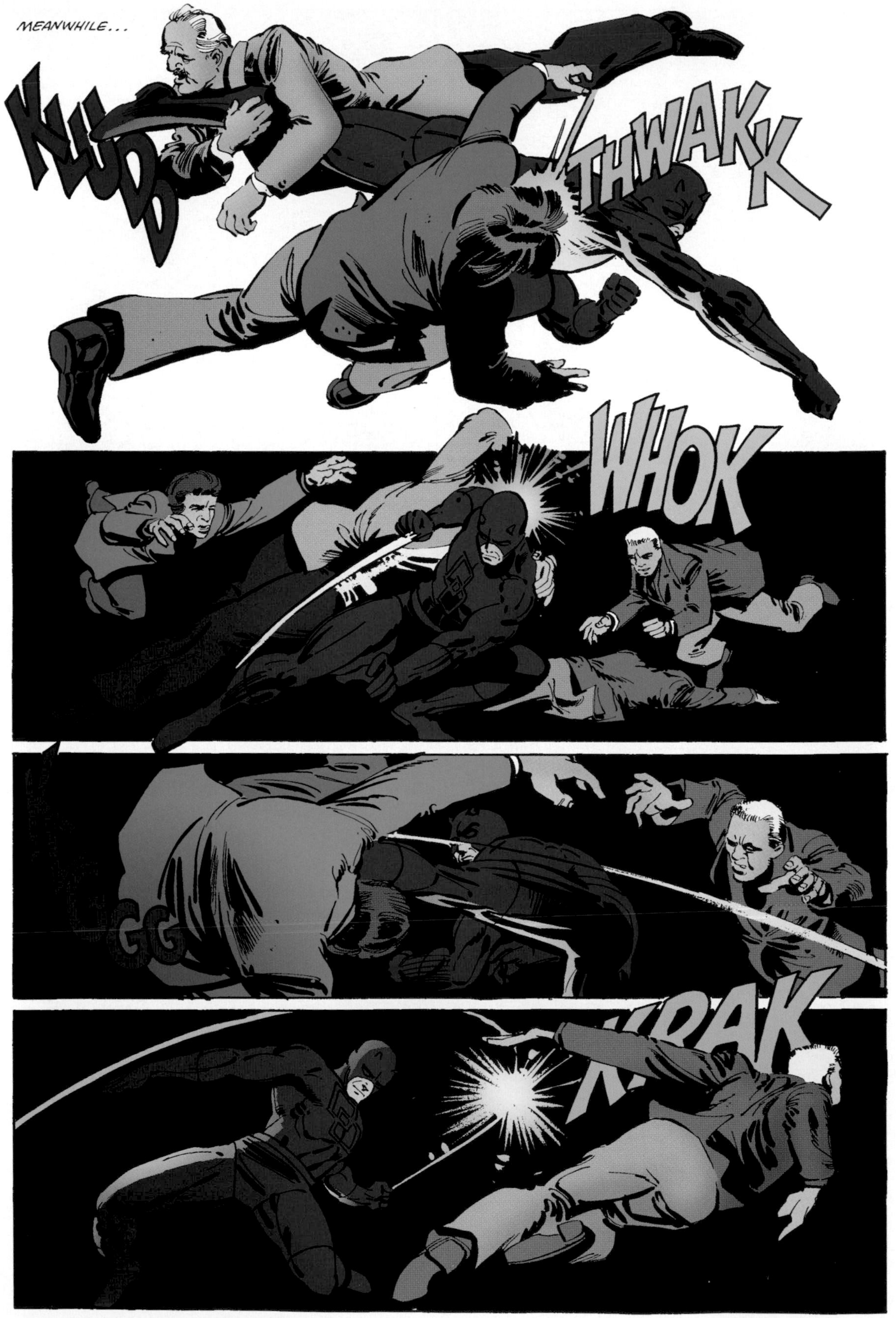
MEANWHILE...
KLUDD
THWAKK
WHOK
GG
RAK

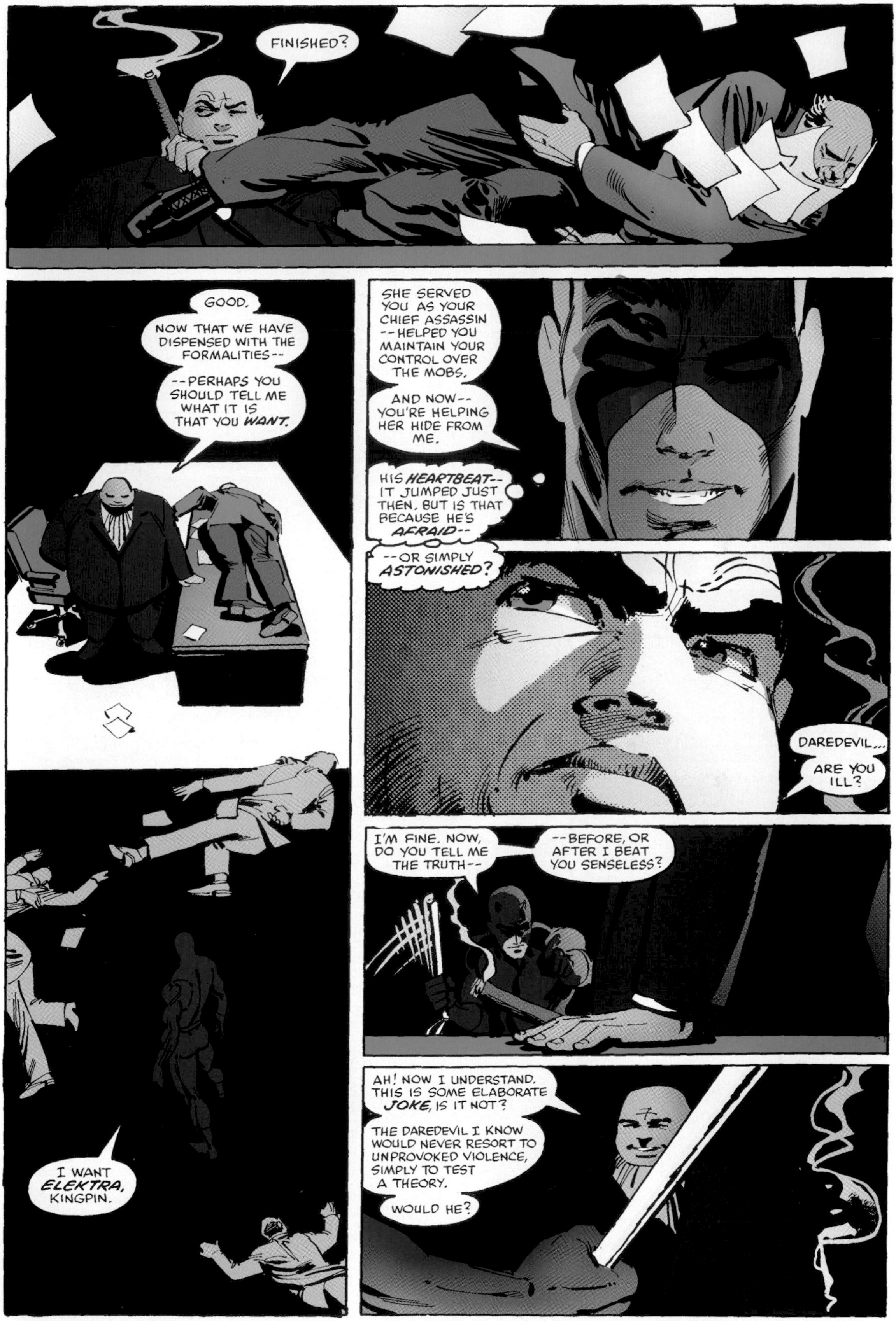
FINISHED?
GOOD.
NOW THAT WE HAVE DISPENSED WITH THE FORMALITIES--
--PERHAPS YOU SHOULD TELL ME WHAT IT IS THAT YOU WANT.
SHE SERVED YOU AS YOUR CHIEF ASSASSIN --HELPED YOU MAINTAIN YOUR CONTROL OVER THE MOBS.
AND NOW-- YOU'RE HELPING HER HIDE FROM ME.
HIS HEARTBEAT-- IT JUMPED JUST THEN. BUT IS THAT BECAUSE HE'S AFRAID--
--OR SIMPLY ASTONISHED?
DAREDEVIL...
ARE YOU ILL?
I WANT ELEKTRA, KINGPIN.
I'M FINE. NOW, DO YOU TELL ME THE TRUTH--
--BEFORE, OR AFTER I BEAT YOU SENSELESS?
AH! NOW I UNDERSTAND. THIS IS SOME ELABORATE JOKE, IS IT NOT?
THE DAREDEVIL I KNOW WOULD NEVER RESORT TO UNPROVOKED VIOLENCE, SIMPLY TO TEST A THEORY.
WOULD HE?

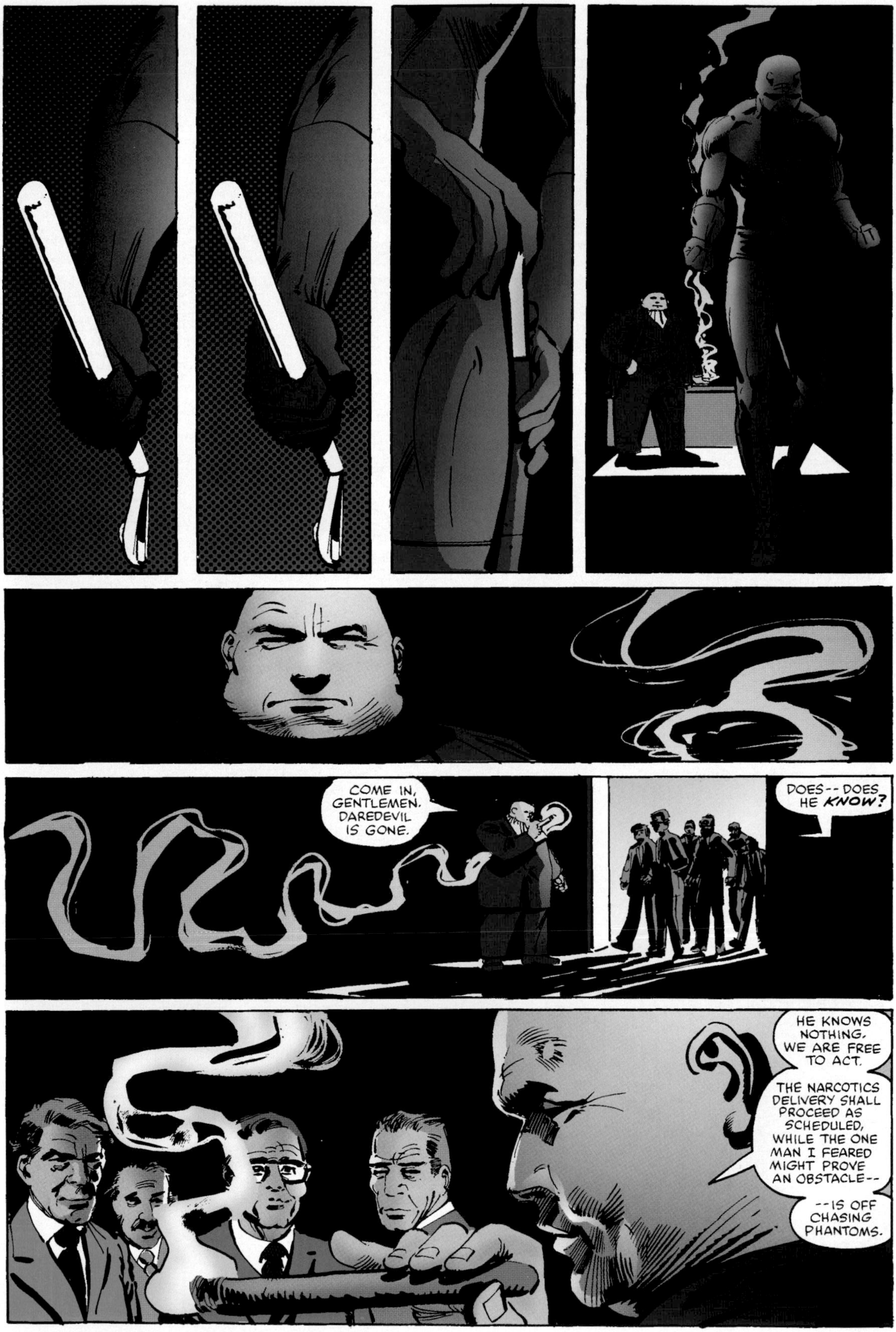

COME IN, GENTLEMEN. DAREDEVIL IS GONE.
DOES-- DOES HE KNOW?
HE KNOWS NOTHING. WE ARE FREE TO ACT.
THE NARCOTICS DELIVERY SHALL PROCEED AS SCHEDULED, WHILE THE ONE MAN I FEARED MIGHT PROVE AN OBSTACLE--
--IS OFF CHASING PHANTOMS.

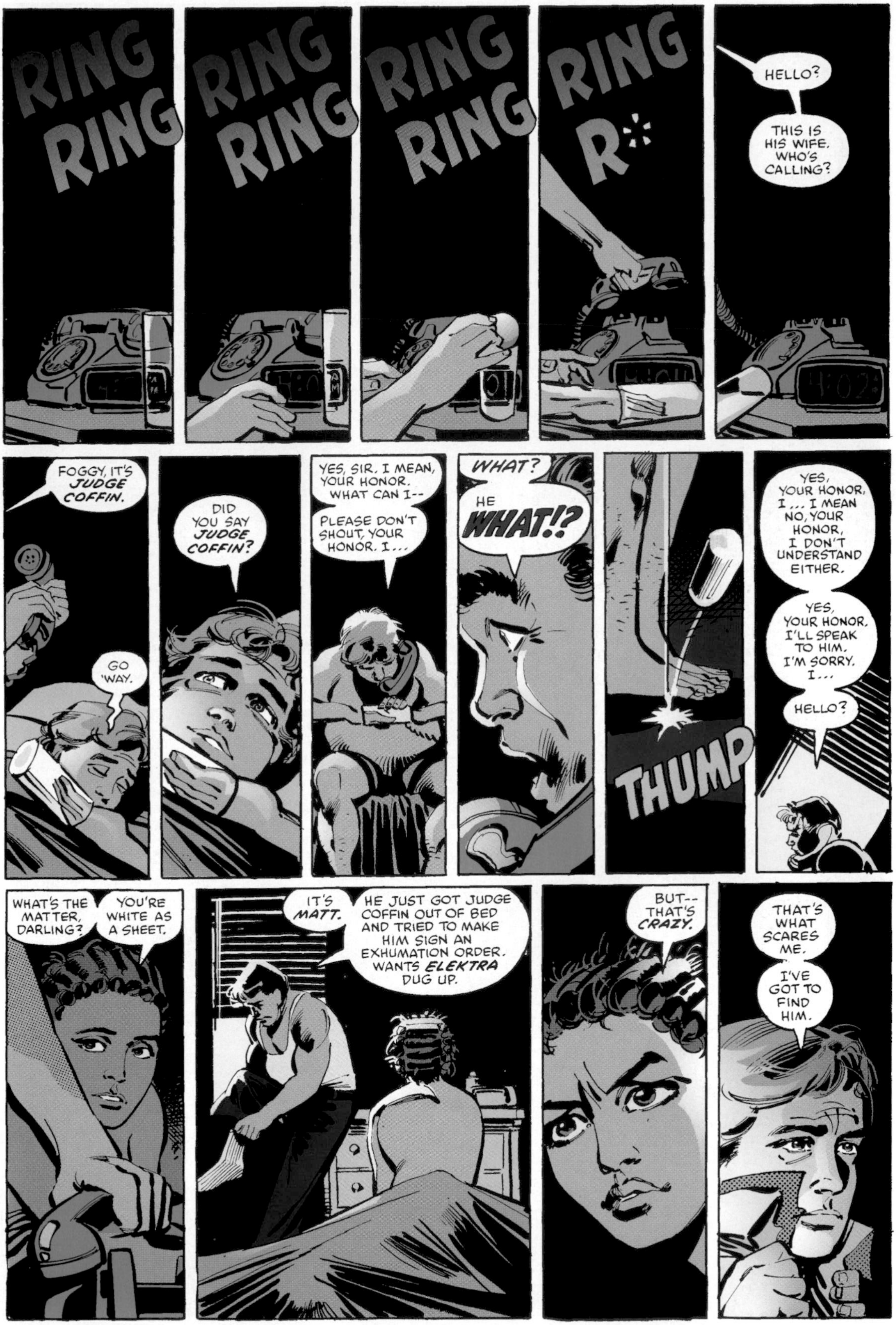
RING
RING
RING
RING
RING
RING
RING
R
HELLO?
THIS IS HIS WIFE. WHO'S CALLING?
FOGGY, IT'S *JUDGE COFFIN*.
GO 'WAY.
DID YOU SAY *JUDGE COFFIN?*
YES, SIR. I MEAN, YOUR HONOR. WHAT CAN I--
PLEASE DON'T SHOUT, YOUR HONOR. I...
WHAT?
HE *WHAT!?*
THUMP
YES, YOUR HONOR, I... I MEAN NO, YOUR HONOR, I DON'T UNDERSTAND EITHER.
YES, YOUR HONOR, I'LL SPEAK TO HIM. I'M SORRY. I...
HELLO?
WHAT'S THE MATTER, DARLING?
YOU'RE WHITE AS A SHEET.
IT'S *MATT*.
HE JUST GOT JUDGE COFFIN OUT OF BED AND TRIED TO MAKE HIM SIGN AN EXHUMATION ORDER. WANTS *ELEKTRA* DUG UP.
BUT-- THAT'S *CRAZY*.
THAT'S WHAT SCARES ME.
I'VE GOT TO FIND HIM.

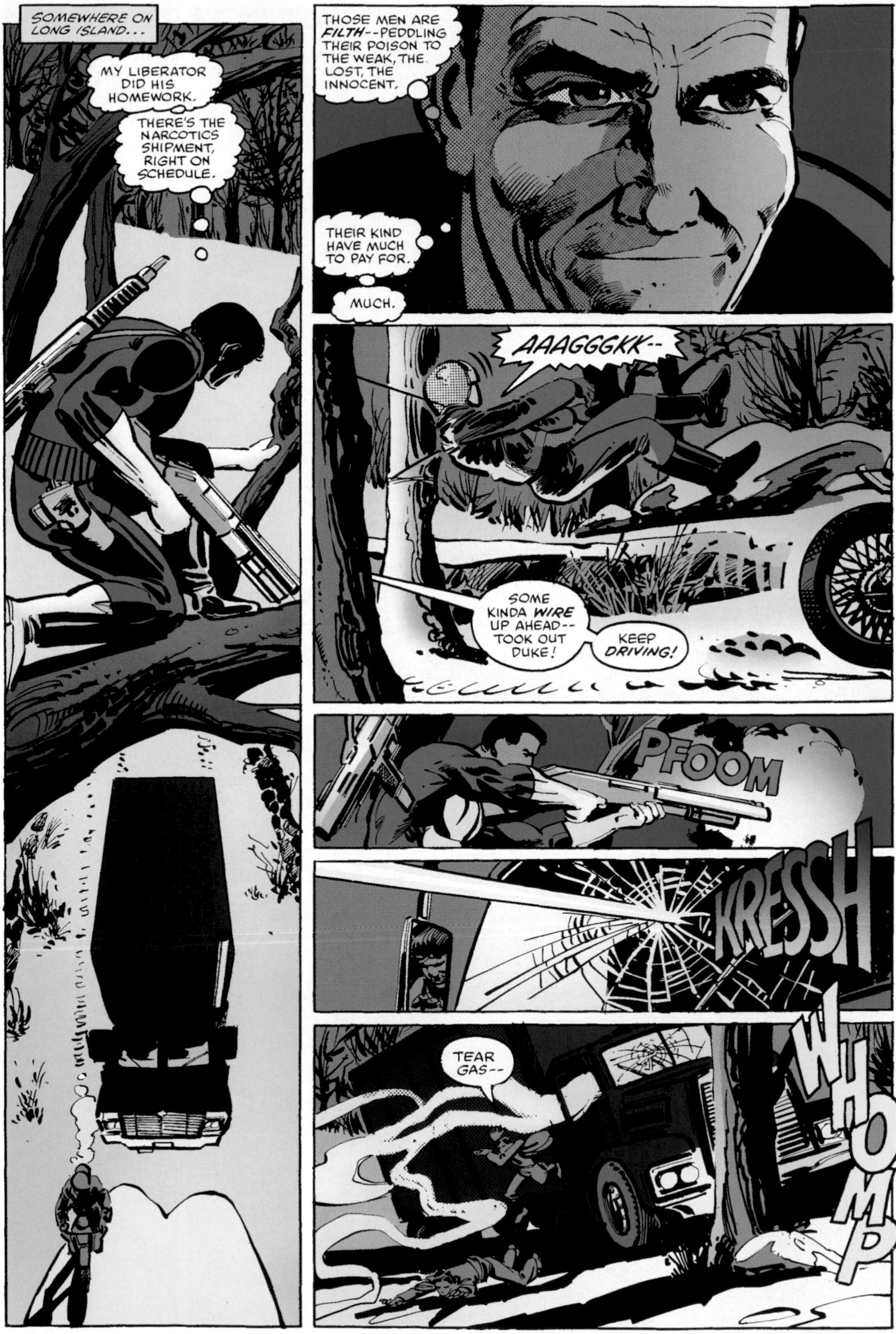
SOMEWHERE ON LONG ISLAND...
MY LIBERATOR DID HIS HOMEWORK.
THERE'S THE NARCOTICS SHIPMENT, RIGHT ON SCHEDULE.
THOSE MEN ARE FILTH--PEDDLING THEIR POISON TO THE WEAK, THE LOST, THE INNOCENT.
THEIR KIND HAVE MUCH TO PAY FOR.
MUCH.
AAAGGGKK--
SOME KINDA WIRE UP AHEAD-- TOOK OUT DUKE!
KEEP DRIVING!
PFOOM
KRESSH
TEAR GAS--
WHOMP

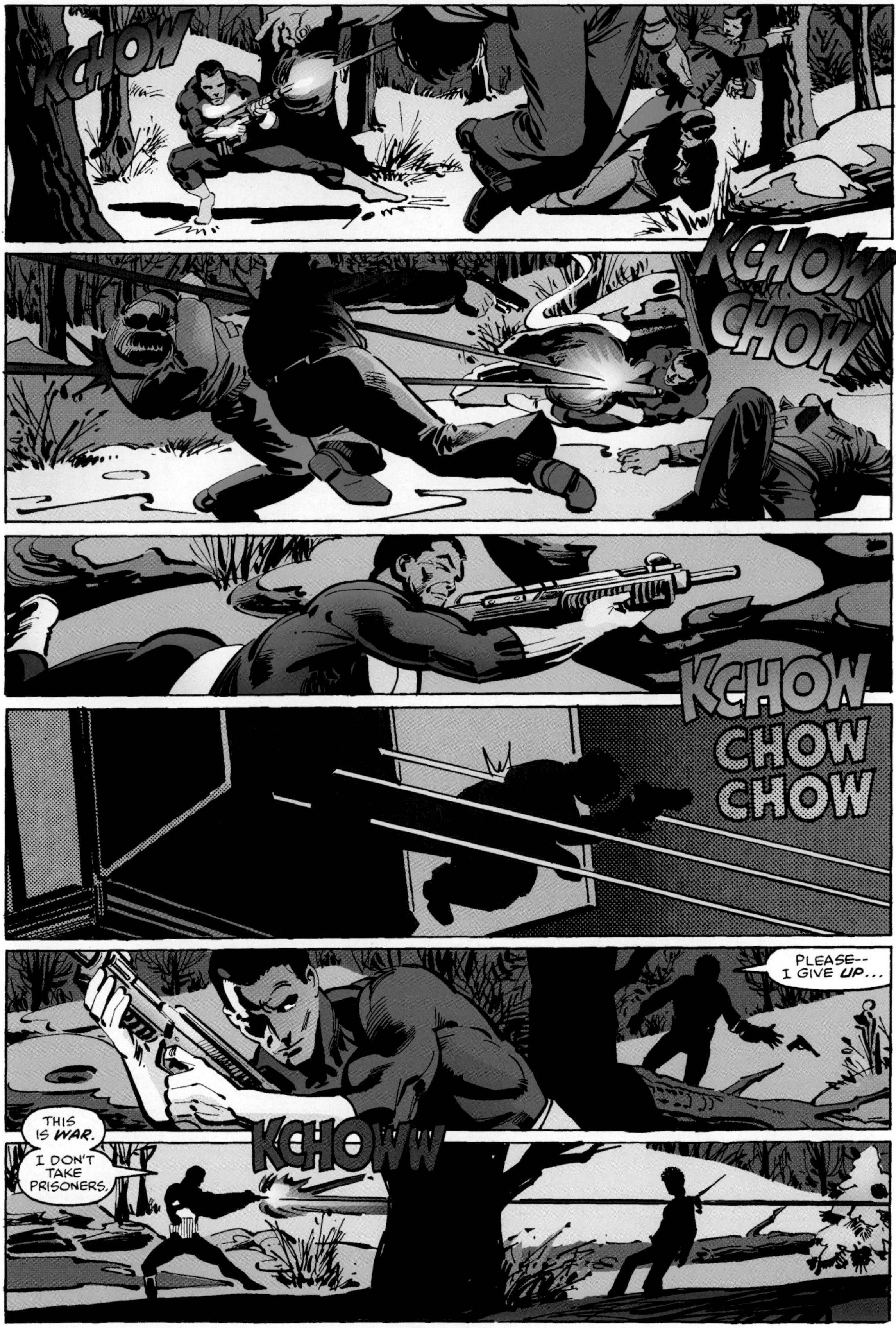
KCHOW
KCHOW
CHOW
KCHOW
CHOW
CHOW
PLEASE--
I GIVE UP...
THIS IS WAR.
I DON'T TAKE PRISONERS.
KCHOWW

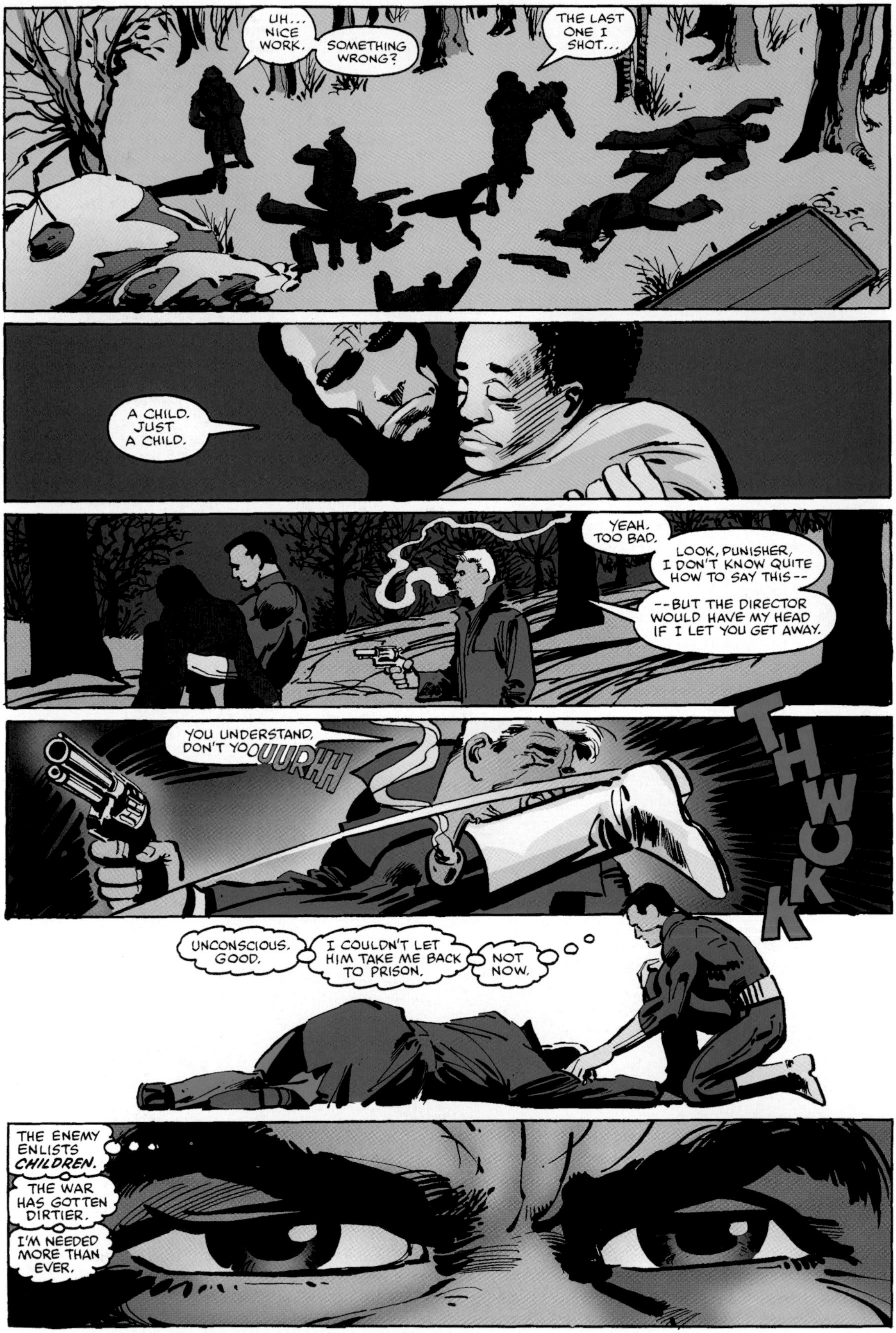
UH... NICE WORK.
SOMETHING WRONG?
THE LAST ONE I SHOT...
A CHILD. JUST A CHILD.
YEAH. TOO BAD.
LOOK, PUNISHER, I DON'T KNOW QUITE HOW TO SAY THIS--
--BUT THE DIRECTOR WOULD HAVE MY HEAD IF I LET YOU GET AWAY.
YOU UNDERSTAND, DON'T YOOUURHH
THWOKK
UNCONSCIOUS. GOOD.
I COULDN'T LET HIM TAKE ME BACK TO PRISON.
NOT NOW.
THE ENEMY ENLISTS CHILDREN.
THE WAR HAS GOTTEN DIRTIER.
I'M NEEDED MORE THAN EVER.

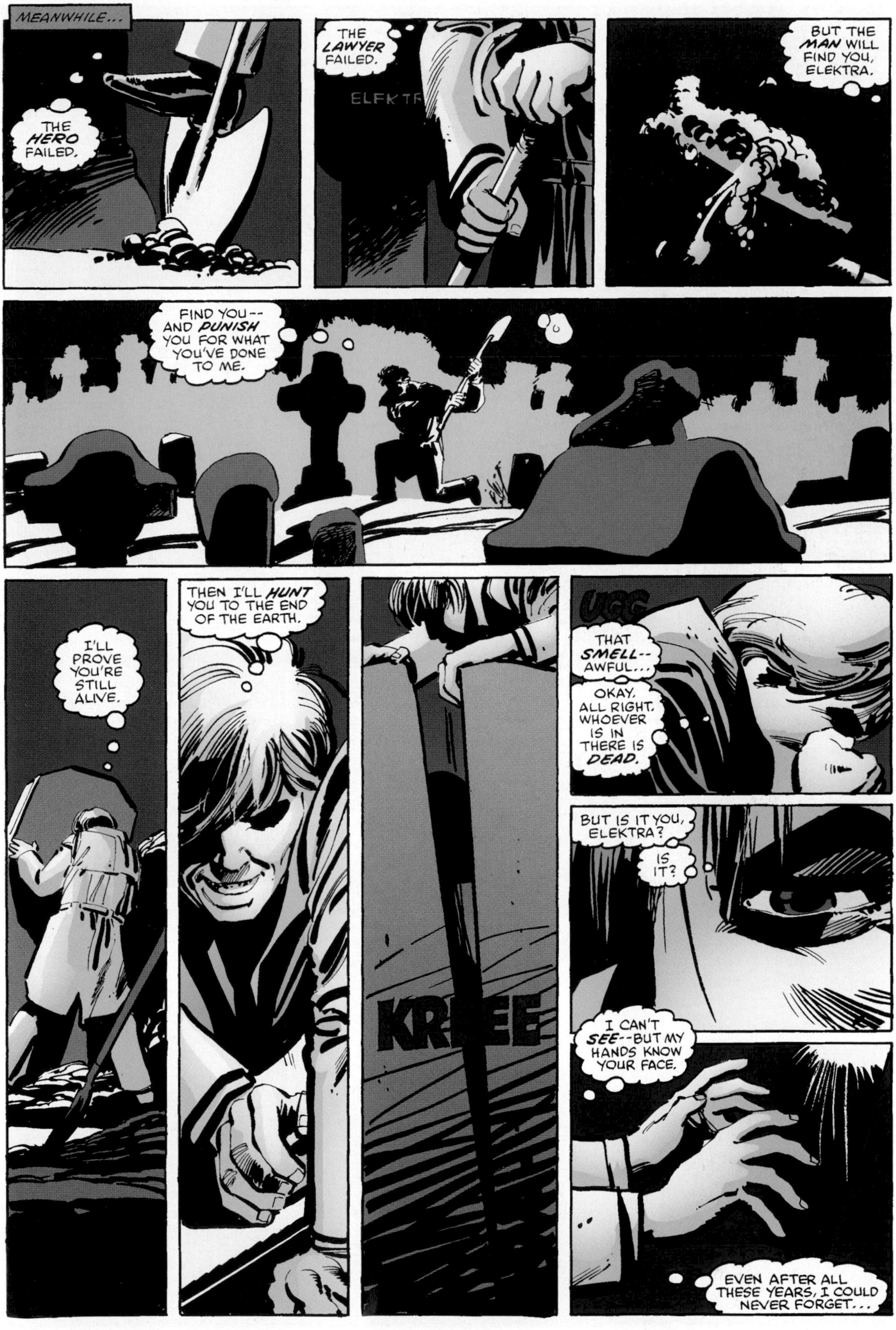
MEANWHILE...
THE HERO FAILED.
THE LAWYER FAILED.
ELEKTR
BUT THE MAN WILL FIND YOU, ELEKTRA.
FIND YOU-- AND PUNISH YOU FOR WHAT YOU'VE DONE TO ME.
I'LL PROVE YOU'RE STILL ALIVE.
THEN I'LL HUNT YOU TO THE END OF THE EARTH.
KREEE
UGG
THAT SMELL-- AWFUL...
OKAY. ALL RIGHT. WHOEVER IS IN THERE IS DEAD.
BUT IS IT YOU, ELEKTRA?
IS IT?
I CAN'T SEE--BUT MY HANDS KNOW YOUR FACE.
EVEN AFTER ALL THESE YEARS, I COULD NEVER FORGET...

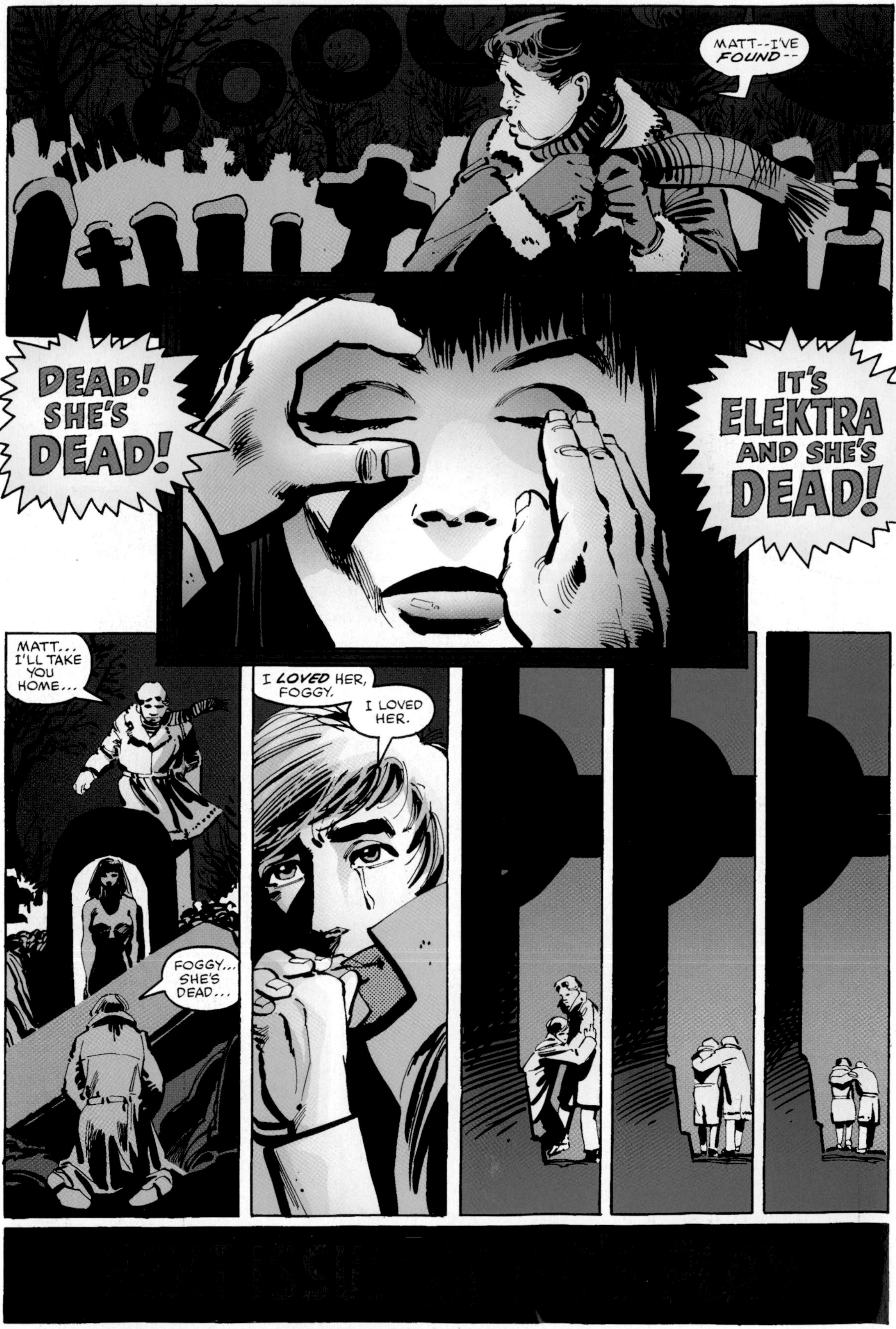
MATT--I'VE FOUND--
DEAD! SHE'S DEAD!
IT'S ELEKTRA AND SHE'S DEAD!
MATT... I'LL TAKE YOU HOME...
FOGGY... SHE'S DEAD...
I LOVED HER, FOGGY.
I LOVED HER.